# National Flood Insurance Program
# Flood
# Insurance
# Manual
# April 2021

edited by
Brian Greul

The NFIP (National Flood Insurance Program) and FEMA (Federal Emergency Management Administration) do a pretty good job later in this book of explaining the purpose and uses of this book. Flood is an inconvenient event that seeps in and destroys families, structures, and communities. The NFIP is the primary insurer for those who wish to insure against the devestation and financial damage caused by flood.

This manual is used by policy holders, insurers, adjusters, and others who have a role in helping protect our communities from flood loss. As a publisher based in Houston, Texas I've seen my fair share of what flood can do first hand. The government does not print and distribute copies of this manual. So I've stepped in as a publisher, recognizing that sometims a written book is better than e-reader. It is my hope that this book will aid those who do the hard work of writing the flood insurance policies, adjusting the claims after an event, and rebuilding their lives to understand and benefit from the National Flood Insurance Program.

An 8.5x11 3 hole punched loose leaf copy may be purchased for your 3 ring binder. Email books@ocotillopress.com for current information.

Should you have suggestions or feedback on ways to improve this book please send email to Books@OcotilloPress.com

---

Edited 2021 Ocotillo Press
ISBN 978-1-954285-31-6



Printed in the United States of America

Ocotillo Press
Houston, TX 77017
Books@OcotilloPress.com

Cover photos courtesy of Flickr User Revolution Messaging - public domain image.

NATIONAL FLOOD INSURANCE PROGRAM

# FLOOD INSURANCE MANUAL

April 2021

FEMA

NATIONAL FLOOD INSURANCE PROGRAM

This page is intentionally left blank.

**U.S. Department of Homeland Security**
Washington, DC 20472

FEMA

April 1, 2021

Dear *National Flood Insurance Program Flood Insurance Manual* User:

FEMA's regular updates to the *National Flood Insurance Program (NFIP) Flood Insurance Manual* reflect an ongoing effort to enhance the customer experience and evolve the NFIP into a world-class organization. FEMA has revised the document to incorporate program changes announced Oct. 1, 2020 and updated Oct. 27, 2020, replace outdated content and clarify existing guidance. Red text on the amended pages identifies updated information and all footers reflect the April 1, 2021 effective date. Revisions in the April 2021 edition include the following:

Section 1 – Reference

- Clarifies that the term "FEMA" includes its contractors and changes instances of "NFIP Bureau" to "FEMA."

Section 3 – How to Write

- Updates rating examples.
- Corrects an inadvertent change to a definition in Table 7 Building Occupancy Types for "Other Residential."
- Deletes an incorrect note regarding Residential Condominium Building Association Policy limits in an Emergency Program community.
- Updates the link to the list of insurers participating in the Mortgage Portfolio Protection Program to https://nfipservices.floodsmart.gov/mortgage-portfolio-protection-program.

Section 4 – How to Endorse

- Updates rating examples.
- Changes instances of "NFIP Bureau."

Section 6 – How to Cancel

- Corrects signature requirements in table.
- Changes instances of "NFIP Bureau."

Appendix C – Lowest Floor Guide

- Corrects "Use Pre-FIRM rate table With Enclosure category" to "Use Pre-FIRM rate table Elevated on Crawlspace category" on pages C-10, C-20, C-42, and C-47.

Appendix D – Coastal Barrier Resources System

- Changes instances of "NFIP Bureau."

Appendix F Community Rating System

- There are no changes to this section, but the list of Community Rating System eligible communities effective April 1, 2021 was updated at the link.

Appendix I – Severe Repetitive Loss Properties

- Changes instances of "NFIP Bureau."

Appendix J – Rate Tables

- Update premium rates for policies written or renewed on or after April 1, 2021.
- Update base premiums for Preferred Risk Policies and Newly Mapped rated policies written or renewed on or after Jan. 1, 2022.
- Update premium multiplier tables for policies rated under the Newly Mapped procedure written or renewed on or after Jan. 1, 2022.
- Corrects Footnote 6 from "For an elevated building on a crawlspace with an attached garage without openings, use "With Enclosure" rates" to "For an elevated building on a crawlspace with an attached garage without openings, use "Elevated on Crawlspace" rates" on pages J-2, J-4, J-5, and J-6.
- Corrects Footnote 7 from "For an elevated building on a crawlspace with an attached garage without openings, use "With Enclosure" rates" to "For an elevated building on a crawlspace with an attached garage without openings, use "Elevated on Crawlspace" rates" on pages J-3
- Corrects Footnote 4 from referring Table 3A to Table 5A.

Appendix L – Definitions and Acronyms

- Adds a definition for "agricultural structure" and clarifies other definitions.
- Removes definition for "NFIP Bureau."

The updated edition of the *NFIP Flood Insurance Manual* does not change flood insurance coverage or supersede the terms and conditions of the Standard Flood Insurance Policy. The guidance and premium rates in this edition reflect the NFIP's existing underwriting requirements and its current rating methodology. They do not represent changes in methodology due to FEMA's planned Risk Rating 2.0 initiative. FEMA continues its preliminary analyses and internal review on how the methodology for determining premium rates may change in the future. Once completed, FEMA will provide additional guidance and updates.

FEMA's goal is to make NFIP products and processes easy to understand and enable insurance professionals to provide policyholders with consistent and reliable service.

Thank you for your continued support for the NFIP and for your service to our policyholders. Together, we can make America more flood resilient and build a culture of preparedness by closing the nation's insurance gap.

Sincerely,

Jeffrey Jackson
Acting, Assistant Administrator for Federal Insurance
Federal Insurance and Mitigation Administration

# Message to National Flood Insurance Program Agents and Insurers

The fight against COVID-19 continues throughout the United States and across the world as the vaccine rollout continues during this pandemic. A record setting 30 named storms swept over the Atlantic during the 2020 hurricane season, leaving paths of destruction and flooding to add more economic hardship. FEMA's National Flood Insurance Program (NFIP) proactively adapted existing authorities to ensure the safety of policyholders, improve the program and reduce disaster suffering.

The NFIP received a one-year reauthorization extension to Sept. 30, 2021. The reauthorization of the NFIP for a full year gives policyholders confidence FEMA can pay flood insurance claims and minimizes the uncertainty of buying and selling homes located in high risk flooding areas. I believe FEMA's mission is tied to our efforts to reshape what it means to build a culture of preparedness in an age of more intense and frequent weather events. The NFIP and our partners at all levels are uniquely positioned to gain new ground to make communities more resilient.

Thank you for representing the NFIP and supporting our policyholders during this time. Your expertise helps us transform our program. We continue our focus on closing the insurance gap, building a culture of preparedness and ensuring the equitable treatment of our current and prospective policyholders.

Together, we will advance service to our customers as 2021 unfolds.

Sincerely,

David I. Maurstad
Deputy Associate Administrator
for Insurance and Mitigation

This page is intentionally left blank.

# Change Record Page

## April 2021 Edition

FEMA updates the *National Flood Insurance Program (NFIP) Flood Insurance Manual* periodically. Red text on the amended pages identifies updated information. All footers have an April 1, 2021 effective date.

This page provides the page numbers for changes made in the April 2021 edition of the *NFIP Flood Insurance Manual*.

---


**Contents** . . . . . . . . . . . . . . . . . . . . . . . . i, vii, xi, xii

**Section 1. Reference** . . . . . . . . . . . . . . . . 1.1–1.5

**Section 3. How to Write** . . . . . . . . . . . . . 3.1–3.60, 3.63–3.64, 3.69–3.70, 3.73–3.106

**Section 4. How to Endorse** . . . . . . . . . . . 4.1–4.16

**Section 6. How to Cancel** . . . . . . . . . . . . 6.1, 6.20

**Appendix C. Lowest Floor Guide** . . . . . . . C.1–C.4

**Appendix D. Coastal Barrier Resources System** . . . . . . . . . . . . . . . . . . D.2

**Appendix I. Severe Repetitive Loss Properties** . . . . . . . . . . . . . . . . . . . . I.1–I.9

**Appendix J. Rate Tables** . . . . . . . . . . . . . J.1–J.14, J.16–J.17, J.21–J.53

**Appendix L. Definitions and Acronyms** . . . L.1–L.12

This page is intentionally left blank.

# Table of Contents

**NOTE:** This document represents the current FEMA guidance on the covered topics and may assist NFIP insurers, vendors, agents, adjusters, and policyholders apply applicable statutory and regulatory requirements, as well as the terms and conditions of the Standard Flood Insurance Policy. This document is not a substitute for applicable legal requirements, nor is it itself a rule. It is not intended to, nor does it impose, legally-binding requirements on any party, except where parties have voluntarily entered into an agreement requiring compliance with FEMA guidance. FEMA's discussion of any brand, trademark, or registered mark is not an endorsement.


Cover Memo

Message to National Flood Insurance Program Agents and Insurers

Change Record

1. Reference ..... 1-1
   - I. **NFIP History** ..... **1-1**
   - II. **Flood Insurance Placement and Technical Assistance** ..... **1-2**
     - A. Placing Flood Business through the NFIP ..... 1-2
     - B. Technical Assistance ..... 1-3
   - III. **NFIP Topics and Contact Information** ..... **1-3**
   - IV. **NFIP Regional Support Offices** ..... **1-4**

2. Before You Start ..... 2-1
   - I. **Policy Forms** ..... **2-1**
   - II. **Eligibility of Property Locations, Buildings, and Contents** ..... **2-2**
     - A. Eligibility of Property Locations ..... 2-2
       1. Where the NFIP Offers Insurance ..... 2-2
       2. Where the NFIP Does Not Offer Insurance ..... 2-3
     - B. Building Eligibility ..... 2-4
       1. Eligible Types of Buildings ..... 2-4
       2. Ineligible Types of Buildings ..... 2-7
     - C. Contents Eligibility ..... 2-8
       1. Eligible Contents ..... 2-8
       2. Ineligible Contents ..... 2-9
     - D. NFIP Coverage Exclusions and Limitations ..... 2-9
   - III. **Coverage D – Increased Cost of Compliance (ICC) Coverage** ..... **2-10**
   - IV. **Insurance Products** ..... **2-10**
   - V. **Effective Dates for New Policies** ..... **2-11**
     - A. Waiting Periods ..... 2-11
       1. Standard 30-day Waiting Period ..... 2-11
       2. Map Revision Exception (1-Day Waiting Period) ..... 2-12
       3. Loan Exception (No Waiting Period) ..... 2-13
       4. Post-Wildfire Exception ..... 2-14
          - a. Application of the Post-Wildfire Exception, 2-14

## 2. Before You Start *continued*

- **VI. Delivery of the Policy** .......... **2-14**
- **VII. Evidence of Insurance** .......... **2-14**
- **VIII. Duplicate Policies** .......... **2-14**
- **IX. Assignment** .......... **2-15**
- **X. Transfer of Business** .......... **2-15**
- **XI. Reforming the Policy** .......... **2-15**
  - A. Increasing Coverage after Reforming a Policy .......... 2-16
  - B. Exceptions for Incorrect Flood Zone or BFE after a Loss .......... 2-16
  - C. Incorrect Policy Form .......... 2-17

## 3. How to Write .......... 3-1

- **I. Rating** .......... **3-1**
  - A. General Information .......... 3-1
    1. Writing a Flood Insurance Policy .......... 3-1
    2. Amount of Insurance Available .......... 3-2
    3. Application Forms .......... 3-3
  - B. Preliminary Rating Information .......... 3-4
    1. Determine the Property Location .......... 3-4
       - a. Street Address, 3-4
       - b. Legal Description, 3-4
       - c. Geographic Location, 3-4
    2. Determine the Flood Zone .......... 3-4
       - a. General Information, 3-4
       - b. Special Considerations, 3-5
    3. Determine Pre- or Post-FIRM Construction .......... 3-5
       - a. Post-FIRM Construction, 3-5
       - b. Pre-FIRM Construction, 3-5
       - c. Date of Construction for Manufactured Homes/Travel Trailers, 3-5
    4. Substantial Improvement .......... 3-6
       - a. Post-FIRM 3-6
       - b. Pre-FIRM 3-6
    5. Determine the Most Beneficial Premium/Coverage .......... 3-6
       - a. Eligibility for Grandfathered Rating, 3-7
       - b. Disqualification for Pre-FIRM Subsidized or Newly Mapped Rating, 3-8
    6. Determine Building Occupancy .......... 3-10
    7. Determine Single Building Eligibility .......... 3-11
    8. Primary Residence .......... 3-12
       - a. General Information, 3-12
       - b. Documentation of Primary Residence, 3-13
       - c. Primary Residence and Trusts, 3-13
  - C. Determine if Elevated or Non-Elevated Building .......... 3-13
    1. Non-Elevated versus Elevated Buildings .......... 3-13
       - a. Non-Elevated Building, 3-13
       - b. Elevated Building, 3-14
    2. Enclosures .......... 3-14
       - a. Enclosure Wall Types, 3-15
       - b. Finished or Unfinished Enclosure, 3-15

## 3. How to Write *continued*


c. Proper Flood Openings Requirement, 3-15
d. Engineered Openings Certified by a Design Professional, 3-16
e. Engineered Openings Certified by the International Code Council Evaluation Service, 3-16

3. Building Partially or Entirely Over Water ........ 3-17
a. Buildings Entirely Over Water, 3-17
b. Buildings Partially Over Water, 3-17
c. Boathouses Located Partially Over Water, 3-17

D. Determine Type of Rating ........ 3-17
1. Rating without an EC ........ 3-17
a. Non-Elevated Building without an EC, 3-18
b. Elevated Building without an EC, 3-18
2. EC Rating ........ 3-19
a. Non-Elevated Building Rated with EC, 3-19
b. Elevated Building Rated with EC, 3-20
c. Hanging Floors and Mid-level Entries (A Zones and V Zones), 3-23

E. Determine Elevation Difference ........ 3-24
1. Guidelines for Elevation Datum Conversion ........ 3-24
2. Elevation Truncation Rule ........ 3-25
3. Elevation Difference Rounding Rule ........ 3-25
4. Elevation Difference Calculation by Flood Zone ........ 3-25
a. Zones A1–A30, AE, AH, AR, AR Dual Zones, A (with BFE), V1–V30, VE, and V, 3-25
b. Zone AO, 3-25
c. Zone A (No estimated BFE), 3-26
d. Zone A (Estimated BFE) 3-26
5. FIRMs with Wave Heights ........ 3-26
a. Wave Height Adjustment Procedure, 3-26
b. Wave Height Adjustment Examples, 3-27
6. Buildings Eligible for Floodproofing Premium Discount ........ 3-27

F. Contents Location ........ 3-28
1. Single-Family Dwellings ........ 3-28
2. Multi-Family and Non-Residential Buildings ........ 3-28

G. Calculate the Premium ........ 3-31
1. Replacement Cost Ratio for V-zone Rating ........ 3-31
2. Standard-Rated Policy ........ 3-31

H. Tenant's Coverage ........ 3-32
1. Contents Coverage ........ 3-32
2. Building Coverage ........ 3-32

I. Special Rating Situations ........ 3-33
1. Alternative Rates ........ 3-33
2. Special Rates ........ 3-33
3. Tentative Rates ........ 3-34

II. **Preferred Risk Policy ........ 3-34**

A. General Information ........ 3-34
1. Maximum Coverage Limits ........ 3-34
2. Deductibles ........ 3-34
3. Incomplete PRP Applications ........ 3-35

## 3. How to Write *continued*


B. Determining Eligibility ..... 3-35
1. Flood Zone ..... 3-35
2. Loss History ..... 3-35
C. Types of Buildings Ineligible for the PRP ..... 3-36
D. Renewal ..... 3-36
E. Policy Conversions ..... 3-37
1. Standard-Rated Policy to PRP Due to Misrating ..... 3-37
2. Standard-Rated Policy to PRP due to a Map Revision, LOMA, or LOMR ..... 3-37
3. PRP to Standard-Rated Policy ..... 3-37
a. Underwriting Information, 3-37
b. Premium Due, 3-38
F. Coverage Limitations ..... 3-38
G. Condominium PRP Eligibility ..... 3-38
1. Residential Single-Unit Building or Townhouse/Rowhouse Type Building with a Separate Entrance for Each Unit ..... 3-38
H. PRP Premium Calculation ..... 3-40

**III. Newly Mapped ..... 3-40**
A. General Information ..... 3-40
1. Maximum Coverage Limits ..... 3-40
2. Deductibles ..... 3-41
3. Incomplete Newly Mapped Rated Policy Applications ..... 3-41
B. Determining Eligibility ..... 3-41
1. Flood Zone ..... 3-41
2. Loss History ..... 3-42
3. FIRM Revision Date versus Policy Effective Date ..... 3-42
C. Ineligibility ..... 3-42
D. Renewal ..... 3-43
1. Renewal Payment ..... 3-44
2. Transition to Full-Risk Rates ..... 3-44
E. Policy Conversions ..... 3-44
1. Standard-Rated Policy to Newly Mapped Due to Misrating ..... 3-44
2. Newly Mapped-Rated Policy to a Standard-Rated Policy ..... 3-45
a. Underwriting Information ..... 3-45
b. Premium Due ..... 3-45
F. Coverage Limitations ..... 3-45
G. Condominium Newly Mapped Rating Eligibility ..... 3-46
1. Residential Single Unit Building or Townhouse/Rowhouse Type Building – Separate Entrance for Each Unit ..... 3-46
2. Multi-Unit Residential Building – 2 to 4 Units per Building ..... 3-46
3. Multi-Unit Residential Building – 5 or More Units per Building ..... 3-46
4. Non-Residential Business, Other Non-Residential Building ..... 3-47
H. Newly Mapped Rated Premium Calculation ..... 3-47

**IV. Condominiums ..... 3-48**
A. Insuring Condominiums ..... 3-48
B. Residential Condominium – Association Coverage ..... 3-48

## 3. How to Write *continued*


C. Residential Condominium – Unit Owners Coverage ........ 3-51

D. Non-Residential Condominium – Association Coverage ........ 3-52

E. Non-Residential Condominium – Unit Owners Coverage ........ 3-52

F. General Concepts ........ 3-53

1. High-Rise versus Low-Rise Condominiums ........ 3-53
2. Basic Limits of Insurance for RCBAP ........ 3-54
3. Condominium Eligibility for Pre-FIRM Subsidized or Newly Mapped Rating ........ 3-54
4. Condominium Pre-FIRM Rate Table Hierarchy ........ 3-55
5. RCBAP Federal Policy Fee Table ........ 3-55
6. RCBAP Premium Calculation ........ 3-55
7. Duplicate Policies ........ 3-56
8. Tentative Rates and Scheduled Buildings ........ 3-56
9. Assessments ........ 3-56
10. Condominium Rating Tables ........ 3-57
    a. Low-Rise Residential Condominiums, 3-58
    b. High-Rise Residential Condominiums, 3-59

G. Sample Replacement Cost Value Letter ........ 3-61

**V. Submit-for-Rate ........ 3-62**

A. Documentation ........ 3-62

B. Additional Guidance ........ 3-63

C. Effective Date ........ 3-63

**VI. Provisional Rating ........ 3-63**

A. General Information ........ 3-63

B. Eligibility Requirements ........ 3-63

C. Reformation ........ 3-64

1. Receipt of Required Elements Within 60 Days of the Policy Effective Date ........ 3-64
2. Receipt of Required Elements More Than 60 Days from the Policy Effective Date ........ 3-64
3. Reformation after Receipt of Required Elements ........ 3-64

D. Endorsements ........ 3-64

E. Notification ........ 3-65

F. Provisional Rating Documents ........ 3-65

1. National Flood Insurance Program Provisional Rating Questionnaire ........ 3-65
2. Provisional Rating Example ........ 3-65
3. Sample Notification ........ 3-65

**VII. Certifications ........ 3-67**

A. General Information ........ 3-67

B. EC ........ 3-67

1. The NFIP Requires ECs For SFHAs ........ 3-67
2. Optional Full-Risk Rating ........ 3-67

C. Completing an EC ........ 3-67

1. Required Certification ........ 3-67
2. Photographs ........ 3-68
3. Other Elevation Information ........ 3-68

## 3. How to Write *continued*


D. Troubleshooting ........ 3-69
E. Floodproofing ........ 3-69
1. Eligibility for a Premium Discount ........ 3-69
2. Requirements for a Premium Discount ........ 3-70
3. Residential Buildings with Basements ........ 3-70
4. Non-Residential Buildings ........ 3-70

**VIII. Mortgage Portfolio Protection Program Policy ........ 3-71**
A. Background ........ 3-71
B. General Information ........ 3-71
1. Eligibility ........ 3-71
2. Policy Form ........ 3-71
3. Underwriting Application ........ 3-71
C. Required Notifications ........ 3-72
1. Notification to Lenders ........ 3-72
2. Notification to Borrowers ........ 3-72
D. Policy Term and Coverage ........ 3-73
1. Waiting Period ........ 3-73
2. Policy Term ........ 3-73
3. Coverage ........ 3-73
4. Deductible ........ 3-74
5. Duplicate Coverage ........ 3-74
6. Coverage Basis ........ 3-74
7. Dual Interest ........ 3-74
E. Premium and Fees ........ 3-74
1. Rates ........ 3-74
F. Policy Administration ........ 3-75
1. Policy Reformation ........ 3-75
2. Renewal ........ 3-75
3. Cancellation ........ 3-75
4. Endorsement ........ 3-76
G. MPPP WYO Insurers ........ 3-76
1. MPPP Expense Allowance ........ 3-76
2. Use of WYO Allowance ........ 3-76

**IX. Rating Examples ........ 3-76**
Table of Contents for Examples ........ 3-76

## 4. How to Endorse ........ 4-1

**I. General Information ........ 4-1**
**II. Endorsement Process ........ 4-1**
**III. Changing the Amount of Coverage ........ 4-1**
A. Adding or Increasing Coverage ........ 4-1
1. Waiting Periods ........ 4-1
a. 30-Day Waiting Period, 4-2
b. 1-Day Waiting Period, 4-2
c. No Waiting Period, 4-3

## 4. How to Endorse *continued*


B. Reducing Coverage .......... 4-4
1. Reduction in Building Coverage .......... 4-4
2. Reduction in Contents Coverage .......... 4-4
C. Removing Coverage .......... 4-4

IV. **Rating Endorsements .......... 4-5**
A. Rate Decreases .......... 4-5
B. Rating Adjustment .......... 4-5
C. Revision of an Alternative Rating .......... 4-5
D. Map Revision .......... 4-6
E. Change in Program Status .......... 4-6
F. Change in Community Rating System (CRS) Status .......... 4-7

V. **Correcting a Misrated Policy .......... 4-7**
VI. **Changing Deductibles .......... 4-7**
A. Deductible Increases .......... 4-8
B. Deductible Decreases .......... 4-8

VII. **Duplicate Coverage .......... 4-8**
VIII. **Property Address Corrections .......... 4-8**
IX. **Assignment of Policy .......... 4-9**
A. Assignment with Building Purchase .......... 4-9
B. Assignment without Building Purchase .......... 4-9

X. **Endorsement Processing Prior to Renewal .......... 4-9**
A. During the Last 90 Days of Policy Term .......... 4-9
B. During the Last 75 Days of Policy Term .......... 4-9
C. Return Premium Generated from Endorsement Processing .......... 4-10

XI. **Completing the General Change Endorsement Form .......... 4-10**
XII. **Return Premium Processing Procedures .......... 4-10**
A. Insurer Processing .......... 4-10
B. Prior Term Refund Processing .......... 4-11

XIII. **Endorsement Rating Examples .......... 4-11**
Table of Contents for Examples .......... 4-11

## 5. How to Renew .......... 5-1

I. **General Information .......... 5-1**
II. **Renewal Process .......... 5-1**
A. Renewal Notice .......... 5-1
1. Amounts of Insurance on the Renewal Notice .......... 5-1
B. Final Notice .......... 5-2
C. Renewal Notification Requirements .......... 5-2
D. Premium Payment .......... 5-2
1. Check .......... 5-3
2. Credit Cards .......... 5-3

## 5. How to Renew *continued*

3. Electronic Transfers ........ 5-3
4. Certified Mail ........ 5-3

E. Premium Receipt ........ 5-3
1. Underpayment of Renewal Premium ........ 5-3

F. Determine the Renewal Effective Date ........ 5-4
G. Renewal by an Application or Recertification Questionnaire ........ 5-4
H. Nonrenewal and Cancellation ........ 5-5
I. Newly Mapped ........ 5-5
J. Coverage Endorsements during the Renewal Cycle ........ 5-6
K. Transfer of Business at Renewal ........ 5-6

**III. Sample Documents ........ 5-8**
A. Renewal Notice ........ 5-8
B. Final Notice ........ 5-11

## 6. How to Cancel ........ 6-1

**I. General Information ........ 6-1**
**II. Cancellation/Nullification ........ 6-1**
A. Processing a Cancellation or Nullification Request ........ 6-1
1. Signatures ........ 6-1
a. Insured's Signature, 6-1
b. Agent Signature, 6-1
2. Receipt Date ........ 6-2

**III. Premium Refunds ........ 6-2**
**IV. Valid Cancellation Reason Codes/Nullification of NFIP Policies ........ 6-2**
**V. Processing Outcomes for Cancellation/Nullification of a Flood Insurance Policy ........ 6-19**
**VI. Sample Verification Letter ........ 6-20**

## Appendix A: Policy ........ A-1

**Dwelling Form ........ A-3**
**General Property Form ........ A-31**
**Residential Condominium Building Association Policy Form ........ A-55**

## Appendix B: Forms ........ B-1

**I. NFIP Flood Insurance Application ........ B-1**
**II. NFIP Preferred Risk Policy and Newly Mapped Application ........ B-4**
**III. NFIP Flood Insurance General Change Endorsement ........ B-7**
**IV. NFIP Flood Insurance Cancellation/Nullification Request Form ........ B-10**
**V. NFIP Residential Basement Floodproofing Certificate ........ B-12**
**VI. NFIP Floodproofing Certificate for Non-Residential Structures ........ B-16**
**VII. NFIP Elevation Certificate and Instructions ........ B-20**

## Appendix C: Lowest Floor Guide ........ C-1

**Lowest Floor Guide for Zones AO and A (without Estimated BFE) ........ C-1**

## Appendix C: Lowest Floor Guide *continued*

**Lowest Floor Guide for Zones A, AE, A1–A30, AH, AR, AR Dual** .......... C-2

**Lowest Floor Guide for Zones V, VE, V1–V30** .......... C-4

I. **Specific Building Drawings** .......... C-7

Elevated Buildings for Pre- and Post-FIRM Risks in Flood Zones B, C, X, A99, and D (Drawings 1–4) .......... C-8

Non-Elevated Buildings for Pre- and Post-FIRM Risks in Flood Zones B, C, X, A99, and D (Drawings 5 to 8) .......... C-12

Elevated Buildings for Pre- and Post-FIRM Risks in Flood Zones A, AO, and AH (Drawings 9 to 15) .......... C-16

Non-Elevated Buildings for Pre- and Post-FIRM Risks in Flood Zones A, AO, and AH (Drawings 16 to 20) .......... C-23

Non-Elevated Buildings for Pre- and Post-FIRM Risks in Flood Zones AE and A1–A30 (Drawings 21 to 29) .......... C-28

Elevated Buildings for Pre- and Post-FIRM Risks in Flood Zones AE and A1–A30 (Drawings 30 to 44) .......... C-37

Non-Elevated Buildings for Pre- and Post-FIRM Risks with Construction Dates of 1975 to September 30, 1981, in Flood Zones VE and V1–V30 (Drawings 45 to 50) .......... C-52

Elevated Buildings for Pre- and Post-FIRM Risks with Construction Dates of 1975 to September 30, 1981, in Flood Zones VE and V1–V30 (Drawings 51 to 63) .......... C-58

Elevated Buildings for Post-FIRM Risks in Flood Zone VE and V1–V30, Construction Date October 1, 1981, and After (Drawings 64 to 75) .......... C-71

Non-Elevated Buildings for Post-FIRM Risks in Flood Zones VE and V1–V30, Construction Date October 1, 1981, and After (Drawing 76) .......... C-83

## Appendix D: Coastal Barrier Resources System .......... D-1

I. **General Information** .......... D-1

II. **Determining Eligibility** .......... D-1

A. Determine if Community has a System Unit or OPA .......... D-1

B. Determine if the Property is Located in a System Unit or OPA .......... D-2

1. Unable to Determine Building Location .......... D-2
2. Building Located in the CBRS Buffer Zone .......... D-2

C. Determine Building Eligibility .......... D-3

D. Proof of Eligibility .......... D-3

1. Buildings Not Located in System Unit or OPA .......... D-3
2. Buildings Located in a System Unit or OPA .......... D-4
3. Buildings Eligible Because of Conforming Use .......... D-5

## Appendix E: Claims .......... E-1

I. **Information for Insureds after a Flood** .......... E-1

II. **Claim Process** .......... E-1

A. Damage Estimate .......... E-1

B. Claim Payment .......... E-2

III. **Disputed Claims** .......... E-2

A. Work with the Adjuster .......... E-2

B. Contact the Adjusting Firm .......... E-2

## Appendix E: Claims *continued*

C. Work with the Insurer ........ E-2
D. File a Proof of Loss with the Insurer ........ E-2
IV. **Appealing a Claim** ........ **E-3**
A. Filing an Appeal ........ E-3
B. Appeal Process ........ E-4
V. **Litigation** ........ **E-4**
VI. **Increased Cost of Compliance (ICC) Claims** ........ **E-5**

## Appendix F: Community Rating System ........ F-1

I. **General Information** ........ **F-1**
II. **Community Eligibility** ........ **F-1**
III. **CRS Premium Discount Eligibility** ........ **F-1**
A. Premium Discount Eligibility by Policy Rating Category ........ F-1
B. Ineligible for CRS Premium Discounts ........ F-2
IV. **CRS Classes and Discounts** ........ **F-2**
V. **Elevation Certificates and Map Information for Agents** ........ **F-3**
VI. **CRS Eligible Communities** ........ **F-3**

## Appendix G: Leased Federal Properties ........ G-1

I. **General Information** ........ **G-1**
II. **Requirements** ........ **G-1**
III. **Correcting an LFP Designation** ........ **G-2**
IV. **Settling a Claim** ........ **G-2**
V. **Sample Letters** ........ **G-3**
A. Sample Insured Notification Letter ........ G-3
B. Sample Agent Notification Letter ........ G-4
C. Sample Lender Notification Letter ........ G-5

## Appendix H: Flood Maps ........ H-1

I. **Flood Map Service Center** ........ **H-1**
II. **Flood Hazard Maps** ........ **H-1**
A. Map Information ........ H-1
B. Communities with Unpublished Maps ........ H-2
C. Unmapped Areas in Communities with Maps ........ H-2
III. **Map Zones** ........ **H-2**
A. SFHAs ........ H-2
1. Zone A ........ H-2
2. Zones A1–A30 ........ H-2
3. Zone AE ........ H-2
4. Zone AH ........ H-3
5. Zone AO ........ H-3
6. Zone A99 ........ H-3
7. Zone AR ........ H-3
8. Zones AR/AE, AR/AH, AR/AO, AR/A1–A30, AR/A ........ H-3

Appendix H: Flood Maps *continued*

9. Zone V .......... H-3
10. Zones V1–V30 .......... H-3
11. Zone VE .......... H-4

B. Moderate or Minimal Hazard Areas .......... H-4
1. Zones B, C, and X .......... H-4
2. Zone D .......... H-4

IV. **Locating Property on a Map** .......... **H-4**

V. **Changing or Correcting a Flood Map** .......... **H-4**

A. Letter of Map Amendment (LOMA) .......... H-4
1. Compare the location of the property to the SFHA .......... H-5
2. Compare the elevation of the property to the 1-percent-annual-chance flood elevation .......... H-5

B. Letter of Map Revision (LOMR) .......... H-5

C. Physical Map Revision .......... H-5

Appendix I: Severe Repetitive Loss Properties .......... I-1

I. **General Information** .......... **I-1**

II. **New Business** .......... **I-1**

III. **Notification Requirements** .......... **I-1**

IV. **Underwriting Requirements** .......... **I-2**

V. **Process for Correcting or Updating a Property's SRL Status** .......... **I-2**

A. Required Documentation .......... I-2

B. SDF Process After FEMA Determination .......... I-3

VI. **Flood Mitigation Assistance (FMA) Program** .......... **I-4**

VII. **Sample Letters** .......... **I-5**

A. Agent Notification Letter .......... I-5

B. Lender Notification Letter .......... I-7

C. Insured Notification Letter .......... I-9

Appendix J: Rate Tables .......... J-1

I. **Effective Date of Rates** .......... **J-1**

II. **Rates for Standard NFIP Policies** .......... **J-1**

III. **Preferred Risk Policy (PRP) Rates** .......... **J-22**

IV. **Newly Mapped Procedure Rates** .......... **J-28**

V. **Mortgage Portfolio Protection Program (MPPP) Rates** .......... **J-36**

VI. **Residential Condominium Building Association Policy (RCBAP) Rates** .......... **J-37**

Appendix K: Residential Basement Floodproofing Premium Discount .......... K-1

I. **Approved Communities for Residential Basement Floodproofing Premium Discount** .......... **K-1**

Appendix L: Definitions and Acronyms .......... L-1

I. **Definitions** .......... **L-1**

II. **Acronyms** .......... **L-11**

# Tables


1. Reference Tables ........ 1-2

Table 1. Major NFIP Reform Legislation ........ 1-2

Table 2. NFIP Topics and Contact Information ........ 1-3

Table 3. NFIP Bureau and Statistical Agent Regional Offices ........ 1-4

2. Before You Start Tables ........ 2-1

Table 1. Standard Flood Insurance Policy Forms ........ 2-1

Table 2. Where the NFIP Offers Insurance ........ 2-2

Table 3. Where the NFIP Does Not Offer Insurance ........ 2-3

Table 4. Buildings the NFIP Insures ........ 2-4

Table 5. Buildings the NFIP Does Not Insure ........ 2-7

Table 6. NFIP Coverage Exclusions and Limitations ........ 2-9

Table 7. NFIP Insurance Products Available ........ 2-10

Table 8. Effective Date of a New Policy with a 30-Day Waiting Period ........ 2-12

Table 9. Effective Date of a New Policy with a 1-Day Waiting Period ........ 2-13

Table 10. Effective Date of a New Policy with No Waiting Period ........ 2-13

Table 11. Reformation ........ 2-16

3. How to Write Tables ........ 3-1

Table 1. Rating a Flood Insurance Policy ........ 3-1

Table 2. Maximum Amount of Insurance Available for the Emergency and Regular Programs ........ 3-3

Table 3. Date of Construction – Manufactured Home/Travel Trailer ........ 3-5

Table 4. Types of Rating ........ 3-6

Table 5. Buildings Eligible for Grandfathered Rating ........ 3-8

Table 5A. Documentation to Verify Grandfathering Eligibility ........ 3-8

Table 6. Pre-FIRM Subsidized Rates Ineligibility Determination ........ 3-9

Table 7. Building Occupancy Types ........ 3-10

Table 8. Elevated Buildings – Elevating Foundation Types ........ 3-14

Table 9. Rating Classes for Non-Elevated Buildings without an EC ........ 3-18

Table 10. Rating Classes for Elevated Buildings without an EC ........ 3-18

Table 11. Considerations when Rating Non-Elevated Buildings with an EC ........ 3-20

Table 12. Elevated Buildings in A Zones Rated with an EC ........ 3-20

Table 13. Elevated Buildings in V Zones Rated with an EC ........ 3-22

Table 14. FIRMs with Wave Height Conversion ........ 3-26

Table 15. Examples of Wave Height Adjustment Calculations ........ 3-27

Table 16. Calculating Floodproofing Premium Discount Eligibility ........ 3-27

Table 17. Contents Location in Non-Elevated Buildings ........ 3-29

Table 18. Contents Location in Elevated Buildings ........ 3-30

Table 19. Calculate Premium for a Standard-Rated Policy ........ 3-31

Table 20. Maximum Coverage Limits by Occupancy Type ........ 3-34

### 3. How to Write Tables *continued*


Table 21. Conditions for Ineligibility for the PRP ....3-36
Table 22. Single Family Residential Building ....3-38
Table 23. Multi-Unit Residential Building – 2 to 4 Units per Building ....3-38
Table 24. Multi-Unit Residential Building – 5 or More Units per Building ....3-39
Table 25. Non-Residential Business, Other Non-Residential Building ....3-39
Table 26. Calculate Premium for a PRP ....3-40
Table 27. Maximum Coverage Limits by Occupancy Type ....3-40
Table 28. Loss History Ineligibility for the Newly Mapped Procedure ....3-42
Table 29. Renewal Payment Requirements ....3-44
Table 30. Single-Family Unit Residential Building ....3-46
Table 31. Multi-Unit Residential Building – 2 to 4 Units per Building ....3-46
Table 32. Multi-Unit Residential Building – 5 or More Units per Building ....3-46
Table 33. Non-Residential Business, Other Non-Residential Building ....3-47
Table 34. Calculate Premium for a Newly Mapped Rated Policy ....3-47
Table 35. Residential Condominium Association Coverage Under the RCBAP ....3-49
Table 36. Residential Condominium Unit Owners Coverage Under the Dwelling Form ....3-51
Table 37. Non-Residential Condominium Association Coverage ....3-52
Table 38. Non-Residential Condominium Unit Owners Coverage ....3-53
Table 39. Basic Limits of Insurance for RCBAP ....3-54
Table 40. Pre-FIRM Subsidized Rates Ineligibility Determination ....3-55
Table 41. Pre-FIRM Rate Table Hierarchy ....3-55
Table 42. RCBAP Federal Policy Fee Table ....3-55
Table 43. Calculate Premium for an RCBAP ....3-56
Table 44. Assessment Coverage After a Loss ....3-57
Table 45. Single-Unit Building or Townhouse/Rowhouse Type – Building with Separate Entrance for Each Unit ....3-58
Table 46. Multi-Unit Building – 2–4 Units per Building – Regardless of Number of Floors (Non-Townhouse) ....3-58
Table 47. Multi-Unit Building – 5 or More Units Per Building, Fewer Than 3 Floors ....3-59
Table 48. Multi-Unit Building – 5 or More Units Per Building, 3 or More Floors ....3-59
Table 49. Non-Residential Condominiums ....3-60
Table 50. Calculate Premium for an MPPP Policy ....3-75


### 4. How to Endorse Tables ....4-2


Table 1. Endorsement Effective Date with a 30-day Waiting Period ....4-2
Table 2. Endorsement Effective Date with a 1-day Waiting Period ....4-3
Table 3. Endorsement Effective Date with No Waiting Period ....4-4
Table 4. Endorsement Effective Dates for Current Term Rating Adjustments ....4-5
Table 5. Endorsement Effective Dates for Map Revisions ....4-6


### 5. How to Renew Tables ....5-2


Table 1. Renewal Notification Requirements ....5-2

## 5. How to Renew Tables *continued*


Table 2. Determine the Renewal Effective Date ....5-4

Table 3. Renewal Payments ....5-5

## 6. How to Cancel Tables ....6-3

Table 1. Valid Cancellation Reason Code 01 ....6-3

Table 2. Valid Cancellation Reason Code 02 ....6-3

Table 3. Valid Cancellation Reason Code 03 ....6-4

Table 4. Valid Cancellation Reason Code 04 ....6-5

Table 5. Valid Cancellation Reason Code 05 ....6-6

Table 6. Valid Cancellation Reason Code 06 ....6-7

Table 7. Valid Cancellation Reason Code 07 ....6-8

Table 8. Valid Cancellation Reason Code 08 ....6-8

Table 9. Valid Cancellation Reason Code 09 ....6-9

Table 10. Valid Cancellation Reason Code 10 ....6-10

Table 11. Valid Cancellation Reason Code 12 ....6-11

Table 12. Valid Cancellation Reason Code 13 ....6-12

Table 13. Valid Cancellation Reason Code 15 ....6-12

Table 14. Valid Cancellation Reason Code 18 ....6-13

Table 15. Valid Cancellation Reason Code 19 ....6-14

Table 16. Valid Cancellation Reason Code 20 ....6-15

Table 17. Valid Cancellation Reason Code 21 ....6-15

Table 18. Valid Cancellation Reason Code 22 ....6-16

Table 19. Valid Cancellation Reason Code 23 ....6-17

Table 20. Valid Cancellation Reason Code 24 ....6-17

Table 21. Valid Cancellation Reason Code 25 ....6-18

Table 22. Valid Cancellation Reason Code 26 ....6-18

## Appendix F Tables ....F-1

Table 1. CRS Premium Discount Eligibility by Policy Rating Category....F-1

Table 2. CRS Premium Discounts by Class and Flood Zone ....F-3

## Appendix G Tables ....G-1

Table 1. Requirements for LFP Properties ....G-1

## Appendix J Tables ....J-1

Rate Table 1. Emergency Program Rates.... J-1

Rate Table 2A. Regular Program – Pre-FIRM Construction Rates .... J-2

Rate Table 2B. Regular Program – Pre-FIRM Construction Rates Non-Primary Residence .... J-3

Rate Table 2C. Regular Program – Pre-FIRM Construction Rates Severe Repetitive Loss Properties.... J-4

Rate Table 2D. Regular Program – Pre-FIRM Construction Rates Substantial Improvement On or After April 1, 2015 .... J-5

## Appendix J Tables *continued*

Rate Table 3A. Regular Program – Post-FIRM Construction Rates: FIRM Zones A99, B, C, X; FIRM Zone D; and FIRM Zones AO, AH .................................... J-6

Rate Table 3B. Regular Program – Post-FIRM Construction Rates: FIRM Zones AE, A1–A30 — Building Rates.......................................................................... J-7

Rate Table 3B. Regular Program – Post-FIRM Construction Rates: FIRM Zones AE, A1–A30 — Contents Rates........................................................................ J-8

Rate Table 3C. Regular Program – Post-FIRM Construction Rates: Unnumbered Zone A — Without Basement/Enclosure/Crawlspace/Subgrade Crawlspace ..................... J-9

Rate Table 3D. Regular Program – Post-FIRM Construction Rates: FIRM Zones '75–'81, V1–V30, VE.......................................................................... J-10

Rate Table 3E. Regular Program – Post-FIRM Construction Rates: 1981 Post-FIRM V1–V30, VE Zone Rates – Elevated Buildings Free of Obstruction .................................... J-11

Rate Table 3F. Regular Program – Post-FIRM Construction Rates: 1981 Post-FIRM V1–V30, VE Zone Rates – Elevated Buildings With Obstruction........................................ J-12

Rate Table 4. Regular Program – FIRM Zone AR and AR Dual Zones Not Elevation-Rated Rates .......................................................................... J-13

Rate Table 5. Regular Program – Pre-FIRM and Post-FIRM Elevation-Related Rates ............ J-14

Rate Table 6. Tentative Rates .......................................................................... J-15

Rate Table 7A. Federal Policy Fee and Probation Surcharge............................................. J-16

Rate Table 7B. Reserve Fund Assessment.......................................................................... J-16

Rate Table 7C. HFIAA Surcharge.......................................................................... J-16

Rate Table 7D. Severe Repetitive Loss Premium.......................................................................... J-16

Rate Table 8A. Minimum Deductibles .......................................................................... J-17

Rate Table 8B. Deductible Factors .......................................................................... J-18

Rate Table 9. Standard Flood Insurance Policy Increased Cost of Compliance (ICC) Coverage.......................................................................... J-19

Rate Table 10. Pre-FIRM Subsidized Rates Ineligibility Determination............................... J-20

Rate Table 11. Pre-FIRM Rate Table Hierarchy.......................................................................... J-20

National Flood Insurance Program Provisional Rating Questionnaire ................................ J-21

PRP Table 3A. Effective January 1, 2020, PRP Coverage Limits and Base Premiums for Properties Currently Mapped in B, C, X, AR, or A99 Zones: 1–4 Family Residential ............ J-22

PRP Table 3A. Effective January 1, 2021, PRP Coverage Limits and Base Premiums for Properties Currently Mapped in B, C, X, AR, or A99 Zones: 1–4 Family Residential ........... J-23

PRP Table 3B. Effective January 1, 2020, PRP Coverage Limits and Base Premiums for Properties Currently Mapped in B, C, X, AR, or A99 Zones: Other Residential.................... J-24

PRP Table 3B. Effective January 1, 2021, PRP Coverage Limits and Base Premiums for Properties Currently Mapped in B, C, X, AR, or A99 Zones: Other Residential.................... J-25

PRP Table 3C. Effective January 1, 2020, PRP Coverage Limits and Base Premiums for Properties Currently Mapped in B, C, X, AR, or A99 Zones: Non-Residential Business or Other Non-Residential .......................................................................... J-26

PRP Table 3C. Effective January 1, 2021, PRP Coverage Limits and Base Premiums for Properties Currently Mapped in B, C, X, AR, or A99 Zones: Non-Residential Business or Other Non-Residential .......................................................................... J-27

## Appendix J Tables *continued*


Newly Mapped Table 3. Effective January 1, 2020, Coverage Limits and Base Premiums for Properties Newly Mapped into an SFHA On or After October 1, 2008: 1–4 Family Residential ........ J-28

Newly Mapped Table 3. Effective January 1, 2021, Coverage Limits and Base Premiums for Properties Newly Mapped into an SFHA On or After October 1, 2008: 1–4 Family Residential ........ J-29

Newly Mapped Table 4. Effective January 1, 2020, Coverage Limits and Base Premiums for Properties Newly Mapped into an SFHA On or After October 1, 2008: Other Residential ........ J-30

Newly Mapped Table 4. Effective January 1, 2021, Coverage Limits and Base Premiums for Properties Newly Mapped into an SFHA On or After October 1, 2008: Other Residential ........ J-31

Newly Mapped Table 5. Effective January 1, 2020, Coverage Limits and Base Premiums for Properties Newly Mapped into an SFHA On or After October 1, 2008: Non-Residential Business or Other Non-Residential ........ J-32

Newly Mapped Table 5. Effective January 1, 2021, Coverage Limits and Base Premiums for Properties Newly Mapped into an SFHA On or After October 1, 2008: Non-Residential Business or Other Non-Residential ........ J-33

Newly Mapped Table 6A. Newly Mapped Multiplier for Policies Effective April 1, 2016 Through December 31, 2016 ........ J-34

Newly Mapped Table 6B. Newly Mapped Multiplier for Policies Effective January 1, 2017 Through December 31, 2017 ........ J-34

Newly Mapped Table 6C. Newly Mapped Multiplier for Policies Effective January 1, 2018 Through December 31, 2018 ........ J-34

Newly Mapped Table 6D. Newly Mapped Multiplier for Policies Effective January 1, 2019 Through December 31, 2019 ........ J-34

Newly Mapped Table 6E. Newly Mapped Multiplier for Policies Effective January 1, 2020 through December 31, 2020 ........ J-35

Newly Mapped Table 6F. Newly Mapped Multiplier for Policies Effective January 1, 2021 Through December 31, 2021 ........ J-35

MPPP Rate and Increased Cost of Compliance (ICC) ........ J-36

Condo Table 2B. Pre-FIRM Subsidized Rate Ineligibility Determination ........ J-37

Condo Table 2C. Condominium Pre-FIRM Rate Table Hierarchy ........ J-37

Condo Table 3A. RCBAP High-Rise Condominium Rates Building and Contents for Pre-FIRM, all zones; Post-FIRM Zones A99,B,C,X,D,A1–30 and AE ........ J-38

Condo Table 3B. RCBAP High-Rise Condominium Rates Pre-FIRM Substantial Improvement On or After April 1, 2015 ........ J-39

Condo Table 3C. RCBAP High-Rise Condominium Rates: AO, AH Post-FIRM; Post-FIRM Unnumbered A Zone ........ J-40

Condo Table 3D. RCBAP High-Rise Condominium Rates: AR and AR Dual Zones ........ J-41

Condo Table 3E. RCBAP High-Rise Condominium Rates: Regular Program – 1975–1981 Post-FIRM Construction FIRM Zones V1–V30, VE ........ J-42

Condo Table 4A. RCBAP Low-Rise Condominium Rates: Regular Program – Pre-FIRM Construction Rates and Regular Program – Post-FIRM Construction Rates ........ J-43

Condo Table 4B. RCBAP Low-Rise Condominium Rates 1–4 Family SRL Properties ........ J-44

## Appendix J Tables *continued*


Condo Table 4C. RCBAP Low-Rise Condominium Rates Pre-FIRM Substantial Improvement On or After April 1, 2015 ... J-45

Condo Table 4D. RCBAP Low-Rise Condominium Rates: Post-FIRM A1–A30, AE — Building and Contents ... J-46

Condo Table 4E. RCBAP Low-Rise Condominium Rates: Regular Program – Post-FIRM Construction Rates Unnumbered Zone A ... J-47

Condo Table 4F. RCBAP Low-Rise Condominium Rates: AR and AR Dual Zones ... J-48

Condo Table 4G. RCBAP Low-Rise Condominium Rates: Regular Program — 1975–1981 Post-FIRM Construction FIRM Zones V1–V30, VE ... J-49

Condo Table 5A. RCBAP High-Rise and Low-Rise Condominium Rates: 1981 Post-FIRM V1–V30, VE Zone Rates, Elevated Buildings Free of Obstruction ... J-50

Condo Table 5B. RCBAP High-Rise and Low-Rise Condominium Rates: 1981 Post-FIRM V1–V30, VE Zone Rates, Elevated Buildings With Obstruction ... J-51

Condo Table 6. RCBAP High-Rise and Low-Rise Condominium Rates: Increased Cost of Compliance (ICC) Coverage ... J-52

Condo Table 7. RCBAP Deductible Factors – All Zones ... J-53


# Figures


## 3. How to Write Figures ... 3-61

Sample Replacement Cost Value Letter ... 3-61

Sample Notice To Accompany Provisionally Rated Policies ... 3-66

## 5. How to Renew Figures ... 5-8

A. Renewal Notice, page 1 ... 5-8

Renewal Notice, page 2 ... 5-9

Renewal Notice, page 3 ... 5-10

B. Final Notice, page 1 ... 5-11

Final Notice, page 2 ... 5-12

Final Notice, page 3 ... 5-13

## 6. How to Cancel Figures ... 6-20

Sample Verification Letter ... 6-20

## Appendix A Figures ... A-3

Dwelling Form ... A-3

General Property Form ... A-31

Residential Condominium Building Association Policy Form ... A-55

## Appendix B Figures ... B-1

NFIP Flood Insurance Application ... B-1

NFIP Preferred Risk Policy and Newly Mapped Application ... B-4

### Appendix B Figures *continued*


NFIP Flood Insurance General Change Endorsement........B-7

NFIP Flood Insurance Cancellation/Nullification Request Form........B-10

NFIP Residential Basement Floodproofing Certificate........B-12

NFIP Floodproofing Certificate for Non-Residential Structures........B-16

NFIP Elevation Certificate and Instructions........B-20

**Appendix G Figures........G-3**

Sample Insured Notification Letter........G-3

Sample Agent Notification Letter........G-4

Sample Lender Notification Letter........G-5

**Appendix H Figures........H-6**

Example FIRM........H-6

**Appendix I Figures........I-4**

Agent Notification Letter........I-4

Lender Notification Letter........I-6

Insured Notification Letter........I-8


# Rating Examples


**3. How to Write Examples........3-76**

Provisional Rating Example 1: Regular Program, Post-FIRM Construction........3-78

Rate Example 1: Emergency Program, $1,500/$1,500 Deductible, Primary Residence........3-79

Rate Example 2: Regular Program, Pre-FIRM Construction, $1,250/$1,250 Deductible Option, Zone B, Primary Residence........3-80

Rate Example 3: Regular Program, Pre-FIRM Construction, $2,000/$2,000 Deductible Option, Zone AE, Primary Residence........3-81

Rate Example 4: Regular Program, Pre-FIRM Construction, $3,000/$2,000 Deductible Option, Zone A15, Non-Primary Residence........3-82

Rate Example 5: Regular Program, Pre-FIRM Construction, $2,000/$2,000 Deductible Option, Zone AE, Severe Repetitive Loss Property, Primary Residence........3-83

Rate Example 6: Regular Program, Pre-FIRM Construction, $2,000/$2,000 Deductible Option, Zone AE, Building Substantially Improved, Primary Residence........3-84

Rate Example 7: Regular Program, Pre-FIRM Construction Rated with Full-Risk Rates, $1,500/$1,500 Deductible, Zone AE, Primary Residence........3-85

Rate Example 8: Regular Program, Post-FIRM, Elevation Rated, $5,000/$5,000 Deductible Option, Zone AE, Non-Residential Business........3-86

Rate Example 9: Regular Program, 1975-'81 Post-FIRM V1–V30, $2,000/$2,000 Deductible Option, Elevation Rated, Zone V13, Non-Primary Residence........3-87

## 3. How to Write Examples *continued*

Rate Example 10: Regular Program, Post-1981 VE or V1–V30, $3,000/$3,000 Deductible Option, With Enclosure, Zone VE, Primary Residence ....................................3-88

Rate Example 11: Regular Program, Post-FIRM Construction, $1,000 Deductible Option, Contents-Only Policy, Zone A17, Primary Residence............................................3-89

Rate Example 12: Regular Program, Post-FIRM, Elevation Rated, $5,000/$5,000 Deductible Option, Zone AO (Without Certification of Compliance or Elevation Certificate), Other Non-Residential ................................................................................3-90

Rate Example 13: Regular Program, Post-FIRM, Elevation Rated, $1,250/$1,250 Deductible Option, Zone AO (With Certification of Compliance or Elevation Certificate), Primary Residence .......................................................................................3-91

Rate Example 14: Regular Program, Post-FIRM, Elevation Rated, $3,000/$2,000 Deductible Option, Zone AH (Without Certification of Compliance or Elevation Certificate), Primary Residence .......................................................................................3-92

Rate Example 15: Regular Program, Post-FIRM, Elevation Rated, $1,250/$1,250 Deductible Option, Zone AH (With Certification of Compliance or Elevation Certificate), 2–4 Family ..................................................................................3-93

Rate Example 16: Regular Program Post-Firm, Elevation Rated, $1,250/$1,250 Deductible Option, Zone A (With BFE), 2–4 Family.........................................................3-94

Rate Example 17: Regular Program, Post-FIRM, Elevation Rated, $1,250/$1,250 Deductible Option, Zone A (Without BFE), Primary Residence .........................................3-95

PRP Rating Example: Preferred Risk Policy, $1,250/$1,250 Deductible, Zone X, Primary Residence ...........................................................................................................3-96

Newly Mapped Rating Example: Zone X, Newly Mapped into SFHA on 11/16/2016, $1,250/$1,250 Deductible, Primary Residence .............................................................3-97

Condo Rating Example 1: Pre-FIRM, Low-Rise, With Enclosure, Coinsurance Penalty, Zone A.........................................................................................................3-98

Condo Rating Example 2: Pre-FIRM, Low-Ride, No Basement/Enclosure, Zone AE ............3-99

Condo Rating Example 3: Pre-FIRM, Low-Rise, No Basement/Enclosure, Zone AE, Building Substantially Improved.......................................................................3-100

Condo Rating Example 4: Post-FIRM, Low-Rise, Coinsurance Penalty, Zone AE ..................3-101

Condo Rating Example 5: Post-Firm, Low-Rise, Zone AE ..................................................3-102

Condo Rating Example 6: Pre-FIRM, High-Rise, Coinsurance Penalty, Zone A.....................3-103

Condo Rating Example 7: Pre-FIRM, High-Rise, Basement, Maximum Deductible Discount, Zone AE.........................................................................................................3-104

Condo Rating Example 8: Post-FIRM, High-Rise, Maximum Deductible Discount, Zone AE.........................................................................................................3-105

Condo Rating Example 9: Pre-FIRM, High-Rise, Enclosure, Maximum Deductible Discount, Coinsurance Penalty, Zone AE .........................................................................3-106

4. How to Endorse Examples ........ 4-11

Endorsement Example 1: Increasing Coverage on a Preferred Risk Policy ........ 4-12

Endorsement Example 2: Increasing Coverage ........ 4-13

Endorsement Example 3: Increasing Coverage After a Rate Change ........ 4-14

Endorsement Example 4: Reducing Building Coverage ........ 4-15

Endorsement Example 5: Change of Primary Residence Status ........ 4-16

# 1. Reference

This section includes a brief history and description of the National Flood Insurance Program (NFIP), which is administered by the Federal Emergency Management Agency (FEMA), and a number of helpful references for flood insurance agents and insurance companies. Please note: the term "FEMA" includes its contractors.

## I. NFIP History

The origins of the NFIP date back to the 1800s.[1] However, it wasn't until 1968 that Congress passed the National Flood Insurance Act of 1968 (NFIA) to address the increasing cost of federal disaster assistance by providing flood insurance to property owners in flood-prone areas where such insurance was either not available or prohibitively expensive.[2] To participate in the program, communities must adopt and enforce floodplain management regulations to reduce future flood damage. In exchange, the Federal Emergency Management Agency (FEMA) makes available flood insurance to residents in those communities and provides certain properties with subsidized premiums to encourage community and property owner participation.[3]

Congress subsequently enacted legislation modifying the NFIP and strengthening certain aspects of the program (see Table 1 on the next page). The Flood Disaster Protection Act of 1973 (FDPA) made the purchase of flood insurance mandatory for properties in Special Flood Hazard Areas (SFHAs)—areas that are at high risk for flooding—that are located in NFIP participating communities and either secure mortgages from federally-backed lenders or received federal assistance for acquisition or construction.[4] This mandatory purchase requirement expanded the overall number of insured properties, including those that qualified for subsidized premiums.

In 1983, to better market NFIP flood insurance and achieve other goals, FEMA adopted regulations establishing the Write Your Own (WYO) Program. Private insurance companies participating in the WYO Program, referred to as WYO companies, may sell NFIP policies next to their own insurance lines and adjust and pay claims arising under the NFIP policies. Likewise, WYO companies are responsible for all aspects of servicing the NFIP policies, including issuing, endorsing, underwriting, renewing, and cancelling policies. WYO companies may withhold administrative and operating expenses from written premiums for selling and servicing NFIP policies. If consistent with NFIP rules and regulations, individual WYO companies may align their flood business to their normal business practices for other lines of insurance. Many agents elect to place their flood policies with WYO companies.

**Table 1** lists the most significant legislation and highlights notable revisions to the program.

---

1. For a brief history of the NFIP through 2005, see: *A Chronology of Major Events Affecting the National Flood Insurance Program*, December 2005. Completed for the Federal Emergency Management Agency Under Contract Number 282-98=0029. The American Institutes for Research. Available at: https://www.fema.gov/media-library/assets/documents/9612.
2. National Flood Insurance Act of 1968, Pub. L. No. 90-448, Title XIII, 82 Stat. 476, 572; 42 U.S.C. 4001 et seq.
3. From 1968 until 1979, the U.S. Department of Housing and Urban Development administered the NFIP. In 1979, FEMA's Federal Insurance and Mitigation Administration (FIMA) began administering the NFIP. In March 2003, FEMA became part of the U.S. Department of Homeland Security (DHS).
4. Flood Disaster Protection Act of 1973, Pub. L. No. 93-234, 87 Stat. 975; 42 U.S.C. 4001 et seq. The Housing and Community Development Act of 1977, Pub. L. No. 93-383, 88 Stat. 633, amended the 1973 act to permit regulated lending institutions to make conventional loans in SFHAs of nonparticipating communities.

**Table 1. Major NFIP Reform Legislation**

| ACT | PROVISIONS |
|---|---|
| **Flood Disaster Protection Act of 1973** | • Prohibited federal assistance for the acquisition or construction of structures located in an SFHA unless the community is participating in the NFIP (unless the assistance is related to disaster assistance provided during a non-flood event)<br>• Prohibited such federal assistance unless the structure is covered by flood insurance<br>• Prohibited federally-backed lenders from making loans secured by buildings located in an SFHA unless the building is covered by flood insurance (collectively referred to as the "mandatory purchase requirement") |
| **National Flood Insurance Reform Act of 1994**[5] | • Expanded and strengthened the FDPA's mandatory purchase requirement.<br>• Required FEMA to offer insurance to cover the cost of complying with state and local floodplain management ordinances (referred to as Increased Cost of Compliance (ICC)).<br>• Established a grant program to fund activities designed to reduce the risk of flood damage to structures covered by an NFIP policy (referred to as the Flood Mitigation Assistance Program or FMA)<br>• Required a mandatory 30-day waiting period before a new NFIP policy becomes effective. |
| **Bunning-Bereuter-Blumenauer Flood Insurance Reform Act of 2004**[6] | • Required FEMA to create a process to enable insureds to appeal claims decisions.<br>• Required FEMA to provide enhanced disclosure to insureds, to include explanation of policy coverages and other terms. |
| **Biggert-Waters Flood Insurance Reform Act of 2012 (BW-12)**[7] | • Required FEMA to phase out premium discounts on an accelerated time frame.<br>• Required establishment of a National Flood Insurance Reserve Fund to be available to pay claims, repay debt owed to the U.S.Treasury, and meet the future obligations of the NFIP.<br>• Increased and adjusted the annual premium increase caps. |
| **Homeowner Flood Insurance Affordability Act of 2014 (HFIAA)**[8] | • Repealed and limited many premium increases required by BW-12.<br>• Imposed a surcharge based on occupancy and primary residence status (referred to as the HFIAA surcharge).<br>• With limited exceptions, reduced the cap on annual increases for flood insurance premiums to 18 percent.<br>• Authorized FEMA to secure reinsurance for the NFIP from the traditional reinsurance and capital markets. |

## II. Flood Insurance Placement and Technical Assistance

### A. Placing Flood Business through the NFIP

Agents may place their business three ways, through:

- One or more WYO insurance companies;
- FEMA's servicing contractor, NFIP Direct; *or*
- A combination of WYO insurance companies and the NFIP Direct.

5. National Flood Insurance Reform Act of 1994, Pub. L. No. 103-325, Title V, 108 Stat. 2255; 42 U.S.C. 4001 et seq.
6. Bunning-Bereuter-Blumenauer Flood Insurance Reform Act of 2004, Pub. L. No. 108-264, 118 Stat. 712; 42 U.S.C. 4001 et seq.
7. Biggert-Waters Flood Insurance Reform Act of 2012, Pub. L. No. 112-141, Div. F, Title II, Subtitle A, 126 Stat. 916; 42 U.S.C. 4001 et seq.
8. Homeowner Flood Insurance Affordability Act of 2014, Pub. L. No. 113-89, 128 Stat. 1020; 42 U.S.C. 4001 et seq.

### B. Technical Assistance

Questions and requests for technical assistance should follow the flow shown in the diagram below.

- The FEMA Mapping and Insurance eXchange (FMIX) can answer general inquiries about flood insurance, call 1-877-336-2627 (1-877-FEMA-MAP).
- Contact Ask the Expert by email, at floodsmart@fema.dhs.gov.
- Office of the Flood Insurance Advocate (OFIA)
  - If additional assistance is needed after using the above resources and those in Table 2 below, please contact the OFIA. The OFIA advocates for the fair treatment of policyholders and property owners by providing education and guidance on all aspects of the NFIP, identifying trends affecting the public, and making recommendations for program improvements to FEMA leadership.
  - Contact the OFIA by visiting http://www.fema.gov/flood-insurance-advocate and clicking on the "Ask the Advocate" button.

## III. NFIP Topics and Contact Information

**Table 2. NFIP Topics and Contact Information**

| Topic | Website and Email Addresses | Telephone |
|---|---|---|
| Agent Marketing, Selling, Servicing information | https://agents.floodsmart.gov | N/A |
| Coastal Barrier Resources System (CBRS) | https://www.fema.gov/coastal-barrier-resources-system | N/A |
| Community Status Book | https://www.fema.gov/national-flood-insurance-program-community-status-book | N/A |
| FEMA Document and Resource Library | https://www.fema.gov/media-library/resources-documents | N/A |
| Flood Map Information from FEMA Map Specialists on:<br>• Letters of Map Change<br>• Other Technical Issues | FEMA Mapping and Insurance eXchange (FMIX)<br>https://www.floodmaps.fema.gov/fhm/fmx_main.html<br>femamapspecialist@riskmapcds.com | Phone:<br>1-877-336-2627<br>(1-877-FEMA-MAP) |
| Flood Maps and Related Products | FEMA Flood Map Service Center<br>https://msc.fema.gov/portal/home | N/A |
| Flood Zone Determination Companies, List of | https://www.fema.gov/flood-zone-determination-companies | N/A |
| General Information for Agents & Consumers | https://www.floodsmart.gov/ | N/A |

**Table 2. NFIP Topics and Contact Information** *continued*

| Topic | Website and Email Addresses | Telephone |
|---|---|---|
| General Flood Insurance Inquiries | FEMA Mapping and Insurance eXchange (FMIX)<br>https://www.floodmaps.fema.gov/fhm/fmx_main.html<br>femamapspecialist@riskmapcds.com | Phone:<br>1-877-336-2627<br>(1-877-FEMA-MAP) |
| Order Forms:<br>Claims & Underwriting | Underwriting forms are only available online and may not be ordered from the warehouse. Download claims and underwriting forms at:<br>https://www.fema.gov/national-flood-insurance-program/national-flood-insurance-program-forms | N/A |
| Public Awareness Materials | fema-publications-warehouse@fema.gov | Phone:<br>1-800-480-2520 |
| Training | https://nfipservices.floodsmart.gov/home/training | N/A |
| WYO Companies, List of | https://www.fema.gov/wyo_company | N/A |
| WYO Companies Writing Mortgage Portfolio Protection Program, List of | https://nfipservices.floodsmart.gov/mortgage-portfolio-protection-program | N/A |

## IV. NFIP Regional Support Offices

The NFIP operates a network of regional offices within the continental United States. The regional staff can assist with problems and answer general questions. However, the regional offices do not handle processing of NFIP insurance activities, such as writing policies or handling claims or appeals, nor do they have records of these actions at their locations.

**Table 3** shows contact information for the NFIP regional support offices. The most current information is available at https://nfipservices.floodsmart.gov/NFIP-Regional-Support-Offices.

**Table 3. NFIP Regional Support Offices**

| NFIP Regional Support Offices | Contact Numbers | Service Area |
|---|---|---|
| **NFIP IT Service & Support (NFIP IT S&S) Headquarters**<br>8400 Corporate Dr., Suite 350<br>Hyattsville, MD 20785 | Phone: 301-386-6332<br>Fax: 267-560-5057 | Entire Country |
| **Region 1**<br>PO Box 16321<br>Hooksett, NH 03106 | Phone: 603-625-5125<br>Fax: 603-625-5125 | Connecticut, Maine, Massachusetts, New Hampshire, Rhode Island, Vermont |

**Table 3. NFIP Regional Support Offices** *continued*

| NFIP Regional Support Offices | Contact Numbers | Service Area |
|---|---|---|
| **Region 2**<br>PO Box 7342<br>Penndel, PA 19047 | Phone: 267-560-5057<br>Fax: 267-560-5057 | New Jersey, New York, Puerto Rico, Virgin Islands |
| **Region 3**<br>PO Box 7342<br>Penndel, PA 19047 | Phone: 267-560-5057<br>Fax: 267-560-5057 | Delaware, District of Columbia, Maryland, Pennsylvania, Virginia, West Virginia |
| **Region 4**<br>PO Box 282<br>Marble Hill, GA 30148 | Phone: 770-893-1480 or 571-389-4762 | Alabama, Florida, Georgia, Kentucky, Mississippi, North Carolina, South Carolina, Tennessee |
| **Region 5**<br>PO Box 443<br>Gates Mills, OH 44040 | Phone: 202-774-7108 | Illinois, Indiana, Michigan, Minnesota, Ohio, Wisconsin |
| **Region 6**<br>PO Box 399<br>Pipe Creek, TX 78063 | Phone: 210-393-7857 | Arkansas, Louisiana, New Mexico, Oklahoma, Texas |
| **Region 6**<br>PO Box 4210<br>Abilene, TX 79608 | Phone: 325-269-3566<br>Fax: 325-202-3300 | Arkansas, Louisiana, New Mexico, Oklahoma, Texas |
| **Region 7**<br>PO Box 252<br>Louisburg, KS 66053 | Phone: 913-837-5220 | Iowa, Kansas, Missouri, Nebraska |
| **Region 8**<br>PO Box 150172<br>Lakewood, CO 80215 | Phone: 303-674-1449 | Colorado, Montana, North Dakota, South Dakota, Utah, Wyoming |
| **Region 9**<br>PO Box 1323<br>Twain Harte, CA 95383 | Phone: 571-424-0611 | American Samoa, Arizona, California, Guam, Hawaii, Mariana Islands, Marshall Islands, Micronesia, Nevada, Palau |
| **Region 10**<br>9300 50th Ave. NE<br>Marysville, WA 98270 | Phone: 360-658-8188<br>Fax: 360-658-8188 | Alaska, Idaho, Oregon, Washington |

This page is intentionally left blank.

# 2. Before You Start

This section provides important information needed prior to writing an NFIP flood insurance policy.

## I. Policy Forms

NFIP insurers may only use the Standard Flood Insurance Policy (SFIP) established by FEMA in federal regulation to sell NFIP flood insurance policies. The SFIP defines the coverages, limitations, and exclusions for NFIP flood insurance policies and includes terms and conditions that are unique to the NFIP. The SFIP outlines flood insurance coverage for a one-year policy term under three different forms: the Dwelling Form, the General Property Form, and the Residential Condominium Building Association Policy (RCBAP) Form.

**Table 1** shows when to use the three SFIP forms to insure a variety of residential and non-residential building and contents risks.

### Table 1. Standard Flood Insurance Policy Forms

| SFIP Form | When and Where To Use |
|---|---|
| **Dwelling Form**<br><br>Available to a homeowner, residential renter, or owner of a residential building containing 1 to 4 units | In a Regular Program community or Emergency Program community, the NFIP provides building and/or contents coverage for:<br>• Single-family, non-condominium residence with incidental occupancy limited to less than 50 percent of the total floor area;<br>• 2–4 family, non-condominium building with incidental occupancy limited to less than 25 percent of the total floor area;<br>• Unit in residential condominium building;<br>• Residential townhouse/rowhouse; *and*<br>• Personal contents in a non-residential building. |
| **General Property Form**<br><br>Available to an owner or lessee of non-residential business or other non-residential buildings or units | In a Regular Program community or Emergency Program community, the NFIP provides building coverage and/or contents coverage for these and similar non-residential risks:<br>• Hotel or motel;<br>• Licensed bed-and-breakfast inn;<br>• Retail shop, restaurant, or other business;<br>• Mercantile building;<br>• Grain bin, silo, or other farm building;<br>• Agricultural or industrial processing facility;<br>• Factory;<br>• Warehouse;<br>• Pool house, clubhouse, or other recreational building;<br>• House of worship;<br>• School;<br>• Nursing home;<br>• Non-residential condominium;<br>• Condominium building with less than 75 percent of its total floor area in residential use;<br>• Detached garage;<br>• Shed; *and*<br>• Stock, inventory, or other commercial contents. |

**Table 1. Standard Flood Insurance Policy Forms** *continued*

| SFIP Form | When and Where To Use |
|---|---|
| **General Property Form**<br>Available to an owner of residential building with 5 or more units | In a Regular Program community or Emergency Program community, the NFIP provides building and/or contents coverage for these residential risks with 5 or more units:<br>• Apartment buildings;<br>• Residential cooperative buildings;<br>• Dormitories;<br>• Assisted-living facilities; *and*<br>• Hotels, motels, tourist homes, and rooming houses that have 5 or more units where the normal guest occupancy/stay is 6 months or more. |
| **RCBAP**<br>Issued to a residential condominium association on behalf of association and unit owners | In a Regular Program community only, the NFIP provides building coverage and, if desired, coverage of commonly owned contents for a residential condominium building with 75 percent or more of its total floor area in residential use. |

## II. Eligibility of Property Locations, Buildings, and Contents

An individual property's eligibility for an NFIP flood insurance policy depends on:

1. The location of the building;
2. Having an insurable building; *and*
3. Having insurable contents.

### A. Eligibility of Property Locations

#### *1. Where the NFIP Offers Insurance*

The NFIP offers insurance for buildings and contents located within participating NFIP communities or located on federal land.

**Table 2** explains what an NFIP participating community is and provides a list of the stages of a participating community.

**Table 2. Where the NFIP Offers Insurance**

| Location | Description |
|---|---|
| **NFIP Participating Communities** | The NFIP insures buildings and contents located within participating NFIP communities or located on federal land.<br>A community must adopt a floodplain management ordinance that meets or exceeds the minimum NFIP criteria and have a Flood Insurance Rate Map (FIRM) or a Flood Hazard Boundary Map (FHBM) for the community to participate in the NFIP. Check with the insurer to determine the community status or refer to the Community Status Book at https://www.fema.gov/national-flood-insurance-program-community-status-book. |

### Table 2. Where the NFIP Offers Insurance *continued*

| Location | Description |
|---|---|
| Emergency Program | The Emergency Program represents the initial phase of a community's participation in the NFIP in which limited amounts of coverage are available.<br>**Note:** Participating communities in the Emergency Program remain in the Emergency Program if an FHBM is rescinded. |
| Regular Program | The Regular Program is the final phase of a community's participation in the NFIP. In this phase, the completed FIRM is in effect and full coverage limits are available. |
| NFIP Participating Communities on Probation | FEMA may place a participating NFIP community on probation when it does not comply with the NFIP's floodplain management requirements. Probation ends when the community remedies all deficiencies. Insurance is available while the community is on probation.<br>FEMA applies a $50 Probation Surcharge to all policies in the community, issued on or after the probation effective date. The NFIP exempts the Group Flood Insurance Policy (GFIP) from the surcharge. FEMA may suspend the community if it does not remedy the violations during the probationary period. |
| Federal Land | NFIP flood insurance is available on land owned by the Federal Government when the local community meets the floodplain management requirements. The NFIP records all federal land under a local community number even if that local community does not have jurisdiction. |

### 2. *Where the NFIP Does Not Offer Insurance*

**Table 3** shows the locations where the NFIP does not offer insurance.

### Table 3. Where the NFIP Does Not Offer Insurance

| Location | Description |
|---|---|
| **Non-Participating Communities** | The NFIP may not sell or renew flood insurance in a community that does not participate in the NFIP. Once FEMA provides a community with an FHBM or a FIRM delineating its flood-prone areas, the community has one year from that date to qualify as an NFIP participating community before this prohibition becomes effective. Check with the insurer to determine the community status or refer to the Community Status Book at https://www.fema.gov/national-flood-insuranceprogram-community-status-book. |
| **Suspended NFIP Community** | The NFIP may not sell or renew flood insurance in a community suspended from the NFIP. Current policies in the suspended community remain in effect until policy expiration.<br>• The NFIP may not renew a policy while the community is suspended.<br>• Insurers must cancel any policies issued in error or any policy renewed after the date of a community suspension.<br>• To obtain coverage after the NFIP reinstates a community, property owners should contact their agent or insurer to submit a new application.<br>• Insurers must use the applicable waiting period required to obtain coverage. |

**Table 3. Where the NFIP Does Not Offer Insurance** *continued*

| Location | Description |
|---|---|
| **Areas Covered by the Coastal Barrier Resources Act** | Flood insurance may not be available in System Units or Otherwise Protected Areas (OPAs) identified under the Coastal Barrier Resources System (CBRS). Such areas designated under the CBRS are typically undeveloped coastal barriers within the boundaries of areas established under federal, state, or local law, or held by a qualified organization, primarily for wildlife refuge, sanctuary, recreational, or natural resource conservation purposes. Refer to the CBRS appendix of this manual for additional information. |

## B. Building Eligibility

The NFIP will insure a building affixed to a permanent site that:

- Has two or more outside rigid walls with a fully secured roof;
- Resists flotation, collapse, and lateral movement; *and*
- Has at least 51 percent of the Actual Cash Value (ACV) of the building, including machinery and equipment that are a part of the building, above ground level unless the lowest level of the affixed structure is at or above the Base Flood Elevation (BFE) and is below ground using earth as insulation material in conjunction with energy-efficient building techniques.

### *1. Eligible Types of Buildings*

**Table 4** describes the types of buildings the NFIP insures.

**Table 4. Buildings the NFIP Insures**

| Building Type | Description |
|---|---|
| **Detached Garage** | In general, the SFIP can only cover one building. However, the Dwelling Form includes limited coverage for a detached garage servicing a 1–4 family dwelling. Coverage is limited to no more than 10 percent of the limit of liability on the 1–4 family dwelling. This coverage does not apply to garages used for residential, business, or farming purposes. |
| **Manufactured Home/Travel Trailer Without Wheels** | A manufactured home (also known as a mobile home) is a structure built on a permanent chassis, transported to a site in one or more sections, and affixed to a permanent foundation.<br><br>A travel trailer without wheels, built on a chassis and affixed to a permanent foundation, is eligible for flood coverage where regulated under the community's floodplain management and building ordinances or laws.<br><br>Manufactured (mobile) homes and travel trailers must meet the following requirements to be eligible for NFIP coverage:<br>• Be affixed to a permanent foundation that may be a poured masonry slab, foundation walls, piers, or blocks so that the wheels and axles of the mobile home do not support its weight; and<br>• Be anchored to a permanent foundation to resist flotation, collapse, or lateral movement by providing over-the-top or frame ties to ground anchors; or in accordance with manufacturer's specifications; or in compliance with the community's floodplain management requirements. |

**Table 4. Buildings the NFIP Insures** *continued*

| Building Type | Description |
| --- | --- |
| **Manufactured Home/Travel Trailer Without Wheels,** *continued* | Manufactured (mobile) homes continuously insured since September 30, 1982, can renew under the previously existing requirements if they meet the following conditions:<br>• Are affixed to a permanent foundation in compliance with the foundation and anchoring requirements at the time of placement.<br>• To be adequately anchored, the foundation support system must secure the manufactured or mobile home into the ground sufficiently to resist flotation, collapse, and lateral movement caused by flood forces, including wind forces in coastal areas.<br>**Note:** All references in this manual to manufactured (mobile) homes are specific to manufactured (mobile) homes and travel trailers without wheels when affixed to a permanent foundation. |
| **Condominium Building** | A condominium is a building or a complex of buildings containing a number of individually owned apartments or houses where each unit owner has an undivided interest in common elements of the building. Residential condominium buildings must be insured under the RCBAP. |
| **Cooperative Building** | Corporations own and manage cooperative buildings, and their ownership differs from the condominium form of ownership. Residents within cooperative buildings buy shares of the corporation, rather than the real estate (building, land, or both building and land). To qualify as a residential occupancy, a cooperative building must have at least 75 percent of the total floor area used for residential purposes. Cooperative buildings are not eligible for the RCBAP. |
| **Homeowners' Association (Non-Condominium)** | A Homeowners' Association not in the condominium form of ownership owns the common areas and individual building owners have a right to use and enjoy the common areas. A Homeowners' Association can purchase a policy for an individual building in the building owner's name when the Association's by-laws require the Association to purchase flood insurance building coverage for its members. A Homeowners' Association not in the condominium form of ownership is not eligible for the RCBAP. |
| **Timeshare Building** | A timeshare is an arrangement where several joint owners have the right to use a property under a time-sharing agreement and where the corporation owns the building. The NFIP insures individual units in a timeshare building in the condominium form of ownership under the Dwelling Form. These buildings are eligible for coverage under the RCBAP if 75 percent of the total floor area of the building is for residential purposes. If the 75% criteria is not met, refer to IV. Condominiums in the How To Write section. |
| **Building Partially Underground** | The NFIP insures buildings or units and eligible contents if 49 percent or less of the ACV, including machinery, is below ground when an energy efficient building technique uses earth as an insulator. The lowest floor must be at or above the BFE. |
| **Agricultural Structure** | A structure used exclusively in connection with the production, harvesting, storage, raising, or drying of agricultural commodities. Examples of eligible agricultural structures include barns, silos, and grain storage buildings. |
| **Building Entirely Over Water before October 1, 1982** | The NFIP will insure a building located entirely in, on, or over water, or seaward of mean high tide, that was not constructed or substantially improved after September 30, 1982. Refer to the How to Write section of this manual for rating information. |

**Table 4. Buildings the NFIP Insures** *continued*

| Building Type | Description |
|---|---|
| **Building Partially Over Water** | The NFIP may insure a building not "entirely" over water, i.e., when part of the exterior perimeter walls and foundation of the building are on land or on the landward side of mean high tide (mean high water). Refer to the How to Write section of this manual for rating information.<br><br>**Note:** When the exterior perimeter walls of the building are completely over water, but the support system or foundation underneath the building extends onto land, or the extension of any mechanism for access into the building (including, but not limited to, stairs, decks, walkways, piers, posts, pilings, docks, or driveways) is fully or partially on land, the building and the access are ineligible for coverage. |
| **Building Becomes Entirely Over Water** | A building originally constructed on land or partially over water that later becomes entirely over water because of erosion is eligible for coverage if the building has had continuous coverage. Coverage must have been in place for at least one year prior to the building being located entirely over water (regardless of any changes in the ownership of the building) or from the date of construction if less than one year. Refer to the How to Write section of this manual for rating information. |
| **Boathouse Located Partially Over Water** | The NFIP insures the non-boathouse parts of a building into which boats are floated, if the building is partly over land and also used for residential, commercial, or municipal purposes and is eligible for flood coverage. The NFIP does not insure boat repair docks or boat storage over water.<br><br>The NFIP will insure the area above the boathouse used for purposes unrelated to the boathouse use (e.g., residential use) from the floor joists to the roof, including walls, and a common wall between the boathouse area and other parts of the building.<br><br>The following items are not covered (refer to the SFIP for the limitations on coverage):<br>• The ceiling and roof over the boathouse portions of the building into which boats are floated;<br>• Floors, walkways, decking, etc., within the boathouse area, or outside the area, but pertaining to boathouse use;<br>• Exterior walls and doors of the boathouse area not common to the rest of the building;<br>• Interior walls and coverings within the boathouse area; and<br>• Contents located within the boathouse area, including furnishings and equipment, relating to the operation and storage of boats and other boathouse uses. |
| **Building in the Course of Construction** | The NFIP will insure a building in the course of construction before it is walled and roofed using the NFIP-issued rates based on the construction designs and the intended use of the building.<br><br>Buildings in the course of construction that are not walled and roofed are not eligible for coverage when construction stops for more than 90 days and/or if the lowest floor for rating purposes is below the BFE. The NFIP will not insure materials or supplies intended for use in such construction, alteration, or repair unless they are contained within an enclosed building on the premises or adjacent to the premises.<br><br>**Important:** If a building under construction, alteration, or repair does not have at least two rigid exterior walls and a fully secured roof at the time of loss, then the deductible amount will be two times the deductible that would otherwise apply to a completed building. See SFIP Sec. VI.A. |

**Table 4. Buildings the NFIP Insures** *continued*

| Building Type | Description |
|---|---|
| Additions and Extensions | When insuring a building with multiple additions, the applicant must choose between purchasing one policy or separate policies for the building and each addition and extension.<br>Additions and extensions attached to and in contact with the building by the following methods may be insured under a separate policy:<br>• Rigid exterior wall<br>• Solid load-bearing interior wall<br>• Stairway<br>• Elevated walkway<br>• Roof<br>The NFIP requires an application for each addition and extension insured separately.<br>The application must:<br>• Clearly describe the separately insured addition and extension;<br>• Contain the rating information specific to the addition and extension; *and*<br>• Request building and/or contents coverage for the addition and extension.<br>The application for the main building should reference the policy number or quote number for the policy covering the addition or extension separately.<br>**Note:** Additions and extensions cannot be excluded from building coverage under the main building's policy unless the additions and extensions are insured separately. |

### 2. *Ineligible Types of Buildings*

NFIP does not insure the buildings shown in **Table 5**.

**Table 5. Buildings the NFIP Does Not Insure**

| Building Type | Description |
|---|---|
| Building Declared in Violation of Floodplain Management Requirements | The NFIP may not insure buildings (or their contents) declared to be constructed or altered in violation of state or local floodplain management laws, regulations, or ordinances. Section 1316 of the National Flood Insurance Act of 1968 (NFIA) allows state or local governments to make this declaration. Insurance becomes available when the owner corrects the violation and the state or local government rescinds the Section 1316 declaration. |
| Container-Type Building | The NFIP does not insure containers used to store gas and liquids, chemical or reactor container tanks or enclosures, brick kilns, and similar units, and their contents. |
| Building Entirely Over Water On or After October 1, 1982 | The NFIP does not insure buildings constructed or substantially improved on or after October 1, 1982, located entirely in, on, or over water, or seaward of mean high tide. |
| Water Treatment Plant | The NFIP does not insure a water treatment plant unless 51% or more of its ACV is above ground. |

**Table 5. Buildings the NFIP Does Not Insure** *continued*

| Building Type | Description |
|---|---|
| **Building Used for the Manufacture or Distribution of a Controlled Substance** | The NFIP may not knowingly insure a building or its contents used for the manufacture or distribution of a controlled substance in violation of federal law. Doing so would directly promote, effectuate, or encourage a violation of the law, which would violate public policy and general principles of insurance. This restriction includes buildings or contents used to grow or dispense marijuana in locations where this activity is legal under state law because governing federal law makes it unlawful to use any place for the manufacture or distribution of a controlled substance. FEMA can provide additional information on the application of this guidance to specific circumstances. |

## C. Contents Eligibility

The NFIP only insures contents located in a building that is eligible for building coverage.

- **Dwelling Form:** Contents must be located inside a building at the described location. If the building is not fully enclosed, contents must be secured to prevent flotation out of the building.
- **General Property Form:** Contents must be located inside the fully enclosed insured building.
- **RCBAP Form:** Contents must be located inside the fully enclosed insured building.

### *1. Eligible Contents*

Examples of eligible contents include:

- Personal property inside a building at the described location, if:
  - The property is owned by the insured or the insured's household family members; *or*
  - At the insured's option, the property is owned by guests or servants;
- Equipment;
- Self-propelled vehicles or machines, not licensed for use on public roads, *and*
  - Used mainly to service the described location; *or*
  - Designed and used to assist handicapped persons while the vehicles or machines are inside a building at the described location;
- Parts and equipment as open stock, not part of a specific vehicle or motorized equipment;
- Contents located in silos, grain storage buildings, and cisterns;
- Commercial contents;
- Contents in units in a cooperative building:
  - Residents of a unit within a cooperative building may purchase contents coverage under the Dwelling Form;
  - Shareholders may apply 10 percent of the contents coverage for betterments and improvements at the time of loss;
- Contents in a non-residential condominium unit; *and*
- Personal property removed to safety at another location to protect it from flood or the imminent danger of flood, for a period of 45 days.

### 2. *Ineligible Contents*

Examples of ineligible contents under certain NFIP policy forms include:

- Automobiles including assembled and unassembled dealer's stock;
- Motorcycles including assembled and unassembled dealer's stock;
- Motorized Equipment including assembled and unassembled dealer's stock; *and*
- Bailee customer's goods including contractors, cleaners, repair shops, processors of goods belonging to others, and similar risks.

## D. NFIP Coverage Exclusions and Limitations

**Table 6** shows examples of NFIP coverage exclusions and limitations.

**Table 6. NFIP Coverage Exclusions and Limitations**

| Types of Exclusion and Limitations | Comment |
|---|---|
| **Basement** | The SFIP limits coverage for basement improvements, such as finished walls, floors, ceilings, or personal belongings kept in a basement. |
| **Elevated Building with Enclosure** | The SFIP limits coverage for enclosed, walled-in areas below the lowest floor of a Post-FIRM elevated building located in a Special Flood Hazard Area (SFHA), including finished walls, floors, ceilings, or personal belongings kept in an enclosure. |
| **Swimming Pool** | The SFIP excludes coverage for indoor or outdoor swimming pools. |
| **Deck** | The SFIP limits coverage for decks except for steps and landings to a maximum landing area of 16 square feet. |
| **Hot Tub or Spa** | The SFIP excludes coverage for hot tubs or spas except where used as bathroom fixtures. |
| **Building Coverage for a Unit in a Cooperative Building** | The NFIP does not provide building coverage for shareholder units in a cooperative building.<br>Residents or tenants of a cooperative building may purchase contents coverage under the Dwelling Form. |
| **Non-Residential Condominium Unit** | The NFIP does not provide building coverage for owners of non-residential units in residential or non-residential buildings. |
| **Timeshare Unit in a Multi-Unit Building** | The NFIP does not provide coverage for these units unless they are in a condominium form of ownership. |
| **Flood in Progress** | The SFIP excludes coverage of losses caused directly or indirectly by a flood that is already in progress at the time and date:<br>1. The policy's first term begins; *or*<br>2. Coverage is added at the policyholder's request.<br>Therefore, damage from a flood that begins before the policy's first term begins is not covered even if the flood does not damage the insured property until after the policy term begins. When coverage is added to an existing policy at the request of the policyholder and a flood is already in progress, damage that occurs to insured property from that same flood event after the effective date of the increased coverage will only be covered under the lesser policy limits. |

## III. Coverage D – Increased Cost of Compliance (ICC) Coverage

The SFIP includes ICC coverage that pays up to $30,000, subject to eligibility, towards the cost to repair or rebuild a flood-damaged structure in compliance with state or local floodplain management ordinances or laws. ICC coverage is not available for:

- Emergency Program policies;
- Contents-only policies;
- Dwelling Form policies on individual condominium units including townhouse/rowhouse condominiums (The condominium association is responsible for complying with mitigation requirements.);
- GFIPs; *or*
- Detached garages, unless covered by a separate policy.

The ICC premium is not eligible for the deductible discount.

ICC coverage is in addition to the amount of building coverage purchased and the total cannot exceed the maximum program limits.

Compliance activities eligible for payment are elevation, floodproofing, relocation, demolition, or any combination of these activities. Eligible floodproofing activities apply only to non-residential structures and residential structures with basements that satisfy FEMA's standards published at 44 CFR 60.6.

## IV. Insurance Products

**Table 7** shows the NFIP insurance products that are currently available.

**Table 7. NFIP Insurance Products Available**

| Policy Type | Description |
|---|---|
| **Preferred Risk Policy (PRP)** | The PRP is a lower cost policy available for properties located in B, C, X, AR, or A99 zones on the current FIRM that have limited loss history. See the How To Write section for more information. |
| **Newly Mapped Rating Procedure** | The Newly Mapped rating procedure applies to properties previously located in Zones B, C, X, D, AR, or A99 and newly mapped into an SFHA on the current map. |
| **Mortgage Portfolio Protection Program (MPPP) Policy** | The MPPP is a force-placed policy available only through a Write Your Own (WYO) Company. See the MPPP section of this manual for more information. |
| **Scheduled Building Policy** | The Scheduled Building Policy provides a group of policies for buildings that have the same ownership and the same location; the properties where the buildings are located must be contiguous. The policy is available to cover 2 to 10 buildings and requires the insured to designate a specific amount of insurance for each building.<br>NFIP requires a separate application for each building and/or contents policy;<br>• The Federal Policy Fee is $50 per building; *and*<br>• The HFIAA Surcharge is charged for each building. |

**Table 7. NFIP Insurance Products Available** *continued*

| Policy Type | Description |
|---|---|
| Group Flood Insurance Policy (GFIP) | A GFIP is a policy covering all individuals named by a State as recipients under section 408 of the Robert T. Stafford Disaster Relief and Emergency Assistance Act[1] of an Individuals and Households Program award for flood damage as a result of a major disaster declaration by the President. The amount of coverage is equivalent to the maximum grant amount established under section 408. The term of the GFIP is for 36 months and begins 60 days after the date of the disaster declaration. Coverage for individual grantees begins on the thirtieth day after the NFIP receives the required data for individual grantees and their premium payments. An insured may cancel a GFIP at any time and secure a regular SFIP through the NFIP. |

1. Pub. L. No. 93-288, 88 Stat. 143; 42 U.S.C. 5174

## V. Effective Dates for New Policies

### A. Waiting Periods

In general, new policies for flood insurance become effective following a 30-day waiting period. However, there are three exceptions listed below and detailed later in this section:

1. **Map Revision Exception (Sec. VI.A.2):** Coverage becomes effective after a one-day waiting period during the first 13 months following the revision of a flood map in the property's community.
2. **Mortgage Loan Exception (Sec. VI.A.3):** Coverage becomes effective at the time of the closing when the initial purchase of flood insurance is in connection with a mortgage loan transaction.
3. **Post-Wildfire Exception (Sec. VI.B):** Coverage becomes effective immediately if:
   a. The covered property experiences damage caused by flood that originated on federal land;
   b. Post-wildfire conditions on federal lands caused or worsened the flooding; *and*
   c. The insured purchased the policy either:
      i. Before the fire containment date; *or*
      ii. During the 60-calendar day period following the fire containment date.

Insurers must follow the applicable waiting period and effective date rules for all policies, including submit-for-rate submissions and policies issued in conjunction with a community's initial entry into the Regular Program or conversion from the Emergency Program to the Regular Program.

Contents-only policies are subject to a 30-day waiting period unless the contents are part of the security for a loan.

#### *1. Standard 30-day Waiting Period*

A 30-day waiting period applies to new policies not otherwise eligible for the exceptions provided above. The date the waiting period begins varies based on:

- The date the insurer receives the application and payment;
- The date of the application; *and*
- The method of sending the application and payment.

For the purposes of determining a waiting period start date, "certified mail" includes certified mail sent through the U.S. Postal Service or reputable third-party delivery services that provides proof of the actual mailing date and delivery date to the insurer.

**Table 8** shows how to determine the effective date of a new policy with a 30-day waiting period.

### Table 8. Effective Date of a New Policy with a 30-day Waiting Period

| Receipt Date | Effective Date |
|---|---|
| If the insurer receives the application and payment ***within*** 10 calendar days from the application date (application date plus 9 days) | The effective date will be 12:01 a.m. (local time) on the 30th calendar day after the application date. |
| **If the application and payment are mailed by certified mail within 4 calendar days from the application date (application date plus 3 days), regardless of when the insurer receives them** | The effective date will be 12:01 a.m. (local time) on the 30th calendar day after the application date. |
| **If the insurer receives the application and payment after 10 or more calendar days from the application date (application date plus 9 days) and the application and payment were NOT mailed by certified mail within 4 calendar days from the application date (application date plus 3 days)** | The effective date will be 12:01 a.m. (local time) on the 30th calendar day after the insurer's receipt date. |

The insurer may not use the receipt date of an invalid payment to determine the effective date of a policy transaction.

A payment is invalid if there are non-sufficient funds (NSF) in the account, a reversal (dispute) is successfully completed on an electronic payment, or the payment is non-negotiable for any other reason.

Upon notification that the payment is invalid, the insurer must:

- Cancel/nullify the transaction associated with that payment; *and*
- Send notification of the cancellation/nullification to the insured, agent, and lender(s), if applicable.
- If the insurer receives a new payment, the insurer must process the transaction based on the new premium receipt date. The insurer must determine the effective date of the transaction based on the new payment receipt date, subject to the effective date rules.
- Note: A new application or endorsement request is not required for this transaction as long as the insurer still has the original request.

### *2. Map Revision Exception (1-Day Waiting Period)*

A 1-day waiting period applies when the NFIP revises an FHBM or a FIRM to show that the building is now in an SFHA when it was not previously. The 1-day waiting period may only apply if the insurer receives the application and payment within 13 months from the effective date of the map revision. If the insurer receives the application and payment after 13 months from the effective date of the map revision, the 30-day waiting period applies. The 1-day waiting period rule applies for all buildings, including those owned by condominium associations.

**Table 9** shows how to determine the effective date of a new policy with a 1-day waiting period.

### Table 9. Effective Date of a New Policy with a 1-day Waiting Period

| Receipt Date | Effective Date |
|---|---|
| If the insurer receives the application and payment ***within*** 10 calendar days from the application date (application date plus 9 days) | The effective date will be 12:01 a.m. (local time) on the next calendar day after the application date. |
| **If the application and payment are mailed by certified mail within 4 calendar days from the application date (application date plus 3 days), regardless of when the insurer receives them** | The effective date will be 12:01 a.m. (local time) on the next calendar day after the application date |
| **If the insurer receives the application and payment after 10 or more calendar days from the application date (application date plus 9 days) and the application and payment were NOT mailed by certified mail within 4 calendar days from the application date (application date plus 3 days)** | The effective date will be 12:01 a.m. (local time) on the next calendar day after the insurer's receipt date. |

### 3. *Loan Exception (No Waiting Period)*

New policies purchased when making, extending, increasing, or renewing a loan are not subject to the 30-day waiting period. This includes condominium association policies purchased in conjunction with loan transactions in the name of the condominium association. See **Table 10**.

The insured must apply for flood insurance on or before the closing date of the loan transaction. If the insured requests the policy after the closing date, the 30-day waiting period applies. A valid application includes all the information necessary to calculate the NFIP policy premium.

The insurer may rely on an agent's representation on the application that there is no waiting period. The insurer must obtain documentation of the loan transaction (such as settlement papers) to validate that a loan transaction occurred before paying the loss if a loss occurs during the first 30 days of the policy.

### Table 10. Effective Date of a New Policy with No Waiting Period

| Receipt Date | Effective Date |
|---|---|
| **If the lender, title company, or settlement attorney pays the premium** | |
| If the insured requests the policy on or before the loan transaction closing and the insurer receives the application and payment ***within*** 30 calendar days from the closing (closing date plus 29 days) | The effective date will be the loan closing date. |
| If the insured requests the policy on or before the loan transaction closing, and the insurer receives the application and payment ***after*** 30 calendar days from the closing (closing date plus 29 days or more) | The effective date will be the insurer's receipt date. |
| **If the insured or other party not listed above pays the premium** | |
| If the insured requests the policy on or before the loan transaction closing, and the insurer receives the application and payment ***within*** 10 calendar days from the loan transaction closing (closing date plus 9 days) | The effective date will be the loan closing date. |
| If the insured requests the policy on or before the loan transaction closing, and the insurer receives the application and payment ***after*** 10 calendar days from the closing (closing date plus 9 days or more) | The effective date will be the insurer's receipt date. |

**NOTE:** When an agent submits an agency check, it must be accompanied by settlement paperwork or a photocopy of the original check from the lender, title company, or settlement attorney to be eligible for the waiting period exception.

#### *4. Post-Wildfire Exception*

The 30-day waiting period may not apply to property (building and contents) affected by flooding from federal land caused by post-wildfire conditions under the following circumstances:

1. The covered property experiences damage caused by flood that originated on federal land;
2. Post-wildfire conditions on federal lands caused or worsened the flooding; *and*
3. The policyholder purchased the policy either:
   a. Before the fire containment date; or
   b. During the 60-calendar-day period following the fire containment date.

The federal agency responsible for the land on which the post-wildfire conditions existed determines the fire containment date.

##### a. Application of the Post-Wildfire Exception

FEMA supports the application of the Post-Wildfire Exception by tracking containment dates for wildfires occurring on federal lands and consulting when necessary with appropriate federal agencies to determine whether post-wildfire conditions caused or exacerbated a flood. WYO companies and NFIP Direct may request assistance with the proper application of the Post-Wildfire Exception by contacting FEMA-FIDClaimsMailbox@fema.dhs.gov.

## VI. Delivery of the Policy

The insurer must send:

- The policy form (i.e., contract) to the insured at the time of policy issuance or after any change made to the policy contract; *and*
- The policy declarations page to the insured, agent, and, if applicable, lender(s).

## VII. Evidence of Insurance

A copy of the Flood Insurance Application and premium payment or a copy of the declarations page is sufficient evidence of proof of purchase for new policies.

## VIII. Duplicate Policies

The NFIP does not allow multiple building policies on a single building. The only exception is for residential condominium buildings. The insurer may issue a Dwelling Form policy to a residential condominium unit owner in a building covered by an RCBAP. The combined coverage between the Dwelling Form policy and the RCBAP cannot exceed $250,000 for the unit.

## IX. Assignment

The owner of an insured building may, with their written consent, assign a flood insurance building policy to the purchaser of the building. The seller must sign the assignment endorsement on or before the closing date. If the building is a primary residence, the insurer must validate the primary residence status at the time of assignment in order for the assignee to be eligible for the primary residence status.

Owners may not assign policies on buildings in the course of construction or on contents only.

## X. Transfer of Business

A transfer of business occurs when an agent moves any or all of his or her business from one insurer to another. The insurer must collect all underwriting information to verify the correct rating and issuance of the policies, including:

- Documentation of primary residence status;
- Documentation of PRP eligibility including verification of the current flood zone;
- Documentation of current and prior flood zone for a policy using the Newly Mapped rating procedure;
- Documentation of all information needed to issue and rate an RCBAP including photos and replacement cost value;
- Photographs of all elevation-rated policies (NFIP will accept photographs from the previous insurer if there is no evidence of structural changes that affect rating); *and*
- All elevation information.

The insurer may use the elevation information on the previous insurer's declaration page if it displays the BFE and the lowest floor elevation.

The insurer must validate the information when there is a discrepancy between the building descriptions in the application and the prior insurer's declarations page. For example:

- If the application indicates a basement or enclosure and it is not shown on the declarations page; or
- If the application describes a non-elevated building and the declarations page describes an elevated building.

**IMPORTANT**

A transfer of business does not include conversions of an entire book of business from one insurer or third-party administrator to another. When an insurer acquires another insurer's book of business, all underwriting files must transfer in their entirety to the new insurer.

## XI. Reforming the Policy

If the premium the insurer receives will not purchase the amounts of insurance requested, then the insurer must issue the policy for the insurance coverage amounts the premium will purchase for a one-year policy term.

The SFIP provisions for reduction of coverage limits or reformation are available at:

- Dwelling Form, section VII, paragraph G;
- General Property Form, section VII, paragraph G; *and*
- RCBAP, section VIII, paragraph G.

## A. Increasing Coverage after Reforming a Policy

**Table 11** describes how an insurer can increase coverage after a policy reformation.

**Table 11. Reformation**

| BEFORE A LOSS | |
|---|---|
| **Complete Rating Information** | If the insurer has all of the information to rerate the policy, the insurer will send a bill for the required additional premium.<br>If the insurer receives the premium within 30 days from the date of the bill, the insurer will increase the policy limits to the originally requested amount effective the beginning of the current policy term.<br>If the insurer does not receive the additional premium within 30 days of the date of the bill, the insurer may only increase coverage by endorsement with a 30-day waiting period. |
| **Incomplete Rating Information** | When the insurer has incomplete rating information and cannot calculate the correct policy premium, the insurer will send a request for additional information. The insurer must receive the additional information within 60 days of the request.<br>If the insurer receives the additional information within 60 days, the insurer will bill the insured for the additional premium.<br>If the insurer does not receive the additional premium within 30 days of the date of the bill, or the additional information within 60 days of the request, the insurer may only increase coverage by endorsement with a 30-day waiting period. |
| **AFTER A LOSS** | |
| **Complete Rating Information** | The insurer will send a bill for the required additional premium for the current policy term only. This is an exception to the SFIP provisions requiring additional premium for the current and the prior policy terms.<br>If the insurer receives the premium within 30 days from the date of the bill, the insurer should increase the policy limits to the originally requested amount effective to the beginning of the current policy term.<br>If the insurer does not receive the additional premium by the due date, the insurer must settle the claim based on the previously submitted premium and reduced policy limits. |

## B. Exceptions for Incorrect Flood Zone or BFE after a Loss

When the insurer discovers after a loss that an incorrect flood zone or BFE resulted in insufficient premium, the following applies:

- The insurer must calculate any additional premium due prospectively from the date of discovery; *and*
- The insurer must apply the automatic reduction in policy limits effective on the date of discovery.

The insurer must pay the claim based on the limits in place before the date of discovery of the incorrect flood zone or BFE. The insured need not pay any additional premium at this time when the flood zone or BFE is incorrect. However, the insurer must bill the insured for the additional premium to restore the originally requested limits effective the date of discovery for the remainder of the policy term. The insurer must receive the additional premium within 30 days to increase the coverage without a waiting period. Otherwise, the insurer will reduce the policy limits to the amount the previously received premium will purchase.

If the insurer must obtain additional rating information, it must receive that information within 60 days. Upon receipt of the information, if it is determined additional premium is due, the insurer will then bill the insured for the additional premium required to maintain the original policy limits for the remainder of the term. The insurer must receive the additional premium within 30 days of the bill to increase the coverage without a waiting period. If the insurer does not receive the additional information within 60 days of the request or the additional premium within 30 days of the date of the bill, there will be a 30 day waiting period to return to the original policy limits.

### C. Incorrect Policy Form

The insurer must use the correct policy form before making a loss payment. When the insurer issues coverage using an incorrect SFIP form, the policy is void and the insurer must cancel and rewrite the coverage under the correct form. The provisions of the correct SFIP form apply.

- The insurer must reform the coverage limits according to the provisions of the correct SFIP form.
- The coverage amounts on the correct SFIP form must equal the coverage amounts on the canceled SFIP form. Coverage cannot exceed:
  - The coverage amounts issued under the incorrect policy form.
  - The maximum coverage amounts available on the correct SFIP form.
- If additional premium is due the insurer must:
  - Send an additional premium notice.
  - Receive the premium within 30 days of the date of the additional premium notice or reduce the coverage to the amount that can be purchased for a one-year term with the premium already submitted.
- If the incorrect policy form is discovered after a claim, any additional premium due can be deducted from the claim settlement.
- Requests to increase coverage above the existing coverage amounts are subject to the endorsement effective date rules.

This page is intentionally left blank.

# 3. How To Write

## I. Rating

### A. General Information

#### *1. Writing a Flood Insurance Policy*

Writing a flood insurance policy properly involves gathering a lot of information and following prescribed steps for different types of coverage. **Table 1** outlines the requirements, which this section discusses in detail.

**Table 1. Rating a Flood Insurance Policy**

| Step | Decision | Options |
|---|---|---|
| **Initial Determinations** | Community Information | • Participating versus Non-Participating<br>• Emergency versus Regular Program |
| | Building | • Meets the definition of an eligible building |
| | Amount and Type of Coverage | • Building coverage, contents coverage, or both |
| | Application Form to Use | • Flood Insurance Application<br>• Preferred Risk Policy and Newly Mapped Application |
| **Gather Preliminary Rating Information** | Property Location | • Street address<br>• Legal description<br>• Geographic location |
| | Flood Zone | • Special Flood Hazard Area (SFHA) zones are: A, AE, A1–A30, AH, AO, AR, A99, V, VE, V1–V30<br>• Non–SFHA zones are: B, C, X, D |
| | Date of Construction | • Pre-FIRM<br>• Post-FIRM |
| | Rating Considerations | • Preferred Risk Policy (PRP)<br>• Newly Mapped rating procedure<br>• Post-FIRM (Full Risk)<br>• Optional Post-FIRM Rating<br>• Grandfathering<br>• Pre-FIRM<br>• Pre-FIRM subsidized<br>• Residential Condominium Building Association Policy (RCBAP) |
| | Building Occupancy | • Single family<br>• 2–4 family<br>• Other residential<br>• Non-residential business<br>• Other non-residential |
| | Primary Residence | • Yes<br>• No |

**Table 1. Rating a Flood Insurance Policy** *continued*

| Step | Decision | Options | |
|---|---|---|---|
| **Gather Preliminary Rating Information** *continued* | Number of Floors | • 1 Floor<br>• 2 Floors<br>• 3 or More Floors<br>• Split Level | • Townhouse/Rowhouse (RCBAP low-rise only)<br>• Manufactured (mobile) home/travel trailer on foundation |
| **Determine Non-elevated or Elevated Building** | Make determination based on foundation type | • Non-elevated building<br>• Elevated building | |
| **Determine Type of Rating** | Rating without an Elevation Certificate (EC) | • Non-elevated building<br>• Elevated building | |
| | Rating with an EC | • Non-elevated building<br>• Elevated building<br>• Any flood zone beginning with A<br>• Any flood zone beginning with V | |
| **Determine Elevation Difference if Rating with an EC** | Calculate difference between Lowest Floor Elevation (LFE) and Base Flood Elevation (BFE) or grade elevation | • Building LFE<br>• BFE or grade elevation | |
| **Determine Premium** | Calculate premium and add fees, surcharges, etc. | • Standard-rated policy<br>• PRP<br>• Newly Mapped rating procedure<br>• RCBAP<br>**Note:** Instructions for premium calculations will appear after each of the sections listed above. | |

### *2. Amount of Insurance Available*

**Table 2** shows the maximum coverage amounts available under the Emergency and the Regular Programs.

- The amount of insurance may not exceed the maximum coverage limits in Table 2.
- Emergency and Regular Program limits are not combinable to provide a higher limit.
- The limits apply to all single condominium units and all other buildings not in a condominium form of ownership, including cooperatives and timeshares.
- Refer to the Condominiums heading in this section for the basic insurance limits and maximum amount of insurance available under the RCBAP.

**NOTE**

If the building's value is less than the minimum deductible available, then the amount of any building loss will be less than the minimum deductible.

**Table 2. Maximum Amount of Insurance Available for the Emergency and Regular Programs[1,2]**

| Building Occupancy | Emergency Program | Regular Program Basic Insurance Limits | Regular Program Additional Insurance Limits | Regular Program Total Insurance Limits |
|---|---|---|---|---|
| **Building Coverage** | | | | |
| Single-Family Dwelling | $35,000[3] | $60,000 | $190,000 | $250,000 |
| 2–4 Family Building | $35,000[3] | $60,000 | $190,000 | $250,000 |
| Other Residential Building | $100,000[5] | $175,000 | $325,000 | $500,000 |
| Non-Residential Building (including Business Buildings and Other Non-Residential Buildings)[4] | $100,000[5] | $175,000 | $325,000 | $500,000 |
| **Contents Coverage** | | | | |
| Residential Property[6] | $10,000 | $25,000 | $75,000 | $100,000 |
| Non-Residential Business, Other Non-Residential Property[4] | $100,000 | $150,000 | $350,000 | $500,000 |

1. Table 2 provides the maximum coverage amounts available under the Emergency Program and the Regular Program, and the columns cannot be aggregated to exceed the limits in the Regular Program, which are established by statute. The aggregate limits for building coverage are the maximum coverage amounts allowed by statute for each building included in the relevant occupancy category.
2. These limits apply to all single condominium units and all other buildings not in a condominium form of ownership, including cooperatives and timeshares. Refer to the Condominiums heading in this section for the basic insurance limits and maximum amount of insurance available under the RCBAP.
3. In Alaska, Guam, Hawaii, and the U.S. Virgin Islands, the amount available is $50,000.
4. For further guidance on Non-Residential Business and Other Non-Residential occupancies, refer to Table 7. Building Occupancy Types in this section of the manual.
5. In Alaska, Guam, Hawaii, and the U.S. Virgin Islands, the amount available is $150,000.
6. The Residential Property occupancy category includes the Single Family, 2–4 Family, Other Residential, and Residential Condominium occupancies.

### *3. Application Forms*

Write a policy using one of two different application forms, selecting the appropriate form based on the guidance below.

- Flood Insurance Application:
  - Use this application to write most policies, including RCBAPs.
- Preferred Risk Policy and Newly Mapped Application:
  - Use this application for buildings located outside of an SFHA (zones B, C, X, D), or in an AR or A99 zone on the current effective Flood Insurance Rate Map (FIRM) that are eligible for PRPs.
  - Use this application for buildings newly mapped from a non-SFHA into an SFHA that are eligible for the Newly Mapped rating procedure.
  - See the PRP and Newly Mapped headings in this section for eligibility requirements.

## B. Preliminary Rating Information

### *1. Determine the Property Location*

There are three ways to determine property location, listed in the subsections below. Note that a P.O. Box address is not a valid identification of the insured property's location.

**NOTE**

For property locations that contain multiple buildings, or if applying for insurance separately for a building with additions and extensions, provide a description of the building to be insured.

*Example:* Maintenance Building #1

#### a. Street Address

A street address is the preferred method and it includes:

- Street number;
- Street name;
- Unit or apartment number;
- City or county name;
- State; *and*
- ZIP code.

*Example:* 4200 Parkview Drive, Unit 6B, Carnegie, PA 15106

#### b. Legal Description

A legal description is the description of the property on the deed or other legal document and may include the community name, subdivision name, and lot number. The insurer may use a legal description only when a building or a subdivision is in the course of construction, or prior to it having an established street address. The insurer must endorse the policy to indicate the street address as soon as it is available.

*Example:* Westmoreland Square, subdivision 3, lot 142

#### c. Geographic Location

A geographic location is a written description of the property's location using location or other identifying markers. If a property is rural and a standard street address is not available, the insurer can enter a detailed description of the property's location.

*Example:* The grain silo behind the barn at the intersection of route 50 and highway 68

### *2. Determine the Flood Zone*

#### a. General Information

To begin the rating process, obtain the flood zone from one of the following sources (some of which are available at the FEMA Flood Map Service Center at https://msc.fema.gov/portal/home):

- FIRM;
- Standard Flood Hazard Determination Form (SFHDF);
- Letter of Determination Review (LODR);
- EC;
- Letter of Map Amendment (LOMA); *or*
- Letter of Map Revision (LOMR).

The rating process defines flood zones as either SFHAs or non-SFHAs.

- SFHA zones are: A, AE, A1–A30, AH, AO, AR, A99, V, VE, V1–V30.
- Non–SFHA zones are: B, C, X, D.

### b. Special Considerations

Below are items to consider when writing a policy:

- Choose the rating method that provides the most favorable premium (lower rate) or flood coverage to the insured.
- When presented with documentation that includes conflicting flood zones or BFEs, and the conflict cannot be resolved, use the more hazardous flood zone or BFE where the building foundation is located. For example, if presented with an EC and SFHDF with conflicting flood zones or BFEs, use the more hazardous information.
- When an attached deck or a portion of the building overhangs a more hazardous flood zone/BFE, but the building foundation system does not extend into the more hazardous flood zone/BFE, rate the building using the flood zone/BFE where the building foundation is located.

## *3. Determine Pre- or Post-FIRM Construction*

### a. Post-FIRM Construction

For insurance rating purposes, buildings are Post-FIRM construction when the start of construction or substantial improvement was **after December 31, 1974**, or on or after the effective date of the initial FIRM for the community, whichever is later.

**NOTE**

Find the effective date of the initial FIRM for the community in the NFIP Community Status Book at https://www.fema.gov/national-flood-insurance-program-community-status-book.

### b. Pre-FIRM Construction

For insurance rating purposes, buildings are Pre-FIRM construction when the start of construction or substantial improvement was **on or before December 31, 1974**, or before the effective date of the initial FIRM for the community.

### c. Date of Construction for Manufactured Homes/Travel Trailers

Determining the date of construction differs for manufactured homes/travel trailers located in a manufactured home park or subdivision versus those on individually owned lots or tracts of land. See **Table 3** for more detailed guidance.

**Table 3. Date of Construction — Manufactured Home/Travel Trailer**

| Manufactured (Mobile) Home/ Travel Trailer Location | Determine Construction Date |
|---|---|
| **Manufactured Home Park or Subdivision** | • The date facilities were constructed for servicing the manufactured home site; *or*<br>• The date of the permit, provided that construction began within 180 days of the permit date. |
| **Individually Owned Lots or Tracts of Land** | • The date the manufactured home was permanently affixed to the site; *or*<br>• The permit date if affixed to the site within 180 days of the permit date. |

### *4. Substantial Improvement*

The agent must confirm if a local community official has declared the building substantially improved and, if so, the substantial improvement date.

#### a. Post-FIRM

For buildings that were originally Post-FIRM construction, the substantial improvement date becomes the date of construction for rating purposes. Rate the policy using the FIRM in effect at the time that the substantial improvement occurred or the current map, whichever is later.

#### b. Pre-FIRM

For buildings that were originally Pre-FIRM construction, if the building is substantially improved on or after April 1, 2015, the date of construction for rating purposes will be the date the building was originally constructed. It is eligible for Pre-FIRM subsidized rates as long as there has been no lapse in coverage (see Pre-FIRM Eligibility Table). Always use full-risk rates for Pre-FIRM buildings when the full-risk rate is lower than the appropriate Pre-FIRM subsidized rates.

For buildings that were originally Pre-FIRM construction, if the building is substantially improved before April 1, 2015, the substantial improvement date becomes the date of construction for rating purposes. Rate the policy using the full-risk rates based on the FIRM in effect at the time of the substantial improvement or the current map, whichever is later.

**NOTE**

All historic buildings are Pre-FIRM if they meet the definition of "historic building" provided in the Definitions appendix.

### *5. Determine the Most Beneficial Premium/Coverage*

Insurers may rate the same building different ways, resulting in different premiums/coverage. Insurers must determine the most beneficial premium/coverage for the insured. Coverage limitations may apply based on the method used to rate a building. Consider the following options from **Table 4** to determine the most beneficial premiums/coverage.

**Table 4. Types of Rating**

| Rating Type | Requirements |
|---|---|
| PRP or Newly Mapped Rating | **PRP**<br>• Buildings in a B, C, X, AR, or A99 Zone.<br>**Newly Mapped**<br>• Buildings recently mapped into an SFHA other than Zone AR or A99.<br>**Both PRP and Newly Mapped**<br>• Must meet eligibility requirements.<br>• Not available for condominium associations.<br>• See the PRP and Newly Mapped headings later in this section. |
| Pre-FIRM Subsidized Rating | • Eligible Pre-FIRM buildings.<br>• Insurers should use full-risk rates for Pre-FIRM buildings ineligible for Pre-FIRM subsidized rates because of a lapse in coverage.<br>• Refer to Table 6, Pre-FIRM Subsidized Rates Ineligibility Determination in this section, to determine eligibility for Pre-FIRM subsidized rates. |

**Table 4. Types of Rating** *continued*

| Rating Type | Requirements |
|---|---|
| **Optional Post-FIRM Rating for a Pre-FIRM Building** | • Full-risk rates may be lower than Pre-FIRM subsidized rates for Pre-FIRM buildings located in SFHAs.<br>• Insured may submit an EC and request full-risk rating for:<br>– Pre-FIRM buildings located in an SFHA;<br>– Pre-FIRM buildings located in an AR or AR Dual Zone.<br>**Note:** See the Floodproofing and Elevation Certificate forms and instructions in Appendix B: Forms. |
| **Post-FIRM Rating** | • The NFIP requires an EC to determine the rate for Post-FIRM buildings located in zones A (with or without BFEs), AE, A1–A30, AH, AO, V (with BFEs), VE, and V1–V30.<br>• The NFIP does not require an EC to determine premium rates for Post-FIRM buildings located in zones AR and AR Dual, A99, B, C, D, and X.<br>• Use for Pre-FIRM buildings located in SFHAs not eligible for the Pre-FIRM subsidized rates because of a lapse in coverage. |
| **Grandfathered Rating** | • Built in compliance<br>• Continuous coverage.<br>• See **Table 5** for more details. |
| **Submit for Rate** | See the Submit-for-Rate heading in this section. For risks requiring submission to the insurer for rating purposes refer to the *NFIP Specific Rating Guidelines* at https://www.fema.gov/media-library/assets/documents/34620. |

### a. Eligibility for Grandfathered Rating

When a FIRM is revised and republished, new or existing policyholders affected by changes to the BFE and/or flood zones may be eligible for grandfathering. Grandfathering gives policyholders the option of having their premium rate determined using either the rating criteria for that property under the current effective FIRM (new map) or the BFE and/or flood zone on a prior FIRM (old map). Insurers should choose the rating method that provides the most favorable premium or flood coverage to the insured. Buildings built in compliance with the FIRM in effect at the time of construction may be eligible for "built-in-compliance" grandfathering. Buildings that have had continuous NFIP flood insurance coverage may be eligible for "continuous coverage" grandfathering. **Table 5** provides information about grandfathering eligibility, and **Table 5A** provides examples of acceptable documentation to verify grandfathering eligibility.

**Table 5. Buildings Eligible for Grandfathered Rating**

| Type | Eligibility | Special Requirements |
|---|---|---|
| **Built-in-Compliance** | Buildings built in compliance with the FIRM in effect at the time of construction | In an elevated building, an enclosure below the elevated floor must be compliant with the FIRM in effect at the time of construction. An enclosure with the lowest floor at or above the BFE at the time of construction is compliant. An enclosure with the lowest floor below the BFE (for example, the lowest floor is 0.1 to 0.5 feet below the BFE) at the time of construction is not compliant if any of the following conditions exist (see the Enclosures heading in this section):<br>• The enclosure is finished;<br>• The enclosure is used for other than parking, storage, *or* building access;<br>• For A zones, the enclosure does not have proper openings;<br>• For V zones, the enclosure does not have breakaway walls; *or*<br>• For V zones, there is machinery and equipment below the elevated floor.<br>**Note:** Do not apply the rounding rule first to determine grandfathering eligibility. |
| **Continuous Coverage** | Continuous coverage under the NFIP maintained on the building | • Continuous NFIP coverage maintained since purchasing the initial policy on the building.<br>• When changing insurers, the receiving insurer must obtain the prior insurer's declaration page for the expiring term to document continuous coverage.<br>• Condominium unit owners are eligible for continuous coverage grandfathering if the condominium association has maintained a master policy.<br>• Policy assignment does not affect eligibility.<br>**Note:** In addition to removing eligibility for continuous coverage grandfathering, a policy lapse may impact eligibility for Pre-FIRM subsidized rates or Newly Mapped rating. |

**Table 5A. Documentation to Verify Grandfathering Eligibility**

| EXAMPLES OF DOCUMENTATION |
|---|
| • A copy of the map panel showing the location of the building.<br>– Must show the date and zone in which the building is located.<br>– The BFE, if any, for that zone.<br>• The rating elements that are to be grandfathered.<br>• A letter from a community official verifying this information, an EC, or a certified SFHDF.<br>• An RCBAP declaration page may be used as supporting documentation for a unit owner policy within that building. |

### b. Disqualification for Pre-FIRM Subsidized or Newly Mapped Rating

If a policy on a Pre-FIRM building eligible for Pre-FIRM subsidized rates lapses, the building is no longer eligible for this subsidy or the Newly Mapped rating procedure under the following conditions:

- The insured wants to reinstate expired or canceled coverage on a previously covered building.
- One or more of the named insureds on the new policy was either a named insured on the expired or canceled policy or had an ownership interest in the building at the time of cancellation or expiration.
- The insured reinstated coverage with premium received on or after April 1, 2016:
  - The second time the insurer receives the renewal payment more than 30 days after expiration but within 90 days from the date of the policy expiration date, the coverage will be reinstated with a 30-day waiting period upon receipt of the renewal payment. **Note:** The policy remains eligible to renew using Pre-FIRM subsidized rates or the Newly Mapped rating procedure for only the first occurrence.
  - The insurer receives the renewal payment more than 90 days following the expiration date. The insurer must require a new application with the full annual premium and apply the 30-day waiting period.
- The insured is no longer eligible if the policy expiration or cancellation was for a reason other than:
  - The insured's lender no longer required the insured to obtain and maintain flood insurance.
  - The property was in a community suspended from the NFIP and the insured reinstated the policy within 180 days of the community's reinstatement as a participating NFIP community.

**Note:** This restriction applies to all lapses that occur on or after April 1, 2016.

Refer to the guidance in **Table 6** to determine when to use Pre-FIRM Subsidized Rates.

### Table 6. Pre-FIRM Subsidized Rates Ineligibility Determination[1,2]

| Was there a prior NFIP policy for this property in the insured's name? | Did a lender require the prior NFIP policy? | Did the prior NFIP policy lapse while required by a lender? | Was the lapse the result of a community suspension? | Was the community reinstated within the last 180 days? | Eligible for Pre-FIRM subsidized rates? |
|---|---|---|---|---|---|
| Yes | Yes | Yes | Yes | No | No |
| Yes | Yes | Yes | No | Yes | No |
| Yes | Yes | Yes | No | No | No |

1. Use this table for all applications for Pre-FIRM buildings.
2. Also use this table for policy reinstatements by means of renewal, where coverage has lapsed more than 30 days after the prior policy expiration or cancellation date, and where the named insured has **not** maintained continuous coverage on the property from April 1, 2016 to the prior policy expiration or cancellation date.

### 6. *Determine Building Occupancy*

There are five different building occupancies. The maximum available coverage limits depend in part on the building occupancy. Refer to **Table 7** for occupancy types. For information regarding manufactured homes and travel trailers refer to the note below Table 7.

**Table 7. Building Occupancy Types**

| Occupancy | Definition |
| --- | --- |
| **Single Family** | 1. A residential single-family building in which the total floor area devoted to non-residential uses is less than 50 percent of the building's total floor area; *or*<br>2. A residential unit within a 2–4 family building, other-residential building, or non-residential building, in which non-residential uses within the unit are limited to less than 50 percent of the unit's total floor area.<br>Examples of non-residential uses within the unit include offices, private schools, studios, or small service operations within a residential building.<br>Single Family includes a residential townhouse/rowhouse, which is a multi-floor unit, divided from similar units by solid, vertical, load-bearing walls, dividing the building from its lowest level to its highest ceiling and having no openings in the walls between units and with no horizontal divisions between any of the units.<br>**Note:** A residential building or unit rented out short term or seasonally is considered residential. |
| **2–4 Family** | A residential building containing 2–4 residential units, with non-residential uses limited to less than 25 percent of the building's total floor area. This category includes apartment buildings and condominium buildings. It excludes hotels and motels with normal room rentals for less than 6 months. |
| **Other Residential** | A residential building containing 5 or more residential units, or a mixed-use building with non-residential uses limited to less than 25 percent of the building's total floor area.<br>This category includes the following buildings where the normal occupancy of a guest is 6 months or more:<br>• Dormitories;<br>• Assisted-living facilities;<br>• Condominium buildings;<br>• Cooperative buildings;<br>• Apartment buildings;<br>• Hotels and motels;<br>• Tourist homes; *and*<br>• Rooming houses.<br>**Note:** Condominium associations may be eligible for the RCBAP. Refer to the Condominium heading in this section for more information. |

**Table 7. Building Occupancy Types** *continued*

| Occupancy | Definition |
|---|---|
| **Non-Residential Business** | A building in which the named insured is a commercial enterprise primarily carried out to generate income and the coverage is for:<br>1. A building not designed for habitation or residential uses;<br>2. A mixed-use building in which the total floor area devoted to residential uses is:<br>– 50 percent or less of the total floor area within the building if the residential building is a single-family property; *or*<br>– 75 percent or less of the total floor area within the building for all other residential properties.<br>3. A building designed for use as office, retail space, wholesale space, hospitality space, or for similar uses; *or*<br>4. The following buildings where the normal occupancy of a guest is less than 6 months:<br>– Condominium buildings;<br>– Apartment buildings;<br>– Hotels and motels;<br>– Tourist homes; *or*<br>– Rooming houses. |
| **Other Non-Residential** | A building not designed for habitation that does not qualify as a non-residential business building, or a mixed-use building that does not qualify as a residential building. This category includes, but is not limited to:<br>• Houses of worship;<br>• Schools;<br>• Agricultural structures;<br>• Garages;<br>• Pool houses;<br>• Clubhouses; *and*<br>• Recreational buildings.<br>A small business cannot use this category. |

**NOTE**

The occupancy for manufactured homes and travel trailers eligible for NFIP coverage (see the Types of Eligible Buildings the NFIP Insures heading in Section 2) may be residential or non-residential depending on their use.

### *7. Determine Single Building Eligibility*

To qualify as a single-building structure, subject to the single-building limits of coverage, a building must be:

- Separated from other buildings by intervening clear space; *or*
- Separated into divisions by solid vertical load-bearing walls.
  - These walls must divide the building from its lowest level to its highest ceiling and have no openings.
  - If there is access through the division wall by a doorway or other opening, the structure must be insured as one building unless it meets all of the following criteria:

**NOTE**

Insurers can submit requests to FEMA seeking single-building determinations for complex structures with multiple building owners.

> It is a separately titled building contiguous to the ground;

> It has a separate legal description; *and*

> It is regarded as a separate property for other real estate purposes, meaning that it has most of its own utilities and may be deeded, conveyed, and taxed separately.

### *8. Primary Residence*

#### a. General Information

A primary residence is a single-family building, 2–4 family building, condominium unit, apartment unit, or unit within a cooperative building in which the insured or the insured's spouse lives. An insured or the insured's spouse may have no more than one primary residence per person. Where the insured or the insured's spouse identify different primary residences, the insured must submit the appropriate documentation for each person's primary residence.

For a single-family building, 2–4 family building, or unit to qualify as a primary residence, the insured or the insured's spouse must live in the residence:

- More than 50 percent of the 365 calendar days following the current policy effective date; *or*
- 50 percent or less of the 365 calendar days following the current policy effective date if the insured has only one residence and does not lease that residence to another party, or use it as rental or income property at any time during the policy term.
  - Examples include, but are not limited to:
    - Active-duty military personnel deployed for 50 percent or more of the policy year in compliance with military orders;
    - Persons displaced from a primary residence and living in a temporary residence due to a federally declared disaster or a loss event on the primary residence claimed on any line of insurance for 50 percent or more of the policy year; *or*
    - Persons absent from a primary residence for reasons such as routine business travel, hospitalizations, and/or vacation for 50 percent or more of the policy year.

**NOTE**

NFIP uses the term **primary residence** for **rating** purposes only.

NFIP uses the term principal residence to determine loss settlement as defined in the Standard Flood Insurance Policy (SFIP). A principal residence is a single-family dwelling in which, at the time of loss, the named insured or the named insured's spouse has lived for either 80 percent of the 365 days immediately preceding the loss, or 80 percent of the period of ownership, if the dwelling was owned less than 365 days. If the dwelling does not meet the definition of principal residence in the SFIP, the NFIP will settle the building losses using actual cash value.

#### b. Documentation of Primary Residence

If the policy or application indicates that coverage is for a primary residence, the insurer must verify that the address is the primary residence. When the mailing address and the property address match, that provides sufficient verification and no further documentation is required. If the addresses do not match, the insurer must obtain supporting documentation. The NFIP accepts the following documentation of primary residence:

- Homestead Tax Credit form for primary residence;
- Driver's license;
- Automobile registration;
- Proof of insurance for a vehicle;
- Voter's registration;
- Documents showing where children attend school; *or*
- A signed and dated primary residence verification statement with the text below:

  <Insured Property Address>

  The above address is my primary residence, and I and/or my spouse will live at this location for more than 50 percent of the 365 days following the policy effective date.

  PURSUANT TO 28 U.S.C. § 1746 I CERTIFY UNDER PENALTY OF PERJURY UNDER THE LAWS OF THE UNITED STATES OF AMERICA THAT THE FOREGOING IS TRUE AND CORRECT. I UNDERSTAND THAT ANY FALSE STATEMENTS MAY CAUSE MY POLICY TO BE VOID, AND MAY BE PUNISHABLE BY FINE OR IMPRISONMENT UNDER APPLICABLE FEDERAL LAW.

#### c. Primary Residence and Trusts

If the policy names a trust, and a beneficiary of the trust is using the building as a primary residence, the beneficiary of the trust must provide documentation of primary residence outlined above. In addition, the insurer must obtain documentation that the person using the home as a primary residence is a beneficiary of the trust named as the insured.

The grantor of a trust may also be eligible for the primary residence status if the trust documents support that the grantor is a beneficiary of the trust with the right to live in the home. The grantor must submit both the trust documents and documentation of primary residence outlined above. The insurer must obtain documentation that the grantor is a beneficiary of the trust named as the insured with the right to live in the home as a benefit.

## C. Determine if Elevated or Non-Elevated Building

For more information regarding ECs, please refer to the Certifications heading in this section.

### *1. Non-Elevated versus Elevated Buildings*

#### a. Non-Elevated Building

A non-elevated building is a building with a:

- Slab-on-grade foundation with wood frame walls on the lowest level; *or*
- Basement or below grade (subgrade) crawlspace foundation.

**NOTE**

**A non-elevated building has a basement** if any area of the building, including any sunken room or sunken portion of a room, has its floor below ground level (subgrade) on all sides.

**A non-elevated building has a subgrade crawlspace** if the subgrade under-floor area is no more than 5 feet below the top of the next higher floor (living floor) and no more than 2 feet below the lowest adjacent grade (LAG) (ground) level on all sides.

### b. Elevated Building

An elevated building is a building that:

- Has no basement; *and*
- Has its lowest elevated floor raised above ground level by foundation walls, shear walls, posts, piers, pilings, or columns.

**Table 8** describes the types of walls associated with elevated buildings.

**Table 8. Elevated Buildings – Elevating Foundation Types**

| Type of Wall | Description |
|---|---|
| **Foundation walls** are masonry walls, poured concrete walls, or precast concrete walls, regardless of height, that extend above grade and support the weight of a building. | Buildings with knee foundation walls below the elevated floor (e.g., foundation walls not constructed the full height of the area between the lowest elevated floor and the grade, with wood-frame or studs attached above the foundation wall) are elevated buildings for rating purposes.<br>The building is non-elevated if a slab foundation supports the foundation walls. |
| | Solid (perimeter) foundation walls may be used to elevate the building in A Zones.<br>Solid (perimeter) foundation walls are not an acceptable way to elevate buildings in V/VE Zones. |
| **Shear walls** are for structural support and not structurally joined or enclosed at the ends, except by breakaway walls. | Reinforced concrete or wood shear walls used as the method of elevating a building are normally parallel (or nearly parallel) to the expected flow of floodwaters. |
| **Piers, posts, piles, and columns** | This includes reinforced masonry piers, concrete piers or columns. |

### *2. Enclosures*

An enclosure is the portion of an elevated building below the lowest elevated floor partially or fully enclosed by rigid walls. Examples of an enclosure are:

- A garage, storage, or utility room below the elevated floor of an elevated building;
- A garage, storage, or utility room attached and next to an elevated building with the enclosure floor lower than the elevated floor
- An enclosed crawlspace below the lowest elevated floor.

FEMA does not consider an enclosed area below the lowest elevated floor to be an enclosure if all the following criteria are met:

- It is the minimum size necessary to protect the building's utilities (i.e., plumbing, pipes, wiring, HVAC supply/return lines);
- It is constructed with flood damage resistant materials;
- There are no mechanical or electrical equipment inside the enclosed area; *and*
- There is not enough space for a person to enter into the enclosed area.

### a. Enclosure Wall Types

- Insect screening with no additional support.
- Plastic lattice.
- Wooden or plastic slats or shutters.
- Solid wood frame walls.
- Masonry walls.
- Breakaway walls:
  - For an enclosure's walls to qualify as breakaway walls, they must meet all of the following criteria:
    - Above ground level;
    - Below the elevated floor of an elevated structure;
    - Non-structurally supporting (non-load-bearing walls); *and*
    - Designed to fail under certain wave force conditions and cause no damage to the elevated portions of the elevated building or its supporting foundation system as a result of failure.

### b. Finished or Unfinished Enclosure

An enclosure is a finished enclosure if any of the following apply:

- It is habitable.
- It has more than 20 linear feet of interior finished wall or paneling. A finished wall is:
  - Drywall taped, mudded, and painted; *or*
  - Painted plywood or similar material.
- It has uses other than building access (stairwells, elevators, etc.), parking, or storage.

FEMA considers an enclosure that complies with NFIP flood damage-resistant materials regulations (44 CFR 60.3(a)(3)) to be an unfinished enclosure. See FEMA Technical Bulletin 2, "Flood Damage-Resistant Materials Requirements."

### c. Proper Flood Openings Requirement

Proper flood openings (flood vents) allow the hydrostatic flood forces on the walls to equalize and minimize foundation damage to the building.

For elevated buildings in any flood zone beginning with an A, the NFIP minimum floodplain management ordinances require enclosures (including crawlspaces, attached garages, and elevator shafts) below the lowest elevated floor be designed with proper openings.

To satisfy the proper openings requirement for rating purposes:

- There must be a minimum of two openings positioned on at least two exterior walls. For partially subgrade floors, there must be a minimum of two openings positioned on a single exterior wall adjacent to the lowest grade next to the building.
- The bottom of all openings must be no higher than one foot above the higher of the exterior or interior adjacent grade or floor immediately below the openings.
- The openings must have a total net area of not less than one square inch for every one square foot of enclosed area.

### d. Engineered Openings Certified by a Design Professional

An alternative to the proper openings requirement is engineered openings. If used, the insured must provide to the insurer a copy of the certification validating that the openings meet NFIP requirements. FEMA Technical Bulletin 1-08, "Openings in Foundation Walls and Walls of Enclosures below Elevated Buildings in Special Flood Hazard Areas" provides technical guidance for these requirements.

The certification statement must identify the building with the installed engineered openings and include:

- The design professional's name, title address, type of license, license number, the state issuing the license, and the signature and applied seal of the certifying registered design professional;
- A statement certifying that the design of the openings will automatically equalize hydrostatic flood loads on exterior walls by allowing for the automatic entry and exit of floodwaters; *and*
- A description of the range of flood characteristics tested or computed for which the certification is valid, such as rates of rise and fall of floodwaters.

### e. Engineered Openings Certified by the International Code Council Evaluation Service

Engineered openings identified by the International Code Council Evaluation Service, Inc., can be used to satisfy the proper opening requirements. The International Code Council Evaluation Service publishes an evaluation report for each specific engineered opening product (make and model) that it certifies, specifying the square footage of the area for which it is certified. If these openings are used, documentation to confirm the installation and model number of the opening is required. Reference the evaluation report information to confirm whether the engineered openings satisfy the proper openings requirement. Examples of documentation that can be used are:

- Documentation to confirm installation should specify the number of openings installed, the square footage of the area for which they are certified, and the model number of the engineered opening; *or*
- An EC may have information that confirms the use of engineered openings.

FEMA Technical Bulletin 1-08, "Openings in Foundation Walls and Walls of Enclosures below Elevated Buildings in Special Flood Hazard Areas" provides technical guidance for these requirements.

### *3. Building Partially or Entirely Over Water*

#### a. Buildings Entirely Over Water

Follow Submit-for-Rate procedures in this section if the building is located entirely over water (i.e., entirely in, on, or over water or seaward of mean high tide) and was not constructed or substantially improved after September 30, 1982. If the building is Pre-FIRM, the Submit-for-Rate procedure may be used to determine optional full-risk rates; otherwise, Pre-FIRM buildings remain eligible for Pre-FIRM subsidized rates. If the building was constructed or substantially improved on or after October 1, 1982, the building is ineligible for coverage.

**Exception:** If a building was originally constructed on land or partially over water, and later becomes entirely over water because of erosion, then the property owner must establish eligibility for NFIP coverage by submitting all of the following documentation:

- A letter from the community official stating that the building originally was constructed on land or only partially over water;
- Photographs of the building over land, if available;
- The approximate date when the building became located entirely over water; *and*
- Proof of continuous flood insurance coverage from the period beginning 1 year prior to the building being located entirely over water (regardless of any changes in the ownership of the building), or from the date of construction if less than 1 year.

#### b. Buildings Partially Over Water

Follow Submit-for-Rate procedures in this section if the building is partially over water. If the building is Pre-FIRM construction, it is eligible for Pre-FIRM subsidized rates or optional full-risk rates under the Submit-for-Rate procedure. Refer to the Before You Start section of this manual for information on coverage the NFIP provides for such buildings.

#### c. Boathouses Located Partially Over Water

When rating a boathouse located partially over water, submit the Flood Insurance Application form with photographs, but no premium, to the NFIP for premium determination. No coverage becomes effective until the NFIP approves the insurance application, determines the rate, and receives the premium. However, buildings constructed prior to October 1, 1982, may continue to be rated using the published rate. Refer to the Before You Start section of this manual for information on coverage the NFIP provides for such buildings.

## D. Determine Type of Rating

### *1. Rating without an EC*

The NFIP does not require an EC for:

- Pre- and Post-FIRM buildings in B, C, X, A99, AR/AR Dual, and D zones;
- Pre-FIRM buildings in A, AE, A1–A30, AO, AH, V, VE, and V1–V30 zones; *or*
- PRP and Newly Mapped rated policies.

### a. Non-Elevated Building without an EC

The rating classes for non-elevated buildings rated without an EC are: No Basement, With Basement, and Non-Elevated with Subgrade Crawlspace. These classes are described in **Table 9** below.

#### Table 9. Rating Classes for Non-Elevated Buildings without an EC

| Rating Class | Description |
|---|---|
| **No Basement** | Non-elevated building without a basement or subgrade crawlspace with slab-on-grade foundation. |
| **With Basement** | Non-elevated buildings have a basement if any area of the building, including any sunken room or sunken portion of a room, has a floor below ground level (subgrade) on all sides. |
| **Non-elevated with Subgrade Crawlspace** | A non-elevated building has a subgrade crawlspace if the subgrade under-floor area is no more than 5 feet below the top of the next higher floor (living floor) and no more than 2 feet below the LAG (ground) level on all sides. |

### b. Elevated Building without an EC

For elevated buildings rated without an EC, the rating classes are No Enclosure, With Enclosure, and Elevated on Crawlspace. These classes are described in **Table 10** below.

**Note:** FEMA considers an enclosure that complies with NFIP flood damage-resistant materials regulations (44 CFR 60.3(a)(3)) to be an unfinished enclosure. See FEMA Technical Bulletin 2, "Flood Damage-Resistant Materials Requirements."

#### Table 10. Rating Classes for Elevated Buildings without an EC

| Rating Class | Description |
|---|---|
| **No Enclosure** | An elevated building with no enclosure below the lowest elevated floor.<br>Use the No Enclosure rates if (see the Enclosures heading in this section):<br>• There is no enclosure below the lowest elevated floor;<br>• The area below the lowest elevated floor is enclosed by lattice or screening; *or*<br>• The enclosure has proper flood openings. |
| **With Enclosure** | An elevated building with an enclosure (including garage, elevator shaft) below the lowest elevated floor.<br>Use the With Enclosure rates if any of the following conditions exists:<br>• The enclosure is finished;<br>• The enclosure is unfinished and does not have proper openings;<br>• The enclosure is used for other than building access, parking, or storage; *or*<br>• There is an elevator below the lowest elevated floor. |
| **Elevated on Crawlspace** | An elevated building with a crawlspace below the elevated floor has an enclosure where the difference between the crawlspace floor and the top of the next highest floor (living floor) is no more than 5 feet and the crawlspace floor is not below grade on all sides. Use Elevated on Crawlspace rates if the crawlspace does not have proper openings. Use the No Enclosure rates if the crawlspace has proper openings. |

**Table 10. Rating Classes for Elevated Buildings without an EC** *continued*

| Rating Class | Description |
|---|---|
| Elevated on Crawlspace with Attached Garage | For an elevated building in any zone beginning with an "A," a crawlspace and garage are separate enclosures for an elevated building. Each enclosure must meet the proper flood opening requirements to exclude the enclosure floor for rating purposes. If the crawlspace and garage share two exterior walls not separated by a foundation wall, the crawlspace and garage are a single enclosure. Use the following guidelines to determine the rating class:<br>• Use Elevated on Crawlspace if either the crawlspace or garage does not have proper openings; *or*<br>• Use No Enclosure if both the crawlspace and garage have proper openings. |

### *2. EC Rating*

The NFIP requires an EC for all Post-FIRM buildings in A, AE, A1–A30, AO, AH, V, VE, V1–V30 zones. ECs are also used in optional rating of buildings in zones AR and AR Dual, and Pre-FIRM buildings using optional Post-FIRM rating.

For a building rated with an EC, the NFIP determines the rate by comparing the LFE of the building to the BFE or grade elevation to establish an elevation difference. Additional information about ECs and determining the elevation difference is included in this section of the manual. See Appendix C: Lowest Floor Guide for additional information.

#### a. Non-Elevated Building Rated with EC

The LFE used for rating a non-elevated building with an EC is the elevation of the building's lowest floor, including basement or subgrade crawlspace. Refer to **Table 11**.

In V zones, the LFE used for rating is the elevation of the lowest horizontal member (bottom of the slab). For all non-elevated buildings in V zones constructed on or after October 1, 1981, follow the procedures outlined in the *NFIP Specific Rating Guidelines* manual at https://www.fema.gov/media-library/assets/documents/34620.

## Table 11. Considerations when Rating Non-Elevated Buildings with an EC

| Characteristic | Description |
|---|---|
| Attached garage | In any zone beginning with the letter "A" where the floor of the attached garage is below the top of the bottom floor of the building:<br>**Single Family (including a condominium unit within a multi-unit residential building that qualifies as a single building)**<br>• The garage floor can be excluded from rating in the following situations:<br>– The garage floor is at or above the BFE;<br>– The garage has proper openings (see the Proper Flood Openings Requirement heading in this section);<br>– The garage is below the BFE and there is no machinery or equipment; *or*<br>– The garage has machinery or equipment below the BFE, and the garage has proper openings.<br>**All Other Occupancies**<br>• Use the garage floor as the lowest floor for rating when the garage floor is below the bottom floor of the building. |
| Basement | Use the elevation of the basement floor, including any sunken room or sunken portion of a room, having its floor below ground level (subgrade) on all sides. |
| Subgrade crawlspace | Use the elevation of the subgrade crawlspace floor where the subgrade under-floor area is no more than 5 feet below the top of the next higher floor and no more than 2 feet below the LAG on all sides. |

### b. Elevated Building Rated with EC

For an elevated building rated with an EC, the LFE used for rating depends on the flood zone and the presence of an enclosure below the lowest elevated floor.

**Note:** FEMA considers an enclosure that complies with NFIP flood damage-resistant materials regulations (44 CFR 60.3(a)(3)) to be an unfinished enclosure. See FEMA Technical Bulletin 2, "Flood Damage-Resistant Materials Requirements."

#### Any Flood Zone Beginning with A

For buildings located in any flood zone beginning with A, the LFE used for rating can be the lowest elevated floor or the enclosure floor depending on the characteristic of the enclosure area. See **Table 12** for how the characteristics of the enclosure area determine what elevation to use.

## Table 12. Elevated Buildings in A Zones Rated with an EC

| Characteristic | Description |
|---|---|
| No Enclosure | Use the elevation of the lowest elevated floor if:<br>• There is no enclosure below the lowest elevated floor;<br>• The area below the lowest elevated floor is enclosed by lattice or screening; *or*<br>• The enclosure has proper flood openings (see the Proper Flood Openings Requirement heading in this section). |

**Table 12. Elevated Buildings in A Zones Rated with an EC** *continued*

| Characteristic | Description |
|---|---|
| **With Enclosure** | For an elevated building with an enclosure (including crawlspace, attached garage, elevator shaft) below the elevated floor:<br>• Use the enclosure floor for rating if any of the following conditions exists (see the Enclosures heading in this section):<br>– The enclosure is finished;<br>– The enclosure is unfinished and does not have proper openings;<br>– The enclosure is used for other than parking, storage, or building access; *or*<br>– There is an elevator below the BFE.<br>• Use the No Enclosure rates if none of the above conditions exists. |
| **Elevated on Crawlspace with Attached Garage** | For an elevated building on a crawlspace with an attached garage, the crawlspace and garage are separate enclosures if foundation walls separate the main building and garage. Use the lowest elevated floor as the LFE for rating if all the following conditions exist:<br>• Each enclosure is unfinished;<br>• Each enclosure is used only for parking, storage or access;<br>• Each enclosure has proper openings; *and*<br>• There is no elevator below the BFE.<br>The crawlspace and garage are a single enclosure if the crawlspace and garage share two exterior walls not separated by a foundation wall. Use the following guidelines to determine the lowest floor for rating:<br>• Use the top of the crawlspace floor or the garage floor, whichever is lower, if neither the crawlspace nor garage has proper openings;<br>• Use the top of the crawlspace floor if the garage is the only area with proper openings;<br>• Use the top of the garage floor if the crawlspace is the only area with proper openings; *or*<br>• Use the top of the finished floor (lowest elevated floor) if both the crawlspace and garage have proper openings.<br>**Note:** If a residential structure built on a crawlspace foundation has an attached garage and the garage floor is at the same elevation or below the crawlspace floor and the garage is converted into a living space, then the building is considered non-elevated and must be rated as non-elevated. The LFE for rating is the floor of the converted living area. |
| **Elevated with an Enclosure and Garage under the Elevated Floor** | If a building is elevated with an enclosure, and the garage is within the enclosure beneath the elevated floor, the garage area is part of the enclosure area. It is not necessary for the garage area to have its own flood openings, as long as the openings in the enclosure meet the NFIP proper openings requirements.<br>• The garage area is part of the enclosed area when the garage shares exterior walls with other enclosed areas, and there is no foundation wall between them.<br>• When a foundation wall separates the garage from other enclosed areas, the garage must meet the proper openings requirement to exclude it in rating. |

### Any Flood Zone Beginning with V

In any flood zone beginning with V, the LFE used for rating can be the lowest elevated floor when there is no enclosure, or the enclosure floor, depending on the characteristics of the enclosure area.

See **Table 13** for how such characteristics determine what LFE to use. The LFE is measured from the bottom of the lowest horizontal structural member as identified on C.2.c on the EC.

**Table 13. Elevated Buildings in V Zones Rated with an EC**

| Characteristic | Description |
|---|---|
| **With Enclosure** | For an elevated building with an enclosure (including attached garage, elevator shaft) below the elevated floor:<br>• Use the bottom of the enclosure floor as the LFE for rating if any of the following conditions exist (see the Enclosures heading in this section):<br>– The enclosure is used for other than parking, storage, and building access;<br>– The enclosure is finished;<br>– There is machinery and equipment below the BFE that provides utility services to the building;<br>– There is an elevator below the BFE;<br>– The enclosure is constructed with non-breakaway walls;<br>– The enclosure is constructed with breakaway walls but is more than 300 square feet in area<br>– The enclosure has load-bearing, supporting walls that provide more than 25% of the building's structural support. |
| **1975 – 1981 Post-FIRM Elevated Buildings** | A 1975-1981 Post-FIRM V-Zone construction refers to any elevated building constructed on or after January 1, 1975, and before October 1, 1981<br><br>**No Enclosure**<br>Use the No Enclosure rates in Rate Table 3D in Appendix J if there is no enclosure or an unfinished enclosure under 300 square feet:<br>• With breakaway walls; *and*<br>• Without machinery or equipment.<br><br>**With Enclosure**<br>Use the With Enclosure rates in Rate Table 3D in Appendix J if there is an enclosure:<br>• With non-breakaway walls;<br>• With breakaway walls 300 square feet or larger; *or*<br>• That is finished (Refer to Enclosure section). |
| **1981 Post-FIRM Elevated Buildings** | A 1981 Post-FIRM V-Zone construction refers to any V-Zone Post-FIRM building for which the:<br>• Permit application date for the construction or substantial improvement is on or after October 1, 1981, *or*<br>• Permit issue date was before October 1, 1981, and the actual start date of construction did not begin within 180 days of the permit date.<br>There are two different rate tables for 1981 Post-FIRM V-Zone elevated buildings. Use of these tables depends on whether the building is Free of Obstruction or With Obstruction. The bottom of the lowest horizontal structural member is the lowest floor for rating purposes. Buildings built prior to October 1, 1981 can use these rate tables if the building complies with Post-1981 standards and it benefits the insured.<br><br>**Free of Obstruction**<br>Use the Free of Obstruction rate table (Rate Table 3E in Appendix J) and the bottom of the elevated floor's lowest horizontal structural member as the LFE for rating if all of the following conditions exist:<br>• There is no elevator, machinery, or equipment below the BFE; *and*<br>• There is no enclosure.<br><br>**With Obstruction**<br>Use the With Obstruction rate table (Rate Table 3F in Appendix J) with the bottom of the elevated floor's lowest horizontal structural member as the LFE for rating, if all of the following conditions exist:<br>• The enclosure is unfinished; |

**Table 13. Elevated Buildings in V Zones Rated with an EC** *continued*

| Characteristic | Description | |
|---|---|---|
| **1981 Post-FIRM Elevated Buildings** *continued* | If there is an enclosure, use the Free of Obstruction rate table if all of the following conditions exist:<br>• There is no elevator, machinery, or equipment below the BFE; *and*<br>• The walls of the enclosure are made of any of the following:<br>– Insect screening with no additional support;<br>– Wooden or plastic lattice with at least 40% of its area open and made with material no more than 1/2 inch thick;<br>– Wooden or plastic slats or shutters with at least 40% of their area open and made with material no more than 1 inch thick; *or*<br>– One solid breakaway wall or a garage door with the remaining walls of the enclosure constructed with screening, lattice, slats, or shutters.<br>Otherwise, use the With Obstruction rate table. | • There is no machinery and equipment below the BFE that provides utility services to the building;<br>• There is no elevator below the BFE;<br>• The enclosure has breakaway walls; *and*<br>• The enclosure is less than 300 square feet in area.<br>Otherwise, the bottom of the enclosure slab is the LFE for rating and rating the building will most likely require following the Submit-for-Rate procedure in this section. |
| **Post-'81 V-Zone Optional Rating** | Elevated buildings in Zones VE and V1–V30 that are Pre-FIRM construction or 1975-1981 Post-FIRM V-Zone Elevated construction can, optionally, be rated using the 1981 Post-FIRM V-Zone rate tables (Table 3E or 3F in Appendix J) if the rates are more favorable to the insured.<br>To qualify, all the following criteria must apply:<br>• The policy must be rated using the BFE printed on the FIRM panel that includes wave height;<br>• The building rates are determined based on the ratio of the estimated building replacement cost and the amount of insurance purchased; *and*<br>• The building must be elevated and either:<br>– Be free of obstructions<br>– Have an enclosure of less than 300 square feet with breakaway walls and no other obstructions.<br>**Note:** Any machinery or equipment located below the BFE are considered obstructions, requiring rating through the Submit-for-Rate procedures in this section. | |

### c. Hanging Floors and Mid-level Entries (A Zones and V Zones)

Hanging floors and mid-level entries are walled-in floor areas beneath an elevated building that do not extend to the ground. For rating purposes:

- In A zones, the top of the hanging floor or mid-level entry is the lowest floor for rating.
- For V zones, the bottom of the hanging floor or mid-level entry's lowest horizontal structural member is the lowest floor for rating.

Refer to the *NFIP Specific Rating Guidelines* for more information at https://www.fema.gov/media-library/assets/documents/34620.

**NOTE**

Floodplain management guidance may refer to hanging floors and mid-level entries as "above-grade enclosures."

## E. Determine Elevation Difference

When determining the full-risk premium rate for a building in an SFHA, calculate the elevation difference in feet between the building's LFE used for rating and the BFE, Base Flood Depth (BFD), or grade elevation, depending on the flood zone. Refer to the "Determine Type of Rating" heading in this section and Lowest Floor Guide in Appendix C of this manual to determine the building's LFE for rating purposes.

For policies outside the SFHA or rated with Pre-FIRM subsidized rates, the NFIP does not require the elevation difference to identify a rate.

### *1. Guidelines for Elevation Datum Conversion*

When determining the elevation difference, verify all elevation data used the datum reflected on the most current FIRM. The insurer must use elevations in the same datum to calculate the elevation difference.

Elevations are typically provided using either National Geodetic Vertical Datum (NGVD) of 1929 or North American Vertical Datum (NAVD) of 1988.

Unless specifically noted on the EC, assume that line items C2.a-h are in the same datum as the BFE in box B9.

If the datum requires conversion, you may use the tool developed by the National Geodetic Survey (NGS) to convert the LFE and BFE to the current datum. The tool is located on the NGS website at http://www.ngs.noaa.gov/cgi-bin/VERTCON/vert_con.prl.

- Enter the north latitude and west longitude of the structure.
- Enter the elevation requiring conversion in the orthometric height field. If the elevation is in feet (most places other than Puerto Rico) make sure to enter "ft" after the elevation.
- Specify the datum of the entered elevation.
- The tool will then provide the conversion factor and the elevation in the other datum.

Conversion Example:

- A property with a latitude of 35° 15' and a longitude of 121° 22' 30" from NGVD 29 to NAVD 88.
- Enter the latitude and longitude in the format specified by the tool.
- Enter the elevation requiring conversion to NAVD 88 and "ft" (for this example, "54.2 ft").
- Select Vertical Datum NGVD 29.
- Click on Submit.
- The VERTCON result will display a conversion factor of 2.726 feet and a building elevation of 56.926 feet NAVD 88.

Alternatively, refer to the Flood Insurance Study or FIRM, which generally list datum conversion factors for specific NFIP communities.

**NOTE**

**NGVD:** National standard reference datum for elevations, formerly referred to as Mean Sea Level (MSL) of 1929.

**NAVD:** The vertical control datum established for vertical control surveying in the United States of America based upon the General Adjustment of the North American Datum of 1988. It replaces the National Geodetic Vertical Datum (NGVD) of 1929.

### 2. Elevation Truncation Rule

If any elevations (BFE, LFE, etc.) are shown in hundredths or greater (ex. 10.572), first truncate all decimals beyond tenths before calculating the elevation difference.

- If the LFE is 10.572 truncate the elevation to 10.5
- If the BFE is 8.45 truncate the elevation to 8.4

### 3. Elevation Difference Rounding Rule

If the elevation difference is shown in tenths (ex. 10.5), apply the rounding rules.

- If the difference is **negative**, round up from .5 and down from .6
  9.5 – 12 = –2.5 (round up to –2)
  8.1 – 10.8 = –2.7 (round down to –3)
- If the difference is **positive**, round up from .5 and down from .4
  12.4 – 8.8 = 3.6 (round up to 4)
  9.8 – 3.5 = 6.3 (round down to 6)

### 4. Elevation Difference Calculation by Flood Zone

#### a. Zones A1–A30, AE, AH, AR, AR Dual Zones, A (with BFE), V1–V30, VE, and V

For A zones, the LFE for rating purposes is the top of the lowest floor. For V zones, the LFE for rating purposes is the lowest horizontal structural member.

**LFE - BFE = Elevation Difference**

*Examples:*

- 10 – 6 = 4
- 8.3 – 6 = 2.3 (round to 2)

**Note:** For zone AH, if the elevation difference is greater than or equal to 0, use With Certification of Compliance rates. See Rate Table 3A in Appendix J.

#### b. Zone AO

For Zone AO, the difference between the building's LFE and the highest adjacent grade (HAG) is the LFE used for rating.

If the LFE is equal to or greater than the BFD, use With Certification of Compliance rate. Otherwise, use Without Certification of Compliance rate.

If the BFD does not appear on the FIRM, use a BFD of 2 for rating purposes.

**(LFE - HAG) - BFD = Elevation Difference**

*Example:*

- LFE is 10.9
- HAG is 8.0
- BFD is 3.0
  - 10.9 – 8.0 = 2.9 = Elevation Difference
  - 2.9 – 3.0 = 0 (Use With Certification of Compliance rates)

#### c. Zone A (No estimated BFE)

In Zone A where there is no established BFE, the difference between the top of the bottom floor and the HAG is the LFE used for rating.

**LFE – HAG = Elevation Difference**

*Examples:*

- 10 – 6 = 4
- 8.3 – 6 = 2.3 (rounded to 2)
- 12.4 – 8.8 = 3.6 (rounded to 4)
- 9.5 – 12 = –2.5 (rounded to –2)

#### d. Zone A (Estimated BFE)

In Zone A with an estimated BFE, the difference between the top of the bottom floor and the estimated BFE is the elevation difference.

**LFE – Estimated BFE = Elevation Difference**

*Examples:*

- 10 – 6 = 4
- 8.3 – 6 = 2.3 (round to 2)

### *5. FIRMs with Wave Heights*

When calculating elevation differences, agents must determine if the BFEs on the FIRM include wave heights. Wave height applies to buildings located in Zones V1–V30 and VE. To determine the rate using an EC, the BFE must include the wave height. Refer to **Table 14** for the conversion requirement.

**Table 14. FIRMs with Wave Height Conversion**

| FIRM Date | Wave Height Conversion |
|---|---|
| **Before January 1, 1981** | Convert the BFE to reflect wave height. |
| **January 1, 1981 and after** | FIRMs may include the wave height.<br>When the wave height is included in the BFE, the following statement appears on the map legend: "Coastal base flood elevations shown on this map include the effects of wave action." |

#### a. Wave Height Adjustment Procedure

A registered professional engineer, architect, or surveyor must complete and sign the EC used to calculate the wave height adjustment. The procedure requires the following information:

- A completed EC.
- BFE from the EC (Item B9) or from the FIRM.
- LAG from Item C2.f of the EC completed by a registered professional engineer, architect, or surveyor.
- Depth of Still Water Flooding (subtract the LAG from the BFE).

  The additional elevation due to wave crest in V-Zone areas will normally vary from a minimum of 2.1 feet to 0.55 times the still water depth at the site. (BFE including wave height adjustment = still water BFE + 0.55 × [still water BFE – LAG elevation].)

### b. Wave Height Adjustment Examples

A building's site is located in Zone V8 with a BFE of 14' NGVD on the appropriate FIRM. Using the information from the EC, calculate the BFE as noted in **Table 15**.

### Table 15. Examples of Wave Height Adjustment Calculations

| Steps | Example 1 | Example 2 |
|---|---|---|
| BFE | 14 | 14 |
| Subtract LAG | −6 | −11 |
| Still Water BFE | 8 | 3 |
| Factor | × 0.55 | × 0.55 |
| Wave Height Adjustment | 4.4 | 1.65 (2.1)* |
| Add BFE | 14 | 14 |
| BFE adjusted | 18.4 | 16.1 |

**Note:** In Example 2, if the calculation results in less than the minimum 2.1 feet, use 2.1 feet in the calculation of the BFE adjusted.

### *6. Buildings Eligible for Floodproofing Premium Discount*

Not all buildings are eligible for the floodproofing premium discount. The Floodproofing heading in this section provides a detailed description of floodproofing and the completion of the Floodproofing Certificate.

- To be eligible for the floodproofing premium discount, a registered professional engineer or architect must certify that the building is floodproofed to at least one foot above the BFE.
- Section I on the Floodproofing Certificate provides the BFE or BFD.
- Section II on the Floodproofing Certificate provides the building floodproofed elevation information.
- Calculate the elevation difference by subtracting the BFE from the building floodproofed elevation.

### Table 16. Calculating Floodproofing Premium Discount Eligibility

| Steps | Example 1 | Example 2 | Example 3 |
|---|---|---|---|
| Building Floodproofed Elevation | 14 | 13 | 12 |
| Subtract BFE | 12 | 12 | 12 |
| Elevation Difference | 2 | 1 | 0 |
| Eligible for Floodproofing Discount | YES | YES | NO |

## F. Contents Location

### *1. Single-Family Dwellings*

For rating purposes, contents in a single-family dwelling are considered to be located throughout the entire building regardless of the building type, with limited coverage in a basement and an enclosed area beneath the lowest elevated floor. Refer to the SFIP for additional details.

### *2. Multi-Family and Non-Residential Buildings*

The shaded areas in the illustrations in **Tables 17 and 18** identify the location of the contents when completing the application. The rates for contents located in the area indicated will be established based on the zone, construction date, and building description.

## Table 17. Contents Location in Non-Elevated Buildings

| | ON APPLICATION FORM | | |
|---|---|---|---|
| CONTENTS IN SHADED AREAS | BUILDING TYPE (INCLUDING BASEMENT, IF ANY) | BASEMENT | CONTENTS LOCATION |
| 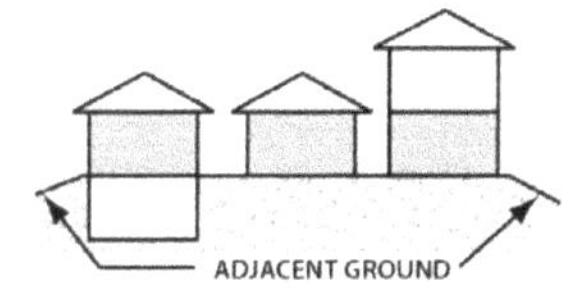 | 1 Floor or 2 Floors | None or Finished or Unfinished | Lowest Floor Only Above Ground Level |
| 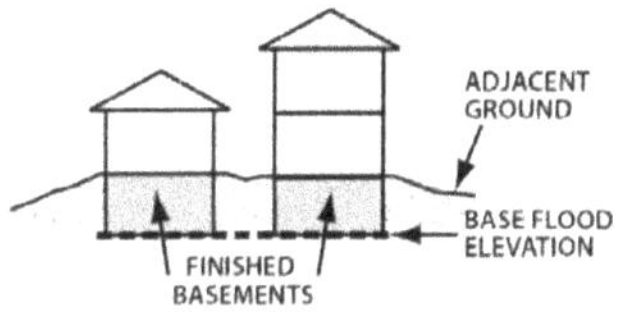 | 2 Floors or 3 or More Floors | Finished | Basement Only |
| | | LIMITED COVERAGE IN BASEMENT | |
| 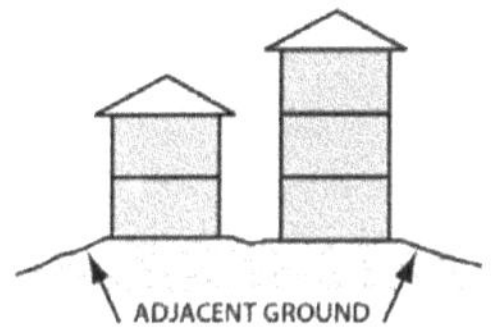 | 2 Floors or 3 or More Floors | None | Lowest Floor Above Ground Level and Higher Floors |
| 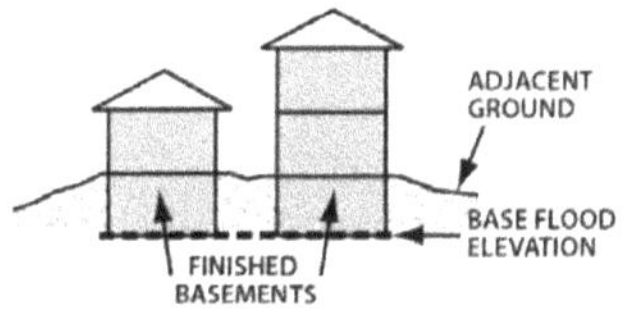 | 2 Floors or 3 or More Floors | Finished | Basement and Above |
| | | LIMITED COVERAGE IN BASEMENT | |
| 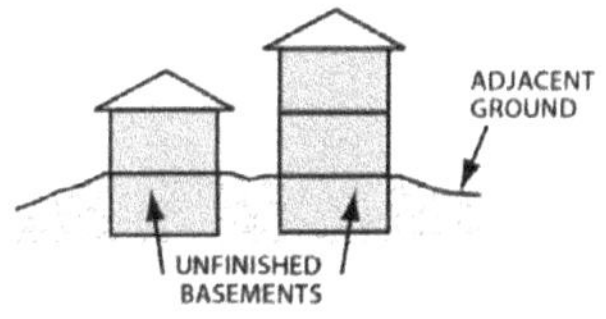 | 2 Floors or 3 or More Floors | Unfinished | Basement and Above |
| | | LIMITED COVERAGE IN BASEMENT | |
| 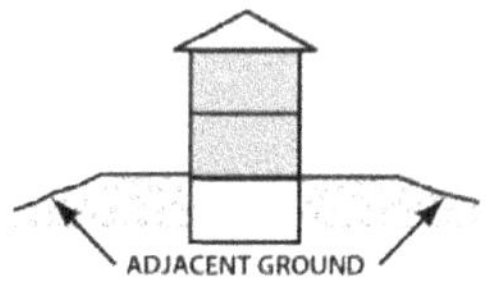 | 3 or More Floors | Finished or Unfinished | Lowest Floor Above Ground Level and Higher Floors |
| 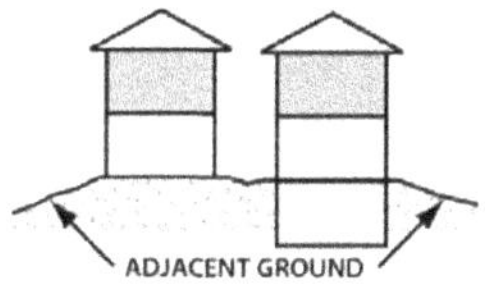 | 2 Floors or 3 or More Floors | None or Finished or Unfinished | Above Ground Level More Than 1 Full Floor |

**Table 18. Contents Location in Elevated Buildings**

| CONTENTS IN SHADED AREAS | ON APPLICATION FORM | | |
|---|---|---|---|
| | BUILDING TYPE (INCLUDING ENCLOSURE, IF ANY) | ENCLOSURE | CONTENTS LOCATION |
| 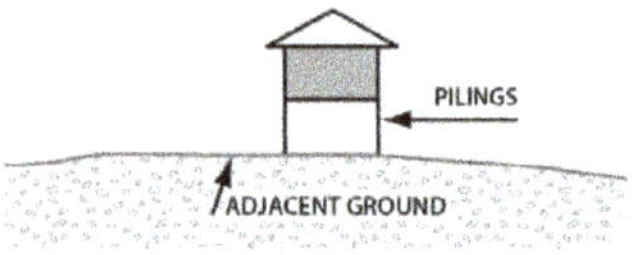  Elevated building free of obstruction | 1 floor | None | Lowest Floor Only Above Ground Level |
| 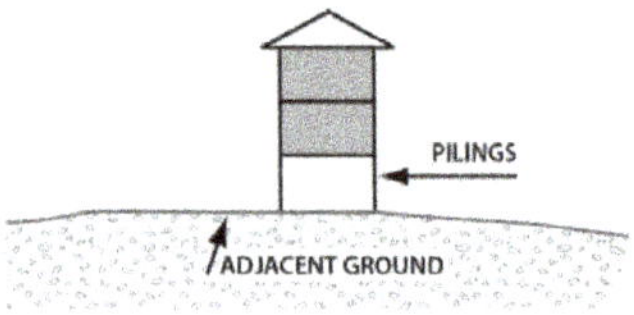  Elevated building free of obstruction | 2 floors | None | Lowest Floor Above Ground Level And Higher Floor |
| 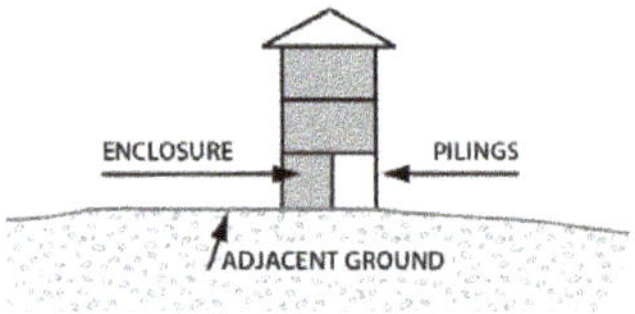  Elevated building with enclosure below lowest elevated floor | 3 or more floors | Unfinished | Basement/ Enclosure and Above |
| | | MAY HAVE LIMITED COVERAGE IN ENCLOSED AREA | |
| 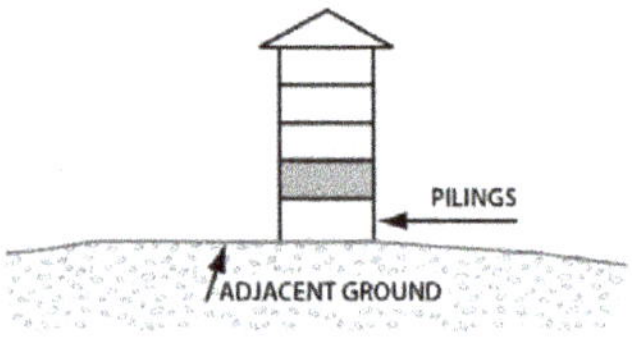  Elevated building, multiple occupancy, no enclosure | 3 or more floors | None | Lowest Floor Only Above Ground Level |
| 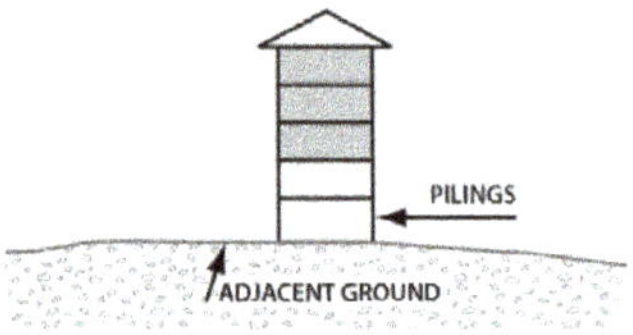  Elevated building, multiple occupancy, no enclosure | 3 or more floors | None | Above Ground Level More Than 1 Full Floor |
| 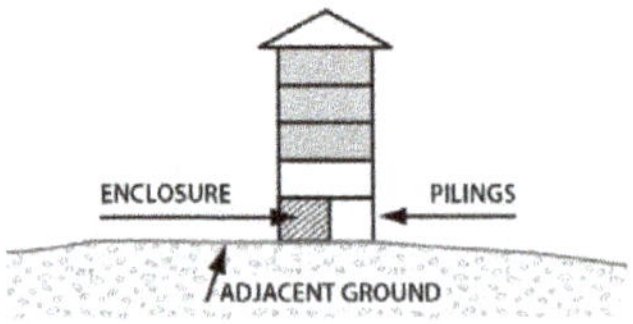  Elevated building, multiple occupancy, with enclosure | 3 or more floors | Unfinished | Above Ground Level More Than 1 Full Floor |

## G. Calculate the Premium

The NFIP only accepts premium in whole dollars. If the discount for an optional deductible does not result in a whole-dollar premium, round up if 50 cents or more; round down if less. Always submit the total amount due.

### *1. Replacement Cost Ratio for V-zone Rating*

The replacement cost ratio is needed to select the proper rate for insurance on buildings in V, V1–V30, and VE zones. The estimated building replacement cost is used in conjunction with the amount of the building insurance desired to determine the insurance-to-replacement-cost ratio.

Replacement cost is defined as the amount of money required to replace or repair the insured building in the event of loss or damage, without a deduction for depreciation. The replacement cost ratio is determined by dividing the amount of building coverage purchased by the replacement cost of the building.

If the replacement cost of the building exceeds the maximum statutory building limit, use the replacement cost, not the maximum statutory building limit, in calculating the ratio. For example, if the residential building replacement cost is $1,000,000 and the amount of building coverage requested is the maximum statutory building limit of $250,000, the ratio is .25; use the rate listed for "Replacement Cost Ratio Under .50."

### *2. Standard-Rated Policy*

For standard-rated policies excluding RCBAPs, calculate the premium by applying a rate per hundred to the amount of coverage requested. Most policies have basic and additional coverage limits with separate rates applied. All rate tables, deductible factors, fees, and surcharges are located in Appendix J. Follow the steps in **Table 19** to determine the total amount due. **Note:** See the Condominium section for premium calculation information for an RCBAP.

**Table 19. Calculate Premium for a Standard-Rated Policy**

| Step | Action | Reference/Guidance |
|---|---|---|
| 1 | **Identify the rate** | Rate tables. |
| 2 | **Apply the deductible factor** | Deductible Factors table for deductible amounts and factors. |
| 3 | **Apply SRL premium (if appropriate)** | See Rate Table 7D. Severe Repetitive Loss Premium in Appendix J for applicable percentage. |
| 4 | **Add Increased Cost of Compliance (ICC) premium** | ICC Premium table for ICC premium amount.<br>Do not apply ICC premium to contents-only policies or to policies for individual condominium units in a multi-unit building. |
| 5 | **Apply CRS discount** | CRS Eligible Communities table for participating communities and CRS discounts.<br>Buildings built in compliance and Pre-FIRM buildings in these communities receive the CRS discount. |

**Table 19. Calculate Premium for a Standard-Rated Policy** *continued*

| Step | Action | Reference/Guidance |
|---|---|---|
| 6 | **Apply Reserve Fund Assessment** | See the Reserve Fund Assessment table for applicable percentage. |
| 7 | **Add Probation Surcharge** | Community Master File or insurer to determine if community is on probation<br>Add a $50 Probation Surcharge if community is on NFIP probation. |
| 8 | **Add HFIAA Surcharge** | A $25 HFIAA surcharge applies to:<br>• Policies covering single-family residences, 2–4 family residences, or individual residential condominium units used as a primary residence by the named insured; *and*<br>• Contents-only policies for apartments used as a primary residence by the named insured.<br>All other policies have a $250 HFIAA surcharge. |
| 9 | **Add Federal Policy Fee** | Federal Policy Fee Table.<br>The Federal Policy Fee for tenant's contents-only policy is $25; for all other policies the Federal Policy Fee is $50. |

## H. Tenant's Coverage

Information is provided below regarding coverage for tenants.

### *1. Contents Coverage*

Tenants may purchase contents coverage that includes coverage for building improvements and betterments. Coverage for contents solely owned by the tenant must be on a separate policy in the name of the tenant only.

The maximum amount payable for improvements and betterments in a building occupied by the insured tenant is 10 percent of the contents coverage amount shown on the declarations page. Improvements and betterments:

- Include fixtures, alterations, installations, and additions that become part of the tenant- occupied building acquired or made solely at the tenant's expense; *and*
- Are not an additional amount of insurance over the amount of contents coverage shown on the declarations page.

### *2. Building Coverage*

Tenants may purchase building coverage if required by the lease agreement, and the policy must include the building owner as a named insured. However, tenants may not purchase building coverage if the owner or another party has purchased NFIP coverage on the same building. Residential condominium buildings are an exception to this condition.

## I. Special Rating Situations

### 1. Alternative Rates

Alternative rating is a rating method available only in communities without V Zones on their FIRM. The NFIP will assume the building is located in a SFHA.

Insurers may only use the alternative rating procedure in the following two instances:

- A building is Pre-FIRM and the FIRM zone is unknown. The FIRM zone should be shown as Zone AA representing the rating method.
- Renewal of policies in communities that convert from the Emergency Program to the Regular Program during a policy's term. The NFIP assigns an AS Zone designation.

Use Pre-FIRM A Zone rates to determine the premium.

Once the FIRM zone is known, the agent or insured must submit a change endorsement correcting the zone and any additional premium necessary. Alternative rates are available for one policy term. Insurers cannot issue a Renewal Premium Notice with alternative rates.

### 2. Special Rates

Certain risks may be eligible for FEMA Special Rates consideration. Special Rates consideration requires the agent or insurer to submit additional information to FEMA that may result in a reduction to the rate based on specific characteristics that are not common to similarly classified buildings. Until FEMA reviews the Special Rate application and provides rates, the rates published in this manual or the *NFIP Specific Rating Guidelines* (SRG) manual apply.

Risks eligible for consideration include the following:

- Subgrade crawlspace when the distance between the subgrade crawlspace floor and the top of the next higher floor is greater than 5 feet or the top of the bottom floor elevation is more than 2 feet below the LAG;
- High-rise residential condominium buildings with basements, eligible under the RCBAP, where the LFE is below the BFE, unfinished, and used for building access, parking, or storage only;
- Pre-FIRM buildings with partial enclosures below the BFE (where a partial enclosure does not enclose the entire area under the elevated floor, is unfinished and used solely for parking, storage, and building access); *or*
- Non-elevated 2–4 family dwellings with an attached garage, where the floor level of the garage is below the level of the building.

To request FEMA Special Rates, the insurer must submit all appropriate documentation listed in the SRG manual to FEMA through the Submit-for-Rate link in UCORT at www.nfip.fema.gov/Default/Login.

#### 3. Tentative Rates

Insurers can issue policies using tentative rates (Appendix J: Rate Tables) when agents fail to provide the required full-risk rating information. Tentative rates are generally higher than other published rates. The insurer should issue the policy, based on tentative rates, with the coverage limits that the premium received can purchase, if the premium payment received is not sufficient to purchase the coverage limits requested.

The insurer will forward a declarations page and a Tentative Rate Letter to the insured and agent requesting the information necessary to determine the proper rate. Insurers may not endorse tentatively-rated policies to increase coverage limits, or renew for another policy term, until the insurer receives the required actuarial rating information and full premium payment.

The insurer may not process claims relating to a tentatively-rated policy until the insurer receives the underwriting information establishing a full-risk rate for the policy. A tentatively-rated policy loss payment cannot exceed the lower coverage amount that the initially submitted premium purchased (using the correct full-risk rating information), or the amount requested by application.

## II. Preferred Risk Policy

### A. General Information

The PRP offers fixed policy combination limits for building/contents or contents-only coverage. The PRP is available for properties located in Zones B, C, X, AR, or A99 in a Regular Program NFIP community that meet certain loss history requirements.

#### 1. Maximum Coverage Limits

**Table 20. Maximum Coverage Limits by Occupancy Type**

| Coverage Type | 1–4 Family | Other Residential | Non-Residential Business, Other Non-Residential |
|---|---|---|---|
| Combined Building/ Contents | $250,000/$100,000 | $500,000/$100,000 | $500,000/$500,000 |
| Contents Only | $100,000 | $100,000 | $500,000 |

#### 2. Deductibles

The deductible for a PRP is $1,000 each for both building and contents coverage if the building coverage is less than or equal to $100,000; if the building coverage is over $100,000, the deductible is $1,250, regardless of the insured building's construction date compared to the initial FIRM date. A contents-only policy will have a $1,000 deductible.

### *3. Incomplete PRP Applications*

The insurer must not issue a PRP when:

- The PRP application is incomplete;
- The information submitted is incomplete or inconsistent; *or*
- There is no premium submitted with the application.

The insurer must issue the policy for coverage equal to the premium payment received even where there is a different (higher) requested amount of coverage.

## B. Determining Eligibility

These factors determine PRP purchase eligibility.

- Flood Zone;
- Loss History; *and*
- Community Status.

### *1. Flood Zone*

Buildings must be located within a B, C, X, A99, or AR flood zone on the current effective FIRM to be eligible for a PRP.

New business applications must include one of the following to document the flood zone:

- An SFHDF that guarantees the accuracy of community and zone information.
- Copy of current effective flood map at time of application marked to show the building's exact location and flood zone. The insurer may require additional documentation if the building is close to the flood zone boundary line.
- Letter signed by a local community official specifying the property address and building's flood zone.
- EC signed and dated by a surveyor, an engineer, an architect, or a local community official specifying the exact location and flood zone of the building.
- LOMA.
- LOMR.
- LODR.

### *2. Loss History*

A building may be ineligible for the PRP based on the building's flood loss history. Refer to **Table 21** for conditions.

**Table 21. Conditions for Ineligibility for the PRP**

| Building's Flood Loss History | Conditions |
|---|---|
| Buildings for which:<br>• Flood-related federal disaster benefits have been provided within any 10-year period, without regard to ownership of the building; *and/or*<br>• Flood insurance claim payments have been made within any 10-year period, without regard to ownership of the building;<br>are ***ineligible*** for the PRP if any of the conditions to the right exist. | • Multiple flood insurance claim payments:<br>– Two separate payments exceeding $1,000 for separate losses.<br>– Three (or more) payments for separate losses, regardless of amount.<br>• Multiple Federal flood disaster relief payments (including loans and grants):<br>– Two separate payments exceeding $1,000 for separate occurrences.<br>– Three separate payments for separate occurrences, regardless of amount,<br>• One flood insurance claim payment and one Federal flood disaster relief payment (including loans and grants), each for separate losses and each more than $1,000. |

**Notes:**

- Count multiple losses at the same location within ten days of each other as one loss and add the payment amounts together.
- Only count Federal flood disaster relief payments (including loans and grants) if the building sustained flood damage.

## C. Types of Buildings Ineligible for the PRP

The following buildings are not eligible for a PRP:

- Buildings or contents located in Emergency Program communities;
- Buildings or contents located in SFHAs except Zones AR and A99;
- Multi-unit residential condominium buildings eligible under the RCBAP; *or*
- Any building located on Leased Federal Property (LFP) where the Administrator determines the building's location to be on the river-facing side of any dike, levee, or other riverine flood-control structure, or seaward of any seawall or other coastal flood-control structure.

## D. Renewal

A policy must meet all PRP eligibility requirements to renew as a PRP. The insurer may not renew a PRP during a policy term when the property no longer meets the loss history requirement. Likewise, a PRP may not renew during a policy term where the property becomes ineligible due to a map revision. The FIRM available at the time of the renewal offer determines a building's continued eligibility for the PRP. If a property is no longer eligible for a PRP, it may be eligible to renew using the Newly Mapped rating procedure if it meets all eligibility criteria (see the Newly Mapped heading in this section). Otherwise, the insurer must rewrite the policy as a standard-rated policy. Refer to the How to Cancel section for information regarding the cancellation or rewriting of a PRP to a standard-rated policy.

**Note:** If the policy is not eligible to renew as a PRP, it may still be endorsed during the current policy term to increase coverage mid-term or to correct misratings, such as an incorrect building description or community number.

## E. Policy Conversions

### *1. Standard-Rated Policy to PRP Due To Misrating*

To convert a standard-rated policy to a PRP when a building is located in a B, C, X, AR, or A99 zone on the current FIRM and qualifies for a PRP:

- The request to endorse, cancel, or rewrite must be for a policy that is in effect.
- The amount of coverage issued under the PRP is the combination of coverage limits equal to the standard-rated policy limits for building or contents, or the next higher limit where there is no PRP combination of equivalent coverage limit.
- There can be no pending or paid claim during the standard-rated policy's term when endorsing, canceling, or rewriting a policy as a PRP.
- The insurer may refund the difference in premium from the standard-rated to PRP for up to 5 years. **Note:** Zones AR and A99 became eligible for the PRP effective October 1, 2016.
- Refer to the How to Cancel section of this manual for the appropriate Cancellation/Rewrite reason code.

**NOTE**

If the standard-rated policy is a contents-only policy and the insured requests building coverage under the PRP, add building coverage by endorsement.
The 30-day waiting period applies to the endorsement.

### *2. Standard-Rated Policy to PRP due to a Map Revision, LOMA, or LOMR*

To convert a standard-rated policy to a PRP as a result of a map revision, LOMA, or LOMR:

- The insurer must receive a request to endorse, cancel, or rewrite the standard-rated policy to a PRP during the active policy term.
- The insurer may endorse, cancel, or rewrite a standard-rated policy as a PRP for up to five policy years.
- There is no paid or pending claim on canceled policy term(s).
- The property meets all other PRP requirements.

The effective date of the request to endorse, cancel or rewrite is the beginning of the policy term in which the map revision, LOMA, or LOMR occurred.

Refer to the How to Cancel section of this manual for the appropriate Cancellation/Rewrite reason code.

### *3. PRP to Standard-Rated Policy*

A PRP must convert to a standard-rated policy on the effective date of the renewal if the property no longer qualifies for PRP rating.

#### a. Underwriting Information

- The insurer must obtain all of the necessary underwriting information from the agent to issue a standard-rated policy.
- The insured/agent will submit additional information needed to rate the policy within 60 days of the insurer's notification.
- The insurer must send a bill to the payor for the standard-rated policy premium due once the insurer has the information necessary to compute the premium.
- Any addition or increase in coverage from the canceled PRP to the rewritten standard-rated policy requires a 30-day waiting period.

### b. Premium Due

- The payor has 30 days from the date the insurer sends the bill to pay the additional premium due.
- The premium due is calculated using the same coverage amounts as shown on the PRP from the beginning of the policy term.
- The insured has the option to reduce or delete coverage to reduce the additional premium due amount.

## F. Coverage Limitations

The following limitations apply to policies issued under a PRP:

- Basement coverage limitations as described in Appendix A: Policy.
- Individual condominium units located in non-residential condominium buildings are not eligible for building coverage.
- Condominium units insured under the Dwelling or General Property form are ineligible for ICC coverage.

> **NOTE**
>
> Elevated building coverage limitations do not apply to a policy issued under the PRP.

## G. Condominium PRP Eligibility

### *1. Residential Single-Unit Building or Townhouse/Rowhouse Type Building With a Separate Entrance for Each Unit*

**Table 22. Single Family Residential Building**

| Purchaser of Policy | Building Occupancy[1] | Condo Unit Indicator[1] | PRP Eligibility | Rate Table | Policy/Form |
|---|---|---|---|---|---|
| **Unit Owner** | Single family | Yes | Yes | 1–4 Family residential | Dwelling |
| **Association (association-owned single unit)** | Single family | Yes | Yes | 1–4 Family residential | Dwelling |
| **Association (entire building)** | N/A | N/A | No | N/A | N/A |

**Table 23. Multi-Unit Residential Building — 2 to 4 Units per Building**

| Purchaser of Policy | Building Occupancy[1] | Condo Unit Indicator[1] | PRP Eligibility | Rate Table | Policy/Form |
|---|---|---|---|---|---|
| **Unit Owner** | 2–4 | Yes | Yes | 1–4 Family residential | Dwelling |
| **Association (association-owned single unit)** | 2–4 | Yes | Yes | 1–4 Family residential | Dwelling |
| **Association (entire building)** | N/A | N/A | No | N/A | N/A |
| **Owner of Non-Residential Contents** | Non-residential business, Other Non-residential | Yes (Building coverage not available) | Yes | Non-residential business, Other Non-residential contents-only | General Property |

### Table 24. Multi-Unit Residential Building — 5 or More Units Per Building

| Purchaser of Policy | Building Occupancy[1] | Condo Unit Indicator[1] | PRP Eligibility | Rate Table | Policy Form |
|---|---|---|---|---|---|
| **Unit Owner** | Other residential | Yes | Yes | Other residential | Dwelling |
| **Association (association-owned single unit)** | Other residential | Yes | Yes | Other residential | Dwelling |
| **Association (entire building)** | N/A | N/A | No | N/A | N/A |
| **Owner of Non-Residential Contents** | Non-residential business, Other Non-residential | Yes (Building coverage not available) | Yes | Non-residential business, Other Non-residential contents-only | General Property |

1. When there is a mix of residential and non-residential usage within a single building, refer to the Before You Start section of this manual

### Table 25. Non-Residential Business, Other Non-Residential Building

| Purchaser of Policy | Building Occupancy[1] | Condo Unit Indicator[1] | PRP Eligibility | Rate Table | Policy Form |
|---|---|---|---|---|---|
| **Owner of Non-Residential Contents** | Non-residential business, Other Non-residential | Yes (Building coverage not available) | Yes | Non-residential business, Other Non-residential contents-only | General Property |
| **Owner of Residential Contents** | Single family | Yes (Building coverage not available) | Yes | Residential contents-only | Dwelling |
| **Association (entire building)** | Non-residential business, Other Non-residential | N/A | Yes | Non-residential business, Other Non-residential building and contents | General Property |

1. When there is a mix of residential and non-residential usage within a single building, refer to the Before You Start section of this manual

## H. PRP Premium Calculation

Follow the steps outlined in **Table 26** to calculate the premium for PRPs. The total amount due equals the total premium plus applicable fees and surcharges.

**Table 26. Calculate Premium for a PRP**

| Step | Action | Reference |
|---|---|---|
| 1 | **Identify the base premium** | PRP premium table corresponding to the building occupancy type and description. |
| 2 | **Apply multiplier** | Apply a multiplier of 1.00 for PRPs. |
| 3 | **Add ICC premium** | ICC Premium table for ICC premium amount.<br>Do not apply ICC premium to contents-only policies or to policies for individual condominium units in a multi-unit building. |
| 4 | **Apply Reserve Fund Assessment** | See the Reserve Fund Assessment table for applicable percentage. |
| 5 | **Add Probation Surcharge** | Community Master File or insurer to determine if community is on probation.<br>Add a $50 Probation Surcharge if community is on NFIP probation. |
| 6 | **Add HFIAA Surcharge** | A $25 HFIAA surcharge applies to:<br>• Policies covering single-family residences, 2-4 family residences, or individual residential condominium units used as a primary residence by the named insured; *and*<br>• Contents-only policies for apartments used as a primary residence by the named insured.<br>All other policies have a $250 HFIAA surcharge. |
| 7 | **Add Federal Policy Fee** | For PRP and contents-only: Add the $25 Federal Policy Fee to the Total Premium. |

# III. Newly Mapped

## A. General Information

The Newly Mapped procedure offers fixed combinations of building and contents coverage limits for properties previously located in Zones B, C, or X that have been newly mapped into a SFHA and meet certain loss history requirements. This procedure also applies to properties in Zones D, AR or A99 that have been newly mapped into a different SFHA zone and meet certain loss history requirements. The Newly Mapped procedure does not apply to properties mapped into the SFHA on the initial FIRM.

### *1. Maximum Coverage Limits*

**Table 27. Maximum Coverage Limits by Occupancy Type**

| Coverage Type | 1–4 Family | Other Residential | Non-Residential Business, Other Non-Residential |
|---|---|---|---|
| Combined Building/ Contents | $250,000/$100,000 | $500,000/$100,000 | $500,000/$500,000 |
| Contents Only | $100,000 | $100,000 | $500,000 |

### 2. Deductibles

Separate but equivalent deductibles apply to both the building and contents coverage. If the building coverage amount exceeds $100,000, the deductible is $1,250. Otherwise, the deductible is $1,000.

### 3. Incomplete Newly Mapped Rated Policy Applications

The insurer may not issue a Newly Mapped rated policy when:

- The Newly Mapped rated policy application is incomplete.
- The information submitted is incomplete or inconsistent.
- There is no premium submitted with the application.

The insurer must issue the policy for coverage equal to the premium payment received even where there is a different (higher) requested amount of coverage.

## B. Determining Eligibility

These factors determine eligibility to follow the Newly Mapped procedure.

- Flood Zone;
- Loss History; *and*
- FIRM Revision Date versus Policy Effective Date.

### 1. Flood Zone

Buildings must be located in a B, C, or X flood zone on the previous flood map and newly mapped into the SFHA, or in Zones D, A99 or AR newly mapped into a different SFHA zone to be eligible for the Newly Mapped procedure. A building located in a D, AR, or A99 zone insured under the PRP and then later remapped to an SFHA (excluding D, AR and A99) is eligible to use the Newly Mapped procedure. New business applications must include documentation validating the current and previous flood zone. To determine the current flood zone, use the FIRM in effect at the time of application and presentment of premium.

New business applications must include one or more of the following to document the previous and current flood zones:

- An SFHDF that guarantees the accuracy of the community and zone information.
- Copy of the most recent effective flood map marked to show the exact location and flood zone of the building. The NFIP may require additional documentation if the building is close to the zone boundary.
- Letter signed by a local community official indicating the property address and flood zone of the building.
- EC signed and dated by a surveyor, an engineer, an architect, or a local community official indicating the exact location and flood zone of the building.
- LOMA.
- LOMR.
- LODR.

### *2. Loss History*

If any of the conditions in the following table exist, the property is ineligible for the Newly Mapped rating procedure.

**Table 28. Loss History Ineligibility for the Newly Mapped Procedure**

| Building's Flood Loss History | Conditions |
|---|---|
| Buildings for which:<br>• Flood-related federal disaster benefits have been provided within any 10-year period, without regard to ownership; *and/or*<br>• Flood insurance claim payments have been made within any 10-year period, without regard to ownership of the building<br>are ***ineligible*** for the Newly Mapped procedure if any of the conditions to the right exist. | • Multiple flood insurance claim payments:<br>– Two separate payments exceeding $1,000 for separate losses<br>– Three (or more) payments for separate losses, regardless of amount<br>• Multiple Federal flood disaster relief payments (including loans and grants):<br>– Two separate payments exceeding $1,000 for separate occurrences<br>– Three separate payments for separate occurrences, regardless of amount<br>• One flood insurance claim payment and one Federal flood disaster relief payment (including loans and grants), each for separate losses and each more than $1,000. |

**Notes:**

- Count multiple losses at the same location within ten days of each other as one loss and add the payment amounts together.
- Only count Federal flood disaster relief payments (including loans and grants) if the building sustained flood damage.

### *3. FIRM Revision Date versus Policy Effective Date*

Properties newly mapped into the SFHA after April 1, 2015, are eligible for the Newly Mapped rating procedure if:

- The policy effective date is within 12 months of the effective FIRM revision date; *or*
- The insured applied for the policy within 45 days of initial lender notification if the notification occurred within 24 months of the effective FIRM revision date. **Note:** The insurer must retain a copy of the lender notification in the underwriting file.

In these cases, use the Newly Mapped multiplier located in Appendix J: Rate Tables based on the map effective date and the policy effective date for the new business transaction.

## C. Ineligibility

The following are ineligible for the Newly Mapped rating procedure:

- Properties mapped into the SFHA by the initial FIRM for a community entering the Regular Program.
- Properties whose first policy effective date is more than 12 months after the effective date of the FIRM that revised or changed the zone from a B, C, or X zone to an SFHA zone, or in the case of a D, A99,

or AR zone, to a different SFHA zone unless following the lender notification guidance provided above.

- Buildings and/or contents in Emergency Program communities.
- Multi-unit residential condominium buildings eligible under the RCBAP.
- Any building on leased federal property determined by the Administrator to be located on the river facing side of any dike, levee, or other riverine flood-control structure, or seaward of any seawall or other coastal flood-control structure.
- Lapsed policies, which may not reinstate by means of a new Preferred Risk Policy and Newly Mapped Application under the following conditions:
  - The insured reinstates coverage on a building for an expired or canceled SFIP.
  - One or more of the named insureds on the new policy was either a named insured on the expired or canceled policy or had an ownership interest in the building at the time the policy expired or the insured canceled the policy.
  - The insurer reinstates a policy issued using the Newly Mapped procedure with premium received:
    - More than 90 days after prior policy expiration or cancellation where the named insured has maintained continuous coverage on the property from April 1, 2016, to the prior policy expiration or cancellation date; *or*
    - More than 30 days after the prior policy expiration or cancellation date, where the named insured has not maintained continuous coverage on the property from April 1, 2016, to the prior policy expiration or cancellation date; *and*
  - The policy expiration or cancellation was for a reason other than:
    - The insured was no longer legally required to obtain and maintain flood insurance; *or*
    - The insured property was in a community suspended from the NFIP and the insurer issued the policy within 180 days of the community's reinstatement in the NFIP.

**Note:** This restriction applies to all lapses that occur on or after April 1, 2016.

## D. Renewal

The property must continue to meet the eligibility requirements at each renewal to maintain a policy rated under the Newly Mapped procedure.

A policy issued using the Newly Mapped procedure may not renew under the Newly Mapped procedure if during a policy term the property no longer meets the loss history requirement. The policy must renew as a standard-rated policy.

The insurer should not renew the policy issued using the Newly Mapped procedure and should rewrite the policy to a PRP if during a policy term the property is mapped from an SFHA to a B, C, X, D, A99, or AR flood zone.

### *1. Renewal Payment*

**Table 29. Renewal Payment Requirements**

| Premium Receipt Date | Eligible for Newly Mapped Procedure | Apply Waiting Period |
|---|---|---|
| Within 30 days of the expiration date | Yes | No |
| Greater than 30 days but less than 90 days following the expiration date | • Yes, for the first occurrence.<br>• No, for a subsequent occurrence. | Yes, the standard 30-day waiting period applies. |
| 90 or more days following the expiration date | No | N/A |

### *2. Transition to Full-Risk Rates*

The rates for a policy using the Newly Mapped procedure will incrementally increase and may eventually be higher than a standard-rated policy (full-risk) at the point of each renewal. To evaluate which rate is more favorable (i.e., policy using the Newly Mapped procedure versus standard-rated policy), insureds can provide the insurer with an EC. The insurer uses the EC to determine when it is beneficial to convert a Newly Mapped rated policy to a standard-rated policy. The insurer may use the current map or a grandfathered zone and/or BFE to determine the full-risk rate for a standard-rated policy.

## E. Policy Conversions

There are two types of policy conversions involving a Newly Mapped rated policy:

- Conversion of a standard-rated policy to a Newly Mapped rated policy due to misrating.
- Conversion of a Newly Mapped rated policy to a standard-rated policy.

### *1. Standard-Rated Policy To Newly Mapped Due To Misrating*

To convert a standard-rated policy to a Newly Mapped rated policy:

- The insurer must receive the request to endorse or cancel/rewrite the policy during the current policy term.
- The building meets all other Newly Mapped rated requirements.
- To cancel/rewrite, there can be no pending or paid claim on the policy term canceled.
- The insurer may refund premium for up to 5 years from the date of the map revision for a standard-rated policy in a B, C, X, D, AR or A99 zone later determined to be eligible for the Newly Mapped rating procedure. Use the multiplier from the map revision date to determine the amount due.

The coverage limits on the converted Newly Mapped rated policy are:

- Equal to either the building and/or contents limits issued under the standard-rated policy; *or*
- The next higher limit if there is no option equal to the standard-rated policy building and/or contents limit.

**NOTE**

If the standard-rated policy is a contents-only policy and the insured requests building coverage under the Newly Mapped rating procedure, add building coverage by endorsement.

The 30-day waiting period applies to the endorsement.

Refer to the How to Cancel section of the manual for the appropriate cancellation/rewrite reason code.

### *2. Newly Mapped Rated Policy to a Standard-rated Policy*

A Newly Mapped rated policy must convert to a standard-rated policy if the property no longer meets the eligibility requirements on the effective date of the policy.

#### a. Underwriting Information

- The insurer must obtain all of the necessary underwriting information from the agent to issue a standard-rated policy.
- The insurer will notify the insured/agent they have 60 days to obtain any missing information and provide it to the insurer.
- The insurer must send a bill to the payor for the standard-rated policy premium due once the insurer has the information necessary to compute the premium.

#### b. Premium Due

- The payor has 30 days from the date the insurer sends the bill to pay the additional premium due.
- The premium due is calculated using the same coverage amounts as shown on the Newly Mapped rated policy from the beginning of the policy term.
- The insured has the option to reduce or delete coverage to reduce the additional premium due amount.
- Any addition or increase in coverage from the canceled Newly Mapped rated policy to the rewritten standard-rated policy requires a 30-day waiting period.

## F. Coverage Limitations

The following limitations apply to policies written using the Newly Mapped rating procedure:

- Basement coverage limitations as described in Appendix A: Policy.
- Individual condominium units located in non-residential condominium buildings are not eligible for building coverage.
- Condominium units insured under the Dwelling or General Property form are ineligible for ICC coverage.

**NOTE**

Elevated building coverage limitations do not apply to a policy issued under the Newly Mapped procedure.

## G. Condominium Newly Mapped Rating Eligibility

The insurer should use these tables for properties newly mapped into SFHA flood zones, excluding AR and A99 on or after October 1, 2016.

### *1. Residential Single Unit Building or Townhouse/Rowhouse Type Building – Separate Entrance for Each Unit*

**Table 30. Single-Family Unit Residential Building**

| Purchaser of Policy | Building Occupancy | Condo Unit Indicator | Newly Mapped | Rate Table | Policy/Form |
|---|---|---|---|---|---|
| Unit Owner | Single family | Yes | Yes | 1–4 Family residential | Dwelling |
| Association (association-owned single unit) | Single family | Yes | Yes | 1–4 Family residential | Dwelling |
| Association (entire building) | N/A | N/A | No | N/A | N/A |

### *2. Multi-Unit Residential Building – 2 To 4 Units per Building*

**Table 31. Multi-Unit Residential Building – 2 to 4 Units per Building**

| Purchaser of Policy | Building Occupancy | Condo Unit Indicator | Newly Mapped | Rate Table | Policy/Form |
|---|---|---|---|---|---|
| Unit Owner | 2–4 | Yes | Yes | 1–4 Family residential | Dwelling |
| Association (association-owned single unit) | 2–4 | Yes | Yes | 1–4 Family residential | Dwelling |
| Association (entire building) | N/A | N/A | No | N/A | N/A |
| Owner of Non-Residential Contents | Non-residential business, Other Non-residential | Yes (Building coverage not available) | Yes | Non-residential business, Other Non-residential contents-only | General Property |

### *3. Multi-Unit Residential Building – 5 or More Units per Building*

**Table 32. Multi-Unit Residential Building – 5 or More Units per Building**

| Purchaser of Policy | Building Occupancy | Condo Unit Indicator | Newly Mapped | Rate Table | Policy Form |
|---|---|---|---|---|---|
| Unit Owner | Other residential | Yes | Yes | Other residential | Dwelling |
| Association (association-owned single unit) | Other residential | Yes | Yes | Other residential | Dwelling |
| Association (entire building) | N/A | N/A | No | N/A | N/A |
| Owner of Non-Residential Contents | Non-residential business, Other Non-residential | Yes (Building coverage not available) | Yes | Non-residential business, Other Non-residential contents-only | General Property |

### 4. Non-Residential Business, Other Non-Residential Building

**Table 33. Non-Residential Business, Other Non-Residential Building**

| Purchaser of Policy | Building Occupancy | Condo Unit Indicator | Newly Mapped | Rate Table | Policy Form |
|---|---|---|---|---|---|
| Owner of Non- Residential Contents | Non-residential business, Other Non-residential | Yes (Building coverage not available) | Yes | Non-residential business, Other Non-residential contents-only | General Property |
| Owner of Residential Contents | Single family | Yes (Building coverage not available) | Yes | Residential contents-only | Dwelling |
| Association (Entire Building) | Non-residential business, Other Non-residential | N/A | Yes | Non-residential business, Other Non-residential building and contents | General Property |

1. When there is a mix of residential and non-residential usage within a single building, refer to the Before You Start section of this manual

## H. Newly Mapped Rated Premium Calculation

Follow the steps outlined in **Table 34** to calculate the premium for Newly Mapped rated policies. The total amount due equals the total premium plus applicable fees and surcharges.

**Table 34. Calculate Premium for a Newly Mapped Rated Policy**

| Step | Action | Reference |
|---|---|---|
| 1 | Identify the base premium | Newly Mapped premium table corresponding to the building occupancy type and description. |
| 2 | Apply multiplier | Refer to the Multiplier tables in Appendix J: Rate Tables.<br>Apply a Multiplier based on the map revision and policy effective date for Newly Mapped rated policies. |
| 3 | Add ICC premium | ICC Premium table for ICC premium amount.<br>Do not apply ICC premium to contents-only policies or to policies for individual condominium units in a multi-unit building. |
| 4 | Apply Reserve Fund Assessment | Refer to the Reserve Fund Assessment table. |
| 5 | Add Probation Surcharge | Community Master File or insurer to determine if community is on probation.<br>Add a $50 Probation Surcharge if community is on NFIP probation. |
| 6 | Add HFIAA Surcharge | A $25 HFIAA surcharge applies to:<br>• Policies covering single-family residences, 2-4 family residences, or individual residential condominium units used as a primary residence by the named insured; *and*<br>• Contents-only policies for apartments used as a primary residence by the named insured.<br>All other policies have a $250 HFIAA surcharge. |

**Table 34. Calculate Premium for a Newly Mapped Rated Policy** *continued*

| Step | Action | Reference |
|---|---|---|
| 7 | **Add Federal Policy Fee** | Add the $50 Federal Policy Fee to the Total Premium. |

# IV. Condominiums

## A. Insuring Condominiums

There are four ways to insure condominiums, and each method has its own eligibility requirement. The methods below illustrate the differing insurance scenarios:

- Residential Condominium Association Coverage on Building and Contents
  - Use the RCBAP to insure a residential condominium building and the contents owned by a condominium association.
- Residential Condominium Unit Owners Coverage on Building and Contents
  - Use the Dwelling Form to insure an individual condominium unit and contents. The owner must be the named insured.
- Non-Residential Condominium Coverage on Building and Contents
  - Use the General Property Form to insure a non-residential condominium building and commonly owned contents.
- Non-Residential Condominium Unit Owner Coverage on Contents only
  - Use the Dwelling Form to insure residential condominium unit owner's contents in non-residential condominium buildings.
  - Use the General Property Form to insure non-residential condominium unit owner's contents in non-residential buildings.

## B. Residential Condominium – Association Coverage

Use the RCBAP to insure a residential condominium building and contents when owned by a condominium association.

The NFIP defines a condominium association as an entity where membership is a required condition of unit ownership and unit owners are responsible for the maintenance and operation of:

- Common elements owned in undivided shares by unit owners.
- Other real property in which the unit owners have use rights.

**Table 35. Residential Condominium Association Coverage Under the RCBAP**

<table>
<tr><th>Policy Form</th><th>RCBAP</th></tr>
<tr><td>Maximum Coverage Limits</td><td>Building: The lesser of the following:<br>• Building's replacement cost; or<br>• Total number of units × $250,000.<br>Contents: Actual cash value (ACV) of commonly owned contents to a maximum of $100,000 per building.</td></tr>
<tr><td>Eligible Insureds</td><td>• Insured must be a residential condominium association.<br>• If the named insured is other than a condominium association, the insurer must have legal documentation confirming the entity is a condominium association. Acceptable examples of condominium association documentation include:<br>– A copy of the condominium association by-laws; or<br>– A statement signed by an officer or representative of the condominium association confirming the building is in a condominium form of ownership.<br>• Insured may be a building owner in a Homeowners Association (HOA) having a condominium form of ownership. The HOA by-laws require purchase of flood insurance building coverage for its members.</td></tr>
<tr><td>Ineligible Insureds</td><td>• Cooperative ownership buildings.<br>• Non-condominium homeowners associations.</td></tr>
<tr><td>Building Eligibility</td><td>• Community must be in Regular Program.<br>• Building must have one or more residential units.<br>• At least 75% of floor area must be residential.<br>• Residential condominium buildings used as a hotel or motel, or rented either short or long-term.<br>• Homeowners Association having a condominium form of ownership.<br>• Timeshare buildings having a condominium form of ownership.</td></tr>
<tr><td>Property Insured</td><td>• Condominium building.<br>• Individually owned units within the building.<br>• Improvements within unit.<br>• Additions and extensions attached or connected to the insured building.<br>• Fixtures, machinery, and equipment within building.<br>• Contents owned by the association.<br>Note: The NFIP requires a separate policy for each building owned by a condominium association. Coverage applies to the single building described in the property location of the Flood Insurance Application and Declarations.</td></tr>
<tr><td>Special Underwriting Requirements</td><td>• The insured or agent must provide the Replacement Cost Value (RCV) of the building in the Application, including the cost of the building's foundation.<br>• The insured or agent must provide evidence of the RCV of the building. Insurers may use a recent property valuation report stating the value of the building and its foundation on a RCV basis to meet this requirement.<br>• The insurer must update the RCV information at least every 3 years. See sample letter at the end of this section.</td></tr>
</table>

**Table 35. Residential Condominium Association Coverage Under the RCBAP** *continued*

| Policy Form | RCBAP | |
|---|---|---|
| **Other Considerations** | • The unit owner may purchase a Dwelling Form policy with building coverage in a condominium building insured under the RCBAP. However, the NFIP will not pay more than $250,000 for combined coverage for a single unit under the Dwelling Form policy and the RCBAP. Insureds may not claim the same damaged items on more than one NFIP policy. | |
| **Replacement Cost Coverage** | • Yes, for the building only, subject to policy provisions.<br>• RCV is the cost to replace property with the same type of material and construction without deduction for depreciation. | |
| **Deductibles** | Condo Table 7 in the Condominium section of Appendix J: Rate Tables shows the available optional deductibles and deductible factors. | |
| **Coinsurance Penalty** | • The RCBAP coinsurance penalty applies to building coverage only. To receive full replacement cost, the insured must have purchased insurance in an amount equal to 80% of the full replacement cost of the building at the time of loss or the maximum amount of insurance available for that building under the NFIP, whichever is less.<br>• The coinsurance penalty calculation is:<br>$\frac{\textbf{Insurance Carried}}{\textbf{Insurance Required}}$ **× Amount of Loss = Limit of Recovery** | |
| **ICC Coverage** | • Yes | |
| **Building Becomes Ineligible** | • If an insurer discovers that a building is not eligible for the RCBAP, the insurer must void the policy and rewrite it using the correct form.<br>• The provisions of the correct SFIP form apply.<br>• The insurer must reform the coverage limits according to the provisions of the correct SFIP form.<br>• Coverage cannot exceed the limits issued on the incorrectly issued RCBAP.<br>• In the event of a loss, if a building is ineligible for a RCBAP, the insurer must rewrite the policy using the correct form for up to the maximum amount of building coverage allowed for the type of building insured. Coverage may not exceed the coverage purchased under the RCBAP. | |
| **Owner Becomes Ineligible** | • If, during a policy term, the risk fails to meet the eligibility requirements due to a change in the form of ownership, it becomes ineligible for coverage under the RCBAP.<br>• The insurer must cancel and rewrite the policy using the correct SFIP form.<br>• The effective date of the cancellation is the date that the form of ownership changed. | |
| **Assessment Coverage** | • No | |
| **Federal Policy Fee** | Number of Units | Federal Policy Fee |
| | 1 | $50 per policy |
| | 2 – 4 | $150 per policy |
| | 5 – 10 | $400 per policy |
| | 11 – 20 | $800 per policy |
| | 21+ | $2,000 per policy |

## C. Residential Condominium – Unit Owners Coverage

Use the Dwelling form to insure an individual condominium unit and its contents. The owner must be the named insured.

**Table 36. Residential Condominium Unit Owners Coverage Under the Dwelling Form**

| Policy Form | Dwelling Form |
|---|---|
| Maximum Coverage Limits | **Emergency Program**<br>• Building $35,000<br>• Contents $10,000<br>**Regular Program**<br>• Building $250,000<br>• Contents $100,000 |
| Insured | • Unit owner;<br>• Association in the name of the unit owner and the association as their interests may appear;<br>• Association for an individual unit owned by the association; *or*<br>• Non-residential unit owner for contents-only coverage. |
| Property Insured | • Building elements.<br>• Individually-owned contents. |
| Eligibility | • Emergency and Regular Programs |
| Other Considerations | • NFIP considers a residential condominium unit in a high-rise or low-rise building, including a townhouse or rowhouse, as a single-family residence.<br>• Unit may purchase a Dwelling Form policy with building coverage in a condominium building insured under the RCBAP. However, the NFIP will not pay more than $250,000 for combined coverage for a single unit under the Dwelling Form policy and the RCBAP. Insureds may not claim the same damaged items on more than one NFIP policy.<br>• In the event of a loss, owners may apply up to 10% of the stated contents coverage amount for betterments and improvements. The 10% is not an additional limit of insurance.<br>• When the applicant is the condominium association, the lenders for the individual unit owners should not appear on the declarations page. |
| Replacement Cost | Yes, subject to policy provisions |
| ICC Coverage | No |
| Assessment Coverage | Yes |
| Federal Policy Fee | $50 |

## D. Non-Residential Condominium — Association Coverage

Use the General Property Form to insure a non-residential condominium building and the commonly owned contents.

### Table 37. Non-Residential Condominium Association Coverage

| Policy Form | General Property Form |
|---|---|
| **Maximum Coverage Limits** | **Emergency Program**<br>• Non-residential<br>• Building $100,000<br>• Contents $100,000<br>**Regular Program**<br>• Building $500,000<br>• Contents $500,000 |
| **Insured Entity** | Non-residential condominium association. |
| **Property Insured** | The property insured includes:<br>• Condominium building.<br>• Individually owned units within the building.<br>• Improvements within unit.<br>• Additions and extensions attached or connected to the insured building.<br>• Fixtures, machinery, and equipment within building.<br>• Contents owned by the association.<br>• Non-residential common building elements and the contents.<br>**Note:** The NFIP requires a separate policy for each building owned by a condominium association. Coverage applies to the single building described in the property location of the Flood Insurance Application and the Declarations. |
| **Eligible Condominiums Types** | Condominium building in a Regular Program community where less than 75% of its floor area is residential use. |
| **Replacement Cost** | No |
| **ICC Coverage** | Yes |
| **Assessment Coverage** | No |
| **Federal Policy Fee** | $50 |

## E. Non-Residential Condominium – Unit Owners Coverage

- Use the Dwelling Form to insure residential condominium unit owner's contents in non-residential condominium buildings. Condominium unit owners in a non-residential condominium may not purchase building coverage.
- Use the General Property Form to insure non-residential condominium unit owner's contents in non-residential buildings.

**Table 38. Non-Residential Condominium Unit Owners Coverage**

| Policy Form | General Property Form or Dwelling Form |
|---|---|
| Maximum Coverage Limits | **Emergency Program**<br>• Contents $100,000<br>**Regular Program**<br>• Contents $500,000 |
| Insured Parties | • Unit owner<br>• Tenant |
| Definition | The NFIP considers a residential condominium unit in a high-rise or low-rise building, including a townhouse or rowhouse, as a single-family residence. |
| Property Insured | Contents of non-residential condominium units. |
| Program Eligibility | Emergency and Regular Programs |
| Other Considerations | In the event of a loss, owners may apply up to 10% of the stated contents coverage amount for betterments and improvements. The 10% is not an additional limit of insurance. |
| Replacement Cost | No |
| ICC Coverage | No |
| Assessment Coverage | No |
| Federal Policy Fee | $50 |

## F. General Concepts

### *1. High-Rise versus Low-Rise Condominiums*

Residential condominium buildings are grouped into 2 different types, low-rise and high-rise, because of the difference in the exposures to the risk that typically exists.

- High-rise buildings have five or more units and at least three floors excluding an enclosure even if it is the lowest floor for rating.
- Low-rise buildings have fewer than five units regardless of the number of floors, or five or more units with fewer than three floors, including the basement.
  - A townhouse/rowhouse is a multi-floor unit divided from similar units by solid, vertical, load-bearing walls, having no openings in the walls between units and with no horizontal divisions between any of the units.
  - Townhouse/rowhouse buildings are always low-rise buildings for rating purposes. The number of floors or units does not change the low-rise designation.

### 2. *Basic Limits of Insurance for RCBAP*

Maximum amount of insurance allowed under the RCBAP is $250,000 × the number of units. **Table 39** shows basic limits of insurance.

**Table 39. Basic Limits of Insurance for RCBAP**

| Building Type | Basic Limit of Insurance |
|---|---|
| High-Rise | $175,000 |
| Low-Rise | $60,000 x Number of Units |

### 3. *Condominium Eligibility for Pre-FIRM Subsidized or Newly Mapped Rating*

If a policy on a Pre-FIRM building eligible for Pre-FIRM subsidized rates lapses, the building is no longer eligible for this subsidy under the following conditions:

- The insured wants to reinstate expired or canceled coverage on a previously covered building;
- One or more of the named insureds on the new policy was either a named insured on the expired or canceled policy or had an ownership interest in the building at the time of cancellation or expiration;
- The insured reinstated coverage with premium received on or after April 1, 2016:
  - The insurer receives the renewal payment more than 30 days after expiration but within the 90-day date of the policy expiration. The insurer reinstates coverage with a 30-day waiting period upon receipt of the renewal payment. The policy remains eligible to renew using Pre-FIRM subsidized rates or the Newly Mapped rating procedure for only the first instance.
  - The insurer receives the renewal payment more than 90 days following the expiration date. The insurer must require a new application with the full annual premium and apply the 30-day waiting period; *or*
- The policy expiration or cancellation was for a reason other than:
  - The insured's lender no longer required the insured to obtain and maintain flood insurance.
  - The property was in a community suspended from the NFIP and the insured reinstated the policy within 180 days of the community's reinstatement as a participating NFIP community.

**Note:** This restriction applies to all lapses that occur on or after April 1, 2016.

Refer to the guidance in **Table 40** to determine if the building is ineligible to use Pre-FIRM Subsidized Rates.

### Table 40. Pre-FIRM Subsidized Rates Ineligibility Determination

| Was there a prior NFIP policy for this property in the insured's name? | Did a lender require the prior NFIP policy? | Did the prior NFIP policy lapse while required by a lender? | Was the lapse the result of a community suspension? | Was the community reinstated within the last 180 days? | Eligible for Pre-FIRM subsidized rates? |
|---|---|---|---|---|---|
| YES | YES | YES | YES | NO | NO |
| YES | YES | YES | NO | YES | NO |
| YES | YES | YES | NO | NO | NO |

#### *4. Condominium Pre-FIRM Rate Table Hierarchy*

Use **Table 41** to determine which Pre-FIRM rate table to use.

### Table 41. Pre-FIRM Rate Table Hierarchy

| Pre-FIRM | Pre-FIRM SRL | Pre-FIRM Substantially Improved | High-Rise Table For Rating | Low-Rise Table For Rating |
|---|---|---|---|---|
| YES | YES | NO | N/A | 4B |
| YES | NO | YES | 3B | 4C |
| YES | YES | YES | N/A | 4B |

#### *5. RCBAP Federal Policy Fee Table*

The Federal Policy Fees for the RCBAP are shown in **Table 42**.

### Table 42. RCBAP Federal Policy Fee Table

| Number of Units | Federal Policy Fee |
|---|---|
| 1 unit | $50 per policy |
| 2–4 units | $150 per policy |
| 5–10 units | $400 per policy |
| 11–20 units | $800 per policy |
| 21 or more units | $2,000 per policy |

#### *6. RCBAP Premium Calculation*

Follow the steps outlined in **Table 43** to calculate the premium. Refer to **Table 39** for the basic limits. Please note, the number of units impacts the Federal Policy Fee and HFIAA surcharge.

**Table 43. Calculate Premium for an RCBAP**

| Step | Action | Reference |
|---|---|---|
| 1 | Identify the rate | Separate rate tables and different basic coverage limits for Low-rise and High-Rise condominium buildings. |
| 2 | Apply the deductible factor | Deductible Factors table for deductible amounts and factors. |
| 3 | Apply SRL premium (if appropriate) | See Rate Table 7D. Severe Repetitive Loss Premium in Appendix J for applicable percentage. |
| 4 | Add ICC premium | ICC Premium table for ICC premium amount. |
| 5 | Apply CRS discount | CRS Eligible Communities table for participating communities and CRS discounts.<br>Buildings built in compliance and Pre-FIRM buildings in these communities receive the CRS discount. |
| 6 | Apply Reserve Fund Assessment | Reserve Fund Assessment table for applicable percentage. |
| 7 | Add Probation Surcharge | Community Master File or insurer to determine if community is on probation.<br>Add a $50 Probation Surcharge if community is on NFIP probation. |
| 8 | Add HFIAA Surcharge | The surcharge is $250 for these policies. |
| 9 | Add Federal Policy Fee | Federal Policy Fee table for RCBAP. |

### *7. Duplicate Policies*

Multiple policies with building coverage may not insure a single building with one exception. The insurer may issue a Dwelling Form policy to a unit owner insuring a condominium unit with building coverage in a condominium building also covered by an RCBAP. However, combined coverage between the Dwelling Form policy and the RCBAP may not exceed $250,000. Insureds may not claim damaged items under more than one policy. NFIP will only pay for damaged items under one policy.

### *8. Tentative Rates and Scheduled Buildings*

Tentative Rates may be applied to rate the RCBAP. For additional guidance on tentative rates, refer to the Tentative Rates subsection within this section of the manual.

The Scheduled Building Policy is not available for the RCBAP.

### *9. Assessments*

The RCBAP and General Property Forms do not provide assessment coverage.

Assessment coverage is only available under the Dwelling Form.

- The insured cannot use the assessment coverage under the Dwelling Form to meet the 80% coinsurance provision of the RCBAP.
- The assessment coverage under the Dwelling form does not apply to ICC coverage or to buildings subject to continuous flooding from closed basin lakes.

Application of assessment coverage after a loss is shown in **Table 44**.

**Table 44. Assessment Coverage After a Loss**

| Condition at Time of Loss | Assessment Coverage Under the Dwelling Form |
|---|---|
| No RCBAP | The unit owner has purchased building coverage.<br>• Responds to a loss assessment against the unit owner for damages to common areas, up to the building limit under the Dwelling Form.<br>• If there is also damage to the building elements of the unit:<br>– Coverage combination cannot exceed the maximum coverage limits available for a single-family dwelling.<br>– Settlement of the unit building damages applies first and then the loss assessment. |
| RCBAP Insured to at Least 80% of the Building Replacement Cost | The unit owner has purchased building coverage:<br>• The loss assessment coverage under the Dwelling Form will pay that part of a loss that exceeds 80% of the association's building replacement cost.<br>• The loss assessment coverage under the Dwelling Form will not cover the association's policy deductible purchased by the condominium association.<br>• The RCBAP is primary and the Dwelling Form is considered excess after exhausting the RCBAP limits.<br>• Coverage combination cannot exceed the maximum coverage limits available for a single-family dwelling. |
| RCBAP Insured to Less Than 80% of the Building Replacement Cost | The unit owner has purchased building coverage:<br>• The RCBAP is primary and the Dwelling Form is considered excess after exhausting the RCBAP limits.<br>• The Dwelling Form will respond to a loss assessment resulting from the coinsurance penalty under the RCBAP even if the loss did not meet the RCBAP limits. |

### *10. Condominium Rating Tables*

Below are tables that provide information regarding rating a condominium.

### a. Low-Rise Residential Condominiums

**Table 45. Single-Unit Building or Townhouse/Rowhouse Type – Building with Separate Entrance for Each Unit**

| Purchaser of Policy | Building Occupancy[1] | Building Indicator[1] | Contents Indicator[2] | Type of Coverage | Rating Classification | Policy Form[3] |
|---|---|---|---|---|---|---|
| **Unit owner** | Single family | Single unit | Household | RC[4] | Single family | Dwelling |
| **Association (association-owned single unit only)** | Single family | Single unit | Household | RC[4] | Single family | Dwelling |
| **Association (entire building)** | Determined by the number of units, i.e., Single family, 2–4 family, other residential | Low-rise | Household | RC | RCBAP low-rise | RCBAP |

1. When there is a mixture of residential and non-residential usage within a single building, refer to the Condominium Association Coverage tables in this section of this manual.
2. In determining the contents location, refer to **Tables 17 and 18** in this section of the manual.
3. RCBAP must be used to insure residential condominium buildings owned by the association that are in a Regular Program community and in which at least 75% of the total floor area within the building is residential. Use the General Property Form if ineligible for the RCBAP.
4. Replacement Cost if the RC eligibility requirements are met (building only).

**Table 46. Multi-Unit Building – 2–4 Units Per Building – Regardless of Number of Floors (Non-Townhouse)**

| Purchaser of Policy | Building Occupancy[1] | Building Indicator[1] | Contents Indicator[2] | Type of Coverage | Rating Classification | Policy Form[3] |
|---|---|---|---|---|---|---|
| **Unit Owner** | 2–4 | Single unit | Household | RC[4] | Single family for building; 2–4 family for contents | Dwelling |
| **Association (association-owned single unit only)** | 2–4 | Single unit | Household | RC[4] | Single family for building; 2–4 family for contents | Dwelling |
| **Association (entire building)** | 2–4 | Low-rise | Household | RC | RCBAP low-rise | RCBAP |
| **Owner of Non-Residential Contents** | Non-residential | Single unit (Building coverage not available) | Other than household | ACV | Non-residential | General Property |

## Table 47. Multi-Unit Building – 5 or More Units Per Building, Fewer Than 3 Floors

| Purchaser of Policy | Building Occupancy[1] | Building Indicator[1] | Contents Indicator[2] | Type of Coverage | Rating Classification | Policy Form[3] |
|---|---|---|---|---|---|---|
| Unit Owner | Other residential | Single unit | Household | RC[4] | Single family for building; other residential for contents | Dwelling |
| Association (association-owned single unit only) | Other residential | Single unit | Household | RC[4] | Single family for building; other residential for contents | Dwelling |
| Association (entire building) | Other residential | Low-rise | Household | RC | RCBAP low-rise | RCBAP |
| Owner of Non-Residential Contents | Non-residential | Single unit (Building coverage not available) | Other than household | ACV | Non-residential | General Property |

1. When there is a mixture of residential and non-residential usage within a single building, refer to the Condominium Association Coverage tables in this section of this manual.
2. In determining the contents location, refer to **Tables 17 and 18** in this section of the manual.
3. RCBAP must be used to insure residential condominium buildings owned by the association that are in a Regular Program community and in which at least 75% of the total floor area within the building is residential. Use the General Property Form if ineligible for the RCBAP.
4. Replacement Cost if the RC eligibility requirements are met (building only).

### b. High-rise Residential Condominiums

## Table 48. Multi-Unit Building – 5 or More Units Per Building, 3 or More Floors[1]

| Purchaser of Policy | Building Occupancy[2] | Building Indicator[2] | Contents Indicator[3] | Type of Coverage | Rating Classification | Policy Form[4] |
|---|---|---|---|---|---|---|
| Unit Owner | Other residential | Single unit | Household | RC[5] | Single family for building; other residential for contents | Dwelling |
| Association (association-owned single unit only) | Other residential | Single unit | Household | RC[5] | Single family for building; other residential for contents | Dwelling |
| Association (entire building) | Other residential | High-rise | Household | RC | RCBAP High-rise | RCBAP |

**Table 49. Non-Residential Condominiums**

| Purchaser of Policy | Building Occupancy[2] | Building Indicator[2] | Contents Indicator[3] | Type of Coverage | Rating Classification | Policy Form[4] |
|---|---|---|---|---|---|---|
| Owner of Non-Residential Contents | Non-residential | Single unit (Building coverage not available) | Other than household | ACV | Non-residential | General Property |
| Owner of Residential Contents | Single family (In a 2–4 unit building) | Single unit (Building coverage not available) | Household | ACV | Single family | Dwelling |
| Owner of Residential Contents | Other residential (In a 5-or-more-unit building) | Single unit (Building coverage not available) | Household | ACV | Single family | Dwelling |
| Association | Non-residential | Low-rise or high-rise | Other than household | ACV | Non-residential | General property |

1. Enclosure/crawlspace, even if it is the lowest floor for rating, cannot be counted as a floor for the purpose of classifying the building as a high-rise.
2. When there is a mixture of residential and non-residential usage within a single building, refer to the Condominium Association Coverage tables in this section.
3. In determining the contents location, refer to **Tables 17 and 18** in this section of the manual.
4. RCBAP must be used to insure residential condominium buildings owned by the association that are in a Regular Program community and in which at least 75% of the total floor area within the building is residential. Use the General Property Form if ineligible under RCBAP.
5. Replacement Cost if the RC eligibility requirements are met (building only).

## G. Sample Replacement Cost Value Letter

Every 3 years the insurer must update the RCV. Below is a sample letter the insurer may use to obtain the RCV for an insured building.

***IMPORTANT FLOOD INSURANCE POLICY INFORMATION***

Agent's Name:
Agent's Address:
Re: Insured's Name:
Property Address:
Policy Number:

Dear Agent:

This letter is to inform you that the Replacement Cost Value (RCV) on file for the building referenced above, insured under the Residential Condominium Building Association Policy (RCBAP), must now be updated. The National Flood Insurance Program (NFIP) requires that the RCV be evaluated every 3 years; it has been at least 3 years since the RCV for the building has been updated.

The RCV as currently listed on the above-referenced policy is <INSERT CURRENT RCV>. The amount of building coverage on the policy is <INSERT CURRENT BUILDING COVERAGE>.

If the RCV indicated above needs to be revised, you must provide new documentation showing the revised RCV. Acceptable documentation of the building's RCV is a recent property valuation report that states the building's value, including the foundation, on an RCV basis.

If the RCV has not changed, you must provide either new RCV documentation or a statement signed by an officer or a representative of the Condominium Association confirming that the RCV is still valid.

Please be aware that to the extent that the amount of building coverage on the policy is not in an amount equal to the lesser of 80 percent or more of the full replacement cost of the building at the time of a loss or the maximum amount of insurance available under the NFIP, the Condominium Association may not be fully reimbursed for the loss.

If you have any questions about the information in this letter, please contact < INSERT CONTACT NAME AND TELEPHONE NUMBER>.

cc: Insured, Lender

## V. Submit-for-Rate

Due to their unique underwriting characteristics and high flood risk, some risks require submission to the insurer for rating purposes. This category includes high-risk properties with no published rates in the *NFIP Flood Insurance Manual*, as well as certain high-risk properties with published rates. Footnotes in the rate tables identify the risks in the Submit-for-Rate category.

### A. Documentation

Insurers must receive the following documentation for Submit-for-Rates:

- Submit-for-Rate Worksheet.
- NFIP Flood Insurance Application.
- EC form.
- Non-Residential Floodproofing Certificate, if applicable.
- If the building is Post-FIRM and has its LFE below the BFE, a copy of the variance issued by the local community stating that it granted permission to construct the building. If the community did not grant a variance, a statement to that effect signed by the applicant or the applicant's representative is required.
- Recent photographs of the building (front and back), or a blueprint (layout of the building) if the building is in the course of construction.
- The square footage of any enclosures (including elevators) or crawlspaces below the elevated floor, the use of the enclosure/crawlspace, a list of machinery and equipment servicing the building in the enclosure/crawlspace, and the approximate value of each.
- The value of the above-grade enclosure (hanging floor or mid-level entry).
- If the area below the elevated floor is enclosed using masonry walls and these walls are represented on the application as being breakaway walls in V Zones, or if the walls appear to be masonry in photographs, a signed letter from a local building official, an engineer, or an architect verifying that the walls are indeed breakaway walls.
- The number of elevators located below the lowest elevated floor of an elevated building and below the BFE.
  **Note:** Do not include chair lifts.
- A statement from the applicant or the applicant's representative that the enclosure was built at the time that the building was originally constructed, or at a later date; must provide that date.
- If the building has a basement, a list of machinery and equipment servicing the building located in the basement and the approximate value of each.
- For elevated buildings, an Elevated Building Determination Form signed by the insured.
- For all Post-1981 V-Zone, non-elevated buildings provide the foundation/structural plans. If the foundation/structural plans are not available, the applicant or agent may provide a written statement to that effect.

- For a non-residential building with an interior pit (oil pit), provide a photo of the interior of the pit.
- For a building with an above-grade enclosure (hanging floor, mid-level entry), provide a photo of the interior of the enclosed area.

### B. Additional Guidance

For additional guidance, refer to the *NFIP Specific Rating Guidelines* manual. If FEMA has not published rates, please submit all documentation via UCORT to FEMA's Underwriting Department to obtain a rate.

If the insurer cannot determine the rate, do not submit premium on these risks until FEMA has determined the appropriate rate.

Submit-for-Rate quotations, excluding the ICC Premium, Federal Policy Fee, Reserve Fund Assessment, HFIAA Surcharge, and Probation Surcharge, if applicable, are valid for 90 days. After 90 days, the agent must resubmit the Flood Insurance Application and supporting documentation to rate the policy. **Please note:** The rates may change based on the policy effective date.

### C. Effective Date

- Follow the effective date guidance provided in the Before You Start section of the manual.

## VI. Provisional Rating

### A. General Information

Provisional rates apply to newly insured risks, enabling coverage placement without the required EC.

- The insurer should receive the EC and apply full-risk rates within 60 days of the policy effective date.
- Provisionally-rated policies are valid for 1 year. However, the insurer must apply full-risk rates prior to any claim payment in the event of a loss.
- Use the effective date rules in the Before You Start section of this manual.
- Provisionally-rated policies cannot be rewritten or renewed.
- The insured may purchase only one provisionally-rated policy per property.

### B. Eligibility Requirements

The newly insured risk must meet all of the following criteria:

- Must be Post-FIRM.
- Must be a 1- to 4-family residential building, excluding mobile homes.
- Must be a property located in Zones AE, A1–A30, AO, AH or A where the community provides BFEs.

## C. Reformation

A provisionally-rated policy has limited reformation rights. The reformation rights depend upon the submission of a valid EC, photographs, and additional premium (if required).

### 1. *Receipt of Required Elements within 60 Days of the Policy Effective Date*

If the insurer receives the required elements within 60 days of the policy effective date and additional premium is due, the insurer must send an underpayment letter. If the insurer receives the additional premium within 30 days of the underpayment letter, the insurer must restore the originally requested limits without a 30-day waiting period. The increased coverage will apply to a loss that occurs before the insurer receives the EC and additional premium.

### 2. *Receipt of Required Elements More Than 60 Days from the Policy Effective Date*

Before a loss, there are two options if additional premium is due after the policy effective date:

- Submit the additional premium for the full policy term. The coverage limits increase to the originally requested limits as of the beginning of the policy term; *or*
- Submit pro-rata additional premium. The additional premium increases the coverage limits with a 30-day waiting period. The increased limits apply only to losses occurring after the 30-day waiting period. Reduced coverage limits apply to losses occurring within the 30-day waiting period.

### 3. *Reformation after Receipt of Required Elements*

- The insurer must determine full-risk rates before issuing payment for a loss.
- The insurer will reduce the coverage to the amount that the received premium purchases, if the cost of the full-risk-rated policy is more than the cost of a provisionally-rated policy.
- A 30-day waiting period applies after the insurer receives the additional premium if the insured wishes to increase coverage.

In all cases, coverage may not exceed the originally requested coverage limits when the full-risk premium is less than the provisional premium.

## D. Endorsements

The insurer may not endorse a provisionally-rated policy to increase coverage until it reforms the policy using full-risk rates.

The agent should submit the following to reform a provisionally-rated policy to a full-risk-rated policy:

- A general change request;
- A valid EC;
- Photographs; *and*
- Additional premium due, if applicable.

## E. Notification

The insurer must provide a notice to the insured, agent, and lender (if applicable) explaining the nature of the coverage, the limited reformation rights, and the full-risk rating requirements. The sample notification letter at the end of this section provides an example to follow.

## F. Provisional Rating Documents

The agent must submit a Provisional Rating Questionnaire (shown in Appendix J: Rate Tables) to the insurer in addition to the application for insurance. One question included in the form asks if the building is located on fill and the four questions below assist in determining if the building is located on fill. If the answer to any of the questions is "yes", the building is elevated on fill.

- Does the building's construction rest on a mound of earth? Examples: The land demonstrates significant slope down and away from the building in the front and rear and/or the driveway exhibits significant slope down and toward the street.
- Is the front door threshold at least 3 feet above the crown of the street?
- Do steps up from the street to the house provide at least a 3-foot rise?
- Is the lower floor of the house at least 2 feet above the floor of the garage?

### *1. National Flood Insurance Program Provisional Rating Questionnaire*

A copy of the Provisional Rating Questionnaire can be found in Appendix J: Rate Tables.

### *2. Provisional Rating Example*

A Provisional Rating example is shown at the beginning of the Rating examples in this section.

### *3. Sample Notification*

A sample notification letter for provisionally-rated policies is shown on the next page.

**SAMPLE NOTICE TO ACCOMPANY PROVISIONALLY RATED POLICIES**

At the request of you and your agent/producer, the enclosed Standard Flood Insurance Policy has been issued using provisional rates because an Elevation Certificate was not available at the time of application. An Elevation Certificate is necessary to determine a premium that accurately reflects the flood risk (i.e., full-risk rates). By accepting this provisionally rated policy, you agree to submit an Elevation Certificate and the required photographs within 60 days of your policy becoming effective. Failure to comply with this requirement may result in lower coverage limits than those shown on the enclosed declarations page and may affect other aspects of your coverage. This policy is issued for a 1-year term and cannot be renewed using provisional rates.

It is likely that after you submit a valid Elevation Certificate, the resulting full-risk premium will be determined to be lower than the provisional premium. In that case, you will receive a refund of the difference for the policy term.

If the full-risk premium is determined to be higher, the following rules apply:

(1) If we receive from you a valid Elevation Certificate and the required photographs within 60 days of the policy effective date, the coverage limits on the declarations page will be revised as of the policy effective date. If any additional premium is due because the full-risk premium is more than the provisional premium, you will then have 30 days to pay the additional premium for the entire term to restore the originally requested limits without a waiting period. Those coverage limits will apply even to a loss occurring before we receive the Elevation Certificate and additional premium. Full-risk rating will be completed before the loss payment is made.

(2) If we receive from you a valid Elevation Certificate and any additional premium due as a result of using full-risk rates more than 60 days after the policy effective date but before a loss occurs, you have 2 options. You may submit the additional premium for the entire policy term, in which case the coverage limits on the enclosed declarations page will be in force from the effective date. Alternatively, you may submit the additional premium, computed for the remainder of the policy term with a 30-day waiting period. In this latter case, the originally requested coverage limits will only apply to any loss occurring after the waiting period. Reduced coverage limits as described in number (3) below will apply to any loss occurring within the waiting period.

(3) If neither (1) nor (2) above applies, full-risk rates must be determined before any loss payment will be made. If the full-risk premium is more than the provisional premium, the coverage limits will be less than those shown on the enclosed declarations page. In that case, the loss payment will be subject to the reduced coverage limits, which will be the coverage limits that the provisional premium would buy using the full-risk rates. If you want to increase your reduced coverage limits, a 30-day waiting period will apply to the additional coverage.

In all instances, if the full-risk premium is less than the provisional premium, the amount of coverage may not exceed the amount originally requested.

If you have any questions, please contact your insurance agent/producer for assistance.

# VII. Certifications

## A. General Information

This section provides information about the NFIP EC and NFIP Floodproofing Certificate.

## B. EC

The EC provides elevation information required:

- To ensure compliance with community floodplain management ordinances;
- To determine the proper insurance premium rate; *and*
- To support a request for a LOMA or LOMR-F.

A sample EC can be found in Appendix B: Forms.

> **NOTE**
>
> A LOMR-F is FEMA's modification of the SFHA shown on the FIRM based on the placement of fill outside the existing regulatory floodway. https://www.fema.gov/letter-map-revision-based-fill

### *1. The NFIP Requires ECs for SFHAs*

For rating purposes, the NFIP requires an EC for buildings in the SFHA:

- Post-FIRM buildings; *and*
- Full-risk elevation-rated Pre-FIRM buildings.

### *2. Optional Full-Risk Rating*

- SFHA full-risk rates may be lower than SFHA Pre-FIRM rates for some buildings. The decision to obtain an EC and request full-risk rating is at the insured's discretion.

The insured may choose to obtain an EC and request full-risk rating for:

- Pre-FIRM Buildings in an SFHA:
  - The insurer may endorse the policy for only the current policy year if the full-risk rating provides a lower premium.
  - The policy continues with the Pre-FIRM subsidized premium rates, if the full-risk rates are not favorable, until the full-risk rating provides a lower premium.
- AR and AR Dual Zones:
  - The EC is optional for both Pre- and Post-FIRM buildings.

## C. Completing an EC

### *1. Required Certification*

The NFIP requires a legally authorized land surveyor, engineer, or architect to certify elevations in all SFHAs except for zones AO and A (without BFEs). The surveyor, engineer, or architect must sign and include their identification number and/or seal in Section D.

A building official, a property owner, or an owner's representative may provide the EC for zones AO and A (without BFEs). The property owner or owner's representative must complete Section F when they prepare the EC for a building in Zones AO or A (without BFEs).

### 2. Photographs

The NFIP will not accept an EC for rating purposes without photographs, except for a building in the course of construction. The photograph requirements apply to all policies rated with an EC.

- Photograph Requirements:
  - A minimum of two clear/legible photographs that show the front and back of the building.
  - Photographs dated within 90 days of submitting the EC to the insurer (not the certification date, if that date is earlier).
  - Photographs must be at least 3"×3" and may be analog (film) or digital. The NFIP prefers color photographs.
- Building in the course of construction:
  - The NFIP waives the photograph requirement when the building is in the course of construction.
  - The NFIP requires a revised EC with photographs when the construction is complete.
  - The NFIP requires as-built building elevations when construction is complete.
- Additional photograph requirements:
  - Buildings with flood openings (flood vents) must have one or more photographs that clearly show the flood vent openings.
  - Split or multi-level buildings must have at least two additional photographs showing both sides of the building.

**NOTE**

The NFIP requires photographs when an agent moves his or her business from one insurer to another.

### 3. Other Elevation Information

Existing documentation containing elevation information (e.g., an older Elevation Certification form, or surveyor letterhead) may transfer to Section C of the EC.

- Only a local official authorized by law or ordinance to administer the community's floodplain management ordinance may complete this transaction.
- The official must certify the information and provide a statement documenting the transfer of information in Section G of the EC.
- NFIP requires the LAG and diagram number for all new business if the elevation certification date is on or after October 1, 1997.
- For zones AO and A (without BFEs), a building official, a property owner, or an owner's representative may provide the information in Sections A, B and E on the EC.
- In Community Rating System (CRS) communities, building elevation information may be available through the community.

## D. Troubleshooting

- Fields not applicable to the surveyed property should be marked as N/A (not applicable).
- The insured or insured's representative must return the EC to the surveyor, engineer, architect or community official to provide missing information and ensure that they complete the critical Section A of the EC.
- The insurer should contact the surveyor, engineer, or architect completing the form to provide missing data in any part of Section C.
- The building elevation information contained in Section C (Survey Required) appears in feet, except in Puerto Rico, where it appears in meters. Before calculating the elevation difference, convert all metric elevation measurements to feet (1m = 3.28084 ft.).
- Section C2a. of the EC may remain blank if the surveyor, engineer, or architect cannot gain access to the crawlspace to obtain the elevation of the crawlspace floor. Preparers should enter the estimated measurements in the comments area of Section D.
- In Section E – Building Elevation Information (Survey Not Required) for Zone AO and Zone A (without BFE), preparers must compute and enter the elevation differences between the lowest floor and the LAG along with lowest floor and HAG.
- The NFIP requires the elevation information of machinery and equipment servicing the building such as water heater, furnace, A/C compressor, heat pump, and water pump, regardless of its location.

## E. Floodproofing

Floodproofing may be an alternative to elevating a building to or above the BFE; however, the NFIP requires a Floodproofing Certificate prior to considering floodproofing mitigation measures in rating a structure. Certified floodproofing may result in lower rates because floodproofing ensures:

- A watertight building;
- Waterproof non-collapsing walls; *and*
- The floor at the base of the floodproofed walls will resist flotation during a flood.

**NOTE**

Allowable methods for floodproofing non-residential buildings differ from those allowed for residential buildings. Contact the local government for the specific requirements.

### *1. Eligibility for a Premium Discount*

- Insureds may receive a premium discount for floodproofing a residential building if all of the following apply:
  - The building has a basement;
  - The building is located in a community where FEMA approved the residential basement floodproofing premium discount; *and*
  - The building is located in zone A1–A30, AE, AR, AR Dual, AO, AH, or A with a BFE.
- Insureds may receive a premium discount for floodproofing a non-residential building if:
  - The building is in any zone other than a V zone; *and*
  - The building is in any participating NFIP community.
- Refer to Appendix K for the list of communities approved for residential basement floodproofing.

**NOTE**

For the non-residential floodproofing premium discount, FEMA will establish the base rate from the elevation difference between the LFE of the building and the BFE. FEMA will apply a discount to that rate based on the information provided for the floodproofing components.

### 2. Requirements for a Premium Discount

A registered professional engineer or architect must certify that the building is floodproofed to at least one foot above the BFE.

### 3. Residential Buildings with Basements

- Insurers must submit a completed Residential Basement Floodproofing Certificate and at least two photographs of the building to obtain a premium discount.
- The NFIP grandfathers a residential floodproofing premium discount if the building was constructed:
  - In a community approved for the residential floodproofing premium discount at the time of construction; *or*
  - Before the date the NFIP removed the community's residential floodproofing premium discount approval.

### 4. Non-Residential Buildings

- The insurer must receive the Floodproofing Certificate with the application and at least two photographs of the building. The photographs must show the floodproofing measures in place.
- All non-residential floodproofed buildings must follow submit-for-rate procedures.
- Insurers must submit the following to FEMA:
  - Completed Flood Insurance Application;
  - Completed EC;
  - Completed Floodproofing Certificate;
  - Photographs of the exterior of the building (all sides);
  - Photographs of the components used to provide floodproofing protection (shields, gates, barriers);
  - Flood Emergency Plan that includes:
    - Chain of command;
    - Notification procedures;
    - Personnel duties;
    - Location of floodproofing components, install procedures, repair procedures;
    - Evacuation procedures for building occupants;
    - Component maintenance procedures during flooding event;
    - Drill and training program (at least once a year);
    - Regular review/update of Flood Emergency Plan; *and*
  - Inspection and Maintenance Plan that includes:
    - Inspection procedures for the entire floodproofing system: wall systems, floor slab, openings, floodproofing components, valve operation, drainage/pump systems, equipment/tools required to engage floodproofing measures; *and*
    - Cadence of the Inspection and Maintenance Plan.

# VIII. Mortgage Portfolio Protection Program Policy

## A. Background

The Mortgage Portfolio Protection Program (MPPP) is a tool to help the mortgage lending and servicing industries bring their mortgage portfolios into compliance with the flood insurance requirements of the Flood Disaster Protection Act of 1973 and the National Flood Insurance Reform Act of 1994 (NFIRA). The law requires flood insurance for all buildings located in a SFHA carrying a mortgage loan issued by a federally regulated lender or servicer. The MPPP does not replace the need for mortgagees to review all mortgage loan applications at the time of loan origination and comply with flood insurance requirements as appropriate.

When property owners receive notice that their building requires flood insurance, they must either show evidence of such a policy to the lender or purchase the necessary coverage. When property owners do not purchase the required flood insurance coverage, lenders can obtain flood insurance policies for these properties under the MPPP. NFIP insurers make this coverage available only as a last resort, and only on mortgages for which property owners did not purchase the required insurance.

## B. General Information

Lenders should encourage all property owners required to purchase flood insurance to obtain a flood insurance policy from their agent or insurer. The MPPP is only available when property owners fail to purchase the required insurance.

NFIP Direct cannot offer the MPPP. Only WYO insurers participating in the MPPP have the ability to service policies for lenders/servicers who have force-placement capability.

### *1. Eligibility*

- The property is determined to be located within the SFHA of a community participating in the NFIP;
- The property is not covered by a flood insurance policy even after a required series of notices from the lender regarding the flood insurance requirement for obtaining and maintaining such coverage; *and*
- The borrower has failed to respond.

### *2. Policy Form*

Insurers should use the current SFIP Dwelling Form and General Property Form for MPPP policies, depending upon the type of structure insured. In the absence of building occupancy information, use the Dwelling Form.

### *3. Underwriting Application*

The MPPP requires the following underwriting data for rating and processing:

- Name and mailing address of insured borrower (see Dual Interest under D in this section);
- Insured property address;

- Lender's name and address;
- Mortgage loan number;
- Community name, number, map panel number and suffix, and program type (Emergency or Regular);
- Lender-verified NFIP flood zone where the property is located;
- Occupancy type;
- Whether the building is the insured's primary residence (Yes or No);
- Whether the building is walled and roofed (Yes or No);
- Whether the building is over water (Yes, Partially, or Entirely); *and*
- Coverage amount.

## C. Required Notifications

### *1. Notification to Lenders*

An insurer providing flood insurance and participating in the MPPP must provide a detailed implementation package to any lending institution that, on a voluntary basis, chooses to participate in the MPPP as required by NFIP regulations in Title 44 of the Code of Federal Regulations §62.23(l). The insurer must maintain evidence documenting that each lender or servicer received the notification.

### *2. Notification to Borrowers*

The lender must send the borrower three notification letters so the borrower is protected against the lending institution arbitrarily placing flood insurance for which the borrower will be billed.

The lender or its authorized representative providing coverage through the MPPP must send an initial notification letter to notify the borrower of the following:

- The Flood Disaster Protection Act of 1973 requirements;
- The determination that the borrower's property is in an identified SFHA on the appropriate FEMA map, necessitating flood insurance coverage for the duration of the loan;
- Describe the procedure to follow should the borrower wish to challenge the determination;
- Request evidence of a valid flood insurance policy or, if there is none, encourage the borrower to obtain SFIP promptly from a local insurance agent or WYO company;
- Advise that the premium for an MPPP policy is significantly higher than a conventional SFIP policy and advise as to the option for obtaining less costly flood insurance; *and*
- Advise that the lender will purchase an MPPP policy at the borrower's expense, if the lender does not receive evidence of flood insurance coverage by a certain date.

The second notification letter must remind the borrower of the previous notice and provide the same information.

The final notification letter must:

- Enclose a copy of the flood insurance policy purchased under the MPPP on the borrower's behalf, together with the Declarations page;
- Advise that the lender purchased the policy because of the borrower's failure to respond to previous notices;
- Remind the insured that similar coverage may be available at significantly lower cost; *and*
- Advise that if the insured purchases another NFIP policy that satisfies the requirement in Federal law, the policy can be canceled and a pro rata refund provided for the unearned portion of the premium.

This is a sample of the final notification the insurer may send to the insured:

> Your lender notified you of the requirement in Federal law to have flood insurance on your property. We are providing the federally mandated flood insurance policy at your lender's request because your lender has not received proof of flood insurance coverage on your property despite previous notices. The rates charged for this policy can be considerably higher than rates available through a conventionally written flood insurance policy. The amounts of insurance coverage may not be sufficient in the event of a flood loss to protect your full interest in the property. You may contact your insurance agent or company at any time to replace this policy with a conventionally underwritten flood insurance policy, typically at a significant savings in premium. If you purchase another NFIP policy that satisfies the requirement in Federal law, a pro rata refund for the unearned portion of the premium will be provided.

The insurer may modify this language to conform to its practices, but the notice must meet the requirements in the NFIP regulations at 44 C.F.R. 62.23(l)(6).

## D. Policy Term and Coverage

### *1. Waiting Period*

The NFIP waiting period and effective dates rules apply to the MPPP.

### *2. Policy Term*

MPPP policies are for a one-year term only and subject to the renewal notification process. The insurer must notify the lender and borrower of all coverage limitations at the inception of coverage. The insurer must also impose any applicable coverage limitations at the time of the loss adjustment.

### *3. Coverage*

Both building and contents coverages are available under the MPPP.

- The available coverage limits for residential occupancies under the Regular Program are $250,000 for building coverage and $100,000 for contents.
- The coverage limits available for residential occupancies in Emergency Program communities are $35,000 for building coverage and $10,000 for contents.

- The insurer may sell higher amounts of insurance to other occupancy types such as other residential, non-residential business or other non-residential business but the insurer must verify the building occupancy type. The verification must occur before any loss.

### 4. Deductible

The MPPP policy deductible is $1,000 each for both building and contents if the building coverage is less than or equal to $100,000. The deductible is $1,250 regardless of the insured building's construction date compared to the initial FIRM date if the building coverage is over $100,000. A contents-only policy has a $1,000 deductible.

### 5. Duplicate Coverage

The NFIP does not allow duplicate building coverage. If more than one policy with building coverage for the same property exists, cancellation or endorsement removing building coverage from all but one of the policies must occur. The NFIP does not consider an RCBAP and a condominium unit owner Dwelling Form policy duplicate policies. However, in the event of a claim, a payment of no more than $250,000 for a single unit may occur in combined coverage under the Dwelling Form policy and the RCBAP.

### 6. Coverage Basis

There are no changes from the standard NFIP practices for these provisions. The coverage basis – actual cash value or replacement cost – depends on the covered building occupancy type and the coverage amount.

### 7. Dual Interest

MPPP policies cover both the lender and the borrower's interests and must include the recorded name of the borrower on the Application Form. It is not necessary to include the lender as a named insured because the Mortgage Clause (section VII.Q. of the Dwelling Form and the General Property Form) affords building coverage to any lender named on the Flood Insurance Application. However, insurers should include the borrower as a named insured if the borrower purchases contents coverage.

## E. Premium and Fees

### 1. Rates

The MPPP requires limited underwriting information and provides special flood insurance rates. See Appendix J: Rate Tables for the rates applicable to MPPP policies. Note the following:

- MPPP policies are not eligible for CRS premium discounts.
- Refer to **Table 2** in this section for basic and additional insurance limits.
- ICC coverage does not apply to contents-only policies or to individually owned condominium units insured under the Dwelling Form or General Property Form.
- The ICC premium is not eligible for the deductible discount. First, calculate the deductible discount, and then add in the ICC premium.

Follow the steps outlined in **Table 50** to calculate the premium for an MPPP policy. The total amount due equals the total premium plus applicable fees and surcharges.

### Table 50. Calculate Premium for an MPPP Policy

| Step | Action | Reference/Guidance |
|---|---|---|
| 1 | Identify the rate | Rate tables – MPPP Rates |
| 2 | Apply the deductible factor | Deductible Factors table for deductible amounts and factors |
| 3 | Add ICC premium | ICC Premium table for ICC premium amount<br>Do not apply ICC premium to contents-only policies or to policies for individual condominium units in a multi-unit building. |
| 4 | Apply CRS discount | N/A |
| 5 | Apply Reserve Fund Assessment | Reserve Fund Assessment table for applicable percentage |
| 6 | Add Probation Surcharge | Community Master File or insurer to determine if community is on probation<br>Add a $50 Probation Surcharge if community is on NFIP probation. |
| 7 | Add HFIAA Surcharge | A $25 HFIAA surcharge applies to:<br>• Policies covering single-family residences, 2–4 family residences, or individual residential condominium units used as a primary residence by the named insured; *and*<br>• Contents-only policies for apartments used as a primary residence by the named insured.<br>All other policies have a $250 HFIAA Surcharge. |
| 8 | Add Federal Policy Fee | Federal Policy Fee Table<br>The Federal Policy Fee for tenant's contents-only policy is $25; for all other policies the Federal Policy Fee is $50. |

## F. Policy Administration

### *1. Policy Reformation*

The provisions for reduction of coverage limits or reformation are described in:

- Dwelling Form, section VII, paragraph G.
- General Property Form, section VII, paragraph G.
- RCBAP, section VIII, paragraph G.

For additional information refer to Reforming the Policy in the Before You Start section of this manual.

### *2. Renewal*

If the insured failed to provide evidence of a flood insurance policy, the full notification process must take place between the lender or authorized representative and the insured before the insurer can renew a policy.

### *3. Cancellation*

Refer to the How to Cancel section for policy cancellation/nullification guidance.

#### *4. Endorsement*

An MPPP policy may be endorsed to:

- Increase coverage;
- Make a lender change; *or*
- Assign another lender or borrower.

Insurers may not endorse an MPPP policy to convert it to a conventionally underwritten SFIP. Rather, insurers must complete a new policy application with a new policy number and follow the underwriting requirements of the SFIP, as contained in this manual.

### G. MPPP WYO Insurers

The following URL links to a list of insurers participating in the MPPP: https://nfipservices.floodsmart.gov/mortgage-portfolio-protection-program.

#### *1. MPPP Expense Allowance*

WYO insurers retain the same expense allowance for MPPP business as they do for all other flood insurance they write.

#### *2. Use of WYO Allowance*

WYO insurers may not use any portion of the allowance retained for MPPP policies under the WYO Financial Assistance/Subsidy Arrangement to pay, reimburse, or otherwise compensate a lending institution, mortgage servicing company, or other similar type of company the WYO insurer might work with to assist in its flood insurance compliance efforts.

The only exception to this rule is when the lender or servicer may be due a commission on a flood insurance policy written on any portion of the institution's portfolio because a licensed property insurance agent on their staff or a licensed insurance agency owned by the institution or servicing company wrote the policy.

## IX. Rating Examples

This section provides 29 illustrative "how to" rating examples for NFIP insurance.

**TABLE OF CONTENTS**

EXAMPLE — PAGE

Provisional Rating Example 1: Regular Program, Post-Firm Construction . . . . . 3-78

Rate Example 1: Emergency Program, $1,500/$1,500 Deductible, Primary Residence . . . . . 3-79

Rate Example 2: Regular Program, Pre-FIRM Construction, $1,250/$1,250 Deductible Option, Zone B, Primary Residence . . . . . 3-80

Rate Example 3: Regular Program, Pre-FIRM Construction, $2,000/$2,000 Deductible Option, Zone AE, Primary Residence . . . . . 3-81

Rate Example 4: Regular Program, Pre-FIRM Construction, $3,000/$2,000 Deductible Option, Zone A15, Non-Primary Residence . . . . . 3-82

Rate Example 5: Regular Program, Pre-FIRM Construction, $2,000/$2,000 Deductible Option, Zone AE, Severe Repetitive Loss Property, Primary Residence . . . . . 3-83

## TABLE OF CONTENTS

EXAMPLE PAGE

Rate Example 6: Regular Program, Pre-FIRM Construction, $2,000/$2,000 Deductible Option, Zone AE, Building Substantially Improved, Primary Residence . . . . 3-84

Rate Example 7: Regular Program, Pre-FIRM Construction Rated With Full-Risk Rates, $1,500/$1,500 Deductible, Zone AE, Primary Residence . . . . 3-85

Rate Example 8: Regular Program, Post-FIRM, Elevation Rated, $5,000/$5,000 Deductible Option, Zone AE, Non-Residential Business . . . . 3-86

Rate Example 9: Regular Program, 1975–'81 Post-FIRM V1–V30, $2,000/$2,000 Deductible Option, Elevation Rated, Zone V13, Non-Primary Residence . . . . 3-87

Rate Example 10: Regular Program, Post-1981 VE Or V1–V30, $3,000/$3,000 Deductible Option, With Enclosure, Zone VE, Primary Residence . . . . 3-88

Rate Example 11: Regular Program, Post-FIRM Construction, $1,000 Deductible Option, Contents-Only Policy, Zone A17, Primary Residence . . . . 3-89

Rate Example 12: Regular Program, Post-FIRM, Elevation Rated, $5,000/$5,000 Deductible Option, Zone AO (Without Certification of Compliance or EC), Other Non-Residential . . . . 3-90

Rate Example 13: Regular Program, Post-FIRM, Elevation Rated, $1,250/$1,250 Deductible Option, Zone AO (With Certification of Compliance or EC), Primary Residence . . . . 3-91

Rate Example 14: Regular Program, Post-FIRM, Elevation Rated, $3,000/$2,000 Deductible Option, Zone Ah (Without Certification of Compliance or EC), Primary Residence . . . . 3-92

Rate Example 15: Regular Program, Post-FIRM, Elevation Rated, $1,250/$1,250 Deductible Option, Zone AH (With Certification of Compliance or EC), 2–4 Family . . . . 3-93

Rate Example 16: Regular Program, Post-FIRM, Elevation Rated, $1,250/$1,250 Deductible Option, Zone A (With BFE), 2–4 Family . . . . 3-94

Rate Example 17: Regular Program, Post-FIRM, Elevation Rated, $1,250/$1,250 Deductible Option, Zone A (Without BFE), Primary Residence . . . . 3-95

PRP Rating Example: Preferred Risk Policy, $1,250/$1,250 Deductible, Zone X, Primary Residence . . . . 3-96

Newly Mapped Rating Example: Zone X, Newly Mapped Into SFHA on 8/1/2019, $1,250/$1,250 Deductible, Primary Residence . . . . 3-97

Condo Rating Example 1: Pre-FIRM, Low-Rise, With Enclosure, Coinsurance Penalty, Zone A . . . . 3-98

Condo Rating Example 2: Pre-FIRM, Low-Rise, No Basement/Enclosure, Zone AE . . . . 3-99

Condominium Rating Example 3: Pre-FIRM, Low-Rise, No Basement/Enclosure, Zone AE, Building Substantially Improved . . . . 3-100

Condo Rating Example 4: Post-FIRM, Low-Rise, Coinsurance Penalty, Zone AE . . . . 3-101

Condo Rating Example 5: Post-FIRM, Low-Rise, Zone AE . . . . 3-102

Condo Rating Example 6: Pre-FIRM, High-Rise, Coinsurance Penalty, Zone A . . . . 3-103

Condo Rating Example 7: Pre-FIRM, High-Rise, Basement, Maximum Deductible Discount, Zone AE . . . . 3-104

Condo Rating Example 8: Post-FIRM, High-Rise, Maximum Deductible Discount, Zone AE . . . . 3-105

Condo Rating Example 9: Pre-FIRM, High-Rise, Enclosure, Maximum Deductible Discount, Coinsurance Penalty, Zone AE . . . . 3-106

## PROVISIONAL RATING EXAMPLE 1
## REGULAR PROGRAM, POST-FIRM CONSTRUCTION

Essential Data to Determine Appropriate Rates and Premium:

**REGULAR PROGRAM:**

- Flood Zone: A with BFE, AE, A1–A30, AO, or AH
- Occupancy: Single-Family Dwelling
- Number of Floors: 3 or More Floors
- Basement/Enclosure: Basement
- Deductible: $3,000/$2,000
- Deductible Factor: .900
- Contents Location: Basement and Above
- Date of Construction: Post-FIRM
- Elevation Difference: N/A
- Floodproofed (Yes/No): No
- Building Coverage: $250,000
- Contents Coverage: $100,000
- ICC Premium: $6
- CRS Rating: N/A
- CRS Discount: N/A
- Reserve Fund Assessment $1,273
- Probation Surcharge: $50
- HFIAA Surcharge: Primary Residence $25
- Federal Policy Fee $50

**DETERMINED RATES:**

Building: 3.00 / 2.00 Contents: 3.00 / 2.00

| ESTIMATED BUILDING REPLACEMENT COST (INCLUDING FOUNDATION): $ | DEDUCTIBLE: | BUILDING $ 3,000 | CONTENTS $ 2,000 |
|---|---|---|---|

| INSURANCE COVERAGE | TOTAL AMOUNT OF INSURANCE | BASIC LIMITS | | | ADDITIONAL LIMITS (REGULAR PROGRAM ONLY) | | | DEDUCTIBLE | TOTAL PREMIUM |
|---|---|---|---|---|---|---|---|---|---|
| | | AMOUNT OF INSURANCE | RATE | ANNUAL PREMIUM | AMOUNT OF INSURANCE | RATE | ANNUAL PREMIUM | PREMIUM REDUCTION/ INCREASE | |
| BUILDING | $250,000 | $60,000 | 3.00 | $1,800 | $190,000 | 2.00 | $3,800 | –$560 | $5,040 |
| CONTENTS | $100,000 | $25,000 | 3.00 | $750 | $75,000 | 2.00 | $1,500 | –$225 | $2,025 |

RATE CATEGORY: ☐ MANUAL ☐ SUBMIT FOR RATE ☐ PROVISIONAL RATING

PAYMENT METHOD: ☐ CHECK ☐ CREDIT CARD ☐ OTHER: ____________

| | |
|---|---|
| ANNUAL SUBTOTAL | $7,065 |
| ICC PREMIUM | $6 |
| SUBTOTAL | $7,071 |
| CRS PREMIUM DISCOUNT ___ % | $0 |
| SUBTOTAL | $7,071 |
| RESERVE FUND ___ % | $1,273 |
| SUBTOTAL | $8,344 |
| PROBATION SURCHARGE | $50 |
| HFIAA SURCHARGE | $25 |
| FEDERAL POLICY FEE | $50 |
| **TOTAL AMOUNT DUE** | **$8,469** |

**NOTICE:** BUILDING COVERAGE BENEFITS – EXCEPT FOR A RESIDENTIAL CONDOMINIUM BUILDING – ARE NOT AVAILABLE IF OTHER NFIP BUILDING COVERAGE HAS BEEN PURCHASED BY THE APPLICANT OR ANY OTHER PARTY FOR THE SAME BUILDING.

THE ABOVE STATEMENTS ARE CORRECT TO THE BEST OF MY KNOWLEDGE. I UNDERSTAND THAT ANY FALSE STATEMENTS MAY BE PUNISHABLE BY FINE AND/OR IMPRISONMENT UNDER APPLICABLE FEDERAL LAW. SEE REVERSE SIDE OF COPIES.

SIGNATURE OF INSURANCE AGENT/PRODUCER ______ DATE (MM/DD/YYYY) ___/___/___

SIGNATURE OF INSURED (OPTIONAL) ______ DATE (MM/DD/YYYY) ___/___/___

**PREMIUM CALCULATION:**

1. Multiply Rate × $100 of Coverage: Building: $5,600 / Contents: $2,250
2. Apply Deductible Factor: Building: .900 × $5,600 = $5,040 / Contents: .900 × $2,250 = $2,025
3. Premium Reduction: Building: $5,600 – $5,040 = $560 / Contents: $2,250 – $2,025 = $225
4. Subtotal: $7,065
5. Add ICC Premium: $6
6. Subtotal: $7,071
7. Subtract CRS Discount: N/A
8. Subtotal: $7,071
9. Add Reserve Fund Assessment: $1,273 (18%)
10. Subtotal: $8,344
11. Add Probation Surcharge: $50
12. Add HFIAA Surcharge: $25
13. Add Federal Policy Fee: $50
14. **Total Amount Due: $8,469**

## RATE EXAMPLE 1
## EMERGENCY PROGRAM, $1,500/$1,500 DEDUCTIBLE, PRIMARY RESIDENCE

Essential Data to Determine Appropriate Rates and Premium:

### Emergency Program:

- Flood Zone: N/A
- Occupancy: Single-Family Dwelling
- Number of Floors: 1 Floor
- Basement/Enclosure: None
- Deductible: $1,500/$1,500
- Deductible Factor: 1.050
- Contents Location: Lowest Floor Above Ground Level
- Date of Construction: Pre-FIRM
- Elevation Difference: N/A
- Floodproofed (Yes/No): No
- Building Coverage: $35,000
- Contents: $10,000
- ICC Premium: N/A
- CRS Rating: N/A
- CRS Discount: N/A
- Reserve Fund Assessment: $114
- Probation Surcharge: N/A
- HFIAA Surcharge: Primary Residence $25
- Federal Policy Fee: $50

### Determined Rates:

Building: 1.27 Contents: 1.60

ESTIMATED BUILDING REPLACEMENT COST (INCLUDING FOUNDATION): $ — DEDUCTIBLE: BUILDING $ 1,500 — CONTENTS $ 1,500

| INSURANCE COVERAGE | TOTAL AMOUNT OF INSURANCE | BASIC LIMITS | | | ADDITIONAL LIMITS (REGULAR PROGRAM ONLY) | | | DEDUCTIBLE | TOTAL PREMIUM |
|---|---|---|---|---|---|---|---|---|---|
| | | AMOUNT OF INSURANCE | RATE | ANNUAL PREMIUM | AMOUNT OF INSURANCE | RATE | ANNUAL PREMIUM | PREMIUM REDUCTION/ INCREASE | |
| BUILDING | $35,000 | $35,000 | 1.27 | $445 | | | | $22 | $467 |
| CONTENTS | $10,000 | $10,000 | 1.60 | $160 | | | | $8 | $168 |

RATE CATEGORY: ☐ MANUAL ☐ SUBMIT FOR RATE ☐ PROVISIONAL RATING

PAYMENT METHOD: ☐ CHECK ☐ CREDIT CARD ☐ OTHER: ____________

| | |
|---|---|
| ANNUAL SUBTOTAL | $635 |
| ICC PREMIUM | $0 |
| SUBTOTAL | $635 |
| CRS PREMIUM DISCOUNT ___ % | $0 |
| SUBTOTAL | $635 |
| RESERVE FUND ___ % | $114 |
| SUBTOTAL | $749 |
| PROBATION SURCHARGE | $0 |
| HFIAA SURCHARGE | $25 |
| FEDERAL POLICY FEE | $50 |
| **TOTAL AMOUNT DUE** | **$824** |

**NOTICE:** BUILDING COVERAGE BENEFITS – EXCEPT FOR A RESIDENTIAL CONDOMINIUM BUILDING – ARE NOT AVAILABLE IF OTHER NFIP BUILDING COVERAGE HAS BEEN PURCHASED BY THE APPLICANT OR ANY OTHER PARTY FOR THE SAME BUILDING.

THE ABOVE STATEMENTS ARE CORRECT TO THE BEST OF MY KNOWLEDGE. I UNDERSTAND THAT ANY FALSE STATEMENTS MAY BE PUNISHABLE BY FINE AND/OR IMPRISONMENT UNDER APPLICABLE FEDERAL LAW. SEE REVERSE SIDE OF COPIES.

____________________ SIGNATURE OF INSURANCE AGENT/PRODUCER ____/____/____ DATE (MM/DD/YYYY)

____________________ SIGNATURE OF INSURED (OPTIONAL) ____/____/____ DATE (MM/DD/YYYY)

### Premium Calculation:

1. Multiply Rate × $100 of Coverage: Building: $445 / Contents: $160
1. Apply Deductible Factor: Building: 1.050 × $445 = $467 / Contents: 1.050 × $160 = $168
1. Premium Increase: Building: $445 – $467 = $22 / Contents: $160 – $168 = $8
1. Annual Subtotal: $635
2. Add ICC Premium: N/A
3. Subtotal: $635
4. Subtract CRS Discount: N/A
5. Subtotal: $635
6. Add Reserve Fund Assessment: $114 (18%)
7. Subtotal: $749
8. Add Probation Surcharge: N/A
9. Add HFIAA Surcharge: $25
10. Add Federal Policy Fee: $50
11. **Total Amount Due:** **$824**

## RATE EXAMPLE 2
## REGULAR PROGRAM, PRE-FIRM CONSTRUCTION, $1,250/$1,250 DEDUCTIBLE OPTION, ZONE B, PRIMARY RESIDENCE

Essential Data to Determine Appropriate Rates and Premium:

**Regular Program:**

- Flood Zone: B
- Occupancy: Single-Family Dwelling
- Number of Floors: 2 Floors
- Basement/Enclosure: None
- Deductible: $1,250/$1,250
- Deductible Factor: .980
- Contents Location: Lowest Floor Above Ground Level and Higher Floors
- Date of Construction: Pre-FIRM
- Elevation Difference: N/A
- Floodproofed (Yes/No): No
- Building Coverage: $150,000
- Contents Coverage: $60,000
- ICC Premium: $8
- CRS Rating: N/A
- CRS Discount: N/A
- Reserve Fund Assessment: $281
- Probation Surcharge: N/A
- HFIAA Surcharge: Primary Residence $25
- Federal Policy Fee: $50

**Determined Rates:**

Building: 1.12 / .32 Contents: 1.73 / .55

ESTIMATED BUILDING REPLACEMENT COST (INCLUDING FOUNDATION): $ DEDUCTIBLE: BUILDING $ 1,250 CONTENTS $ 1,250

| INSURANCE COVERAGE | TOTAL AMOUNT OF INSURANCE | BASIC LIMITS | | | ADDITIONAL LIMITS (REGULAR PROGRAM ONLY) | | | DEDUCTIBLE | TOTAL PREMIUM |
|---|---|---|---|---|---|---|---|---|---|
| | | AMOUNT OF INSURANCE | RATE | ANNUAL PREMIUM | AMOUNT OF INSURANCE | RATE | ANNUAL PREMIUM | PREMIUM REDUCTION/ INCREASE | |
| BUILDING | $150,000 | $60,000 | 1.12 | $672 | $90,000 | .32 | $288 | −$19 | $941 |
| CONTENTS | $60,000 | $25,000 | 1.73 | $433 | $35,000 | .55 | $193 | −$12 | $613 |

RATE CATEGORY: ☐ MANUAL ☐ SUBMIT FOR RATE ☐ PROVISIONAL RATING

PAYMENT METHOD: ☐ CHECK ☐ CREDIT CARD ☐ OTHER: ____________

| | |
|---|---|
| ANNUAL SUBTOTAL | $1,554 |
| ICC PREMIUM | $8 |
| SUBTOTAL | $1,562 |
| CRS PREMIUM DISCOUNT ___ % | $0 |
| SUBTOTAL | $1,562 |
| RESERVE FUND ___ % | $281 |
| SUBTOTAL | $1,843 |
| PROBATION SURCHARGE | $0 |
| HFIAA SURCHARGE | $25 |
| FEDERAL POLICY FEE | $50 |
| **TOTAL AMOUNT DUE** | **$1,918** |

**NOTICE:** BUILDING COVERAGE BENEFITS – EXCEPT FOR A RESIDENTIAL CONDOMINIUM BUILDING – ARE NOT AVAILABLE IF OTHER NFIP BUILDING COVERAGE HAS BEEN PURCHASED BY THE APPLICANT OR ANY OTHER PARTY FOR THE SAME BUILDING.

THE ABOVE STATEMENTS ARE CORRECT TO THE BEST OF MY KNOWLEDGE. I UNDERSTAND THAT ANY FALSE STATEMENTS MAY BE PUNISHABLE BY FINE AND/OR IMPRISONMENT UNDER APPLICABLE FEDERAL LAW. SEE REVERSE SIDE OF COPIES.

______________________ ___/___/______
SIGNATURE OF INSURANCE AGENT/PRODUCER DATE (MM/DD/YYYY)

______________________ ___/___/______
SIGNATURE OF INSURED (OPTIONAL) DATE (MM/DD/YYYY)

**Premium Calculation:**

| | | |
|---|---|---|
| 1. | Multiply Rate × $100 of Coverage: | Building: $960 / Contents: $626 |
| 1. | Apply Deductible Factor: | Building: .980 × $960 = $941 / Contents: .980 × $626 = $613 |
| 2. | Premium Reduction: | Building: $960 – $941 = $19 / Contents: $626 – $613 = $13 |
| 3. | Annual Subtotal: | $1,554 |
| 4. | Add ICC Premium: | $8 |
| 5. | Subtotal: | $1,562 |
| 6. | Subtract CRS Discount: | N/A |
| 7. | Subtotal: | $1,562 |
| 8. | Add Reserve Fund Assessment: | $281 (18%) |
| 9. | Subtotal: | $1,843 |
| 10. | Add Probation Surcharge: | N/A |
| 11. | Add HFIAA Surcharge: | $25 |
| 12. | Add Federal Policy Fee: | $50 |
| **13.** | **Total Amount Due:** | **$1,918** |

## RATE EXAMPLE 3
## REGULAR PROGRAM, PRE-FIRM CONSTRUCTION, $2,000/$2,000 DEDUCTIBLE OPTION, ZONE AE, PRIMARY RESIDENCE

Essential Data to Determine Appropriate Rates and Premium:

**Regular Program:**

- Flood Zone: AE
- Occupancy: Single-Family Dwelling
- Number of Floors: 2 Floors
- Basement/Enclosure
- Deductible: $2,000/$2,000
- Deductible Factor: 1.000
- Contents Location: Enclosure and Above
- Date of Construction: Pre-FIRM
- Elevation Difference: N/A
- Floodproofed (Yes/No): No
- Building Coverage: $200,000
- Contents Coverage: $75,000
- ICC Premium: $56
- CRS Rating: N/A
- CRS Discount: N/A
- Reserve Fund Assessment: $933
- Probation Surcharge: N/A
- HFIAA Surcharge: Primary Residence $25
- Federal Policy Fee: $50

**Determined Rates:**

Building: 1.36 / 2.05 Contents: 1.60 / 2.08

| ESTIMATED BUILDING REPLACEMENT COST (INCLUDING FOUNDATION): $ | | | | | | DEDUCTIBLE: | BUILDING $ 2,000 | CONTENTS $ 2,000 | |
|---|---|---|---|---|---|---|---|---|---|
| | | BASIC LIMITS | | | ADDITIONAL LIMITS (REGULAR PROGRAM ONLY) | | | DEDUCTIBLE | |
| INSURANCE COVERAGE | TOTAL AMOUNT OF INSURANCE | AMOUNT OF INSURANCE | RATE | ANNUAL PREMIUM | AMOUNT OF INSURANCE | RATE | ANNUAL PREMIUM | PREMIUM REDUCTION/ INCREASE | TOTAL PREMIUM |
| BUILDING | $200,000 | $60,000 | 1.36 | $816 | $140,000 | 2.05 | $2,870 | $0 | $3,686 |
| CONTENTS | $75,000 | $25,000 | 1.60 | $400 | $50,000 | 2.08 | $1,040 | $0 | $1,440 |

| | |
|---|---|
| ANNUAL SUBTOTAL | $5,126 |
| ICC PREMIUM | $56 |
| SUBTOTAL | $5,182 |
| CRS PREMIUM DISCOUNT ___ % | $0 |
| SUBTOTAL | $5,182 |
| RESERVE FUND ___ % | $933 |
| SUBTOTAL | $6,115 |
| PROBATION SURCHARGE | $0 |
| HFIAA SURCHARGE | $25 |
| FEDERAL POLICY FEE | $50 |
| **TOTAL AMOUNT DUE** | **$6,190** |

RATE CATEGORY:
☐ MANUAL ☐ SUBMIT FOR RATE ☐ PROVISIONAL RATING

PAYMENT METHOD:
☐ CHECK ☐ CREDIT CARD
☐ OTHER: ______________

**NOTICE:** BUILDING COVERAGE BENEFITS – EXCEPT FOR A RESIDENTIAL CONDOMINIUM BUILDING – ARE NOT AVAILABLE IF OTHER NFIP BUILDING COVERAGE HAS BEEN PURCHASED BY THE APPLICANT OR ANY OTHER PARTY FOR THE SAME BUILDING.

THE ABOVE STATEMENTS ARE CORRECT TO THE BEST OF MY KNOWLEDGE. I UNDERSTAND THAT ANY FALSE STATEMENTS MAY BE PUNISHABLE BY FINE AND/OR IMPRISONMENT UNDER APPLICABLE FEDERAL LAW. SEE REVERSE SIDE OF COPIES.

______________________________ ____/____/____
SIGNATURE OF INSURANCE AGENT/PRODUCER DATE (MM/DD/YYYY)

______________________________ ____/____/____
SIGNATURE OF INSURED (OPTIONAL) DATE (MM/DD/YYYY)

**Premium Calculation:**

1. Multiply Rate × $100 of Coverage: Building: $3,686 / Contents: $1,440
2. Apply Deductible Factor: Building: 1.000 × $3,686 = $3,686 / Contents: 1.000 × $1,440 = $1,440
3. Premium Reduction/Increase: Building: $0 / Contents: $0
4. Annual Subtotal: $5,126
5. Add ICC Premium: $56
6. Subtotal: $5,182
7. Subtract CRS Discount: N/A
8. Subtotal: $5,182
9. Add Reserve Fund Assessment: $933 (18%)
10. Subtotal: $6,115
11. Add Probation Surcharge: N/A
12. Add HFIAA Surcharge: $25
13. Add Federal Policy Fee: $50
14. **Total Amount Due: $6,190**

## RATE EXAMPLE 4
## REGULAR PROGRAM, PRE-FIRM CONSTRUCTION, $3,000/$2,000 DEDUCTIBLE OPTION, ZONE A15, NON-PRIMARY RESIDENCE

Essential Data to Determine Appropriate Rates and Premium:

**Regular Program:**

- Flood Zone: A15
- Occupancy: Single-Family Dwelling
- Number of Floors: 3 or More Floors
- Basement/Enclosure: Basement
- Deductible: $3,000/$2,000
- Deductible Factor: .975
- Contents Location: Basement and Above
- Date of Construction: Pre-FIRM
- Elevation Difference: N/A
- Floodproofed (Yes/No): No
- Building Coverage: $250,000
- Contents Coverage: $100,000
- ICC Premium: $49
- CRS Rating: 4
- CRS Discount: 30%
- Reserve Fund Assessment: $2,594
- Probation Surcharge: N/A
- HFIAA Surcharge: Non-Primary Residence $250
- Federal Policy Fee: $50

**Determined Rates:**

Building: 5.17 / 6.17 Contents: 6.11 / 6.28

ESTIMATED BUILDING REPLACEMENT COST (INCLUDING FOUNDATION): $ DEDUCTIBLE: BUILDING $ 3,000 CONTENTS $ 3,000

| INSURANCE COVERAGE | TOTAL AMOUNT OF INSURANCE | BASIC LIMITS | | | ADDITIONAL LIMITS (REGULAR PROGRAM ONLY) | | | DEDUCTIBLE | |
|---|---|---|---|---|---|---|---|---|---|
| | | AMOUNT OF INSURANCE | RATE | ANNUAL PREMIUM | AMOUNT OF INSURANCE | RATE | ANNUAL PREMIUM | PREMIUM REDUCTION/ INCREASE | TOTAL PREMIUM |
| BUILDING | $250,000 | $60,000 | 5.17 | $3,102 | $190,000 | 6.11 | $11,723 | –$371 | $14,454 |
| CONTENTS | $100,000 | $25,000 | 6.17 | $1,528 | $75,000 | 6.28 | $4,710 | –$156 | $6,082 |

RATE CATEGORY: ☐ MANUAL ☐ SUBMIT FOR RATE ☐ PROVISIONAL RATING

PAYMENT METHOD: ☐ CHECK ☐ CREDIT CARD ☐ OTHER: ____________

| | |
|---|---|
| ANNUAL SUBTOTAL | $20,536 |
| ICC PREMIUM | $49 |
| SUBTOTAL | $20,585 |
| CRS PREMIUM DISCOUNT ____ % | –$6,176 |
| SUBTOTAL | $14,409 |
| RESERVE FUND ____ % | $2,594 |
| SUBTOTAL | $17,003 |
| PROBATION SURCHARGE | $0 |
| HFIAA SURCHARGE | $250 |
| FEDERAL POLICY FEE | $50 |
| **TOTAL AMOUNT DUE** | **$17,003** |

**NOTICE:** BUILDING COVERAGE BENEFITS – EXCEPT FOR A RESIDENTIAL CONDOMINIUM BUILDING – ARE NOT AVAILABLE IF OTHER NFIP BUILDING COVERAGE HAS BEEN PURCHASED BY THE APPLICANT OR ANY OTHER PARTY FOR THE SAME BUILDING.

THE ABOVE STATEMENTS ARE CORRECT TO THE BEST OF MY KNOWLEDGE. I UNDERSTAND THAT ANY FALSE STATEMENTS MAY BE PUNISHABLE BY FINE AND/OR IMPRISONMENT UNDER APPLICABLE FEDERAL LAW. SEE REVERSE SIDE OF COPIES.

SIGNATURE OF INSURANCE AGENT/PRODUCER ______ DATE (MM/DD/YYYY) ____/____/____

SIGNATURE OF INSURED (OPTIONAL) ______ DATE (MM/DD/YYYY) ____/____/____

**Premium Calculation:**

1. Multiply Rate × $100 of Coverage: Building: $14,825 / Contents: $6,238
1. Apply Deductible Factor: Building: .975 × $14,825 = $14,454 / Contents: .975 × $6,238 = $6,082
2. Premium Reduction: Building: $14,825 – $14,454 = $371 / Contents: $6,238 – $6,082 = $156
1. Annual Subtotal: $20,536
1. Add ICC Premium: $49
1. Subtotal: $20,585
1. Subtract CRS Discount: –$6,176 (30%)
1. Subtotal: $14,409
2. Add Reserve Fund Assessment: $2,594 (18%)
1. Subtotal: $17,003
2. Add Probation Surcharge: N/A
3. Add HFIAA Surcharge: $250
4. Add Federal Policy Fee: $50
5. **Total Amount Due:** **$17,303**

## RATE EXAMPLE 5
## REGULAR PROGRAM, PRE-FIRM CONSTRUCTION, $2,000/$2,000 DEDUCTIBLE OPTION, ZONE AE, SEVERE REPETITIVE LOSS PROPERTY, PRIMARY RESIDENCE

Essential Data to Determine Appropriate Rates and Premium:

### Regular Program:

- Flood Zone: AE
- Occupancy: Single-Family Dwelling
- Number of Floors: 2 Floors
- Basement/Enclosure: None
- Deductible: $2,000/$2,000
- Deductible Factor: 1.000
- Contents Location: Lowest Floor Above Ground Level and Higher Floors
- Date of Construction: Pre-FIRM
- Elevation Difference: N/A
- Floodproofed (Yes/No): No
- Building Coverage: $200,000
- Contents Coverage: $40,000
- SRL Premium: $1,311
- ICC Premium: $56
- CRS Rating: N/A
- CRS Discount: N/A
- Reserve Fund Assessment: $1,819
- Probation Surcharge: N/A
- HFIAA Surcharge: Primary Residence $25
- Federal Policy Fee: $50

### Determined Rates:

Building: 3.33 / 3.40 Contents: 4.25 / 6.12

ESTIMATED BUILDING REPLACEMENT COST (INCLUDING FOUNDATION): $ DEDUCTIBLE: BUILDING $ 2,000 CONTENTS $ 2,000

| INSURANCE COVERAGE | TOTAL AMOUNT OF INSURANCE | BASIC LIMITS AMOUNT OF INSURANCE | BASIC LIMITS RATE | BASIC LIMITS ANNUAL PREMIUM | ADDITIONAL LIMITS (REGULAR PROGRAM ONLY) AMOUNT OF INSURANCE | ADDITIONAL LIMITS RATE | ADDITIONAL LIMITS ANNUAL PREMIUM | DEDUCTIBLE PREMIUM REDUCTION/ INCREASE | TOTAL PREMIUM |
|---|---|---|---|---|---|---|---|---|---|
| BUILDING | $200,000 | $60,000 | 3.33 | $1,998 | $140,000 | 3.40 | $4,760 | $0 | $6,758 |
| CONTENTS | $40,000 | $25,000 | 4.25 | $1,063 | $15,000 | 6.12 | $918 | $0 | $1,981 |

| | |
|---|---|
| ANNUAL SUBTOTAL | $8,739 |
| SEVERE REPETITIVE LOSS PREMIUM | $1,311 |
| ICC PREMIUM | $56 |
| SUBTOTAL | $10,106 |
| CRS PREMIUM DISCOUNT ___ % | $0 |
| SUBTOTAL | $10,106 |
| RESERVE FUND ___ % | $1,819 |
| SUBTOTAL | $11,925 |
| PROBATION SURCHARGE | $0 |
| HFIAA SURCHARGE | $25 |
| FEDERAL POLICY FEE | $50 |
| **TOTAL AMOUNT DUE** | **$12,000** |

RATE CATEGORY: ☐ MANUAL ☐ SUBMIT FOR RATE ☐ PROVISIONAL RATING

PAYMENT METHOD: ☐ CHECK ☐ CREDIT CARD ☐ OTHER: ____________

**NOTICE:** BUILDING COVERAGE BENEFITS – EXCEPT FOR A RESIDENTIAL CONDOMINIUM BUILDING – ARE NOT AVAILABLE IF OTHER NFIP BUILDING COVERAGE HAS BEEN PURCHASED BY THE APPLICANT OR ANY OTHER PARTY FOR THE SAME BUILDING.

THE ABOVE STATEMENTS ARE CORRECT TO THE BEST OF MY KNOWLEDGE. I UNDERSTAND THAT ANY FALSE STATEMENTS MAY BE PUNISHABLE BY FINE AND/OR IMPRISONMENT UNDER APPLICABLE FEDERAL LAW. SEE REVERSE SIDE OF COPIES.

____________ SIGNATURE OF INSURANCE AGENT/PRODUCER ___/___/___ DATE (MM/DD/YYYY)

____________ SIGNATURE OF INSURED (OPTIONAL) ___/___/___ DATE (MM/DD/YYYY)

### Premium Calculation:

1. Multiply Rate × $100 of Coverage: Building: $6,758 / Contents: $1,981
2. Apply Deductible Factor: Building: 1.000 × $6,758 = $6,758 / Contents: 1.000 × $1,981 = $1,981
3. Premium Reduction/Increase: Building: $0 / Contents: $0
4. Annual Subtotal: $8,739
5. Add SRL Premium: $1,311 (18%)
6. Add ICC Premium: $56
7. Subtotal: $10,106
8. Subtract CRS Discount: N/A
9. Subtotal: $10,106
10. Add Reserve Fund Assessment: $1,819 (18%)
11. Subtotal: $11,925
12. Add Probation Surcharge: N/A
13. Add HFIAA Surcharge: $25
14. Add Federal Policy Fee: $50
15. **Total Amount Due: $12,000**

## RATE EXAMPLE 6
## REGULAR PROGRAM, PRE-FIRM CONSTRUCTION, $2,000/$2,000 DEDUCTIBLE OPTION, ZONE AE, BUILDING SUBSTANTIALLY IMPROVED, PRIMARY RESIDENCE

Essential Data to Determine Appropriate Rates and Premium:

**Regular Program:**

- Flood Zone: AE
- Occupancy: Single-Family Dwelling
- Number of Floors: 2 Floors
- Basement/Enclosure: None
- Deductible: $2,000/$2,000
- Deductible Factor: 1.000
- Contents Location: Lowest Floor Above Ground Level and Higher Floors
- Date of Construction: Pre-FIRM
- Elevation Difference: N/A
- Floodproofed (Yes/No): No
- Building Coverage: $250,000
- Contents Coverage: $100,000
- ICC Premium: $49
- CRS Rating: N/A
- CRS Discount: N/A
- Reserve Fund Assessment: $2,530
- Probation Surcharge: N/A
- HFIAA Surcharge: Primary Residence $25
- Federal Policy Fee: $50

**Determined Rates:**

Building: 3.60 / 3.30 Contents: 4.52 / 5.93

ESTIMATED BUILDING REPLACEMENT COST (INCLUDING FOUNDATION): $ — DEDUCTIBLE: BUILDING $ 2,000 CONTENTS $ 2,000

| INSURANCE COVERAGE | TOTAL AMOUNT OF INSURANCE | BASIC LIMITS | | | ADDITIONAL LIMITS (REGULAR PROGRAM ONLY) | | | DEDUCTIBLE | |
|---|---|---|---|---|---|---|---|---|---|
| | | AMOUNT OF INSURANCE | RATE | ANNUAL PREMIUM | AMOUNT OF INSURANCE | RATE | ANNUAL PREMIUM | PREMIUM REDUCTION/ INCREASE | TOTAL PREMIUM |
| BUILDING | $250,000 | $60,000 | 3.60 | $2,160 | $190,000 | 3.30 | $6,270 | $0 | $8,430 |
| CONTENTS | $100,000 | $25,000 | 4.52 | $1,130 | $75,000 | 5.93 | $4,448 | $0 | $5,578 |

RATE CATEGORY: ☐ MANUAL ☐ SUBMIT FOR RATE ☐ PROVISIONAL RATING

PAYMENT METHOD: ☐ CHECK ☐ CREDIT CARD ☐ OTHER: ____

| | |
|---|---|
| ANNUAL SUBTOTAL | $14,008 |
| ICC PREMIUM | $49 |
| SUBTOTAL | $14,057 |
| CRS PREMIUM DISCOUNT ___ % | $0 |
| SUBTOTAL | $14,057 |
| RESERVE FUND ___ % | $2,530 |
| SUBTOTAL | $16,587 |
| PROBATION SURCHARGE | $0 |
| HFIAA SURCHARGE | $25 |
| FEDERAL POLICY FEE | $50 |
| **TOTAL AMOUNT DUE** | **$16,662** |

**NOTICE:** BUILDING COVERAGE BENEFITS – EXCEPT FOR A RESIDENTIAL CONDOMINIUM BUILDING – ARE NOT AVAILABLE IF OTHER NFIP BUILDING COVERAGE HAS BEEN PURCHASED BY THE APPLICANT OR ANY OTHER PARTY FOR THE SAME BUILDING.

THE ABOVE STATEMENTS ARE CORRECT TO THE BEST OF MY KNOWLEDGE. I UNDERSTAND THAT ANY FALSE STATEMENTS MAY BE PUNISHABLE BY FINE AND/OR IMPRISONMENT UNDER APPLICABLE FEDERAL LAW. SEE REVERSE SIDE OF COPIES.

____________________ SIGNATURE OF INSURANCE AGENT/PRODUCER ___/___/___ DATE (MM/DD/YYYY)

____________________ SIGNATURE OF INSURED (OPTIONAL) ___/___/___ DATE (MM/DD/YYYY)

**Premium Calculation:**

1. Multiply Rate × $100 of Coverage: Building: $8,430 / Contents: $5,578
2. Apply Deductible Factor: Building: 1.000 × $8,430 = $8,430 / Contents: 1.000 × $5,578 = $5,578
3. Premium Reduction/Increase: Building: $0 / Contents: $0
4. Annual Subtotal: $14,008
5. Add ICC Premium: $49
6. Subtotal: $14,057
7. Subtract CRS Discount: N/A
8. Subtotal: $14,057
9. Add Reserve Fund Assessment: $2,530 (18%)
10. Subtotal: $16,587
11. Add Probation Surcharge: N/A
12. Add HFIAA Surcharge: $25
13. Add Federal Policy Fee: $50
14. **Total Amount Due: $16,662**

## RATE EXAMPLE 7
## REGULAR PROGRAM, PRE-FIRM CONSTRUCTION RATED WITH FULL-RISK RATES, $1,500/$1,500 DEDUCTIBLE, ZONE AE, PRIMARY RESIDENCE

Essential Data to Determine Appropriate Rates and Premium:

### Regular Program:

- Flood Zone: AE
- Occupancy: Single-Family Dwelling
- Number of Floors: 2 Floors
- Basement/Enclosure: None
- Deductible: $1,500/$1,500
- Deductible Factor: 0.965
- Contents Location: Above Ground Level and Higher Floors
- Date of Construction: Pre-FIRM
- Elevation Difference: +1
- Floodproofed (Yes/No): No
- Building Coverage: $150,000
- Contents Coverage: $50,000
- ICC Premium: $8
- CRS Rating: 8
- CRS Discount: 10%
- Reserve Fund Assessment: $108
- Probation Surcharge: N/A
- HFIAA Surcharge: Primary Residence $25
- Federal Policy Fee: $50

### Determined Rates:

Building: .80 / .08 Contents: .41 / .12

| ESTIMATED BUILDING REPLACEMENT COST (INCLUDING FOUNDATION): $ | | DEDUCTIBLE: | | BUILDING $ 1,500 | | CONTENTS $ 1,500 | | |
|---|---|---|---|---|---|---|---|---|
| | | BASIC LIMITS | | | ADDITIONAL LIMITS (REGULAR PROGRAM ONLY) | | | DEDUCTIBLE | |
| INSURANCE COVERAGE | TOTAL AMOUNT OF INSURANCE | AMOUNT OF INSURANCE | RATE | ANNUAL PREMIUM | AMOUNT OF INSURANCE | RATE | ANNUAL PREMIUM | PREMIUM REDUCTION/ INCREASE | TOTAL PREMIUM |
| BUILDING | $150,000 | $60,000 | .80 | $468 | $90,000 | .08 | $72 | –$19 | $533 |
| CONTENTS | $50,000 | $25,000 | .41 | $100 | $25,000 | .12 | $30 | –$5 | $128 |

RATE CATEGORY: ☐ MANUAL ☐ SUBMIT FOR RATE ☐ PROVISIONAL RATING

PAYMENT METHOD: ☐ CHECK ☐ CREDIT CARD ☐ OTHER: ____

| | |
|---|---|
| ANNUAL SUBTOTAL | $661 |
| ICC PREMIUM | $8 |
| SUBTOTAL | $669 |
| CRS PREMIUM DISCOUNT ___ % | –$67 |
| SUBTOTAL | $602 |
| RESERVE FUND ___ % | $108 |
| SUBTOTAL | $710 |
| PROBATION SURCHARGE | $0 |
| HFIAA SURCHARGE | $25 |
| FEDERAL POLICY FEE | $50 |
| **TOTAL AMOUNT DUE** | **$785** |

**NOTICE:** BUILDING COVERAGE BENEFITS – EXCEPT FOR A RESIDENTIAL CONDOMINIUM BUILDING – ARE NOT AVAILABLE IF OTHER NFIP BUILDING COVERAGE HAS BEEN PURCHASED BY THE APPLICANT OR ANY OTHER PARTY FOR THE SAME BUILDING.

THE ABOVE STATEMENTS ARE CORRECT TO THE BEST OF MY KNOWLEDGE. I UNDERSTAND THAT ANY FALSE STATEMENTS MAY BE PUNISHABLE BY FINE AND/OR IMPRISONMENT UNDER APPLICABLE FEDERAL LAW. SEE REVERSE SIDE OF COPIES.

SIGNATURE OF INSURANCE AGENT/PRODUCER ____ DATE (MM/DD/YYYY) ___/___/___

SIGNATURE OF INSURED (OPTIONAL) ____ DATE (MM/DD/YYYY) ___/___/___

### Premium Calculation:

1. Multiply Rate × $100 of Coverage: Building: $540 / Contents: $130
2. Apply Deductible Factor: Building: .965 × $540 = $521 / Contents: .965 × $130 = $125
3. Premium Reduction/Increase: Building: $540 – $521 = $19 / Contents: $130 – $125 = $5
4. Annual Subtotal: $646
5. Add ICC Premium: $8
6. Subtotal: $654
7. Subtract CRS Discount: –$65 (10%)
8. Subtotal: $589
9. Add Reserve Fund Assessment: $106 (18%)
10. Subtotal: $695
11. Add Probation Surcharge: N/A
12. Add HFIAA Surcharge: $25
13. Add Federal Policy Fee: $50
14. **Total Amount Due:** **$770**

## RATE EXAMPLE 8
## REGULAR PROGRAM, POST-FIRM, ELEVATION RATED, $5,000/$5,000 DEDUCTIBLE OPTION, ZONE AE, NON-RESIDENTIAL BUSINESS

Essential Data to Determine Appropriate Rates and Premium:

### Regular Program:

- Flood Zone: AE
- Occupancy: Non-Residential Business
- Number of Floors: 2 Floors
- Basement/Enclosure: None
- Deductible: $5,000/$5,000
- Deductible Factor: .890
- Contents Location: Above Ground Level and Higher Floors
- Date of Construction: Post-FIRM
- Elevation Difference: +4
- Floodproofed (Yes/No): No
- Building Coverage: $500,000
- Contents Coverage: $500,000
- ICC Premium: $6
- CRS Rating: 5
- CRS Discount: 25%
- Reserve Fund Assessment: $168
- Probation Surcharge: N/A
- HFIAA Surcharge: Non-Residential Business $250
- Federal Policy Fee: $50

### Determined Rates:

Building: .22 / .08 Contents: .22 / .12

ESTIMATED BUILDING REPLACEMENT COST (INCLUDING FOUNDATION): $ | DEDUCTIBLE: BUILDING $ 5,000 | CONTENTS $ 5,000

| INSURANCE COVERAGE | TOTAL AMOUNT OF INSURANCE | BASIC LIMITS: AMOUNT OF INSURANCE | BASIC LIMITS: RATE | BASIC LIMITS: ANNUAL PREMIUM | ADDITIONAL LIMITS (REGULAR PROGRAM ONLY): AMOUNT OF INSURANCE | ADDITIONAL LIMITS: RATE | ADDITIONAL LIMITS: ANNUAL PREMIUM | DEDUCTIBLE: PREMIUM REDUCTION/ INCREASE | TOTAL PREMIUM |
|---|---|---|---|---|---|---|---|---|---|
| BUILDING | $500,000 | $175,000 | .22 | $385 | $325,000 | .08 | $260 | –$71 | $574 |
| CONTENTS | $500,000 | $150,000 | .22 | $330 | $350,000 | .12 | $420 | –$82 | $668 |

RATE CATEGORY: ☐ MANUAL ☐ SUBMIT FOR RATE ☐ PROVISIONAL RATING

PAYMENT METHOD: ☐ CHECK ☐ CREDIT CARD ☐ OTHER: ____________

| | |
|---|---|
| ANNUAL SUBTOTAL | $1,242 |
| ICC PREMIUM | $6 |
| SUBTOTAL | $1,248 |
| CRS PREMIUM DISCOUNT ___ % | –$312 |
| SUBTOTAL | $936 |
| RESERVE FUND ___ % | $168 |
| SUBTOTAL | $1,104 |
| PROBATION SURCHARGE | $0 |
| HFIAA SURCHARGE | $250 |
| FEDERAL POLICY FEE | $50 |
| **TOTAL AMOUNT DUE** | **$1,404** |

**NOTICE:** BUILDING COVERAGE BENEFITS – EXCEPT FOR A RESIDENTIAL CONDOMINIUM BUILDING – ARE NOT AVAILABLE IF OTHER NFIP BUILDING COVERAGE HAS BEEN PURCHASED BY THE APPLICANT OR ANY OTHER PARTY FOR THE SAME BUILDING.

THE ABOVE STATEMENTS ARE CORRECT TO THE BEST OF MY KNOWLEDGE. I UNDERSTAND THAT ANY FALSE STATEMENTS MAY BE PUNISHABLE BY FINE AND/OR IMPRISONMENT UNDER APPLICABLE FEDERAL LAW. SEE REVERSE SIDE OF COPIES.

SIGNATURE OF INSURANCE AGENT/PRODUCER ____/____/____ DATE (MM/DD/YYYY)

SIGNATURE OF INSURED (OPTIONAL) ____/____/____ DATE (MM/DD/YYYY)

### Premium Calculation:

1. Multiply Rate × $100 of Coverage: Building: $645 / Contents: $750
2. Apply Deductible Factor: Building: .890 × $645 = $574 / Contents: .890 × $750 = $668
3. Premium Reduction: Building: $645 – $574 = $71 / Contents: $750 – $668 = $82
4. Annual Subtotal: $1,242
5. Add ICC Premium: $6
6. Subtotal: $1,248
7. Subtract CRS Discount: –$312 (25%)
8. Subtotal: $936
9. Add Reserve Fund Assessment: $168 (18%)
10. Subtotal: $1,104
11. Add Probation Surcharge: N/A
12. Add HFIAA Surcharge: $250
13. Add Federal Policy Fee: $50
14. **Total Amount Due: $1,404**

## RATE EXAMPLE 9
## REGULAR PROGRAM, 1975–'81 POST-FIRM V1–V30, $2,000/$2,000 DEDUCTIBLE OPTION, ELEVATION RATED, ZONE V13, NON-PRIMARY RESIDENCE

Essential Data to Determine Appropriate Rates and Premium:

**Regular Program:**

- Flood Zone: V13
- Occupancy: Single-Family Dwelling
- Number of Floors: 2 Floors
- Basement/Enclosure: None
- Deductible: $2,000/$2,000
- Deductible Factor: .925
- Contents Location: Lowest Floor Above Ground Level and Higher Floors
- Date of Construction: 1975–'81 (Post-FIRM)
- Elevation Difference: +1
- Floodproofed (Yes/No): No
- Building Coverage: $150,000
- Contents Coverage: $100,000
- ICC Premium: $33
- CRS Rating: 8
- CRS Discount: 10%
- Reserve Fund Assessment: $1,347
- Probation Surcharge: N/A
- HFIAA Surcharge: Non-Primary Residence $250
- Federal Policy Fee: $50

**Determined Rates:**

Building: 6.97 / 1.50 Contents: 4.71 / 2.99

ESTIMATED BUILDING REPLACEMENT COST (INCLUDING FOUNDATION): $ — DEDUCTIBLE: BUILDING $ 2,000 CONTENTS $ 2,000

| INSURANCE COVERAGE | TOTAL AMOUNT OF INSURANCE | BASIC LIMITS: AMOUNT OF INSURANCE | BASIC LIMITS: RATE | BASIC LIMITS: ANNUAL PREMIUM | ADDITIONAL LIMITS (REGULAR PROGRAM ONLY): AMOUNT OF INSURANCE | ADDITIONAL LIMITS: RATE | ADDITIONAL LIMITS: ANNUAL PREMIUM | DEDUCTIBLE: PREMIUM REDUCTION/ INCREASE | TOTAL PREMIUM |
|---|---|---|---|---|---|---|---|---|---|
| BUILDING | $150,000 | $60,000 | 6.97 | $4,182 | $90,000 | 1.50 | $1,350 | –$415 | $5,117 |
| CONTENTS | $100,000 | $25,000 | 4.71 | $1,178 | $75,000 | 2.99 | $2,243 | –$257 | $3,164 |

RATE CATEGORY: ☐ MANUAL ☐ SUBMIT FOR RATE ☐ PROVISIONAL RATING

PAYMENT METHOD: ☐ CHECK ☐ CREDIT CARD ☐ OTHER: ______

| | |
|---|---|
| ANNUAL SUBTOTAL | $8,281 |
| ICC PREMIUM | $33 |
| SUBTOTAL | $8,314 |
| CRS PREMIUM DISCOUNT ___ % | –$831 |
| SUBTOTAL | $7,483 |
| RESERVE FUND ___ % | $1,347 |
| SUBTOTAL | $8,830 |
| PROBATION SURCHARGE | $0 |
| HFIAA SURCHARGE | $250 |
| FEDERAL POLICY FEE | $50 |
| **TOTAL AMOUNT DUE** | **$9,130** |

**NOTICE:** BUILDING COVERAGE BENEFITS – EXCEPT FOR A RESIDENTIAL CONDOMINIUM BUILDING – ARE NOT AVAILABLE IF OTHER NFIP BUILDING COVERAGE HAS BEEN PURCHASED BY THE APPLICANT OR ANY OTHER PARTY FOR THE SAME BUILDING.

THE ABOVE STATEMENTS ARE CORRECT TO THE BEST OF MY KNOWLEDGE. I UNDERSTAND THAT ANY FALSE STATEMENTS MAY BE PUNISHABLE BY FINE AND/OR IMPRISONMENT UNDER APPLICABLE FEDERAL LAW. SEE REVERSE SIDE OF COPIES.

______ SIGNATURE OF INSURANCE AGENT/PRODUCER ___/___/___ DATE (MM/DD/YYYY)

______ SIGNATURE OF INSURED (OPTIONAL) ___/___/___ DATE (MM/DD/YYYY)

**Premium Calculation:**

1. Multiply Rate × $100 of Coverage: Building: $5,532 / Contents: $3,421
2. Apply Deductible Factor: Building: .925 × $5,532 = $5,117 / Contents: .925 × $3,421 = $3,164
3. Premium Reduction: Building: $5,532 – $5,117 = $368 / Contents: $3,421 – $3,164 = $257
4. Annual Subtotal: $8,281
5. Add ICC Premium: $33
6. Subtotal: $8,314
7. Subtract CRS Discount: –$831 (10%)
8. Subtotal: $7,483
9. Add Reserve Fund Assessment: $1,347 (18%)
10. Subtotal: $8,830
11. Add Probation Surcharge: N/A
12. Add HFIAA Surcharge: $250
13. Add Federal Policy Fee: $50
14. **Total Amount Due: $9,130**

### RATE EXAMPLE 10
### REGULAR PROGRAM, POST-1981 VE OR V1–V30, $3,000/$3,000 DEDUCTIBLE OPTION, WITH ENCLOSURE, ZONE VE, PRIMARY RESIDENCE

Essential Data to Determine Appropriate Rates and Premium:

**Regular Program:**

- Flood Zone: VE
- Occupancy: Single-Family Dwelling
- Number of Floors: 3 or More Floors
- Basement/Enclosure: Enclosure (< 300 sq. ft., w/o M&E)
- Deductible: $3,000/$3,000
- Deductible Factor: .850
- Contents Location: Lowest Floor Above Ground Level and Higher Floors
- Date of Construction: Post-'81
- Elevation Difference: –1
- Floodproofed (Yes/No): No
- Building Coverage: $250,000
- Contents Coverage: $100,000
- Replacement Cost Ratio: 75% or more
- ICC Premium: $16
- CRS Rating: 9
- CRS Discount: 5%
- Reserve Fund Assessment: $2,409
- Probation Surcharge: N/A
- HFIAA Surcharge: Primary Residence $25
- Federal Policy Fee: $50

**Determined Rates:**

Building: 5.03 / 5.03 Contents: 3.98 / 3.98

ESTIMATED BUILDING REPLACEMENT COST (INCLUDING FOUNDATION): $ DEDUCTIBLE: BUILDING $ 3,000 CONTENTS $ 3,000

| INSURANCE COVERAGE | TOTAL AMOUNT OF INSURANCE | BASIC LIMITS | | | ADDITIONAL LIMITS (REGULAR PROGRAM ONLY) | | | DEDUCTIBLE | TOTAL PREMIUM |
|---|---|---|---|---|---|---|---|---|---|
| | | AMOUNT OF INSURANCE | RATE | ANNUAL PREMIUM | AMOUNT OF INSURANCE | RATE | ANNUAL PREMIUM | PREMIUM REDUCTION/ INCREASE | |
| BUILDING | $250,000 | $60,000 | 5.03 | $3,018 | $190,000 | 5.03 | $9,557 | –$1,886 | $10,689 |
| CONTENTS | $100,000 | $25,000 | 3.98 | $995 | $75,000 | 3.98 | $2,985 | –$597 | $3,383 |

RATE CATEGORY: ☐ MANUAL ☐ SUBMIT FOR RATE ☐ PROVISIONAL RATING

PAYMENT METHOD: ☐ CHECK ☐ CREDIT CARD ☐ OTHER: ______

| | |
|---|---|
| ANNUAL SUBTOTAL | $14,072 |
| ICC PREMIUM | $16 |
| SUBTOTAL | $14,088 |
| CRS PREMIUM DISCOUNT ___ % | –$704 |
| SUBTOTAL | $13,384 |
| RESERVE FUND ___ % | $2,409 |
| SUBTOTAL | $15,793 |
| PROBATION SURCHARGE | $0 |
| HFIAA SURCHARGE | $25 |
| FEDERAL POLICY FEE | $50 |
| **TOTAL AMOUNT DUE** | $15,868 |

**NOTICE:** BUILDING COVERAGE BENEFITS – EXCEPT FOR A RESIDENTIAL CONDOMINIUM BUILDING – ARE NOT AVAILABLE IF OTHER NFIP BUILDING COVERAGE HAS BEEN PURCHASED BY THE APPLICANT OR ANY OTHER PARTY FOR THE SAME BUILDING.

THE ABOVE STATEMENTS ARE CORRECT TO THE BEST OF MY KNOWLEDGE. I UNDERSTAND THAT ANY FALSE STATEMENTS MAY BE PUNISHABLE BY FINE AND/OR IMPRISONMENT UNDER APPLICABLE FEDERAL LAW. SEE REVERSE SIDE OF COPIES.

______ SIGNATURE OF INSURANCE AGENT/PRODUCER ___/___/___ DATE (MM/DD/YYYY)

______ SIGNATURE OF INSURED (OPTIONAL) ___/___/___ DATE (MM/DD/YYYY)

**Premium Calculation:**

1. Multiply Rate × $100 of Coverage: Building: $12,575 / Contents: $3,980
2. Apply Deductible Factor: Building: .850 × $12,575 = $10,689 / Contents: .850 × $3,980 = $3,383
3. Premium Reduction: Building: $12,575 – $10,689 = $1,886 / Contents: $3,980 – $3,383 = $597
4. Annual Subtotal: $14,072
5. Add ICC Premium: $16
6. Subtotal: $14,088
7. Subtract CRS Discount: –$704 (5%)
8. Subtotal: $13,384
9. Add Reserve Fund Assessment: $2,409 (18%)
10. Subtotal: $15,793
11. Add Probation Surcharge: N/A
12. Add HFIAA Surcharge: $25
13. Add Federal Policy Fee: $50
14. **Total Amount Due: $15,868**

## RATE EXAMPLE 11
## REGULAR PROGRAM, POST-FIRM CONSTRUCTION, $1,000 DEDUCTIBLE OPTION, CONTENTS-ONLY POLICY, ZONE A17, PRIMARY RESIDENCE

Essential Data to Determine Appropriate Rates and Premium:

**Regular Program:**

- Flood Zone: A17
- Occupancy: 2–4 Family Dwelling (Renter's Policy)
- Number of Floors: 2 Floors
- Basement/Enclosure: None
- Deductible: $1,000 Contents-Only
- Deductible Factor: 1.000
- Contents Location: Above Ground Level More Than 1 Full Floor
- Date of Construction: Post-FIRM
- Elevation Difference: +2
- Floodproofed (Yes/No): No
- Building Coverage: N/A
- Contents Coverage: $100,000
- ICC Premium: N/A
- CRS Rating: N/A
- CRS Discount: N/A
- Reserve Fund Assessment: $33
- Probation Surcharge: N/A
- HFIAA Surcharge: Primary Residence $25
- Federal Policy Fee: $25

**Determined Rates:**

Building: N/A Contents: .38 / .12

ESTIMATED BUILDING REPLACEMENT COST (INCLUDING FOUNDATION): $ — DEDUCTIBLE: BUILDING — CONTENTS $ 1,000

| INSURANCE COVERAGE | TOTAL AMOUNT OF INSURANCE | BASIC LIMITS: AMOUNT OF INSURANCE | BASIC LIMITS: RATE | BASIC LIMITS: ANNUAL PREMIUM | ADDITIONAL LIMITS (REGULAR PROGRAM ONLY): AMOUNT OF INSURANCE | ADDITIONAL LIMITS: RATE | ADDITIONAL LIMITS: ANNUAL PREMIUM | DEDUCTIBLE: PREMIUM REDUCTION/ INCREASE | TOTAL PREMIUM |
|---|---|---|---|---|---|---|---|---|---|
| BUILDING | | | | | | | | | |
| CONTENTS | $100,000 | $25,000 | .38 | $95 | $75,000 | .12 | $90 | $0 | $185 |

RATE CATEGORY: ☐ MANUAL ☐ SUBMIT FOR RATE ☐ PROVISIONAL RATING

PAYMENT METHOD: ☐ CHECK ☐ CREDIT CARD ☐ OTHER: ______

**NOTICE:** BUILDING COVERAGE BENEFITS – EXCEPT FOR A RESIDENTIAL CONDOMINIUM BUILDING – ARE NOT AVAILABLE IF OTHER NFIP BUILDING COVERAGE HAS BEEN PURCHASED BY THE APPLICANT OR ANY OTHER PARTY FOR THE SAME BUILDING.

THE ABOVE STATEMENTS ARE CORRECT TO THE BEST OF MY KNOWLEDGE. I UNDERSTAND THAT ANY FALSE STATEMENTS MAY BE PUNISHABLE BY FINE AND/OR IMPRISONMENT UNDER APPLICABLE FEDERAL LAW. SEE REVERSE SIDE OF COPIES.

______ SIGNATURE OF INSURANCE AGENT/PRODUCER ____/____/____ DATE (MM/DD/YYYY)

______ SIGNATURE OF INSURED (OPTIONAL) ____/____/____ DATE (MM/DD/YYYY)

| | |
|---|---|
| ANNUAL SUBTOTAL | $185 |
| ICC PREMIUM | $0 |
| SUBTOTAL | $185 |
| CRS PREMIUM DISCOUNT ___ % | $0 |
| SUBTOTAL | $185 |
| RESERVE FUND ___ % | $33 |
| SUBTOTAL | $218 |
| PROBATION SURCHARGE | $0 |
| HFIAA SURCHARGE | $25 |
| FEDERAL POLICY FEE | $25 |
| **TOTAL AMOUNT DUE** | **$268** |

**Premium Calculation:**

1. Multiply Rate × $100 of Coverage: Building: N/A / Contents: $185
2. Apply Deductible Factor: Building: N/A / Contents: 1.000 × $185 = $185
3. Premium Reduction/Increase: Building: N/A / Contents: $0
4. Annual Subtotal: $185
5. Add ICC Premium: N/A
6. Subtotal: $185
7. Subtract CRS Discount: N/A
8. Subtotal: $185
9. Add Reserve Fund Assessment: $32 (18%)
10. Subtotal: $218
11. Add Probation Surcharge: N/A
12. Add HFIAA Surcharge: $25
13. Add Federal Policy Fee: $25
14. **Total Amount Due: $268**

## RATE EXAMPLE 12
## REGULAR PROGRAM, POST-FIRM, ELEVATION RATED, $5,000/$5,000 DEDUCTIBLE OPTION, ZONE AO (WITHOUT CERTIFICATION OF COMPLIANCE OR ELEVATION CERTIFICATE), OTHER NON-RESIDENTIAL

Essential Data to Determine Appropriate Rates and Premium:

**Regular Program:**

- Flood Zone: AO (Without Certification of Compliance or Elevation Certificate)
- Occupancy: Other Non-Residential
- Number of Floors: 2 Floors
- Basement/Enclosure: None
- Deductible: $5,000/$5,000
- Deductible Factor: .890
- Contents Location: Lowest Floor Above Ground Level and Higher Floors
- Date of Construction: Post-FIRM
- Elevation Difference: –1
- Floodproofed (Yes/No): No
- Building Coverage: $500,000
- Contents Coverage: $500,000
- ICC Premium: $6
- CRS Rating: N/A
- CRS Discount: N/A
- Reserve Fund Assessment: $952
- Probation Surcharge: N/A
- HFIAA Surcharge: Other Non-Residential $250
- Federal Policy Fee: $50

**Determined Rates:**

Building: 1.56 / .26 Contents: 1.20 / .16

| ESTIMATED BUILDING REPLACEMENT COST (INCLUDING FOUNDATION): $ | | DEDUCTIBLE: BUILDING $ 5,000 | | | | | CONTENTS $ 5,000 | | |
|---|---|---|---|---|---|---|---|---|---|
| | | BASIC LIMITS | | | ADDITIONAL LIMITS (REGULAR PROGRAM ONLY) | | | DEDUCTIBLE | |
| INSURANCE COVERAGE | TOTAL AMOUNT OF INSURANCE | AMOUNT OF INSURANCE | RATE | ANNUAL PREMIUM | AMOUNT OF INSURANCE | RATE | ANNUAL PREMIUM | PREMIUM REDUCTION/ INCREASE | TOTAL PREMIUM |
| BUILDING | $500,000 | $175,000 | 1.56 | $2,730 | $325,000 | .26 | $845 | –$393 | $3,182 |
| CONTENTS | $500,000 | $150,000 | 1.20 | $1,800 | $350,000 | .16 | $560 | –$260 | $2,100 |

RATE CATEGORY: ☐ MANUAL ☐ SUBMIT FOR RATE ☐ PROVISIONAL RATING

PAYMENT METHOD: ☐ CHECK ☐ CREDIT CARD ☐ OTHER: ____________

| | |
|---|---|
| ANNUAL SUBTOTAL | $5,282 |
| ICC PREMIUM | $6 |
| SUBTOTAL | $5,288 |
| CRS PREMIUM DISCOUNT ___ % | $0 |
| SUBTOTAL | $5,288 |
| RESERVE FUND ___ % | $952 |
| SUBTOTAL | $6,240 |
| PROBATION SURCHARGE | $0 |
| HFIAA SURCHARGE | $250 |
| FEDERAL POLICY FEE | $50 |
| **TOTAL AMOUNT DUE** | **$6,540** |

**NOTICE:** BUILDING COVERAGE BENEFITS – EXCEPT FOR A RESIDENTIAL CONDOMINIUM BUILDING – ARE NOT AVAILABLE IF OTHER NFIP BUILDING COVERAGE HAS BEEN PURCHASED BY THE APPLICANT OR ANY OTHER PARTY FOR THE SAME BUILDING.

THE ABOVE STATEMENTS ARE CORRECT TO THE BEST OF MY KNOWLEDGE. I UNDERSTAND THAT ANY FALSE STATEMENTS MAY BE PUNISHABLE BY FINE AND/OR IMPRISONMENT UNDER APPLICABLE FEDERAL LAW. SEE REVERSE SIDE OF COPIES.

____________________ ____/____/____
SIGNATURE OF INSURANCE AGENT/PRODUCER DATE (MM/DD/YYYY)

____________________ ____/____/____
SIGNATURE OF INSURED (OPTIONAL) DATE (MM/DD/YYYY)

**Premium Calculation:**

1. Multiply Rate × $100 of Coverage: Building: $3,575 / Contents: $2,360
2. Apply Deductible Factor: Building: .890 × $3,575 = $3,182 / Contents: .890 × $2,360 = $2,100
3. Premium Reduction: Building: $3,575 – $3,182 = $393 / Contents: $2,360 – $2,100 = $260
4. Annual Subtotal: $5,282
5. Add ICC Premium: $6
6. Subtotal: $5,288
7. Subtract CRS Discount: N/A
8. Subtotal: $5,288
9. Add Reserve Fund Assessment: $952 (18%)
10. Subtotal: $6,240
11. Add Probation Surcharge: N/A
12. Add HFIAA Surcharge: $250
13. Add Federal Policy Fee: $50
14. **Total Amount Due: $6,540**

## RATE EXAMPLE 13
## REGULAR PROGRAM, POST-FIRM, ELEVATION RATED, $1,250/$1,250 DEDUCTIBLE OPTION, ZONE AO (WITH CERTIFICATION OF COMPLIANCE OR ELEVATION CERTIFICATE), PRIMARY RESIDENCE

Essential Data to Determine Appropriate Rates and Premium:

**Regular Program:**

- Flood Zone: AO (With Certification of Compliance or Elevation Certificate)
- Occupancy: Single-Family Dwelling
- Number of Floors: 2 Floors
- Basement/Enclosure: None
- Deductible: $1,250/$1,250
- Deductible Factor: .980
- Contents Location: Above Ground Level and Higher Floors
- Date of Construction: Post-FIRM
- Elevation Difference: +1
- Floodproofed (Yes/No): No
- Building Coverage: $250,000
- Contents Coverage: $100,000
- ICC Premium: $6
- CRS Rating: N/A
- CRS Discount: N/A
- Reserve Fund Assessment: $96
- Probation Surcharge: N/A
- HFIAA Surcharge: Primary Residence $25
- Federal Policy Fee: $50

**Determined Rates:**

Building: .30 / .09 Contents: .38 / .12

| ESTIMATED BUILDING REPLACEMENT COST (INCLUDING FOUNDATION): $ | | DEDUCTIBLE: BUILDING $ 1,250 | | | CONTENTS $ 1,250 | | | | |
|---|---|---|---|---|---|---|---|---|---|
| | | BASIC LIMITS | | | ADDITIONAL LIMITS (REGULAR PROGRAM ONLY) | | | DEDUCTIBLE | |
| INSURANCE COVERAGE | TOTAL AMOUNT OF INSURANCE | AMOUNT OF INSURANCE | RATE | ANNUAL PREMIUM | AMOUNT OF INSURANCE | RATE | ANNUAL PREMIUM | PREMIUM REDUCTION/ INCREASE | TOTAL PREMIUM |
| BUILDING | $250,000 | $60,000 | .30 | $180 | $190,000 | .09 | $171 | –$7 | $344 |
| CONTENTS | $100,000 | $25,000 | .38 | $95 | $75,000 | .12 | $90 | –$4 | $181 |

RATE CATEGORY: ☐ MANUAL ☐ SUBMIT FOR RATE ☐ PROVISIONAL RATING

PAYMENT METHOD: ☐ CHECK ☐ CREDIT CARD ☐ OTHER: ______

| | |
|---|---|
| ANNUAL SUBTOTAL | $525 |
| ICC PREMIUM | $6 |
| SUBTOTAL | $531 |
| CRS PREMIUM DISCOUNT ___ % | $0 |
| SUBTOTAL | $531 |
| RESERVE FUND ___ % | $96 |
| SUBTOTAL | $627 |
| PROBATION SURCHARGE | $0 |
| HFIAA SURCHARGE | $25 |
| FEDERAL POLICY FEE | $50 |
| **TOTAL AMOUNT DUE** | **$702** |

**NOTICE:** BUILDING COVERAGE BENEFITS – EXCEPT FOR A RESIDENTIAL CONDOMINIUM BUILDING – ARE NOT AVAILABLE IF OTHER NFIP BUILDING COVERAGE HAS BEEN PURCHASED BY THE APPLICANT OR ANY OTHER PARTY FOR THE SAME BUILDING.

THE ABOVE STATEMENTS ARE CORRECT TO THE BEST OF MY KNOWLEDGE. I UNDERSTAND THAT ANY FALSE STATEMENTS MAY BE PUNISHABLE BY FINE AND/OR IMPRISONMENT UNDER APPLICABLE FEDERAL LAW. SEE REVERSE SIDE OF COPIES.

______________________ ____/____/____
SIGNATURE OF INSURANCE AGENT/PRODUCER DATE (MM/DD/YYYY)

______________________ ____/____/____
SIGNATURE OF INSURED (OPTIONAL) DATE (MM/DD/YYYY)

**Premium Calculation:**

1. Multiply Rate × $100 of Coverage: Building: $351 / Contents: $185
2. Apply Deductible Factor: Building: .980 × $351 = $344 / Contents: .980 × $185 = $181
3. Premium Reduction: Building: $351 – $344 = $6 / Contents: $185 – $181 = $4
4. Annual Subtotal: $525
5. Add ICC Premium: $6
6. Subtotal: $531
7. Subtract CRS Discount: N/A
8. Subtotal: $531
9. Add Reserve Fund Assessment: $96 (18%)
10. Subtotal: $627
11. Add Probation Surcharge: N/A
12. Add HFIAA Surcharge: $25
13. Add Federal Policy Fee: $50
14. **Total Amount Due:** $702

## RATE EXAMPLE 14
## REGULAR PROGRAM, POST-FIRM, ELEVATION RATED, $3,000/$2,000 DEDUCTIBLE OPTION, ZONE AH (WITHOUT CERTIFICATION OF COMPLIANCE OR ELEVATION CERTIFICATE), PRIMARY RESIDENCE

Essential Data to Determine Appropriate Rates and Premium:

**Regular Program:**

- Flood Zone: AH (Without Certification of Compliance or Elevation Certificate)
- Occupancy: Single-Family Dwelling
- Number of Floors: 1 Floor
- Basement/Enclosure: None
- Deductible: $3,000/$2,000
- Deductible Factor: .900
- Contents Location: Lowest Floor Above Ground Level
- Date of Construction: Post-FIRM
- Elevation Difference: –1
- Floodproofed (Yes/No): No
- Building Coverage: $250,000
- Contents Coverage: $25,000
- ICC Premium: $6
- CRS Rating: N/A
- CRS Discount: N/A
- Reserve Fund Assessment: $263
- Probation Surcharge: N/A
- HFIAA Surcharge: Primary Residence $25
- Federal Policy Fee: $50

**Determined Rates:**

Building: 1.71 / .20 Contents: .84 / .15

ESTIMATED BUILDING REPLACEMENT COST (INCLUDING FOUNDATION): $ DEDUCTIBLE: BUILDING $ 3,000 CONTENTS $ 2,000

| INSURANCE COVERAGE | TOTAL AMOUNT OF INSURANCE | BASIC LIMITS: AMOUNT OF INSURANCE | BASIC LIMITS: RATE | BASIC LIMITS: ANNUAL PREMIUM | ADDITIONAL LIMITS (REGULAR PROGRAM ONLY): AMOUNT OF INSURANCE | ADDITIONAL LIMITS: RATE | ADDITIONAL LIMITS: ANNUAL PREMIUM | DEDUCTIBLE: PREMIUM REDUCTION/ INCREASE | TOTAL PREMIUM |
|---|---|---|---|---|---|---|---|---|---|
| BUILDING | $250,000 | $60,000 | 1.71 | $1,026 | $190,000 | .20 | $380 | –$141 | $1,265 |
| CONTENTS | $25,000 | $25,000 | .84 | $210 | $0 | .15 | $0 | –$21 | $189 |

RATE CATEGORY: ☐ MANUAL ☐ SUBMIT FOR RATE ☐ PROVISIONAL RATING

PAYMENT METHOD: ☐ CHECK ☐ CREDIT CARD ☐ OTHER: ______

| | |
|---|---|
| ANNUAL SUBTOTAL | $1,454 |
| ICC PREMIUM | $6 |
| SUBTOTAL | $1,460 |
| CRS PREMIUM DISCOUNT ___ % | $0 |
| SUBTOTAL | $1,460 |
| RESERVE FUND ___ % | $263 |
| SUBTOTAL | $1,723 |
| PROBATION SURCHARGE | $0 |
| HFIAA SURCHARGE | $25 |
| FEDERAL POLICY FEE | $50 |
| **TOTAL AMOUNT DUE** | **$1,798** |

**NOTICE:** BUILDING COVERAGE BENEFITS – EXCEPT FOR A RESIDENTIAL CONDOMINIUM BUILDING – ARE NOT AVAILABLE IF OTHER NFIP BUILDING COVERAGE HAS BEEN PURCHASED BY THE APPLICANT OR ANY OTHER PARTY FOR THE SAME BUILDING.

THE ABOVE STATEMENTS ARE CORRECT TO THE BEST OF MY KNOWLEDGE. I UNDERSTAND THAT ANY FALSE STATEMENTS MAY BE PUNISHABLE BY FINE AND/OR IMPRISONMENT UNDER APPLICABLE FEDERAL LAW. SEE REVERSE SIDE OF COPIES.

______ SIGNATURE OF INSURANCE AGENT/PRODUCER ___/___/___ DATE (MM/DD/YYYY)

______ SIGNATURE OF INSURED (OPTIONAL) ___/___/___ DATE (MM/DD/YYYY)

**Premium Calculation:**

1. Multiply Rate × $100 of Coverage: Building: $1,406 / Contents: $210
2. Apply Deductible Factor: Building: .900 × $1,406 = $1,265 / Contents: .900 × $210 = $189
3. Premium Reduction: Building: $1,406 – $1,265 = $141 / Contents = $210 – $189 = $21
4. Annual Subtotal: $1,454
5. Add ICC Premium: $6
6. Subtotal: $1,460
7. Subtract CRS Discount: N/A
8. Subtotal: $1,460
9. Add Reserve Fund Assessment: $263 (18%)
10. Subtotal: $1,723
11. Add Probation Surcharge: N/A
12. Add HFIAA Surcharge: $25
13. Add Federal Policy Fee: $50
14. **Total Amount Due: $1,798**

## RATE EXAMPLE 15
## REGULAR PROGRAM, POST-FIRM, ELEVATION RATED, $1,250/$1,250 DEDUCTIBLE OPTION, ZONE AH (WITH CERTIFICATION OF COMPLIANCE OR ELEVATION CERTIFICATE), 2–4 FAMILY

Essential Data to Determine Appropriate Rates and Premium:

**Regular Program:**

- Flood Zone: AH (With Certification of Compliance or Elevation Certificate)
- Occupancy: 2–4 Family Dwelling
- Number of Floors: 2 Floors
- Basement/Enclosure: None
- Deductible: $1,250/$1,250
- Deductible Factor: .980
- Contents Location: Lowest Floor Above Ground Level and Higher Floors
- Date of Construction: Post-FIRM
- Elevation Difference: +3
- Floodproofed (Yes/No): No
- Building Coverage: $200,000
- Contents Coverage: $40,000
- ICC Premium: $6
- CRS Rating: N/A
- CRS Discount: N/A
- Reserve Fund Assessment: $75
- Probation Surcharge: N/A
- HFIAA Surcharge: 2–4 Family $250
- Federal Policy Fee: $50

**Determined Rates:**

Building: .30 / .09 Contents: .38 / .12

ESTIMATED BUILDING REPLACEMENT COST (INCLUDING FOUNDATION): $ DEDUCTIBLE: BUILDING $ 1,250 CONTENTS $ 1,250

| INSURANCE COVERAGE | TOTAL AMOUNT OF INSURANCE | BASIC LIMITS: AMOUNT OF INSURANCE | RATE | ANNUAL PREMIUM | ADDITIONAL LIMITS (REGULAR PROGRAM ONLY): AMOUNT OF INSURANCE | RATE | ANNUAL PREMIUM | DEDUCTIBLE: PREMIUM REDUCTION/ INCREASE | TOTAL PREMIUM |
|---|---|---|---|---|---|---|---|---|---|
| BUILDING | $200,000 | $60,000 | .30 | $180 | $140,000 | .09 | $126 | –$6 | $300 |
| CONTENTS | $40,000 | $25,000 | .38 | $95 | $15,000 | .12 | $19 | –$2 | $111 |

RATE CATEGORY: ☐ MANUAL ☐ SUBMIT FOR RATE ☐ PROVISIONAL RATING

PAYMENT METHOD: ☐ CHECK ☐ CREDIT CARD ☐ OTHER: ____________

| | |
|---|---|
| ANNUAL SUBTOTAL | $411 |
| ICC PREMIUM | $6 |
| SUBTOTAL | $417 |
| CRS PREMIUM DISCOUNT ___ % | $0 |
| SUBTOTAL | $417 |
| RESERVE FUND ___ % | $75 |
| SUBTOTAL | $492 |
| PROBATION SURCHARGE | $0 |
| HFIAA SURCHARGE | $250 |
| FEDERAL POLICY FEE | $50 |
| **TOTAL AMOUNT DUE** | **$792** |

**NOTICE:** BUILDING COVERAGE BENEFITS – EXCEPT FOR A RESIDENTIAL CONDOMINIUM BUILDING – ARE NOT AVAILABLE IF OTHER NFIP BUILDING COVERAGE HAS BEEN PURCHASED BY THE APPLICANT OR ANY OTHER PARTY FOR THE SAME BUILDING.

THE ABOVE STATEMENTS ARE CORRECT TO THE BEST OF MY KNOWLEDGE. I UNDERSTAND THAT ANY FALSE STATEMENTS MAY BE PUNISHABLE BY FINE AND/OR IMPRISONMENT UNDER APPLICABLE FEDERAL LAW. SEE REVERSE SIDE OF COPIES.

____________________ SIGNATURE OF INSURANCE AGENT/PRODUCER ____/____/____ DATE (MM/DD/YYYY)

____________________ SIGNATURE OF INSURED (OPTIONAL) ____/____/____ DATE (MM/DD/YYYY)

**Premium Calculation:**

1. Multiply Rate × $100 of Coverage: Building: $306 / Contents: $113
2. Apply Deductible Factor: Building: .980 × $306 = $300 / Contents: .980 × $113 = $111
3. Premium Reduction: Building: $306 – $300 = $6 / Contents = $113 – $111 = $2
4. Annual Subtotal: $411
5. Add ICC Premium: $6
6. Subtotal: $417
7. Subtract CRS Discount: N/A
8. Subtotal: $417
9. Add Reserve Fund Assessment: $75 (18%)
10. Subtotal: $492
11. Add Probation Surcharge: N/A
12. Add HFIAA Surcharge: $250
13. Add Federal Policy Fee: $50
14. **Total Amount Due: $792**

## RATE EXAMPLE 16
## REGULAR PROGRAM, POST-FIRM, ELEVATION RATED, $1,250/$1,250 DEDUCTIBLE OPTION, ZONE A (WITH BFE), 2–4 FAMILY

Essential Data to Determine Appropriate Rates and Premium:

### Regular Program:

- Flood Zone: A
- Occupancy: 2–4 Family Dwelling
- Number of Floors: 2 Floors
- Basement/Enclosure: None
- Deductible: $1,250/$1,250
- Deductible Factor: .980
- Contents Location: Lowest Floor Above Ground Level and Higher Floors
- Date of Construction: Post-FIRM
- Elevation Difference: +6 (with BFE)
- Floodproofed (Yes/No): No
- Building Coverage: $140,000
- Contents Coverage: $70,000
- ICC Premium: $8
- CRS Rating: N/A
- CRS Discount: N/A
- Reserve Fund Assessment: $98
- Probation Surcharge: N/A
- HFIAA Surcharge: 2–4 Family $250
- Federal Policy Fee: $50

### Determined Rates:

Building: .58 / .10 Contents: .33 / .08

ESTIMATED BUILDING REPLACEMENT COST (INCLUDING FOUNDATION): $ DEDUCTIBLE: BUILDING $ 1,250 CONTENTS $ 1,250

| INSURANCE COVERAGE | TOTAL AMOUNT OF INSURANCE | BASIC LIMITS | | | ADDITIONAL LIMITS (REGULAR PROGRAM ONLY) | | | DEDUCTIBLE | TOTAL PREMIUM |
|---|---|---|---|---|---|---|---|---|---|
| | | AMOUNT OF INSURANCE | RATE | ANNUAL PREMIUM | AMOUNT OF INSURANCE | RATE | ANNUAL PREMIUM | PREMIUM REDUCTION/ INCREASE | |
| BUILDING | $140,000 | $60,000 | .58 | $348 | $80,000 | .10 | $80 | –$9 | $419 |
| CONTENTS | $70,000 | $25,000 | .33 | $83 | $45,000 | .08 | $36 | –$2 | $117 |

RATE CATEGORY: ☐ MANUAL ☐ SUBMIT FOR RATE ☐ PROVISIONAL RATING

PAYMENT METHOD: ☐ CHECK ☐ CREDIT CARD ☐ OTHER: ____________

| | |
|---|---|
| ANNUAL SUBTOTAL | $536 |
| ICC PREMIUM | $8 |
| SUBTOTAL | $544 |
| CRS PREMIUM DISCOUNT ___ % | $0 |
| SUBTOTAL | $544 |
| RESERVE FUND ___ % | $98 |
| SUBTOTAL | $642 |
| PROBATION SURCHARGE | $0 |
| HFIAA SURCHARGE | $250 |
| FEDERAL POLICY FEE | $50 |
| **TOTAL AMOUNT DUE** | **$942** |

**NOTICE:** BUILDING COVERAGE BENEFITS – EXCEPT FOR A RESIDENTIAL CONDOMINIUM BUILDING – ARE NOT AVAILABLE IF OTHER NFIP BUILDING COVERAGE HAS BEEN PURCHASED BY THE APPLICANT OR ANY OTHER PARTY FOR THE SAME BUILDING.

THE ABOVE STATEMENTS ARE CORRECT TO THE BEST OF MY KNOWLEDGE. I UNDERSTAND THAT ANY FALSE STATEMENTS MAY BE PUNISHABLE BY FINE AND/OR IMPRISONMENT UNDER APPLICABLE FEDERAL LAW. SEE REVERSE SIDE OF COPIES.

________________________________ ____/____/____
SIGNATURE OF INSURANCE AGENT/PRODUCER DATE (MM/DD/YYYY)

________________________________ ____/____/____
SIGNATURE OF INSURED (OPTIONAL) DATE (MM/DD/YYYY)

### Premium Calculation:

1. Multiply Rate × $100 of Coverage: Building: $428 / Contents: $119
2. Apply Deductible Factor: Building: .980 × $4282 = $419 / Contents: .980 × $119 = $117
3. Premium Reduction: Building: $428 – $419 = $9 / Contents = $119 – $117 = $2
4. Annual Subtotal: $536
5. Add ICC Premium: $8
6. Subtotal: $544
7. Subtract CRS Discount: N/A
8. Subtotal: $544
9. Add Reserve Fund Assessment: $98 (18%)
10. Subtotal: $642
11. Add Probation Surcharge: N/A
12. Add HFIAA Surcharge: $250
13. Add Federal Policy Fee: $50
14. **Total Amount Due: $942**

## RATE EXAMPLE 17
## REGULAR PROGRAM, POST-FIRM, ELEVATION RATED, $1,250/$1,250 DEDUCTIBLE OPTION, ZONE A (WITHOUT BFE), PRIMARY RESIDENCE

Essential Data to Determine Appropriate Rates and Premium:

**Regular Program:**

- Flood Zone: A
- Occupancy: Single-Family Dwelling
- Number of Floors: 2 Floors
- Basement/Enclosure: None
- Deductible: $1,250/$1,250
- Deductible Factor: .980
- Contents Location: Lowest Floor Above Ground Level and Higher Floors
- Date of Construction: Post-FIRM
- Elevation Difference: +5 (without BFE)
- Floodproofed (Yes/No): No
- Building Coverage: $135,000
- Contents Coverage: $60,000
- ICC Premium: $8
- CRS Rating: N/A
- CRS Discount: N/A
- Reserve Fund Assessment: $100
- Probation Surcharge: N/A
- HFIAA Surcharge: Primary Residence $25
- Federal Policy Fee: $50

**Determined Rates:**

Building: .59 / .12 Contents: .34 / .08

ESTIMATED BUILDING REPLACEMENT COST (INCLUDING FOUNDATION): $

DEDUCTIBLE: BUILDING $ 1,250 CONTENTS $ 1,250

| INSURANCE COVERAGE | TOTAL AMOUNT OF INSURANCE | BASIC LIMITS: AMOUNT OF INSURANCE | BASIC LIMITS: RATE | BASIC LIMITS: ANNUAL PREMIUM | ADDITIONAL LIMITS (REGULAR PROGRAM ONLY): AMOUNT OF INSURANCE | ADDITIONAL LIMITS: RATE | ADDITIONAL LIMITS: ANNUAL PREMIUM | DEDUCTIBLE: PREMIUM REDUCTION/ INCREASE | TOTAL PREMIUM |
|---|---|---|---|---|---|---|---|---|---|
| BUILDING | $135,000 | $60,000 | .59 | $354 | $75,000 | .12 | $90 | –$9 | $435 |
| CONTENTS | $60,000 | $25,000 | .34 | $85 | $35,000 | .08 | $28 | –$2 | $111 |

RATE CATEGORY: ☐ MANUAL ☐ SUBMIT FOR RATE ☐ PROVISIONAL RATING

PAYMENT METHOD: ☐ CHECK ☐ CREDIT CARD ☐ OTHER: ____________

**NOTICE:** BUILDING COVERAGE BENEFITS – EXCEPT FOR A RESIDENTIAL CONDOMINIUM BUILDING – ARE NOT AVAILABLE IF OTHER NFIP BUILDING COVERAGE HAS BEEN PURCHASED BY THE APPLICANT OR ANY OTHER PARTY FOR THE SAME BUILDING.

THE ABOVE STATEMENTS ARE CORRECT TO THE BEST OF MY KNOWLEDGE. I UNDERSTAND THAT ANY FALSE STATEMENTS MAY BE PUNISHABLE BY FINE AND/OR IMPRISONMENT UNDER APPLICABLE FEDERAL LAW. SEE REVERSE SIDE OF COPIES.

______________________ SIGNATURE OF INSURANCE AGENT/PRODUCER ____/____/____ DATE (MM/DD/YYYY)

______________________ SIGNATURE OF INSURED (OPTIONAL) ____/____/____ DATE (MM/DD/YYYY)

| | |
|---|---|
| ANNUAL SUBTOTAL | $546 |
| ICC PREMIUM | $8 |
| SUBTOTAL | $554 |
| CRS PREMIUM DISCOUNT ___ % | $0 |
| SUBTOTAL | $554 |
| RESERVE FUND ___ % | $100 |
| SUBTOTAL | $654 |
| PROBATION SURCHARGE | $0 |
| HFIAA SURCHARGE | $25 |
| FEDERAL POLICY FEE | $50 |
| **TOTAL AMOUNT DUE** | **$729** |

**Premium Calculation:**

1. Multiply Rate × $100 of Coverage: Building: $444 / Contents: $113
2. Apply Deductible Factor: Building: .980 × $444 = $435 / Contents: .980 × $113 = $111
3. Premium Reduction: Building: $444 – $435 = $9 / Contents = $113 – $111 = $2
4. Annual Subtotal: $546
5. Add ICC Premium: $8
6. Subtotal: $554
7. Subtract CRS Discount: N/A
8. Subtotal: $554
9. Add Reserve Fund Assessment: $100 (18%)
10. Subtotal: $654
11. Add Probation Surcharge: N/A
12. Add HFIAA Surcharge: $25
13. Add Federal Policy Fee: $50
14. **Total Amount Due: $729**

## PRP RATING EXAMPLE
## PREFERRED RISK POLICY, $1,250/$1,250 DEDUCTIBLE, ZONE X, PRIMARY RESIDENCE

Essential Data to Determine Appropriate Rates and Premium:

### REGULAR PROGRAM:

- Flood Zone: X
- Policy Effective Date: 1/8/2021
- Occupancy: Single-Family Dwelling
- Number of Floors: 2 Floors
- Basement/Enclosure: None
- Deductible: $1,250/$1,250
- Contents Location: Lowest Floor Above Ground Level and Higher Floors
- Date of Construction: Post-FIRM
- Replacement Cost $200,000
- Building Coverage: $200,000
- Contents Coverage: $80,000
- Multiplier: 1.000
- ICC Premium: $8
- Reserve Fund Percent 18%
- Reserve Fund Assessment $83
- Probation Surcharge: N/A
- HFIAA Surcharge: Primary Residence $25
- Federal Policy Fee $25

### COVERAGE AND PREMIUM:

**ESTIMATED BUILDING REPLACEMENT COST (INCLUDING FOUNDATION):**

**$** ______________________________

**ENTER SELECTED OPTION FOR COVERAGE LIMIT AND PREMIUM FROM THE TABLES IN THIS MANUAL.**

**BUILDING AND CONTENTS COVERAGE COMBINATION**

| REQUESTED COVERAGE | |
|---|---|
| BUILDING COVERAGE | $200,000 |
| CONTENTS COVERAGE / CONTENTS ONLY | $80,000 |
| **PREMIUM CALCULATION** | |
| BASE PREMIUM | $452 |
| MULTIPLIER | 1.000 |
| ADJUSTED PREMIUM | $452 |
| ICC PREMIUM | $8 |
| **PREMIUM SUBTOTAL** | **$460** |
| RESERVE FUND ASSESSMENT PERCENT | 18% |
| RESERVE FUND ASSESSMENT AMOUNT | $83 |
| **TOTAL PREMIUM** | **$543** |
| **FEES AND SURCHARGES** | |
| HFIAA SURCHARGE | $25 |
| PROBATION SURCHARGE | $0 |
| FEDERAL POLICY FEE | $25 |
| **TOTAL AMOUNT DUE** | **$593** |

INDICATE THE RATE TABLE USED FOR THE BASE PREMIUM: 3A
RISK RATING METHOD: ☐ 7 - PRP ☐ R - NEWLY MAPPED

### PREMIUM CALCULATION:

| | | |
|---|---|---|
| 1. | Enter the coverage amounts: Building: $200,000 / Contents: $80,000 | |
| 2. | Select Base Premium: | $452 |
| 3. | Apply the Multiplier: | 1.000 |
| 4. | Adjusted Premium: | $452 |
| 5. | Add ICC Premium: | $8 |
| 6. | Subtotal: | $460 |
| 7. | Enter Reserve Fund Assessment Percentage: | 18% |
| 8. | Add Reserve Fund Assessment Amount: | $83 |
| 9. | Subtotal: | $543 |
| 10. | HFIAA Surcharge: | $25 |
| 11. | Add Federal Policy Fee: | $25 |
| **12.** | **Total Prepaid Amount:** | **$593** |

## NEWLY MAPPED RATING EXAMPLE
## ZONE X, NEWLY MAPPED INTO SFHA ON 8/1/2020, $1,250/$1,250 DEDUCTIBLE, PRIMARY RESIDENCE

Essential Data to Determine Appropriate Rates and Premium:

**REGULAR PROGRAM:**

- Flood Zone: X
- Policy Effective Date: 1/3/2021
- Occupancy: Single-Family Dwelling
- Number of Floors: 2 Floors
- Basement/Enclosure: None
- Deductible: $1,250/$1,250
- Contents Location: Lowest Floor Above Ground Level and Higher Floors
- Replacement Cost $150,000
- Building Coverage: $150,000
- Contents Coverage: $60,000
- Multiplier: 1.000
- ICC Premium: $8
- Reserve Fund Percent 18%
- Reserve Fund Assessment $68
- Probation Surcharge: N/A
- HFIAA Surcharge: Primary Residence $25
- Federal Policy Fee $50

**COVERAGE AND PREMIUM:**

**ESTIMATED BUILDING REPLACEMENT COST (INCLUDING FOUNDATION):**

**$** ______________________

**ENTER SELECTED OPTION FOR COVERAGE LIMIT AND PREMIUM FROM THE TABLES IN THIS MANUAL.**

**BUILDING AND CONTENTS COVERAGE COMBINATION**

| REQUESTED COVERAGE | |
|---|---|
| BUILDING COVERAGE | $150,000 |
| CONTENTS COVERAGE / CONTENTS ONLY | $60,000 |
| **PREMIUM CALCULATION** | |
| BASE PREMIUM | $367 |
| MULTIPLIER | 1.000 |
| ADJUSTED PREMIUM | $367 |
| ICC PREMIUM | $8 |
| **PREMIUM SUBTOTAL** | **$375** |
| RESERVE FUND ASSESSMENT PERCENT | 18% |
| RESERVE FUND ASSESSMENT AMOUNT | $68 |
| **TOTAL PREMIUM** | **$443** |
| **FEES AND SURCHARGES** | |
| HFIAA SURCHARGE | $25 |
| PROBATION SURCHARGE | $0 |
| FEDERAL POLICY FEE | $50 |
| **TOTAL AMOUNT DUE** | **$518** |

INDICATE THE RATE TABLE USED FOR THE BASE PREMIUM: 3
RISK RATING METHOD: ☐ 7 - PRP ☒ R - NEWLY MAPPED

**PREMIUM CALCULATION:**

| | | |
|---|---|---|
| 1 | Enter the coverage amounts: Building: $150,000 / Contents: $60,000 | |
| 2 | Select Base Premium: | $367 |
| 3 | Apply the Multiplier: | 1.000 |
| 4 | Adjusted Premium: | $367 |
| 5 | Add ICC Premium: | $8 |
| 6 | Subtotal: | $375 |
| 7 | Enter Reserve Fund Assessment Percentage: | 18% |
| 8 | Add Reserve Fund Assessment Amount: | $68 |
| 9 | Subtotal: | $443 |
| 10 | HFIAA Surcharge: | $25 |
| 11 | Add Federal Policy Fee: | $50 |
| **12** | **Total Prepaid Amount:** | **$518** |

## CONDO RATING EXAMPLE 1
## PRE-FIRM, LOW-RISE, WITH ENCLOSURE, COINSURANCE PENALTY, ZONE A

**REGULAR PROGRAM:**

| | |
|---|---|
| • Building Coverage: | $140,000 |
| • Contents Coverage: | $100,000 |
| • Condominium Type: | Low-rise |
| • Flood Zone: | A |
| • Occupancy: | Other Residential |
| • Number of Units: | 6 |
| • Date of Construction: | Pre-FIRM |
| • Building Type: | 3 or More Floors, Including Enclosure |
| • Deductible: | $2,000/$2,000 |
| • Deductible Factor: | 1.000 |
| • Replacement Cost: | $600,000 |
| • Elevation Difference: | N/A |
| • 80% Coinsurance Amount: | $480,000 |
| • ICC Premium: | $56 ($30,000 Coverage) |
| • CRS Rating: | N/A |
| • CRS Discount: | N/A |
| • Reserve Fund Assessment | $705 |
| • Probation Surcharge: | N/A |
| • HFIAA Surcharge: RCBAP | $250 |
| • Federal Policy Fee | $400 |

**DETERMINED RATES:**

Building: 1.29 / 1.69 Contents: 1.64 / 2.19

ESTIMATED BUILDING REPLACEMENT COST (INCLUDING FOUNDATION): $600,000 — DEDUCTIBLE: BUILDING $2,000 CONTENTS $2,000

| INSURANCE COVERAGE | TOTAL AMOUNT OF INSURANCE | BASIC LIMITS: AMOUNT OF INSURANCE | RATE | ANNUAL PREMIUM | ADDITIONAL LIMITS (REGULAR PROGRAM ONLY): AMOUNT OF INSURANCE | RATE | ANNUAL PREMIUM | DEDUCTIBLE: PREMIUM REDUCTION/ INCREASE | TOTAL PREMIUM |
|---|---|---|---|---|---|---|---|---|---|
| BUILDING | $140,000 | $140,000 | 1.29 | $1,806 | $0 | 1.69 | $0 | $0 | $1,806 |
| CONTENTS | $100,000 | $25,000 | 1.64 | $410 | $75,000 | 2.19 | $1,643 | $0 | $2,053 |

RATE CATEGORY: ☐ MANUAL ☐ SUBMIT FOR RATE ☐ PROVISIONAL RATING

PAYMENT METHOD: ☐ CHECK ☐ CREDIT CARD ☐ OTHER: ______

| | |
|---|---|
| ANNUAL SUBTOTAL | $3,859 |
| ICC PREMIUM | $56 |
| SUBTOTAL | $3,915 |
| CRS PREMIUM DISCOUNT ___ % | $0 |
| SUBTOTAL | $3,915 |
| RESERVE FUND ___ % | $705 |
| SUBTOTAL | $4,620 |
| PROBATION SURCHARGE | $0 |
| HFIAA SURCHARGE | $250 |
| FEDERAL POLICY FEE | $400 |
| **TOTAL AMOUNT DUE** | **$5,270** |

**NOTICE:** BUILDING COVERAGE BENEFITS – EXCEPT FOR A RESIDENTIAL CONDOMINIUM BUILDING – ARE NOT AVAILABLE IF OTHER NFIP BUILDING COVERAGE HAS BEEN PURCHASED BY THE APPLICANT OR ANY OTHER PARTY FOR THE SAME BUILDING.

THE ABOVE STATEMENTS ARE CORRECT TO THE BEST OF MY KNOWLEDGE. I UNDERSTAND THAT ANY FALSE STATEMENTS MAY BE PUNISHABLE BY FINE AND/OR IMPRISONMENT UNDER APPLICABLE FEDERAL LAW. SEE REVERSE SIDE OF COPIES.

______ SIGNATURE OF INSURANCE AGENT/PRODUCER ___/___/___ DATE (MM/DD/YYYY)

______ SIGNATURE OF INSURED (OPTIONAL) ___/___/___ DATE (MM/DD/YYYY)

**PREMIUM CALCULATION:**

| | |
|---|---|
| 1. Multiply Rate × $100 of Coverage: | Building: $1,806 / Contents: $2,053 |
| 2. Apply Deductible Factor: | Building: 1.000 × $1,806 = $1,806 / Contents: 1.000 × $2,053 = $2,053 |
| 3. Premium Reduction/Increase: | Building: $0 / Contents: $0 |
| 4. Annual Subtotal: | $3,859 |
| 5. Add ICC Premium: | $56 |
| 6. Subtotal: | $3,915 |
| 7. Subtract CRS Discount: | N/A |
| 8. Subtotal: | $3,915 |
| 9. Add Reserve Fund Assessment: | $705 (18%) |
| 10. Subtotal: | $4,620 |
| 11. Add Probation Surcharge: | N/A |
| 12. Add HFIAA Surcharge: | $250 |
| 13. Add Federal Policy Fee: | $400 |
| **14. Total Amount Due:** | **$5,270** |

**CLAIMS ADJUSTMENT WITH COINSURANCE PROVISION:**

Claim Payment is determined as follows:

$$\frac{\text{(Insurance Carried) } \$140{,}000}{\text{(Insurance Required) } \$480{,}000} \times \text{(Amount of Loss) } \$100{,}000 = \text{(Limit of Recovery) } \$29{,}167 - \text{Less Deductible}$$

(Coinsurance Penalty applies because minimum insurance amount of $480,000 was not met.)

## CONDO RATING EXAMPLE 2
## PRE-FIRM, LOW-RISE, NO BASEMENT/ENCLOSURE, ZONE AE

### REGULAR PROGRAM:

| | | | |
|---|---|---|---|
| • Building Coverage: | $480,000 | • Replacement Cost: | $600,000 |
| • Contents Coverage: | $50,000 | • Elevation Difference: | N/A |
| • Condominium Type: | Low-rise | • 80% Coinsurance Amount: | $480,000 |
| • Flood Zone: | AE | • ICC Premium: | $56 ($30,000 Coverage) |
| • Occupancy: | Other Residential | • CRS Rating: | N/A |
| • Number of Units: | 6 | • CRS Discount: | N/A |
| • Date of Construction: | Pre-FIRM | • Reserve Fund Assessment | $1,191 |
| • Building Type: | 1 Floor, No Basement | • Probation Surcharge: | N/A |
| • Deductible: | $2,000/$2,000 | • HFIAA Surcharge: RCBAP | $250 |
| • Deductible Factor: | 1.000 | • Federal Policy Fee | $400 |

### DETERMINED RATES:

Building: 1.17 / 1.16 Contents: 1.64 / 2.19

ESTIMATED BUILDING REPLACEMENT COST (INCLUDING FOUNDATION): $600,000 — DEDUCTIBLE: BUILDING $2,000 CONTENTS $2,000

| INSURANCE COVERAGE | TOTAL AMOUNT OF INSURANCE | BASIC LIMITS: AMOUNT OF INSURANCE | RATE | ANNUAL PREMIUM | ADDITIONAL LIMITS (REGULAR PROGRAM ONLY): AMOUNT OF INSURANCE | RATE | ANNUAL PREMIUM | DEDUCTIBLE: PREMIUM REDUCTION/ INCREASE | TOTAL PREMIUM |
|---|---|---|---|---|---|---|---|---|---|
| BUILDING | $480,000 | $360,000 | 1.17 | $4,212 | $120,000 | 1.16 | $1,392 | $0 | $5,604 |
| CONTENTS | $50,000 | $25,000 | 1.64 | $410 | $25,000 | 2.19 | $548 | $0 | $958 |

RATE CATEGORY: ☐ MANUAL ☐ SUBMIT FOR RATE ☐ PROVISIONAL RATING

PAYMENT METHOD: ☐ CHECK ☐ CREDIT CARD ☐ OTHER: ____________

| | |
|---|---|
| ANNUAL SUBTOTAL | $6,562 |
| ICC PREMIUM | $56 |
| SUBTOTAL | $6,618 |
| CRS PREMIUM DISCOUNT ___ % | $0 |
| SUBTOTAL | $6,618 |
| RESERVE FUND ___ % | $1,191 |
| SUBTOTAL | $7,809 |
| PROBATION SURCHARGE | $0 |
| HFIAA SURCHARGE | $250 |
| FEDERAL POLICY FEE | $400 |
| **TOTAL AMOUNT DUE** | **$8,459** |

**NOTICE:** BUILDING COVERAGE BENEFITS – EXCEPT FOR A RESIDENTIAL CONDOMINIUM BUILDING – ARE NOT AVAILABLE IF OTHER NFIP BUILDING COVERAGE HAS BEEN PURCHASED BY THE APPLICANT OR ANY OTHER PARTY FOR THE SAME BUILDING.

THE ABOVE STATEMENTS ARE CORRECT TO THE BEST OF MY KNOWLEDGE. I UNDERSTAND THAT ANY FALSE STATEMENTS MAY BE PUNISHABLE BY FINE AND/OR IMPRISONMENT UNDER APPLICABLE FEDERAL LAW. SEE REVERSE SIDE OF COPIES.

______________________ ____/____/______
SIGNATURE OF INSURANCE AGENT/PRODUCER DATE (MM/DD/YYYY)

______________________ ____/____/______
SIGNATURE OF INSURED (OPTIONAL) DATE (MM/DD/YYYY)

### PREMIUM CALCULATION:

1. Multiply Rate × $100 of Coverage: Building: $5,604 / Contents: $958
2. Apply Deductible Factor: Building: 1.00 × $5,604 = $5,604 / Contents: 1.00 × $958 = $958
3. Premium Reduction/Increase: Building: $0 / Contents: $0
4. Annual Subtotal: $6,562
5. Add ICC Premium: $56
6. Subtotal: $6,618
7. Subtract CRS Discount: N/A
8. Subtotal: $6,618
9. Add Reserve Fund Assessment: $1,191 (18%)
10. Subtotal: $7,809
11. Add Probation Surcharge: N/A
12. Add HFIAA Surcharge: $250
13. Add Federal Policy Fee: $400
14. **Total Amount Due: $8,469**

### CLAIMS ADJUSTMENT WITH COINSURANCE PROVISION:

Coinsurance Penalty does not apply since minimum insurance amount of 80% was met.

## CONDO RATING EXAMPLE 3
## PRE-FIRM, LOW-RISE, NO BASEMENT/ENCLOSURE, ZONE AE, BUILDING SUBSTANTIALLY IMPROVED

**REGULAR PROGRAM:**

- Building Coverage: $1,000,000
- Contents Coverage: $40,000
- Condominium Type: Low-rise
- Flood Zone: AE
- Occupancy: 2–4 Family
- Number of Units: 4
- Date of Construction: Pre-FIRM
- Building Type: 2 Floors, No Basement/ Enclosure
- Deductible: $2,000/$2,000
- Deductible Factor: 1.000
- Replacement Cost: $1,200,000
- Elevation Difference: N/A
- ICC Premium: $56 ($30,000 Coverage)
- CRS Rating: N/A
- CRS Discount: N/A
- Reserve Fund Assessment $6,172
- Probation Surcharge: N/A
- HFIAA Surcharge: RCBAP $250
- Federal Policy Fee $150

**DETERMINED RATES:**

Building: 3.28 / 3.20 Contents: 4.52 / 6.06

ESTIMATED BUILDING REPLACEMENT COST (INCLUDING FOUNDATION): $1,200,000 — DEDUCTIBLE: BUILDING $2,000 CONTENTS $2,000

| INSURANCE COVERAGE | TOTAL AMOUNT OF INSURANCE | BASIC LIMITS AMOUNT OF INSURANCE | BASIC LIMITS RATE | BASIC LIMITS ANNUAL PREMIUM | ADDITIONAL LIMITS (REGULAR PROGRAM ONLY) AMOUNT OF INSURANCE | ADDITIONAL LIMITS RATE | ADDITIONAL LIMITS ANNUAL PREMIUM | DEDUCTIBLE PREMIUM REDUCTION/ INCREASE | TOTAL PREMIUM |
|---|---|---|---|---|---|---|---|---|---|
| BUILDING | $1,000,000 | $240,000 | 3.28 | $7,872 | $760,000 | 3.20 | $24,320 | $0 | $32,192 |
| CONTENTS | $40,000 | $25,000 | 4.52 | $1,130 | $15,000 | 6.06 | $909 | $0 | $2,039 |

RATE CATEGORY: ☐ MANUAL ☐ SUBMIT FOR RATE ☐ PROVISIONAL RATING

PAYMENT METHOD: ☐ CHECK ☐ CREDIT CARD ☐ OTHER: ____

| | |
|---|---|
| ANNUAL SUBTOTAL | $34,231 |
| ICC PREMIUM | $56 |
| SUBTOTAL | $34,287 |
| CRS PREMIUM DISCOUNT ___ % | $0 |
| SUBTOTAL | $34,287 |
| RESERVE FUND ___ % | $6,172 |
| SUBTOTAL | $40,459 |
| PROBATION SURCHARGE | $0 |
| HFIAA SURCHARGE | $250 |
| FEDERAL POLICY FEE | $150 |
| **TOTAL AMOUNT DUE** | **$40,859** |

**NOTICE:** BUILDING COVERAGE BENEFITS – EXCEPT FOR A RESIDENTIAL CONDOMINIUM BUILDING – ARE NOT AVAILABLE IF OTHER NFIP BUILDING COVERAGE HAS BEEN PURCHASED BY THE APPLICANT OR ANY OTHER PARTY FOR THE SAME BUILDING.

THE ABOVE STATEMENTS ARE CORRECT TO THE BEST OF MY KNOWLEDGE. I UNDERSTAND THAT ANY FALSE STATEMENTS MAY BE PUNISHABLE BY FINE AND/OR IMPRISONMENT UNDER APPLICABLE FEDERAL LAW. SEE REVERSE SIDE OF COPIES.

SIGNATURE OF INSURANCE AGENT/PRODUCER ____ DATE (MM/DD/YYYY) ___/___/____

SIGNATURE OF INSURED (OPTIONAL) ____ DATE (MM/DD/YYYY) ___/___/____

**PREMIUM CALCULATION:**

1. Multiply Rate × $100 of Coverage: Building: $32,192 / Contents: $2,039
2. Apply Deductible Factor: Building: 1.000 × $32,192 = $32,192 / Contents: 1.000 × $2,039 = $2,039
3. Premium Reduction: Building: $0 / Contents: $0
4. Annual Subtotal: $34,231
5. Add ICC Premium: $56
6. Subtotal: $34,287
7. Subtract CRS Discount: N/A
8. Subtotal: $34,287
9. Add Reserve Fund Assessment: $6,172 (18%)
10. Subtotal: $40,459
11. Add Probation Surcharge: N/A
12. Add HFIAA Surcharge: $250
13. Add Federal Policy Fee: $150
14. **Total Amount Due: $40,859**

**CLAIMS ADJUSTMENT WITH COINSURANCE PROVISION:**

Coinsurance Penalty does not apply as the maximum amount of insurance was purchased.

## CONDO RATING EXAMPLE 4
## POST-FIRM, LOW-RISE, COINSURANCE PENALTY, ZONE AE

**REGULAR PROGRAM:**

- Building Coverage: $750,000
- Contents Coverage: $100,000
- Condominium Type: Low-rise
- Flood Zone: AE
- Occupancy: Other Residential
- Number of Units: 14
- Date of Construction: Post-FIRM
- Building Type: 2 Floors, No Basement/ Enclosure
- Deductible: $1,500/$1,500
- Deductible Factor: .990
- Contents Location: Lowest Floor Above Ground Level & Higher
- Replacement Cost: $1,120,000
- Elevation Difference: +1
- 80% Coinsurance Amount: $896,000
- ICC Premium: $8 ($30,000 Coverage)
- CRS Rating: N/A
- CRS Discount: N/A
- Reserve Fund Assessment $1,107
- Probation Surcharge: N/A
- HFIAA Surcharge: $250
- Federal Policy Fee $800

**DETERMINED RATES:**

Building: .80 / .08 Contents: .46 / .12

| ESTIMATED BUILDING REPLACEMENT COST (INCLUDING FOUNDATION): $1,120,000 | | DEDUCTIBLE: | BUILDING $1,500 | | CONTENTS $1,500 | | | | |
|---|---|---|---|---|---|---|---|---|---|
| | | BASIC LIMITS | | | ADDITIONAL LIMITS (REGULAR PROGRAM ONLY) | | | DEDUCTIBLE | |
| INSURANCE COVERAGE | TOTAL AMOUNT OF INSURANCE | AMOUNT OF INSURANCE | RATE | ANNUAL PREMIUM | AMOUNT OF INSURANCE | RATE | ANNUAL PREMIUM | PREMIUM REDUCTION/ INCREASE | TOTAL PREMIUM |
| BUILDING | $750,000 | $750,000 | .80 | $6,000 | $0 | .08 | $0 | –$60 | $5,940 |
| CONTENTS | $100,000 | $25,000 | .46 | $115 | $75,000 | .12 | $90 | –$2 | $203 |

RATE CATEGORY: ☐ MANUAL ☐ SUBMIT FOR RATE ☐ PROVISIONAL RATING

PAYMENT METHOD: ☐ CHECK ☐ CREDIT CARD ☐ OTHER: ____________

**NOTICE:** BUILDING COVERAGE BENEFITS – EXCEPT FOR A RESIDENTIAL CONDOMINIUM BUILDING – ARE NOT AVAILABLE IF OTHER NFIP BUILDING COVERAGE HAS BEEN PURCHASED BY THE APPLICANT OR ANY OTHER PARTY FOR THE SAME BUILDING.

THE ABOVE STATEMENTS ARE CORRECT TO THE BEST OF MY KNOWLEDGE. I UNDERSTAND THAT ANY FALSE STATEMENTS MAY BE PUNISHABLE BY FINE AND/OR IMPRISONMENT UNDER APPLICABLE FEDERAL LAW. SEE REVERSE SIDE OF COPIES.

____________________ SIGNATURE OF INSURANCE AGENT/PRODUCER ____/____/____ DATE (MM/DD/YYYY)

____________________ SIGNATURE OF INSURED (OPTIONAL) ____/____/____ DATE (MM/DD/YYYY)

| | |
|---|---|
| ANNUAL SUBTOTAL | $6,143 |
| ICC PREMIUM | $8 |
| SUBTOTAL | $6,151 |
| CRS PREMIUM DISCOUNT ____ % | $0 |
| SUBTOTAL | $6,151 |
| RESERVE FUND ____ % | $1,107 |
| SUBTOTAL | $7,258 |
| PROBATION SURCHARGE | $0 |
| HFIAA SURCHARGE | $250 |
| FEDERAL POLICY FEE | $800 |
| **TOTAL AMOUNT DUE** | **$8,308** |

**PREMIUM CALCULATION:**

1. Multiply Rate × $100 of Coverage: Building: $6,000 / Contents: $205
2. Apply Deductible Factor: Building: .990 × $6,000 = $5,940 / Contents: .990 × $205 = $203
3. Premium Reduction: Building: $6,000 – $5,940 = $60 / Contents: $205 – $203 = $2
4. Annual Subtotal: $6,143
5. Add ICC Premium: $8
6. Subtotal: $6,151
7. Subtract CRS Discount: N/A
8. Subtotal: $6,151
9. Add Reserve Fund Assessment: $1,107 (18%)
10. Subtotal: $7,258
11. Add Probation Surcharge: N/A
12. Add HFIAA Surcharge: $250
13. Add Federal Policy Fee: $800
14. **Total Amount Due: $8,308**

**CLAIMS ADJUSTMENT WITH COINSURANCE PROVISION:**

Claim Payment is determined as follows:

$$\frac{\text{(Insurance Carried) } \$750{,}000}{\text{(Insurance Required) } \$896{,}000} \times \text{(Amount of Loss) } \$300{,}000 = \text{(Limit of Recovery) } \$251{,}116 - \text{Less Deductible}$$

(Coinsurance Penalty applies because minimum insurance amount of $896,000 was not met.)

## CONDO RATING EXAMPLE 5
## POST-FIRM, LOW-RISE, ZONE AE

**REGULAR PROGRAM:**

- Building Coverage: $600,000
- Contents Coverage: $15,000
- Condominium Type: Low-rise
- Flood Zone: AE
- Occupancy: Other Residential
- Number of Units: 6
- Date of Construction: Post-FIRM
- Building Type: 3 or More Floors, Townhouse, No Basement/Enclosure
- Deductible: $2,000/$2,000
- Deductible Factor: .975
- Contents Location: Lowest Floor Above Ground Level and Higher.
- Replacement Cost: $600,000
- Elevation Difference: +2
- 80% Coinsurance Amount: $480,000
- ICC Premium: $8 ($30,000 Coverage)
- CRS Rating: N/A
- CRS Discount: N/A
- Reserve Fund Assessment $321
- Probation Surcharge: N/A
- HFIAA Surcharge: RCBAP $250
- Federal Policy Fee $400

**DETERMINED RATES:**

Building: .44 / .08 Contents: .31 / .12

ESTIMATED BUILDING REPLACEMENT COST (INCLUDING FOUNDATION): $600,000 — DEDUCTIBLE: BUILDING $2,000 — CONTENTS $2,000

| INSURANCE COVERAGE | TOTAL AMOUNT OF INSURANCE | BASIC LIMITS: AMOUNT OF INSURANCE | RATE | ANNUAL PREMIUM | ADDITIONAL LIMITS (REGULAR PROGRAM ONLY): AMOUNT OF INSURANCE | RATE | ANNUAL PREMIUM | DEDUCTIBLE: PREMIUM REDUCTION/ INCREASE | TOTAL PREMIUM |
|---|---|---|---|---|---|---|---|---|---|
| BUILDING | $600,000 | $360,000 | .44 | $1,584 | $240,000 | .08 | $192 | –$443 | $1,732 |
| CONTENTS | $15,000 | $15,000 | .31 | $47 | $0 | .12 | $0 | –$1 | $46 |

| | |
|---|---|
| ANNUAL SUBTOTAL | $1,778 |
| ICC PREMIUM | $8 |
| SUBTOTAL | $1,786 |
| CRS PREMIUM DISCOUNT ___ % | $0 |
| SUBTOTAL | $1,786 |
| RESERVE FUND ___ % | $321 |
| SUBTOTAL | $2,107 |
| PROBATION SURCHARGE | $0 |
| HFIAA SURCHARGE | $250 |
| FEDERAL POLICY FEE | $400 |
| **TOTAL AMOUNT DUE** | **$2,757** |

RATE CATEGORY: ☐ MANUAL ☐ SUBMIT FOR RATE ☐ PROVISIONAL RATING

PAYMENT METHOD: ☐ CHECK ☐ CREDIT CARD ☐ OTHER: ____________

**NOTICE:** BUILDING COVERAGE BENEFITS – EXCEPT FOR A RESIDENTIAL CONDOMINIUM BUILDING – ARE NOT AVAILABLE IF OTHER NFIP BUILDING COVERAGE HAS BEEN PURCHASED BY THE APPLICANT OR ANY OTHER PARTY FOR THE SAME BUILDING.

THE ABOVE STATEMENTS ARE CORRECT TO THE BEST OF MY KNOWLEDGE. I UNDERSTAND THAT ANY FALSE STATEMENTS MAY BE PUNISHABLE BY FINE AND/OR IMPRISONMENT UNDER APPLICABLE FEDERAL LAW. SEE REVERSE SIDE OF COPIES.

______________________ ___/___/____
SIGNATURE OF INSURANCE AGENT/PRODUCER — DATE (MM/DD/YYYY)

______________________ ___/___/____
SIGNATURE OF INSURED (OPTIONAL) — DATE (MM/DD/YYYY)

**PREMIUM CALCULATION:**

1. Multiply Rate × $100 of Coverage: Building: $1,776 / Contents: $47
2. Apply Deductible Factor: Building: .975 × $1,776 = $1,732 / Contents: .975 × $47 = $46
3. Premium Reduction: Building: $1,776 – $1,732 = $44 / Contents: $47 – $46 = $1
4. Annual Subtotal: $1,778
5. Add ICC Premium: $8
6. Subtotal: $1,786
7. Subtract CRS Discount: N/A
8. Subtotal: $1,786
9. Add Reserve Fund Assessment: $321 (18%)
10. Subtotal: $2,107
11. Add Probation Surcharge: N/A
12. Add HFIAA Surcharge: $250
13. Add Federal Policy Fee: $400
14. **Total Amount Due: $2,757**

**CLAIMS ADJUSTMENT WITH COINSURANCE PROVISION:**

Coinsurance Penalty does not apply since the minimum insurance amount of 80% was met.

## CONDO RATING EXAMPLE 6
## PRE-FIRM, HIGH-RISE, COINSURANCE PENALTY, ZONE A

**REGULAR PROGRAM:**

- Building Coverage: $1,110,000
- Contents Coverage: $100,000
- Condominium Type: High-rise
- Flood Zone: A
- Occupancy: Other Residential
- Number of Units: 50
- Date of Construction: Pre-FIRM
- Building Type: 3 or More Floors, No Basement/ Enclosure
- Deductible: $2,000/$2,000
- Deductible Factor: 1.000
- Contents Location: Lowest Floor Above Ground Level Only
- Replacement Cost: $1,500,000
- Elevation Difference: N/A
- 80% Coinsurance Amount: $1,200,000
- ICC Premium: $56 ($30,000 Coverage)
- CRS Rating: 5
- CRS Discount: 25%
- Reserve Fund Assessment $1,135
- Probation Surcharge: N/A
- HFIAA Surcharge: RCBAP $250
- Federal Policy Fee $2,000

**DETERMINED RATES:**

Building: 1.45 / .412 Contents: 1.60 / 2.08

ESTIMATED BUILDING REPLACEMENT COST (INCLUDING FOUNDATION): $1,500,000 — DEDUCTIBLE: BUILDING $2,000 CONTENTS $2,000

| INSURANCE COVERAGE | TOTAL AMOUNT OF INSURANCE | BASIC LIMITS AMOUNT OF INSURANCE | BASIC LIMITS RATE | BASIC LIMITS ANNUAL PREMIUM | ADDITIONAL LIMITS (REGULAR PROGRAM ONLY) AMOUNT OF INSURANCE | ADDITIONAL LIMITS RATE | ADDITIONAL LIMITS ANNUAL PREMIUM | DEDUCTIBLE PREMIUM REDUCTION/ INCREASE | TOTAL PREMIUM |
|---|---|---|---|---|---|---|---|---|---|
| BUILDING | $1,110,000 | $175,000 | 1.45 | $2,538 | $935,000 | .412 | $3,852 | $0 | $6,390 |
| CONTENTS | $100,000 | $25,000 | 1.60 | $400 | $75,000 | 2.08 | $1,560 | $0 | $1,960 |

RATE CATEGORY: ☐ MANUAL ☐ SUBMIT FOR RATE ☐ PROVISIONAL RATING

PAYMENT METHOD: ☐ CHECK ☐ CREDIT CARD ☐ OTHER: ____

| | |
|---|---|
| ANNUAL SUBTOTAL | $8,350 |
| ICC PREMIUM | $56 |
| SUBTOTAL | $8,406 |
| CRS PREMIUM DISCOUNT ___ % | −$2,102 |
| SUBTOTAL | $6,304 |
| RESERVE FUND ___ % | $1,135 |
| SUBTOTAL | $7,439 |
| PROBATION SURCHARGE | $0 |
| HFIAA SURCHARGE | $250 |
| FEDERAL POLICY FEE | $2,000 |
| **TOTAL AMOUNT DUE** | **$9,689** |

**NOTICE:** BUILDING COVERAGE BENEFITS – EXCEPT FOR A RESIDENTIAL CONDOMINIUM BUILDING – ARE NOT AVAILABLE IF OTHER NFIP BUILDING COVERAGE HAS BEEN PURCHASED BY THE APPLICANT OR ANY OTHER PARTY FOR THE SAME BUILDING.

THE ABOVE STATEMENTS ARE CORRECT TO THE BEST OF MY KNOWLEDGE. I UNDERSTAND THAT ANY FALSE STATEMENTS MAY BE PUNISHABLE BY FINE AND/OR IMPRISONMENT UNDER APPLICABLE FEDERAL LAW. SEE REVERSE SIDE OF COPIES.

____ SIGNATURE OF INSURANCE AGENT/PRODUCER ___/___/___ DATE (MM/DD/YYYY)

____ SIGNATURE OF INSURED (OPTIONAL) ___/___/___ DATE (MM/DD/YYYY)

**PREMIUM CALCULATION:**

1. Multiply Rate × $100 of Coverage: Building: $6,390 / Contents: $1,960
2. Apply Deductible Factor: Building: 1.000 × $6,390 = $6,390 / Contents: 1.000 × $1,960 = $1,960
3. Premium Reduction/Increase: Building: $0 / Contents: $0
4. Annual Subtotal: $8,350
5. Add ICC Premium: $56
6. Subtotal: $8,406
7. Subtract CRS Discount: −$2,103 (25%)
8. Subtotal: $6,304
9. Add Reserve Fund Assessment: $1,135 (18%)
10. Subtotal: $7,439
11. Add Probation Surcharge: N/A
12. Add HFIAA Surcharge: $250
13. Add Federal Policy Fee: $2,000
14. **Total Amount Due: $9,689**

**CLAIMS ADJUSTMENT WITH COINSURANCE PROVISION:**

Claim Payment is determined as follows:

$$\frac{\text{(Insurance Carried) } \$1{,}110{,}000}{\text{(Insurance Required) } \$1{,}200{,}000} \times \text{(Amount of Loss) } \$200{,}000 = \text{(Limit of Recovery) } \$185{,}000 - \text{Less Deductible}$$

(Coinsurance Penalty applies because minimum insurance amount of $1,200,000 was not met.)

## CONDO RATING EXAMPLE 7
## PRE-FIRM, HIGH-RISE, BASEMENT, MAXIMUM DEDUCTIBLE DISCOUNT, ZONE AE

**REGULAR PROGRAM:**

- Building Coverage: $3,000,000
- Contents Coverage: $100,000
- Condominium Type: High-rise
- Flood Zone: AE
- Occupancy: Other Residential
- Number of Units: 50
- Date of Construction: Pre-FIRM
- Building Type: 3 or More Floors, including Basement
- Deductible: $5,000/$5,000
- Deductible Factor: .940 (Maximum Total Discount of $221 applies)
- Replacement Cost: $3,750,000
- Elevation Difference: N/A
- 80% Coinsurance Amount: $3,000,000
- ICC Premium: $56 ($30,000 Coverage)
- CRS Rating: 8
- CRS Discount: 10%
- Reserve Fund Assessment: $3,033
- Probation Surcharge: N/A
- HFIAA Surcharge: RCBAP $250
- Federal Policy Fee: $2,000

**DETERMINED RATES:**

Building: 1.56 / .550 Contents: 1.60 / 1.76

ESTIMATED BUILDING REPLACEMENT COST (INCLUDING FOUNDATION): $3,750,000 — DEDUCTIBLE: BUILDING $5,000 CONTENTS $5,000

| INSURANCE COVERAGE | TOTAL AMOUNT OF INSURANCE | BASIC LIMITS AMOUNT OF INSURANCE | BASIC LIMITS RATE | BASIC LIMITS ANNUAL PREMIUM | ADDITIONAL LIMITS (REGULAR PROGRAM ONLY) AMOUNT OF INSURANCE | ADDITIONAL LIMITS RATE | ADDITIONAL LIMITS ANNUAL PREMIUM | DEDUCTIBLE PREMIUM REDUCTION/ INCREASE | TOTAL PREMIUM |
|---|---|---|---|---|---|---|---|---|---|
| BUILDING | $3,000,000 | $175,000 | 1.56 | $2,730 | $2,825,000 | .550 | $14,435 | –$221 | $16,994 |
| CONTENTS | $100,000 | $25,000 | 1.60 | $400 | $75,000 | 1.76 | $1,320 | $0 | $1,720 |

RATE CATEGORY: ☐ MANUAL ☐ SUBMIT FOR RATE ☐ PROVISIONAL RATING

PAYMENT METHOD: ☐ CHECK ☐ CREDIT CARD ☐ OTHER: ______

| | |
|---|---|
| ANNUAL SUBTOTAL | $18,664 |
| ICC PREMIUM | $56 |
| SUBTOTAL | $18,720 |
| CRS PREMIUM DISCOUNT ___ % | –$1,872 |
| SUBTOTAL | $16,848 |
| RESERVE FUND ___ % | $3,033 |
| SUBTOTAL | $19,881 |
| PROBATION SURCHARGE | $0 |
| HFIAA SURCHARGE | $250 |
| FEDERAL POLICY FEE | $2,000 |
| **TOTAL AMOUNT DUE** | **$22,131** |

**NOTICE:** BUILDING COVERAGE BENEFITS – EXCEPT FOR A RESIDENTIAL CONDOMINIUM BUILDING – ARE NOT AVAILABLE IF OTHER NFIP BUILDING COVERAGE HAS BEEN PURCHASED BY THE APPLICANT OR ANY OTHER PARTY FOR THE SAME BUILDING.

THE ABOVE STATEMENTS ARE CORRECT TO THE BEST OF MY KNOWLEDGE. I UNDERSTAND THAT ANY FALSE STATEMENTS MAY BE PUNISHABLE BY FINE AND/OR IMPRISONMENT UNDER APPLICABLE FEDERAL LAW. SEE REVERSE SIDE OF COPIES.

SIGNATURE OF INSURANCE AGENT/PRODUCER ____ DATE (MM/DD/YYYY) ___/___/___

SIGNATURE OF INSURED (OPTIONAL) ____ DATE (MM/DD/YYYY) ___/___/___

**PREMIUM CALCULATION:**

1. Multiply Rate × $100 of Coverage: Building: $17,165 / Contents: $1,720
2. Apply Deductible Factor: Building: .940 × $17,165 = $16,944 / Maximum Total Discount of $221 applies
3. Premium Reduction: Building: $17,165 - $16,944 = $221 / Contents: $0
4. Annual Subtotal: $18,664
5. Add ICC Premium: $56
6. Subtotal: $18,720
7. Subtract CRS Discount: –$1,872 (10%)
8. Subtotal: $16,848
9. Add Reserve Fund Assessment: $3,033 (18%)
10. Subtotal: $19,881
11. Add Probation Surcharge: N/A
12. Add HFIAA Surcharge: $250
13. Add Federal Policy Fee: $2,000
14. **Total Amount Due: $22,131**

**CLAIMS ADJUSTMENT WITH COINSURANCE PROVISION:**

Coinsurance Penalty does not apply since the minimum insurance amount of 80% was met.

**NOTE:** The NFIP accepts premium only in whole dollars. If the discount for an optional deductible does not result in a whole-dollar premium, round up if 50¢ or more; round down if less. Always submit gross premium.

## CONDO RATING EXAMPLE 8
## POST-FIRM, HIGH-RISE, MAXIMUM DEDUCTIBLE DISCOUNT, ZONE AE

**REGULAR PROGRAM:**

- Building Coverage: $12,000,000
- Contents Coverage: $100,000
- Condominium Type: High-rise
- Flood Zone: AE
- Occupancy: Other Residential
- Number of Units: 100
- Date of Construction: Post-FIRM
- Building Type: 3 or More Floors, No Basement/Enclosure
- Deductible: $5,000/$5,000
- Deductible Factor: .920 (Maximum Total Discount of $221 applies)
- Contents Location: Lowest Floor Above Ground Level and Higher
- Replacement Cost: $15,000,000
- Elevation Difference: 0
- 80% Coinsurance Amount: $12,000,000
- ICC Premium: $8 ($30,000 Coverage)
- CRS Rating: 9
- CRS Discount: 5%
- Reserve Fund Assessment $2,307
- Probation Surcharge: N/A
- HFIAA Surcharge: RCBAP $250
- Federal Policy Fee $2,000

**DETERMINED RATES:**

Building: 2.40 / .078 Contents: .77 / .12

ESTIMATED BUILDING REPLACEMENT COST (INCLUDING FOUNDATION): $15,000,000 — DEDUCTIBLE: BUILDING $5,000 CONTENTS $5,000

| INSURANCE COVERAGE | TOTAL AMOUNT OF INSURANCE | BASIC LIMITS: AMOUNT OF INSURANCE | BASIC LIMITS: RATE | BASIC LIMITS: ANNUAL PREMIUM | ADDITIONAL LIMITS (REGULAR PROGRAM ONLY): AMOUNT OF INSURANCE | ADDITIONAL LIMITS: RATE | ADDITIONAL LIMITS: ANNUAL PREMIUM | DEDUCTIBLE: PREMIUM REDUCTION/ INCREASE | TOTAL PREMIUM |
|---|---|---|---|---|---|---|---|---|---|
| BUILDING | $12,000,000 | $175,000 | 2.40 | $4,200 | $11,825,000 | .078 | $9,224 | −$221 | $13,203 |
| CONTENTS | $100,000 | $25,000 | .77 | $193 | $75,000 | .12 | $90 | $0 | $283 |

RATE CATEGORY: ☐ MANUAL ☐ SUBMIT FOR RATE ☐ PROVISIONAL RATING

PAYMENT METHOD: ☐ CHECK ☐ CREDIT CARD ☐ OTHER: ____________

| | |
|---|---|
| ANNUAL SUBTOTAL | $13,486 |
| ICC PREMIUM | $8 |
| SUBTOTAL | $13,494 |
| CRS PREMIUM DISCOUNT ___ % | −$675 |
| SUBTOTAL | $12,819 |
| RESERVE FUND ___ % | $2,307 |
| SUBTOTAL | $15,126 |
| PROBATION SURCHARGE | $0 |
| HFIAA SURCHARGE | $250 |
| FEDERAL POLICY FEE | $2,000 |
| **TOTAL AMOUNT DUE** | **$17,375** |

**NOTICE:** BUILDING COVERAGE BENEFITS – EXCEPT FOR A RESIDENTIAL CONDOMINIUM BUILDING – ARE NOT AVAILABLE IF OTHER NFIP BUILDING COVERAGE HAS BEEN PURCHASED BY THE APPLICANT OR ANY OTHER PARTY FOR THE SAME BUILDING.

THE ABOVE STATEMENTS ARE CORRECT TO THE BEST OF MY KNOWLEDGE. I UNDERSTAND THAT ANY FALSE STATEMENTS MAY BE PUNISHABLE BY FINE AND/OR IMPRISONMENT UNDER APPLICABLE FEDERAL LAW. SEE REVERSE SIDE OF COPIES.

____________________ SIGNATURE OF INSURANCE AGENT/PRODUCER ____/____/____ DATE (MM/DD/YYYY)

____________________ SIGNATURE OF INSURED (OPTIONAL) ____/____/____ DATE (MM/DD/YYYY)

**PREMIUM CALCULATION:**

1. Multiply Rate × $100 of Coverage: Building: $13,424 / Contents: $283
2. Apply Deductible Factor: Building: .920 × $13,424 = $13,203 / Maximum Total Discount of $221 applies
3. Premium Reduction: Building: $13,424 – $13,203 = $221 / Contents: $0
4. Annual Subtotal: $13,486
5. Add ICC Premium: $8
6. Subtotal: $13,494
7. Subtract CRS Discount: –$675 (5%)
8. Subtotal: $12,819
9. Add Reserve Fund Assessment: $2,307 (18%)
10. Subtotal: $15,126
12. Add Probation Surcharge: N/A
12. Add HFIAA Surcharge: $250
13. Add Federal Policy Fee: $2,000
14. **Total Amount Due: $17,376**

**CLAIMS ADJUSTMENT WITH COINSURANCE PROVISION:**

Coinsurance Penalty does not apply since the minimum insurance amount of 80% was met.

**NOTE:** The NFIP accepts premium only in whole dollars. If the discount for an optional deductible does not result in a whole-dollar premium, round up if 50¢ or more; round down if less. Always submit gross premium.

## CONDO RATING EXAMPLE 9

## PRE-FIRM, HIGH-RISE, ENCLOSURE, MAXIMUM DEDUCTIBLE DISCOUNT, COINSURANCE PENALTY, ZONE AE

**REGULAR PROGRAM:**

- Building Coverage: $4,000,000
- Contents Coverage: $100,000
- Condominium Type: High-rise
- Flood Zone: AE
- Occupancy: Other Residential
- Number of Units: 200
- Date of Construction: Pre-FIRM
- Building Type: 3 or More Floors, Including Enclosure
- Deductible: $3,000/$3,000
- Deductible Factor: .980 (Maximum Total Discount of $111 applies)
- Replacement Cost: $18,000,000
- Elevation Difference: N/A
- 80% Coinsurance Amount: $14,400,000
- ICC Premium: $56 ($30,000 Coverage)
- CRS Rating: N/A
- CRS Discount: N/A
- Reserve Fund Assessment $3,671
- Probation Surcharge: N/A
- HFIAA Surcharge: RCBAP $250
- Federal Policy Fee $2,000

**DETERMINED RATES:**

Building: 1.56 / .412 Contents: 1.60 / 2.08

ESTIMATED BUILDING REPLACEMENT COST (INCLUDING FOUNDATION): $18,000,000 — DEDUCTIBLE: BUILDING $3,000 CONTENTS $3,000

| INSURANCE COVERAGE | TOTAL AMOUNT OF INSURANCE | BASIC LIMITS: AMOUNT OF INSURANCE | BASIC LIMITS: RATE | BASIC LIMITS: ANNUAL PREMIUM | ADDITIONAL LIMITS (REGULAR PROGRAM ONLY): AMOUNT OF INSURANCE | ADDITIONAL LIMITS: RATE | ADDITIONAL LIMITS: ANNUAL PREMIUM | DEDUCTIBLE: PREMIUM REDUCTION/ INCREASE | TOTAL PREMIUM |
|---|---|---|---|---|---|---|---|---|---|
| BUILDING | $4,000,000 | $175,000 | 1.56 | $2,730 | $3,825,000 | .412 | $15,759 | –$111 | $18,378 |
| CONTENTS | $100,000 | $25,000 | 1.60 | $400 | $75,000 | 2.08 | $1,560 | $0 | $1,960 |

RATE CATEGORY: ☐ MANUAL ☐ SUBMIT FOR RATE ☐ PROVISIONAL RATING

PAYMENT METHOD: ☐ CHECK ☐ CREDIT CARD ☐ OTHER: ________

| | |
|---|---|
| ANNUAL SUBTOTAL | $20,338 |
| ICC PREMIUM | $56 |
| SUBTOTAL | $20,394 |
| CRS PREMIUM DISCOUNT ___ % | $0 |
| SUBTOTAL | $20,394 |
| RESERVE FUND ___ % | $3,671 |
| SUBTOTAL | $24,065 |
| PROBATION SURCHARGE | $0 |
| HFIAA SURCHARGE | $250 |
| FEDERAL POLICY FEE | $2,000 |
| **TOTAL AMOUNT DUE** | **$26,315** |

**NOTICE:** BUILDING COVERAGE BENEFITS – EXCEPT FOR A RESIDENTIAL CONDOMINIUM BUILDING – ARE NOT AVAILABLE IF OTHER NFIP BUILDING COVERAGE HAS BEEN PURCHASED BY THE APPLICANT OR ANY OTHER PARTY FOR THE SAME BUILDING.

THE ABOVE STATEMENTS ARE CORRECT TO THE BEST OF MY KNOWLEDGE. I UNDERSTAND THAT ANY FALSE STATEMENTS MAY BE PUNISHABLE BY FINE AND/OR IMPRISONMENT UNDER APPLICABLE FEDERAL LAW. SEE REVERSE SIDE OF COPIES.

SIGNATURE OF INSURANCE AGENT/PRODUCER ________ DATE (MM/DD/YYYY) ___/___/___

SIGNATURE OF INSURED (OPTIONAL) ________ DATE (MM/DD/YYYY) ___/___/___

**PREMIUM CALCULATION:**

1. Multiply Rate × $100 of Coverage: Building: $18,489 / Contents: $1,960
2. Apply Deductible Factor: Building: .980 × $18,489 = $18,378 / Maximum Total Discount of $111 applies
3. Premium Reduction: Building: $18,489 – $18,378 = $111 / Contents: $0
4. Annual Subtotal: $20,338
5. Add ICC Premium: $56
6. Subtotal: $20,394
7. Subtract CRS Discount: $0
8. Subtotal: $20,394
9. Add Reserve Fund Assessment: $3,671 (18%)
10. Subtotal: $24,065
11. Add Probation Surcharge: N/A
12. Add HFIAA Surcharge: $250
13. Add Federal Policy Fee: $2,000
14. **Total Amount Due: $26,315**

**CLAIMS ADJUSTMENT WITH COINSURANCE PROVISION:**

Claim Payment is determined as follows:

$$\frac{\text{(Insurance Carried) } \$4{,}000{,}000}{\text{(Insurance Required) } \$14{,}400{,}000} \times \text{(Amount of Loss) } \$1{,}000{,}000 = \text{(Limit of Recovery) } \$277{,}778 - \text{Less Deductible}$$

(Coinsurance Penalty applies because minimum insurance amount of $14,400,000 was not met.)

# 4. How to Endorse

## I. General Information

An endorsement is a change or correction to an existing NFIP policy.

The General Change Endorsement form cannot be used to:

- Renew a policy;
- Extend or change a policy year; *or*
- Change the effective date of the policy.

## II. Endorsement Process

Agents must submit a General Change Endorsement form or a similar request to the insurer to endorse a policy. A copy of the form is located in Appendix B.

Examples of premium-bearing endorsements:

- Increasing, adding, reducing, or removing coverage amounts.
- Changing a building description.
- Adjusting rates.
- Revising maps.
- Correcting a misrated policy.
- Changing Primary Residence status.

Examples of non-premium endorsements:

- Changing a mortgagee.
- Changing the mailing address.
- Changing insured information.
- Changing the agent of record.
- Assigning the policy.

## III. Changing the Amount of Coverage

### A. Adding or Increasing Coverage

Insureds may add or increase coverage on their policy any time during the policy term. Insurers must calculate the additional premium pro rata using the rates in effect as of the policy effective date for the balance of the policy term or the rate in effect as of the endorsement effective date, in accordance with each insurer's standard business practice. Insurers must receive the full additional premium prior to processing endorsements to add or increase coverage.

#### *1. Waiting Periods*

The NFIP applies a 30-day waiting period, a 1-day waiting period, or no waiting period for endorsements that add or increase coverage, depending on the circumstances of the endorsement as described in III.A.1a, b, and c.

Waiting period determinations may differ for submissions sent via certified mail. The term certified mail extends to certified mail sent via the U.S. Postal

Service or reputable third-party delivery services that provide proof of the actual mailing and delivery date to the insurer.

The insurer may not use the receipt date of an invalid payment to determine the effective date of a policy transaction (endorsement).

A payment is invalid if there are non-sufficient funds (NSF) in the account, a successfully completed reversal (dispute) of an electronic payment, or the payment is non-negotiable for any other reason.

Upon notification that the payment is invalid, the insurer must:

- Cancel/nullify the transaction associated with that payment; *and*
- Send notification of the cancellation/nullification to the insured, agent, and lender(s), if applicable.

If the insurer receives a new payment, the insurer must process the transaction based on the new premium receipt date. The insurer must determine the effective date of the transaction based on the new payment receipt date, subject to the effective date rules.

**Note:** A new endorsement request is not required for this transaction as long as the insurer still has the original request.

### a. 30-Day Waiting Period

A 30-day waiting period applies to endorsements that add or increase coverage not associated with a loan transaction (i.e., making, extending, increasing, or renewing a loan).

**Table 1** shows how to determine the effective date of an endorsement with a 30-day waiting period.

**Table 1. Endorsement Effective Date with a 30-day Waiting Period**

| RECEIPT DATE | EFFECTIVE DATE |
|---|---|
| If the insurer receives the endorsement and payment ***within*** 10 calendar days from the endorsement request date (endorsement request date plus 9 days). | The effective date will be 12:01 a.m. (local time) on the 30th calendar day after the **endorsement request date** |
| If the endorsement request and payment are mailed by certified mail ***within*** 4 calendar days from the endorsement request date (endorsement request date plus 3 days) regardless of when the insurer receives them. | The effective date will be 12:01 a.m. (local time) on the 30th calendar day after the **endorsement request date** |
| If the insurer receives the endorsement request and payment ***after*** 10 or more calendar days from the endorsement request date (endorsement request date plus 9 days) and the endorsement request and payment were **NOT** mailed by certified mail within 4 calendar days from the endorsement request date (endorsement request date plus 3 days). | The effective date will be 12:01 a.m. (local time) on the 30th calendar day after the **insurer's receipt date** |

### b. 1-Day Waiting Period

A 1-day waiting period applies when the NFIP revises a Flood Hazard Boundary Map (FHBM) or a Flood Insurance Rate Map (FIRM) showing that the building is now in the Special Flood Hazard Area (SFHA) where it was not previously. To qualify for the 1-day waiting period, the insurer must receive the endorsement request and payment within 13 months from the effective date of the map revision. If the insurer receives the endorsement request and payment after 13 months from the effective date of the map revision, the 30-day waiting period applies. The 1-day waiting period rule applies for all buildings, including those owned by condominium associations.

**Table 2** shows how to determine the effective date of an endorsement with a 1-day waiting period.

### Table 2. Endorsement Effective Date with a 1-day Waiting Period

| RECEIPT DATE | EFFECTIVE DATE |
| --- | --- |
| The insurer receives the endorsement and payment ***within*** 10 calendar days from the endorsement request date (endorsement request date plus 9 days). | The effective date will be 12:01 a.m. (local time) on the next calendar day after the **endorsement request date**. |
| If the endorsement request and payment are mailed by certified mail ***within*** 4 calendar days from the endorsement request date (endorsement request date plus 3 days) regardless of when the insurer receives them. | The effective date will be 12:01 a.m. (local time) on the next calendar day after the **endorsement request date**. |
| If the insurer receives the endorsement request and payment ***after*** 10 or more calendar days from the endorsement request date (endorsement request date plus 9 days) and the endorsement request and payment were **NOT** mailed by certified mail within 4 calendar days from the endorsement request date (endorsement request date plus 3 days). | The effective date will be 12:01 a.m. (local time) on the next calendar day after the **insurer's receipt date**. |

#### c. No Waiting Period

No waiting period applies to endorsements purchased when making, extending, increasing, or renewing a loan with a federally regulated lender. This includes condominium association endorsements purchased in conjunction with loan transactions in the name of the condominium association.

The insured must request the flood insurance endorsement prior to the closing of the loan transaction. **The 30-day waiting period applies when the insured requests the endorsement after the loan closing.** A valid endorsement request includes all the information necessary to calculate the NFIP policy premium.

The insurer may rely on an agent's representation on the endorsement that there is no waiting period. The insurer must obtain documentation of the loan transaction (such as settlement papers) to validate no waiting period before paying the loss if a loss occurs during the first 30 days of the change in coverage.

**Table 3. Endorsement Effective Date with No Waiting Period**

| RECEIPT DATE | EFFECTIVE DATE |
|---|---|
| **If the lender, title company or settlement attorney pays the premium** | |
| If the insured requests the endorsement on or before the loan transaction closing, and the insurer receives the endorsement request and payment ***within*** 30 calendar days from the closing (closing date plus 29 days). | The effective date will be on the date of the loan closing. |
| If the insured requests the endorsement on or before the loan transaction closing, and the insurer receives the endorsement request and payment ***after*** 30 or more calendar days from the closing (closing date plus 29 days). | The effective date will be on the **insurer's receipt date**. |
| **If the insured or other party not listed above pays the premium** | |
| If the insured requests the endorsement on or before the loan transaction closing, and the insurer receives the endorsement request and payment ***within*** 10 calendar days from the loan closing (closing date plus 9 days). | The effective date will be on the date of the loan closing. |
| If the insured requests the endorsement on or before the loan transaction closing, and the insurer receives the endorsement and payment ***after*** 10 or more calendar days from the closing (closing date plus 9 days). | The effective date will be on the **insurer's receipt date**. |

## B. Reducing Coverage

### *1. Reduction in Building Coverage*

Insureds may only reduce building coverage to align the coverage amount with the current replacement cost of the insured building or due to the removal of a portion of the building. The effective date of the endorsement cannot be earlier than the day after the occurrence causing the request to reduce coverage. Insurers may not accept a reduction in building coverage endorsement without a valid explanation. For example, a valid explanation would be, "A wing of a building damaged by fire and the building is repaired without the wing."

### *2. Reduction in Contents Coverage*

Insureds may reduce contents coverage only when they sell or remove a portion of the contents, reducing the contents' value to less than the amount insured. Insurers may not accept a contents coverage reduction endorsement without a valid explanation. For example, a valid explanation would be, "Insured moved out of house and a limited amount of insured contents remain at the described location."

## C. Removing Coverage

Insurers may only remove coverage upon the insured's request in the following instances:

- The building or contents are no longer at the described location;

- The insured no longer owns the property;
- There is more than one NFIP policy with building coverage insuring the same building; *or*
- Building coverage may be removed while retaining contents coverage for a policy insuring a condominium unit only if there is a Residential Condominium Building Association Policy (RCBAP) in force.

## IV. Rating Endorsements

Insurers should use the current rate tables as of the effective date of a policy or the rate in effect as of the endorsement effective date, in accordance with each insurer's standard business practice to determine the revised premium for coverage changes (i.e., premium-bearing endorsements). Insurers may refund premiums where an endorsement to a policy results in a lowered premium. Insurers may not process refunds for canceled or inactive policies.

### A. Rate Decreases

Insurers may not revise a policy's premium to account for rate decreases during a policy term. Insurers may adjust premium to account for a rate decrease at renewal if the rate table is in effect as of the effective date of the policy renewal.

### B. Rating Adjustment

**Table 4** shows how to determine the endorsement effective date when applying a rating adjustment in various situations.

**Table 4. Endorsement Effective Dates for Current Term Rating Adjustments**

| RATING ADJUSTMENT | ENDORSEMENT EFFECTIVE DATE |
|---|---|
| Use of the grandfathering rating procedure for a policy previously not eligible for grandfathering. | The effective date of the current policy term. |
| Use of FEMA Special Rates (refer to the How to Write section). | The date FEMA provided the rates to the insurer. |
| Revision of alternative rates (rates used for Pre-FIRM-rated risks where the zone is unknown). | The effective date of the current policy term. |
| Use of an Elevation Certificate (EC) for Post-FIRM/full-risk rating for a Pre-FIRM building. | The effective date of the current policy term. The insurer applies the valid EC and issues a refund if the rates are more favorable. |
| Use of an EC on Post-FIRM buildings rated using "Without Certification of Compliance or Elevation Certificate" for zones AO and AH, or "No Elevation Certificate or No BFE" for Unnumbered A Zone. | The effective date of the current policy term. |
| Use of an updated EC. | The effective date of the current policy term. |

### C. Revision of an Alternative Rating

Insurers may endorse an active policy to reflect the premium based on the known flood zone for a policy rated using alternative rates (when the flood zone was unknown). The endorsement effective date is the effective date of the current policy term.

**Alternative Rating**

Insurers must rate policies using Alternative Rating when all of the following conditions apply:

- The building is Pre-FIRM;
- The FIRM flood zone is unknown; *and*
- The building is in a community that has no V Zones.

Insurers can use Alternative Rating for renewal policies in communities that convert from the Emergency Program to the Regular Program when the listed conditions apply.

## D. Map Revision

The insurer may endorse a policy to revise the flood zone or Base Flood Elevation (BFE) when FEMA issues a revised FIRM, Letter of Map Amendment (LOMA), or Letter of Map Revision (LOMR).

The insurer must receive the endorsement request during the policy period; otherwise, no refund is available. Refer to **Table 5** for guidance on the endorsement effective date.

Prior to submitting an endorsement request, an agent must:

- Verify the consistency of the elevation datum on the revised FIRM and the EC used to determine the building elevations.
- Use the Flood Map Status Information Service to verify the LOMA/LOMR applies to the most recent map revision.

**NOTE**

If a LOMA/LOMR results in a less beneficial rate for a policy, it may be eligible for grandfathering. See the heading Eligibility for Grandfathered Rating in the How to Write section.

**Table 5. Endorsement Effective Dates for Map Revisions**

| DATE OF MAP REVISION OR AMENDMENT | ENDORSEMENT EFFECTIVE DATE |
| --- | --- |
| Revision or amendment became effective during the current policy term. | Use the map revision or LOMA/LOMR date as the endorsement effective date. |
| Revision or amendment became effective during a previous policy term. | Use the map revision or LOMA/LOMR date as the endorsement effective date, or up to 5 years from the current policy year to the date of the map revision or amendment, whichever date is later. |
| Revision effective during an expired policy term. | Use the map revision or LOMA/LOMR date as the endorsement effective date, or up to 5 years from the current policy year to the date of the map revision, whichever date is later. |

## E. Change in Program Status

Insurers must revise the policy rating to reflect the correct flood zone when a community converts from the Emergency Program to the Regular Program. No premium refund is allowed on premium previously paid.

### F. Change in Community Rating System (CRS) Status

If a community's CRS class changes or a given policy's eligibility for a CRS discount changes midway through a policy term, any resulting adjustment to the CRS discount applies only at the next policy renewal.

## V. Correcting a Misrated Policy

A misrated policy occurs when a policy premium is incorrect because one or more rating characteristics are incorrect.

Rating characteristics used to determine premium include items such as: loss history, building occupancy, building use, primary residency status, physical alteration of the building, replacement cost, community number, Lowest Floor Elevation (LFE) used for rating, flood zone, BFE, and the presence of enclosures, basements, or crawlspaces (including below-grade crawlspaces).

Examples of misrated policies may include but are not limited to:

- A Preferred Risk Policy (PRP) with more than one paid claim that exceeds $1,000 and renews as a PRP;
- A standard rated policy found to be eligible may be endorsed or rewritten to a PRP (please refer to Cancellation Reason Code 22 in How to Cancel);
- A policy rated based upon the incorrect building occupancy;
- The building's construction date is incorrect;
- The original EC data is mistyped or misinterpreted; *or*
- The information provided on the application proves to be incorrect by valid documentation.

If the insurer receives the endorsement request for an active policy, and:

- The event that triggered the misrating became effective during the current policy term, use the event date as the endorsement effective date.
- The event that triggered the misrating became effective during a previous policy term, use the event date as the endorsement effective date or up to 5 years from the current policy year to the date of misrating, whichever date is later.

Insurers must include any lapse in coverage when determining the number of years allowed for a premium refund due to a misrating occurrence. The insurer must provide proper documentation. The insurer must reimburse the NFIP for any endorsement-issued refunds exceeding the allowable amount.

Lapses in coverage do not extend the number of policy terms allowed for return premiums.

> **Misrating Does Not Include**
>
> **Map Revisions**
> Changes due to a revised flood map, LOMA, or LOMR do not cause misratings. Refer to the IV. D Map Revision section for rules related to map change endorsements.
>
> **Optional Post-FIRM Rates**
> Changes due to the use of optional Post-FIRM rates are not a misrating. For example, if an insured provides an EC to change the policy to the full-risk rate because it is less expensive than Pre-FIRM subsidized rates, the original policy was not misrated.

## VI. Changing Deductibles

Insurers can increase or decrease deductibles during the current policy term and must apply the appropriate premium surcharge or discount.

Increased Cost of Compliance (ICC) premium, however, is not eligible for deductible discounts or surcharges. Insurers must add the ICC premium after calculating the revised premium with the modified deductible.

### A. Deductible Increases

Insurers may increase deductibles during the current policy term. The earliest effective date of the increased deductible is the date the insurer receives the endorsement request.

### B. Deductible Decreases

Insurers may not decrease deductibles during the current policy term unless the property has a mortgage and the lender requires a lower deductible. The earliest effective date of the decreased deductible is:

- 30 days from the date the insurer receives the endorsement request; *or*
- The date the insurer receives the endorsement request if the lender requests the change in connection with making, increasing, extending, or renewing a loan.

## VII. Duplicate Coverage

The NFIP does not permit duplicate coverage. Insurers may issue one building coverage policy per building.

Only one building policy may remain in force where there is more than one policy with building coverage for the same building. The policy that remains in force must list all building owners as named insureds, and insurers must cancel or remove building coverage on all other policies for that building.

**Condominium Coverage**

Insurers may issue more than one building coverage policy for the same building for condominium association and condominium unit owners. Condominium units, however, shall not receive duplicate coverage or coverage that exceeds the program maximum limits.

Insurers must specify the individual unit insured in the property description for all unit policies.

If an insurer determines that the insured(s) did not knowingly create a duplicate policy, the insurer must provide written notice to the insured(s) of duplicate coverage.

The notice must advise the insured(s) of their options to:

- Keep the policy with the **earlier effective date**. The insured may increase coverage up to the coverage limits of the policy with a later effective date. The endorsement effective date for increased coverage is the effective date of the later policy.
- Keep the policy with the **later effective date**. The insured may increase coverage up to the coverage limits of the policy with an earlier effective date. The endorsement effective date for increased coverage is the effective date of the later policy.

The insurer may endorse the policy to remove duplicate building coverage for up to 5 years. Refer to the How to Cancel section of this manual for further guidance on canceling a duplicate policy.

## VIII. Property Address Corrections

Insurers may endorse a policy to correct a property address without FEMA approval but may not insure a different building at the same or another location. If this occurs, the insurer must include documentation substantiating this change in the underwriting file. Examples include a typographical error correction, a specific unit number addition, or a U.S. Postal Service address revision. Insureds must purchase a new policy for each additional building identified, and each building must carry insurance.

If a claim is pending, the insurer must obtain authorization from FEMA prior to correcting the address and making a claim payment. The waiver must indicate that the:

- Building description, coverage, and rating elements belong to the building at the address indicated on the correction endorsement; *and*
- Insured has no insurable interest in the building at the incorrect address.

**US Postal Service address revision (911)**

An insurer may endorse a policy to correct a property address due to a US Postal Service address revision (911) without FEMA approval. If this occurs, the insurer must include documentation substantiating the change in the underwriting file.

Insurers may not endorse or transfer a flood policy to change the insured building, location, or unit. Examples include relocating to a different unit within the same building, or moving a mobile home/travel trailer to a new location.

## IX. Assignment of a Policy

Insureds may assign policies for insured buildings due to transfers of ownership. Insureds may not assign policies that cover buildings in the course of construction or for contents only. The seller must sign the endorsement assigning the policy on or before the closing date. The insurer must receive the seller's signature and documentation authorizing the assignment.

### A. Assignment with Building Purchase

The owner/seller of an insured building may assign the flood policy to the purchaser of the insured building. The assignment becomes effective on the date of the ownership transfer.

### B. Assignment without Building Purchase

The owner of an insured building may assign the flood policy to the new building owner effective on the date of the ownership transfer. Examples include inheritance, gifting, divorce, estate, trust, or foreclosure.

## X. Endorsement Processing Prior to Renewal

### A. During the Last 90 Days of Policy Term

- The insurer will issue a revised Renewal Notice if the insurer has not processed the renewal premium payment, and the agent submits a General Change Endorsement.
- The payor may pay the premium for the revised Renewal Notice if the insurer has not received the premium for the original Renewal Notice.

### B. During the Last 75 Days of Policy Term

When the payor ***has not*** paid the original Renewal Notice premium, the agent must submit:

- A General Change Endorsement for the current policy term.
- An upcoming policy term Renewal Application.

The payor must submit a separate premium payment for each transaction. The agent must advise the payor not to pay the original Renewal Notice or related Final Notice if the agent has already submitted a Renewal Application with premium.

If the payor ***has*** paid the premium for the original Renewal Notice, the agent must:

- Submit the General Change Endorsement and the required additional premium for the renewal policy term.
- Submit a separate General Change Endorsement and the required additional premium for the remainder of the current policy term, if applicable.

The endorsement to increase coverage (up to the inflation factor) will be effective as of the renewal date only when the insurer receives the endorsement and additional premium within the 30-day grace period.

### C. Return Premium Generated from Endorsement Processing

The insurer will calculate return premium using rates in effect on the effective date of the change or the policy effective date in accordance with each insurer's standard business practice. Revise the rate effective from the inception date of the current policy term, provided the inception date is on or after the endorsement date.

The Federal Policy Fee and Probation Surcharge (if applicable) are not subject to calculation of return premiums.

## XI. Completing the General Change Endorsement Form

The agent/insured must provide the policy number, the reason for change, and the endorsement effective date. The agent must only complete the remaining sections associated with the change.

Insurers may accept electronic endorsement submissions. Insurers must determine the business practices and transaction authentication methods they will use to ensure the security and integrity of such transactions.

A signature is required for all endorsements. The insurer must receive a dated General Change Endorsement form or similar document, signed by the insured, whenever there is a request to reduce policy limits, increase the deductible, assign the policy, or change the agent of record.

## XII. Return Premium Processing Procedures

### A. Insurer Processing

Insurers must process the return premium on policy terms for which they are the insurer of record.

## B. Prior Term Refund Processing

Agents must contact the insurer to determine the handling of return premiums that cover more than 2 years. Some insurers may choose to process return premium requests that cover more than 2 years; other insurers may submit the request and documentation to FEMA for processing. The documentation must include the following:

- The insurer's statistical records or declarations pages for each policy term with evidence of premium payments.
- An endorsement request for each policy term and the premium refund calculation for each insurer policy term.
- For a LOMA, LOMR, or Letter of Determination Review (LODR):
  - A copy of the most recent flood map marked showing the exact location and flood zone of the building.
  - Letter signed and dated by a local community official indicating the exact location and flood zone of the building.
  - EC signed and dated by a surveyor, an engineer, an architect, or a local community official indicating the exact location and flood zone of the building.
  - Flood zone determination certification guaranteeing the accuracy of the information.

Insurers may send requests and documentation to the FEMA by emailing NFIPUnderwritingMailbox@fema.dhs.gov.

FEMA will notify insurers of the premium refunded and the Expense Allowance due to the NFIP. The insurers must maintain this documentation as part of their underwriting files. FEMA will return rejected refund requests.

# XIII. Endorsement Rating Examples

**TABLE OF CONTENTS**


| EXAMPLE | PAGE |
| --- | --- |
| Example 1: Increasing Coverage on a Preferred Risk Policy | 4-12 |
| Example 2: Increasing Coverage | 4-13 |
| Example 3: Increasing Coverage After a Rate Change | 4-14 |
| Example 4: Reducing Building Coverage | 4-15 |
| Example 5: Change of Primary Residence Status | 4-16 |

**ENDORSEMENT EXAMPLE 1**
**INCREASING COVERAGE ON A PREFERRED RISK POLICY**

- Policy term is August 12, 2021–2022
- Single Family with basement.
- Property Currently Mapped in Zone X.
- Present coverage: Building $75,000/ Contents $30,000.
- Adjusted Premium at policy effective date was $394. Adjusted Premium includes the multiplier calculation.
- Endorsement effective date is November 11, 2021.
- Coverages added are $125,000 on the building and $50,000 on the contents for a total of $200,000 on the building and $80,000 on the contents for a total adjusted premium of $543.
- Rates in effect on the effective date of the policy are to be used in calculating the premiums.
- Add the ICC Premium and calculate the New Premium Subtotal.
- Add the Reserve Fund Amount and calculate the New Premium Subtotal.
- The Premium Previously Paid is $394 (excluding Probation Surcharge/HFIAA Surcharge/Federal Policy Fee), which is the total current annual premium including ICC Premium and Reserve Fund Assessment.
- Subtract the Premium Previously Paid from the Premium Total to obtain the Difference (should be additional/return premium).
- The difference between these 2 premiums is $149.
- Prorate the Difference.

  Time period is November 11, 2021, to August 12, 2022;
  Number of days is 274;
  Pro-rata factor is .751

TO INCREASE/DECREASE COVERAGE, COMPLETE SECTIONS A & B. FOR RATE CHANGE, COMPLETE SECTION A ONLY.

INDICATE THE RATE TABLE USED: ____________ RISK RATING METHOD: ☐ 7 - PRP ☐ R - NEWLY MAPPED

| INSURANCE COVERAGE | SECTION A - CURRENT LIMITS | | | SECTION B - NEW LIMITS | | | A + B PREMIUM |
|---|---|---|---|---|---|---|---|
| | AMOUNT | RATE | PREMIUM | AMOUNT | RATE | PREMIUM | |
| BUILDING BASIC LIMIT | — | — | — | — | — | — | — |
| BUILDING ADDITIONAL LIMIT | — | — | — | — | — | — | — |
| CONTENTS BASIC LIMIT | — | — | — | — | — | — | — |
| CONTENTS ADDITIONAL LIMIT | — | — | — | — | — | — | — |
| FOR PRP AND NEWLY MAPPED ONLY, ENTER LIMITS FROM THE *NFIP FLOOD INSURANCE MANUAL* | BUILDING | CONTENTS | PREMIUM | BUILDING | CONTENTS | PREMIUM | |
| | $75,000 | $30,000 | $326 | $125,000 | $50,000 | $452 | $452 |

**IF CHANGING AMOUNT OF INSURANCE, ENTER NEW TOTAL AMOUNT BELOW**

| BUILDING COVERAGE | | | CONTENTS COVERAGE | | |
|---|---|---|---|---|---|
| BASIC | ADDITIONAL | TOTAL | BASIC | ADDITIONAL | TOTAL |
| — | — | $200,000 | — | — | $80,000 |

**IF RETURN PREMIUM, MAIL REFUND TO:** ☐ **INSURED** ☐ **AGENT/PRODUCER** ☐ **PAYOR**

**PAYMENT METHOD:** ☐ CHECK ☐ CREDIT CARD ☐ OTHER: ________

| | |
|---|---|
| SUBTOTAL | $452 |
| DEDUCTIBLE DISCOUNT/SURCHARGE | — |
| SUBTOTAL | $452 |
| ICC PREMIUM | $8 |
| SUBTOTAL | $460 |
| CRS PREMIUM DISCOUNT ___ % | — |
| SUBTOTAL | $460 |
| RESERVE FUND 18 % | $83 |
| SUBTOTAL | $543 |
| PREMIUM PREVIOUSLY PAID (Excludes Probation Surcharge/Federal Policy Fee) | $394 |
| HFIAA SURCHARGE | — |
| DIFFERENCE ________ (+/-) | $149 |
| PRO-RATA FACTOR | .751 |
| **TOTAL AMOUNT DUE** (+/-) | **$112** |

**NOTICE:** BUILDING COVERAGE BENEFITS – EXCEPT FOR A RESIDENTIAL CONDOMINIUM BUILDING – ARE NOT AVAILABLE IF OTHER NFIP BUILDING COVERAGE HAS BEEN PURCHASED BY THE APPLICANT OR ANY OTHER PARTY FOR THE SAME BUILDING.

THE ABOVE STATEMENTS ARE CORRECT TO THE BEST OF MY KNOWLEDGE. I UNDERSTAND THAT ANY FALSE STATEMENTS MAY BE PUNISHABLE BY FINE AND/OR IMPRISONMENT UNDER APPLICABLE FEDERAL LAW. SEE REVERSE SIDE OF COPIES.

______________________________ ____/____/____
SIGNATURE OF INSURANCE AGENT/PRODUCER DATE (MM/DD/YYYY)

______________________________ ____/____/____
SIGNATURE OF INSURED (IF APPLICABLE) DATE (MM/DD/YYYY)

______________________________ ____/____/____
SIGNATURE OF ASSIGNEE (FOR ASSIGNMENT ONLY) DATE (MM/DD/YYYY)

## ENDORSEMENT EXAMPLE 2
## INCREASING COVERAGE

- Policy term is April 4, 2021–2022.
- Single-family dwelling, no basement.
- Pre-FIRM Building.
- Building located in Zone C.
- Present coverage: Building $35,000 / Contents $10,000.
- Endorsement is effective on October 10, 2021, to add additional coverage of $65,000 on the building and $15,000 on the contents for a total of $100,000 building coverage and $25,000 contents coverage.
- Premium rates are: Building 1.12 / .32, Contents 1.73 / .55.
- To increase coverage, complete Sections A and B. Section A is for current coverage. Section B should show the amount of the coverage increase only.
- $25,000 of the $60,000 coverage and the $40,000 additional coverage to be added on the building must be calculated in the "Amount" column under Section B, "Increased/Decreased Coverage Only" (using the applicable rate) to amend the present coverage to the threshold for the Regular Program basic limits.
- $10,000 of the $15,000 coverage to be added on the contents must be calculated under the "Amount" column under Section B, "Increased/Decreased Coverage Only" (using the applicable rate) to amend the present coverage to the threshold for the Regular Program basic limits.
- Add Section A and B premiums to obtain the New Premium Totals.
- Add the New Premium Totals to calculate the Premium Subtotal.
- Add the ICC Premium and calculate the New Premium Subtotal.
- Add the Reserve Fund Amount and calculate the New Premium Subtotal.
- The Premium Previously Paid is $673 (excluding Probation Surcharge/HFIAA Surcharge/Federal Policy Fee), which is the total current annual premium including ICC Premium and Reserve Fund Assessment.
- Subtract the Premium Previously Paid from the Premium Total to obtain the Difference (should be additional/return premium).
- Prorate the Difference.

  Time period is October 10, 2021, to April 4, 2022;
  Number of days is 176;
  Pro-rata factor is .482

TO INCREASE/DECREASE COVERAGE, COMPLETE SECTIONS A & B. FOR RATE CHANGE, COMPLETE SECTION A ONLY.

INDICATE THE RATE TABLE USED: ______ RISK RATING METHOD: ☐ 7 - PRP ☐ R - NEWLY MAPPED

| INSURANCE COVERAGE | SECTION A – CURRENT LIMITS | | | SECTION B – NEW LIMITS | | | A + B PREMIUM |
|---|---|---|---|---|---|---|---|
| | AMOUNT | RATE | PREMIUM | AMOUNT | RATE | PREMIUM | |
| BUILDING BASIC LIMIT | $35,000 | 1.12 | $392 | $25,000 | 1.12 | $280 | $672 |
| BUILDING ADDITIONAL LIMIT | — | — | — | $40,000 | .32 | $128 | $128 |
| CONTENTS BASIC LIMIT | $10,000 | 1.73 | $173 | $15,000 | 1.73 | $260 | $433 |
| CONTENTS ADDITIONAL LIMIT | — | — | — | — | — | — | — |
| FOR PRP AND NEWLY MAPPED ONLY, ENTER LIMITS FROM THE *NFIP FLOOD INSURANCE MANUAL* | BUILDING | CONTENTS | PREMIUM | BUILDING | CONTENTS | PREMIUM | |
| | — | — | — | — | — | — | — |

| IF CHANGING AMOUNT OF INSURANCE, ENTER NEW TOTAL AMOUNT BELOW | | | | | |
|---|---|---|---|---|---|
| BUILDING COVERAGE | | | CONTENTS COVERAGE | | |
| BASIC | ADDITIONAL | TOTAL | BASIC | ADDITIONAL | TOTAL |
| $60,000 | $40,000 | $100,000 | $25,000 | — | $25,000 |

IF RETURN PREMIUM, MAIL REFUND TO: ☐ INSURED ☐ AGENT/PRODUCER ☐ PAYOR

PAYMENT METHOD: ☐ CHECK ☐ CREDIT CARD ☐ OTHER: ______

| | |
|---|---|
| SUBTOTAL | $1,233 |
| DEDUCTIBLE DISCOUNT/SURCHARGE | — |
| SUBTOTAL | $1,233 |
| ICC PREMIUM | $8 |
| SUBTOTAL | $1,241 |
| CRS PREMIUM DISCOUNT ___ % | — |
| SUBTOTAL | $1,241 |
| RESERVE FUND 18 % | $223 |
| SUBTOTAL | $1,464 |
| PREMIUM PREVIOUSLY PAID (Excludes Probation Surcharge/Federal Policy Fee) | $673 |
| HFIAA SURCHARGE | — |
| DIFFERENCE ______ (+/-) | $791 |
| PRO-RATA FACTOR | .482 |
| **TOTAL AMOUNT DUE** (+/-) | $381 |

**NOTICE:** BUILDING COVERAGE BENEFITS – EXCEPT FOR A RESIDENTIAL CONDOMINIUM BUILDING – ARE NOT AVAILABLE IF OTHER NFIP BUILDING COVERAGE HAS BEEN PURCHASED BY THE APPLICANT OR ANY OTHER PARTY FOR THE SAME BUILDING.

THE ABOVE STATEMENTS ARE CORRECT TO THE BEST OF MY KNOWLEDGE. I UNDERSTAND THAT ANY FALSE STATEMENTS MAY BE PUNISHABLE BY FINE AND/OR IMPRISONMENT UNDER APPLICABLE FEDERAL LAW. SEE REVERSE SIDE OF COPIES.

______________________ SIGNATURE OF INSURANCE AGENT/PRODUCER ____/____/____ DATE (MM/DD/YYYY)

______________________ SIGNATURE OF INSURED (IF APPLICABLE) ____/____/____ DATE (MM/DD/YYYY)

______________________ SIGNATURE OF ASSIGNEE (FOR ASSIGNMENT ONLY) ____/____/____ DATE (MM/DD/YYYY)

## ENDORSEMENT EXAMPLE 3
## INCREASING COVERAGE AFTER A RATE CHANGE

- Policy term is March 12, 2021–2022.
- Single-family dwelling, Regular Program.
- 1 floor, no basement.
- Current policy limits: Building $30,000 / Contents $8,000.
- Building located in an AE Zone, Post-FIRM.
- Premium rates are: Building 2.25, Contents 1.03. **Note:** The rates used are the rates in effect on the policy effective date.
- Post-FIRM construction with a 0 elevation difference.
- Endorsement effective date is May 9, 2021.
- The coverages being added are $15,000 on the building and $7,000 on contents for a total of $45,000 building coverage and $15,000 contents coverage.
- A rate increase takes effect on April 1, 2021.
- Rates in effect on the effective date of the policy are to be used.
- In Section A, enter the basic limits and rates for building and contents in effect at the beginning of the policy term.
- In Section B, enter the $15,000 basic building amount, and the applicable rate (2.25). (See page END 1, "Addition of Coverage or Increase in Amount of Insurance." Companies are allowed to use either rates in effect at policy inception or rates in effect at endorsement effective date.)
- In Section B, enter the $7,000 basic contents amount and the applicable rate (1.03).
- Add Sections A and B premiums to obtain the New Premium Totals.
- Add the New Premium Totals to calculate the Premium Subtotal.
- Add in the ICC Premium and calculate the New Premium Subtotal.
- Add the Reserve Fund Amount and calculate the New Premium Subtotal.
- The Premium Previously Paid is $858 (excluding Probation Surcharge/HFIAA Surcharge/Federal Policy Fee), which is the total current annual premium including ICC Premium and Reserve Fund Assessment.
- Subtract the Premium Previously Paid from the Premium Total to obtain the Difference (should be additional/return premium).
- Prorate the Difference.

  Time period is May 9, 2021, to March 12, 2022;
  Number of days is 307;
  Pro-rata factor is .841

TO INCREASE/DECREASE COVERAGE, COMPLETE SECTIONS A & B. FOR RATE CHANGE, COMPLETE SECTION A ONLY.

INDICATE THE RATE TABLE USED: ______________ RISK RATING METHOD: ☐ 7 - PRP ☐ R - NEWLY MAPPED

| INSURANCE COVERAGE | SECTION A - CURRENT LIMITS | | | SECTION B - NEW LIMITS | | | A + B PREMIUM |
|---|---|---|---|---|---|---|---|
| | AMOUNT | RATE | PREMIUM | AMOUNT | RATE | PREMIUM | |
| BUILDING BASIC LIMIT | $30,000 | 2.25 | $675 | $15,000 | 2.25 | $338 | $1,013 |
| BUILDING ADDITIONAL LIMIT | — | — | — | — | — | — | — |
| CONTENTS BASIC LIMIT | $8,000 | 1.03 | $82 | $7,000 | 1.03 | $72 | $154 |
| CONTENTS ADDITIONAL LIMIT | — | — | — | — | — | — | — |
| FOR PRP AND NEWLY MAPPED ONLY, ENTER LIMITS FROM THE *NFIP FLOOD INSURANCE MANUAL* | BUILDING | CONTENTS | PREMIUM | BUILDING | CONTENTS | PREMIUM | |
| | — | — | — | — | — | — | — |

IF CHANGING AMOUNT OF INSURANCE, ENTER NEW TOTAL AMOUNT BELOW

| BUILDING COVERAGE | | | CONTENTS COVERAGE | | |
|---|---|---|---|---|---|
| BASIC | ADDITIONAL | TOTAL | BASIC | ADDITIONAL | TOTAL |
| $45,000 | — | $45,000 | $15,000 | — | $15,000 |

IF RETURN PREMIUM, MAIL REFUND TO: ☐ INSURED ☐ AGENT/PRODUCER ☐ PAYOR

PAYMENT METHOD: ☐ CHECK ☐ CREDIT CARD ☐ OTHER: ______

| | |
|---|---|
| SUBTOTAL | $1,167 |
| DEDUCTIBLE DISCOUNT/SURCHARGE | — |
| SUBTOTAL | $1,167 |
| ICC PREMIUM | $6 |
| SUBTOTAL | $1,173 |
| CRS PREMIUM DISCOUNT ___ % | — |
| SUBTOTAL | $1,173 |
| RESERVE FUND 18 % | $211 |
| SUBTOTAL | $1,384 |
| PREMIUM PREVIOUSLY PAID (Excludes Probation Surcharge/Federal Policy Fee) | $858 |
| HFIAA SURCHARGE | — |
| DIFFERENCE ________ (+/-) | $526 |
| PRO-RATA FACTOR | .841 |
| **TOTAL AMOUNT DUE** (+/-) | **$442** |

**NOTICE:** BUILDING COVERAGE BENEFITS – EXCEPT FOR A RESIDENTIAL CONDOMINIUM BUILDING – ARE NOT AVAILABLE IF OTHER NFIP BUILDING COVERAGE HAS BEEN PURCHASED BY THE APPLICANT OR ANY OTHER PARTY FOR THE SAME BUILDING.

THE ABOVE STATEMENTS ARE CORRECT TO THE BEST OF MY KNOWLEDGE. I UNDERSTAND THAT ANY FALSE STATEMENTS MAY BE PUNISHABLE BY FINE AND/OR IMPRISONMENT UNDER APPLICABLE FEDERAL LAW. SEE REVERSE SIDE OF COPIES.

________________________ SIGNATURE OF INSURANCE AGENT/PRODUCER ____/____/____ DATE (MM/DD/YYYY)

________________________ SIGNATURE OF INSURED (IF APPLICABLE) ____/____/____ DATE (MM/DD/YYYY)

________________________ SIGNATURE OF ASSIGNEE (FOR ASSIGNMENT ONLY) ____/____/____ DATE (MM/DD/YYYY)

## ENDORSEMENT EXAMPLE 4
## REDUCING BUILDING COVERAGE

- Policy term is June 6, 2021–2022.
- Single-family dwelling, with basement.
- Regular Program, Zone B, Post-FIRM.
- Policy limits: Building $150,000 / Contents $0.
- A wing of the building was destroyed by fire on December 10, 2021, and the building was repaired without the wing, reducing the value of the dwelling to $100,000. (This explanation should be recorded in the Reason for Change section of the General Change Endorsement form.)
- Present rates are: Building 1.25 / .44
- Endorsement effective date is December 10, 2021.
- In Section A, enter the basic building amount ($60,000) and the applicable rate (1.25).
- In Section B, enter the new additional building amount at the same rate of .44.
- Add Sections A and B to obtain the New Premium Totals.
- Add the New Premium Totals to obtain the Premium Subtotal.
- Add in the ICC Premium and calculate the New Premium Subtotal.
- Add the Reserve Fund Amount and calculate the New Premium Subtotal.
- The Premium Previously Paid is $1,362 (excluding the Probation Surcharge/HFIAA Surcharge/Federal Policy Fee), which is the total current annual premium including ICC Premium and Reserve Fund Assessment.
- Subtract the Premium Previously Paid from the Premium Total to obtain the Difference (should be additional/return premium).
- Prorate the Difference.

  Time period is December 10, 2021, to June 6, 2022;
  Number of days is 178;
  Pro-rata factor is .488

TO INCREASE/DECREASE COVERAGE, COMPLETE SECTIONS A & B. FOR RATE CHANGE, COMPLETE SECTION A ONLY.

INDICATE THE RATE TABLE USED: ____________ RISK RATING METHOD: ☐ 7 - PRP ☐ R - NEWLY MAPPED

| INSURANCE COVERAGE | SECTION A - CURRENT LIMITS | | | SECTION B - NEW LIMITS | | | A + B PREMIUM |
|---|---|---|---|---|---|---|---|
| | AMOUNT | RATE | PREMIUM | AMOUNT | RATE | PREMIUM | |
| BUILDING BASIC LIMIT | $60,000 | 1.25 | $750 | — | — | — | $750 |
| BUILDING ADDITIONAL LIMIT | $90,000 | .44 | $386 | –$50,000 | .44 | –$220 | $176 |
| CONTENTS BASIC LIMIT | — | — | — | — | — | — | — |
| CONTENTS ADDITIONAL LIMIT | — | — | — | — | — | — | — |
| FOR PRP AND NEWLY MAPPED ONLY, ENTER LIMITS FROM THE *NFIP FLOOD INSURANCE MANUAL* | BUILDING | CONTENTS | PREMIUM | BUILDING | CONTENTS | PREMIUM | |
| | — | — | — | — | — | — | — |

IF CHANGING AMOUNT OF INSURANCE, ENTER NEW TOTAL AMOUNT BELOW

| BUILDING COVERAGE | | | CONTENTS COVERAGE | | |
|---|---|---|---|---|---|
| BASIC | ADDITIONAL | TOTAL | BASIC | ADDITIONAL | TOTAL |
| $60,000 | $40,000 | $100,000 | — | — | — |

IF RETURN PREMIUM, MAIL REFUND TO: ☐ INSURED ☐ AGENT/PRODUCER ☐ PAYOR

PAYMENT METHOD: ☐ CHECK ☐ CREDIT CARD ☐ OTHER: ________

| | |
|---|---|
| SUBTOTAL | $926 |
| DEDUCTIBLE DISCOUNT/SURCHARGE | — |
| SUBTOTAL | $926 |
| ICC PREMIUM | $8 |
| SUBTOTAL | $934 |
| CRS PREMIUM DISCOUNT ____ % | — |
| SUBTOTAL | $934 |
| RESERVE FUND 18 % | $168 |
| SUBTOTAL | $1,102 |
| PREMIUM PREVIOUSLY PAID (Excludes Probation Surcharge/Federal Policy Fee) | $1,362 |
| HFIAA SURCHARGE | — |
| DIFFERENCE ________ (+/-) | –$260 |
| PRO-RATA FACTOR | .488 |
| **TOTAL AMOUNT DUE** (+/-) | **–$126** |

**NOTICE:** BUILDING COVERAGE BENEFITS – EXCEPT FOR A RESIDENTIAL CONDOMINIUM BUILDING – ARE NOT AVAILABLE IF OTHER NFIP BUILDING COVERAGE HAS BEEN PURCHASED BY THE APPLICANT OR ANY OTHER PARTY FOR THE SAME BUILDING.

THE ABOVE STATEMENTS ARE CORRECT TO THE BEST OF MY KNOWLEDGE. I UNDERSTAND THAT ANY FALSE STATEMENTS MAY BE PUNISHABLE BY FINE AND/OR IMPRISONMENT UNDER APPLICABLE FEDERAL LAW. SEE REVERSE SIDE OF COPIES.

________________________ ____/____/____
SIGNATURE OF INSURANCE AGENT/PRODUCER DATE (MM/DD/YYYY)

________________________ ____/____/____
SIGNATURE OF INSURED (IF APPLICABLE) DATE (MM/DD/YYYY)

________________________ ____/____/____
SIGNATURE OF ASSIGNEE (FOR ASSIGNMENT ONLY) DATE (MM/DD/YYYY)

## ENDORSEMENT EXAMPLE 5
## CHANGE OF PRIMARY RESIDENCE STATUS

- Policy term May 15, 2021–2022.
- Single-family dwelling, no basement.
- Post-FIRM construction with a +4 elevation difference.
- Building located in Zone AE
- Present coverage: Building $150,000 / Contents $15,000.
- Endorsement is effective on October 30, 2021, to change Residence status from Non-Primary to Primary.
- Full-risk premium rates are: Building .31 / .09, Contents .38 / .12
- Complete Section A for current coverage
- Add Section A premiums to obtain the New Premium Totals.
- Add the New Premium Totals to calculate the Premium Subtotal.
- Add the ICC Premium and calculate the New Premium Subtotal.
- Add the Reserve Fund Amount and calculate the New Premium Subtotal.
- The Premium Previously Paid is $642 (excluding Probation Surcharge/Federal Policy Fee), which is the total current annual premium including ICC Premium and Reserve Fund Assessment and HFIAA Surcharge.
- Enter the applicable HFIAA Surcharge Amount.
- Subtract the new HFIAA Surcharge of $25 from the previously paid HFIAA Surcharge of $250 and enter the difference.
- Prorate the Difference.

  Time period is October 30, 2021, to May 15, 2022;
  Number of days is 197;
  Pro-rata factor is .540

TO INCREASE/DECREASE COVERAGE, COMPLETE SECTIONS A & B. FOR RATE CHANGE, COMPLETE SECTION A ONLY.

INDICATE THE RATE TABLE USED: ____________ RISK RATING METHOD: ☐ 7 - PRP ☐ R - NEWLY MAPPED

| INSURANCE COVERAGE | SECTION A - CURRENT LIMITS | | | SECTION B - NEW LIMITS | | | A + B PREMIUM |
|---|---|---|---|---|---|---|---|
| | AMOUNT | RATE | PREMIUM | AMOUNT | RATE | PREMIUM | |
| BUILDING BASIC LIMIT | $60,000 | .31 | $186 | — | — | — | $186 |
| BUILDING ADDITIONAL LIMIT | $90,000 | .09 | $81 | — | — | — | $81 |
| CONTENTS BASIC LIMIT | $15,000 | .38 | $57 | — | — | — | $57 |
| CONTENTS ADDITIONAL LIMIT | — | — | — | — | — | — | — |
| FOR PRP AND NEWLY MAPPED ONLY, ENTER LIMITS FROM THE *NFIP FLOOD INSURANCE MANUAL* | BUILDING | CONTENTS | PREMIUM | BUILDING | CONTENTS | PREMIUM | |
| | — | — | — | — | — | — | — |

**IF CHANGING AMOUNT OF INSURANCE, ENTER NEW TOTAL AMOUNT BELOW**

| BUILDING COVERAGE | | | CONTENTS COVERAGE | | |
|---|---|---|---|---|---|
| BASIC | ADDITIONAL | TOTAL | BASIC | ADDITIONAL | TOTAL |
| — | — | — | — | — | — |

**IF RETURN PREMIUM, MAIL REFUND TO:** ☐ INSURED ☐ AGENT/PRODUCER ☐ PAYOR

PAYMENT METHOD: ☐ CHECK ☐ CREDIT CARD ☐ OTHER: ________

| | |
|---|---|
| SUBTOTAL | $324 |
| DEDUCTIBLE DISCOUNT/SURCHARGE | — |
| SUBTOTAL | $324 |
| ICC PREMIUM | $8 |
| SUBTOTAL | $332 |
| CRS PREMIUM DISCOUNT ___ % | — |
| SUBTOTAL | $332 |
| RESERVE FUND 18 % | $60 |
| SUBTOTAL | $392 |
| PREMIUM PREVIOUSLY PAID (Excludes Probation Surcharge/Federal Policy Fee) | $642 |
| HFIAA SURCHARGE | $25 |
| DIFFERENCE ________ (+/-) | –$225 |
| PRO-RATA FACTOR | .540 |
| **TOTAL AMOUNT DUE** (+/-) | **–$122** |

**NOTICE:** BUILDING COVERAGE BENEFITS – EXCEPT FOR A RESIDENTIAL CONDOMINIUM BUILDING – ARE NOT AVAILABLE IF OTHER NFIP BUILDING COVERAGE HAS BEEN PURCHASED BY THE APPLICANT OR ANY OTHER PARTY FOR THE SAME BUILDING.

THE ABOVE STATEMENTS ARE CORRECT TO THE BEST OF MY KNOWLEDGE. I UNDERSTAND THAT ANY FALSE STATEMENTS MAY BE PUNISHABLE BY FINE AND/OR IMPRISONMENT UNDER APPLICABLE FEDERAL LAW. SEE REVERSE SIDE OF COPIES.

| | |
|---|---|
| SIGNATURE OF INSURANCE AGENT/PRODUCER | ____/____/____ DATE (MM/DD/YYYY) |
| SIGNATURE OF INSURED (IF APPLICABLE) | ____/____/____ DATE (MM/DD/YYYY) |
| SIGNATURE OF ASSIGNEE (FOR ASSIGNMENT ONLY) | ____/____/____ DATE (MM/DD/YYYY) |

# 5. How to Renew

## I. General Information

- The Standard Flood Insurance Policy (SFIP) contract is for one year only.
- All policies expire at 12:01 a.m. on the last day of the one-year policy term.
- A new policy term and new contractual agreement between the insured and the insurer begins when an expiring policy renews.
- All policies renew using the rates in effect on the policy renewal effective date.
- The insurer must receive the premium in full to renew the policy at the coverage amount offered on the renewal bill.
- Paying the premium more than 30 days after the expiration date of the policy causes a lapse in coverage that may affect policy rating.
- All references to days are calendar days, not business days.

> **NOTE**
>
> **Severe Repetitive Loss (SRL) Properties**
>
> The NFIP Special Direct Facility, operated by NFIP Direct, processes the policy renewals for SRL properties. (Refer to Appendix I: SRL of this manual for more information.)

## II. Renewal Process

### A. Renewal Notice

The insurer must mail a Renewal Notice at least 45 days before the policy expires to the payor listed on the policy declarations page, using first-class mail. The insurer must also mail a copy of the Renewal Notice to all parties listed on the policy declarations page, stating "THIS IS NOT A BILL."

#### *1. Amounts of Insurance on the Renewal Notice*

Insurers must use the rates that will be in effect on the policy renewal date to calculate the premium to renew the policy. The insurer may present the payor with two coverage options:

- **Option A** – Renewing for the Same Amounts of Insurance:
  - This option provides the current amounts of insurance and applicable deductibles.
- **Option B** – Renewing for Higher Amounts of Insurance:
  - This option provides an inflation option of 10 percent for the building and 5 percent for the contents with applicable deductibles.
  - The amount of insurance offered cannot exceed the maximum limits.
  - The minimum deductible may change based on the amount of insurance offered at renewal.
  - For Preferred Risk Policies (PRPs) and Newly Mapped policies, the insurer must use the next higher amounts of insurance available. For more information on the combinations of insurance amounts, refer to Appendix J: Rate Tables.
  - The amount of insurance cannot exceed the replacement cost of the building.

## B. Final Notice

If the insurer does not receive the premium payment by the policy expiration date, the insurer must send a Final Notice on the policy expiration date to all parties listed on the prior policy declarations page.

The Final Notice must include the same information printed on the Renewal Notice and state that coverage has expired.

**Lender Protection**

Coverage will continue for lenders listed on the declarations page for 30 days from the Final Notice mailing date, as required under the Mortgage Clause of the SFIP (see Appendix A: Policy).

- The Final Notice to the lender must indicate that coverage will terminate if premium is not received within this 30-day period;
- Insurers must be able to reproduce copies of the Final Notice to the mortgagee; *and*
- The insurer must have processes in place to verify the Final Notice mailing date.

## C. Renewal Notification Requirements

Refer to **Table 1** below for renewal notification requirements.

### Table 1. Renewal Notification Requirements

| Notice Type | Payor | All Other Parties Listed on the Declarations Page |
|---|---|---|
| **Renewal Notice** | Insurer mails Renewal Notice for payment 45 days prior to the policy expiration date. | Insurer mails a copy of Renewal Notice for payment 45 days prior to the policy expiration date. |
| **Final Notice** | Insurer mails Final Notice on the policy expiration date. | Insurer mails a copy of Final Notice on the policy expiration date. |
| **Policy Declarations Page** | Insurer mails policy declarations page after receiving payment. | Insurer mails the policy declarations page after receiving payment. |

## D. Premium Payment

The payor may pay the premium by check, credit card, or electronically. The insurer must receive the premium within 30 days of the policy expiration date (includes policy expiration date plus 29 days).

The insurer may not use the receipt date of an invalid payment to determine the effective date of a policy renewal.

A payment is invalid if there are non-sufficient funds (NSF) in the account, a successfully completed reversal (dispute) of an electronic payment, or the payment is non-negotiable for any other reason.

Upon notification that the payment is invalid, the insurer must:

- Cancel/nullify the transaction associated with that payment; *and*
- Send notification of the cancellation/nullification to the insured, agent, and lender(s), if applicable.

If the insurer receives a new payment, the insurer must process the transaction based on the new premium receipt date. The insurer must determine the effective date of the transaction based on the new payment receipt date, subject to the effective date rules.

**Note:** A new application or endorsement request is not required for this transaction as long as the insurer still has the original request.

### *1. Check*

The payor can pay by a check payable to the insurer.

### *2. Credit Cards*

The payor can make a payment by credit card, if the insurer accepts credit card payments.

### *3. Electronic Transfers*

The insurer may use electronic transfers if its process includes authentication of signatures and dates of receipt of premium.

### *4. Certified Mail*

- For valid payments sent via certified mail, the payment receipt date is the certified mail date:
  - If the certified mail date is within 30 days of the policy expiration date there is no lapse in coverage.
  - If the certified mail date is outside the grace period there will be a lapse in coverage. Calculate the new effective date based on the certified mail date.
- The term certified mail extends to certified mail sent via the U.S. Postal Service or reputable third-party delivery services that provide proof of the actual mailing and delivery date to the insurer.

## E. Premium Receipt

Upon receipt of the full premium, the insurer must send the policy declarations page to the insured and all parties listed on the policy.

### *1. Underpayment of Renewal Premium*

- If the insurer receives a payment less than the amount shown on the bill, the insurer must send an underpayment notice for the additional premium.
- If the insurer receives the additional premium within 30 days of the underpayment notice, the policy will renew at the original requested amount.

- If the insurer does not receive the additional premium within 30 days of the underpayment notice, then the insurer must reduce the coverage to the amount that the premium received will purchase.
- If the insurer receives the additional premium more than 30 days from the underpayment notice, the amount of insurance must increase by endorsement using the applicable waiting period. Please refer to the How to Endorse section for the effective date rules.

## F. Determine the Renewal Effective Date

The date the insurer receives the premium will determine the effective date except for payments sent by certified mail. (Refer to **II.D.4 Certified Mail** for more information). Use **Table 2** to determine the renewal effective date.

**Table 2. Determine the Renewal Effective Date**

| RECEIPT DATE | RENEWAL DATE | EXAMPLE |
|---|---|---|
| ***Within 30 days of*** **the policy expiration date** | The insurer renews the policy with the same effective date and policy number as the previous term without a lapse in coverage. | If the policy expires on May 1 and the insurer receives payment before May 30, then the effective date of the policy is May 1. |
| ***On or after 30 days but within 90 days*** **following the policy expiration date** | The insurer renews the policy with the same policy number as the previous term. However, the effective date of the policy will be 30 days from the date the insurer receives the payment, which results in a lapse in coverage. | If the policy expires on May 1 and the insurer receives payment on June 15, the effective date of the policy is July 15. |
| ***On or after 90 days*** **following the policy expiration date** | The insurer cannot renew the expired policy. The insurer must receive a new Application with payment after validating the rate. The standard 30-day waiting period will apply and there will be a lapse in coverage. | If the policy expires on May 1 and the insurer receives the payment on August 15, determine the effective date based on the applicable effective date rule for the standard 30-day waiting period. |

**Note:** If the 30th day falls on a Saturday, Sunday, or holiday, the deadline does not extend to the next business day.

## G. Renewal by an Application or Recertification Questionnaire

- If the insurer does not have sufficient underwriting information to renew or rate a policy, the insurer may require an Application or Recertification Questionnaire.
- The insurer may not generate a Renewal Notice if the insurer does not have all the required information to underwrite or rate a policy, unless the insurer discovers mid-term that an existing policy was incorrectly written and chooses to renew the policy for a single policy term using tentative rates.
- The insurer must notify any lender listed on the declarations page of the requirement to renew by means of an Application or Recertification Questionnaire no less than 45 days prior to policy expiration.
- The insurer must mail the Final Notice within 5 days of the policy expiration date and send a final notice to all parties listed on the prior policy declarations page.

Examples of situations that may require an Application or Recertification Questionnaire are:

- Tentatively rated policies;
- Provisionally rated policies;
- FEMA reunderwriting requirements resulting from an audit, quality review, or program changes;
- Misrating discovered by the insurer at the time of loss or during an internal quality review;
- Substantial improvements;
- New additions or extensions to the building (even when not a substantial improvement);
- Buildings in the course of construction during a previous policy term;
- PRP ineligibility; *or*
- Loss of eligibility for NFIP grandfathering rules.

## H. Nonrenewal and Cancellation

- The insurer may not renew a policy for an ineligible risk.
- The insurer may not generate Renewal Notices or renew policies when a building becomes ineligible for flood insurance. Examples include but are not limited to when:
  - The NFIP suspended the community in which the building is located;
  - A state or local authority declared the property in violation of its floodplain management regulations (Section 1316 property); *or*
  - A property has been identified as being in a System Unit or Otherwise Protected Area under the Coastal Barrier Resources System (CBRS) after the designation date.
- Within five days of the policy expiration date, the insurer must notify all parties listed on the prior policy declarations page of the nonrenewal and cancellation by sending a Final Notice.
- Existing tentatively rated policies are subject to non-renewal if the insurer does not receive the required full-risk rating information.

## I. Newly Mapped

The policy renewal premium receipt date may impact continued eligibility for the newly mapped rating procedure. Please see **Table 3** below.

**Table 3. Renewal Payments**

| Premium Receipt Date | Eligible for Newly Mapped Procedure | Apply Waiting Period |
|---|---|---|
| **Within 30 Days of the Expiration Date** | Yes | No |
| **Greater than 30 Days but less than 90 Days following the Expiration Date** | Yes, for the first occurrence.<br>No, for a subsequent occurrence | Yes, the standard 30-day waiting period applies. |
| **90 or more days following the Expiration Date** | No | N/A |

## J. Coverage Endorsements during the Renewal Cycle

The renewal bill may not reflect endorsements received close to the expiration date (example: within 75 days of the policy expiration date). When the insurer receives the request for coverage endorsements close to renewal, follow the guidelines below:

- If the insurer receives a request to increase coverage after sending a Renewal Notice, but more than 30 days prior to the current policy expiration date, the insurer shall issue a revised Renewal Notice. If the insurer receives the premium for the increased coverage before the end of the 30-day grace period, the increased coverage becomes effective at 12:01 a.m. on the date of the policy renewal.
- If the insurer receives a request to increase coverage less than 30 days prior to the current policy expiration date, the following rules apply:
  - If the requested coverage is less than Option B, the insurer must receive the premium for the increased coverage before the expiration of the 30-day grace period for the new coverage to become effective at 12:01 a.m. on the date of the policy renewal.
  - If the requested coverage amount of insurance is greater than Option B, the insurer must issue the renewal policy using the Option B coverage amounts, and then endorse the policy to the requested amount with the appropriate waiting period. Refer to the How to Endorse section for questions regarding the waiting period.

## K. Transfer of Business at Renewal

- A transfer of business occurs when an insured or an agent moves any or all of their existing business from one insurer to another.
- When the transfer occurs, the insurer must obtain, either from the insured or the agent, the following:
  - The declaration page from the prior insurer, an Application, and all underwriting information to verify the correct rating of the policy.
  - Documentation of primary/non-primary residence status.
  - If the policy is rated using elevation information, then a copy of the Elevation Certificate (EC) is required when the declarations page issued by the previous insurer does not include the Lowest Floor Elevation (LFE) and Base Flood Elevation (BFE).
  - A PRP requires documentation of eligibility that includes verification of the flood zone.
  - Documentation of both the current and previous flood zones for Newly Mapped properties.
  - A Residential Condominium Building Association Policy (RCBAP) requires all information needed to issue and rate the policy, including photos and Replacement Cost Value (RCV) documentation.
  - All transferred elevation-rated policies require photographs. The new insurer may use the photographs on file with the previous insurer if there have been no structural changes that affect the building's rating.

- The insurer must validate elevation information on the previous declarations page when there is a discrepancy in the building description (e.g., the Application shows a basement and the declarations page describes an elevated building).

| Insurer or Third-Party Conversion |
| --- |
| Transfer of business does not include conversions of all business from one insurer or third-party administrator to another insurer or third-party administrator. When an insurer acquires another insurer's book of business, all underwriting files must transfer in their entirety to the new insurer. |

## III. Sample Documents

### A. Renewal Notice, page 1

National Flood Insurance Program
*U.S. Department of Homeland Security*
PO Box 913111
Denver, CO 80291

**FEMA**

Mail To :

Agent :

**RENEWAL NOTICE**

Your flood insurance policy will expire on 07/15/2019. Please follow renewal instructions on the remittance coupon below.

**Policy Number :**
**Policy Expiration Date :**
**Loan Number :**
**Billing Date :**
**Payor :**
**Insured Property Location :**

| Coverage Options | Coverage Amounts | | Deductibles | | Premium |
|---|---|---|---|---|---|
| | Building | Contents | Building | Contents | |
| A. Current coverage | | | | | |
| B. Increased coverage | | | | | |

This renewal offer is being made on behalf of NFIP Direct Servicing Agent

**Follow the instructions below to pay your renewal premium online with a credit card or electronic check.**

- Log on to **https://my.nfipdirect.fema.gov** and select "Pay Renewal Online".
- Enter your policy information and follow the instructions to select your payment type and available coverage amounts if applicable.
- You will immediately receive a copy of your renewal declarations page.

**See reverse of this notice for important additional information**

IF PAYING BY CHECK OR MONEY ORDER PLEASE DETACH HERE AND SEND THIS PORTION WITH YOUR PAYMENT.

Insured Name :
Renewal Date :
Policy No :
Bill ID :

**To pay by check or money order :**

- Make payment for the exact amount of the coverage option you selected.
- Full payment is required for the option selected.
- Write your policy number on your check or money order.
- Return this portion in the attached return envelope.

Select One:   ◯ Option A   ◯ Option B

Amount Enclosed:   $ ☐☐☐☐☐☐☐ .00

**Make check or money order payable to :**

NFIP Direct Servicing Agent
PO BOX 913111
DENVER, CO 80291-3111

00000        0000

## A. Renewal Notice, page 2

MORTGAGEE, ADDITIONAL INTEREST, DISASTER AGENCY INFORMATION

1st Mortgagee: 2nd Mortgagee: Additional Interest: Disaster Agency:

1. Provided your payment is received within 30 days of the expiration of your policy (expiration date + 29 days), it will be renewed without a lapse in coverage. Any payment received after the 30 day grace period and prior to 90 days will still renew your policy, however there will be a 30 day waiting period for coverage to become effective. The 30 day waiting period begins the day the premium is received. When there is a lapse in coverage you will be subject to the rates and underwriting requirements on the date the policy goes into effect.

   To ensure that your policy is renewed without a lapse in coverage you may use the electronic payment options (e-check or credit card) available to you. You may also mail your premium via USPS certified mail or other third party delivery services that provides either a proof of mailing, or that provides documentation showing the actual mailing date and the delivery date, to us at the remittance address shown on this form. In these instances the mailing date will be used as the cash receipts date even though delivery may be after the expiration date.

2. You are encouraged to insure your property for at least 80% of the structures replacement cost to ensure adequate coverage in the event of a loss. Contact your insurance agent/producer for details.

3. If the mortgagee listed on the bill is not the current mortgagee, please forward the bill to the new financial institution (if they are responsible for premium payment) and have your agent/producer send a General Change Endorsement to correct the policy.

4. Please note if this policy is a Preferred Risk Policy (PRP): If the flood zone listed on your policy is not the zone on the current Flood Insurance Rate Map (FIRM), you may no longer be eligible for the PRP. Please contact your insurance agent/producer to verify if you are still eligible for this policy and/or to obtain an updated quote.

5. Effective April 1, 2015 a $10,000 deductible option will be available for all residential buildings. If selected, the $10,000 deductible will apply separately to building coverage and to contents coverage. Before requesting your deductible be increased, please contact your lender for approval. With the approval of your lender, your agent will assist you in submitting the endorsement request for the deductible increase.

   Contact your agent if you have questions related to your deductible options.

**FOR QUESTIONS ON ANY OF THIS INFORMATION, PLEASE CONTACT YOUR INSURANCE AGENT/PRODUCER.**

This policy is not subject to cancellation for reasons other than those set forth in the National Flood Insurance Program rules and regulations. In matters involving billing disputes, cancellation is not available other than for billing processing error or fraud.

00000 0000

## A. Renewal Notice, page 3

May 16, 2019

**IMPORTANT NOTICE TO RESIDENTIAL POLICYHOLDERS**

As you were previously advised, the HFIAA Surcharge was implemented as part of the Homeowners Flood Insurance Affordability Act of 2014. Effective April 1, 2015, this mandatory surcharge is added to all flood policies. It is used to offset the subsidized premiums for some policies, and help achieve the financial sustainability goals of the NFIP as mandated by Congress under the BW12 legislation. The fee will be included each year until the policy premium subsidies are eliminated. **The fee is $25.00 for a primary residence and $250.00 for all other buildings. To date we have not received documentation to indicate that the building insured on this policy is your primary residence.**

**A primary residence is described as a building that will be lived in by an insured or an insured's spouse for more than 50% of the 365 days following the policy effective date. In addition, the insured must not establish or acquire another residence or use the residence as a rental or income property any time during the policy term.**

**Effective April 1, 2019: Some two to four family buildings now qualify for the $25.00 HFIAA Surcharge.**

**If the building insured on this policy is your primary residence, please complete the information on the form below, subtract $225.00 from your renewal payment and return the form with your renewal notice and payment.**

If your mortgage company is responsible for the payment of your renewal premium and your primary residence status needs updating, please complete and return this form by either:

**Uploading directly to your policy:**

Go to: https://my.nfipdirect.fema.gov
Select: "Upload documents"
Follow the instructions on the web site

**Or mail to:**

NFIP Direct Servicing Agent
PO BOX 913111
DENVER, CO 80291-3111

If the building insured on this policy is not your primary residence, please disregard this message.

---

**VERIFICATION OF PRIMARY RESIDENCE STATUS FOR NFIP POLICY RATING**

Property Address:

The above address is my primary residence, and I and/or my spouse will live at this location for more than 50 percent of the 365 days following the policy effective date. In addition, I will not establish or acquire another residence or use this residence as a rental or income property any time during the policy term.

Insured Name (Printed): ______________________________

Insured Signature: ______________________________ Date: ______________

PURSUANT TO 28 U.S.C. § 1746 I CERTIFY UNDER PENALTY OF PERJURY UNDER THE LAWS OF THE UNITED STATES OF AMERICA THAT THE FOREGOING IS TRUE AND CORRECT. I UNDERSTAND THAT ANY FALSE STATEMENTS MAY CAUSE MY POLICY TO BE VOID, AND MAY BE PUNISHABLE BY FINE OR IMPRISONMENT UNDER APPLICABLE FEDERAL LAW.

File: Page 1 of 1 DocID:

## B. Final Notice, page 1

National Flood Insurance Program
*U.S. Department of Homeland Security*
PO Box 913111
Denver, CO 80291

FEMA

Mail To :

Agent :

**FINAL NOTICE**

Your flood insurance policy expired on 07/15/2019. It may be reinstated 30 days after premium is received. Please see the online payment options described below to make an immediate payment.

**Policy Number :**
**Policy Expiration Date :**
**Loan Number :**
**Billing Date :**
**Payor :**
**Insured Property Location :**

| Coverage Options | Coverage Amounts: Building | Coverage Amounts: Contents | Deductibles: Building | Deductibles: Contents | Premium |
|---|---|---|---|---|---|
| A. Current coverage | | | | | |
| B. Increased coverage | | | | | |

This renewal offer is being made on behalf of NFIP DIRECT SERVICING AGENT

**Follow the instructions below to pay your renewal premium online with a credit card or electronic check.**

- Visit **https://my.nfipdirect.fema.gov** and select "Pay Renewal Online".
- Enter your policy information and follow the instructions to select your payment type and available coverage amounts if applicable.
- You will immediately receive a copy of your renewal declarations page.

**See reverse of this notice for important additional information**

IF PAYING BY CHECK OR MONEY ORDER PLEASE DETACH HERE AND SEND THIS PORTION WITH YOUR PAYMENT.

Insured Name :
Renewal Date :
Policy No :
Bill ID :
Select One: ◯ Option A ◯ Option B

**To pay by check or money order :**

- Make payment for the exact amount of the coverage option you selected.
- Full payment is required for the option selected.
- Write your policy number on your check or money order.
- Return this portion in the attached return envelope.

Amount Enclosed: $ ☐☐☐☐☐☐☐ .00

**Make check or money order payable to :**

NFIP DIRECT SERVICING AGENT
PO BOX 913111
DENVER, CO 80291-3111

00000 0000

## B. Final Notice, page 2

**MORTGAGEE, ADDITIONAL INTEREST, DISASTER AGENCY INFORMATION**

| 1st Mortgagee: | 2nd Mortgagee: | Additional Interest: | Disaster Agency: |
|---|---|---|---|

1. Provided your payment is received within 30 days of the expiration of your policy (expiration date + 29 days), it will be renewed without a lapse in coverage. Any payment received after the 30 day grace period and prior to 90 days will still renew your policy, however there will be a 30 day waiting period for coverage to become effective. The 30 day waiting period begins the day the premium is received. When there is a lapse in coverage you will be subject to the rates and underwriting requirements on the date the policy goes into effect.

   To ensure that your policy is renewed without a lapse in coverage you may use the electronic payment options (e-check or credit card) available to you. You may also mail your premium via USPS certified mail or other third party delivery services that provides either a proof of mailing, or that provides documentation showing the actual mailing date and the delivery date, to us at the remittance address shown on this form. In these instances the mailing date will be used as the cash receipts date even though delivery may be after the expiration date.

2. You are encouraged to insure your property for at least 80% of the structures replacement cost to ensure adequate coverage in the event of a loss. Contact your insurance agent/producer for details.

3. If the mortgagee listed on the bill is not the current mortgagee, please forward the bill to the new financial institution (if they are responsible for premium payment) and have your agent/producer send a General Change Endorsement to correct the policy.

4. Please note if this policy is a Preferred Risk Policy (PRP): If the flood zone listed on your policy is not the zone on the current Flood Insurance Rate Map (FIRM), you may no longer be eligible for the PRP. Please contact your insurance agent/producer to verify if you are still eligible for this policy and/or to obtain an updated quote.

5. Effective April 1, 2015 a $10,000 deductible option will be available for all residential buildings. If selected, the $10,000 deductible will apply separately to building coverage and to contents coverage. Before requesting your deductible be increased, please contact your lender for approval. With the approval of your lender, your agent will assist you in submitting the endorsement request for the deductible increase.

   Contact your agent if you have questions related to your deductible options.

**FOR QUESTIONS ON ANY OF THIS INFORMATION, PLEASE CONTACT YOUR INSURANCE AGENT/PRODUCER.**

This policy is not subject to cancellation for reasons other than those set forth in the National Flood Insurance Program rules and regulations. In matters involving billing disputes, cancellation is not available other than for billing processing error or fraud.

□□□□□ □□□□

## B. Final Notice, page 3

July 15, 2019

**IMPORTANT NOTICE TO RESIDENTIAL POLICYHOLDERS**

As you were previously advised, the HFIAA Surcharge was implemented as part of the Homeowners Flood Insurance Affordability Act of 2014. Effective April 1, 2015, this mandatory surcharge is added to all flood policies. It is used to offset the subsidized premiums for some policies, and help achieve the financial sustainability goals of the NFIP as mandated by Congress under the BW12 legislation. The fee will be included each year until the policy premium subsidies are eliminated. **The fee is $25.00 for a primary residence and $250.00 for all other buildings. To date we have not received documentation to indicate that the building insured on this policy is your primary residence.**

**A primary residence is described as a building that will be lived in by an insured or an insured's spouse for more than 50% of the 365 days following the policy effective date. In addition, the insured must not establish or acquire another residence or use the residence as a rental or income property any time during the policy term.**

**Effective April 1, 2019: Some two to four family buildings now qualify for the $25.00 HFIAA Surcharge.**

**If the building insured on this policy is your primary residence, please complete the information on the form below, subtract $225.00 from your renewal payment and return the form with your renewal notice and payment.**

If your mortgage company is responsible for the payment of your renewal premium and your primary residence status needs updating, please complete and return this form by either:

**Uploading directly to your policy:**

Go to: https://my.nfipdirect.fema.gov
Select: "Upload documents"
Follow the instructions on the web site

**Or mail to:**

NFIP DIRECT SERVICING AGENT
PO BOX 913111
DENVER, CO 80291-3111

If the building insured on this policy is not your primary residence, please disregard this message.

**VERIFICATION OF PRIMARY RESIDENCE STATUS FOR NFIP POLICY RATING**

Property Address:

The above address is my primary residence, and I and/or my spouse will live at this location for more than 50 percent of the 365 days following the policy effective date. In addition, I will not establish or acquire another residence or use this residence as a rental or income property any time during the policy term.

Insured Name (Printed): ______________________________

Insured Signature: ______________________________ Date: ______________

PURSUANT TO 28 U.S.C. § 1746 I CERTIFY UNDER PENALTY OF PERJURY UNDER THE LAWS OF THE UNITED STATES OF AMERICA THAT THE FOREGOING IS TRUE AND CORRECT. I UNDERSTAND THAT ANY FALSE STATEMENTS MAY CAUSE MY POLICY TO BE VOID, AND MAY BE PUNISHABLE BY FINE OR IMPRISONMENT UNDER APPLICABLE FEDERAL LAW.

File: Page 1 of 1 DocID:

This page is intentionally left blank.

# 6. How to Cancel

## I. General Information

Flood policies may be terminated mid-term or full-term by cancellation, or full-term by nullification. The insured may request a cancellation or nullification of an NFIP policy for the specific reasons outlined within this section. The insured may be entitled to a full, partial, or no refund.

## II. Cancellation/Nullification

- To cancel a policy, agents must submit a completed Cancellation/Nullification Request Form with proper documentation to the insurer.
- Upon completion of the cancellation/nullification request the insurer must provide the insured and all interested parties with a notice of cancellation/nullification. Interested parties include any additional insureds, additional lenders, loss payees, trustees, or disaster assistance agencies.
- Prior to processing a cancellation request for reason codes 8, 9, 15, and 19, the insurer must inform eligible insureds with standard-rated policies for property located in a non-Special Flood Hazard Area (SFHA) of their option to convert to a Preferred Risk Policy (PRP).

**Note:** A copy of the Cancellation/Nullification Request form is located in Appendix B: Forms.

### A. Processing a Cancellation or Nullification Request

The insurer may accept electronic submissions if their business process includes signature authentication and records receipt dates. Insurers are responsible for the security and integrity of electronic transactions.

#### *1. Signatures*

#### a. Insured's Signature

All named insureds must provide the insurer with a signed and dated cancellation/nullification request except for reason codes 5, 6, 21, 22, 23, and 25.

Below are specific exceptions when the insured's signature is not required:

- When using cancellation reason code 1:
  - In the event of foreclosure when the court documentation confirms the unearned premium belongs to the lender.
  - For a policy covering property that was eligible for coverage, but became ineligible midterm due to physical alteration of the structure.
- When using cancellation reason code 4:
  - When there is deliberately created duplicate coverage, the insurer must cancel the policy with the later effective date.

#### b. Agent Signature

The agent must sign and date the cancellation/nullification request for all cancellation reason codes except 6, 21, 22, 23, and 25.

### 2. Receipt Date

The receipt date of a cancellation/nullification request is either:

- The date the insurer initially receives the cancellation/nullification request if the insurer receives all required documentation 60 days or less from the insurer's request for additional documentation; *or*
- The date the insurer receives the required documentation if the insurer receives all required documentation more than 60 days from the insurer's request for documentation.

## III. Premium Refunds

Insurers must process the return premium on policy terms for which they are the insurer of record.

For a return premium request that covers more than two policy terms, the insurer may submit the request and documentation to FEMA for processing. The documentation must include the following:

- A policy cancellation request and the premium refund calculation for each policy term.
- The insurer's statistical records or declarations pages for each policy term and evidence of premium payments obtained from the insured if these documents are not available from the insurer's records.
- Photographs verifying ineligible risks.

Insurers may send requests and documentation to FEMA by email to: NFIPUnderwritingMailbox@fema.dhs.gov.

FEMA notifies the insurers of the premium refunded and the Expense Allowance due to the NFIP. The insurers must maintain this documentation as part of their underwriting files. FEMA will return rejected refund requests.

## IV. Valid Cancellation Reason Codes/Nullification of NFIP Policies

The valid reason codes for canceling/nullifying a flood policy are shown in **Tables 1–22 below.** Unless otherwise stated, all conditions for each separate reason code must be met in order to cancel a policy.

**Note:** The valid reason codes are not in sequence as some numbers have been retired over time.

### Table 1: Valid Cancellation Reason Code 01

| Reason Code 01 | Building sold, removed, destroyed, or physically altered and no longer meets the definition of an eligible building |
|---|---|
| Valid Reasons | 1. The insured sells or transfers ownership of the insured building and does not have an insurable interest in the insured building.<br>2. Relocation or destruction of the insured building.<br>3. Alteration of the insured building rendering it ineligible for coverage. (An example is the insured removes a mobile home from a permanent foundation and places it on wheels.)<br>4. The builder or developer requests to cancel a policy mid-term because ownership transfers to a newly created condominium association, and the association purchased a policy under its name.<br>5. The building is a total loss because the building damage is greater than or equal to the replacement cost of the building.<br>6. The lienholder foreclosed on the building. |
| Cancellation Effective Date | The date the insured ceased to have an insurable interest in the building or the building became ineligible for coverage. Examples include the date of the sale of the building or the date the insured removed the building from the described location. |
| Type of Refund | 1. Pro-rata (pro-rated) premium refund, including Increased Cost of Compliance (ICC) premium, Reserve Fund Assessment, and Homeowner Flood Insurance Affordability Act of 2014 (HFIAA) Surcharge, will apply to the policy term in which the cancellation became effective. The refund does not include the Federal Policy Fee and Probation Surcharge.<br>2. Full premium refunds apply to any subsequent policy term(s), including fees and surcharges. |
| Cancellation Request | The insurer must receive the cancellation request within 1 year of the policy expiration date. |
| Required Documentation | Bill of sale, settlement statement, closing disclosure statement, proof of removal, proof of total loss, court documentation for foreclosed buildings, or photographs to verify ineligible risks. |
| Policy Terms Eligible for Refund | Up to 5 years prior to the receipt date of the cancellation request. |

### Table 2: Valid Cancellation Code Reason 02

| Reason Code 02 | Contents sold, removed, or destroyed |
|---|---|
| Valid Reasons | 1. The insured sells or transfers ownership of the insured contents;<br>2. Contents completely removed or relocated from the described location; *or*<br>3. Contents destroyed by any peril. |
| Cancellation Effective Date | The date the insured ceased to have an insurable interest in the contents at the described location, or the removal date of the contents from the described location. |

**Table 2: Valid Cancellation Code Reason 02,** *continued*

| Reason Code 02 | Contents sold, removed, or destroyed |
|---|---|
| Type of Refund | 1. Pro-rata (pro-rated) premium refund, including ICC premium, Reserve Fund Assessment, and HFIAA Surcharge, will apply to the policy term in which the cancellation became effective. The refund does not include the Federal Policy Fee and Probation Surcharge.<br>2. Full premium refunds apply to any subsequent policy term(s), including fees and surcharges. |
| Cancellation Request | The insurer must receive the cancellation request within 1 year of the policy expiration date. |
| Required Documentation | Bill of sale, inventory record, proof of total loss, or, in the case of residential contents, a signed statement from the insured. |
| Policy Terms Eligible for Refund | Up to 5 years prior to the receipt date of the cancellation request. |

**Table 3: Valid Cancellation Reason Code 03**

| Reason Code 03 | Policy canceled and rewritten to establish a common expiration date with other insurance coverage for same building |
|---|---|
| Conditions | 1. The insurer must remain the same for the new flood policy with the same or higher amounts of coverage. The agent must submit a new application and premium.<br>2. The other insurance coverage for which the common expiration date is established must be for building coverage on the same building insured by the current in-force flood policy. |
| Cancellation Effective Date | The effective date of the new flood policy is subject to the 30-day waiting period. Additional or increases in coverage limits beyond the limits on the canceled policy are subject to the 30-day waiting period. |
| Type of Refund | Pro-rata (pro-rated) premium refund, including ICC premium, Reserve Fund Assessment, and HFIAA Surcharge, will apply to the policy term in which the cancellation<br>became effective. The refund does not include the Federal Policy Fee and Probation Surcharge. |
| Cancellation Request | The insurer must receive the cancellation request within 1 year of the new policy effective date. |
| Required Documentation | 1. A new application and premium.<br>2. The agent must request cancellation of the prior policy upon receipt of the new policy declarations page.<br>3. The insurer must retain a copy of the new policy declarations page and the other perils policy declarations that show the building address and policy effective dates. |
| Policy Terms Eligible for Refund | Current policy term. |

### Table 4: Valid Cancellation Reason Code 04

| Reason Code 04 | Duplicate NFIP policies |
|---|---|
| Conditions for Duplicate Policies for Same Named Insured | Only one policy may be active for the same named insured for the same coverage on the building and/or contents. If there are duplicate policies, the insured may choose which policy to keep as long as there has not been a deliberate creation of duplicate policies.<br>If deliberately created duplicate policies are active, the insurer must cancel the policy with the later effective date. If a loss occurs while deliberately created duplicate policies are active, the insurer must adjust the claim according to the terms of the policy with the earlier effective date. There are five exceptions to the rule about canceling the deliberately created duplicate policy with the later effective date:<br>1. Cancellation of the earlier policy to establish a common expiration date with other policies (see Reason Code 3).<br>2. Cancellation of a Dwelling Policy because coverage is being provided under an Residential Condominium Building Association Policy (RCBAP) (see Reason Code 10).<br>3. Cancellation of an NFIP lender force-placed Mortgage Portfolio Protection Program (MPPP) policy because the borrower purchased an NFIP flood policy. The insurer must receive a copy of the lender's force-placement letter and the new flood policy declarations page with the Cancellation/Nullification Request form.<br>4. The policy with the earlier effective date has been expired for more than 30 days.<br>5. Cancellation of a Group Flood Insurance Policy (GFIP) replaced by a standard-rated policy. |
| Conditions for Duplicate Policies for Different Named Insureds | Only one flood policy may be active for different named insureds for the same building. If there are duplicate policies, the building owner must choose which policy to keep and the building owner must be a named insured. For example, if a tenant purchased building coverage, the insurer must remove the building coverage, endorse the policy to add the building owner as a named insured, or cancel the policy. Only 1 policy with building coverage may remain in effect. |
| Cancellation Effective Date | 1. For policies with the same effective date, the cancellation effective date is the date of the policy chosen by the insured.<br>2. For policies with different effective dates, the policy with the later effective date must be canceled unless it is one of the following exceptions:<br>• An MPPP policy replaced by a standard-rated policy;<br>• The policy with the earlier effective date that has been expired for more than 30 days; *or*<br>• A Group Flood Insurance Policy replaced by a standard-rated policy. |
| Type of Refund | 1. Full premium refunds apply when the cancellation is effective at the inception of the term, and for the renewal terms when the cancellation request applies to the policy with the later effective date. A full refund of the fees and surcharges applies for these conditions.<br>2. Pro-rata (pro-rated) premium refunds apply, including ICC premium, Reserve Fund Assessment, and HFIAA Surcharge, when the cancellation is effective mid-term. The exception to allow cancellation of the earlier policy applies. The refund does not include the Federal Policy Fee and Probation Surcharge.<br>3. No premium refunds apply to a canceled GFIP. |

**Table 4: Valid Cancellation Reason Code 04** *continued*

| Reason Code 04 | Duplicate NFIP policies |
|---|---|
| Cancellation Request | The insurer must receive the cancellation request within 1 year of the policy expiration date. |
| Required Documentation | Copy of the declarations page(s) and, for the standard force-placed policy, a copy of the force-placement letter from the lender. |
| Policy Terms Eligible for Refund | Up to 5 years prior to the date of the cancellation request. |

**Table 5: Valid Cancellation Reason Code 05**

| Reason Code 05 | Nonpayment of premium |
|---|---|
| Valid Reasons | Valid reasons to nullify the policy for nonpayment of premium include:<br>1. An insured's check payment to the agent or insurer is returned for non-sufficient funds or rejected.<br>2. An insured's credit card payment to the agent or insurer is rejected or disputed.<br>Reason Code 5 is not valid if an agent advances insurance agency funds without first receiving payment from the insured. |
| Cancellation Effective Date | The cancellation effective date is the policy inception date. |
| Type of Refund | The insurer must provide a full refund to the agent, including all fees and surcharges for returned or rejected insured payments to the agent. There is no refund for returned or rejected payments made by the insured directly to the insurer. |
| Cancellation Request | The insurer must receive the cancellation request during the policy term. |
| Required Documentation | The bank or credit card notice of returned or rejected payment. |
| Policy Terms Eligible for Refund | Current policy term. |

**Table 6: Valid Cancellation Reason Code 06**

| Reason Code 06 | Risk not eligible for coverage |
|---|---|
| Valid Reasons | An insurer issues a policy for an ineligible property. Refer to the Standard Flood Insurance Policy (SFIP) for a list of risks not eligible for coverage. A cancellation explanation must accompany the request.<br><br>Examples of risks not eligible at the time of application include:<br>1. Structures that do not meet the definition of a building.<br>2. Contents not located in an eligible building.<br>3. Policies issued under an incorrect community number for buildings not located in an NFIP participating community.<br>4. Buildings located in a Coastal Barrier Resources System (CBRS).<br>5. Buildings declared as a 1316 property prior to the flood policy application.<br><br>Examples of risks that were eligible at the time of application but are not eligible at the time of renewal include:<br>1. Buildings determined to be a 1316 property after the time of application.<br>2. Buildings located in an NFIP participating community suspended after the issuance of the flood policy.<br>3. Annexation of the property to a non-participating community after issuance of the flood policy. |
| Cancellation Effective Date | The effective date of the first full policy term the property became ineligible for coverage. |
| Type of Refund | Full premium refund including fees and surcharges will apply to the first full policy term in which the property became ineligible for policy coverage and any subsequent policy terms, provided there are no paid claims.<br><br>If there are paid claims the insurer must verify the loss history of the property with FEMA before issuing refunds for more than two policy terms:<br>1. The net refund paid to the insured is the difference between the premium refund and the amount of the paid claims if the premium refund is greater than the amount of any paid claims.<br>2. The insurer must reimburse the NFIP for the difference between the premium refund amount and the paid claims if the premium refund is less than the amount of any paid claims. |
| Cancellation Request | The insurer must receive the cancellation request within 1 year of the policy expiration date. |
| Required Documentation | An explanation describing the valid reason for the cancellation request, along with the appropriate supporting documentation. Supporting documentation should include information as to when the property became ineligible for NFIP coverage.<br><br>Examples of supporting documentation that may demonstrate ineligibility include property tax records, Section 1316 declaration, Coastal Barrier Resources Act (CBRA) determination, photographs, or other supporting documentation. |
| Policy Terms Eligible for Refund | All prior terms the property was ineligible for NFIP coverage. |

**Table 7: Valid Cancellation Reason Code 07**

| Reason Code 07 | Property closing did not occur |
|---|---|
| **Conditions** | The insurer may nullify the policy when:<br>1. An insurer issues a policy and the anticipated transfer of the property does not take place.<br>2. The insured does not acquire an insurable interest in the property. |
| **Cancellation Effective Date** | The cancellation effective date will be the policy inception date. |
| **Type of Refund** | Full premium refund including fees and surcharges. |
| **Cancellation Request** | The insurer must receive the cancellation request within 1 year of the new flood policy effective date. |
| **Required Documentation** | Signed statement from the insured indicating that the property closing did not occur. See sample verification letter regarding the requirement to maintain flood insurance coverage. |
| **Policy Terms Eligible for Refund** | Current policy term. |

**Table 8: Valid Cancellation Reason Code 08**

| Reason Code 08 | Policy not required by lender |
|---|---|
| **Conditions** | 1. A lender determines a flood policy is required for a loan closing, but later it is discovered that the building was not located in an SFHA at the time of closing and flood insurance should not have been required by the lender; *and*<br>2. There are no paid or pending claims.<br>3. Insurers may use this cancellation reason even for non-SFHA-rated policies.<br>4. The insurer must inform eligible insureds with standard-rated policies for a property in a non-SFHA of their option to convert to a PRP prior to canceling the policy. |
| **Cancellation Effective Date** | The date the insurer receives the cancellation request and all appropriate supporting documentation. |
| **Type of Refund** | Pro-rata (pro-rated) premium refund, including ICC premium, Reserve Fund Assessment, and HFIAA Surcharge, will apply when the cancellation effective date is during the policy term. The refund does not include the Federal Policy Fee and Probation Surcharge. |
| **Cancellation Request** | The insurer must receive the cancellation request within the initial policy term. |

### Table 8: Valid Cancellation Reason Code 08 *continued*

| Reason Code 08 | Policy not required by lender |
|---|---|
| **Required Documentation** | 1. A revised flood zone determination from the lender showing that the property is not in an SFHA.<br>2. If there is a discrepancy between the lender and insured's determinations, a FEMA Out-As-Shown Determination because of a Letter of Map Amendment (LOMA) application must accompany the request.<br>3. A signed statement from the insured that the lender does not require a flood policy based on the revised flood zone determination. See the sample verification letter regarding the requirement to maintain flood insurance coverage. |
| **Policy Terms Eligible for Refund** | Current policy term. |

### Table 9: Valid Cancellation Reason Code 09

| Reason Code 09 | Insurance no longer required by lender because property is no longer located in an SFHA because of a map revision or LOMR |
|---|---|
| **Conditions** | 1. A lender determines a flood policy is required because the building is located in an SFHA.<br>2. After the insurer issues the flood policy, FEMA issues a map revision or Letter of Map Revision (LOMR) that removes the building from the SFHA.<br>3. The lender determines coverage is no longer required for a structure on a residential property, detached from the primary residential structure, and that is not a residence.<br>4. Insurers must inform eligible insureds with standard-rated policies for a property in a non-SFHA of their option to convert to a PRP prior to canceling the policy.<br>Insurers may also use this cancellation reason if:<br>1. The building is rated in a non-SFHA due to grandfathering or issued as a newly mapped policy.<br>**Note:** If the insurer receives a Letter of Map Revision Based on Fill (LOMR-F) or a Letter of Map Revision Floodway (LOMR-FW) with the cancellation request use Reason Code 19. |
| **Cancellation Effective Date** | The date the insurer receives the cancellation request and all appropriate supporting documentation. |
| **Type of Refund** | Pro-rata (pro-rated) premium refund, including ICC premium, Reserve Fund Assessment, and HFIAA Surcharge, applies when the cancellation effective date is during the policy term. The refund does not include the Federal Policy Fee and Probation Surcharge. |
| **Cancellation Request** | The insurer must receive the cancellation request during the policy year. |

### Table 9: Valid Cancellation Reason Code 09 *continued*

| Reason Code 09 | Insurance no longer required by lender because property is no longer located in an SFHA because of a map revision or LOMR |
|---|---|
| **Required Documentation** | A signed statement from the insured that the lender no longer requires the policy because the property is no longer in an SFHA due to a map revision, or coverage is no longer required by the lender for a detached structure.<br>A copy of the revised map or LOMR; or, in the case of multi-property LOMRs that do not list the property's specific building, street address, lot number, or rural address, any of the following and a copy of the LOMR:<br>1. A letter that the insured received from the applicable community official, stating that their building was removed from the SFHA by a multi-property LOMR;<br>2. A letter from the applicable community official, on official letterhead, stating that the building was included in the area removed from the SFHA by the multi-property LOMR, which listed only boundaries/ intersections of streets, lot numbers, or rural addresses; *or*<br>3. In cases, and only in cases, where (1) a community official could not or would not provide a letter, or (2) the building has a rural address, the following set of two documents may be submitted:<br>• A copy of a legal notice, such as a real estate assessment notice or a water/sewer notice, that shows the lot number, street or rural address, or other legal designation of the location of the building; *and*<br>• A letter from the mortgage lender that (1) shows the lot number, street or rural address, or other legal designation of the location of the building, and (2) states that the building was within the boundaries of the area removed from the SFHA by the LOMR. Letters from community officials must match the street address and lot number with a specific multi-property LOMR, stating that the individual building street address, lot number, or rural address (e.g., RR, Box #, Hwy) was included in the area covered by the LOMR. The insurer may accept zone determinations in lieu of the documentation cited above for these situations.<br>4. When a condominium association seeks to cancel a RCBAP, the condominium association must provide a signed letter that lists the number of units and specifies the owner of each unit. Each unit owner must provide a release from the lender or sign a statement that there is no lender.<br>See sample verification letter regarding no requirement to maintain flood insurance coverage. |
| **Policy Terms Eligible for Refund** | Current policy term. |

### Table 10: Valid Cancellation Reason Code 10

| Reason Code 10 | Condominium unit or association policy converting to RCBAP |
|---|---|
| **Conditions** | 1. A standard-rated policy with only building coverage for a condominium unit that is replaced by an RCBAP.<br>2. The unit owner policy and the RCBAP building limits are more than the cost of the unit or over the program maximum limits of coverage. |
| **Cancellation Effective Date** | The cancellation effective date is the effective date of the RCBAP. |

### Table 10: Valid Cancellation Reason Code 10 *continued*

| Reason Code 10 | Condominium unit or association policy converting to RCBAP |
|---|---|
| Type of Refund | 1. Pro-rata (pro-rated) premium refund, including ICC premium, Reserve Fund Assessment, and HFIAA Surcharge will apply when coverage provided under the RCBAP during the first policy term is duplicate. The refund does not include the Federal Policy Fee and Probation Surcharge.<br>2. For policy terms after the first term, full premium refunds will apply including fees and surcharges. |
| Cancellation Request | The insurer must receive the cancellation request within 1 year of the policy expiration date. |
| Required Documentation | A copy of the RCBAP and documentation showing the replacement cost value of the unit. |
| Policy Terms Eligible for Refund | Up to 5 years prior to the receipt date of the cancellation request. |

### Table 11: Valid Cancellation Reason Code 12

| Reason Code 12 | Mortgage paid off |
|---|---|
| Conditions | 1. A lender determines a flood policy is required for a mortgage loan closing.<br>2. After an insurer issues the flood policy, the mortgage loan is paid off.<br>3. There are no paid or pending claims for the policy term(s) in process of cancellation. |
| Cancellation Effective Date | The date the insurer receives the cancellation request. |
| Type of Refund | 1. Pro-rata (pro-rated) premium refund, including ICC premium and Reserve Fund Assessment and HFIAA Surcharge, will apply when the cancellation effective date is during the policy term. The refund does not include the Federal Policy Fee and Probation Surcharge.<br>2. A full premium refund, including fees and surcharges, will apply to a renewal policy if the policy renewed after a payoff of the mortgage because it was in the renewal billing cycle. |
| Cancellation Request | The insurer must receive the cancellation request during the policy year. |
| Required Documentation | A signed statement from the insured that the mortgage has been paid off and the lender no longer requires flood insurance. See sample verification letter regarding the requirement to maintain flood insurance coverage. |
| Policy Terms Eligible for Refund | The pro-rata portion of the policy term in which the mortgage payoff occurred, and the full renewal term if the policy renewed after the mortgage payoff. |

### Table 12: Valid Cancellation Reason Code 13

| Reason Code 13 | Voidance prior to effective date |
|---|---|
| Conditions | 1. The insured pays the premium for a new policy subject to the 30-day waiting period or for a renewal policy.<br>2. Prior to the effective date of the new or renewal policy, the insured does not want the policy to go into effect. |
| Cancellation Effective Date | The policy effective date of the new or renewed policy (voided). |
| Type of Refund | Full premium refund including fees and surcharges. |
| Cancellation Request | The request must be made prior to the policy effective date. The insurer may receive the cancellation request after the policy effective date. |
| Required Documentation | A request from the insured to cancel the pending new or renewal policy. |
| Policy Terms Eligible for Refund | Current year. |

### Table 13: Valid Cancellation Reason Code 15

| Reason Code 15 | Insurance no longer required based on FEMA review of lender's SFHA determination |
|---|---|
| Conditions | 1. A lender determines a building is located in an SFHA and requires a flood policy.<br>2. The borrower and/or lender sends a request for a Letter of Determination Review (LODR) to FEMA within 45 days of the lender's notification to the borrower that the building is in an SFHA.<br>3. FEMA issues a LODR indicating the building is not located in an SFHA.<br>4. There are no paid or pending claims for the canceled policy term(s).<br>5. Insurers must inform eligible insureds with standard-rated policies for a property in a non-SFHA of their option to convert to a PRP prior to canceling the policy.<br>Insurers may also use this cancellation reason, for a policy rated in a non-SFHA due to grandfathering, or issued as a newly mapped policy. |
| Cancellation Effective Date | The date the insurer receives the cancellation request and all required documentation. |
| Type of Refund | 1. Pro-rata (pro-rated) premium refund, including ICC premium, Reserve Fund Assessment and HFIAA Surcharge, will apply when the cancellation effective date is during the policy term. The refund does not include the Federal Policy Fee and Probation Surcharge.<br>2. A full premium refund, including fees and surcharges, will apply in those cases where the policy renewed after receipt of the cancellation request because it was in the renewal billing cycle. |
| Cancellation Request | The insurer must receive the cancellation request during the policy term. |

**Table 13: Valid Cancellation Reason Code 15** *continued*

| Reason Code 15 | Insurance no longer required based on FEMA review of lender's SFHA determination |
|---|---|
| Required Documentation | 1. A copy of FEMA's LODR.<br>2. A signed statement from the insured that the lender no longer requires flood insurance. See the sample verification letter detailing the requirement to maintain flood insurance coverage. |
| Policy Terms Eligible for Refund | The pro-rata (pro-rated) portion of the policy term in which the insurer received the cancellation request, and the full renewal term if the policy renewed after the insurer received the cancellation request. |

**Table 14: Valid Cancellation Reason Code 18**

| Reason Code 18 | Mortgage paid off on an MPPP policy |
|---|---|
| Conditions | 1. The lender determines a flood policy is required as part of a mortgage loan closing.<br>2. The lender applies for a policy under the MPPP.<br>3. The mortgage loan is paid off after an insurer issues the MPPP flood policy,<br>4. There are no paid or pending claims for the canceled policy term(s). |
| Cancellation Effective Date | The date the insurer receives the cancellation request. |
| Type of Refund | 1. Pro-rata (pro-rated) premium refund, including ICC premium, Reserve Fund Assessment, and HFIAA Surcharge, applies when the cancellation effective date occurs during the policy term. The refund does not include the Federal Policy Fee and Probation Surcharge.<br>2. A full premium refund, including fees and surcharges, will apply in those cases where the policy renewed after the lender considers the mortgage paid in full and the insurer receives the cancellation request during the renewal billing cycle. |
| Cancellation Request | The insurer must receive the cancellation request during the policy term. |
| Required Documentation | A written statement acknowledging the paid-in-full mortgage from the lender. A signed statement from the insured that the lender no longer requires flood insurance. See the sample verification letter regarding the requirement to maintain flood insurance coverage. |
| Policy Terms Eligible for Refund | The pro-rata (pro-rated) portion of the policy term in which the mortgage payoff occurred, and the full renewal term if the policy renewed after the mortgage payoff. |

**Table 15: Valid Cancellation Reason Code 19**

| Reason Code 19 | Insurance no longer required by the lender because the building has been removed from the SFHA by means of a LOMA, including LOMR-F and LOMR-FW |
|---|---|
| **Conditions** | 1. A lender determines a flood policy is required because the building is located in an SFHA.<br>2. FEMA issues a LOMA, including LOMR-F and LOMR-FW, that removes the building from the SFHA after the insurer issues the flood policy.<br>3. The lender confirms in writing that a flood policy is no longer required.<br>4. There are no paid or pending claims for the canceled policy term(s).<br>Insurers may also use this cancellation reason for a policy rated in a non-SFHA due to grandfathering, or issued as a newly mapped policy.<br>Insurers must inform eligible insureds with standard-rated policies for a property in a non-SFHA of their option to convert to a PRP prior to canceling the policy.<br>**Note:** The RCBAP requires a signed letter from the condominium association listing the number of units and specifying the owner of each unit. Every unit owner must provide a lender release or a statement that there is no lender. See sample verification letter at the end of this section. |
| **Cancellation Effective Date** | Current policy term and 1 prior policy term provided the LOMA issuance occurred within 60 days before the current policy's effective date and there are no pending or issued claim payments during the canceled terms. |
| **Type of Refund** | A premium refund, including ICC, Reserve Fund Assessment, and HFIAA Surcharge. The refund does not include the Federal Policy Fee and Probation Surcharge. |
| **Cancellation Request** | Insurer must receive the request during the policy term or within 6 months of the policy expiration date. |
| **Required Documentation** | Statement from the mortgagee that flood insurance is no longer required or a signed statement from the insured that the lender no longer requires flood insurance. See the sample verification letter regarding the requirement to maintain flood insurance coverage. Also, include a copy of the LOMA. |
| **Policy Terms Eligible for Refund** | Current policy term and 1 prior policy term provided the LOMA issuance took place within 60 days before the current policy's effective date. There are no paid or pending claims during the year of the policy term cancellation.<br>*Example:* The flood policy was effective from January 1, 2015, to January 1, 2016, and renewed January 1, 2016, to January 1, 2017. The effective date of the LOMA is December 1, 2015. The cancellation will be effective January 1, 2015.<br>**Note:** There will be no refund if the date of the LOMA is more than 60 days prior to the most recent renewal or for a policy term that ended prior to the LOMA effective date. |

### Table 16: Valid Cancellation Reason Code 20

| Reason Code 20 | Policy written to the wrong facility |
|---|---|
| Conditions | The wrong insurer issues a policy with building coverage for an SRL. |
| Cancellation Effective Date | The cancellation effective date will be the effective date of the current policy (nullified). |
| Type of Refund | Full premium refund including fees and surcharges. |
| Cancellation Request | The insurer must receive the cancellation request during the current policy term. |
| Required Documentation | A report from the NFIP that lists the building as an SRL Property. |
| Policy Terms Eligible for Refund | Current policy term. |

### Table 17: Valid Cancellation Reason Code 21

| Reason Code 21 | Continuous lake flooding or closed basin lakes |
|---|---|
| Conditions | 1. FEMA notification of a continuous lake flooding or closed basin lakes property.<br>2. The cancellation can be for only 1 term of a policy. |
| Cancellation Effective Date | Must be after the date of loss. |
| Type of Refund | No premium refund allowed. |
| Cancellation Request | N/A |
| Required Documentation | FEMA notification. |
| Policy Terms Eligible for Refund | N/A |

**Table 18: Valid Cancellation Reason Code 22**

| Reason Code 22 | Cancel/rewrite due to misrating |
| --- | --- |
| Valid Reasons | 1. To correct a policy effective date;<br>2. To cancel and rewrite ineligible PRPs or MPPP policies within the same company;<br>3. To cancel a standard-rated policy that is eligible for a PRP due to misrating, as defined in the How to Endorse section of this manual. This includes a standard-rated policy incorrectly rated in an SFHA, or failure to apply for a Newly Mapped property;<br>4. The property was eligible for continuous coverage or built-in-compliance grandfathering discovered after the time of application; *and*<br>5. System constraints prevent a legitimate correction. |
| Conditions | There are no paid or pending claims for the canceled policy term(s). |
| Cancellation/ Rewrite Effective Dates | The cancellation date and the rewritten policy effective date must be the effective date of the first eligible policy term. |
| Type of Refund | Full premium refund including fees and surcharges. Apply the refund to the newly rewritten policy. |
| Cancellation Request | N/A |
| Required Documentation | The insurer must retain documentation supporting the misrating. For a standard-rated policy eligible for the PRP, submit one of the following:<br>1. A LOMA.<br>2. A LOMR.<br>3. A letter indicating the property address and flood zone of the building, and signed and dated by a local community official.<br>4. An EC indicating the exact location and flood zone of the building signed and dated by a surveyor, an engineer, an architect, or a local community official.<br>5. A flood zone determination certification that guarantees the accuracy of the information; *or*<br>6. A copy of the most recent flood map marked to show the exact location and flood zone of the building, though additional documentation may be required if the building is close to the zone boundary. |
| Policy Terms Eligible for Refund | 1. Going back a maximum of 5 years from the current term when converting a standard-rated B, C, or X zone policy to a PRP; or a policy misrated in an SFHA that is eligible for a PRP.<br>2. In determining the number of policy years for refund eligibility, do not include terms that expired before a lapse in coverage. |

**Table 19: Valid Cancellation Reason Code 23**

| Reason Code 23 | Fraud |
|---|---|
| Valid Reasons | FEMA determines that an insured or agent committed fraud or misrepresented a material fact. |
| Cancellation Effective Date | The cancellation effective date will be the effective date of the policy term during which the fraudulent act or misrepresentation of material fact was committed. |
| Type of Refund | 1. There is no premium refund for this reason code.<br>2. If the agent did not commit or participate in the fraud, the agent will retain the full commission and there is no reduction to the insurer's expense allowance. |
| Cancellation Request | N/A |
| Required Documentation | FEMA notification. |
| Policy Terms Eligible for Refund | N/A |

**Table 20: Valid Cancellation Reason Code 24**

| Reason Code 24 | Cancel/rewrite due to map revision, LOMA, or LOMR |
|---|---|
| Valid Reasons | To cancel a standard-rated flood insurance policy and rewrite to a PRP within the same company as the result of a map revision, LOMA, or LOMR. |
| Conditions | There are no paid or pending claims for the canceled policy term(s). |
| Cancellation/ Rewrite Effective Dates | The cancellation date and the rewritten policy effective date must be the effective date of the first eligible policy term. |
| Type of Refund | Full premium refund including fees and surcharges. The insurer must apply the refund to the new rewritten policy. |
| Cancellation Request | The insurer must receive the request during the policy term. |
| Required Documentation | 1. A copy of the revised map, LOMA, or LOMR.<br>2. A signed and dated cancellation/nullification request. |
| Policy Terms Eligible for Refund | Up to five policy years from receipt date of cancellation request provided there are no paid or pending claims for the canceled policy term(s). |

### Table 21: Valid Cancellation Reason Code 25

| Reason Code 25 | HFIAA Section 28 refund |
| --- | --- |
| Valid Reasons | To cancel and rewrite policies subject to the HFIAA. |
| Cancellation Effective Date | The policy term affected by HFIAA Section 28 reunderwriting on or after October 1, 2016 or renewing on or after October 1, 2017. |
| Type of Refund | Full premium refund including fees and surcharges. The insurer must apply the refund to the new rewritten policy. |
| Cancellation Request | N/A |
| Required Documentation | 1. Declarations page; *and*<br>2. Flood zone determination, a copy of the current map, or any other applicable documentation. |
| Policy Terms Eligible for Refund | Up to five years. |

### Table 22: Valid Cancellation Reason Code 26

**Note: Cancellation request must be submitted to FEMA for review.**

| Reason Code 26 | Duplicate policy from source other than NFIP |
| --- | --- |
| Valid Reasons | To cancel an NFIP policy when the insured obtained a duplicate policy from sources other than the NFIP. This reason can only be used when the insured did not intend to renew or purchase the NFIP policy because they purchased duplicate flood insurance coverage from a non-NFIP insurer. The NFIP will presume that an insured did not intend to renew their policy if they purchased a duplicate non-NFIP policy prior to the NFIP policy's purchase or renewal date.<br>If the insured requested to cancel or not renew the NFIP policy prior to the NFIP policy effective date, refer to Table 12: Reason Code 13 Voidance prior to effective date. |
| Cancellation Effective Date | The effective date of the NFIP policy (nullified). |
| Type of Refund | Full premium refund including fees and surcharges. |
| Cancellation Request | An NFIP insurer may cancel (nullify) a policy using this reason code without further approval from FEMA if: (1) the policyholder purchased a duplicate non-NFIP policy prior to the NFIP policy's purchase or renewal date, and (2) submitted the request to the NFIP insurer within 30 days of the NFIP policy becoming effective. FEMA must review and approve all other requests under this reason code.<br>These requests can be sent to NFIPUnderwritingmailbox@fema.dhs.gov with an explanation explaining the circumstances and a copy of both the NFIP and non-NFIP policy. |
| Required Documentation | Evidence of valid duplicate non-NFIP flood insurance policy, such as a declaration page. |
| Policy Terms Eligible for Refund | Current year. |

## V. Processing Outcomes for Cancellation/Nullification of a Flood Insurance Policy

| REASON CODE for Cancellation/ Nullification | SIGNATURE REQUIRED | PREMIUM REFUND (Including ICC, Reserve Fund Assessment, and HFIAA Surcharge) | | PROBATION SURCHARGE | | FEDERAL POLICY FEE | | PRODUCER COMMISSION (Direct Business Only) | | |
|---|---|---|---|---|---|---|---|---|---|---|
| | Insured, Agent or Both | Full | Pro Rata | Full Refund | Fully Earned | Full Refund | Fully Earned | Full Deduction | Pro Rata | Retained |
| 1 | * | | × | | × | | × | | × | |
| 2 | Both | | × | | × | | × | | × | |
| 3 | Both | | × | | × | | × | | × | |
| 4 | * | | × | | × | | × | | × | |
| 5 | Agent | × | | × | | × | | × | | |
| 6 | * | × | | × | | × | | × | | |
| 7 | Both | × | | × | | × | | × | | |
| 8 | Both | | × | | × | | × | | × | |
| 9 | Both | | × | | × | | × | | | × |
| 10 | Both | | × | | × | | × | | × | |
| 12 | Both | | × | | × | | × | | × | |
| 13 | Both | × | | × | | × | | × | | |
| 15 | Both | | × | | × | | × | | × | |
| 18 | Both | | × | | × | | × | | × | |
| 19 | Both | × | | | × | | × | | | × |
| 20 | Both | × | | × | | × | | × | | |
| 21 | * | NO REFUND OF PREMIUM, FEDERAL POLICY FEE, RESERVE FUND ASSESSMENT AND HFIAA SURCHARGE ALLOWED | | | | | | | | × |
| 22 | * | × | | × | | × | | × | | |
| 23 | * | NO REFUND OF PREMIUM, FEDERAL POLICY FEE, RESERVE FUND ASSESSMENT AND HFIAA SURCHARGE ALLOWED | | | | | | | | × |
| 24 | Both | × | | × | | × | | | | × |
| 25 | * | × | | × | | × | | | | × |
| 26 | Both | × | | × | | × | | × | | |

* Refer to the signature section at the beginning of How to Cancel.

## VI. Sample Verification Letter

**SAMPLE VERIFICATION LETTER**

**VERIFICATION THAT THERE IS NO REQUIREMENT TO MAINTAIN FLOOD INSURANCE COVERAGE WITH THE NATIONAL FLOOD INSURANCE PROGRAM**

**<Insured Property Address>**

I, ______________________________, am not required by a lender, loss payee, landlord, or any Federal agency to maintain flood insurance through the National Flood Insurance Program for the above referenced property pursuant to any statute, regulation, or contract, and I am aware that by canceling my coverage, I may lose eligibility for any subsidized premium rates made available through the National Flood Insurance Program.

Check the reason that best applies:

☐ Property Closing Did Not Occur

☐ Policy Not Required by Mortgagee Due to a Revised Zone Determination by Mortgagee

☐ Insurance No Longer Required by Mortgagee Because Property is no Longer in a Special Flood Hazard Area due to Physical Map Revision

☐ Coverage No Longer Required by Mortgagee for a Detached Structure

☐ Mortgage Paid Off

☐ Insurance No Longer Required Based on FEMA Review of Lender's Determination by Means of a Letter of Determination Review

☐ Insurance No Longer Required by the Mortgagee Because the Building is Determined Outside of the Special Flood Hazard Area by means of a Letter of Map Amendment

I CERTIFY UNDER PENALTY OF PERJURY THAT THE FOREGOING IS TRUE AND CORRECT. I UNDERSTAND THAT ANY FALSE STATEMENTS MAY CAUSE MY POLICY TO BE VOID.

______________________________

Insured Name (Printed)

______________________________ ______________________

Insured Signature Date

# Appendix A: Policy

NFIP insurers may only use the Standard Flood Insurance Policy (SFIP) established by FEMA in federal regulation to sell NFIP flood insurance policies. The SFIP defines the coverages, limitations, and exclusions for NFIP flood insurance policies and includes terms and conditions that are unique to the NFIP.

There are three policy forms:

- The Dwelling Form (see page A-3)
- The General Property Form (see page A-31)
- The Residential Condominium Building Association Policy (RCBAP) Form (see page A-55)

See the Policy Forms heading in the Before You Start section for guidance on when to use each form.

This page is intentionally left blank.

National Flood Insurance Program

# Dwelling Form

Standard Flood Insurance Policy

F-122 / October 2015

FEMA

ONLINE The NFIP Dwelling Form, SFIP FEMA Form 122, is available at https://www.fema.gov/media-library/assets/documents/18118?id=4099

FEDERAL EMERGENCY MANAGEMENT AGENCY
FEDERAL INSURANCE ADMINISTRATION

STANDARD FLOOD INSURANCE POLICY

**DWELLING FORM**

PLEASE READ THE POLICY CAREFULLY. THE FLOOD INSURANCE PROVIDED IS SUBJECT TO LIMITATIONS, RESTRICTIONS, AND EXCLUSIONS. THIS POLICY COVERS ONLY:

1. A NON-CONDOMINIUM RESIDENTIAL BUILDING DESIGNED FOR PRINCIPAL USE AS A DWELLING PLACE OF ONE TO FOUR FAMILIES, OR
2. A SINGLE FAMILY DWELLING UNIT IN A CONDOMINIUM BUILDING.

**I. AGREEMENT**

The Federal Emergency Management Agency (FEMA) provides flood insurance under the terms of the National Flood Insurance Act of 1968 and its Amendments, and Title 44 of the Code of Federal Regulations.

**We will pay you for direct physical loss by or from flood to your insured property if you:**

**1. Have paid the correct premium;**

**2. Comply with all terms and conditions of this policy; and**

**3. Have furnished accurate information and statements.**

We have the right to review the information you give us at any time and to revise your policy based on our review.

**II. DEFINITIONS**

**A.** In this policy, "you" and "your" refer to the insured(s) shown on the Declarations Page of this policy and your spouse, if a resident of the same household. Insured(s) includes: Any mortgagee and loss payee named in the Application and Declarations Page, as well as any other mortgagee or loss payee determined to exist at the time of loss in the order of precedence. "We," "us," and "our" refer to the insurer.

Some definitions are complex because they are provided as they appear in the law or regulations, or result from court cases. The precise definitions are intended to protect you.

**Flood**, as used in this flood insurance policy, means:

**1.** A general and temporary condition of partial or complete inundation of two or more acres of normally dry land area or of two or more properties (one of which is your property) from:

   **a.** Overflow of inland or tidal waters,

   **b.** Unusual and rapid accumulation or runoff of surface waters from any source,

   **c.** Mudflow.

**2.** Collapse or subsidence of land along the shore of a lake or similar body of water as a result of erosion or undermining caused by waves or currents of water exceeding anticipated cyclical levels that result in a flood as defined in A.1.a. above.

**B.** The following are the other key definitions we use in this policy:

**1.** **Act.** The National Flood Insurance Act of 1968 and any amendments to it.

**2.** **Actual Cash Value.** The cost to replace an insured item of property at the time of loss, less the value of its physical depreciation.

**3.** **Application.** The statement made and signed by you or your agent in applying for this policy. The application gives information we use to determine the eligibility of the risk, the kind of policy to be issued, and the correct premium payment. The application is part of this flood insurance policy. For us to issue you a policy, the correct premium payment must accompany the application.

**4.** **Base Flood.** A flood having a one percent chance of being equaled or exceeded in any given year.

**5.** **Basement.** Any area of the building, including any sunken room or sunken portion of a room, having its floor below ground level (subgrade) on all sides.

**6.** **Building.**

   **a.** A structure with two or more outside rigid walls and a fully secured roof, that is affixed to a permanent site;

b. A manufactured home (a "manufactured home," also known as a mobile home, is a structure: built on a permanent chassis, transported to its site in one or more sections, and affixed to a permanent foundation); or

c. A travel trailer without wheels, built on a chassis and affixed to a permanent foundation, that is regulated under the community's floodplain management and building ordinances or laws.

Building does not mean a gas or liquid storage tank or a recreational vehicle, park trailer or other similar vehicle, except as described in B.6.c. above.

7. **Cancellation.** The ending of the insurance coverage provided by this policy before the expiration date.

8. **Condominium.** That form of ownership of real property in which each unit owner has an undivided interest in common elements.

9. **Condominium Association.** The entity made up of the unit owners responsible for the maintenance and operation of:

   a. Common elements owned in undivided shares by unit owners; and

   b. Other real property in which the unit owners have use rights; where membership in the entity is a required condition of unit ownership.

10. **Declarations Page.** A computer-generated summary of information you provided in the application for insurance. The Declarations Page also describes the term of the policy, limits of coverage, and displays the premium and our name. The Declarations Page is a part of this flood insurance policy.

11. **Described Location.** The location where the insured building(s) or personal property are found. The described location is shown on the Declarations Page.

**12. Direct Physical Loss By or From Flood. Loss or damage to insured property, directly caused by a flood. There must be evidence of physical changes to the property.**

13. **Dwelling.** A building designed for use as a residence for no more than four families or a single-family unit in a building under a condominium form of ownership.

14. **Elevated Building.** A building that has no basement and that has its lowest elevated floor raised above ground level by foundation walls, shear walls, posts, piers, pilings, or columns.

15. **Emergency Program.** The initial phase of a community's participation in the National Flood Insurance Program. During this phase, only limited amounts of insurance are available under the Act.

16. **Expense Constant.** A flat charge you must pay on each new or renewal policy to defray the expenses of the Federal Government related to flood insurance.

17. **Federal Policy Fee.** A flat charge you must pay on each new or renewal policy to defray certain administrative expenses incurred in carrying out the National Flood Insurance Program. This fee covers expenses not covered by the Expense Constant.

18. **Improvements.** Fixtures, alterations, installations, or additions comprising a part of the insured dwelling or the apartment in which you reside.

19. **Mudflow.** A river of liquid and flowing mud on the surface of normally dry land areas, as when earth is carried by a current of water. Other earth movements, such as landslide, slope failure, or a saturated soil mass moving by liquidity down a slope, are not mudflows.

20. **National Flood Insurance Program (NFIP).** The program of flood insurance coverage and floodplain management administered under the Act and applicable Federal regulations in Title 44 of the Code of Federal Regulations, Subchapter B.

21. **Policy.** The entire written contract between you and us. It includes:

    a. This printed form;

    b. The application and Declarations Page;

    c. Any endorsement(s) that may be issued; and

    d. Any renewal certificate indicating that coverage has been instituted for a new policy and new policy term.

**Only one dwelling, which you specifically described in the application, may be insured under this policy.**

22. **Pollutants.** Substances that include, but are not limited to, any solid, liquid, gaseous, or thermal irritant or contaminant, including smoke, vapor, soot, fumes, acids, alkalis, chemicals, and waste. "Waste" includes, but is not limited to, materials to be recycled, reconditioned, or reclaimed.

23. **Post-FIRM Building.** A building for which construction or substantial improvement occurred after December 31, 1974, or on or after the effective date of an initial Flood Insurance Rate Map (FIRM), whichever is later.

24. **Probation Premium.** A flat charge you must pay on each new or renewal policy issued covering property in a community the NFIP has placed on probation under the provisions of 44 CFR 59.24.

25. **Regular Program.** The final phase of a community's participation in the National Flood Insurance Program. In this phase, a Flood Insurance Rate Map is in effect and full limits of coverage are available under the Act.

26. **Special Flood Hazard Area.** An area having special flood or mudflow, and/or flood-related erosion hazards, and shown on a Flood Hazard Boundary Map or Flood Insurance Rate Map as Zone A, AO, A1–A30, AE, A99, AH, AR, AR/A, AR/AE, AR/AH, AR/AO, AR/A1–A30, V1–V30, VE, or V.

27. **Unit.** A single-family unit you own in a condominium building.

28. **Valued Policy.** A policy in which the insured and the insurer agree on the value of the property insured, that value being payable in the event of a total loss. The Standard Flood Insurance Policy is not a valued policy.

## III. PROPERTY COVERED

### A. COVERAGE A—BUILDING PROPERTY

We insure against direct physical loss by or from flood to:

1. The dwelling at the described location, or for a period of 45 days at another location as set forth in III.C.2.b., Property Removed to Safety.

2. Additions and extensions attached to and in contact with the dwelling by means of a rigid exterior wall, a solid load-bearing interior wall, a stairway, an elevated walkway, or a roof. At your option, additions and extensions connected by any of these methods may be separately insured. Additions and extensions attached to and in contact with the building by means of a common interior wall that is not a solid load-bearing wall are always considered part of the dwelling and cannot be separately insured.

3. **A detached garage at the described location. Coverage is limited to no more than 10% of the limit of liability on the dwelling. Use of this insurance is at your option but reduces the building limit of liability. We do not cover any detached garage used or held for use for residential (i.e., dwelling), business, or farming purposes.**

4. Materials and supplies to be used for construction, alteration, or repair of the dwelling or a detached garage while the materials and supplies are stored in a fully enclosed building at the described location or on an adjacent property.

5. A building under construction, alteration, or repair at the described location.

   a. If the structure is not yet walled or roofed as described in the definition for building (see II.B. 6.a.) then coverage applies:

      (1) Only while such work is in progress; or

      (2) If such work is halted, only for a period of up to 90 continuous days thereafter.

   **b. However, coverage does not apply until the building is walled and roofed if the lowest floor, including the basement floor, of a non-elevated building or the lowest elevated floor of an elevated building is:**

      **(1) Below the base flood elevation in Zones AH, AE, A1–A30, AR, AR/AE, AR/AH, AR/A1–A30, AR/A, AR/AO; or**

      **(2) Below the base flood elevation adjusted to include the effect of wave action in Zones VE or V1–V30.**

   The lowest floor levels are based on the bottom of the lowest horizontal structural member of the floor in Zones VE or V1–V30 and the top of the floor in Zones AH, AE, A1–A30, AR, AR/AE, AR/AH, AR/A1–A30, AR/A, AR/AO.

6. **A manufactured home or a travel trailer as described in the Definitions section (see II.B.6.b. and II.B.6.c.).**

   **If the manufactured home or travel trailer is in a special flood hazard area, it must be anchored in the following manner at the time of the loss:**

   **a. By over-the-top or frame ties to ground anchors; or**

b. In accordance with the manufacturer's specifications; or

c. In compliance with the community's floodplain management requirements unless it has been continuously insured by the NFIP at the same described location since September 30, 1982.

7. The following items of property which are covered under Coverage A only:

a. Awnings and canopies;

b. Blinds;

c. Built-in dishwashers;

d. Built-in microwave ovens;

e. Carpet permanently installed over unfinished flooring;

f. Central air conditioners;

g. Elevator equipment;

h. Fire sprinkler systems;

i. Walk-in freezers;

j. Furnaces and radiators;

k. Garbage disposal units;

l. Hot water heaters, including solar water heaters;

m. Light fixtures;

n. Outdoor antennas and aerials fastened to buildings;

o. Permanently installed cupboards, bookcases, cabinets, paneling, and wallpaper;

p. Plumbing fixtures;

q. Pumps and machinery for operating pumps;

r. Ranges, cooking stoves, and ovens;

s. Refrigerators; and

t. Wall mirrors, permanently installed.

8. Items of property in a building enclosure below the lowest elevated floor of an elevated post-FIRM building located in Zones A1–A30, AE, AH, AR, AR/A, AR/AE, AR/AH, AR/A1–A30, V1–V30, or VE, or in a basement, regardless of the zone. Coverage is limited to the following:

a. Any of the following items, if installed in their functioning locations and, if necessary for operation, connected to a power source:

(1) Central air conditioners;

(2) Cisterns and the water in them;

(3) Drywall for walls and ceilings in a basement and the cost of labor to nail it, unfinished and unfloated and not taped, to the framing;

(4) Electrical junction and circuit breaker boxes;

(5) Electrical outlets and switches;

(6) Elevators, dumbwaiters, and related equipment, except for related equipment installed below the base flood elevation after September 30, 1987;

(7) Fuel tanks and the fuel in them;

(8) Furnaces and hot water heaters;

(9) Heat pumps;

(10) Nonflammable insulation in a basement;

(11) Pumps and tanks used in solar energy systems;

(12) Stairways and staircases attached to the building,

not separated from it by elevated walkways;

(13) Sump pumps;

(14) Water softeners and the chemicals in them, water filters, and faucets installed as an integral part of the plumbing system;

(15) Well water tanks and pumps;

(16) Required utility connections for any item in this list; and

(17) Footings, foundations, posts, pilings, piers, or other foundation walls and anchorage systems required to support a building.

b. Clean-up.

B. COVERAGE B—PERSONAL PROPERTY

1. If you have purchased personal property coverage, we insure against direct physical loss by or from flood to personal property inside a building at the described location, if:

a. The property is owned by you or your household family members; and

b. At your option, the property is owned by guests or servants.

Personal property is also covered for a period of 45 days at another location as set forth in III.C.2.b., Property Removed to Safety.

Personal property in a building that is not fully enclosed must be secured to prevent flotation out of the building. If the personal property does float out during a flood, it will be conclusively presumed that it was not reasonably secured. In that case there is no coverage for such property.

2. Coverage for personal property includes the following property, subject to B.1. above, which is covered under Coverage B only:

a. Air conditioning units, portable or window type;

b. Carpets, not permanently installed, over unfinished flooring;

c. Carpets over finished flooring;

d. Clothes washers and dryers;

e. "Cook-out" grills;

f. Food freezers, other than walk-in, and food in any freezer; and

g. Portable microwave ovens and portable dishwashers.

3. Coverage for items of property in a building enclosure below the lowest elevated floor of an elevated post-FIRM building located in Zones A1–A30, AE, AH, AR, AR/A, AR/AE, AR/AH, AR/A1–A30, V1–V30, or VE, or in a basement, regardless of the zone, is limited to the following items, if installed in their functioning locations and, if necessary for operation, connected to a power source:

a. Air conditioning units, portable or window type;

b. Clothes washers and dryers; and

c. Food freezers, other than walk-in, and food in any freezer.

4. If you are a tenant and have insured personal property under Coverage B in this policy, we will cover such

property, including your cooking stove or range and refrigerator. **The policy will also cover improvements made or acquired solely at your expense in the dwelling or apartment in which you reside, but for not more than 10% of the limit of liability shown for personal property on the Declarations Page. Use of this insurance is at your option but reduces the personal property limit of liability.**

5. **If you are the owner of a unit and have insured personal property under Coverage B in this policy, we will also cover your interior walls, floor, and ceiling (not otherwise covered under a flood insurance policy purchased by your condominium association) for not more than 10% of the limit of liability shown for personal property on the Declarations Page. Use of this insurance is at your option but reduces the personal property limit of liability.**

6. **Special Limits. We will pay no more than $2,500 for any one loss to one or more of the following kinds of personal property:**

   a. **Artwork, photographs, collectibles, or memorabilia, including but not limited to, porcelain or other figures, and sports cards;**

   b. **Rare books or autographed items;**

   c. **Jewelry, watches, precious and semi-precious stones, or articles of gold, silver, or platinum;**

   d. **Furs or any article containing fur which represents its principal value; or**

   e. **Personal property used in any business.**

7. **We will pay only for the functional value of antiques.**

C. COVERAGE C—OTHER COVERAGES

1. **Debris Removal**

   a. We will pay the expense to remove non-owned debris that is on or in insured property and debris of insured property anywhere.

   b. If you or a member of your household perform the removal work, the value of your work will be based on the Federal minimum wage.

   c. This coverage does not increase the Coverage A or Coverage B limit of liability.

2. **Loss Avoidance Measures**

   a. Sandbags, Supplies, and Labor

      **(1) We will pay up to $1,000 for costs you incur to protect the insured building from a flood or imminent danger of flood, for the following:**

      **(a) Your reasonable expenses to buy:**

      (i) Sandbags, including sand to fill them;

      (ii) Fill for temporary levees;

      (iii) Pumps; and

      (iv) Plastic sheeting and lumber used in connection with these items.

      (b) The value of work, at the Federal minimum wage, that you or a member of your household perform.

      (2) This coverage for Sandbags, Supplies and Labor only applies if damage to insured property by or from flood is imminent and the threat of flood damage is apparent enough to lead a person of common prudence to anticipate flood damage. One of the following must also occur:

SFIP DWELLING FORM PAGE 6 OF 26

(a) A general and temporary condition of flooding in the area near the described location must occur, even if the flood does not reach the building; or

(b) A legally authorized official must issue an evacuation order or other civil order for the community in which the building is located calling for measures to preserve life and property from the peril of flood.

This coverage does not increase the Coverage A or Coverage B limit of liability.

**b.** Property Removed to Safety

**(1) We will pay up to $1,000 for the reasonable expenses you incur to move insured property to a place other than the described location that contains the property in order to protect it from flood or the imminent danger of flood.**

Reasonable expenses include the value of work, at the Federal minimum wage, you or a member of your household perform.

**(2) If you move insured property to a location other than the described location that contains the property, in order to protect it from flood or the imminent danger of flood, we will cover such property while at that location for a period of 45 consecutive days from the date you begin to move it there. The personal property that is moved must be placed in a fully enclosed building or otherwise reasonably protected from the elements.**

**Any property removed, including a moveable home described in II.6.b. and c., must be placed above ground level or outside of the special flood hazard area.**

This coverage does not increase the Coverage A or Coverage B limit of liability.

**3. Condominium Loss Assessments**

**a.** If this policy insures a unit, we will pay, up to the Coverage A limit of liability, your share of loss assessments charged against you by the condominium association in accordance with the condominium association's articles of association, declarations and your deed.

**The assessment must be made as a result of direct physical loss by or from flood during the policy term, to the building's common elements.**

**b. We will not pay any loss assessment charged against you:**

**(1) And the condominium association by any governmental body;**

**(2) That results from a deductible under the insurance purchased by the condominium association insuring common elements;**

**(3) That results from a loss to personal property, including contents of a condominium building;**

**(4) That results from a loss sustained by the condominium association that was not reimbursed under a flood insurance policy written in the name of the**

association under the Act because the building was not, at the time of loss, insured for an amount equal to the lesser of:

(a) 80% or more of its full replacement cost; or

(b) The maximum amount of insurance permitted under the Act;

(5) To the extent that payment under this policy for a condominium building loss, in combination with payments under any other NFIP policies for the same building loss, exceeds the maximum amount of insurance permitted under the Act for that kind of building; or

(6) To the extent that payment under this policy for a condominium building loss, in combination with any recovery available to you as a tenant in common under any NFIP condominium association policies for the same building loss, exceeds the amount of insurance permitted under the Act for a single-family dwelling.

Loss assessment coverage does not increase the Coverage A limit of liability.

D. COVERAGE D—INCREASED COST OF COMPLIANCE

1. General

This policy pays you to comply with a State or local floodplain management law or ordinance affecting repair or reconstruction of a structure suffering flood damage. Compliance activities eligible for payment are: elevation, floodproofing, relocation, or demolition (or any combination of these activities) of your structure. **Eligible floodproofing activities are limited to:**

a. **Non-residential structures.**

b. **Residential structures with basements that satisfy FEMA's standards published in the Code of Federal Regulations [44 CFR 60.6 (b) or (c)].**

2. Limit of Liability

**We will pay you up to $30,000 under this Coverage D—Increased Cost of Compliance, which only applies to policies with building coverage (Coverage A). Our payment of claims under Coverage D is in addition to the amount of coverage which you selected on the application and which appears on the Declarations Page. But the maximum you can collect under this policy for both Coverage A—Building Property and Coverage D—Increased Cost of Compliance cannot exceed the maximum permitted under the Act.** We do not charge a separate deductible for a claim under Coverage D.

3. Eligibility

a. **A structure covered under Coverage A—Building Property sustaining a loss caused by a flood as defined by this policy must:**

(1) **Be a "repetitive loss structure."** A repetitive loss structure is one that meets the following conditions:

(a) The structure is covered by a contract of flood insurance issued under the NFIP.

(b) The structure has suffered flood damage on two occasions during a 10-year period which ends on the date of the second loss.

(c) The cost to repair the flood damage, on average, equaled or exceeded 25% of the market value of the structure at the time of each flood loss.

(d) In addition to the current claim, the NFIP must have paid the previous qualifying claim, and the State or community must have a cumulative, substantial damage provision or repetitive loss provision in its floodplain management law or ordinance being enforced against the structure; or

(2) **Be a structure that has had flood damage in which the cost to repair equals or exceeds 50% of the market value of the structure at the time of the flood.** The State or community must have a substantial damage provision in its floodplain management law or ordinance being enforced against the structure.

b. This Coverage D pays you to comply with State or local floodplain management laws or ordinances that meet the minimum standards of the National Flood Insurance Program found in the Code of Federal Regulations at 44 CFR 60.3. **We pay for compliance activities that exceed those standards under these conditions:**

(1) **3.a.(1) above.**

(2) **Elevation or floodproofing in any risk zone to preliminary or advisory base flood elevations provided by FEMA which the State or local government has adopted and is enforcing for flood-damaged structures in such areas.** (This includes compliance activities in B, C, X, or D zones which are being changed to zones with base flood elevations. This also includes compliance activities in zones where base flood elevations are being increased, and a flood-damaged structure must comply with the higher advisory base flood elevation.) **Increased Cost of Compliance coverage does not apply to situations in B, C, X, or D zones where the community has derived its own elevations and is enforcing elevation or floodproofing requirements for flood-damaged structures to elevations derived solely by the community.**

(3) **Elevation or floodproofing above the base flood elevation to meet State or local "freeboard" requirements, i.e., that a structure must be elevated above the base flood elevation.**

c. Under the minimum NFIP criteria at 44 CFR 60.3 (b)(4), States and communities must require the elevation or floodproofing of structures in unnumbered A zones to the base flood elevation where elevation data is obtained from a Federal, State, or other source. Such compliance activities are also eligible for Coverage D.

d. This coverage will also pay for the incremental cost, after demolition or relocation, of elevating or floodproofing a structure during its rebuilding at the same or another site to meet State or local floodplain management laws or ordinances, subject to Exclusion D.5.g. below.

e. This coverage will also pay to bring a flood-damaged structure into compliance with state or local floodplain management laws or ordinances even if the structure had received a variance before the present loss from the applicable floodplain management requirements.

4. **Conditions**

a. **When a structure covered under Coverage A—Building Property sustains a loss caused by a flood, our payment for the loss under this Coverage D will be for the increased cost to elevate, floodproof, relocate, or demolish (or any** combination of these activities) caused by the enforcement of current State or local floodplain management ordinances or laws. Our payment for eligible demolition activities will be for the cost to demolish and clear the site of the building debris or a portion thereof caused by the enforcement of current State or local floodplain management ordinances or laws. Eligible activities for the cost of clearing the site will include those necessary to discontinue utility service to the site and ensure proper abandonment of on-site utilities.

b. When the building is repaired or rebuilt, it must be intended for the same occupancy as the present building unless otherwise required by current floodplain management ordinances or laws.

5. Exclusions

Under this Coverage D (Increased Cost of Compliance) we will not pay for:

a. The cost to comply with any floodplain management law or ordinance in communities participating in the Emergency Program.

b. The cost associated with enforcement of any ordinance or law that requires any insured or others to test for, monitor, clean up, remove, contain, treat, detoxify or neutralize, or in any way respond to, or assess the effects of pollutants.

c. The loss in value to any insured building or other structure due to the requirements of any ordinance or law.

d. The loss in residual value of the undamaged portion of a building demolished as a consequence of enforcement of any State or local floodplain management law or ordinance.

e. Any Increased Cost of Compliance under this Coverage D:

(1) Until the building is elevated, floodproofed, demolished, or relocated on the same or to another premises; and

(2) Unless the building is elevated, floodproofed, demolished, or relocated as soon as reasonably possible after the loss, not to exceed two years.

f. Any code upgrade requirements, e.g., plumbing or electrical wiring, not specifically related to the State or local floodplain management law or ordinance.

g. Any compliance activities needed to bring additions or improvements made after the loss occurred into compliance with State or local floodplain management laws or ordinances.

h. Loss due to any ordinance or law that you were required to comply with before the current loss.

i. Any rebuilding activity to standards that do not meet the NFIP's minimum requirements. This includes any situation where the insured has received from the State or community a variance in connection with the current flood loss to rebuild the property to an elevation below the base flood elevation.

j. Increased Cost of Compliance for a garage or carport.

k. Any structure insured under an NFIP Group Flood Insurance Policy.

l. Assessments made by a condominium association on individual condominium unit owners to pay increased costs of repairing commonly owned buildings after a flood in compliance with State or local floodplain management ordinances or laws.

6. Other Provisions

a. Increased Cost of Compliance coverage will not be included in the calculation to determine whether coverage meets the 80% insurance-to-value requirement for replacement cost coverage as set forth in VII. General Conditions, V. Loss Settlement.

b. All other conditions and provisions of the policy apply.

---

IV. PROPERTY NOT COVERED

---

We do not cover any of the following:

1. Personal property not inside a building;
2. A building, and personal property in it, located entirely in, on, or over water or seaward of mean high tide if it was constructed or substantially improved after September 30, 1982;
3. Open structures, including a building used as a boathouse or any structure or building into which boats are floated, and personal property located in, on, or over water;
4. Recreational vehicles other than travel trailers described in the Definitions section (see II.B.6.c.) whether affixed to a permanent foundation or on wheels;
5. Self-propelled vehicles or machines, including their parts and equipment. However, we do cover self-propelled vehicles or machines not licensed for use on public roads that are:

   a. Used mainly to service the described location or

   b. Designed and used to assist handicapped persons, while the vehicles or machines are inside a building at the described location;

SFIP DWELLING FORM PAGE 11 OF 26

6. Land, land values, lawns, trees, shrubs, plants, growing crops, or animals;
7. Accounts, bills, coins, currency, deeds, evidences of debt, medals, money, scrip, stored value cards, postage stamps, securities, bullion, manuscripts, or other valuable papers;
8. Underground structures and equipment, including wells, septic tanks, and septic systems;
9. Those portions of walks, walkways, decks, driveways, patios and other surfaces, all whether protected by a roof or not, located outside the perimeter, exterior walls of the insured building or the building in which the insured unit is located;
10. Containers, including related equipment, such as, but not limited to, tanks containing gases or liquids;
11. Buildings or units and all their contents if more than 49% of the actual cash value of the building is below ground, unless the lowest level is at or above the base flood elevation and is below ground by reason of earth having been used as insulation material in conjunction with energy efficient building techniques;
12. Fences, retaining walls, seawalls, bulkheads, wharves, piers, bridges, and docks;
13. Aircraft or watercraft, or their furnishings and equipment;
14. Hot tubs and spas that are not bathroom fixtures, and swimming pools, and their equipment, such as, but not limited to, heaters, filters, pumps, and pipes, wherever located;
15. Property not eligible for flood insurance pursuant to the provisions of the Coastal Barrier Resources Act and the Coastal Barrier Improvement Act and amendments to these Acts;
16. Personal property you own in common with other unit owners comprising the membership of a condominium association.

## V. EXCLUSIONS

A. We only pay for direct physical loss by or from flood, which means that we do not pay you for:

1. Loss of revenue or profits;
2. Loss of access to the insured property or described location;
3. Loss of use of the insured property or described location;
4. Loss from interruption of business or production;
5. Any additional living expenses incurred while the insured building is being repaired or is unable to be occupied for any reason;
6. The cost of complying with any ordinance or law requiring or

regulating the construction, demolition, remodeling, renovation, or repair of property, including removal of any resulting debris. This exclusion does not apply to any eligible activities we describe in Coverage D—Increased Cost of Compliance; or

7. Any other economic loss you suffer.

B. We do not insure a loss directly or indirectly caused by a flood that is already in progress at the time and date:

1. The policy term begins; or
2. Coverage is added at your request.

C. We do not insure for loss to property caused directly by earth movement even if the earth movement is caused by flood. Some examples of earth movement that we do not cover are:

1. Earthquake;
2. Landslide;
3. Land subsidence;
4. Sinkholes;
5. Destabilization or movement of land that results from accumulation of water in subsurface land area; or
6. Gradual erosion.

We do, however, pay for losses from mudflow and land subsidence as a result of erosion that are specifically covered under our definition of flood (see II.A.1.c. and II.A.2.).

D. We do not insure for direct physical loss caused directly or indirectly by any of the following:

1. The pressure or weight of ice;
2. Freezing or thawing;
3. Rain, snow, sleet, hail, or water spray;
4. Water, moisture, mildew, or mold damage that results primarily from any condition:
   a. Substantially confined to the dwelling; or
   b. That is within your control, including but not limited to:
      (1) Design, structural, or mechanical defects;
      (2) Failure, stoppage, or breakage of water or sewer lines, drains, pumps, fixtures, or equipment; or
      (3) Failure to inspect and maintain the property after a flood recedes;
5. Water or water-borne material that:
   a. Backs up through sewers or drains;
   b. Discharges or overflows from a sump, sump pump or related equipment; or
   c. Seeps or leaks on or through the covered property;

unless there is a flood in the area and the flood is the proximate cause of the sewer or drain backup,

SFIP DWELLING FORM PAGE 13 OF 26

**sump pump discharge or overflow, or the seepage of water;**

6. **The pressure or weight of water unless there is a flood in the area and the flood is the proximate cause of the damage from the pressure or weight of water;**
7. **Power, heating, or cooling failure unless the failure results from direct physical loss by or from flood to power, heating, or cooling equipment on the described location;**
8. **Theft, fire, explosion, wind, or windstorm;**
9. **Anything you or any member of your household do or conspires to do to deliberately cause loss by flood; or**
10. **Alteration of the insured property that significantly increases the risk of flooding.**

E. **We do not insure for loss to any building or personal property located on land leased from the Federal Government, arising from or incident to the flooding of the land by the Federal Government, where the lease expressly holds the Federal Government harmless under flood insurance issued under any Federal Government program.**

F. **We do not pay for the testing for or monitoring of pollutants unless required by law or ordinance.**

## VI. DEDUCTIBLES

A. When a loss is covered under this policy, we will pay only that part of the loss that exceeds your deductible amount, subject to the limit of liability that applies. The deductible amount is shown on the Declarations Page.

**However, when a building under construction, alteration, or repair does not have at least two rigid exterior walls and a fully secured roof at the time of loss, your deductible amount will be two times the deductible that would otherwise apply to a completed building.**

B. In each loss from flood, separate deductibles apply to the building and personal property insured by this policy.

C. The deductible does NOT apply to:

1. III.C.2. Loss Avoidance Measures;
2. III.C.3. Condominium Loss Assessments; or
3. III.D. Increased Cost of Compliance.

## VII. GENERAL CONDITIONS

A. **PAIR AND SET CLAUSE**

In case of loss to an article that is part of a pair or set, we will have the option of paying you:

1. An amount equal to the cost of replacing the lost, damaged, or destroyed article, minus its depreciation, or
2. The amount that represents the fair proportion of the total value of the pair or set that the lost, damaged, or destroyed article bears to the pair or set.

B. **CONCEALMENT OR FRAUD AND POLICY VOIDANCE**

1. **With respect to all insureds under this policy, this policy:**

a. Is void;

b. Has no legal force or effect;

c. Cannot be renewed; and

d. Cannot be replaced by a new NFIP policy, if, before or after a loss, you or any other insured or your agent have at any time:

(1) Intentionally concealed or misrepresented any material fact or circumstance;

(2) Engaged in fraudulent conduct; or

(3) Made false statements; relating to this policy or any other NFIP insurance.

2. This policy will be void as of the date wrongful acts described in B.1. above were committed.

3. Fines, civil penalties, and imprisonment under applicable Federal laws may also apply to the acts of fraud or concealment described above.

4. This policy is also void for reasons other than fraud, misrepresentation, or wrongful act. This policy is void from its inception and has no legal force under the following conditions:

a. If the property is located in a community that was not participating in the NFIP on the policy's inception date and did not join or reenter the program during the policy term and before the loss occurred; or

b. If the property listed on the application is otherwise not eligible for coverage under the NFIP.

C. OTHER INSURANCE

1. If a loss covered by this policy is also covered by other insurance that includes flood coverage not issued under the Act, we will not pay more than the amount of insurance you are entitled to for lost, damaged, or destroyed property insured under this policy subject to the following:

a. We will pay only the proportion of the loss that the amount of insurance that applies under this policy bears to the total amount of insurance covering the loss, unless C.1.b. or c. immediately below applies.

b. If the other policy has a provision stating that it is excess insurance, this policy will be primary.

c. This policy will be primary (but subject to its own deductible) up to the deductible in the other flood policy (except another policy as described in C.1.b. above). When the other deductible amount is reached, this policy will participate in the same proportion that the amount of insurance under this policy bears to the total amount of both policies, for the remainder of the loss.

2. If there is other insurance in the name of your condominium association covering the same property covered by this policy,

**then this policy will be in excess over the other insurance.**

D. AMENDMENTS, WAIVERS, ASSIGNMENT

This policy cannot be changed nor can any of its provisions be waived without the express written consent of the Federal Insurance Administrator. No action we take under the terms of this policy constitutes a waiver of any of our rights. You may assign this policy in writing when you transfer title of your property to someone else except under these conditions:

1. When this policy covers only personal property; or
2. When this policy covers a structure during the course of construction.

E. CANCELLATION OF THE POLICY BY YOU

1. You may cancel this policy in accordance with the applicable rules and regulations of the NFIP.
2. If you cancel this policy, you may be entitled to a full or partial refund of premium also under the applicable rules and regulations of the NFIP.

F. NON-RENEWAL OF THE POLICY BY US

Your policy will not be renewed:

1. If the community where your covered property is located stops participating in the NFIP, or
2. If your building has been declared ineligible under Section 1316 of the Act.

G. REDUCTION AND REFORMATION OF COVERAGE

1. **If the premium we received from you was not enough to buy the kind and amount of coverage you requested, we will provide only the amount of coverage that can be purchased for the premium payment we received.**
2. The policy can be reformed to increase the amount of coverage resulting from the reduction described in G.1. above to the amount you requested as follows:
   a. Discovery of Insufficient Premium or Incomplete Rating Information Before a Loss:
      (1) **If we discover before you have a flood loss that your premium payment was not enough to buy the requested amount of coverage, we will send you and any mortgagee or trustee known to us a bill for the required additional premium for the current policy term (or that portion of the current policy term following any endorsement changing the amount of coverage). If you or the mortgagee or trustee pay the additional premium within 30 days from the date of our bill, we will reform the policy to increase the amount of coverage to the originally requested amount effective to the beginning of the current policy term (or subsequent date of any endorsement changing the amount of coverage).**
      (2) **If we determine before you have a flood loss that the rating information we have is incomplete and prevents us from calculating the additional premium, we will ask you to send the required information. You must submit the information within 60 days of our request. Once we determine the amount of additional premium for the current policy term, we will follow the procedure in G.2.a.(1) above.**
      (3) **If we do not receive the additional premium (or additional information) by**

**the date it is due, the amount of coverage can only be increased by endorsement subject to any appropriate waiting period.**

b. Discovery of Insufficient Premium or Incomplete Rating Information After a Loss:

(1) **If we discover after you have a flood loss that your premium payment was not enough to buy the requested amount of coverage, we will send you and any mortgagee or trustee known to us a bill for the required additional premium for the current and the prior policy terms. If you or the mortgagee or trustee pay the additional premium within 30 days of the date of our bill, we will reform the policy to increase the amount of coverage to the originally requested amount effective to the beginning of the prior policy term.**

(2) **If we discover after you have a flood loss that the rating information we have is incomplete and prevents us from calculating the additional premium, we will ask you to send the required information. You must submit the information before your claim can be paid. Once we determine the amount of additional premium for the current and prior policy terms, we will follow the procedure in G.2.b.(1) above.**

(3) **If we do not receive the additional premium by the date it is due, your flood insurance claim will be settled based on the reduced amount of coverage. The amount of coverage can only be increased by endorsement subject to any appropriate waiting period.**

3. **However, if we find that you or your agent intentionally did not tell us, or falsified, any important fact or circumstance or did anything fraudulent relating to this insurance, the provisions of Condition B. Concealment or Fraud and Policy Voidance apply.**

H. POLICY RENEWAL

1. This policy will expire at 12:01 a.m. on the last day of the policy term.

2. We must receive the payment of the appropriate renewal premium within 30 days of the expiration date.

3. If we find, however, that we did not place your renewal notice into the U.S. Postal Service, or if we did mail it, we made a mistake, e.g., we used an incorrect, incomplete, or illegible address, which delayed its delivery to you before the due date for the renewal premium, then we will follow these procedures:

   a. If you or your agent notified us, not later than 1 year after the date on which the payment of the renewal premium was due, of non-receipt of a renewal notice before the due date for the renewal premium, and we determine that the circumstances in the preceding paragraph apply, we will mail a second bill providing a revised due date, which will be 30 days after the date on which the bill is mailed.

   b. If we do not receive the premium requested in the second bill by the revised due date, then we will not renew the policy. In that case, the policy will remain an expired policy as of the expiration date shown on the Declarations Page.

4. In connection with the renewal of this policy, we may ask you during the policy term to recertify, on a Recertification Questionnaire we will provide to you, the rating information used to rate your most recent application for or renewal of insurance.

I. CONDITIONS SUSPENDING OR RESTRICTING INSURANCE

**We are not liable for loss that occurs while there is a hazard that is increased by any means within your control or knowledge.**

J. REQUIREMENTS IN CASE OF LOSS

**In case of a flood loss to insured property, you must:**

**1. Give prompt written notice to us;**

**2. As soon as reasonably possible, separate the damaged and undamaged property, putting it in the best possible order so that we may examine it;**

**3. Prepare an inventory of damaged property showing the quantity, description, actual cash value, and amount of loss. Attach all bills, receipts, and related documents;**

**4. Within 60 days after the loss, send us a proof of loss, which is your statement of the amount you are claiming under the policy signed and sworn to by you, and which furnishes us with the following information:**

**a. The date and time of loss;**

**b. A brief explanation of how the loss happened;**

**c. Your interest (for example, "owner") and the interest, if any, of others in the damaged property;**

**d. Details of any other insurance that may cover the loss;**

**e. Changes in title or occupancy of the covered property during the term of the policy;**

**f. Specifications of damaged buildings and detailed repair estimates;**

**g. Names of mortgagees or anyone else having a lien, charge, or claim against the insured property;**

**h. Details about who occupied any insured building at the time of loss and for what purpose; and**

**i. The inventory of damaged personal property described in J.3. above.**

**5. In completing the proof of loss, you must use your own judgment concerning the amount of loss and justify that amount.**

**6. You must cooperate with the adjuster or representative in the investigation of the claim.**

**7. The insurance adjuster whom we hire to investigate your claim may furnish you with a proof of loss form, and she or he may help you complete it. However, this is a matter of courtesy only, and you must still send us a proof of loss within 60 days after the loss even if the adjuster does not furnish the form or help you complete it.**

8. We have not authorized the adjuster to approve or disapprove claims or to tell you whether we will approve your claim.

9. At our option, we may accept the adjuster's report of the loss instead of your proof of loss. The adjuster's report will include information about your loss and the damages you sustained. You must sign the adjuster's report. At our option, we may require you to swear to the report.

K. OUR OPTIONS AFTER A LOSS

Options we may, in our sole discretion, exercise after loss include the following:

1. At such reasonable times and places that we may designate, you must:
   a. Show us or our representative the damaged property;
   b. Submit to examination under oath, while not in the presence of another insured, and sign the same; and
   c. Permit us to examine and make extracts and copies of:
      (1) Any policies of property insurance insuring you against loss and the deed establishing your ownership of the insured real property;
      (2) Condominium association documents including the Declarations of the condominium, its Articles of Association or Incorporation, Bylaws, rules and regulations, and other relevant documents if you are a unit owner in a condominium building; and
      (3) All books of accounts, bills, invoices and other vouchers, or certified copies pertaining to the damaged property if the originals are lost.
2. We may request, in writing, that you furnish us with a complete inventory of the lost, damaged or destroyed property, including:
   a. Quantities and costs;
   b. Actual cash values or replacement cost (whichever is appropriate);
   c. Amounts of loss claimed;
   d. Any written plans and specifications for repair of the damaged property that you can reasonably make available to us; and
   e. Evidence that prior flood damage has been repaired.
3. If we give you written notice within 30 days after we receive your signed, sworn proof of loss, we may:
   a. Repair, rebuild, or replace any part of the lost, damaged, or destroyed property with material or property of like kind and quality or its functional equivalent; and

## b. Take all or any part of the damaged property at the value that we agree upon or its appraised value.

L. **NO BENEFIT TO BAILEE**

No person or organization, other than you, having custody of covered property will benefit from this insurance.

M. **LOSS PAYMENT**

1. We will adjust all losses with you. We will pay you unless some other person or entity is named in the policy or is legally entitled to receive payment. Loss will be payable 60 days after we receive your proof of loss (or within 90 days after the insurance adjuster files the adjuster's report signed and sworn to by you in lieu of a proof of loss) and:
   a. We reach an agreement with you;
   b. There is an entry of a final judgment; or
   c. There is a filing of an appraisal award with us, as provided in VII.P.
2. If we reject your proof of loss in whole or in part you may:
   a. Accept our denial of your claim;
   b. Exercise your rights under this policy; or
   c. File an amended proof of loss as long as it is filed within 60 days of the date of the loss.

N. **ABANDONMENT**

You may not abandon to us damaged or undamaged property insured under this policy.

O. **SALVAGE**

## We may permit you to keep damaged property insured under this policy after a loss, and we will reduce the amount of the loss proceeds payable to you under the policy by the value of the salvage.

P. **APPRAISAL**

If you and we fail to agree on the actual cash value or, if applicable, replacement cost of your damaged property to settle upon the amount of loss, then either may demand an appraisal of the loss. In this event, you and we will each choose a competent and impartial appraiser within 20 days after receiving a written request from the other. The two appraisers will choose an umpire. If they cannot agree upon an umpire within 15 days, you or we may request that the choice be made by a judge of a court of record in the State where the covered property is located. The appraisers will separately state the actual cash value, the replacement cost, and the amount of loss to each item. If the appraisers submit a written report of an agreement to us, the amount agreed upon will be the amount of loss. If they fail to agree, they will submit their differences to the umpire. A decision agreed to by any two will set the amount of actual cash value and loss, or if it applies, the replacement cost and loss.

Each party will:

1. Pay its own appraiser; and
2. Bear the other expenses of the appraisal and umpire equally.

Q. **MORTGAGE CLAUSE**

The word "mortgagee" includes trustee.

Any loss payable under Coverage A—Building Property will be paid to any mortgagee of whom we have actual notice, as well as any other mortgagee or loss payee determined to exist at the time of loss, and you, as interests appear. If more than one mortgagee is named, the order of payment will be the same as the order of precedence of the mortgages.

If we deny your claim, that denial will not apply to a valid claim of the mortgagee, if the mortgagee:

1. Notifies us of any change in the ownership or occupancy, or substantial change in risk of which the mortgagee is aware;
2. Pays any premium due under this policy on demand if you have neglected to pay the premium; and
3. Submits a signed, sworn proof of loss within 60 days after receiving notice from us of your failure to do so.

All of the terms of this policy apply to the mortgagee.

The mortgagee has the right to receive loss payment even if the mortgagee has started foreclosure or similar action on the building.

If we decide to cancel or not renew this policy, it will continue in effect for the benefit of the mortgagee only for 30 days after we notify the mortgagee of the cancellation or non-renewal.

If we pay the mortgagee for any loss and deny payment to you, we are subrogated to all the rights of the mortgagee granted under the mortgage on the property. Subrogation will not impair the right of the mortgagee to recover the full amount of the mortgagee's claim.

R. **SUIT AGAINST US**

You may not sue us to recover money under this policy unless you have complied with all the requirements of the policy. If you do sue, you must start the suit within 1 year after the date of the written denial of all or part of the claim, and you must file the suit in the United States District Court of the district in which the covered property was located at the time of loss. This requirement applies to any claim that you may have under this policy and to any dispute that you may have arising out of the handling of any claim under the policy.

**S. SUBROGATION**

Whenever we make a payment for a loss under this policy, we are subrogated to your right to recover for that loss from any other person. That means that your right to recover for a loss that was partly or totally caused by someone else is automatically transferred to us, to the extent that we have paid you for the loss. We may require you to acknowledge this transfer in writing. After the loss, you may not give up our right to recover this money or do anything that would prevent us from recovering it. If you make any claim against any person who caused your loss and recover any money, you must pay us back first before you may keep any of that money.

**T. CONTINUOUS LAKE FLOODING**

1. If an insured building has been flooded by rising lake waters continuously for 90 days or more and it appears reasonably certain that a continuation of this flooding will result in a covered loss to the insured building equal to or greater than the building policy limits plus the deductible or the maximum payable under the policy for any one building loss, we will pay you the lesser of these two amounts without waiting for the further damage to occur if you sign a release agreeing:

   a. To make no further claim under this policy;

   b. Not to seek renewal of this policy;

   c. Not to apply for any flood insurance under the Act for property at the described location; and

   d. Not to seek a premium refund for current or prior terms.

   **If the policy term ends before the insured building has been flooded continuously for 90 days, the provisions of this paragraph T.1. will apply when the insured building suffers a covered loss before the policy term ends.**

2. If your insured building is subject to continuous lake flooding from a closed basin lake, you may elect to file a claim under either paragraph T.1. above or T.2. (A "closed basin lake" is a natural lake from which water leaves primarily through evaporation and whose surface area now exceeds or has exceeded 1 square mile at any time in the recorded past. Most of the nation's closed basin lakes are in the western half of the United States where annual evaporation exceeds annual precipitation and where lake levels and surface areas are subject to considerable fluctuation due to wide variations in the climate. These lakes may overtop their basins on rare occasions.) Under this paragraph T.2. we will pay your claim as if the building is a total loss even though it has not been continuously inundated for 90 days, subject to the following conditions:

   a. **Lake flood waters must damage or imminently threaten to damage your building.**

   b. **Before approval of your claim, you must:**

      (1) **Agree to a claim payment that reflects your buying back the salvage on a negotiated basis; and**

      (2) **Grant the conservation easement described in FEMA's "Policy Guidance for Closed Basin Lakes" to be recorded in the office of the local recorder of deeds.** FEMA, in consultation with the community in which the property is located, will identify on a map an area or areas of special consideration (ASC) in which there is a potential for flood damage from continuous lake flooding. FEMA will give the community the agreed-upon map showing the ASC. This easement will only apply to that portion of the property in the ASC. It will allow certain agricultural and recreational uses of the land. The only structures it will allow on any portion of the property within the ASC are certain simple agricultural and recreational structures. If any of these allowable structures are insurable buildings under the NFIP and are insured under the NFIP, they will not be eligible for the benefits of this paragraph T.2. If a U.S. Army Corps of Engineers certified flood control project or otherwise certified flood control project later protects the property, FEMA will, upon request, amend the ASC to remove areas protected by those projects. The restrictions of the easement will then no longer apply to any portion of the property removed from the ASC; and

      (3) **Comply with paragraphs T.1.a. through T.1.d. above.**

   c. **Within 90 days of approval of your claim, you must move your building to a new location**

**outside the ASC.** FEMA will give you an additional 30 days to move if you show there is sufficient reason to extend the time.

d. Before the final payment of your claim, you must acquire an elevation certificate and a floodplain development permit from the local floodplain administrator for the new location of your building.

e. **Before the approval of your claim, the community having jurisdiction over your building must:**

(1) Adopt a permanent land use ordinance, or a temporary moratorium for a period not to exceed 6 months to be followed immediately by a permanent land use ordinance, that is consistent with the provisions specified in the easement required in paragraph T.2.b. above.

(2) Agree to declare and report any violations of this ordinance to FEMA so that under Section 1316 of the National Flood Insurance Act of 1968, as amended, flood insurance to the building can be denied; and

(3) **Agree to maintain as deed-restricted, for purposes compatible with open space or agricultural or recreational use only, any affected property the community acquires an interest in.** These deed restrictions must be consistent with the provisions of paragraph T.2.b. above, except that, even if a certified project protects the property, the land use restrictions continue to apply if the property was acquired under the Hazard Mitigation Grant Program or the Flood Mitigation Assistance Program. If a non-profit land trust organization receives the property as a donation, that organization must maintain the property as deed-restricted, consistent with the provisions of paragraph T.2.b. above.

f. Before the approval of your claim, the affected State must take all action set forth in FEMA's "Policy Guidance for Closed Basin Lakes."

g. **You must have NFIP flood insurance coverage continuously in effect from a date established by FEMA until you file a claim under paragraph T.2.** If a subsequent owner buys NFIP insurance that goes into effect within 60 days of the date of transfer of title, any gap in coverage during that 60-day period will not be a violation of this continuous coverage requirement. For the purpose of honoring a claim under this paragraph T.2., we will not consider to be in effect any increased coverage that became effective after the date established by FEMA. The exception to this is any increased coverage in the amount suggested by your insurer as an inflation adjustment.

h. This paragraph T.2. will be in effect for a community when the FEMA Regional Administrator for the affected region provides to the community, in writing, the following:

(1) Confirmation that the community and the State are in compliance with the conditions in paragraphs T.2.e. and T.2.f. above, and

(2) The date by which you must have flood insurance in effect.

**U. DUPLICATE POLICIES NOT ALLOWED**

1. **We will not insure your property under more than one NFIP policy.**

If we find that the duplication was not knowingly created, we will give you written notice. The notice will advise you that you may choose one of several options under the following procedures:

a. If you choose to keep in effect the policy with the earlier effective date, you may also choose to add the coverage limits of the later policy to the limits of the earlier policy. The change will become effective as of the effective date of the later policy.

b. If you choose to keep in effect the policy with the later effective date, you may also choose to add the coverage limits of the earlier policy to the limits of the later policy. The change will be effective as of the effective date of the later policy.

In either case, you must pay the pro rata premium for the increased coverage limits within 30 days of the written notice. In no event will the resulting coverage limits exceed the permissible limits of coverage under the Act or your insurable interest, whichever is less.

We will make a refund to you, according to applicable NFIP rules, of the premium for the policy not being kept in effect.

2. Your option under Condition U. Duplicate Policies Not Allowed to elect which NFIP policy to keep in effect does not apply when duplicates have been knowingly created. Losses occurring under such circumstances will be adjusted according to the terms and conditions of the earlier policy. The policy with the later effective date must be canceled.

V. **LOSS SETTLEMENT**

1. **Introduction**

This policy provides three methods of settling losses: Replacement Cost, Special Loss Settlement, and Actual Cash Value. Each method is used for a different type of property, as explained in a–c. below.

a. Replacement Cost loss settlement, described in V.2. below, applies to a single-family dwelling provided:

(1) It is your principal residence, which means that, at the time of loss, you or your spouse lived there for 80% of:

(a) The 365 days immediately preceding the loss; or

(b) The period of your ownership, if you owned the dwelling for less than 365 days; and

(2) At the time of loss, the amount of insurance in this policy that applies to the dwelling is 80% or more of its full replacement cost immediately before the loss, or is the maximum amount of insurance available under the NFIP.

b. Special loss settlement, described in V.3. below, applies to a single-family dwelling that is a manufactured or mobile home or a travel trailer.

c. Actual Cash Value loss settlement applies to a single-family dwelling not subject to replacement cost or special loss settlement, and to the property listed in V.4. below.

2. **Replacement Cost Loss Settlement**

The following loss settlement conditions apply to a single-family dwelling described in V.1.a. above:

a. We will pay to repair or replace the damaged dwelling after application of the deductible and without deduction for depreciation, but not more than the least of the following amounts:

(1) The building limit of liability shown on your Declarations Page;

(2) The replacement cost of that part of the dwelling damaged, with materials of like kind and quality and for like use; or

(3) The necessary amount actually spent to repair or replace the damaged part of the dwelling for like use.

b. If the dwelling is rebuilt at a new location, the cost described above is limited to the cost that would have been incurred if the dwelling had been rebuilt at its former location.

c. When the full cost of repair or replacement is more than $1,000 or more than 5 percent of the whole amount of insurance that applies to the dwelling, we will not be liable for any loss under V.2.a. above or V.4.a.(2) below unless and until actual repair or replacement is completed.

d. You may disregard the replacement cost conditions above and make claim under this policy for loss to dwellings on an actual cash value basis. You may then make claim for any additional liability according to V.2.a., b., and c. above, provided you notify us of your intent to do so within 180 days after the date of loss.

e. If the community in which your dwelling is located has been converted from the Emergency Program to the Regular Program during the current policy term, then we will consider the maximum amount of available NFIP insurance to be the amount that was available at the beginning of the current policy term.

3. Special Loss Settlement

a. The following loss settlement conditions apply to a single-family dwelling that:

(1) Is a manufactured or mobile home or a travel trailer, as defined in II.B.6.b. and c.,

(2) Is at least 16 feet wide when fully assembled and has an area of at least 600 square feet within its perimeter walls when fully assembled, and

(3) Is your principal residence, as specified in V.1.a.(1) above.

b. If such a dwelling is totally destroyed or damaged to such an extent that, in our judgment, it is not economically feasible to repair, at least to its pre-damage condition, we will, at our discretion pay the least of the following amounts:

(1) The lesser of the replacement cost of the dwelling or 1.5 times the actual cash value, or

(2) The building limit of liability shown on your Declarations Page.

c. If such a dwelling is partially damaged and, in our judgment, it is economically feasible to repair it to its pre-damage condition, we will settle the loss according to the Replacement Cost conditions in V.2. above.

4. Actual Cash Value Loss Settlement

The types of property noted below are subject to actual cash value (or in the case of V.4.a.(2), below, proportional) loss settlement.

a. A dwelling, at the time of loss, when the amount of insurance on the dwelling is both less than 80% of its full replacement cost immediately before the loss and less than the maximum amount of insurance available under the NFIP. In that case, we will pay the greater of the following amounts, but not more than the amount of insurance that applies to that dwelling:

(1) The actual cash value, as defined in II.B.2., of the damaged part of the dwelling; or

(2) A proportion of the cost to repair or replace the damaged part of the dwelling, without deduction for physical depreciation and after application of the deductible.

This proportion is determined as follows: If 80% of the full replacement cost of the dwelling is less than the maximum amount of insurance available under the NFIP, then the proportion is determined by dividing the actual amount of insurance on the dwelling by the amount of insurance that represents 80% of its full replacement cost. But if 80% of the full replacement cost of the dwelling is greater than the maximum amount of insurance available under the NFIP, then the proportion is determined by dividing the actual amount of insurance on the dwelling by the maximum amount of insurance available under the NFIP.

b. A two-, three-, or four-family dwelling.

c. A unit that is not used exclusively for single-family dwelling purposes.

d. Detached garages.

e. Personal property.

f. Appliances, carpets, and carpet pads.

g. Outdoor awnings, outdoor antennas or aerials of any type, and other outdoor equipment.

h. Any property covered under this policy that is abandoned after a loss and remains as debris anywhere on the described location.

i. A dwelling that is not your principal residence.

5. **Amount of Insurance Required**

To determine the amount of insurance required for a dwelling immediately before the loss, we do not include the value of:

a. Footings, foundations, piers, or any other structures or devices that are below the undersurface of the lowest basement floor and support all or part of the dwelling;

b. Those supports listed in V.5.a. above, that are below the surface of the ground inside the foundation walls if there is no basement; and

c. Excavations and underground flues, pipes, wiring, and drains.

**NOTE:** The Coverage D—Increased Cost of Compliance limit of liability is not included in the determination of the amount of insurance required.

**VIII. LIBERALIZATION CLAUSE**

If we make a change that broadens your coverage under this edition of our policy, but does not require any additional premium, then that change will automatically apply to your insurance as of the date we implement the change, provided that this implementation date falls within 60 days before or during the policy term stated on the Declarations Page.

**IX. WHAT LAW GOVERNS**

This policy and all disputes arising from the handling of any claim under the policy are governed exclusively by the flood insurance regulations issued by FEMA, the National Flood Insurance Act of 1968, as amended (42 U.S.C. 4001, et seq.), and Federal common law.

IN WITNESS WHEREOF, we have signed this policy below and hereby enter into this Insurance Agreement.

David I. Maurstad
Deputy Associate Administrator
FEMA's Federal Insurance and Mitigation Administration

## CLAIM GUIDELINES IN CASE OF A FLOOD

If you have questions, consult your insurance agent or call the National Flood Insurance Program (NFIP) toll-free at 1-800-638-6620 or on the TDD/TTY relay line at 711.

Know your insurance representative's name and telephone number. List them here for fast reference:

Insurance Agent ______________________________

Agent's Phone Number ______________________________

- Notify us or your agent, in writing, as soon as possible after the flood.
- Your claim will be assigned to an NFIP certified adjuster.
- Identify the claims adjuster assigned to your claim and contact him or her if you have not been contacted within 24 hours after you reported the claim to your insurance representative.
- As soon as possible, separate damaged property from undamaged property so that damage can be inspected and evaluated.
- To help the claims adjuster, take photographs of the outside of the premises showing the flooding and the damage and photographs of the inside of the premises showing the height of the water and the damaged property.
- Place all account books, financial records, receipts, and other loss verification material in a safe place for examination and evaluation by the claims adjuster.
- Work cooperatively with the claims adjuster to promptly determine and document all claim items. Be prepared to advise the claims adjuster of the cause and responsible party(ies) if the flooding resulted from other than natural cause.
- Make sure that the claims adjuster fully explains, and that you fully understand, all allowances and procedures for processing claim payments. This policy requires you to send us a signed and sworn-to, detailed proof of loss within 60 days after the loss.
- Any and all coverage problems and claim allowance restrictions must be communicated directly from the NFIP. Claims adjusters are not authorized to approve or deny claims; their job is to report to the NFIP on the elements of flood cause and damage.

At our option, we may accept an adjuster's report of the loss instead of your proof of loss. The adjuster's report will include information about your loss and the damages to your insured property.

**F-122** (OCT. 2015)

National Flood Insurance Program

# General Property Form

Standard Flood Insurance Policy

F-123 / October 2015

FEMA

ONLINE The NFIP General Property Form, SFIP FEMA Form 123, is available at https://www.fema.gov/media-library/assets/documents/18113?id=4098

FEDERAL EMERGENCY MANAGEMENT AGENCY
FEDERAL INSURANCE ADMINISTRATION

STANDARD FLOOD INSURANCE POLICY

## GENERAL PROPERTY FORM

PLEASE READ THE POLICY CAREFULLY. THE FLOOD INSURANCE COVERAGE PROVIDED IS SUBJECT TO LIMITATIONS, RESTRICTIONS, AND EXCLUSIONS.

**THIS POLICY PROVIDES NO COVERAGE:**

**1. IN A REGULAR PROGRAM COMMUNITY, FOR A RESIDENTIAL CONDOMINIUM BUILDING, AS DEFINED IN THIS POLICY; AND**

**2. EXCEPT FOR PERSONAL PROPERTY COVERAGE, FOR A UNIT IN A CONDOMINIUM BUILDING.**

### I. AGREEMENT

The Federal Emergency Management Agency (FEMA) provides flood insurance under the terms of the National Flood Insurance Act of 1968 and its Amendments, and Title 44 of the Code of Federal Regulations.

**We will pay you for direct physical loss by or from flood to your insured property if you:**

**1. Have paid the correct premium;**

**2. Comply with all terms and conditions of this policy; and**

**3. Have furnished accurate information and statements.**

We have the right to review the information you give us at any time and to revise your policy based on our review.

### II. DEFINITIONS

**A.** In this policy, "you" and "your" refer to the insured(s) shown on the Declarations Page of this policy. Insured(s) includes: Any mortgagee and loss payee named in the Application and Declarations Page, as well as any other mortgagee or loss payee determined to exist at the time of loss in the order of precedence. "We," "us," and "our" refer to the insurer.

Some definitions are complex because they are provided as they appear in the law or regulations, or result from court cases. The precise definitions are intended to protect you.

**Flood**, as used in this flood insurance policy, means:

**1.** A general and temporary condition of partial or complete inundation of two or more acres of normally dry land area or of two or more properties (one of which is your property) from:

   **a.** Overflow of inland or tidal waters;

   **b.** Unusual and rapid accumulation or runoff of surface waters from any source;

   **c.** Mudflow.

**2.** Collapse or subsidence of land along the shore of a lake or similar body of water as a result of erosion or undermining caused by waves or currents of water exceeding anticipated cyclical levels which result in a flood as defined in A.1.a. above.

**B.** The following are the other key definitions we use in this policy:

**1. Act.** The National Flood Insurance Act of 1968 and any amendments to it.

**2. Actual Cash Value.** The cost to replace an insured item of property at the time of loss, less the value of its physical depreciation.

**3. Application.** The statement made and signed by you or your agent in applying for this policy. The application gives information we use to determine the eligibility of the risk, the kind of policy to be issued, and the correct premium payment. The application is part of this flood insurance policy. For us to issue you a policy, the correct premium payment must accompany the application.

4. **Base Flood.** A flood having a one percent chance of being equaled or exceeded in any given year.

5. **Basement.** Any area of the building, including any sunken room or sunken portion of a room, having its floor below ground level (subgrade) on all sides.

6. **Building.**

   a. A structure with two or more outside rigid walls and a fully secured roof, that is affixed to a permanent site;

   b. A manufactured home ("a manufactured home," also known as a mobile home, is a structure: built on a permanent chassis, transported to its site in one or more sections, and affixed to a permanent foundation); or

   c. A travel trailer without wheels, built on a chassis and affixed to a permanent foundation, that is regulated under the community's floodplain management and building ordinances or laws.

   Building does not mean a gas or liquid storage tank or a recreational vehicle, park trailer, or other similar vehicle, except as described in B.6.c., above.

7. **Cancellation.** The ending of the insurance coverage provided by this policy before the expiration date.

8. **Condominium.** That form of ownership of real property in which each unit owner has an undivided interest in common elements.

9. **Condominium Association.** The entity, formed by the unit owners, responsible for the maintenance and operation of:

   a. Common elements owned in undivided shares by unit owners; and

   b. Other real property in which the unit owners have use rights where membership in the entity is a required condition of unit ownership.

10. **Declarations Page.** A computer-generated summary of information you provided in the application for insurance. The Declarations Page also describes the term of the policy, limits of coverage, and displays the premium and our name. The Declarations Page is a part of this flood insurance policy.

11. **Described Location.** The location where the insured building or personal property is found. The described location is shown on the Declarations Page.

## 12.Direct Physical Loss By or From Flood. Loss or damage to insured property, directly caused by a flood. There must be evidence of physical changes to the property.

13. **Elevated Building.** A building that has no basement and that has its lowest elevated floor raised above ground level by foundation walls, shear walls, posts, piers, pilings, or columns.

14. **Emergency Program.** The initial phase of a community's participation in the National Flood Insurance Program. During this phase, only limited amounts of insurance are available under the Act.

15. **Expense Constant.** A flat charge you must pay on each new or renewal policy to defray the expenses of the Federal Government related to flood insurance.

16. **Federal Policy Fee.** A flat charge you must pay on each new or renewal policy to defray certain administrative expenses incurred in carrying out the National Flood Insurance Program. This fee covers expenses not covered by the expense constant.

17. **Improvements.** Fixtures, alterations, installations, or additions comprising a part of the insured building.

18. **Mudflow.** A river of liquid and flowing mud on the surfaces of normally dry land areas, as when earth is carried by a current of water. Other earth movements, such as landslide, slope failure, or a saturated soil mass moving by liquidity down a slope, are not mudflows.

19. **National Flood Insurance Program (NFIP).** The program of flood insurance coverage and floodplain management administered under the Act and applicable Federal regulations in Title 44 of the Code of Federal Regulations, Subchapter B.

20. **Policy.** The entire written contract between you and us. It includes:

    a. This printed form;

    b. The application and Declarations Page;

    c. Any endorsement(s) that may be issued; and,

    d. Any renewal certificate indicating that coverage has been instituted for a new policy and new policy term.

## Only one building, which you specifically described in the application, may be insured under this policy.

21. **Pollutants.** Substances that include, but that are not limited to, any solid, liquid, gaseous or thermal irritant or contaminant, including smoke, vapor, soot, fumes, acids, alkalis, chemicals, and waste. "Waste" includes, but is not limited to, materials to be recycled, reconditioned, or reclaimed.

22. **Post-FIRM Building.** A building for which construction or substantial improvement occurred after December 31, 1974, or on or after the effective date of an initial Flood Insurance Rate Map (FIRM), whichever is later.

23. **Probation Premium.** A flat charge you must pay on each new or renewal policy issued covering property in a community that has been placed on probation under the provisions of 44 CFR 59.24.

24. **Regular Program.** The final phase of a community's participation in the National Flood Insurance Program. In this phase, a Flood Insurance Rate Map is in effect and full limits of coverage are available under the Act.

25. **Residential Condominium Building.** A building, owned and administered as a condominium, containing one or more family units and in which at least 75% of the floor area is residential.

26. **Special Flood Hazard Area.** An area having special flood or mudflow, and/or flood-related erosion hazards, and shown on a Flood Hazard Boundary Map or Flood Insurance Rate Map as Zone A, AO, A1–A30, AE, A99, AH, AR, AR/A, AR/AE, AR/AH, AR/AO, AR/A1–A30, V1–V30, VE, V.

27. **Stock.** means merchandise held in storage or for sale, raw materials, and in-process or finished goods, including supplies used in their packing or shipping.

**Stock does not include any property not covered under Section IV. Property Not Covered**, except the following:

a. Parts and equipment for self-propelled vehicles;

b. Furnishings and equipment for watercraft;

c. Spas and hot-tubs, including their equipment; and

d. Swimming pool equipment.

28. **Unit.** A unit in a condominium building.

29. **Valued Policy.** A policy in which the insured and the insurer agree on the value of the property insured, that value being payable in the event of a total loss. The Standard Flood Insurance Policy is not a valued policy.

## III. PROPERTY COVERED

### A. COVERAGE A—BUILDING PROPERTY

We insure against direct physical loss by or from flood to:

1. The building described on the Declarations Page at the described location. **If the building is a condominium building and the named insured is the condominium association, Coverage A includes all units within the building and the improvements within the units, provided the units are owned in common by all unit owners.**

2. We also insure building property for a period of 45 days at another location, as set forth in III.C.2.b., Property Removed to Safety.

3. Additions and extensions attached to and in contact with the building by means of a rigid exterior wall, a solid load-bearing interior wall, a stairway, an elevated walkway, or a roof. At your option, additions and extensions connected by any of these methods may be separately insured. Additions and extensions attached to and in contact with the building by means of a common interior wall that is not a solid load-bearing wall are always considered part of the building and cannot be separately insured.

4. The following fixtures, machinery, and equipment, which are covered under Coverage A only:

   a. Awnings and canopies;

   b. Blinds;

   c. Carpet permanently installed over unfinished flooring;

   d. Central air conditioners;

   e. Elevator equipment;

   f. Fire extinguishing apparatus;

   g. Fire sprinkler systems;

   h. Walk-in freezers;

   i. Furnaces;

   j. Light fixtures;

   k. Outdoor antennas and aerials attached to buildings;

   l. Permanently installed cupboards, bookcases, paneling, and wallpaper;

   m. Pumps and machinery for operating pumps;

   n. Ventilating equipment; and

   o. Wall mirrors, permanently installed;

   p. In the units within the building, installed:

      (1) Built-in dishwashers;

      (2) Built-in microwave ovens;

      (3) Garbage disposal units;

      (4) Hot water heaters, including solar water heaters;

      (5) Kitchen cabinets;

      (6) Plumbing fixtures;

      (7) Radiators;

      (8) Ranges;

      (9) Refrigerators; and

      (10) Stoves.

5. Materials and supplies to be used for construction, alteration, or repair of the insured building while the materials and supplies are stored in a fully enclosed building at the described location or on an adjacent property.

6. A building under construction, alteration, or repair at the described location.

   a. If the structure is not yet walled or roofed as described in the definition for building (see II.6.a.), then coverage applies:

      (1) Only while such work is in progress; or

      (2) If such work is halted, only for a period of up to 90 continuous days thereafter.

   **b. However, coverage does not apply until the building is walled and roofed if the lowest floor, including the basement floor, of a non-elevated building or the lowest elevated floor of an elevated building is:**

      **(1) Below the base flood elevation in Zones AH, AE, A1–A30, AR, AR/AE, AR/AH, AR/A1–A30, AR/A, AR/AO; or**

      **(2) Below the base flood elevation adjusted to include the effect of wave action in Zones VE or V1–V30.**

   The lowest floor levels are based on the bottom of the lowest horizontal structural member of the floor in Zones VE or V1–V30 and the top of the floor in Zones AH, AE, A1–A30, AR, AR/AE, AR/AH, AR/A1–A30, AR/A, AR/AO.

**7. A manufactured home or a travel trailer as described in the Definitions Section (see II.B.6.b. and II.B.6.c.).**

   **If the manufactured home or travel trailer is in a special flood hazard area, it must be anchored in the following manner at the time of the loss:**

   **a. By over-the-top or frame ties to ground anchors; or**

   **b. In accordance with the manufacturer's specifications; or**

   **c. In compliance with the community's floodplain management requirements unless it has been continuously insured by the NFIP at the same described location since September 30, 1982.**

**8. Items of property in a building enclosure below the lowest elevated floor of an elevated post-FIRM building located in zones A1–A30, AE, AH, AR, AR/A, AR/AE, AR/AH, AR/A1–A30, V1–V30, or VE, or in a basement, regardless of the zone. Coverage is limited to the following:**

   **a. Any of the following items, if installed in their functioning locations and, if necessary for operation, connected to a power source:**

      **(1) Central air conditioners;**

      **(2) Cisterns and the water in them;**

      **(3) Drywall for walls and ceilings in a basement and the cost of labor to nail it, unfinished and unfloated and not taped, to the framing;**

      **(4) Electrical junction and circuit breaker boxes;**

      **(5) Electrical outlets and switches;**

      **(6) Elevators, dumbwaiters, and related equipment, except for related equipment installed below the base flood elevation after September 30, 1987;**

SFIP GENERAL PROPERTY FORM PAGE 4 OF 22

(7) **Fuel tanks and the fuel in them;**

(8) **Furnaces and hot water heaters;**

(9) **Heat pumps;**

(10) **Nonflammable insulation in a basement;**

(11) **Pumps and tanks used in solar energy systems;**

(12) **Stairways and staircases attached to the building, not separated from it by elevated walkways;**

(13) **Sump pumps;**

(14) **Water softeners and the chemicals in them, water filters, and faucets installed as an integral part of the plumbing system;**

(15) **Well water tanks and pumps;**

(16) **Required utility connections for any item in this list; and**

(17) **Footings, foundations, posts, pilings, piers, or other foundation walls and anchorage systems required to support a building.**

**b.** Clean-up.

**B. COVERAGE B—PERSONAL PROPERTY**

**1. If you have purchased personal property coverage, we insure, subject to B.2., 3., and 4. below, against direct physical loss by or from flood to personal property inside the fully enclosed insured building:**

**a. Owned solely by you, or in the case of a condominium, owned solely by the condominium association and used exclusively in the conduct of the business affairs of the condominium association; or**

**b. Owned in common by the unit owners of the condominium association.**

**We also insure such personal property for 45 days while stored at a temporary location, as set forth in III.C.2.b., Property Removed to Safety.**

**2. When this policy covers personal property, coverage will be either for household personal property or other than household personal property, while within the insured building, but not both.**

**a.** If this policy covers household personal property, it will insure household personal property usual to a living quarters, that:

**(1)** Belongs to you, or a member of your household, or at your option:

**(a)** Your domestic worker;

**(b)** Your guest; or

**(2)** You may be legally liable for.

**b.** If this policy covers other than household personal property, it will insure your:

**(1)** Furniture and fixtures;

**(2)** Machinery and equipment;

**(3)** Stock; and

**(4)** Other personal property owned by you and used in your business, subject to IV. Property Not Covered.

**3.** Coverage for personal property includes the following property, subject to B.1.a. and B.1.b. above, which is covered under Coverage B only:

**a.** Air conditioning units installed in the building;

**b.** Carpet, not permanently installed, over unfinished flooring;

c. Carpets over finished flooring;

d. Clothes washers and dryers;

e. "Cook-out" grills;

f. Food freezers, other than walk-in, and food in any freezer;

g. Outdoor equipment and furniture stored inside the insured building;

h. Ovens and the like; and

i. Portable microwave ovens and portable dishwashers.

4. **Items of property in a building enclosure below the lowest elevated floor of an elevated post-FIRM building located in Zones A1–A30, AE, AH, AR, AR/A, AR/AE, AR/AH, AR/A1–A30, V1–V30, or VE, or in a basement, regardless of the zone, is limited to the following items, if installed in their functioning locations and, if necessary for operation, connected to a power source:**

   a. **Air conditioning units—portable or window type;**

   b. **Clothes washers and dryers; and**

   c. **Food freezers, other than walk-in, and food in any freezer.**

5. **Special Limits. We will pay no more than $2,500 for any loss to one or more of the following kinds of personal property:**

   a. **Artwork, photographs, collectibles, or memorabilia, including but not limited to, porcelain or other figures, and sports cards;**

   b. **Rare books or autographed items;**

   c. **Jewelry, watches, precious and semi-precious stones, articles of gold, silver, or platinum;**

   d. **Furs or any article containing fur which represents its principal value; or**

6. **We will pay only for the functional value of antiques.**

7. **If you are a tenant, you may apply up to 10% of the Coverage B limit to improvements:**

   a. **Made a part of the building you occupy; and**

   b. **You acquired, or made at your expense, even though you cannot legally remove.**

   **This coverage does not increase the amount of insurance that applies to insured personal property.**

8. **If you are a condominium unit owner,** you may apply up to 10% of the Coverage B limit to cover loss to interior:

   a. Walls,

   b. Floors, and

   c. Ceilings,

   **that are not covered under a policy issued to the condominium association insuring the condominium building.**

   This coverage does not increase the amount of insurance that applies to insured personal property.

9. **If you are a tenant, personal property must be inside the fully enclosed building.**

C. COVERAGE C—OTHER COVERAGES

1. **Debris Removal**

   a. We will pay the expense to remove non-owned debris that is on or in insured property and debris of insured property anywhere.

   b. If you or a member of your household perform the removal work, the value of your work will be based on the Federal minimum wage.

c. This coverage does not increase the Coverage A or Coverage B limit of liability.

2. **Loss Avoidance Measures**

a. Sandbags, Supplies, and Labor

**(1) We will pay up to $1,000 for the costs you incur to protect the insured building from a flood or imminent danger of flood, for the following:**

**(a) Your reasonable expenses to buy:**

**(i)** Sandbags, including sand to fill them;

**(ii)** Fill for temporary levees;

**(iii)** Pumps; and

**(iv)** Plastic sheeting and lumber used in connection with these items; and

**(b)** The value of work, at the Federal minimum wage, that you perform.

**(2)** This coverage for Sandbags, Supplies, and Labor only applies if damage to insured property by or from flood is imminent and the threat of flood damage is apparent enough to lead a person of common prudence to anticipate flood damage. One of the following must also occur:

**(a)** A general and temporary condition of flooding in the area near the described location must occur, even if the flood does not reach the insured building; or

**(b)** A legally authorized official must issue an evacuation order or other civil order for the community in which the insured building is located calling for measures to preserve life and property from the peril of flood.

This coverage does not increase the Coverage A or Coverage B limit of liability.

b. Property Removed to Safety

**(1) We will pay up to $1,000 for the reasonable expenses you incur to move insured property to a place other than the described location that contains the property in order to protect it from flood or the imminent danger of flood.**

Reasonable expenses include the value of work, at the Federal minimum wage, that you perform.

**(2) If you move insured property to a place other than the described location that contains the property, in order to protect it from flood or the imminent danger of flood, we will cover such property while at that location for a period of 45 consecutive days from the date you begin to move it there. The personal property that is moved must be placed in a fully enclosed building, or otherwise reasonably protected from the elements.**

**Any property removed, including a moveable home described in II.6.b. and c., must be placed above ground level or outside of the special flood hazard area.**

This coverage does not increase the Coverage A or Coverage B limit of liability.

3. **Pollution Damage**

**We will pay for damage caused by pollutants to covered property if the discharge, seepage, migration, release, or escape of the pollutants is caused by or results from flood. The most we will pay under this coverage is $10,000. This coverage does not increase the Coverage A or Coverage B limits of liability. Any payment under this provision when combined with all other**

payments for the same loss cannot exceed the replacement cost or actual cash value, as appropriate, of the covered property. This coverage does not include the testing for or monitoring of pollutants unless required by law or ordinance.

D. COVERAGE D—INCREASED COST OF COMPLIANCE

1. General

This policy pays you to comply with a State or local floodplain management law or ordinance affecting repair or reconstruction of a structure suffering flood damage. Compliance activities eligible for payment are: elevation, floodproofing, relocation, or demolition (or any combination of these activities) of your structure. Eligible floodproofing activities are limited to:

a. Non-residential structures.

b. Residential structures with basements that satisfy FEMA's standards published in the Code of Federal Regulations [44 CFR 60.6 (b) or (c)].

2. Limit of Liability

We will pay you up to $30,000 under this Coverage D—Increased Cost of Compliance, which only applies to policies with building coverage (Coverage A). Our payment of claims under Coverage D is in addition to the amount of coverage which you selected on the application and which appears on the Declarations Page. But the maximum you can collect under this policy for both Coverage A (Building Property) and Coverage D (Increased Cost of Compliance) cannot exceed the maximum permitted under the Act. We do NOT charge a separate deductible for a claim under Coverage D.

3. Eligibility

a. A structure covered under Coverage A—Building Property sustaining a loss caused by a flood as defined by this policy must:

(1) Be a "repetitive loss structure." A "repetitive loss structure" is one that meets the following conditions:

(a) The structure is covered by a contract of flood insurance issued under the NFIP.

(b) The structure has suffered flood damage on 2 occasions during a 10-year period which ends on the date of the second loss.

(c) The cost to repair the flood damage, on average, equaled or exceeded 25% of the market value of the structure at the time of each flood loss.

(d) In addition to the current claim, the NFIP must have paid the previous qualifying claim, and the State or community must have a cumulative, substantial damage provision or repetitive loss provision in its floodplain management law or ordinance being enforced against the structure; or

(2) Be a structure that has had flood damage in which the cost to repair equals or exceeds 50% of the market value of the structure at the time of the flood. The State or community must have a substantial damage provision in its floodplain management law or ordinance being enforced against the structure.

b. This Coverage D pays you to comply with State or local floodplain management laws or ordinances that meet the minimum standards of the National Flood Insurance Program found in the Code of Federal Regulations at 44 CFR 60.3. We pay for compliance activities that exceed those standards under these conditions:

(1) **3.a.(1) above.**

(2) **Elevation or floodproofing in any risk zone to preliminary or advisory base flood elevations provided by FEMA which the State or local government has adopted and is enforcing for flood-damaged structures in such areas.** (This includes compliance activities in B, C, X, or D zones which are being changed to zones with base flood elevations. This also includes compliance activities in zones where base flood elevations are being increased, and a flood-damaged structure must comply with the higher advisory base flood elevation.) **Increased Cost of Compliance coverage does not apply to situations in B, C, X, or D zones where the community has derived its own elevations and is enforcing elevation or floodproofing requirements for flood-damaged structures to elevations derived solely by the community.**

(3) **Elevation or floodproofing above the base flood elevation to meet State or local "freeboard" requirements, i.e., that a structure must be elevated above the base flood elevation.**

c. Under the minimum NFIP criteria at 44 CFR 60.3 (b)(4), States and communities must require the elevation or floodproofing of structures in unnumbered A zones to the base flood elevation where elevation data is obtained from a Federal, State, or other source. Such compliance activities are also eligible for Coverage D.

d. This coverage will also pay for the incremental cost, after demolition or relocation, of elevating or floodproofing a structure during its rebuilding at the same or another site to meet State or local floodplain management laws or ordinances, subject to Exclusion D.5.g. below.

e. This coverage will also pay to bring a flood-damaged structure into compliance with State or local floodplain management laws or ordinances even if the structure had received a variance before the present loss from the applicable floodplain management requirements.

4. **Conditions**

a. **When a structure covered under Coverage A—Building Property sustains a loss caused by a flood, our payment for the loss under this Coverage D will be for the increased cost to elevate, floodproof, relocate, or demolish (or any combination of these activities) caused by the enforcement of current State or local floodplain management ordinances or laws. Our payment for eligible demolition activities will be for the cost to demolish and clear the site of the building debris or a portion thereof caused by the enforcement of current State or local floodplain management ordinances or laws. Eligible activities for the cost of clearing the site will include those necessary to discontinue utility service to the site and ensure proper abandonment of on-site utilities.**

b. **When the building is repaired or rebuilt, it must be intended for the same occupancy as the present building unless otherwise required by current floodplain management ordinances or laws.**

5. **Exclusions**

**Under this Coverage D—Increased Cost of Compliance, we will not pay for:**

a. The cost to comply with any floodplain management law or ordinance in communities participating in the Emergency Program.

b. The cost associated with enforcement of any ordinance or law that requires any insured or others to test for, monitor, clean up, remove, contain, treat, detoxify or neutralize, or in any way respond to, or assess the effects of pollutants.

c. The loss in value to any insured building or other structure due to the requirements of any ordinance or law.

d. The loss in residual value of the undamaged portion of a building demolished as a consequence of enforcement of any State or local floodplain management law or ordinance.

e. Any Increased Cost of Compliance under this Coverage D:

(1) Until the building is elevated, floodproofed, demolished, or relocated on the same or to another premises; and

(2) Unless the building is elevated, floodproofed, demolished, or relocated as soon as reasonably possible after the loss, not to exceed two years.

f. Any code upgrade requirements, e.g., plumbing or electrical wiring, not specifically related to the State or local floodplain management law or ordinance.

g. Any compliance activities needed to bring additions or improvements made after the loss occurred into compliance with State or local floodplain management laws or ordinances.

h. Loss due to any ordinance or law that you were required to comply with before the current loss.

i. Any rebuilding activity to standards that do not meet the NFIP's minimum requirements. This includes any situation where the insured has received from the State or community a variance in connection with the current flood loss to rebuild the property to an elevation below the base flood elevation.

j. Increased Cost of Compliance for a garage or carport.

k. Any structure insured under an NFIP Group Flood Insurance Policy.

l. Assessments made by a condominium association on individual condominium unit owners to pay increased costs of repairing commonly owned buildings after a flood in compliance with State or local floodplain management ordinances or laws.

6. **Other Provisions**

All other conditions and provisions of this policy apply.

## IV. PROPERTY NOT COVERED

We do not cover any of the following property:

1. Personal property not inside the fully enclosed building;
2. A building, and personal property in it, located entirely in, on, or over water or seaward of mean high tide, if it was constructed or substantially improved after September 30, 1982;
3. Open structures, including a building used as a boathouse or any structure or building into which boats are floated, and personal property located in, on, or over water;
4. Recreational vehicles other than travel trailers described in II.B.6.c., whether affixed to a permanent foundation or on wheels;
5. Self-propelled vehicles or machines, including their parts and equipment. However, we do cover self-propelled vehicles or machines, provided they are not licensed for use on public roads and are:
   a. Used mainly to service the described location; or
   b. Designed and used to assist handicapped persons, while the vehicles or machines are inside a building at the described location;
6. Land, land values, lawns, trees, shrubs, plants, growing crops, or animals;
7. Accounts, bills, coins, currency, deeds, evidences of debt, medals, money, scrip, stored value cards, postage stamps, securities, bullion, manuscripts, or other valuable papers;
8. Underground structures and equipment, including wells, septic tanks, and septic systems;
9. Those portions of walks, walkways, decks, driveways, patios, and other surfaces, all whether protected by a roof or not, located outside the perimeter, exterior walls of the insured building;
10. Containers including related equipment, such as, but not limited to, tanks containing gases or liquids;
11. Buildings or units and all their contents if more than 49% of the actual cash value of the building or unit is below ground, unless the lowest level is at or above the base flood elevation and is below ground by reason of earth having been used as insulation material in conjunction with energy efficient building techniques;
12. Fences, retaining walls, seawalls, bulkheads, wharves, piers, bridges, and docks;
13. Aircraft or watercraft, or their furnishings and equipment;
14. Hot tubs and spas that are not bathroom fixtures, and swimming pools, and their equipment such

as, but not limited to, heaters, filters, pumps, and pipes, wherever located;

15. Property not eligible for flood insurance pursuant to the provisions of the Coastal Barrier Resources Act and the Coastal Barrier Improvement Act of 1990 and amendments to these Acts;

16. Personal property owned by or in the care, custody or control of a unit owner, except for property of the type and under the circumstances set forth under III. Coverage B—Personal Property of this policy;

17. A residential condominium building located in a Regular Program community.

V. EXCLUSIONS

A. We only pay for direct physical loss by or from flood, which means that we do not pay you for:

1. Loss of revenue or profits;

2. Loss of access to the insured property or described location;

3. Loss of use of the insured property or described location;

4. Loss from interruption of business or production;

5. Any additional expenses incurred while the insured building is being repaired or is unable to be occupied for any reason;

6. The cost of complying with any ordinance or law requiring or regulating the construction, demolition, remodeling, renovation, or repair of property, including removal of any resulting debris. This exclusion does not apply to any eligible activities we describe in Coverage D—Increased Cost of Compliance; or

7. Any other economic loss you suffer.

B. We do not insure a loss directly or indirectly caused by a flood that is already in progress at the time and date:

1. The policy term begins; or

2. Coverage is added at your request.

C. We do not insure for loss to property caused directly by earth movement even if the earth movement is caused by flood. Some examples of earth movement that we do not cover are:

1. Earthquake;

2. Landslide;

3. Land subsidence;

4. Sinkholes;

5. Destabilization or movement of land that results from accumulation of water in subsurface land areas; or

6. Gradual erosion

We do, however, pay for losses from mudflow and land subsidence as a result of erosion that are specifically covered under our definition of flood (see A.1.c. and II.A.2.).

D. We do not insure for direct physical loss caused directly or indirectly by:

1. The pressure or weight of ice;
2. Freezing or thawing;
3. Rain, snow, sleet, hail, or water spray;
4. Water, moisture, mildew, or mold damage that results primarily from any condition:
   a. Substantially confined to the insured building; or
   b. That is within your control including, but not limited to:
      (1) Design, structural, or mechanical defects;
      (2) Failures, stoppages, or breakage of water or sewer lines, drains, pumps, fixtures, or equipment; or
      (3) Failure to inspect and maintain the property after a flood recedes;
5. Water or water-borne material that:
   a. Backs up through sewers or drains;
   b. Discharges or overflows from a sump, sump pump, or related equipment; or
   c. Seeps or leaks on or through the covered property;

   unless there is a flood in the area and the flood is the proximate cause of the sewer or drain backup, sump pump discharge or overflow, or the seepage of water;
6. The pressure or weight of water unless there is a flood in the area and the flood is the proximate cause of the damage from the pressure or weight of water;
7. Power, heating, or cooling failure unless the failure results from direct physical loss by or from flood to power, heating, or cooling equipment situated on the described location;
8. Theft, fire, explosion, wind, or windstorm;
9. Anything that you or your agents do or conspire to do to cause loss by flood deliberately; or
10. Alteration of the insured property that significantly increases the risk of flooding.

E. We do not insure for loss to any building or personal property located on land leased from the Federal Government, arising from or incident to the flooding of the land by the Federal Government, where the lease expressly holds the Federal Government harmless under flood insurance issued under any Federal Government program.

## VI. DEDUCTIBLES

A. When a loss is covered under this policy, we will pay only that part of the loss that exceeds the applicable deductible amount, subject to the limit of liability that applies. The deductible amount is shown on the Declarations Page.

**However, when a building under construction, alteration, or repair does not have at least two rigid exterior walls and a fully secured roof at the time of loss, your deductible amount will be two times the deductible that would otherwise apply to a completed building.**

B. In each loss from flood, separate deductibles apply to the building and personal property insured by this policy.

C. No deductible applies to:

1. III.C.2. Loss Avoidance Measures; or
2. III.D. Increased Cost of Compliance.

## VII. GENERAL CONDITIONS

A. PAIR AND SET CLAUSE

In case of loss to an article that is part of a pair or set, we will have the option of paying you:

1. An amount equal to the cost of replacing the lost, damaged, or destroyed article, less depreciation, or
2. An amount which represents the fair proportion of the total value of the pair or set that the lost, damaged, or destroyed article bears to the pair or set.

B. CONCEALMENT OR FRAUD AND POLICY VOIDANCE

1. **With respect to all insureds under this policy, this policy:**
   a. **Is void,**
   b. **Has no legal force or effect,**
   c. **Cannot be renewed, and**
   d. **Cannot be replaced by a new NFIP policy, if, before or after a loss, you or any other insured or your agent have at any time:**
      (1) **Intentionally concealed or misrepresented any material fact or circumstance,**
      (2) **Engaged in fraudulent conduct, or**
      (3) **Made false statements relating to this policy or any other NFIP insurance.**
2. This policy will be void as of the date wrongful acts described in B.1. above were committed.
3. Fines, civil penalties, and imprisonment under applicable Federal laws may also apply to the acts of fraud or concealment described above.
4. **This policy is also void for reasons other than fraud, misrepresentation, or wrongful act. This policy is void from its inception and has no legal force under the following conditions:**
   a. **If the property is located in a community that was not participating in the NFIP on the policy's inception date and did not join or re-enter the program during the policy term and before the loss occurred; or**
   b. **If the property listed on the application is otherwise not eligible for coverage under the NFIP.**

C. OTHER INSURANCE

1. **If a loss covered by this policy is also covered by other insurance that includes flood coverage not issued under the Act, we will not pay more than the amount of insurance that you are entitled to for lost, damaged, or destroyed property insured under this policy subject to the following:**

   a. **We will pay only the proportion of the loss that the amount of insurance that applies under this policy bears to the total amount of insurance covering the loss, unless C.1.b. or c. below applies.**

   b. **If the other policy has a provision stating that it is excess insurance, this policy will be primary.**

   c. **This policy will be primary (but subject to its own deductible) up to the deductible in the other flood policy (except another policy as described in C.1.b. above). When the other deductible amount is reached, this policy will participate in the same proportion that the amount of insurance under this policy bears to the total amount of both policies, for the remainder of the loss.**

2. **Where this policy covers a condominium association and there is a flood insurance policy in the name of a unit owner that covers the same loss as this policy, then this policy will be primary.**

D. AMENDMENTS, WAIVERS, ASSIGNMENT

This policy cannot be changed nor can any of its provisions be waived without the express written consent of the Federal Insurance Administrator. No action that we take under the terms of this policy can constitute a waiver of any of our rights. You may assign this policy in writing when you transfer title of your property to someone else except under these conditions:

1. When this policy covers only personal property; or
2. When this policy covers a structure during the course of construction.

E. CANCELLATION OF POLICY BY YOU

1. You may cancel this policy in accordance with the applicable rules and regulations of the NFIP.
2. If you cancel this policy, you may be entitled to a full or partial refund of premium also under the applicable rules and regulations of the NFIP.

F. NON-RENEWAL OF THE POLICY BY US

Your policy will not be renewed:

1. If the community where your covered property is located stops participating in the NFIP; or
2. If your building has been declared ineligible under section 1316 of the Act.

G. REDUCTION AND REFORMATION OF COVERAGE

1. **If the premium we received from you was not enough to buy the kind and amount of coverage that you requested, we will provide only the amount of coverage that can be purchased for the premium payment we received.**

2. The policy can be reformed to increase the amount of coverage resulting from the reduction described in G.1. above to the amount you requested as follows:

   a. Discovery of Insufficient Premium or Incomplete Rating Information Before a Loss.

      (1) **If we discover before you have a flood loss that your premium payment was not enough to buy the requested amount of coverage, we will send you and any mortgagee or trustee known to us a bill for the required**

SFIP GENERAL PROPERTY FORM PAGE 15 OF 22

additional premium for the current policy term (or that portion of the current policy term following any endorsement changing the amount of coverage). If you or the mortgagee or trustee pay the additional premium within 30 days from the date of our bill, we will reform the policy to increase the amount of coverage to the originally requested amount effective to the beginning of the current policy term (or subsequent date of any endorsement changing the amount of coverage).

(2) If we determine before you have a flood loss that the rating information we have is incomplete and prevents us from calculating the additional premium, we will ask you to send the required information. You must submit the information within 60 days of our request. Once we determine the amount of additional premium for the current policy term, we will follow the procedure in G.2.a.(1) above.

(3) If we do not receive the additional premium (or additional information) by the date it is due, the amount of coverage can only be increased by endorsement subject to any appropriate waiting period.

b. Discovery of Insufficient Premium or Incomplete Rating Information After a Loss.

(1) If we discover after you have a flood loss that your premium payment was not enough to buy the requested amount of coverage, we will send you and any mortgagee or trustee known to us a bill for the required additional premium for the current and the prior policy terms. If you or the mortgagee or trustee pay the additional premium within 30 days of the date of our bill, we will reform the policy to increase the amount of coverage to the originally requested amount effective to the beginning of the prior policy term.

(2) If we discover after you have a flood loss that the rating information we have is incomplete and prevents us from calculating the additional premium, we will ask you to send the required information. You must submit the information before your claim can be paid. Once we determine the amount of additional premium for the current and prior policy terms, we will follow the procedure in G.2.b.(1) above.

(3) If we do not receive the additional premium by the date it is due, your flood insurance

claim will be settled based on the reduced amount of coverage. The amount of coverage can only be increased by endorsement subject to any appropriate waiting period.

3. However, if we find that you or your agent intentionally did not tell us, or falsified, any important fact or circumstance or did anything fraudulent relating to this insurance, the provisions of Condition B. above apply.

H. POLICY RENEWAL

1. This policy will expire at 12:01 a.m. on the last day of the policy term.

2. We must receive the payment of the appropriate renewal premium within 30 days of the expiration date.

3. If we find, however, that we did not place your renewal notice into the U.S. Postal Service, or if we did mail it, we made a mistake, e.g., we used an incorrect, incomplete, or illegible address, which delayed its delivery to you before the due date for the renewal premium, then we will follow these procedures:

   a. If you or your agent notified us, not later than one year after the date on which the payment of the renewal premium was due, of nonreceipt of a renewal notice before the due date for the renewal premium, and we determine that the circumstances in the preceding paragraph apply, we will mail a second bill providing a revised due date, which will be 30 days after the date on which the bill is mailed.

   b. If we do not receive the premium requested in the second bill by the revised due date, then we will not renew the policy. In that case, the policy will remain as an expired policy as of the expiration date shown on the Declarations Page.

4. In connection with the renewal of this policy, we may ask you during the policy term to re-certify, on a Recertification Questionnaire that we will provide to you, the rating information used to rate your most recent application for or renewal of insurance.

I. CONDITIONS SUSPENDING OR RESTRICTING INSURANCE

We are not liable for loss that occurs while there is a hazard that is increased by any means within your control or knowledge.

J. REQUIREMENTS IN CASE OF LOSS

In case of a flood loss to insured property, you must:

1. Give prompt written notice to us;

2. As soon as reasonably possible, separate the damaged and undamaged property, putting it in the best possible order so that we may examine it;

3. Prepare an inventory of damaged property showing the quantity, description, actual cash value, and amount of loss. Attach all bills, receipts, and related documents;

4. Within 60 days after the loss, send us a proof of loss, which is your statement of the amount you are claiming under the policy signed and sworn to by you, and which furnishes us with the following information:

   a. The date and time of loss;

   b. A brief explanation of how the loss happened;

   c. Your interest (for example, "owner") and the interest, if any, of others in the damaged property;

   d. Details of any other insurance that may cover the loss;

   e. Changes in title or occupancy of the insured property during the term of the policy;

f. Specifications of damaged buildings and detailed repair estimates;

g. Names of mortgagees or anyone else having a lien, charge, or claim against the insured property;

h. Details about who occupied any insured building at the time of loss and for what purpose; and

i. The inventory of damaged property described in J.3. above.

5. In completing the proof of loss, you must use your own judgment concerning the amount of loss and justify that amount.

6. You must cooperate with the adjuster or representative in the investigation of the claim.

7. The insurance adjuster whom we hire to investigate your claim may furnish you with a proof of loss form, and she or he may help you complete it. However, this is a matter of courtesy only, and you must still send us a proof of loss within sixty days after the loss even if the adjuster does not furnish the form or help you complete it.

8. We have not authorized the adjuster to approve or disapprove claims or to tell you whether we will approve your claim.

9. At our option, we may accept the adjuster's report of the loss instead of your proof of loss. The adjuster's report will include information about your loss and the damages you sustained. You must sign the adjuster's report. At our option, we may require you to swear to the report.

K. OUR OPTIONS AFTER A LOSS

Options we may, in our sole discretion, exercise after loss include the following:

1. At such reasonable times and places that we may designate, you must:

   a. Show us or our representative the damaged property;

   b. Submit to examination under oath, while not in the presence of another insured, and sign the same; and

   c. Permit us to examine and make extracts and copies of:

      (1) Any policies of property insurance insuring you against loss and the deed establishing your ownership of the insured real property;

      (2) Condominium association documents including the Declarations of the condominium, its Articles of Association or Incorporation, Bylaws, and rules and regulations; and

      (3) All books of accounts, bills, invoices, and other vouchers, or certified copies pertaining to the damaged property if the originals are lost.

2. We may request, in writing, that you furnish us with a complete

**inventory of the lost, damaged, or destroyed property, including:**

**a. Quantities and costs;**

**b. Actual cash values;**

**c. Amounts of loss claimed;**

**d. Any written plans and specifications for repair of the damaged property that you can reasonably make available to us; and**

**e. Evidence that prior flood damage has been repaired.**

**3. If we give you written notice within 30 days after we receive your signed, sworn proof of loss, we may:**

**a. Repair, rebuild, or replace any part of the lost, damaged, or destroyed property with material or property of like kind and quality or its functional equivalent; and**

**b. Take all or any part of the damaged property at the value we agree upon or its appraised value.**

**L. NO BENEFIT TO BAILEE**

No person or organization, other than you, having custody of covered property will benefit from this insurance.

**M. LOSS PAYMENT**

1. We will adjust all losses with you. We will pay you unless some other person or entity is named in the policy or is legally entitled to receive payment. Loss will be payable 60 days after we receive your proof of loss (or within 90 days after the insurance adjuster files an adjuster's report signed and sworn to by you in lieu of a proof of loss) and:
   - a. We reach an agreement with you;
   - b. There is an entry of a final judgment; or
   - c. There is a filing of an appraisal award with us, as provided in VII.P.
2. If we reject your proof of loss in whole or in part you may:
   - a. Accept such denial of your claim;
   - b. Exercise your rights under this policy; or
   - c. File an amended proof of loss, as long as it is filed within 60 days of the date of the loss.

**N. ABANDONMENT**

You may not abandon damaged or undamaged insured property to us.

**O. SALVAGE**

**We may permit you to keep damaged insured property after a loss, and we will reduce the amount of the loss proceeds payable to you under the policy by the value of the salvage.**

**P. APPRAISAL**

If you and we fail to agree on the actual cash value of the damaged property so as to determine the amount of loss, either may demand an appraisal of the loss. In this event, you and we will each choose a competent and impartial appraiser within 20 days after receiving a written request from the other. The two appraisers will choose an umpire. If they cannot agree upon an umpire within 15 days, you or we may request that the choice be made by a judge of a court of record in the state where the insured property is located. The appraisers will separately state the actual cash value and the amount of loss to each item. If the appraisers submit a written report of an agreement to us, the amount agreed upon will be the amount of loss. If they fail to agree, they will submit their differences to the umpire. A decision agreed to by any two will set the amount of actual cash value and loss.

Each party will:

1. Pay its own appraiser; and
2. Bear the other expenses of the appraisal and umpire equally.

**Q. MORTGAGE CLAUSE**

The word "mortgagee" includes trustee.

Any loss payable under Coverage A—Building Property will be paid to any mortgagee of whom we have actual notice, as well as any other mortgagee or loss payee determined to exist at the time of loss, and you, as interests appear. If more than one mortgagee is named, the order of payment will be the same as the order of precedence of the mortgages. If we deny your claim, that denial will not apply to a valid claim of the mortgagee, if the mortgagee:

1. Notifies us of any change in the ownership or occupancy, or substantial change in risk of which the mortgagee is aware;

2. Pays any premium due under this policy on demand if you have neglected to pay the premium; and

3. Submits a signed, sworn proof of loss within 60 days after receiving notice from us of your failure to do so.

All terms of this policy apply to the mortgagee.

The mortgagee has the right to receive loss payment even if the mortgagee has started foreclosure or similar action on the building.

If we decide to cancel or not renew this policy, it will continue in effect for the benefit of the mortgagee only for 30 days after we notify the mortgagee of the cancellation or non-renewal.

If we pay the mortgagee for any loss and deny payment to you, we are subrogated to all the rights of the mortgagee granted under the mortgage on the property. Subrogation will not impair the right of the mortgagee to recover the full amount of the mortgagee's claim.

**R. SUIT AGAINST US**

You may not sue us to recover money under this policy unless you have complied with all the requirements of the policy. If you do sue, you must start the suit within one year of the date of the written denial of all or part of the claim, and you must file the suit in the United States District Court of the district in which the insured property was located at the time of loss. This requirement applies to any claim that you may have under this policy and to any dispute that you may have arising out of the handling of any claim under the policy.

**S. SUBROGATION**

Whenever we make a payment for a loss under this policy, we are subrogated to your right to recover for that loss from any other person. That means that your right to recover for a loss that was partly or totally caused by someone else is automatically transferred to us, to the extent that we have paid you for the loss. We may require you to acknowledge this transfer in writing. After the loss, you may not give up our right to recover this money or do anything that would prevent us from recovering it. If you make any claim against any person who caused your loss and recover any money, you must pay us back first before you may keep any of that money.

**T. CONTINUOUS LAKE FLOODING**

1. If an insured building has been flooded by rising lake waters continuously for 90 days or more and it appears reasonably certain that a continuation of this flooding will result in a covered loss to the insured building equal to or greater than the building policy limits plus the deductible or the maximum payable under the policy for any one building loss, we will pay you the lesser of these two amounts without waiting for the further damage to occur if you sign a release agreeing:

   a. To make no further claim under this policy;

   b. Not to seek renewal of this policy;

   c. Not to apply for any flood insurance under the Act for property at the described location; and

   d. Not to seek a premium refund for current or prior terms.

**If the policy term ends before the insured building has been flooded continuously for 90 days, the provisions of this paragraph T.1. will apply when as the insured building suffers a covered loss before the policy term ends.**

2. If your insured building is subject to continuous lake flooding from a closed basin lake, you may elect to file a claim under either paragraph T.1. above or this paragraph T.2. (A "closed basin lake" is a natural lake from which water leaves primarily through evaporation and whose surface area now exceeds or has exceeded one square mile at any time in the recorded past. Most of the nation's closed basin lakes are in the western half of the United States, where annual evaporation exceeds annual precipitation and where lake levels and surface areas are subject to considerable fluctuation due to wide variations in the climate. These lakes may overtop their basins on rare occasions.) Under this paragraph T.2 we will pay your claim as if the building is a total loss even though it has not been continuously inundated for 90 days, subject to the following conditions:

   **a. Lake flood waters must damage or imminently threaten to damage your building.**

   **b. Before approval of your claim, you must:**

      **(1) Agree to a claim payment that reflects your buying back the salvage on a negotiated basis; and**

      **(2) Grant the conservation easement described in FEMA's "Policy Guidance for Closed Basin Lakes," to be recorded in the office of the local recorder of deeds.** FEMA, in consultation with the community in which the property is located, will identify on a map an area or areas of special consideration (ASC) in which there is a potential for flood damage from continuous lake flooding. FEMA will give the community the agreed-upon map showing the ASC. This easement will only apply to that portion of the property in the

ASC. It will allow certain agricultural and recreational uses of the land. The only structures that it will allow on any portion of the property within the ASC are certain, simple agricultural and recreational structures. If any of these allowable structures are insurable buildings under the NFIP and are insured under the NFIP, they will not be eligible for the benefits of this paragraph T.2. If a U.S. Army Corps of Engineers certified flood control project or otherwise certified flood control project later protects the property, FEMA will, upon request, amend the ASC to remove areas protected by those projects. The restrictions of the easement will then no longer apply to any portion of the property removed from the ASC; and

(3) **Comply with paragraphs T.1.a. through T.1.d. above.**

c. **Within 90 days of approval of your claim, you must move your building to a new location outside the ASC.** FEMA will give you an additional 30 days to move if you show that there is sufficient reason to extend the time.

d. Before the final payment of your claim, you must acquire an elevation certificate and a floodplain development permit from the local floodplain administrator for the new location of your building.

e. **Before the approval of your claim, the community having jurisdiction over your building must:**

(1) Adopt a permanent land use ordinance, or a temporary moratorium for a period not to exceed 6 months to be followed immediately by a permanent land use ordinance, that is consistent with the provisions specified in the easement required in paragraph T.2.b. above;

(2) Agree to declare and report any violations of this ordinance to FEMA so that under Sec. 1316 of the National Flood Insurance Act of 1968, as amended, flood insurance to the building can be denied; and

(3) **Agree to maintain as deed-restricted, for purposes compatible with open space or agricultural or recreational use only, any affected property the community acquires an interest in. These deed restrictions must be consistent with the provisions of paragraph T.2.b. above except that even if a certified project protects the property, the land use restrictions continue to apply if the property was acquired under the Hazard Mitigation Grant Program or the Flood Mitigation Assistance Program. If a non-profit land trust organization receives the property as a donation, that organization must maintain the property as deed-restricted, consistent with the provisions of paragraph T.2.b. above.**

f. Before the approval of your claim, the affected State must take all action set forth in FEMA's "Policy Guidance for Closed Basin Lakes."

g. **You must have NFIP flood insurance coverage continuously in effect from a date established by FEMA until you file a claim under this paragraph T.2.** If a subsequent owner buys NFIP insurance that goes into effect within 60 days of the date of transfer of title, any gap in coverage during that 60-day period will not be a violation of this continuous coverage requirement. For the purpose of honoring a claim under this paragraph T.2, we will not consider to be in effect any increased coverage that became effective after the date established by FEMA. The exception to this is any increased coverage in the amount suggested by your insurer as an inflation adjustment.

h. This paragraph T.2. will be in effect for a community when the FEMA Regional Administrator for the affected region provides to the community, in writing, the following:

(1) Confirmation that the community and the State are in compliance with the conditions in paragraphs T.2.e. and T.2.f. above, and

(2) The date by which you must have flood insurance in effect.

**U. Duplicate Policies Not Allowed**

## 1. Property may not be insured under more than one NFIP policy.

If we find that the duplication was not knowingly created, we will give you written notice. The notice will advise you that you may choose one of several options under the following procedures:

**a.** If you choose to keep in effect the policy with the earlier effective date, you may also choose to add the coverage limits of the later policy to the limits of the earlier policy. The change will become effective as of the effective date of the later policy.

**b.** If you choose to keep in effect the policy with the later effective date, you may also choose to add the coverage limits of the earlier policy to the limits of the later policy. The change will be effective as of the effective date of the later policy.

In either case, you must pay the pro rata premium for the increased coverage limits within 30 days of the written notice. In no event will the resulting coverage limits exceed the permissible limits of coverage under the Act or your insurable interest, whichever is less. We will make a refund to you, according to applicable NFIP rules, of the premium for the policy not being kept in effect.

**2.** Your option under this Condition U. Duplicate Policies Not Allowed to elect which NFIP policy to keep in effect does not apply when duplicates have been knowingly created. Losses occurring under such circumstances will be adjusted according to the terms and conditions of the earlier policy. The policy with the later effective date must be canceled.

**V. LOSS SETTLEMENT**

We will pay the least of the following amounts after application of the deductible:

**1.** The applicable amount of insurance under this policy;

**2.** The actual cash value; or

**3.** The amount it would cost to repair or replace the property with material of like kind and quality within a reasonable time after the loss.

### VIII. LIBERALIZATION CLAUSE

If we make a change that broadens your coverage under this edition of our policy, but does not require any additional premium, then that change will automatically apply to your insurance as of the date we implement the change, provided that this implementation date falls within 60 days before, or during, the policy term stated on the Declarations Page.

### IX. WHAT LAW GOVERNS

This policy and all disputes arising from the handling of any claim under the policy are governed exclusively by the flood insurance regulations issued by FEMA, the National Flood Insurance Act of 1968, as amended (42 U.S.C. 4001, et seq.), and Federal common law.

IN WITNESS WHEREOF, we have signed this policy below and hereby enter into this Insurance Agreement.

David I. Maurstad
Deputy Associate Administrator
FEMA's Federal Insurance and Mitigation Administration

## CLAIM GUIDELINES IN CASE OF A FLOOD

If you have questions, consult your insurance agent or call the National Flood Insurance Program (NFIP) toll-free at 1-800-638-6620 or on the TDD/TTY relay line at 711.

Know your insurance representative's name and telephone number. List them here for fast reference:

Insurance Agent ____________________________________________

Agent's Phone Number ______________________________________

- Notify us or your agent, in writing, as soon as possible after the flood.
- Your claim will be assigned to an NFIP certified adjuster.
- Identify the claims adjuster assigned to your claim and contact him or her if you have not been contacted within 24 hours after you reported the claim to your insurance representative.
- As soon as possible, separate damaged property from undamaged property so that damage can be inspected and evaluated.
- To help the claims adjuster, take photographs of the outside of the premises showing the flooding and the damage and photographs of the inside of the premises showing the height of the water and the damaged property.
- Place all account books, financial records, receipts, and other loss verification material in a safe place for examination and evaluation by the claims adjuster.
- Work cooperatively with the claims adjuster to promptly determine and document all claim items. Be prepared to advise the claims adjuster of the cause and responsible party(ies) if the flooding resulted from other than natural cause.
- Make sure that the claims adjuster fully explains, and that you fully understand, all allowances and procedures for processing claim payments. This policy requires you to send us a signed and sworn-to, detailed proof of loss within 60 days after the loss.
- Any and all coverage problems and claim allowance restrictions must be communicated directly from the NFIP. Claims adjusters are not authorized to approve or deny claims; their job is to report to the NFIP on the elements of flood cause and damage.

At our option, we may accept an adjuster's report of the loss instead of your proof of loss. The adjuster's report will include information about your loss and the damages to your insured property.

**F-123** (OCT. 2015)

National Flood Insurance Program

# Residential Condominium Building Association Policy

Standard Flood Insurance Policy

F-144 / October 2015

FEMA

ONLINE The NFIP RCBAP SFIP FEMA Form 144, is available at https://www.fema.gov/media-library/assets/documents/18113?id=4098

FEDERAL EMERGENCY MANAGEMENT AGENCY
FEDERAL INSURANCE ADMINISTRATION

STANDARD FLOOD INSURANCE POLICY

# RESIDENTIAL CONDOMINIUM BUILDING ASSOCIATION POLICY

## I. AGREEMENT

Please read the policy carefully. The flood insurance provided is subject to limitations, restrictions, and exclusions.

**This policy covers only a residential condominium building in a regular program community. If the community reverts to emergency program status during the policy term and remains as an emergency program community at time of renewal, this policy cannot be renewed.**

The Federal Emergency Management Agency (FEMA) provides flood insurance under the terms of the National Flood Insurance Act of 1968 and its Amendments, and Title 44 of the Code of Federal Regulations.

**We will pay you for direct physical loss by or from flood to your insured property if you:**

1. **Have paid the correct premium;**
2. **Comply with all terms and conditions of this policy; and**
3. **Have furnished accurate information and statements.**

We have the right to review the information you give us at any time and to revise your policy based on our review.

## II. DEFINITIONS

**A.** In this policy, "you" and "your" refer to the insured(s) shown on the Declarations Page of this policy. Insured(s) includes: Any mortgagee and loss payee named in the Application and Declarations Page, as well as any other mortgagee or loss payee determined to exist at the time of loss in the order of precedence. "We," "us," and "our" refer to the insurer.

Some definitions are complex because they are provided as they appear in the law or regulations, or result from court cases. The precise definitions are intended to protect you.

Flood, as used in this flood insurance policy, means:

1. A general and temporary condition of partial or complete inundation of two or more acres of normally dry land area or of two or more properties (one of which is your property) from:
   - **a.** Overflow of inland or tidal waters;
   - **b.** Unusual and rapid accumulation or runoff of surface waters from any source;
   - **c.** Mudflow.
2. Collapse or subsidence of land along the shore of a lake or similar body of water as a result of erosion or undermining caused by waves or currents of water exceeding anticipated cyclical levels which result in a flood as defined in A.1.a above.

**B.** The following are the other key definitions that we use in this policy:

1. **Act.** The National Flood Insurance Act of 1968 and any amendments to it.
2. **Actual Cash Value.** The cost to replace an insured item of property at the time of loss, less the value of its physical depreciation.
3. **Application.** The statement made and signed by you or your agent in applying for this policy. The application gives information we use to determine the eligibility of the risk, the kind of policy to be issued, and the correct premium payment. The application is part of this flood insurance policy. For us to issue you a policy, the correct premium payment must accompany the application.
4. **Base Flood.** A flood having a one percent chance of being equaled or exceeded in any given year.
5. **Basement.** Any area of the building, including any sunken room or sunken portion of a room, having its floor below ground level (subgrade) on all sides.

6. **Building**

   a. A structure with two or more outside rigid walls and a fully secured roof, that is affixed to a permanent site;

   b. A manufactured home ("a manufactured home," also known as a mobile home, is a structure: built on a permanent chassis, transported to its site in one or more sections, and affixed to a permanent foundation); or

   c. A travel trailer without wheels, built on a chassis and affixed to a permanent foundation, that is regulated under the community's floodplain management and building ordinances or laws.

   Building does not mean a gas or liquid storage tank or a recreational vehicle, park trailer or other similar vehicle, except as described in B.6.c., above.

7. **Cancellation.** The ending of the insurance coverage provided by this policy before the expiration date.

8. **Condominium.** That form of ownership of real property in which each unit owner has an undivided interest in common elements.

9. **Condominium Association.** The entity, formed by the unit owners, responsible for the maintenance and operation of:

   a. Common elements owned in undivided shares by unit owners; and

   b. Other real property in which the unit owners have use rights; where membership in the entity is a required condition of unit ownership.

10. **Declarations Page.** A computer-generated summary of information you provided in the application for insurance. The Declarations Page also describes the term of the policy, limits of coverage, and displays the premium and our name. The Declarations Page is a part of this flood insurance policy.

11. **Described Location.** The location where the insured building or personal property is found. The described location is shown on the Declarations Page.

## 12. Direct Physical Loss By or From Flood. Loss or damage to insured property, directly caused by a flood. There must be evidence of physical changes to the property.

13. **Elevated Building.** A building that has no basement and that has its lowest elevated floor raised above ground level by foundation walls, shear walls, posts, piers, pilings, or columns.

14. **Emergency Program.** The initial phase of a community's participation in the National Flood Insurance Program. During this phase, only limited amounts of insurance are available under the Act.

15. **Expense Constant.** A flat charge you must pay on each new or renewal policy to defray the expenses of the Federal Government related to flood insurance.

16. **Federal Policy Fee.** A flat charge you must pay on each new or renewal policy to defray certain administrative expenses incurred in carrying out the National Flood Insurance Program. This fee covers expenses not covered by the expense constant.

17. **Improvements.** Fixtures, alterations, installations, or additions comprising a part of the residential condominium building, including improvements in the units.

18. **Mudflow.** A river of liquid and flowing mud on the surfaces of normally dry land areas, as when earth is carried by a current of water. Other earth movements, such as landslide, slope failure, or a saturated soil mass moving by liquidity down a slope, are not mudflows.

19. **National Flood Insurance Program (NFIP).** The program of flood insurance coverage and floodplain management administered under the Act and applicable Federal regulations in Title 44 of the Code of Federal Regulations, Subchapter B.

20. **Policy.** The entire written contract between you and us. It includes:

    a. This printed form;

    b. The application and Declarations Page;

    c. Any endorsement(s) that may be issued; and

    d. Any renewal certificate indicating that coverage has been instituted for a new policy and new policy term.

## Only one building, which you specifically described in the application, may be insured under this policy.

21. **Pollutants.** Substances that include, but are not limited to, any solid, liquid, gaseous, or thermal irritant or contaminant, including smoke, vapor, soot, fumes, acids, alkalis, chemicals, and waste. "Waste" includes, but is not limited to, materials to be recycled, reconditioned, or reclaimed.

22. **Post-FIRM Building.** A building for which construction or substantial improvement occurred after December 31, 1974, or on or after the effective date of an initial Flood Insurance Rate Map (FIRM), whichever is later.

23. **Probation Premium.** A flat charge you must pay on each new or renewal policy issued covering property in a community that the NFIP has placed on probation under the provisions of 44 CFR 59.24.

24. **Regular Program.** The final phase of a community's participation in the National Flood Insurance Program. In this phase, a Flood Insurance Rate Map is in effect and full limits of coverage are available under the Act.

25. **Residential Condominium Building.** A building, owned and administered as a condominium, containing one or more family units and in which at least 75% of the floor area is residential.

26. **Special Flood Hazard Area.** An area having special flood or mudflow, and/or flood-related erosion hazards, and shown on a Flood Hazard Boundary Map or Flood Insurance Rate Map as Zone A, AO, A1–A30, AE, A99, AH, AR, AR/A, AR/AE, AR/AH, AR/AO, AR/A1–A30, V1–V30, VE, or V.

27. **Unit.** A single-family unit in a residential condominium building.

28. **Valued Policy.** A policy in which the insured and the insurer agree on the value of the property insured, that value being payable in the event of a total loss. The Standard Flood Insurance Policy is not a valued policy.

## III. PROPERTY COVERED

### A. COVERAGE A—BUILDING PROPERTY

We insure against direct physical loss by or from flood to:

1. The residential condominium building described on the Declarations Page at the described location, including all units within the building and the improvements within the units.

2. We also insure such building property for a period of 45 days at another location, as set forth in III.C.2.b., Property Removed to Safety.

3. Additions and extensions attached to and in contact with the building by means of a rigid exterior wall, a solid load-bearing interior wall, a stairway, an elevated walkway, or a roof. At your option, additions and extensions connected by any of these methods may be separately insured. Additions and extensions attached to and in contact with the building by means of a common interior wall that is not a solid load-bearing wall are always considered part of the building and cannot be separately insured.

4. The following fixtures, machinery and equipment, including its units, which are covered under Coverage A only:

   a. Awnings and canopies;

   b. Blinds;

   c. Carpet permanently installed over unfinished flooring;

   d. Central air conditioners;

   e. Elevator equipment;

   f. Fire extinguishing apparatus;

   g. Fire sprinkler systems;

   h. Walk-in freezers;

   i. Furnaces;

   j. Light fixtures;

   k. Outdoor antennas and aerials fastened to buildings;

   l. Permanently installed cupboards, bookcases, paneling, and wallpaper;

   m. Pumps and machinery for operating pumps;

   n. Ventilating equipment;

   o. Wall mirrors, permanently installed; and

   p. In the units within the building, installed:

      (1) Built-in dishwashers;

      (2) Built-in microwave ovens;

      (3) Garbage disposal units;

      (4) Hot water heaters, including solar water heaters;

      (5) Kitchen cabinets;

      (6) Plumbing fixtures;

      (7) Radiators;

      (8) Ranges;

      (9) Refrigerators; and

      (10) Stoves.

5. Materials and supplies to be used for construction, alteration or repair of the insured building while the materials and supplies are stored in a fully enclosed building at the described location or on an adjacent property.

6. A building under construction, alteration or repair at the described location.

   a. If the structure is not yet walled or roofed as described in the definition for building (see II.B.6.a.), then coverage applies:

      (1) Only while such work is in progress; or

      (2) If such work is halted, only for a period of up to 90 continuous days thereafter.

   **b. However, coverage does not apply until the building is walled and roofed if the lowest floor, including the basement floor, of a non-elevated building or the lowest elevated floor of an elevated building is:**

      **(1) Below the base flood elevation in Zones AH, AE,**

A1–30, AR, AR/AE, AR/AH, AR/A1–30, AR/A, AR/AO; or

(2) Below the base flood elevation adjusted to include the effect of wave action in Zones VE or V1–30.

The lowest floor levels are based on the bottom of the lowest horizontal structural member of the floor in Zones VE or V1–V30 and the top of the floor in Zones AH, AE, A1–A30, AR, AR/AE, AR/AH, AR/A1–A30, AR/A, AR/AO.

7. A manufactured home or a travel trailer as described in the Definitions Section (See II.B.b. and c.).

   If the manufactured home is in a special flood hazard area, it must be anchored in the following manner at the time of the loss:

   a. By over-the-top or frame ties to ground anchors; or

   b. In accordance with the manufacturer's specifications; or

   c. In compliance with the community's floodplain management requirements unless it has been continuously insured by the NFIP at the same described location since September 30, 1982.

8. Items of property in a building enclosure below the lowest elevated floor of an elevated post-FIRM building located in zones A1–A30, AE, AH, AR, AR/A, AR/AE, AR/AH, AR/A1–A30, V1–V30, or VE, or in a basement, regardless of the zone. Coverage is limited to the following:

   a. Any of the following items, if installed in their functioning locations and, if necessary for operation, connected to a power source:

   (1) Central air conditioners;

   (2) Cisterns and the water in them;

   (3) Drywall for walls and ceilings in a basement and the cost of labor to nail it, unfinished and unfloated and not taped, to the framing;

   (4) Electrical junction and circuit breaker boxes;

   (5) Electrical outlets and switches;

   (6) Elevators, dumbwaiters, and related equipment, except for related equipment installed below the base flood elevation after September 30, 1987;

   (7) Fuel tanks and the fuel in them;

   (8) Furnaces and hot water heaters;

   (9) Heat pumps;

   (10) Nonflammable insulation in a basement;

   (11) Pumps and tanks used in solar energy systems;

   (12) Stairways and staircases attached to the building, not separated from it by elevated walkways;

   (13) Sump pumps;

**(14) Water softeners and the chemicals in them, water filters and faucets installed as an integral part of the plumbing system;**

**(15) Well water tanks and pumps;**

**(16) Required utility connections for any item in this list; and**

**(17) Footings, foundations, posts, pilings, piers, or other foundation walls and anchorage systems required to support a building.**

b. Clean-up.

B. COVERAGE B—PERSONAL PROPERTY

**1. If you have purchased personal property coverage, we insure, subject to B.2. and B.3. below, against direct physical loss by or from flood to personal property that is inside the fully enclosed insured building and is:**

**a. Owned by the unit owners of the condominium association in common, meaning property in which each unit owner has an undivided ownership interest; or**

**b. Owned solely by the condominium association and used exclusively in the conduct of the business affairs of the condominium association.**

**We also insure such personal property for 45 days while stored at a temporary location, as set forth in III.C.2.b., Property Removed to Safety.**

2. Coverage for personal property includes the following property, subject to B.1. above, which is covered under Coverage B only:

a. Air conditioning units—portable or window type;

b. Carpet, not permanently installed, over unfinished flooring;

c. Carpets over finished flooring;

d. Clothes washers and dryers;

e. "Cook-out" grills;

f. Food freezers, other than walk-in, and the food in any freezer;

g. Outdoor equipment and furniture stored inside the insured building;

h. Ovens and the like; and

i. Portable microwave ovens and portable dishwashers.

**3. Coverage for items of property in a building enclosure below the lowest elevated floor of an elevated post-FIRM building located in Zones A1–A30, AE, AH, AR, AR/A, AR/AE, AR/AH, AR/A1–A30, V1–V30, or VE, or in a basement, regardless of the zone, is limited to the following items, if installed in their functioning locations and, if necessary for operation, connected to a power source:**

**a. Air conditioning units—portable or window type;**

**b. Clothes washers and dryers; and**

**c. Food freezers, other than walk-in, and food in any freezer.**

**4. Special Limits. We will pay no more than $2,500 for any one loss to one or more of the following kinds of personal property:**

a. **Artwork, photographs, collectibles, or memorabilia, including but not limited to, porcelain or other figures, and sports cards;**

b. **Rare books or autographed items;**

c. **Jewelry, watches, precious and semi-precious stones, or articles of gold, silver, or platinum;**

d. **Furs or any article containing fur which represents its principal value.**

5. **We will pay only for the functional value of antiques.**

C. COVERAGE C—OTHER COVERAGES

1. **Debris Removal**

a. We will pay the expense to remove non-owned debris that is on or in insured property and debris of insured property anywhere.

b. If you or a member of your household perform the removal work, the value of your work will be based on the Federal minimum wage.

c. This coverage does not increase the Coverage A or Coverage B limit of liability.

2. **Loss Avoidance Measures**

a. Sandbags, Supplies, and Labor

(1) **We will pay up to $1,000 for the costs you incur to protect the insured building from a flood or imminent danger of flood, for the following:**

(a) **Your reasonable expenses to buy:**

(i) Sandbags, including sand to fill them;

(ii) Fill for temporary levees;

(iii) Pumps; and

(iv) Plastic sheeting and lumber used in connection with these items; and

(b) The value of work, at the Federal minimum wage, that you perform.

(2) This coverage for Sandbags, Supplies, and Labor applies only if damage to insured property by or from flood is imminent and the threat of flood damage is apparent enough to lead a person of common prudence to anticipate flood damage. One of the following must also occur:

(a) A general and temporary condition of flooding in the area near the described location must occur, even if the flood does not reach the insured building; or

(b) A legally authorized official must issue an evacuation order or other civil order for the community in which the insured building is located calling for measures to preserve life and property from the peril of flood. This coverage does not increase the Coverage A or Coverage B limit of liability.

b. Property Removed to Safety

(1) **We will pay up to $1,000 for the reasonable expenses you incur to move insured property to a place other than the described location that contains the property in order to protect it from flood or the imminent danger of flood.**

Reasonable expenses include the value of work, at the Federal minimum wage, that you perform.

(2) **If you move insured property to a location other than the described location that contains the property, in order to protect it from flood or the imminent danger of flood, we will cover such property while at that location for a period of 45 consecutive days from the date you begin to move it**

SFIP RESIDENTIAL CONDOMINIUM BUILDING ASSOCIATION POLICY FORM PAGE 6 OF 24

**there. The personal property that is moved must be placed in a fully enclosed building, or otherwise reasonably protected from the elements.**

**Any property removed, including a moveable home described in II.6.b. and c., must be placed above ground level or outside of the special flood hazard area.**

This coverage does not increase the Coverage A or Coverage B limit of liability.

D. COVERAGE D—INCREASED COST OF COMPLIANCE

1. General

This policy pays you to comply with a State or local floodplain management law or ordinance affecting repair or reconstruction of a structure suffering flood damage. Compliance activities eligible for payment are: elevation, floodproofing, relocation, or demolition (or any combination of these activities) of your structure. **Eligible floodproofing activities are limited to:**

**a. Non-residential structures.**

**b. Residential structures with basements that satisfy FEMA's standards published in the Code of Federal Regulations [44 CFR 60.6 (b) or (c)].**

2. Limit of Liability

**We will pay you up to $30,000 under this Coverage D—Increased Cost of Compliance, which only applies to policies with building coverage (Coverage A). Our payment of claims under Coverage D is in addition to the amount of coverage which you selected on the application and which appears on the Declarations Page. But the maximum you can collect under this policy for both Coverage A—Building Property and Coverage D—Increased Cost of Compliance cannot exceed the maximum permitted under the Act.** We do not charge a separate deductible for a claim under Coverage D.

3. Eligibility

**a. A structure covered under Coverage A—Building Property sustaining a loss caused by a flood as defined by this policy must:**

**(1) Be a "repetitive loss structure."** A "repetitive loss structure" is one that meets the following conditions:

(a) The structure is covered by a contract of flood insurance issued under the NFIP.

(b) The structure has suffered flood damage on 2 occasions during a 10-year period which ends on the date of the second loss.

(c) The cost to repair the flood damage, on average, equaled or exceeded 25% of the market value of the structure at the time of each flood loss.

(d) In addition to the current claim, the NFIP must have paid the previous qualifying claim, and the State or community must have a cumulative, substantial damage provision or repetitive loss provision in its floodplain management law or ordinance being enforced against the structure; or

**(2) Be a structure that has had flood damage in which the cost to repair equals or exceeds 50% of the market value of the structure at the time of the flood.** The State or community must have a substantial damage provision in its floodplain management law or ordinance being enforced against the structure.

b. This Coverage D pays you to comply with State or local floodplain management laws or ordinances that meet the minimum standards of the National

Flood Insurance Program found in the Code of Federal Regulations at 44 CFR 60.3. **We pay for compliance activities that exceed those standards under these conditions:**

**(1) 3.a.(1) above.**

**(2) Elevation or floodproofing in any risk zone to preliminary or advisory base flood elevations provided by FEMA which the State or local government has adopted and is enforcing for flood-damaged structures in such areas.** (This includes compliance activities in B, C, X, or D zones which are being changed to zones with base flood elevations. This also includes compliance activities in zones where base flood elevations are being increased, and a flood-damaged structure must comply with the higher advisory base flood elevation.) **Increased Cost of Compliance coverage does not apply to situations in B, C, X, or D zones where the community has derived its own elevations and is enforcing elevation or floodproofing requirements for flood-damaged structures to elevations derived solely by the community.**

**(3) Elevation or floodproofing above the base flood elevation to meet State or local "freeboard" requirements, i.e., that a structure must be elevated above the base flood elevation.**

c. Under the minimum NFIP criteria at 44 CFR 60.3 (b)(4), States and communities must require the elevation or floodproofing of structures in unnumbered A zones to the base flood elevation where elevation data is obtained from a Federal, State, or other source. Such compliance activities are also eligible for Coverage D.

d. This coverage will also pay for the incremental cost, after demolition or relocation, of elevating or floodproofing a structure during its rebuilding at the same or another site to meet State or local floodplain management laws or ordinances, subject to Exclusion D.5.g. below relating to improvements.

e. This coverage will also pay to bring a flood-damaged structure into compliance with State or local floodplain management laws or ordinances even if the structure had received a variance before the present loss from the applicable floodplain management requirements.

4. **Conditions**

**a. When a structure covered under Coverage A—Building Property sustains a loss caused by a flood, our payment for the loss under this Coverage D will be for the increased cost to elevate, floodproof, relocate, or demolish (or any combination of these activities) caused by the enforcement of current State or local floodplain management ordinances or laws. Our payment for eligible demolition activities will be for the cost to demolish and clear the site of the building debris or a portion thereof caused by the enforcement of current State or local floodplain management ordinances or laws. Eligible activities for the cost of clearing the site will include those necessary to discontinue utility service to the site and ensure proper abandonment of on-site utilities.**

**b. When the building is repaired or rebuilt, it must be intended for the same occupancy as**

the present building unless otherwise required by current floodplain management ordinances or laws.

5. Exclusions

Under this Coverage D—Increased Cost of Compliance, we will not pay for:

a. The cost to comply with any floodplain management law or ordinance in communities participating in the Emergency Program.

b. The cost associated with enforcement of any ordinance or law that requires any insured or others to test for, monitor, clean up, remove, contain, treat, detoxify or neutralize, or in any way respond to, or assess the effects of pollutants.

c. The loss in value to any insured building or other structure due to the requirements of any ordinance or law.

d. The loss in residual value of the undamaged portion of a building demolished as a consequence of enforcement of any State or local floodplain management law or ordinance.

e. Any Increased Cost of Compliance under this Coverage D:

(1) Until the building is elevated, floodproofed, demolished, or relocated on the same or to another premises; and

(2) Unless the building is elevated, floodproofed, demolished, or relocated as soon as reasonably possible after the loss, not to exceed two years.

f. Any code upgrade requirements, e.g., plumbing or electrical wiring, not specifically related to the State or local floodplain management law or ordinance.

g. Any compliance activities needed to bring additions or improvements made after the loss occurred into compliance with State or local floodplain management laws or ordinances.

h. Loss due to any ordinance or law that you were required to comply with before the current loss.

i. Any rebuilding activity to standards that do not meet the NFIP's minimum requirements. This includes any situation where the insured has received from the State or community a variance in connection with the current flood loss to rebuild the property to an elevation below the base flood elevation.

j. Increased Cost of Compliance for a garage or carport.

k. Any structure insured under an NFIP Group Flood Insurance Policy.

l. Assessments made by a condominium association on individual condominium unit owners to pay increased costs of repairing commonly owned buildings after a flood in compliance with State or local floodplain management ordinances or laws.

6. **Other Provisions**

   **a.** Increased Cost of Compliance coverage will not be included in the calculation to determine whether coverage meets the coinsurance requirement for replacement cost coverage under VIII. General Conditions, V. Loss Settlement.

   **b.** All other conditions and provisions of this policy apply.

---

**IV. PROPERTY NOT COVERED**

---

**We do not cover any of the following:**

1. **Personal property not inside the fully enclosed building;**
2. **A building, and personal property in it, located entirely in, on, or over water or seaward of mean high tide, if constructed or substantially improved after September 30, 1982;**
3. **Open structures, including a building used as a boathouse or any structure or building into which boats are floated, and personal property located in, on, or over water;**
4. **Recreational vehicles other than travel trailers described in the Definitions Section (see II.B.6.c.) whether affixed to a permanent foundation or on wheels;**
5. **Self-propelled vehicles or machines, including their parts and equipment.**

   **However, we do cover self-propelled vehicles or machines, provided they are not licensed for use on public roads and are:**

   **a. Used mainly to service the described location, or**

   **b. Designed and used to assist handicapped persons, while the vehicles or machines are inside a building at the described location;**
6. **Land, land values, lawns, trees, shrubs, plants, growing crops, or animals;**
7. **Accounts, bills, coins, currency, deeds, evidences of debt, medals, money, scrip, stored value cards, postage stamps, securities, bullion, manuscripts, or other valuable papers;**
8. **Underground structures and equipment, including wells, septic tanks, and septic systems;**
9. **Those portions of walks, walkways, decks, driveways, patios, and other surfaces, all whether protected by a roof or not, located outside the perimeter, exterior walls of the insured building;**
10. **Containers, including related equipment, such as, but not**

limited to, tanks containing gases or liquids;

11. Buildings and all their contents if more than 49% of the actual cash value of the building is below ground, unless the lowest level is at or above the base flood elevation and is below ground by reason of earth having been used as insulation material in conjunction with energy efficient building techniques;

12. Fences, retaining walls, seawalls, bulkheads, wharves, piers, bridges, and docks;

13. Aircraft or watercraft, or their furnishings and equipment;

14. Hot tubs and spas that are not bathroom fixtures, and swimming pools, and their equipment such as, but not limited to, heaters, filters, pumps, and pipes, wherever located;

15. Property not eligible for flood insurance pursuant to the provisions of the Coastal Barrier Resources Act and the Coastal Barrier Improvement Act of 1990 and amendments to these acts;

16. Personal property used in connection with any incidental commercial occupancy or use of the building.

## V. EXCLUSIONS

A. We only pay for direct physical loss by or from flood, which means that we do not pay you for:

1. Loss of revenue or profits;
2. Loss of access to the insured property or described location;
3. Loss of use of the insured property or described location;
4. Loss from interruption of business or production;
5. Any additional living expenses incurred while the insured building is being repaired or is unable to be occupied for any reason;
6. The cost of complying with any ordinance or law requiring or regulating the construction, demolition, remodeling, renovation, or repair of property, including removal of any resulting debris. This exclusion does not apply to any eligible activities that we describe in Coverage D—Increased Cost of Compliance; or
7. Any other economic loss.

B. We do not insure a loss directly or indirectly caused by a flood that is already in progress at the time and date:

1. The policy term begins; or
2. Coverage is added at your request.

C. We do not insure for loss to property caused directly by earth movement even if the earth movement is caused by flood. Some examples of earth movement that we do not cover are:

1. Earthquake;
2. Landslide;
3. Land subsidence;
4. Sinkholes;
5. Destabilization or movement of land that results from accumulation of water in subsurface land areas; or
6. Gradual erosion.

We do, however, pay for losses from mudflow and land subsidence as a result of erosion that are specifically covered under our definition of flood (see II.A.1.c. and II.A.2.).

D. We do not insure for direct physical loss caused directly or indirectly by:

1. The pressure or weight of ice;
2. Freezing or thawing;
3. Rain, snow, sleet, hail, or water spray;
4. Water, moisture, mildew, or mold damage that results primarily from any condition:
   a. Substantially confined to the insured building; or
   b. That is within your control including, but not limited to:
      (1) Design, structural, or mechanical defects;
      (2) Failures, stoppages, or breakage of water or sewer lines, drains, pumps, fixtures, or equipment; or
      (3) Failure to inspect and maintain the property after a flood recedes;
5. Water or water-borne material that:
   a. Backs up through sewers or drains;
   b. Discharges or overflows from a sump, sump pump, or related equipment; or
   c. Seeps or leaks on or through insured property; unless there is a flood in the area and the flood is the proximate cause of the sewer, drain, or sump pump discharge or overflow, or the seepage of water;
6. The pressure or weight of water unless there is a flood in the area and the flood is the proximate cause of the damage from the pressure or weight of water;
7. Power, heating, or cooling failure unless the failure results from direct physical loss by or from flood to power, heating, or cooling equipment situated on the described location;
8. Theft, fire, explosion, wind, or windstorm;
9. Anything you or your agents do or conspire to do to cause loss by flood deliberately; or
10. Alteration of the insured property that significantly increases the risk of flooding.

**E. We do not insure for loss to any building or personal property located on land leased from the Federal Government, arising from or incident to the flooding of the land by the Federal Government, where the lease expressly holds the Federal Government harmless under flood insurance issued under any Federal Government program.**

**F. We do not pay for the testing for or monitoring of pollutants unless required by law or ordinance.**

## VI. DEDUCTIBLES

**A.** When a loss is covered under this policy, we will pay only that part of the loss that exceeds the applicable deductible amount, subject to the limit of insurance that applies. The deductible amount is shown on the Declarations Page.

**However, when a building under construction, alteration, or repair does not have at least two rigid exterior walls and a fully secured roof at the time of loss, your deductible amount will be two times the deductible that would otherwise apply to a completed building.**

**B.** In each loss from flood, separate deductibles apply to the building and personal property insured by this policy.

**C.** No deductible applies to:

**1.** III.C.2. Loss Avoidance Measures; or

**2.** III.D. Increased Cost of Compliance.

## VII. COINSURANCE

**A. This Coinsurance Section applies only to coverage on the building.**

**B. We will impose a penalty on loss payment unless the amount of insurance applicable to the damaged building is:**

**1. At least 80% of its replacement cost; or**

**2. The maximum amount of insurance available for that building under the NFIP, whichever is less.**

**C. If the actual amount of insurance on the building is less than the required amount in accordance with the terms of VII.B. above, then loss payment is determined as follows** (subject to all other relevant conditions in this policy, including those pertaining to valuation, adjustment, settlement, and payment of loss):

**1.** Divide the actual amount of insurance carried on the building by the required amount of insurance.

**2.** Multiply the amount of loss, before application of the deductible, by the figure determined in C.1. above.

**3.** Subtract the deductible from the figure determined in C.2. above.

We will pay the amount determined in C.3. above, or the amount of insurance carried, whichever is less. The amount of insurance carried, if in excess of the applicable maximum amount of insurance available under the NFIP, is reduced accordingly.

***Examples***

**Example #1 (Inadequate Insurance)**

| | |
|---|---|
| Replacement value of the building | $250,000 |
| Required amount of insurance | $200,000 |
| (80% of replacement value of $250,000) | |
| Actual amount of insurance carried | $180,000 |
| Amount of the loss | $150,000 |
| Deductible | $500 |

**Step 1:** 180,000 ÷ 200,000 = .90
(90% of what should be carried.)

**Step 2:** 150,000 X .90 = 135,000

**Step 3:** 135,000 - 500 = 134,500

We will pay no more than $134,500. The remaining $15,500 is not covered due to the coinsurance penalty ($15,000) and application of the deductible ($500).

**Example #2 (Adequate Insurance)**

| | |
|---|---|
| Replacement value of the building | $500,000 |
| Required amount of insurance (80% of replacement value of $500,000) | $400,000 |
| Actual amount of insurance carried | $400,000 |
| Amount of the loss | $200,000 |
| Deductible | $500 |

In this example there is no coinsurance penalty, because the actual amount of insurance carried meets the required amount. We will pay no more than $199,500 ($200,000 amount of loss minus the $500 deductible).

**D.** In calculating the full replacement cost of a building:

**1.** The replacement cost value of any covered building property will be included;

**2.** The replacement cost value of any building property not covered under this policy will not be included; and

**3.** Only the replacement cost value of improvements installed by the condominium association will be included.

## VIII. GENERAL CONDITIONS

### A. PAIR AND SET CLAUSE

In case of loss to an article that is part of a pair or set, we will have the option of paying you:

1. An amount equal to the cost of replacing the lost, damaged, or destroyed article, less depreciation; or
2. An amount which represents the fair proportion of the total value of the pair or set that the lost, damaged, or destroyed article bears to the pair or set.

### B. CONCEALMENT OR FRAUD AND POLICY VOIDANCE

**1. With respect to all insureds under this policy, this policy:**

**a. Is void,**

**b. Has no legal force or effect,**

**c. Cannot be renewed, and**

**d. Cannot be replaced by a new NFIP policy, if, before or after a loss, you or any other insured or your agent have at any time:**

**(1) Intentionally concealed or misrepresented any material fact or circumstance,**

**(2) Engaged in fraudulent conduct, or**

**(3) Made false statements,**

**relating to this policy or any other NFIP insurance.**

2. This policy will be void as of the date the wrongful acts described in B.1. above were committed.

3. Fines, civil penalties, and imprisonment under applicable Federal laws may also apply to the acts of fraud or concealment described above.

**4. This policy is also void for reasons other than fraud, misrepresentation, or wrongful act. This policy is void from its inception and has no legal force under the following conditions:**

**a. If the property is located in a community that was not participating in the NFIP on the policy's inception date and did not join or re-enter the program during the policy term and before the loss occurred; or**

**b. If the property listed on the application is not otherwise eligible for coverage under the NFIP.**

C. OTHER INSURANCE

1. **If a loss covered by this policy is also covered by other insurance that includes flood coverage not issued under the Act, we will not pay more than the amount of insurance that you are entitled to for lost, damaged or destroyed property insured under this policy subject to the following:**

   a. **We will pay only the proportion of the loss that the amount of insurance that applies under this policy bears to the total amount of insurance covering the loss, unless C.1.b. or c. immediately below applies.**

   b. **If the other policy has a provision stating that it is excess insurance, this policy will be primary.**

   c. **This policy will be primary (but subject to its own deductible) up to the deductible in the other flood policy (except another policy as described in C.1.b. above). When the other deductible amount is reached, this policy will participate in the same proportion that the amount of insurance under this policy bears to the total amount of both policies, for the remainder of the loss.**

2. **If there is a flood insurance policy in the name of a unit owner that covers the same loss as this policy, then this policy will be primary.**

D. AMENDMENTS, WAIVERS, ASSIGNMENT

This policy cannot be changed nor can any of its provisions be waived without the express written consent of the Federal Insurance Administrator. No action that we take under the terms of this policy constitutes a waiver of any of our rights. You may assign this policy in writing when you transfer title of your property to someone else except under these conditions:

1. When this policy covers only personal property; or
2. When this policy covers a structure during the course of construction.

E. CANCELLATION OF POLICY BY YOU

1. You may cancel this policy in accordance with the applicable rules and regulations of the NFIP.
2. If you cancel this policy, you may be entitled to a full or partial refund of premium also under the applicable rules and regulations of the NFIP.

F. NON-RENEWAL OF THE POLICY BY US

Your policy will not be renewed:

1. If the community where your covered property is located stops participating in the NFIP, or
2. Your building has been declared ineligible under Section 1316 of the Act.

G. REDUCTION AND REFORMATION OF COVERAGE

1. **If the premium we received from you was not enough to buy the kind and amount of coverage you requested, we will provide only the amount of coverage that can be purchased for the premium payment we received.**

2. The policy can be reformed to increase the amount of coverage resulting from the reduction described in G.1. above the amount that you requested as follows:

   a. Discovery of Insufficient Premium or Incomplete Rating Information Before a Loss.

      (1) **If we discover before you have a flood loss that your premium payment was not enough to buy the requested amount of coverage, we will send you and any mortgagee or**

trustee known to us a bill for the required additional premium for the current policy term (or that portion of the current policy term following any endorsement changing the amount of coverage). If you or the mortgagee or trustee pay the additional premium within 30 days from the date of our bill, we will reform the policy to increase the amount of coverage to the originally requested amount effective to the beginning of the current policy term (or subsequent date of any endorsement changing the amount of coverage).

(2) If we determine before you have a flood loss that the rating information we have is incomplete and prevents us from calculating the additional premium, we will ask you to send the required information. You must submit the information within 60 days of our request. Once we determine the amount of additional premium for the current policy term, we will follow the procedure in G.2.a.(1) above.

(3) If we do not receive the additional premium (or additional information) by the date it is due, the amount of coverage can only be increased by endorsement subject to any appropriate waiting period.

b. Discovery of Insufficient Premium or Incomplete Rating Information After a Loss.

(1) If we discover after you have a flood loss that your premium payment was not enough to buy the requested amount of coverage, we will send you and any mortgagee or trustee known to us a bill for the required additional premium for the current and the prior policy terms. If you or the mortgagee or trustee pay the additional premium within 30 days of the date of our bill, we will reform the policy to increase the amount of coverage to the originally requested amount effective to the beginning of the prior policy term.

(2) If we discover after you have a flood loss that the rating information we have is incomplete and prevents us from calculating the additional premium, we will ask you to send the required information. You must submit the information before your claim can be paid. Once we determine the amount of additional premium for the current and prior policy terms, we

**will follow the procedure in G.2.b.(1) above.**

**(3) If we do not receive the additional premium by the date it is due, your flood insurance claim will be settled based on the reduced amount of coverage. The amount of coverage can only be increased by endorsement subject to any appropriate waiting period.**

**3. However, if we find that you or your agent intentionally did not tell us, or falsified, any important fact or circumstance or did anything fraudulent relating to this insurance, the provisions of Condition B. Concealment or Fraud and Policy Voidance above apply.**

H. POLICY RENEWAL

1. This policy will expire at 12:01 a.m. on the last day of the policy term.

2. We must receive the payment of the appropriate renewal premium within 30 days of the expiration date.

3. If we find, however, that we did not place your renewal notice into the U.S. Postal Service, or if we did mail it, we made a mistake, e.g., we used an incorrect, incomplete, or illegible address, which delayed its delivery to you before the due date for the renewal premium, then we will follow these procedures:

   a. If you or your agent notified us, not later than 1 year after the date on which the payment of the renewal premium was due, of nonreceipt of a renewal notice before the due date for the renewal premium, and we determine that the circumstances in the preceding paragraph apply, we will mail a second bill providing a revised due date, which will be 30 days after the date on which the bill is mailed.

   b. If we do not receive the premium requested in the second bill by the revised due date, then we will not renew the policy. In that case, the policy will remain as an expired policy as of the expiration date shown on the Declarations Page.

4. In connection with the renewal of this policy, we may ask you during the policy term to re-certify, on a Recertification Questionnaire that we will provide you, the rating information used to rate your most recent application for or renewal of insurance.

I. CONDITIONS SUSPENDING OR RESTRICTING INSURANCE

**We are not liable for loss that occurs while there is a hazard that is increased by any means within your control or knowledge.**

J. REQUIREMENTS IN CASE OF LOSS

**In case of a flood loss to insured property, you must:**

**1. Give prompt written notice to us;**

**2. As soon as reasonably possible, separate the damaged and undamaged property, putting it in the best possible order so that we may examine it;**

**3. Prepare an inventory of damaged personal property showing the quantity, description, actual cash value, and amount of loss. Attach all bills, receipts and related documents;**

**4. Within 60 days after the loss, send us a proof of loss, which is your statement of the amount you are claiming under the policy signed and sworn to by you, and which furnishes us with the following information:**

   **a. The date and time of loss;**

   **b. A brief explanation of how the loss happened;**

   **c. Your interest (for example, "owner") and the interest, if**

any, of others in the damaged property;

d. Details of any other insurance that may cover the loss;

e. Changes in title or occupancy of the insured property during the term of the policy;

f. Specifications of damaged insured buildings and detailed repair estimates;

g. Names of mortgagees or anyone else having a lien, charge, or claim against the insured property;

h. Details about who occupied any insured building at the time of loss and for what purpose; and

i. The inventory of damaged personal property described in J.3. above.

5. In completing the proof of loss, you must use your own judgment concerning the amount of loss and justify that amount.

6. You must cooperate with the adjuster or representative in the investigation of the claim.

7. The insurance adjuster whom we hire to investigate your claim may furnish you with a proof of loss form, and she or he may help you complete it. However, this is a matter of courtesy only, and you must still send us a proof of loss within sixty days after the loss even if the adjuster does not furnish the form or help you complete it.

8. We have not authorized the adjuster to approve or disapprove claims or to tell you whether we will approve your claim.

9. At our option, we may accept the adjuster's report of the loss instead of your proof of loss. The adjuster's report will include information about your loss and the damages you sustained. You must sign the adjuster's report. At our option, we may require you to swear to the report.

K. OUR OPTIONS AFTER A LOSS

Options that we may, in our sole discretion, exercise after loss include the following:

1. At such reasonable times and places that we may designate, you must:

   a. Show us or our representative the damaged property;

   b. Submit to examination under oath, while not in the presence of another insured, and sign the same; and

   c. Permit us to examine and make extracts and copies of:

      (1) Any policies of property insurance insuring you against loss and the deed establishing your ownership of the insured real property;

      (2) Condominium association documents including the Declarations of the condo-

**minium, its Articles of Association or Incorporation, Bylaws, and rules and regulations; and**

**(3) All books of accounts, bills, invoices and other vouchers, or certified copies pertaining to the damaged property if the originals are lost.**

**2. We may request, in writing, that you furnish us with a complete inventory of the lost, damaged, or destroyed property, including:**

**a. Quantities and costs;**

**b. Actual cash values or replacement cost (whichever is appropriate);**

**c. Amounts of loss claimed;**

**d. Any written plans and specifications for repair of the damaged property that you can make reasonably available to us; and**

**e. Evidence that prior flood damage has been repaired.**

**3. If we give you written notice within 30 days after we receive your signed, sworn proof of loss, we may:**

**a. Repair, rebuild, or replace any part of the lost, damaged, or destroyed property with material or property of like kind and quality or its functional equivalent; and**

**b. Take all or any part of the damaged property at the value we agree upon or its appraised value.**

L. NO BENEFIT TO BAILEE

No person or organization, other than you, having custody of covered property will benefit from this insurance.

M. LOSS PAYMENT

1. We will adjust all losses with you. We will pay you unless some other person or entity is named in the policy or is legally entitled to receive payment. Loss will be payable 60 days after we receive your proof of loss (or within 90 days after the insurance adjuster files an adjuster's report signed and sworn to by you in lieu of a proof of loss) and:
   a. We reach an agreement with you;
   b. There is an entry of a final judgment; or
   c. There is a filing of an appraisal award with us, as provided in VIII.P.
2. If we reject your proof of loss in whole or in part you may:
   a. Accept such denial of your claim;
   b. Exercise your rights under this policy; or
   c. File an amended proof of loss as long as it is filed within 60 days of the date of the loss.

N. ABANDONMENT

You may not abandon damaged or undamaged insured property to us.

O. SALVAGE

**We may permit you to keep damaged insured property after a loss, and we will reduce the amount of the loss proceeds payable to you under the policy by the value of the salvage.**

P. APPRAISAL

If you and we fail to agree on the actual cash value or, if applicable, replacement cost of the damaged property so as to determine the amount of loss, then either may demand an appraisal of the loss. In this event, you and we will each choose a competent and impartial appraiser within 20 days after receiving a written request from the other. The two appraisers will choose an umpire. If they cannot agree upon an umpire within 15 days, you or we may request that the choice be made by a judge of a court of record in the State where the insured property is located. The appraisers will separately state the actual cash value, the replacement cost, and the amount of loss to each item. If the appraisers submit a written report of an agreement to us, the amount agreed upon will be the amount of loss. If they fail to agree, they will submit their differences to the umpire. A decision agreed to by any two will set the amount of actual cash value and loss, or if it applies, the replacement cost and loss.

Each party will:

1. Pay its own appraiser; and
2. Bear the other expenses of the appraisal and umpire equally.

### Q. MORTGAGE CLAUSE

The word "mortgagee" includes trustee.

Any loss payable under Coverage A—Building will be paid to any mortgagee of whom we have actual notice, as well as any other mortgagee or loss payee determined to exist at the time of loss, and you, as interests appear. If more than one mortgagee is named, the order of payment will be the same as the order of precedence of the mortgages.

If we deny your claim, that denial will not apply to a valid claim of the mortgagee, if the mortgagee:

1. Notifies us of any change in the ownership or occupancy, or substantial change in risk, of which the mortgagee is aware;
2. Pays any premium due under this policy on demand if you have neglected to pay the premium; and
3. Submits a signed, sworn proof of loss within 60 days after receiving notice from us of your failure to do so.

All of the terms of this policy apply to the mortgagee.

The mortgagee has the right to receive loss payment even if the mortgagee has started foreclosure or similar action on the building.

If we decide to cancel or not renew this policy, it will continue in effect for the benefit of the mortgagee only for 30 days after we notify the mortgagee of the cancellation or non-renewal.

If we pay the mortgagee for any loss and deny payment to you, we are subrogated to all the rights of the mortgagee granted under the mortgage on the property. Subrogation will not impair the right of the mortgagee to recover the full amount of the mortgagee's claim.

### R. SUIT AGAINST US

You may not sue us to recover money under this policy unless you have complied with all the requirements of the policy. If you do sue, you must start the suit within one year of the date of the written denial of all or part of the claim and you must file the suit in the United States District Court of the district in which the insured property was located at the time of loss. This requirement applies to any claim that you may have under this policy and to any dispute that you may have arising out of the handling of any claim under the policy.

### S. SUBROGATION

Whenever we make a payment for a loss under this policy, we are subrogated to your right to recover for that loss from any other person. That means that your right to recover for a loss that was partly or totally caused by someone else is automatically transferred to us, to the extent that we have paid you for the loss. We may require you to acknowledge this transfer in writing. After the loss, you may not give up our right to recover this money or do anything that would prevent us from recovering it. If you make any claim against any person who caused your loss and recover any money, you must pay us back first before you may keep any of that money.

### T. CONTINUOUS LAKE FLOODING

1. If an insured building has been flooded by rising lake waters continuously for 90 days or more and it appears reasonably certain that a continuation of this flooding will result in a covered loss to the insured building equal to or greater than the building policy limits plus the deductible or the maximum payable under the policy for any one building loss, we will pay you the lesser of these two amounts without waiting for the further damage to occur if you sign a release agreeing:
   a. To make no further claim under this policy;
   b. Not to seek renewal of this policy;
   c. Not to apply for any flood insurance under the Act for property at the described location; and
   d. Not to seek a premium refund for current or prior terms.

   **If the policy term ends before the insured building has been flooded continuously for 90 days, the provisions of this paragraph T.1. will apply as long as the insured building suffers a covered loss before the policy term ends.**

2. If your insured building is subject to continuous lake flooding from a closed basin lake, you may elect to file a claim under either paragraph T.1. above or this paragraph T.2. (A "closed basin lake" is a natural lake from which water leaves primarily through evaporation and whose surface area now exceeds or has exceeded one square mile at any time in the recorded past. Most of the nation's closed basin lakes are in the western half of the United States, where annual evaporation exceeds annual precipitation and where lake levels and surface areas are subject to considerable fluctuation due to wide variations in the climate. These lakes may overtop their basins on rare occasions.) Under this paragraph T.2., we will pay your claim as if the building is a total loss even though it has not been continuously inundated for 90 days, subject to the following conditions:

a. **Lake flood waters must damage or imminently threaten to damage your building.**

b. **Before approval of your claim, you must:**

(1) **Agree to a claim payment that reflects your buying back the salvage on a negotiated basis; and**

(2) **Grant the conservation easement contained in FEMA's "Policy Guidance for Closed Basin Lakes," to be recorded in the office of the local recorder of deeds.** FEMA, in consultation with the community in which the property is located, will identify on a map an area or areas of special consideration (ASC) in which there is a potential for flood damage from continuous lake flooding. FEMA will give the community the agreed-upon map showing the ASC. This easement will only apply to that portion of the property in the ASC. It will allow certain agricultural and recreational uses of the land. The only structures that it will allow on any portion of the property within the ASC are certain simple agricultural and recreational structures. If any of these allowable structures are insurable buildings under the NFIP and are insured under the NFIP, they will not be eligible for the benefits of this paragraph T.2. If a U.S. Army Corps of Engineers certified flood control project or otherwise certified flood control project later protects the property, FEMA will, upon request, amend the ASC to remove areas protected by those projects. The restrictions of the easement will then no longer apply to any portion of the property removed from the ASC; and

(3) **Comply with paragraphs T.1.a. through T.1.d. above.**

c. **Within 90 days of approval of your claim, you must move your building to a new location outside the ASC.** FEMA will give you an additional 30 days to move if you show there is sufficient reason to extend the time.

d. Before the final payment of your claim, you must acquire an elevation certificate and a floodplain development permit from the local floodplain administrator for the new location of your building.

e. **Before the approval of your claim, the community having jurisdiction over your building must:**

(1) Adopt a permanent land use ordinance, or a temporary moratorium for a period not to exceed 6 months to be followed immediately by a permanent land use ordinance, that is consistent with the provisions specified in the easement required in paragraph T.2.b. above;

(2) Agree to declare and report any violations of this ordinance to FEMA so that under Sec. 1316 of the National Flood Insurance Act of 1968, as amended, flood insurance to the building can be denied; and

(3) **Agree to maintain as deed-restricted, for purposes compatible with open space or agricultural or recreational use only, any affected property the community acquires an interest in.** These deed restrictions must be consistent with the provisions of paragraph T.2.b. above, except that, even if a certified project protects the property, the land use restrictions continue to apply if the property was acquired under the Hazard Mitigation Grant Program or the Flood Mitigation Assistance Program. If a non-profit land trust organization receives the property as a donation, that organization must maintain the property as deed-restricted, consistent with the provisions of paragraph T.2.b. above.

f. Before the approval of your claim, the affected State must take all action set forth in FEMA's "Policy Guidance for Closed Basin Lakes."

g. **You must have NFIP flood insurance coverage continuously in effect from a date established by FEMA until you file a claim under this paragraph T.2.** If a subsequent owner buys NFIP insurance that goes into effect within 60 days of the date of transfer of title, any gap in coverage during that 60-day period will not be a violation of this continuous coverage requirement. For the purpose of honoring a claim under this paragraph T.2., we will not consider to be in effect any increased coverage that became effective after the date established by FEMA. The exception to this is any increased coverage in the amount suggested by your insurer as an inflation adjustment.

**h.** This paragraph T.2. will be in effect for a community when the FEMA Regional Director for the affected region provides to the community, in writing, the following:

**(1)** Confirmation that the community and the State are in compliance with the conditions in paragraphs T.2.e. and T.2.f. above, and

**(2)** The date by which you must have flood insurance in effect.

**U. DUPLICATE POLICIES NOT ALLOWED**

**1. We will not insure your property under more than one NFIP policy.**

If we find that the duplication was not knowingly created, we will give you written notice. The notice will advise you that you may choose one of several options under the following procedures:

**a.** If you choose to keep in effect the policy with the earlier effective date, you may also choose to add the coverage limits of the later policy to the limits of the earlier policy. The change will become effective as of the effective date of the later policy.

**b.** If you choose to keep in effect the policy with the later effective date, you may also choose to add the coverage limits of the earlier policy to the limits of the later policy. The change will be effective as of the effective date of the later policy.

In either case, you must pay the pro rata premium for the increased coverage limits within 30 days of the written notice. In no event will the resulting coverage limits exceed the permissible limits of coverage under the Act or your insurable interest, whichever is less. We will make a refund to you, according to applicable NFIP rules, of the premium for the policy not being kept in effect.

2. The insured's option under this Condition U. Duplicate Policies Not Allowed to elect which NFIP policy to keep in effect does not apply when duplicates have been knowingly created. Losses occurring under such circumstances will be adjusted according to the terms and conditions of the earlier policy. The policy with the later effective date must be canceled.

**V. LOSS SETTLEMENT**

**1. Introduction**

This policy provides three methods of settling losses: Replacement Cost, Special Loss Settlement, and Actual Cash Value. Each method is used for a different type of property, as explained in a.–c. below.

**a. Replacement Cost Loss Settlement described in V.2. below applies to buildings other than manufactured homes or travel trailers.**

**b. Special Loss Settlement described in V.3. below applies to a residential condominium building that is a travel trailer or a manufactured home.**

**c. Actual Cash Value loss settlement applies to all other property covered under this policy, as outlined in V.4. below.**

2. **Replacement Cost Loss Settlement**

**a. We will pay to repair or replace a damaged or destroyed building, after application of the deductible and without deduction for depreciation, but not more than the least of the following amounts:**

**(1) The amount of insurance in this policy that applies to the building;**

**(2) The replacement cost of that part of the building damaged, with materials of like kind and quality, and for like occupancy and use; or**

**(3) The necessary amount actually spent to repair or replace the damaged part of the building for like occupancy and use.**

**b. We will not be liable for any loss on a Replacement Cost**

Coverage basis unless and until actual repair or replacement of the damaged building or parts thereof, is completed.

c. If a building is rebuilt at a location other than the described location, we will pay no more than it would have cost to repair or rebuild at the described location, subject to all other terms of Replacement Cost Loss Settlement.

3. Special Loss Settlement

a. The following loss settlement conditions apply to a residential condominium building that is: (1) a manufactured home or a travel trailer, as defined in II.B.6.b. and c., and (2) at least 16 feet wide when fully assembled and has at least 600 square feet within its perimeter walls when fully assembled.

b. If such a building is totally destroyed or damaged to such an extent that, in our judgment, it is not economically feasible to repair, at least to its pre-damaged condition, we will, at our discretion, pay the least of the following amounts:

(1) The lesser of the replacement cost of the manufactured home or travel trailer or 1.5 times the actual cash value; or

(2) The Building Limit of liability shown on your Declarations Page.

c. If such a manufactured home or travel trailer is partially damaged and, in our judgment, it is economically feasible to repair it to its pre-damaged condition, we will settle the loss according to the Replacement Cost Loss Settlement conditions in V.2. above.

4. Actual Cash Value Loss Settlement

a. The types of property noted below are subject to actual cash value loss settlement:

(1) Personal property;

(2) Insured property abandoned after a loss and that remains as debris at the described location;

(3) Outside antennas and aerials, awnings, and other outdoor equipment;

(4) Carpeting and pads;

(5) Appliances; and

(6) A manufactured home or mobile home or a travel trailer as defined in II.B.6.b. or c. that does not meet the conditions for Special Loss Settlement in V.3. above.

b. We will pay the least of the following amounts:

(1) The applicable amount of insurance under this policy;

(2) The actual cash value (as defined in II.B.2.); or

**(3) The amount it would cost to repair or replace the property with material of like kind and quality within a reasonable time after the loss.**

### IX. LIBERALIZATION CLAUSE

If we make a change that broadens your coverage under this edition of our policy, but does not require any additional premium, then that change will automatically apply to your insurance as of the date we implement the change, provided that this implementation date falls within 60 days before or during the policy term stated on the Declarations Page.

### X. WHAT LAW GOVERNS

This policy and all disputes arising from the handling of any claim under the policy are governed exclusively by the flood insurance regulations issued by FEMA, the National Flood Insurance Act of 1968, as amended (42 U.S.C. 4001, *et seq.*), and Federal common law.

IN WITNESS WHEREOF, we have signed this policy below and hereby enter into this Insurance Agreement.

David I. Maurstad
Deputy Associate Administrator
FEMA's Federal Insurance and Mitigation Administration

## CLAIM GUIDELINES IN CASE OF A FLOOD

If you have questions, consult your insurance agent or call the National Flood Insurance Program (NFIP) toll-free at 1-800-638-6620 or on the TDD/TTY relay line at 711.

Know your insurance representative's name and telephone number. List them here for fast reference:

Insurance Agent ________________________________________________

Agent's Phone Number ___________________________________________

- Notify us or your agent, in writing, as soon as possible after the flood.
- Your claim will be assigned to an NFIP certified adjuster.
- Identify the claims adjuster assigned to your claim and contact him or her if you have not been contacted within 24 hours after you reported the claim to your insurance representative.
- As soon as possible, separate damaged property from undamaged property so that damage can be inspected and evaluated.
- To help the claims adjuster, take photographs of the outside of the premises showing the flooding and the damage and photographs of the inside of the premises showing the height of the water and the damaged property.
- Place all account books, financial records, receipts, and other loss verification material in a safe place for examination and evaluation by the claims adjuster.
- Work cooperatively with the claims adjuster to promptly determine and document all claim items. Be prepared to advise the claims adjuster of the cause and responsible party(ies) if the flooding resulted from other than natural cause.
- Make sure that the claims adjuster fully explains, and that you fully understand, all allowances and procedures for processing claim payments. This policy requires you to send us a signed and sworn-to, detailed proof of loss within 60 days after the loss.
- Any and all coverage problems and claim allowance restrictions must be communicated directly from the NFIP. Claims adjusters are not authorized to approve or deny claims; their job is to report to the NFIP on the elements of flood cause and damage.

At our option, we may accept an adjuster's report of the loss instead of your proof of loss. The adjuster's report will include information about your loss and the damages to your insured property.

**F-144** (OCT. 2015)

# I. NFIP Flood Insurance Application

THIS LAYOUT OF THE REVISED FLOOD INSURANCE APPLICATION IS PROVIDED FOR YOUR REFERENCE.
THE FINAL FORM WILL BE RELEASED UPON O.M.B. APPROVAL.

**U.S. DEPARTMENT OF HOMELAND SECURITY**
**FEDERAL EMERGENCY MANAGEMENT AGENCY**

National Flood Insurance Program

**FLOOD INSURANCE APPLICATION, PAGE 1 (OF 2)**

**IMPORTANT—PLEASE PRINT OR TYPE; ENTER DATES AS MM/DD/YYYY.**

☐ NEW ☐ RENEWAL ☐ TRANSFER (NFIP POLICIES ONLY)
PRIOR POLICY #: ______

**BILLING**
FOR RENEWAL, BILL:
☐ INSURED ☐ LOSS PAYEE
☐ FIRST MORTGAGEE ☐ OTHER (AS SPECIFIED IN THE "2ND MORTGAGEE/OTHER" BOX BELOW)
☐ SECOND MORTGAGEE

**AGENT/PRODUCER INFORMATION**
NAME AND MAILING ADDRESS OF AGENT/PRODUCER:
AGENCY NO.: ______ AGENT'S NO.: ______
PHONE NO.: ______ FAX NO.: ______
EMAIL ADDRESS: ______

**PROPERTY LOCATION**
**NOTE: ONE BUILDING PER POLICY – BLANKET COVERAGE NOT PERMITTED.**
IS BUILDING LOCATED IN A CBRS OR OPA? ☐ YES ☐ NO
IS INSURED PROPERTY LOCATION SAME AS INSURED'S MAILING ADDRESS? ☐ YES ☐ NO
IF NO, ENTER PROPERTY ADDRESS. IF RURAL, ENTER LEGAL DESCRIPTION, OR GEOGRAPHIC LOCATION OF PROPERTY (DO NOT USE P.O. BOX).
IDENTIFY ADDRESS TYPE: ☐ STREET ☐ LEGAL DESCRIPTION* ☐ GEOGRAPHIC LOCATION
FOR AN ADDRESS WITH MULTIPLE BUILDINGS AND/OR FOR A BUILDING WITH ADDITIONS OR EXTENSIONS, DESCRIBE THE INSURED BUILDING: ______
* LEGAL DESCRIPTION MAY BE USED ONLY WHILE A BUILDING OR SUBDIVISION IS IN THE COURSE OF CONSTRUCTION OR PRIOR TO ESTABLISHING A STREET ADDRESS.

**DISASTER ASSISTANCE**
IS INSURANCE REQUIRED FOR DISASTER ASSISTANCE? ☐ YES ☐ NO
IF YES, CHECK THE GOVERNMENT AGENCY: ☐ SBA ☐ FEMA ☐ FHA
☐ OTHER (SPECIFY): ______
CASE FILE NO.: ______

**COMMUNITY**
GRANDFATHERING INFORMATION
GRANDFATHERED? ☐ YES ☐ NO IF YES, ☐ BUILT IN COMPLIANCE *OR*
☐ CONTINUOUS COVERAGE (PROVIDE PRIOR POLICY NUMBER IN BOX ABOVE)
RATING MAP INFORMATION
NAME OF COUNTY/PARISH: ______
COMMUNITY NO./PANEL NO. AND SUFFIX: ______ - ______
FIRM ZONE: ______ MAP DATE: ___/___/_____
COMMUNITY PROGRAM TYPE IS: ☐ REGULAR ☐ EMERGENCY
CURRENT MAP INFORMATION
CURRENT COMMUNITY NO./PANEL NO. AND SUFFIX: ______ - ______
CURRENT FIRM ZONE: ______ CURRENT BFE: ______
MAP DATE: ___/___/_____

**POLICY PERIOD**
POLICY PERIOD IS FROM ___/___/_____ TO ___/___/_____
12:01 A.M. LOCAL TIME AT THE INSURED PROPERTY LOCATION.
WAITING PERIOD:
☐ STANDARD 30-DAY
☐ REQUIRED FOR LOAN TRANSACTION – NO WAITING PERIOD
☐ MAP REVISION (ZONE CHANGE FROM NON-SFHA TO SFHA) – 1 DAY
☐ TRANSFER (NFIP POLICIES ONLY) – NO WAITING PERIOD

**INSURED INFORMATION**
NAME AND MAILING ADDRESS OF INSURED:
PHONE NO.: ______
EMAIL ADDRESS: ______
IS THE INSURED A SMALL BUSINESS? ☐ YES ☐ NO
IS THE INSURED A NON-PROFIT ENTITY? ☐ YES ☐ NO

**1ST MORTGAGEE**
NAME AND MAILING ADDRESS OF FIRST MORTGAGEE:
LOAN NO.: ______
IS INSURANCE REQUIRED UNDER MANDATORY PURCHASE? ☐ YES ☐ NO

**2ND MORTGAGEE/OTHER**
NAME AND MAILING ADDRESS OF: ☐ 2ND MORTGAGEE ☐ LOSS PAYEE ☐ OTHER
IF OTHER, SPECIFY: ______
LOAN NO.: ______
IS INSURANCE REQUIRED UNDER MANDATORY PURCHASE? ☐ YES ☐ NO

**PRIOR NFIP COVERAGE**
COMPLETE THIS SECTION ONLY FOR PRE-FIRM BUILDINGS LOCATED IN AN SFHA.
1. HAS THE APPLICANT HAD A PRIOR NFIP POLICY FOR THIS PROPERTY? ☐ YES ☐ NO
2. WAS THE POLICY REQUIRED BY THE LENDER UNDER MANDATORY PURCHASE? ☐ YES ☐ NO
3. **IF YES**, HAS THE PRIOR NFIP POLICY EVER LAPSED WHILE COVERAGE WAS REQUIRED UNDER MANDATORY PURCHASE BY THE LENDER? ☐ YES ☐ NO
4. **IF YES**, WAS THE LAPSE THE RESULT OF A COMMUNITY SUSPENSION? ☐ YES ☐ NO
   **IF YES, WHAT IS THE SUSPENSION DATE?** ___/___/_____
   WHAT IS THE REINSTATEMENT DATE? ___/___/_____
5. WILL THIS POLICY BE EFFECTIVE WITHIN 180 DAYS OF THE COMMUNITY REINSTATEMENT AFTER SUSPENSION REFERRED TO IN (4) ABOVE? ☐ YES ☐ NO

N F I P C O P Y

**ALL BUILDINGS**
1. BUILDING PURPOSE
☐ 100% RESIDENTIAL
☐ 100% NON-RESIDENTIAL
☐ MIXED-USE – SPECIFY PERCENTAGE OF RESIDENTIAL USE: ____ %
2. BUILDING OCCUPANCY
☐ SINGLE FAMILY
☐ 2-4 FAMILY
☐ OTHER RESIDENTIAL
☐ NON-RESIDENTIAL BUSINESS
☐ OTHER NON-RESIDENTIAL
3. IS THE BUILDING A HOUSE OF WORSHIP? ☐ YES ☐ NO
4. IS THE BUILDING AN AGRICULTURAL STRUCTURE? ☐ YES ☐ NO
5. BUILDING DESCRIPTION (CHECK ONE)
☐ MAIN HOUSE
☐ DETACHED GUEST HOUSE
☐ DETACHED GARAGE
☐ BARN
☐ APARTMENT BUILDING
☐ APARTMENT - UNIT
☐ COOPERATIVE BUILDING
☐ COOPERATIVE - UNIT
☐ WAREHOUSE
☐ TOOL/STORAGE SHED
☐ POOLHOUSE, CLUBHOUSE, RECREATION BUILDING
☐ OTHER: ______
6. CONDOMINIUM INFORMATION
IS BUILDING IN A CONDOMINIUM FORM OF OWNERSHIP? ☐ YES ☐ NO
IS COVERAGE FOR THE ENTIRE BUILDING? ☐ YES ☐ NO
TOTAL NUMBER OF UNITS: ______
☐ HIGH-RISE ☐ LOW-RISE
IS COVERAGE FOR A CONDOMINIUM UNIT? ☐ YES ☐ NO
7. ADDITIONS AND EXTENSIONS (IF APPLICABLE)
DOES THE BUILDING HAVE ANY ADDITIONS OR EXTENSIONS? ☐ YES ☐ NO
(ADDITIONS AND EXTENSIONS MAY BE SEPARATELY INSURED.)
COVERAGE IS FOR:
☐ BUILDING INCLUDING ADDITION(S) AND EXTENSION(S)
☐ BUILDING EXCLUDING ADDITION(S) AND EXTENSION(S). PROVIDE POLICY NUMBER FOR ADDITION OR EXTENSION: ______
☐ ADDITION OR EXTENSION ONLY (INCLUDE DESCRIPTION IN THE PROPERTY LOCATION BOX ABOVE). PROVIDE POLICY NUMBER FOR BUILDING EXCLUDING ADDITION(S) OR EXTENSION(S): ______
8. PRIMARY RESIDENCE, RENTAL PROPERTY, TENANT'S COVERAGE
IS BUILDING INSURED'S PRIMARY RESIDENCE? ☐ YES ☐ NO
IS BUILDING A RENTAL PROPERTY? ☐ YES ☐ NO
IS THE INSURED A TENANT? ☐ YES ☐ NO
**IF YES**, IS THE TENANT REQUESTING BUILDING COVERAGE? ☐ YES ☐ NO
**IF YES**, SEE NOTICE IN SIGNATURE BLOCK ON PAGE 2.
9. BUILDING INFORMATION
IS BUILDING IN THE COURSE OF CONSTRUCTION? ☐ YES ☐ NO
IS BUILDING WALLED AND ROOFED? ☐ YES ☐ NO
IS BUILDING OVER WATER? ☐ NO ☐ PARTIALLY ☐ ENTIRELY
IS BUILDING LOCATED ON FEDERAL LAND? ☐ YES ☐ NO
IS BUILDING A SEVERE REPETITIVE LOSS PROPERTY? ☐ YES ☐ NO
10. IS BUILDING ELEVATED? ☐ YES ☐ NO
11. BASEMENT, ENCLOSURE, CRAWLSPACE
☐ NONE
☐ FINISHED BASEMENT/ENCLOSURE
☐ CRAWLSPACE
☐ UNFINISHED BASEMENT/ENCLOSURE
☐ SUBGRADE CRAWLSPACE
IS THE BASEMENT/SUBGRADE CRAWLSPACE FLOOR BELOW GRADE ON ALL SIDES? ☐ YES ☐ NO
12. NUMBER OF FLOORS IN BUILDING (INCLUDING BASEMENT/ENCLOSED AREA, IF ANY) OR BUILDING TYPE
☐ 1 ☐ 2 ☐ 3 OR MORE
☐ SPLIT LEVEL
☐ TOWNHOUSE/ROWHOUSE (RCBAP LOW-RISE ONLY)
☐ MANUFACTURED (MOBILE) HOME/TRAVEL TRAILER ON FOUNDATION

**NON-ELEVATED BUILDINGS**
1. GARAGE
IS A GARAGE ATTACHED TO THE BUILDING? ☐ YES ☐ NO
TOTAL NET AREA OF THE GARAGE: |_|_|_|_|_| SQUARE FEET.
ARE THERE ANY OPENINGS (EXCLUDING DOORS) THAT ARE DESIGNED TO ALLOW THE PASSAGE OF FLOODWATERS THROUGH THE GARAGE? ☐ YES ☐ NO
**IF YES**, NUMBER OF PERMANENT FLOOD OPENINGS WITHIN 1 FOOT ABOVE THE ADJACENT GRADE: ______
TOTAL AREA OF ALL PERMANENT OPENINGS: |_|_|_|_|_| SQUARE INCHES.
IS THE GARAGE USED SOLELY FOR PARKING OF VEHICLES, BUILDING ACCESS, AND/OR STORAGE? ☐ YES ☐ NO
**IF YES**, DOES THE GARAGE CONTAIN MACHINERY AND/OR EQUIPMENT? ☐ YES ☐ NO
2. BASEMENT/SUBGRADE CRAWLSPACE
DOES THE BASEMENT/SUBGRADE CRAWLSPACE CONTAIN MACHINERY AND/OR EQUIPMENT? ☐ YES ☐ NO
**IF YES**, SELECT THE VALUE BELOW:
☐ UP TO $10,000
☐ $10,001 TO $20,000
☐ IF GREATER THAN $20,000 - INDICATE THE AMOUNT: ______
DOES THE BASEMENT/SUBGRADE CRAWLSPACE CONTAIN A WASHER, DRYER OR FOOD FREEZER? ☐ YES ☐ NO
**IF YES**, SELECT THE VALUE BELOW:
☐ UP TO $5,000
☐ $5,001 TO $10,000
☐ IF GREATER THAN $10,000 - INDICATE THE AMOUNT: ______

**FEMA Form 086-0-1** **F-050** (DEC 2019)

PLEASE SUBMIT TOTAL AMOUNT DUE AND ALL REQUIRED CERTIFICATIONS WITH THE NFIP COPY OF THIS APPLICATION.
IF PAYING BY CHECK OR MONEY ORDER, MAKE PAYABLE TO THE NATIONAL FLOOD INSURANCE PROGRAM.
**IMPORTANT** — COMPLETE PAGE 1 AND PAGE 2 BEFORE SENDING APPLICATION TO THE NFIP. — **IMPORTANT**

**ONLINE** The current approved version of the NFIP Flood Insurance Application, FEMA Form 086-0-1, is available at https://www.fema.gov/media-library/assets/documents/154

THIS LAYOUT OF THE REVISED FLOOD INSURANCE APPLICATION IS PROVIDED FOR YOUR REFERENCE.
THE FINAL FORM WILL BE RELEASED UPON O.M.B. APPROVAL.

**U.S. DEPARTMENT OF HOMELAND SECURITY**
**FEDERAL EMERGENCY MANAGEMENT AGENCY**
National Flood Insurance Program

# FLOOD INSURANCE APPLICATION, PAGE 2 (OF 2)

**IMPORTANT—PLEASE PRINT OR TYPE; ENTER DATES AS MM/DD/YYYY.**
ALL DATA PROVIDED BY THE INSURED OR OBTAINED FROM THE ELEVATION CERTIFICATE SHOULD BE REVIEWED AND TRANSCRIBED BELOW. THIS PART OF THE APPLICATION MUST BE COMPLETED FOR ALL BUILDINGS.

☐ NEW ☐ RENEWAL ☐ TRANSFER (NFIP POLICIES ONLY)
PRIOR POLICY #: ______

## ELEVATED BUILDINGS

ELEVATED BUILDINGS (INCLUDING MANUFACTURED (MOBILE) HOMES/ TRAVEL TRAILERS)

1. IF THE BUILDING IS ELEVATED, IS THE AREA BELOW
- ☐ FREE OF OBSTRUCTION
- ☐ WITH OBSTRUCTION

2. ELEVATING FOUNDATION TYPE
- ☐ PIERS, POSTS, OR PILES
- ☐ REINFORCED MASONRY PIERS OR CONCRETE PIERS OR COLUMNS
- ☐ REINFORCED CONCRETE SHEAR WALLS
- ☐ WOOD SHEAR WALLS
- ☐ SOLID FOUNDATION WALLS

3. MACHINERY AND/OR EQUIPMENT

DOES THE AREA BELOW THE ELEVATED FLOOR CONTAIN MACHINERY AND/OR EQUIPMENT? ☐ YES ☐ NO
IF YES, SELECT THE VALUE BELOW:
- ☐ UP TO $10,000
- ☐ $10,001 TO $20,000
- ☐ IF GREATER THAN $20,000 - INDICATE THE AMOUNT: ______

DOES THE AREA BELOW THE ELEVATED FLOOR CONTAIN A WASHER, DRYER OR FOOD FREEZER? ☐ YES ☐ NO
IF YES, SELECT THE VALUE BELOW:
- ☐ UP TO $5,000
- ☐ $5,001 TO $10,000
- ☐ IF GREATER THAN $10,000 - INDICATE THE AMOUNT: ______

4. AREA BELOW THE ELEVATED FLOOR

IS THE AREA BELOW THE ELEVATED FLOOR ENCLOSED? ☐ YES ☐ NO
IF YES, CHECK ONE OF THE FOLLOWING:
☐ FULLY ☐ PARTIALLY

IS THERE A GARAGE? (CHECK ONE)
- ☐ NO GARAGE
- ☐ BENEATH THE LIVING SPACE
- ☐ NEXT TO THE LIVING SPACE

DOES THE AREA BELOW THE ELEVATED FLOOR CONTAIN ELEVATORS?
☐ YES ☐ NO
IF YES, HOW MANY? ______

**IF THE ANSWER TO ANY OF THE QUESTIONS REGARDING THE AREA BELOW THE ELEVATED FLOOR IS YES, OR THERE IS A GARAGE, ANSWER ALL THE FOLLOWING.**

INDICATE MATERIAL USED FOR ENCLOSURE:
- ☐ INSECT SCREENING
- ☐ LIGHT WOOD LATTICE
- ☐ SOLID WOOD FRAME WALLS (BREAKAWAY)
- ☐ SOLID WOOD FRAME WALLS (NON-BREAKAWAY)
- ☐ MASONRY WALLS (IF BREAKAWAY, SUBMIT CERTIFICATION DOCUMENTATION)
- ☐ MASONRY WALLS (NON-BREAKAWAY)
- ☐ OTHER (DESCRIBE): ______

IF ENCLOSED WITH A MATERIAL OTHER THAN INSECT SCREENING OR LIGHT WOOD LATTICE, PROVIDE THE SIZE OF ENCLOSED AREA:
☐☐☐☐☐ SQUARE FEET

IS THE ENCLOSED AREA/CRAWLSPACE USED FOR ANY PURPOSE OTHER THAN SOLELY FOR PARKING OF VEHICLES, BUILDING ACCESS AND/OR STORAGE? ☐ YES ☐ NO
IF YES, DESCRIBE: ______

DOES THE ENCLOSED AREA HAVE MORE THAN 20 LINEAR FEET OF FINISHED INTERIOR WALL, PANELING, ETC.?
☐ YES ☐ NO

5. FLOOD OPENINGS

IS THE ENCLOSED AREA/CRAWLSPACE CONSTRUCTED WITH OPENINGS (EXCLUDING DOORS) TO ALLOW THE PASSAGE OF FLOODWATERS THROUGH THE ENCLOSED AREA? ☐ YES ☐ NO

IF YES, INDICATE NUMBER OF PERMANENT FLOOD OPENINGS WITHIN 1 FOOT ABOVE ADJACENT GRADE: ______

TOTAL AREA OF ALL PERMANENT FLOOD OPENINGS:
☐☐☐☐☐ SQUARE INCHES.

ARE FLOOD OPENINGS ENGINEERED?
☐ YES ☐ NO
IF YES, SUBMIT CERTIFICATION.

## MANUFACTURED (MOBILE) HOMES/ TRAVEL TRAILERS

NOTE: WHEELS MUST BE REMOVED FOR TRAVEL TRAILER TO BE INSURABLE.

1. MANUFACTURED (MOBILE) HOME/TRAVEL TRAILER DATA

YEAR OF MANUFACTURE: ☐☐☐☐
MAKE: ______
MODEL NUMBER: ______
SERIAL NUMBER: ______
DIMENSIONS: ☐☐☐ × ☐☐☐ FEET
ARE THERE ANY PERMANENT ADDITIONS AND/OR EXTENSIONS? ☐ YES ☐ NO
IF YES, THE DIMENSIONS ARE: ☐☐☐ × ☐☐☐ FEET

2. ANCHORING

THE MANUFACTURED (MOBILE) HOME/TRAVEL TRAILER ANCHORING SYSTEM UTILIZES: (CHECK ALL THAT APPLY.)
- ☐ OVER-THE-TOP TIES ☐ GROUND ANCHORS
- ☐ FRAME TIES ☐ SLAB ANCHORS
- ☐ FRAME CONNECTORS
- ☐ OTHER (DESCRIBE): ______

3. INSTALLATION

THE MANUFACTURED (MOBILE) HOME/TRAVEL TRAILER WAS INSTALLED IN ACCORDANCE WITH: (CHECK ALL THAT APPLY.)
- ☐ MANUFACTURER'S SPECIFICATIONS
- ☐ LOCAL FLOODPLAIN MANAGEMENT STANDARDS
- ☐ STATE AND/OR LOCAL BUILDING STANDARDS

**NFIP COPY**

## CONSTRUCTION INFORMATION

**CHECK ONE OF THE FOLLOWING AND ENTER DATE FOR ORIGINAL CONSTRUCTION:**
☐ BUILDING PERMIT ☐ CONSTRUCTION ____/____/______

**CHECK IF BUILDING HAS BEEN SUBSTANTIALLY IMPROVED AND ENTER DATE:**
☐ SUBSTANTIAL IMPROVEMENT ____/____/______

**CHECK ONE OF THE FOLLOWING FOR MANUFACTURED (MOBILE) HOMES/TRAVEL TRAILERS:**
- ☐ LOCATED OUTSIDE A MOBILE HOME PARK OR SUBDIVISION: DATE OF PERMANENT PLACEMENT
- ☐ LOCATED INSIDE A MOBILE HOME PARK OR SUBDIVISION: CONSTRUCTION DATE OF MOBILE HOME PARK OR SUBDIVISION FACILITIES

## CONTENTS

CONTENTS LOCATED IN:*
- ☐ Basement/Subgrade Crawlspace only
- ☐ Basement/Subgrade Crawlspace and above
- ☐ Enclosure/Crawlspace and above
- ☐ Lowest floor only above ground level
- ☐ Lowest floor above ground level and higher floors
- ☐ Above ground level more than one full floor
- ☐ Manufactured (mobile) home

IS PERSONAL PROPERTY HOUSEHOLD CONTENTS? ☐ YES ☐ NO
IF NO, DESCRIBE: ______
*IF SINGLE FAMILY, CONTENTS ARE RATED THROUGHOUT THE BUILDING.

## ELEVATION DATA

IS BUILDING POST-FIRM CONSTRUCTION?
☐ YES ☐ NO
(IF POST-FIRM CONSTRUCTION IN ZONES A1-A30, AE, AO, AH, V, V1-V30, VE, OR IF PRE-FIRM CONSTRUCTION IS ELEVATION RATED, ATTACH ELEVATION CERTIFICATE.)

ELEVATION CERTIFICATION DATE: ____/____/______
BUILDING DIAGRAM NO.: ______ LOWEST ADJACENT GRADE (LAG): ______
LOWEST FLOOR ELEVATION: ______ (-) BASE FLOOD ELEVATION: ______ (=) DIFFERENCE TO NEAREST FOOT: ______ (+ OR −)
IN ZONES V AND V1-V30 ONLY, DOES BASE FLOOD ELEVATION INCLUDE EFFECTS OF WAVE ACTION? ☐ YES ☐ NO
IS BUILDING FLOODPROOFED? ☐ YES ☐ NO
(SEE THE *NFIP FLOOD INSURANCE MANUAL* FOR CERTIFICATION REQUIREMENTS.)

## COVERAGE AND RATING

**ESTIMATED BUILDING REPLACEMENT COST** (INCLUDING FOUNDATION): $ ______ **DEDUCTIBLE:** BUILDING $ ______ CONTENTS $ ______

| INSURANCE COVERAGE | TOTAL AMOUNT OF INSURANCE | BASIC LIMITS: AMOUNT OF INSURANCE | BASIC LIMITS: RATE | BASIC LIMITS: ANNUAL PREMIUM | ADDITIONAL LIMITS (REGULAR PROGRAM ONLY): AMOUNT OF INSURANCE | ADDITIONAL LIMITS: RATE | ADDITIONAL LIMITS: ANNUAL PREMIUM | DEDUCTIBLE: PREMIUM REDUCTION/INCREASE | TOTAL PREMIUM |
|---|---|---|---|---|---|---|---|---|---|
| BUILDING | | | | .00 | | | .00 | .00 | .00 |
| CONTENTS | | | | .00 | | | .00 | .00 | .00 |

RATE CATEGORY:
☐ MANUAL ☐ SUBMIT FOR RATE ☐ PROVISIONAL RATING
INDICATE THE RATE TABLE USED: ______

PAYMENT METHOD:
☐ CHECK ☐ CREDIT CARD
☐ OTHER: ______

| | |
|---|---|
| ANNUAL SUBTOTAL | $ |
| SRL PREMIUM | |
| ICC PREMIUM | |
| SUBTOTAL | |
| CRS PREMIUM DISCOUNT ____ % | |
| SUBTOTAL | |
| RESERVE FUND ____ % | |
| SUBTOTAL | |
| PROBATION SURCHARGE | |
| HFIAA SURCHARGE | |
| FEDERAL POLICY FEE | |
| **TOTAL AMOUNT DUE** | $ |

## SIGNATURE

**NOTICE:** BUILDING COVERAGE BENEFITS – EXCEPT FOR A RESIDENTIAL CONDOMINIUM BUILDING – ARE NOT AVAILABLE IF OTHER NFIP BUILDING COVERAGE HAS BEEN PURCHASED BY THE APPLICANT OR ANY OTHER PARTY FOR THE SAME BUILDING.

THE ABOVE STATEMENTS ARE CORRECT TO THE BEST OF MY KNOWLEDGE. I UNDERSTAND THAT ANY FALSE STATEMENTS MAY BE PUNISHABLE BY FINE AND/OR IMPRISONMENT UNDER APPLICABLE FEDERAL LAW. SEE LAST PAGE OF FORM.

______ SIGNATURE OF INSURANCE AGENT/PRODUCER ____/____/______ DATE (MM/DD/YYYY)

______ SIGNATURE OF INSURED (OPTIONAL) ____/____/______ DATE (MM/DD/YYYY)

**FEMA Form 086-0-1** **F-050** (DEC 2019)

PLEASE SUBMIT TOTAL AMOUNT DUE AND ALL REQUIRED CERTIFICATIONS WITH THE NFIP COPY OF THIS APPLICATION.
IF PAYING BY CHECK OR MONEY ORDER, MAKE PAYABLE TO THE NATIONAL FLOOD INSURANCE PROGRAM.
**IMPORTANT** — COMPLETE PAGE 1 AND PAGE 2 BEFORE SENDING APPLICATION TO THE NFIP. — **IMPORTANT**

*National Flood Insurance Program*

## FLOOD INSURANCE APPLICATION

**FEMA FORM 086-0-1**

**NONDISCRIMINATION**

No person or organization shall be excluded from participation in, denied the benefits of, or subjected to discrimination under the Program authorized by the Act, on the grounds of race, color, creed, sex, age or national origin.

**PRIVACY ACT**

The information requested is necessary to process your Flood Insurance Application for a flood insurance policy. The authority to collect the information is Title 42, U.S. Code, Sections 4001 to 4028. Disclosures of this information may be made: to federal, state, tribal, and local government agencies, fiscal agents, your agent, mortgage servicing companies, insurance or other companies, lending institutions, and contractors working for us, for the purpose of carrying out the National Flood Insurance Program; to certain property owners for the purpose of property loss history evaluation; to the American Red Cross for verification of nonduplication of benefits following a flooding event or disaster; to law enforcement agencies or professional organizations when there may be a violation or potential violation of law; to a federal, state or local agency when we request information relevant to an agency decision concerning issuance of a grant or other benefit, or in certain circumstances when a federal agency requests such information for a similar purpose from us; to a Congressional office in response to an inquiry made at the request of an individual; to the Office of Management and Budget (OMB) in relation to private relief legislation under OMB Circular A-19; and to the National Archives and Records Administration in records management inspections. Providing the information is voluntary, but failure to do so may delay or prevent issuance of the flood insurance policy.

**GENERAL**

This information is provided pursuant to Public Law 96-511 (Paperwork Reduction Act of 1980, as amended), dated December 11, 1980, to allow the public to participate more fully and meaningfully in the Federal paperwork review process.

**AUTHORITY**

Public Law 96-511, amended, 44 U.S.C. 3507; and 5 CFR 1320.

**PAPERWORK BURDEN DISCLOSURE NOTICE**

Public reporting burden for this form is estimated to average 12 minutes per response. The burden estimate includes the time for reviewing instructions, searching existing data sources, gathering and maintaining the data needed, and completing and submitting the form. This collection of information is required to obtain or retain benefits. You are not required to respond to this collection of information unless a valid OMB control number is displayed in the upper right corner of this form. Send comments regarding the accuracy of the burden estimate and any suggestions for reducing the burden to: Information Collections Management, Department of Homeland Security, Federal Emergency Management Agency, 500 C Street SW, Washington, DC 20742, Paperwork Reduction Project (1660-0006). **NOTE: Do not send your completed form to this address.**

# II. NFIP Preferred Risk Policy and Newly Mapped Application

THIS LAYOUT OF THE REVISED PRP AND NEWLY MAPPED APPLICATION IS PROVIDED FOR YOUR REFERENCE.
THE FINAL FORM WILL BE RELEASED UPON O.M.B. APPROVAL.

**U.S. DEPARTMENT OF HOMELAND SECURITY**
**FEDERAL EMERGENCY MANAGEMENT AGENCY**

National Flood Insurance Program

**PREFERRED RISK POLICY AND NEWLY MAPPED APPLICATION, PAGE 1 (OF 2)**

**IMPORTANT—PLEASE PRINT OR TYPE; ENTER DATES AS MM/DD/YYYY.**

☐ NEW ☐ RENEWAL
☐ TRANSFER (NFIP POLICIES ONLY)
PRIOR POLICY #: ____________

**BILLING**

FOR RENEWAL, BILL:
☐ INSURED
☐ FIRST MORTGAGEE
☐ SECOND MORTGAGEE
☐ LOSS PAYEE
☐ OTHER (AS SPECIFIED IN THE "2ND MORTGAGEE/OTHER" BOX BELOW)

**POLICY PERIOD**

POLICY PERIOD IS FROM ____ /____ /________ TO ____ /____ /________
12:01 A.M. LOCAL TIME AT THE INSURED PROPERTY LOCATION.

WAITING PERIOD:
☐ STANDARD 30-DAY
☐ REQUIRED FOR LOAN TRANSACTION – NO WAITING PERIOD
☐ MAP REVISION (ZONE CHANGE FROM NON-SFHA TO SFHA) – 1 DAY
☐ TRANSFER (NFIP POLICIES ONLY) – NO WAITING PERIOD

**AGENT/PRODUCER INFORMATION**

NAME AND MAILING ADDRESS OF AGENT/PRODUCER:

AGENCY NO.: ____________ AGENT'S NO.: ____________
PHONE NO.: ____________ FAX NO.: ____________
EMAIL ADDRESS: ____________

**INSURED INFORMATION**

NAME AND MAILING ADDRESS OF INSURED:

PHONE NO.: ____________
EMAIL ADDRESS: ____________
IS THE INSURED A SMALL BUSINESS? ☐ YES ☐ NO
IS THE INSURED A NON-PROFIT ENTITY? ☐ YES ☐ NO

**PROPERTY LOCATION**

**NOTE: ONE BUILDING PER POLICY – BLANKET COVERAGE NOT PERMITTED.**
IS BUILDING LOCATED IN A CBRS OR OPA? ☐ YES ☐ NO
IS INSURED PROPERTY LOCATION SAME AS INSURED'S MAILING ADDRESS? ☐ YES ☐ NO
IF NO, ENTER PROPERTY ADDRESS. IF RURAL, ENTER LEGAL DESCRIPTION, OR GEOGRAPHIC LOCATION OF PROPERTY (DO NOT USE P.O. BOX).
IDENTIFY ADDRESS TYPE: ☐ STREET ☐ LEGAL DESCRIPTION* ☐ GEOGRAPHIC LOCATION

FOR AN ADDRESS WITH MULTIPLE BUILDINGS AND/OR FOR A BUILDING WITH ADDITIONS OR EXTENSIONS, DESCRIBE THE INSURED BUILDING:
____________

* LEGAL DESCRIPTION MAY BE USED ONLY WHILE A BUILDING OR SUBDIVISION IS IN THE COURSE OF CONSTRUCTION OR PRIOR TO ESTABLISHING A STREET ADDRESS.

**1ST MORTGAGEE**

NAME AND MAILING ADDRESS OF FIRST MORTGAGEE:

LOAN NO.: ____________
IS INSURANCE REQUIRED UNDER MANDATORY PURCHASE? ☐ YES ☐ NO

**DISASTER ASSISTANCE**

IS INSURANCE REQUIRED FOR DISASTER ASSISTANCE? ☐ YES ☐ NO
**IF YES**, CHECK THE GOVERNMENT AGENCY: ☐ SBA ☐ FEMA ☐ FHA
☐ OTHER (SPECIFY): ____________
CASE FILE NO.: ____________

**2ND MORTGAGEE/OTHER**

NAME AND MAILING ADDRESS OF: ☐ 2ND MORTGAGEE ☐ LOSS PAYEE ☐ OTHER
IF OTHER, SPECIFY: ____________

LOAN NO.: ____________
IS INSURANCE REQUIRED UNDER MANDATORY PURCHASE? ☐ YES ☐ NO

**COMMUNITY**

RATING MAP INFORMATION
NAME OF COUNTY/PARISH: ____________
COMMUNITY NO./PANEL NO. AND SUFFIX: ____________ - ______
FIRM ZONE: ________ MAP DATE: ____ /____ /________
CURRENT MAP INFORMATION
CURRENT COMMUNITY NO./PANEL NO. AND SUFFIX: ____________ - ______
CURRENT FIRM ZONE: ________ CURRENT BFE: ________
MAP DATE: ____ /____ /________
NEWLY MAPPED INFORMATION
DATE THE BUILDING WAS NEWLY MAPPED INTO THE SFHA: ____ /____ /________

**PRIOR NFIP COVERAGE**

COMPLETE THIS SECTION FOR PRE- AND POST-FIRM BUILDINGS LOCATED IN AN SFHA.
1. HAS THE APPLICANT HAD A PRIOR NFIP POLICY FOR THIS PROPERTY? ☐ YES ☐ NO
2. WAS THE POLICY REQUIRED BY THE LENDER UNDER MANDATORY PURCHASE? ☐ YES ☐ NO
3. **IF YES**, HAS THE PRIOR NFIP POLICY EVER LAPSED WHILE COVERAGE WAS REQUIRED UNDER MANDATORY PURCHASE BY THE LENDER? ☐ YES ☐ NO
4. **IF YES**, WAS THE LAPSE THE RESULT OF A COMMUNITY SUSPENSION? ☐ YES ☐ NO
   **IF YES**, WHAT IS THE SUSPENSION DATE? ____ /____ /________
   WHAT IS THE REINSTATEMENT DATE? ____ /____ /________
5. WILL THIS POLICY BE EFFECTIVE WITHIN 180 DAYS OF THE COMMUNITY REINSTATEMENT AFTER SUSPENSION REFERRED TO IN (4) ABOVE? ☐ YES ☐ NO

**NFIP COPY**

**ALL BUILDINGS**

1. BUILDING PURPOSE
☐ 100% RESIDENTIAL
☐ 100% NON-RESIDENTIAL
☐ MIXED-USE – SPECIFY PERCENTAGE OF RESIDENTIAL USE: ______ %

2. BUILDING OCCUPANCY
☐ SINGLE FAMILY
☐ 2-4 FAMILY
☐ OTHER RESIDENTIAL
☐ NON-RESIDENTIAL BUSINESS
☐ OTHER NON-RESIDENTIAL

3. IS THE BUILDING A HOUSE OF WORSHIP? ☐ YES ☐ NO

4. IS THE BUILDING AN AGRICULTURAL STRUCTURE? ☐ YES ☐ NO

5. BUILDING DESCRIPTION (CHECK ONE)
☐ MAIN HOUSE
☐ DETACHED GUEST HOUSE
☐ DETACHED GARAGE
☐ BARN
☐ APARTMENT BUILDING
☐ APARTMENT - UNIT
☐ COOPERATIVE BUILDING
☐ COOPERATIVE - UNIT
☐ WAREHOUSE
☐ TOOL/STORAGE SHED
☐ POOLHOUSE, CLUBHOUSE, RECREATION BUILDING
☐ OTHER: ____________

6. CONDOMINIUM INFORMATION
IS BUILDING IN A CONDOMINIUM FORM OF OWNERSHIP? ☐ YES ☐ NO
IS COVERAGE FOR THE ENTIRE BUILDING? ☐ YES ☐ NO
TOTAL NUMBER OF UNITS: ________ ☐ HIGH-RISE ☐ LOW-RISE
IS COVERAGE FOR A CONDOMINIUM UNIT? ☐ YES ☐ NO

7. ADDITIONS AND EXTENSIONS (IF APPLICABLE)
DOES THE BUILDING HAVE ANY ADDITIONS OR EXTENSIONS? ☐ YES ☐ NO
(ADDITIONS AND EXTENSIONS MAY BE SEPARATELY INSURED.)
COVERAGE IS FOR:
☐ BUILDING INCLUDING ADDITION(S) AND EXTENSION(S)
☐ BUILDING EXCLUDING ADDITION(S) AND EXTENSION(S). PROVIDE POLICY NUMBER FOR ADDITION OR EXTENSION: ____________
☐ ADDITION OR EXTENSION ONLY (INCLUDE DESCRIPTION IN THE PROPERTY LOCATION BOX ABOVE). PROVIDE POLICY NUMBER FOR BUILDING EXCLUDING ADDITION(S) OR EXTENSION(S): ____________

8. PRIMARY RESIDENCE, RENTAL PROPERTY, TENANT'S COVERAGE
IS BUILDING INSURED'S PRIMARY RESIDENCE? ☐ YES ☐ NO
IS BUILDING A RENTAL PROPERTY? ☐ YES ☐ NO
IS THE INSURED A TENANT? ☐ YES ☐ NO
**IF YES**, IS THE TENANT REQUESTING BUILDING COVERAGE? ☐ YES ☐ NO
**IF YES**, SEE NOTICE IN SIGNATURE BLOCK ON PAGE 2.

9. BUILDING INFORMATION
IS BUILDING IN THE COURSE OF CONSTRUCTION? ☐ YES ☐ NO
IS BUILDING WALLED AND ROOFED? ☐ YES ☐ NO
IS BUILDING OVER WATER? ☐ NO ☐ PARTIALLY ☐ ENTIRELY

IS BUILDING LOCATED ON FEDERAL LAND? ☐ YES ☐ NO
IS BUILDING A SEVERE REPETITIVE LOSS PROPERTY? ☐ YES ☐ NO

10. IS BUILDING ELEVATED? ☐ YES ☐ NO

11. BASEMENT, ENCLOSURE, CRAWLSPACE
☐ NONE
☐ FINISHED BASEMENT/ENCLOSURE
☐ CRAWLSPACE
☐ UNFINISHED BASEMENT/ENCLOSURE
☐ SUBGRADE CRAWLSPACE
IS THE BASEMENT/SUBGRADE CRAWLSPACE FLOOR BELOW GRADE ON ALL SIDES? ☐ YES ☐ NO

12. NUMBER OF FLOORS IN BUILDING (INCLUDING BASEMENT/ENCLOSED AREA, IF ANY) OR BUILDING TYPE
☐ 1 ☐ 2 ☐ 3 OR MORE
☐ SPLIT LEVEL
☐ TOWNHOUSE/ROWHOUSE (RCBAP LOW-RISE ONLY)
☐ MANUFACTURED (MOBILE) HOME/TRAVEL TRAILER ON FOUNDATION

**NON-ELEVATED BUILDINGS**

1. GARAGE
IS A GARAGE ATTACHED TO THE BUILDING? ☐ YES ☐ NO
TOTAL NET AREA OF THE GARAGE: |_|_|_|_|_| SQUARE FEET.
ARE THERE ANY OPENINGS (EXCLUDING DOORS) THAT ARE DESIGNED TO ALLOW THE PASSAGE OF FLOODWATERS THROUGH THE GARAGE? ☐ YES ☐ NO
**IF YES**, NUMBER OF PERMANENT FLOOD OPENINGS WITHIN 1 FOOT ABOVE THE ADJACENT GRADE: ______
TOTAL AREA OF ALL PERMANENT OPENINGS: |_|_|_|_|_| SQUARE INCHES.
IS THE GARAGE USED SOLELY FOR PARKING OF VEHICLES, BUILDING ACCESS, AND/OR STORAGE? ☐ YES ☐ NO
**IF YES**, DOES THE GARAGE CONTAIN MACHINERY AND/OR EQUIPMENT? ☐ YES ☐ NO

2. BASEMENT/SUBGRADE CRAWLSPACE
DOES THE BASEMENT/SUBGRADE CRAWLSPACE CONTAIN MACHINERY AND/OR EQUIPMENT? ☐ YES ☐ NO
**IF YES**, SELECT THE VALUE BELOW:
☐ UP TO $10,000
☐ $10,001 TO $20,000
☐ IF GREATER THAN $20,000 - INDICATE THE AMOUNT: ____________

DOES THE BASEMENT/SUBGRADE CRAWLSPACE CONTAIN A WASHER, DRYER OR FOOD FREEZER? ☐ YES ☐ NO
**IF YES**, SELECT THE VALUE BELOW:
☐ UP TO $5,000
☐ $5,001 TO $10,000
☐ IF GREATER THAN $10,000 - INDICATE THE AMOUNT: ____________

**FEMA Form 086-0-5** **F-089** (DEC 2019)

PLEASE SUBMIT TOTAL AMOUNT DUE AND ALL REQUIRED CERTIFICATIONS WITH THE NFIP COPY OF THIS APPLICATION.
IF PAYING BY CHECK OR MONEY ORDER, MAKE PAYABLE TO THE NATIONAL FLOOD INSURANCE PROGRAM.
**IMPORTANT** — COMPLETE PAGE 1 AND PAGE 2 BEFORE SENDING APPLICATION TO THE NFIP. — **IMPORTANT**

**ONLINE** The current approved version of the NFIP Preferred Risk Policy and Newly Mapped Application, FEMA Form 086-0-5, is available at https://www.fema.gov/media-library/assets/documents/209

THIS LAYOUT OF THE REVISED PRP AND NEWLY MAPPED APPLICATION IS PROVIDED FOR YOUR REFERENCE.
THE FINAL FORM WILL BE RELEASED UPON O.M.B. APPROVAL.

**U.S. DEPARTMENT OF HOMELAND SECURITY**
**FEDERAL EMERGENCY MANAGEMENT AGENCY**
**National Flood Insurance Program**

**PREFERRED RISK POLICY AND NEWLY MAPPED APPLICATION, PAGE 2 (OF 2)**

**IMPORTANT—PLEASE PRINT OR TYPE; ENTER DATES AS MM/DD/YYYY.**
ALL DATA PROVIDED BY THE INSURED OR OBTAINED FROM THE ELEVATION CERTIFICATE SHOULD BE REVIEWED AND TRANSCRIBED BELOW. THIS PART OF THE APPLICATION MUST BE COMPLETED FOR ALL BUILDINGS.

☐ NEW ☐ RENEWAL ☐ TRANSFER (NFIP POLICIES ONLY)
PRIOR POLICY #: ____________

## ELEVATED BUILDINGS

ELEVATED BUILDINGS (INCLUDING MANUFACTURED (MOBILE) HOMES/TRAVEL TRAILERS)

1. IF THE BUILDING IS ELEVATED, IS THE AREA BELOW
   - ☐ FREE OF OBSTRUCTION
   - ☐ WITH OBSTRUCTION
2. ELEVATING FOUNDATION TYPE
   - ☐ PIERS, POSTS, OR PILES
   - ☐ REINFORCED MASONRY PIERS OR CONCRETE PIERS OR COLUMNS
   - ☐ REINFORCED CONCRETE SHEAR WALLS
   - ☐ WOOD SHEAR WALLS
   - ☐ SOLID FOUNDATION WALLS
3. MACHINERY AND/OR EQUIPMENT

DOES THE AREA BELOW THE ELEVATED FLOOR CONTAIN MACHINERY AND/OR EQUIPMENT? ☐ YES ☐ NO
**IF YES**, SELECT THE VALUE BELOW:
- ☐ UP TO $10,000
- ☐ $10,001 TO $20,000
- ☐ IF GREATER THAN $20,000 - INDICATE THE AMOUNT: ____________

DOES THE AREA BELOW THE ELEVATED FLOOR CONTAIN A WASHER, DRYER OR FOOD FREEZER? ☐ YES ☐ NO
**IF YES**, SELECT THE VALUE BELOW:
- ☐ UP TO $5,000
- ☐ $5,001 TO $10,000
- ☐ IF GREATER THAN $10,000 - INDICATE THE AMOUNT: ____________

4. AREA BELOW THE ELEVATED FLOOR

IS THE AREA BELOW THE ELEVATED FLOOR ENCLOSED? ☐ YES ☐ NO
**IF YES**, CHECK ONE OF THE FOLLOWING: ☐ FULLY ☐ PARTIALLY

IS THERE A GARAGE? (CHECK ONE)
- ☐ NO GARAGE
- ☐ BENEATH THE LIVING SPACE
- ☐ NEXT TO THE LIVING SPACE

DOES THE AREA BELOW THE ELEVATED FLOOR CONTAIN ELEVATORS? ☐ YES ☐ NO
**IF YES**, HOW MANY? ____________

**IF THE ANSWER TO ANY OF THE QUESTIONS REGARDING THE AREA BELOW THE ELEVATED FLOOR IS YES, OR THERE IS A GARAGE, ANSWER ALL THE FOLLOWING.**

INDICATE MATERIAL USED FOR ENCLOSURE:
- ☐ INSECT SCREENING
- ☐ LIGHT WOOD LATTICE
- ☐ SOLID WOOD FRAME WALLS (BREAKAWAY)
- ☐ SOLID WOOD FRAME WALLS (NON-BREAKAWAY)
- ☐ MASONRY WALLS (IF BREAKAWAY, SUBMIT CERTIFICATION DOCUMENTATION)
- ☐ MASONRY WALLS (NON-BREAKAWAY)
- ☐ OTHER (DESCRIBE): ____________

IF ENCLOSED WITH A MATERIAL OTHER THAN INSECT SCREENING OR LIGHT WOOD LATTICE, PROVIDE THE SIZE OF ENCLOSED AREA: |_|_|_|_|_| SQUARE FEET

IS THE ENCLOSED AREA/CRAWLSPACE USED FOR ANY PURPOSE OTHER THAN SOLELY FOR PARKING OF VEHICLES, BUILDING ACCESS AND/OR STORAGE? ☐ YES ☐ NO

**IF YES**, DESCRIBE: ____________

DOES THE ENCLOSED AREA HAVE MORE THAN 20 LINEAR FEET OF FINISHED INTERIOR WALL, PANELING, ETC.? ☐ YES ☐ NO

5. FLOOD OPENINGS

IS THE ENCLOSED AREA/CRAWLSPACE CONSTRUCTED WITH OPENINGS (EXCLUDING DOORS) TO ALLOW THE PASSAGE OF FLOODWATERS THROUGH THE ENCLOSED AREA? ☐ YES ☐ NO

**IF YES**, INDICATE NUMBER OF PERMANENT FLOOD OPENINGS WITHIN 1 FOOT ABOVE ADJACENT GRADE: ____________.

TOTAL AREA OF ALL PERMANENT FLOOD OPENINGS: |_|_|_|_|_| SQUARE INCHES.

ARE FLOOD OPENINGS ENGINEERED? ☐ YES ☐ NO
**IF YES**, SUBMIT CERTIFICATION.

## MANUFACTURED (MOBILE) HOMES/TRAVEL TRAILERS

**NOTE: WHEELS MUST BE REMOVED FOR TRAVEL TRAILER TO BE INSURABLE.**

1. MANUFACTURED (MOBILE) HOME/TRAVEL TRAILER DATA

YEAR OF MANUFACTURE: |_|_|_|_|

MAKE: |_|_|_|_|_|_|_|_|_|_|_|_|_|_|_|_|_|_|_|_|_|_|_|_|_|

MODEL NUMBER: |_|_|_|_|_|_|_|_|_|_|_|_|_|_|_|_|_|_|_|_|_|_|

SERIAL NUMBER: |_|_|_|_|_|_|_|_|_|_|_|_|_|_|_|_|_|_|_|_|_|_|

DIMENSIONS: |_|_|_| × |_|_|_| FEET

ARE THERE ANY PERMANENT ADDITIONS AND/OR EXTENSIONS? ☐ YES ☐ NO

**IF YES**, THE DIMENSIONS ARE: |_|_|_| × |_|_|_| FEET

2. ANCHORING

THE MANUFACTURED (MOBILE) HOME/TRAVEL TRAILER ANCHORING SYSTEM UTILIZES: (CHECK ALL THAT APPLY.)
- ☐ OVER-THE-TOP TIES
- ☐ GROUND ANCHORS
- ☐ FRAME TIES
- ☐ SLAB ANCHORS
- ☐ FRAME CONNECTORS
- ☐ OTHER (DESCRIBE): ____________

3. INSTALLATION

THE MANUFACTURED (MOBILE) HOME/TRAVEL TRAILER WAS INSTALLED IN ACCORDANCE WITH: (CHECK ALL THAT APPLY.)
- ☐ MANUFACTURER'S SPECIFICATIONS
- ☐ LOCAL FLOODPLAIN MANAGEMENT STANDARDS
- ☐ STATE AND/OR LOCAL BUILDING STANDARDS

## CONSTRUCTION INFORMATION

**CHECK ONE OF THE FOLLOWING AND ENTER DATE FOR ORIGINAL CONSTRUCTION:**
☐ BUILDING PERMIT ☐ CONSTRUCTION ____/____/________

**CHECK IF BUILDING HAS BEEN SUBSTANTIALLY IMPROVED AND ENTER DATE:**
☐ SUBSTANTIAL IMPROVEMENT ____/____/________

**CHECK ONE OF THE FOLLOWING FOR MANUFACTURED (MOBILE) HOMES/TRAVEL TRAILERS:**
- ☐ LOCATED OUTSIDE A MOBILE HOME PARK OR SUBDIVISION: DATE OF PERMANENT PLACEMENT
- ☐ LOCATED INSIDE A MOBILE HOME PARK OR SUBDIVISION: CONSTRUCTION DATE OF MOBILE HOME PARK OR SUBDIVISION FACILITIES

## CONTENTS

**CONTENTS LOCATED IN:***
- ☐ Basement/Subgrade Crawlspace only
- ☐ Basement/Subgrade Crawlspace and above
- ☐ Enclosure/Crawlspace and above
- ☐ Lowest floor only above ground level
- ☐ Lowest floor above ground level and higher floors
- ☐ Above ground level more than one full floor
- ☐ Manufactured (mobile) home

IS PERSONAL PROPERTY HOUSEHOLD CONTENTS? ☐ YES ☐ NO
**IF NO**, DESCRIBE: ____________
*IF SINGLE FAMILY, CONTENTS ARE RATED THROUGHOUT THE BUILDING.

## BUILDING ELIGIBILITY

**THE PREFERRED RISK POLICY (PRP) IS ONLY AVAILABLE IF ALL ANSWERS TO QUESTIONS A AND B ARE NO, EXCEPT FOR BUILDINGS ELIGIBLE UNDER THE NEWLY MAPPED PROCEDURE, FOR WHICH THE ANSWER TO QUESTION A MAY BE YES.**

**ANSWER THE FOLLOWING TO DETERMINE A BUILDING'S ELIGIBILITY FOR A PRP:**

A) IS THE BUILDING LOCATED IN A SPECIAL FLOOD HAZARD AREA (SFHA) EXCLUDING ZONES AR AND A99? ☐ YES ☐ NO

B) DO ANY OF THE FOLLOWING CONDITIONS, ARISING FROM 1 OR MORE OCCURRENCES IN ANY 10-YEAR PERIOD, EXIST?
- 2 LOSS PAYMENTS, EACH MORE THAN $1,000 ☐ YES ☐ NO
- 3 OR MORE LOSS PAYMENTS, REGARDLESS OF AMOUNT ☐ YES ☐ NO
- 2 FEDERAL DISASTER RELIEF PAYMENTS, EACH MORE THAN $1,000 ☐ YES ☐ NO
- 3 FEDERAL DISASTER RELIEF PAYMENTS, REGARDLESS OF AMOUNT ☐ YES ☐ NO
- 1 FLOOD INSURANCE CLAIM PAYMENT AND 1 FLOOD DISASTER RELIEF PAYMENT (INCLUDING LOANS AND GRANTS), EACH MORE THAN $1,000 ☐ YES ☐ NO

## COVERAGE AND PREMIUM

**ESTIMATED BUILDING REPLACEMENT COST (INCLUDING FOUNDATION):**
$ ____________

**ENTER SELECTED OPTION FOR COVERAGE LIMIT AND PREMIUM FROM THE TABLES IN THE *NFIP FLOOD INSURANCE MANUAL***

**BUILDING AND CONTENTS COVERAGE COMBINATION**

| REQUESTED COVERAGE | |
|---|---|
| BUILDING COVERAGE | $ |
| CONTENTS COVERAGE / CONTENTS ONLY | $ |
| **PREMIUM CALCULATION** | |
| BASE PREMIUM | $ |
| MULTIPLIER | |
| ADJUSTED PREMIUM | $ |
| ICC PREMIUM | $ |
| **PREMIUM SUBTOTAL** | **$** |
| RESERVE FUND ASSESSMENT PERCENT | % |
| RESERVE FUND ASSESSMENT AMOUNT | $ |
| **TOTAL PREMIUM** | **$** |
| **FEES AND SURCHARGES** | |
| HFIAA SURCHARGE | $ |
| PROBATION SURCHARGE | $ |
| FEDERAL POLICY FEE | $ |
| **TOTAL AMOUNT DUE** | **$** |

INDICATE THE RATE TABLE USED FOR THE BASE PREMIUM: ____________
RISK RATING METHOD: ☐ 7 - PRP ☐ R - NEWLY MAPPED

## SIGNATURE

**NOTICE:** BUILDING COVERAGE BENEFITS – EXCEPT FOR A RESIDENTIAL CONDOMINIUM BUILDING – ARE NOT AVAILABLE IF OTHER NFIP BUILDING COVERAGE HAS BEEN PURCHASED BY THE APPLICANT OR ANY OTHER PARTY FOR THE SAME BUILDING.

THE ABOVE STATEMENTS ARE CORRECT TO THE BEST OF MY KNOWLEDGE. I UNDERSTAND THAT ANY FALSE STATEMENTS MAY BE PUNISHABLE BY FINE AND/OR IMPRISONMENT UNDER APPLICABLE FEDERAL LAW. SEE LAST PAGE OF FORM.

____________________ SIGNATURE OF INSURANCE AGENT/PRODUCER ____/____/________ DATE (MM/DD/YYYY)

____________________ SIGNATURE OF INSURED (OPTIONAL) ____/____/________ DATE (MM/DD/YYYY)

NFIP COPY

**FEMA Form 086-0-5** **F-089** (DEC 2019)

PLEASE SUBMIT TOTAL AMOUNT DUE AND ALL REQUIRED CERTIFICATIONS WITH THE NFIP COPY OF THIS APPLICATION.
IF PAYING BY CHECK OR MONEY ORDER, MAKE PAYABLE TO THE NATIONAL FLOOD INSURANCE PROGRAM.
**IMPORTANT** — COMPLETE PAGE 1 AND PAGE 2 BEFORE SENDING APPLICATION TO THE NFIP. — **IMPORTANT**

*National Flood Insurance Program*

**PREFERRED RISK POLICY AND NEWLY MAPPED APPLICATION**

**FEMA FORM 086-0-5**

**NONDISCRIMINATION**

No person or organization shall be excluded from participation in, denied the benefits of, or subjected to discrimination under the Program authorized by the Act, on the grounds of race, color, creed, sex, age or national origin.

**PRIVACY ACT**

The information requested is necessary to process your Flood Insurance Application for a flood insurance policy. The authority to collect the information is Title 42, U.S. Code, Sections 4001 to 4028. Disclosures of this information may be made: to federal, state, tribal, and local government agencies, fiscal agents, your agent, mortgage servicing companies, insurance or other companies, lending institutions, and contractors working for us, for the purpose of carrying out the National Flood Insurance Program; to certain property owners for the purpose of property loss history evaluation; to the American Red Cross for verification of nonduplication of benefits following a flooding event or disaster; to law enforcement agencies or professional organizations when there may be a violation or potential violation of law; to a federal, state or local agency when we request information relevant to an agency decision concerning issuance of a grant or other benefit, or in certain circumstances when a federal agency requests such information for a similar purpose from us; to a Congressional office in response to an inquiry made at the request of an individual; to the Office of Management and Budget (OMB) in relation to private relief legislation under OMB Circular A-19; and to the National Archives and Records Administration in records management inspections. Providing the information is voluntary, but failure to do so may delay or prevent issuance of the flood insurance policy.

**GENERAL**

This information is provided pursuant to Public Law 96-511 (Paperwork Reduction Act of 1980, as amended), dated December 11, 1980, to allow the public to participate more fully and meaningfully in the Federal paperwork review process.

**AUTHORITY**

Public Law 96-511, amended, 44 U.S.C. 3507; and 5 CFR 1320.

**PAPERWORK BURDEN DISCLOSURE NOTICE**

Public reporting burden for this form is estimated to average 10 minutes per response. The burden estimate includes the time for reviewing instructions, searching existing data sources, gathering and maintaining the data needed, and completing and submitting the form. This collection of information is required to obtain or retain benefits. You are not required to respond to this collection of information unless a valid OMB control number is displayed in the upper right corner of this form. Send comments regarding the accuracy of the burden estimate and any suggestions for reducing the burden to: Information Collections Management, Department of Homeland Security, Federal Emergency Management Agency, 500 C Street SW, Washington, DC 20742, Paperwork Reduction Project (1660-0006). **NOTE: Do not send your completed form to this address.**

# III. NFIP Flood Insurance General Change Endorsement

THIS LAYOUT OF THE REVISED GENERAL CHANGE ENDORSEMENT IS PROVIDED FOR YOUR REFERENCE.
THE FINAL FORM WILL BE RELEASED UPON O.M.B. APPROVAL.

**U.S. DEPARTMENT OF HOMELAND SECURITY**
**FEDERAL EMERGENCY MANAGEMENT AGENCY**
National Flood Insurance Program
**FLOOD INSURANCE GENERAL CHANGE ENDORSEMENT, PAGE 1 (OF 2)**

POLICY #: ______________

**FOR ALL POLICY TYPES. IMPORTANT—PLEASE PRINT OR TYPE; ENTER DATES AS MM/DD/YYYY.**

**CHANGE**

REASON FOR CHANGE (CHECK ALL THAT APPLY)
☐ MORTGAGEE ☐ MAILING ADDRESS
☐ INCREASE COVERAGE ☐ BILLING
☐ BUILDING INFORMATION ☐ AGENT/PRODUCER
☐ INSURED INFORMATION
☐ OTHER (SPECIFY): ______________

**ASSIGNMENT**

REASON FOR ASSIGNMENT:
☐ NEW PURCHASE
DATE OF PURCHASE: ____ /____ /________
☐ OTHER (SPECIFY): ______________

**AGENT/PRODUCER INFORMATION**

NAME AND MAILING ADDRESS OF AGENT/PRODUCER:

AGENCY NO.: ______________ AGENT'S NO.: ______________
PHONE NO.: ______________ FAX NO.: ______________
EMAIL ADDRESS: ______________

**PROPERTY LOCATION**

**NOTE: ONE BUILDING PER POLICY – BLANKET COVERAGE NOT PERMITTED.**
IS BUILDING LOCATED IN A CBRS OR OPA? ☐ YES ☐ NO
IS INSURED PROPERTY LOCATION SAME AS INSURED'S MAILING ADDRESS? ☐ YES ☐ NO
IF NO, ENTER PROPERTY ADDRESS. IF RURAL, ENTER LEGAL DESCRIPTION, OR GEOGRAPHIC LOCATION OF PROPERTY (DO NOT USE P.O. BOX).
IDENTIFY ADDRESS TYPE: ☐ STREET ☐ LEGAL DESCRIPTION* ☐ GEOGRAPHIC LOCATION

FOR AN ADDRESS WITH MULTIPLE BUILDINGS AND/OR FOR A BUILDING WITH ADDITIONS OR EXTENSIONS, DESCRIBE THE INSURED BUILDING:
______________

* LEGAL DESCRIPTION MAY BE USED ONLY WHILE A BUILDING OR SUBDIVISION IS IN THE COURSE OF CONSTRUCTION OR PRIOR TO ESTABLISHING A STREET ADDRESS.

**COMMUNITY**

GRANDFATHERING INFORMATION
GRANDFATHERED? ☐ YES ☐ NO **IF YES,** ☐ BUILT IN COMPLIANCE *OR*
☐ CONTINUOUS COVERAGE (PROVIDE PRIOR POLICY NO. ______________ )

RATING MAP INFORMATION
NAME OF COUNTY/PARISH: ______________
COMMUNITY NO./PANEL NO. AND SUFFIX: ______________ - ________
FIRM ZONE: ________ MAP DATE: ____ /____ /________
COMMUNITY PROGRAM TYPE IS: ☐ REGULAR ☐ EMERGENCY

CURRENT MAP INFORMATION
CURRENT COMMUNITY NO./PANEL NO. AND SUFFIX: ______________ - ________
CURRENT FIRM ZONE: ________ CURRENT BFE: ________
MAP DATE: ____ /____ /________

NEWLY MAPPED INFORMATION
DATE THE BUILDING WAS NEWLY MAPPED INTO THE SFHA: ____ /____ /________

**BILLING**

FOR RENEWAL, BILL:
☐ INSURED ☐ LOSS PAYEE
☐ FIRST MORTGAGEE ☐ OTHER (AS SPECIFIED IN THE "2ND MORTGAGEE/OTHER" BOX BELOW)
☐ SECOND MORTGAGEE

**POLICY PERIOD**

POLICY PERIOD IS FROM ____ /____ /________ TO ____ /____ /________
12:01 A.M. LOCAL TIME AT THE INSURED PROPERTY LOCATION.
WAITING PERIOD:
☐ STANDARD 30-DAY
☐ REQUIRED FOR LOAN TRANSACTION – NO WAITING PERIOD
☐ MAP REVISION (ZONE CHANGE FROM NON-SFHA TO SFHA) – 1 DAY
☐ TRANSFER (NFIP POLICIES ONLY) – NO WAITING PERIOD

**INSURED INFORMATION**

NAME AND MAILING ADDRESS OF INSURED:

PHONE NO.: ______________
EMAIL ADDRESS: ______________
IS THE INSURED A SMALL BUSINESS? ☐ YES ☐ NO
IS THE INSURED A NON-PROFIT ENTITY? ☐ YES ☐ NO

**1ST MORTGAGEE**

NAME AND MAILING ADDRESS OF FIRST MORTGAGEE:

LOAN NO.: ______________
IS INSURANCE REQUIRED UNDER MANDATORY PURCHASE? ☐ YES ☐ NO

**2ND MORTGAGEE/OTHER**

NAME AND MAILING ADDRESS OF: ☐ 2ND MORTGAGEE ☐ LOSS PAYEE ☐ OTHER
IF OTHER, SPECIFY: ______________

LOAN NO.: ______________
IS INSURANCE REQUIRED UNDER MANDATORY PURCHASE? ☐ YES ☐ NO

**PRIOR NFIP COVERAGE**

COMPLETE THIS SECTION ONLY FOR PRE-FIRM BUILDINGS LOCATED IN AN SFHA.
1. HAS THE APPLICANT HAD A PRIOR NFIP POLICY FOR THIS PROPERTY? ☐ YES ☐ NO
2. WAS THE POLICY REQUIRED BY THE LENDER UNDER MANDATORY PURCHASE? ☐ YES ☐ NO
3. IF YES, HAS THE PRIOR NFIP POLICY EVER LAPSED WHILE COVERAGE WAS REQUIRED UNDER MANDATORY PURCHASE BY THE LENDER? ☐ YES ☐ NO
4. IF YES, WAS THE LAPSE THE RESULT OF A COMMUNITY SUSPENSION? ☐ YES ☐ NO
   IF YES, WHAT IS THE SUSPENSION DATE? ____ /____ /________
   WHAT IS THE REINSTATEMENT DATE? ____ /____ /________
5. WILL THIS POLICY BE EFFECTIVE WITHIN 180 DAYS OF THE COMMUNITY REINSTATEMENT AFTER SUSPENSION REFERRED TO IN (4) ABOVE? ☐ YES ☐ NO

**NFIP COPY**

**ALL BUILDINGS**

1. BUILDING PURPOSE
☐ 100% RESIDENTIAL
☐ 100% NON-RESIDENTIAL
☐ MIXED-USE – SPECIFY PERCENTAGE OF RESIDENTIAL USE: ____ %

2. BUILDING OCCUPANCY
☐ SINGLE FAMILY
☐ 2-4 FAMILY
☐ OTHER RESIDENTIAL
☐ NON-RESIDENTIAL BUSINESS
☐ OTHER NON-RESIDENTIAL

3. IS THE BUILDING A HOUSE OF WORSHIP? ☐ YES ☐ NO

4. IS THE BUILDING AN AGRICULTURAL STRUCTURE? ☐ YES ☐ NO

5. BUILDING DESCRIPTION (CHECK ONE)
☐ MAIN HOUSE
☐ DETACHED GUEST HOUSE
☐ DETACHED GARAGE
☐ BARN
☐ APARTMENT BUILDING
☐ APARTMENT - UNIT
☐ COOPERATIVE BUILDING
☐ COOPERATIVE - UNIT
☐ WAREHOUSE
☐ TOOL/STORAGE SHED
☐ POOLHOUSE, CLUBHOUSE, RECREATION BUILDING
☐ OTHER: ______________

6. CONDOMINIUM INFORMATION
IS BUILDING IN A CONDOMINIUM FORM OF OWNERSHIP? ☐ YES ☐ NO
IS COVERAGE FOR THE ENTIRE BUILDING? ☐ YES ☐ NO
TOTAL NUMBER OF UNITS: ________
☐ HIGH-RISE ☐ LOW-RISE
IS COVERAGE FOR A CONDOMINIUM UNIT? ☐ YES ☐ NO

7. ADDITIONS AND EXTENSIONS (IF APPLICABLE)
DOES THE BUILDING HAVE ANY ADDITIONS OR EXTENSIONS? ☐ YES ☐ NO
(ADDITIONS AND EXTENSIONS MAY BE SEPARATELY INSURED.)
COVERAGE IS FOR:
☐ BUILDING INCLUDING ADDITION(S) AND EXTENSION(S)
☐ BUILDING EXCLUDING ADDITION(S) AND EXTENSION(S). PROVIDE POLICY NUMBER FOR ADDITION OR EXTENSION: ______________
☐ ADDITION OR EXTENSION ONLY (INCLUDE DESCRIPTION IN THE PROPERTY LOCATION BOX ABOVE). PROVIDE POLICY NUMBER FOR BUILDING EXCLUDING ADDITION(S) OR EXTENSION(S): ______________

8. PRIMARY RESIDENCE, RENTAL PROPERTY, TENANT'S COVERAGE
IS BUILDING INSURED'S PRIMARY RESIDENCE? ☐ YES ☐ NO
IS BUILDING A RENTAL PROPERTY? ☐ YES ☐ NO
IS THE INSURED A TENANT? ☐ YES ☐ NO
IF YES, IS THE TENANT REQUESTING BUILDING COVERAGE? ☐ YES ☐ NO
IF YES, SEE NOTICE IN SIGNATURE BLOCK ON PAGE 2.

9. BUILDING INFORMATION
IS BUILDING IN THE COURSE OF CONSTRUCTION? ☐ YES ☐ NO
IS BUILDING WALLED AND ROOFED? ☐ YES ☐ NO
IS BUILDING OVER WATER? ☐ NO ☐ PARTIALLY ☐ ENTIRELY
IS BUILDING LOCATED ON FEDERAL LAND? ☐ YES ☐ NO
IS BUILDING A SEVERE REPETITIVE LOSS PROPERTY? ☐ YES ☐ NO

10. IS BUILDING ELEVATED? ☐ YES ☐ NO

11. BASEMENT, ENCLOSURE, CRAWLSPACE
☐ NONE
☐ FINISHED BASEMENT/ENCLOSURE
☐ CRAWLSPACE
☐ UNFINISHED BASEMENT/ENCLOSURE
☐ SUBGRADE CRAWLSPACE
IS THE BASEMENT/SUBGRADE CRAWLSPACE FLOOR BELOW GRADE ON ALL SIDES? ☐ YES ☐ NO

12. NUMBER OF FLOORS IN BUILDING (INCLUDING BASEMENT/ENCLOSED AREA, IF ANY) OR BUILDING TYPE
☐ 1 ☐ 2 ☐ 3 OR MORE
☐ SPLIT LEVEL
☐ TOWNHOUSE/ROWHOUSE (RCBAP LOW-RISE ONLY)
☐ MANUFACTURED (MOBILE) HOME/TRAVEL TRAILER ON FOUNDATION

**NON-ELEVATED BUILDINGS**

1. GARAGE
IS A GARAGE ATTACHED TO THE BUILDING? ☐ YES ☐ NO
TOTAL NET AREA OF THE GARAGE: |_|_|_|_|_| SQUARE FEET.
ARE THERE ANY OPENINGS (EXCLUDING DOORS) THAT ARE DESIGNED TO ALLOW THE PASSAGE OF FLOODWATERS THROUGH THE GARAGE? ☐ YES ☐ NO
IF YES, NUMBER OF PERMANENT FLOOD OPENINGS WITHIN 1 FOOT ABOVE THE ADJACENT GRADE: ________.
TOTAL AREA OF ALL PERMANENT OPENINGS: |_|_|_|_|_| SQUARE INCHES.
IS THE GARAGE USED SOLELY FOR PARKING OF VEHICLES, BUILDING ACCESS, AND/OR STORAGE? ☐ YES ☐ NO
IF YES, DOES THE GARAGE CONTAIN MACHINERY AND/OR EQUIPMENT? ☐ YES ☐ NO

2. BASEMENT/SUBGRADE CRAWLSPACE
DOES THE BASEMENT/SUBGRADE CRAWLSPACE CONTAIN MACHINERY AND/OR EQUIPMENT? ☐ YES ☐ NO
IF YES, SELECT THE VALUE BELOW:
☐ UP TO $10,000
☐ $10,001 TO $20,000
☐ IF GREATER THAN $20,000 - INDICATE THE AMOUNT: ______________
DOES THE BASEMENT/SUBGRADE CRAWLSPACE CONTAIN A WASHER, DRYER OR FOOD FREEZER? ☐ YES ☐ NO
IF YES, SELECT THE VALUE BELOW:
☐ UP TO $5,000
☐ $5,001 TO $10,000
☐ IF GREATER THAN $10,000 - INDICATE THE AMOUNT: ______________

**FEMA Form 086-0-3** **F-051** (DEC 2019)

PLEASE SUBMIT TOTAL AMOUNT DUE AND ALL REQUIRED CERTIFICATIONS WITH THE NFIP COPY OF THIS ENDORSEMENT.
IF PAYING BY CHECK OR MONEY ORDER, MAKE PAYABLE TO THE NATIONAL FLOOD INSURANCE PROGRAM.
**IMPORTANT** — COMPLETE PAGE 1 AND PAGE 2 BEFORE SENDING ENDORSEMENT TO THE NFIP. — **IMPORTANT**

**ONLINE** The current approved version of the NFIP Flood Insurance General Change Endorsement, FEMA Form 086-0-3, is available at https://www.fema.gov/media-library/assets/documents/144

THIS LAYOUT OF THE REVISED GENERAL CHANGE ENDORSEMENT IS PROVIDED FOR YOUR REFERENCE.
THE FINAL FORM WILL BE RELEASED UPON O.M.B. APPROVAL.

**U.S. DEPARTMENT OF HOMELAND SECURITY**
**FEDERAL EMERGENCY MANAGEMENT AGENCY**
National Flood Insurance Program

## FLOOD INSURANCE GENERAL CHANGE ENDORSEMENT, PAGE 2 (OF 2)

**FOR ALL POLICY TYPES. IMPORTANT—PLEASE PRINT OR TYPE; ENTER DATES AS MM/DD/YYYY.**
ALL DATA PROVIDED BY THE INSURED OR OBTAINED FROM THE ELEVATION CERTIFICATE SHOULD BE REVIEWED AND TRANSCRIBED BELOW. THIS PART OF THE ENDORSEMENT MUST BE COMPLETED FOR ALL BUILDINGS.

POLICY #: ____________

### ELEVATED BUILDINGS

ELEVATED BUILDINGS (INCLUDING MANUFACTURED [MOBILE] HOMES/ TRAVEL TRAILERS)

1. IF THE BUILDING IS ELEVATED, IS THE AREA BELOW
   - ☐ FREE OF OBSTRUCTION
   - ☐ WITH OBSTRUCTION
2. ELEVATING FOUNDATION TYPE
   - ☐ PIERS, POSTS, OR PILES
   - ☐ REINFORCED MASONRY PIERS OR CONCRETE PIERS OR COLUMNS
   - ☐ REINFORCED CONCRETE SHEAR WALLS
   - ☐ WOOD SHEAR WALLS
   - ☐ SOLID FOUNDATION WALLS
3. MACHINERY AND/OR EQUIPMENT

DOES THE AREA BELOW THE ELEVATED FLOOR CONTAIN MACHINERY AND/OR EQUIPMENT? ☐ YES ☐ NO

IF YES, SELECT THE VALUE BELOW:
- ☐ UP TO $10,000
- ☐ $10,001 TO $20,000
- ☐ IF GREATER THAN $20,000 - INDICATE THE AMOUNT: ____________

DOES THE AREA BELOW THE ELEVATED FLOOR CONTAIN A WASHER, DRYER OR FOOD FREEZER? ☐ YES ☐ NO

IF YES, SELECT THE VALUE BELOW:
- ☐ UP TO $5,000
- ☐ $5,001 TO $10,000
- ☐ IF GREATER THAN $10,000 - INDICATE THE AMOUNT: ____________

4. AREA BELOW THE ELEVATED FLOOR

IS THE AREA BELOW THE ELEVATED FLOOR ENCLOSED? ☐ YES ☐ NO

IF YES, CHECK ONE OF THE FOLLOWING: ☐ FULLY ☐ PARTIALLY

IS THERE A GARAGE? (CHECK ONE)
- ☐ NO GARAGE
- ☐ BENEATH THE LIVING SPACE
- ☐ NEXT TO THE LIVING SPACE

DOES THE AREA BELOW THE ELEVATED FLOOR CONTAIN ELEVATORS? ☐ YES ☐ NO

IF YES, HOW MANY? ____________

**IF THE ANSWER TO ANY OF THE QUESTIONS REGARDING THE AREA BELOW THE ELEVATED FLOOR IS YES, OR THERE IS A GARAGE, ANSWER ALL THE FOLLOWING.**

INDICATE MATERIAL USED FOR ENCLOSURE:
- ☐ INSECT SCREENING
- ☐ LIGHT WOOD LATTICE
- ☐ SOLID WOOD FRAME WALLS (BREAKAWAY)
- ☐ SOLID WOOD FRAME WALLS (NON-BREAKAWAY)
- ☐ MASONRY WALLS (IF BREAKAWAY, SUBMIT CERTIFICATION DOCUMENTATION)
- ☐ MASONRY WALLS (NON-BREAKAWAY)
- ☐ OTHER (DESCRIBE): ____________

IF ENCLOSED WITH A MATERIAL OTHER THAN INSECT SCREENING OR LIGHT WOOD LATTICE, PROVIDE THE SIZE OF ENCLOSED AREA: |_|_|_|_|_| SQUARE FEET

IS THE ENCLOSED AREA/CRAWLSPACE USED FOR ANY PURPOSE OTHER THAN SOLELY FOR PARKING OF VEHICLES, BUILDING ACCESS AND/OR STORAGE? ☐ YES ☐ NO

IF YES, DESCRIBE: ____________

DOES THE ENCLOSED AREA HAVE MORE THAN 20 LINEAR FEET OF FINISHED INTERIOR WALL, PANELING, ETC.? ☐ YES ☐ NO

5. FLOOD OPENINGS

IS THE ENCLOSED AREA/CRAWLSPACE CONSTRUCTED WITH OPENINGS (EXCLUDING DOORS) TO ALLOW THE PASSAGE OF FLOODWATERS THROUGH THE ENCLOSED AREA? ☐ YES ☐ NO

IF YES, INDICATE NUMBER OF PERMANENT FLOOD OPENINGS WITHIN 1 FOOT ABOVE ADJACENT GRADE: ______.

TOTAL AREA OF ALL PERMANENT FLOOD OPENINGS: |_|_|_|_|_| SQUARE INCHES.

ARE FLOOD OPENINGS ENGINEERED? ☐ YES ☐ NO

IF YES, SUBMIT CERTIFICATION.

### MANUFACTURED (MOBILE) HOMES/ TRAVEL TRAILERS

NOTE: WHEELS MUST BE REMOVED FOR TRAVEL TRAILER TO BE INSURABLE.

1. MANUFACTURED (MOBILE) HOME/TRAVEL TRAILER DATA

YEAR OF MANUFACTURE: |_|_|_|_|

MAKE: |_|_|_|_|_|_|_|_|_|_|_|_|_|_|_|_|_|_|_|_|_|_|_|_|_|

MODEL NUMBER: |_|_|_|_|_|_|_|_|_|_|_|_|_|_|_|_|_|_|_|_|_|_|

SERIAL NUMBER: |_|_|_|_|_|_|_|_|_|_|_|_|_|_|_|_|_|_|_|_|_|_|

DIMENSIONS: |_|_|_| × |_|_|_| FEET

ARE THERE ANY PERMANENT ADDITIONS AND/OR EXTENSIONS? ☐ YES ☐ NO

IF YES, THE DIMENSIONS ARE: |_|_|_| × |_|_|_| FEET

2. ANCHORING

THE MANUFACTURED (MOBILE) HOME/TRAVEL TRAILER ANCHORING SYSTEM UTILIZES: (CHECK ALL THAT APPLY.)
- ☐ OVER-THE-TOP TIES
- ☐ GROUND ANCHORS
- ☐ FRAME TIES
- ☐ SLAB ANCHORS
- ☐ FRAME CONNECTORS
- ☐ OTHER (DESCRIBE): ____________

3. INSTALLATION

THE MANUFACTURED (MOBILE) HOME/TRAVEL TRAILER WAS INSTALLED IN ACCORDANCE WITH: (CHECK ALL THAT APPLY.)
- ☐ MANUFACTURER'S SPECIFICATIONS
- ☐ LOCAL FLOODPLAIN MANAGEMENT STANDARDS
- ☐ STATE AND/OR LOCAL BUILDING STANDARDS

### CONSTRUCTION INFORMATION

**CHECK ONE OF THE FOLLOWING AND ENTER DATE FOR ORIGINAL CONSTRUCTION:**
☐ BUILDING PERMIT ☐ CONSTRUCTION ____/____/______

**CHECK IF BUILDING HAS BEEN SUBSTANTIALLY IMPROVED AND ENTER DATE:**
☐ SUBSTANTIAL IMPROVEMENT ____/____/______

**CHECK ONE OF THE FOLLOWING FOR MANUFACTURED (MOBILE) HOMES/TRAVEL TRAILERS:**
- ☐ LOCATED OUTSIDE A MOBILE HOME PARK OR SUBDIVISION: DATE OF PERMANENT PLACEMENT
- ☐ LOCATED INSIDE A MOBILE HOME PARK OR SUBDIVISION: CONSTRUCTION DATE OF MOBILE HOME PARK OR SUBDIVISION FACILITIES

### CONTENTS

**CONTENTS LOCATED IN:***
- ☐ Basement/Subgrade Crawlspace only
- ☐ Basement/Subgrade Crawlspace and above
- ☐ Enclosure/Crawlspace and above
- ☐ Lowest floor only above ground level
- ☐ Lowest floor above ground level and higher floors
- ☐ Above ground level more than one full floor
- ☐ Manufactured (mobile) home

IS PERSONAL PROPERTY HOUSEHOLD CONTENTS? ☐ YES ☐ NO

IF NO, DESCRIBE: ____________

*IF SINGLE FAMILY, CONTENTS ARE RATED THROUGHOUT THE BUILDING.

### ELEVATION DATA

IS BUILDING POST-FIRM CONSTRUCTION? ☐ YES ☐ NO

(IF POST-FIRM CONSTRUCTION IN ZONES A, 1-A30, AE, AO, AH, V, V1-V30, VE, OR IF PRE-FIRM CONSTRUCTION IS ELEVATION RATED, ATTACH ELEVATION CERTIFICATE.)

ELEVATION CERTIFICATION DATE: ____/____/______

BUILDING DIAGRAM NO.: ________ LOWEST ADJACENT GRADE (LAG): ________

LOWEST FLOOR ELEVATION: ________ (–) BASE FLOOD ELEVATION: ________ (=) DIFFERENCE TO NEAREST FOOT: ______ (+ OR –)

IN ZONES V AND V1-V30 ONLY, DOES BASE FLOOD ELEVATION INCLUDE EFFECTS OF WAVE ACTION? ☐ YES ☐ NO

IS BUILDING FLOODPROOFED? ☐ YES ☐ NO

(SEE THE *NFIP FLOOD INSURANCE MANUAL* FOR CERTIFICATION REQUIREMENTS.)

### COVERAGE AND RATING

**ESTIMATED BUILDING REPLACEMENT COST** (INCLUDING FOUNDATION): $ ____________ **DEDUCTIBLE:** BUILDING $ ____________ CONTENTS $ ____________

**TO INCREASE/DECREASE COVERAGE, COMPLETE SECTIONS A & B. FOR RATE CHANGE, COMPLETE SECTION A ONLY.**

**INDICATE THE RATE TABLE USED:** ____________ **RISK RATING METHOD:** ☐ 7 - PRP ☐ R - NEWLY MAPPED

| INSURANCE COVERAGE | SECTION A - CURRENT LIMITS | | | SECTION B - NEW LIMITS | | | A + B PREMIUM |
|---|---|---|---|---|---|---|---|
| | AMOUNT | RATE | PREMIUM | AMOUNT | RATE | PREMIUM | |
| BUILDING BASIC LIMIT | | | | | | | |
| BUILDING ADDITIONAL LIMIT | | | | | | | |
| CONTENTS BASIC LIMIT | | | | | | | |
| CONTENTS ADDITIONAL LIMIT | | | | | | | |
| FOR PRP AND NEWLY MAPPED ONLY, ENTER LIMITS FROM THE *NFIP FLOOD INSURANCE MANUAL* | BUILDING | CONTENTS | PREMIUM | BUILDING | CONTENTS | PREMIUM | |

| IF CHANGING AMOUNT OF INSURANCE, ENTER NEW TOTAL AMOUNT BELOW | | | | | |
|---|---|---|---|---|---|
| BUILDING COVERAGE | | | CONTENTS COVERAGE | | |
| BASIC | ADDITIONAL | TOTAL | BASIC | ADDITIONAL | TOTAL |
| | | | | | |

**IF RETURN PREMIUM, MAIL REFUND TO:** ☐ INSURED ☐ AGENT/PRODUCER ☐ PAYOR

**PAYMENT METHOD:**
- ☐ CHECK
- ☐ CREDIT CARD
- ☐ OTHER: ____________

| | |
|---|---|
| SUBTOTAL | |
| DEDUCTIBLE DISCOUNT/SURCHARGE | |
| SUBTOTAL | |
| SRL PREMIUM | |
| ICC PREMIUM | |
| SUBTOTAL | |
| CRS PREMIUM DISCOUNT ____ % | |
| SUBTOTAL | |
| RESERVE FUND ____ % | |
| SUBTOTAL | |
| PREMIUM PREVIOUSLY PAID (Excludes Probation Surcharge/Federal Policy Fee) | |
| HFIAA SURCHARGE | |
| DIFFERENCE ________ (+/-) | |
| PRO-RATA FACTOR | |
| **TOTAL AMOUNT DUE** (+/-) | |

### SIGNATURE

**NOTICE:** BUILDING COVERAGE BENEFITS – EXCEPT FOR A RESIDENTIAL CONDOMINIUM BUILDING – ARE NOT AVAILABLE IF OTHER NFIP BUILDING COVERAGE HAS BEEN PURCHASED BY THE APPLICANT OR ANY OTHER PARTY FOR THE SAME BUILDING.

THE ABOVE STATEMENTS ARE CORRECT TO THE BEST OF MY KNOWLEDGE. I UNDERSTAND THAT ANY FALSE STATEMENTS MAY BE PUNISHABLE BY FINE AND/OR IMPRISONMENT UNDER APPLICABLE FEDERAL LAW. SEE LAST PAGE OF FORM.

____________________ SIGNATURE OF INSURANCE AGENT/PRODUCER ____/____/______ DATE (MM/DD/YYYY)

____________________ SIGNATURE OF INSURED (IF APPLICABLE) ____/____/______ DATE (MM/DD/YYYY)

____________________ SIGNATURE OF ASSIGNEE (FOR ASSIGNMENT ONLY) ____/____/______ DATE (MM/DD/YYYY)

N F I P C O P Y

**FEMA Form 086-0-3** **F-051** (DEC 2019)

PLEASE SUBMIT TOTAL AMOUNT DUE AND ALL REQUIRED CERTIFICATIONS WITH THE NFIP COPY OF THIS ENDORSEMENT.
IF PAYING BY CHECK OR MONEY ORDER, MAKE PAYABLE TO THE NATIONAL FLOOD INSURANCE PROGRAM.
**IMPORTANT** — COMPLETE PAGE 1 AND PAGE 2 BEFORE SENDING ENDORSEMENT TO THE NFIP. — **IMPORTANT**

*National Flood Insurance Program*

## FLOOD INSURANCE GENERAL CHANGE ENDORSEMENT

**FEMA FORM 086-0-3**

**NONDISCRIMINATION**

No person or organization shall be excluded from participation in, denied the benefits of, or subjected to discrimination under the Program authorized by the Act, on the grounds of race, color, creed, sex, age or national origin.

**PRIVACY ACT**

The information requested is necessary to process your Flood Insurance Application for a flood insurance policy. The authority to collect the information is Title 42, U.S. Code, Sections 4001 to 4028. Disclosures of this information may be made: to federal, state, tribal, and local government agencies, fiscal agents, your agent, mortgage servicing companies, insurance or other companies, lending institutions, and contractors working for us, for the purpose of carrying out the National Flood Insurance Program; to certain property owners for the purpose of property loss history evaluation; to the American Red Cross for verification of nonduplication of benefits following a flooding event or disaster; to law enforcement agencies or professional organizations when there may be a violation or potential violation of law; to a federal, state or local agency when we request information relevant to an agency decision concerning issuance of a grant or other benefit, or in certain circumstances when a federal agency requests such information for a similar purpose from us; to a Congressional office in response to an inquiry made at the request of an individual; to the Office of Management and Budget (OMB) in relation to private relief legislation under OMB Circular A-19; and to the National Archives and Records Administration in records management inspections. Providing the information is voluntary, but failure to do so may delay or prevent issuance of the flood insurance policy.

**GENERAL**

This information is provided pursuant to Public Law 96-511 (Paperwork Reduction Act of 1980, as amended), dated December 11, 1980, to allow the public to participate more fully and meaningfully in the Federal paperwork review process.

**AUTHORITY**

Public Law 96-511, amended, 44 U.S.C. 3507; and 5 CFR 1320.

**PAPERWORK BURDEN DISCLOSURE NOTICE**

Public reporting burden for this form is estimated to average 9 minutes per response. The burden estimate includes the time for reviewing instructions, searching existing data sources, gathering and maintaining the data needed, and completing and submitting the form. This collection of information is required to obtain or retain benefits. You are not required to respond to this collection of information unless a valid OMB control number is displayed in the upper right corner of this form. Send comments regarding the accuracy of the burden estimate and any suggestions for reducing the burden to: Information Collections Management, Department of Homeland Security, Federal Emergency Management Agency, 500 C Street SW, Washington, DC 20742, Paperwork Reduction Project (1660-0006). **NOTE: Do not send your completed form to this address.**

## IV. NFIP Flood Insurance Cancellation/Nullification Request Form

THIS LAYOUT OF THE REVISED FLOOD INSURANCE CANCELLATION/NULLIFICATION REQUEST FORM IS PROVIDED FOR YOUR REFERENCE. THE FINAL FORM WILL BE RELEASED UPON O.M.B. APPROVAL.

U.S. DEPARTMENT OF HOMELAND SECURITY
FEDERAL EMERGENCY MANAGEMENT AGENCY

**National Flood Insurance Program**

**Flood Insurance Cancellation/Nullification Request Form**

POLICY #: ____________

**IMPORTANT – Please print or type; enter dates as MM/DD/YYYY.**

**POLICY PERIOD**

Policy Period Is From ____________ To ____________
12:01 A.M. LOCAL TIME AT THE INSURED PROPERTY LOCATION.

Cancellation Effective Date: ____________

**AGENT/PRODUCER INFORMATION**

Agent/Producer information for the policy being canceled::

Agency No.: ____________
Agent's No.: ____________
Phone No.: ____________
FAX No.: ____________
Email Address: ____________

**INSURED MAILING INFORMATION**

Name and Mailing Address of Insured for Mailing Refund:

Phone No.: ____________

**INSURED PROPERTY LOCATION**

Insured Property Location if Different from Insured's Mailing Address:

**FIRST MORTGAGEE INFORMATION**

Name and Mailing Address of First Mortgagee:

Loan No.: ____________

**SECOND MORTGAGEE / OTHER INFORMATION**

Information below is that of: ☐ Second Mortgagee ☐ Loss Payee
☐ Other (specify): ____________

**CANCELLATION REASON CODE**

**Please see all valid cancellation reason codes and requirements for their use in the "How to Cancel" section of the *NFIP Flood Insurance Manual* on the FEMA website.**

**https://www.fema.gov/flood-insurance-manual**

**CANCELLATION REASON CODE: ______**

**REFUND**

**Make Refund Payable To (check one):** ☐ Insured ☐ Payor ☐ Agent (Reason Code 5 Only)

**Mail Refund To (check one):** ☐ Insured ☐ Payor ☐ Agent (Reason Code 5 or at Request of Insured)

**SIGNATURE**

The above statements are correct to the best of my knowledge. I understand that any false statements may be punishable by fine and/or imprisonment under applicable federal law. See second page of form.

SIGNATURE OF INSURED (NOT REQUIRED FOR REASON CODES 5, 6, 22, OR 25) ____________ DATE ____________

SIGNATURE OF OTHER INSURED ____________ DATE ____________ SIGNATURE OF AGENT/PRODUCER ____________ DATE ____________

N F I P C O P Y

**FEMA Form 086-0-2** **REPLACES ALL PREVIOUS EDITIONS.** **F-052** (DEC 2019)

PLEASE ATTACH ALL REQUIRED DOCUMENTS TO NFIP COPY OF CANCELLATION/ NULLIFICATION REQUEST FORM.
SEND ORIGINAL TO NFIP, KEEP A COPY FOR YOUR RECORDS, AND PROVIDE COPIES TO THE INSURED AND MORTGAGEE(S).

**ONLINE** The current approved version of The NFIP Flood Insurance Cancellation/Nullification Request Form, FEMA Form 086-0-2, is available at https://www.fema.gov/media-library/assets/documents/1190

*National Flood Insurance Program*

## FLOOD INSURANCE CANCELLATION/NULLIFICATION REQUEST FORM

**FEMA FORM 086-0-2**

**NONDISCRIMINATION**

No person or organization shall be excluded from participation in, denied the benefits of, or subjected to discrimination under the Program authorized by the Act, on the grounds of race, color, creed, sex, age or national origin.

**PRIVACY ACT**

The information requested is necessary to process your Flood Insurance Application for a flood insurance policy. The authority to collect the information is Title 42, U.S. Code, Sections 4001 to 4028. Disclosures of this information may be made: to federal, state, tribal, and local government agencies, fiscal agents, your agent, mortgage servicing companies, insurance or other companies, lending institutions, and contractors working for us, for the purpose of carrying out the National Flood Insurance Program; to certain property owners for the purpose of property loss history evaluation; to the American Red Cross for verification of nonduplication of benefits following a flooding event or disaster; to law enforcement agencies or professional organizations when there may be a violation or potential violation of law; to a federal, state or local agency when we request information relevant to an agency decision concerning issuance of a grant or other benefit, or in certain circumstances when a federal agency requests such information for a similar purpose from us; to a Congressional office in response to an inquiry made at the request of an individual; to the Office of Management and Budget (OMB) in relation to private relief legislation under OMB Circular A-19; and to the National Archives and Records Administration in records management inspections. Providing the information is voluntary, but failure to do so may delay or prevent issuance of the flood insurance policy.

**GENERAL**

This information is provided pursuant to Public Law 96-511 (Paperwork Reduction Act of 1980, as amended), dated December 11, 1980, to allow the public to participate more fully and meaningfully in the Federal paperwork review process.

**AUTHORITY**

Public Law 96-511, amended, 44 U.S.C. 3507; and 5 CFR 1320.

**PAPERWORK BURDEN DISCLOSURE NOTICE**

Public reporting burden for this form is estimated to average 7.5 minutes per response. The burden estimate includes the time for reviewing instructions, searching existing data sources, gathering and maintaining the data needed, and completing and submitting the form. This collection of information is required to obtain or retain benefits. You are not required to respond to this collection of information unless a valid OMB control number is displayed in the upper right corner of this form. Send comments regarding the accuracy of the burden estimate and any suggestions for reducing the burden to: Information Collections Management, Department of Homeland Security, Federal Emergency Management Agency, 500 C Street SW, Washington, DC 20742, Paperwork Reduction Project (1660-0006). **NOTE: Do not send your completed form to this address.**

## V. NFIP Residential Basement Floodproofing Certificate

DEPARTMENT OF HOMELAND SECURITY
Federal Emergency Management Agency
National Flood Insurance Program

OMB No.: 1660-0033
Expiration: 05/31/2020

### Residential Basement Floodproofing Certificate

PAPERWORK BURDEN DISCLOSURE NOTICE

Public reporting burden for this data collection is estimated to average 3.25 hours per response. The burden estimate includes the time for reviewing instructions, searching existing data sources, gathering and maintaining the data needed, and completing and submitting this Residential Basement Floodproofing Certificate. You are not required to respond to this collection of information unless a valid OMB control number is displayed in the upper right corner of this Residential Basement Floodproofing Certificate. Send comments regarding the accuracy of the burden estimate and any suggestions for reducing the burden to: Information Collections Management, Department of Homeland Security, Federal Emergency Management Agency, 500 C Street, SW, Washington, DC 20472, Paperwork Reduction Project (1660-0033). **NOTE: Do not send your completed form to this address.**

**Privacy Act Statement**

**AUTHORITY**
National Flood Insurance Act of 1968, as amended (42 U.S.C. § 4001 et seq.).

**PRINCIPAL PURPOSE(S)**
This information is being collected for two primary purposes. First, for community use in documenting compliance with floodplain management ordinances, where records are maintained by the community. Second, for flood insurance purposes of estimating the risk premium rates necessary to provide flood insurance for new or substantially improved structures in designated Special Flood Hazard Areas. Records are located at the facility that underwrites and administers the policy (Write Your Own (WYO) companies or the Federal Emergency Management Agency's (FEMA) National Flood Insurance Program (NFIP) Direct).

**ROUTINE USE(S)**
When this form is maintained by FEMA and is used in conjunction with the application and maintenance of a flood insurance policy, the information requested on this form may be shared externally as a "routine use" to authorized WYO companies receiving transferred policies, to assist the Department of Homeland Security (DHS)/FEMA in estimating the risk premium rates necessary to provide flood insurance for new or substantially improved structures in designated Special Flood Hazard Areas. A complete list of the routine uses can be found in the system of records notice associated with this form, "DHS/FEMA-003 - National Flood Insurance Program Files 79 Fed. Reg. 28,747 (May 19, 2014); and upon written request, written consent, by agreement, or as required by law. The Department's full list of system of records notices can be found on the Department's website at http://www.dhs.gov/system-records-notices-sorns.

**DISCLOSURE**
The disclosure of information on this form is voluntary; however, failure to provide the information requested may result in the inability to obtain flood insurance through the National Flood Insurance Program, or the building being subject to higher premium rates for flood insurance. Information will only be released as permitted by law.

FEMA FORM 086-0-24 (12/19) Page 1 of 4

**ONLINE** The NFIP Residential Basement Floodproofing Certificate, FEMA Form 086-0-24, is available at https://www.fema.gov/media-library/assets/documents/215

DEPARTMENT OF HOMELAND SECURITY
Federal Emergency Management Agency
National Flood Insurance Program

OMB No.: 1660-0033
Expiration: 05/31/2020

## Residential Basement Floodproofing Certificate

| BUILDING OWNER'S NAME | **FOR INSURANCE COMPANY USE** POLICY NUMBER |
|---|---|
| BUILDING STREET ADDRESS *(Including Apt., Unit Number)* | COMPANY NAIC NUMBER |
| OTHER DESCRIPTION *(Lot and Block Numbers, etc.)* | |

| CITY | STATE | ZIPCODE |
|---|---|---|
| | | |

**SECTION I - FLOOD INSURANCE RATE MAP (FIRM) INFORMATION**

Provide the following from the FIRM and flood profile *(from Flood Insurance Study)*

| COMMUNITY NUMBER | PANEL NUMBER | SUFFIX | DATE OF FIRM | ZONE | BASE FLOOD ELEVATION (In AO Zones, Use depth) | NAME OF FLOODING SOURCE(S) AFFECTING BUILDING |
|---|---|---|---|---|---|---|
| | | | | | | |

Indicate elevation datum used for Base Flood Elevation shown above: ☐ NGVD 1929 ☐ NAVD 1988 ☐ Other/Source: ____________

**SECTION II - FLOODPROOFED ELEVATION CERTIFICATION** *(By a Registered Professional Land Surveyor, Engineer, or Architect)*

All elevations must be based on finished construction.

**Floodproofing Elevation Information for Zones A1-30, AE, AH, AO:**

Building is floodproofed to an elevation of _______ . _______ feet. (In Puerto Rico only: ______ . _______ meters.)

*(Elevation datum used must be the same as that on the FIRM.)*

Elevation of the top of the basement floor is _______ . _______ feet. (In Puerto Rico only: ______ . _______ meters.)

Lowest adjacent (finished) grade next to the building (LAG): _______ . _______ feet. (In Puerto Rico only: ______ . _______ meters.)

Highest adjacent (finished) grade next to the building (HAG): _______ . _______ feet. (In Puerto Rico only: ______ . _______ meters.)

Indicate elevation datum used for Section II: ☐ NGVD 1929 ☐ NAVD 1988 ☐ Other/Source: ____________

(NOTE: For insurance rating purposes, the building's floodproofed elevation must be at least 1 foot above the Base Flood Elevation to receive rating credit. If the building is floodproofed only to the Base Flood Elevation, then the building's insurance rating will result in a higher premium.)

Section II certification is to be signed and sealed by a land surveyor, engineer, or architect authorized by law to certify elevation information.

*I certify that the information in Section II on this Certificate represents a true and accurate interpretation and determination by the undersigned using the available information and data. I understand that any false statement may be punishable by fine or imprisonment under 18 U.S. Code, Section 1001.*

| CERTIFIER'S NAME | LICENSE NUMBER *(or affix Seal)* | | | Place Seal Here |
|---|---|---|---|---|
| TITLE | COMPANY NAME | | | |
| ADDRESS | CITY | STATE | ZIP CODE | |
| SIGNATURE | PHONE NO. | DATE | | |

FEMA FORM 086-0-24 (12/19)

Page 2 of 4

DEPARTMENT OF HOMELAND SECURITY
Federal Emergency Management Agency
National Flood Insurance Program

OMB No.: 1660-0033
Expiration: 05/31/2020

## Residential Basement Floodproofing Certificate *continued*

| BUILDING STREET ADDRESS *(Including Apt., Unit Number)* | | |
|---|---|---|
| CITY | STATE | ZIPCODE |

**SECTION III - FLOODPROOFING CERTIFICATION** *(By a Registered Professional Engineer or Architect)*

**Residential Floodproofed Basement Construction Certification:**

I certify the structure, based upon development and/or review of the design, specifications, as-built drawings for construction and physical inspection, has been designed and constructed in accordance with the accepted standards of practice (ASCE 24-05, ASCE 24-14, or their equivalent) and any alterations also meet those standards and the following provisions.

- Basement area, together with attendant utilities and sanitary facilities, is watertight to the floodproofing design elevation with walls that are impermeable to the passage of water without human intervention; and
- Basement walls and floor are capable of resisting hydrostatic and hydrodynamic loads and the effects of buoyancy resulting from flooding to the floodproofing design elevation; and have been designed so that minimal damage will occur from floods that exceed the floodproofing design elevation; and
- Building design, including the floodproofing design elevation, complies with community requirements; and
- Soil or fill adjacent to the structure is compacted and protected against erosion and local scour (in accordance with ASCE 24).

I certify that the information in Section III on this certificate represents a true and accurate determination by the undersigned using the available information and data. I understand that any false statement may be punishable by fine or imprisonment under 18 U.S. Code, Section 1001.

| | | | | |
|---|---|---|---|---|
| CERTIFIER'S NAME | LICENSE NUMBER *(or affix Seal)* | | | |
| TITLE | COMPANY NAME | | | |
| ADDRESS | CITY | STATE | ZIP CODE | |
| SIGNATURE | PHONE NO. | DATE | | Place Seal Here |

Copies of this certificate must be given to: 1) the community official: 2) the insurance agent: and 3) the building owner.

FEMA FORM 086-0-24 (12/19)

Page 3 of 4

DEPARTMENT OF HOMELAND SECURITY
Federal Emergency Management Agency
National Flood Insurance Program

OMB No.: 1660-0033
Expiration: 05/31/2020

## Residential Basement Floodproofing Certificate *continued*

**Instructions for Completing the Residential Basement Floodproofing Certificate**

To receive credit for floodproofing, a completed Residential Basement Floodproofing Certificate is required for residential buildings with basements in Regular Program communities, located in zones A1-A30, AE, AR, AR Dual, AO, AH, and A with BFE.

The communities must have been specifically approved and authorized by FEMA to receive residential basement floodproofing rating credit. Approved communities are listed in Appendix K of the *NFIP Flood Insurance Manual*, available on the FEMA website at https://www.fema.gov/flood-insurance-manual.

When applying for flood insurance, the following information must be provided with the completed Residential Basement Floodproofing Certificate:

- The Flood Insurance Application
- At least two photographs of the building.

FEMA FORM 086-0-24 (12/19)

Page 4 of 4

## VI. NFIP Floodproofing Certificate for Non-Residential Structures

DEPARTMENT OF HOMELAND SECURITY
Federal Emergency Management Agency
National Flood Insurance Program

OMB No.: 1660-0008
Expiration: 11/30/2022

### FLOODPROOFING CERTIFICATE FOR NON-RESIDENTIAL STRUCTURES

**Paperwork Burden Disclosure Notice**

Public reporting burden for this data collection is estimated to average 3.25 hours per response. The burden estimate includes the time for reviewing instructions, searching existing data sources, gathering and maintaining the data needed, and completing and submitting this form. You are not required to respond to this collection of information unless a valid OMB control number is displayed on this form. Send comments regarding the accuracy of the burden estimate and any suggestions for reducing the burden to: Information Collections Management, Department of Homeland Security, Federal Emergency Management Agency, 500 C Street SW, Washington, DC 20742, Paperwork Reduction Project (1660-0008). **NOTE: Do not send your completed form to this address.**

**General**: This information is provided pursuant to Public Law 96-511 (the Paperwork Reduction Act of 1980, as amended), dated December 11, 1980, to allow the public to participate more fully and meaningfully in the Federal paperwork review process.

**Authority**: Public Law 96-511, amended; 44 U.S.C. 3507; and 5 CFR 1320.

**Privacy Act Statement**

**Authority**: Title 44 CFR § 61.7 and 61.8.

**Principal Purpose(s)**: This information is being collected for the primary purpose of estimating the risk premium rates necessary to provide flood insurance for new or substantially improved structures in designated Special Flood Hazard Areas.

**Routine Use(s)**: The information on this form may be disclosed as generally permitted under 5 U.S.C. § 552a(b) of the Privacy Act of 1974, as amended. This includes using this information as necessary and authorized by the routine uses published in DHS/FEMA-003 – National Flood Insurance Program Files System or Records Notice 73 Fed. Reg. 77747 (December 19, 2008); DHS/FEMA/NFIP/LOMA-1 – National Flood Insurance Program (NFIP) Letter of Map Amendment (LOMA) System of Records Notice 71 Fed. Reg. 7990 (February 15, 2006); and upon written request, written consent, by agreement, or as required by law.

**Disclosure**: The disclosure of information on this form is voluntary; however, failure to provide the information requested may result in the inability to obtain flood insurance through the National Flood Insurance Program or being subject to higher premium rates for flood insurance. Information will only be released as permitted by law.

**Purpose of the Floodproofing Certificate for Non-Residential Structures**

Under the National Flood Insurance Program (NFIP), the floodproofing of non-residential buildings may be permitted as an alternative to elevating to or above the Base Flood Elevation (BFE). A floodproofing design certification is required for non-residential structures that are floodproofed. This form is to be used for that certification.

A floodproofed building is a building that has been designed and constructed to be watertight (substantially impermeable to floodwaters) below the BFE and with structural components having the capability of resisting hydrostatic and hydrodynamic loads and effects of buoyancy. Before a floodproofed building is designed, numerous planning considerations, including flood warning time, uses of the building, mode of entry to and exit from the building and the site in general, floodwater velocities, flood depths, debris impact potential, and flood frequency, must be addressed to ensure that dry floodproofing will be a viable floodplain management measure.

The minimum NFIP requirement is to floodproof a building to the BFE. However, when it is rated for flood insurance one-foot is subtracted from the floodproofed elevation. Therefore, a building has to be floodproofed to one foot above the BFE to receive the same favorable flood insurance rates as a building elevated to the BFE.

Additional guidance can be found in FEMA Publication 936, Floodproofing Non-Residential Buildings (2013), available on FEMA's website at https://www.fema.gov/media-library/assets/documents/34270.

FEMA Form 086-0-34 (12/19) Page 1 of 4

**ONLINE** The NFIP Floodproofing Certificate for Non-Residential Structures, FEMA Form 086-0-34, is available at https://www.fema.gov/media-library/assets/documents/2748

DEPARTMENT OF HOMELAND SECURITY
Federal Emergency Management Agency
National Flood Insurance Program

OMB No.: 1660-0008
Expiration: 11/30/2022

## FLOODPROOFING CERTIFICATE FOR NON-RESIDENTIAL STRUCTURES

The floodproofing of non-residential buildings may be permitted as an alternative to elevating to or above the Base Flood Elevation; however, a floodproofing design certification is required. This form is to be used for that certification. Floodproofing of a residential building does not alter a community's floodplain management elevation requirements or affect the insurance rating unless the community has been issued an exception by FEMA to allow floodproofed residential basements. The permitting of a floodproofed residential basement requires a separate certification specifying that the design complies with the local floodplain management ordinance.

| | | |
|---|---|---|
| BUILDING OWNER'S NAME | | **FOR INSURANCE COMPANY USE** |
| STREET ADDRESS (Including Apt., Unit, Suite, and/or Bldg. Number) OR P.O. ROUTE AND BOX NUMBER | | POLICY NUMBER |
| OTHER DESCRIPTION (Lot and Block Numbers, etc.) | | COMPANY NAIC NUMBER |
| CITY | STATE | Zip Code |

**SECTION I – FLOOD INSURANCE RATE MAP (FIRM) INFORMATION**

Provide the following from the proper FIRM:

| COMMUNITY NUMBER | PANEL NUMBER | SUFFIX | DATE OF FIRM INDEX | FIRM ZONE | BASE FLOOD ELEVATION (in AO Zones, Use Depth) |
|---|---|---|---|---|---|
| | | | | | |

Indicate elevation datum used for Base Flood Elevation shown above: ☐ NGVD 1929 ☐ NAVD 1988 ☐ Other/Source:

**SECTION II – FLOODPROOFED ELEVATION CERTIFICATION (By a Registered Professional Land Surveyor, Engineer, or Architect)**

All elevations must be based on finished construction.

**Floodproofing Elevation Information:**

Building is floodproofed to an elevation of . feet (In Puerto Rico only: . meters).

☐ NGVD 1929 ☐ NAVD 1988 ☐ Other/Source:

(Elevation datum used must be the same as that used for the Base Flood Elevation.)

Height of floodproofing on the building above the lowest adjacent grade is feet (In Puerto Rico only: meters).

**For Unnumbered A Zones Only:**

Highest adjacent (finished) grade next to the building (HAG) . feet (In Puerto Rico only: . meters)

☐ NGVD 1929 ☐ NAVD 1988 ☐ Other/Source:

(NOTE: For insurance rating purposes, the building's floodproofed design elevation must be at least 1 foot above the Base Flood Elevation to receive rating credit. If the building is floodproofed only to the Base Flood Elevation, then the building's insurance rating will result in a higher premium. See the Instructions section for information on documentation that must accompany this certificate if being submitted for flood insurance rating purposes.)

FEMA Form 086-0-34 (12/19)

Page 2 of 4

DEPARTMENT OF HOMELAND SECURITY
Federal Emergency Management Agency
National Flood Insurance Program

OMB No.: 1660-0008
Expiration: 11/30/2022

## FLOODPROOFING CERTIFICATE FOR NON-RESIDENTIAL STRUCTURES

**Non-Residential Floodproofed Elevation Information Certification:**

Section II certification is to be signed and sealed by a land surveyor, engineer, or architect authorized by law to certify elevation information

*I certify that the information in Section II on this Certificate represents a true and accurate interpretation and determination by the undersigned using the available information and data. I understand that any false statement may be punishable by fine or imprisonment under 18 U.S. Code, Section 1001.*

| | | | | |
|---|---|---|---|---|
| CERTIFIER'S NAME | LICENSE NUMBER (or Affix Seal) | | | PLACE SEAL HERE |
| TITLE | COMPANY NAME | | | |
| ADDRESS | CITY | STATE | ZIP CODE | |
| SIGNATURE | DATE | PHONE | | |

**SECTION III – FLOODPROOFED CERTIFICATION (By a Registered Professional Engineer or Architect)**

**Non-Residential Floodproofed Construction Certification:**

*I certify the structure, based upon development and/or review of the design, specifications, as-built drawings for construction and physical inspection, has been designed and constructed in accordance with the accepted standards of practice (ASCE 24-05, ASCE 24-14 or their equivalent) and any alterations also meet those standards and the following provisions.*

The structure, together with attendant utilities and sanitary facilities is watertight to the floodproofed design elevation indicated above, is substantially impermeable to the passage of water, and shall perform in accordance with the 44 Code of Federal Regulations (44 CFR 60.3(c)(3).

All structural components are capable of resisting hydrostatic and hydrodynamic flood forces, including the effects of buoyancy, and anticipated debris impact forces.

*I certify that the information in Section III on this certificate represents a true and accurate determination by the undersigned using the available information and data. I understand that any false statement may be punishable by fine or imprisonment under 18 U.S. Code, Section 1001.*

| | | | | |
|---|---|---|---|---|
| CERTIFIER'S NAME | LICENSE NUMBER (or Affix Seal) | | | PLACE SEAL HERE |
| TITLE | COMPANY NAME | | | |
| ADDRESS | CITY | STATE | ZIP CODE | |
| SIGNATURE | DATE | PHONE | | |

Copy all pages of this Floodproofing Certificate and all attachments for 1) community official, 2) insurance agent/company, and 3) building owner.

FEMA Form 086-0-34 (12/19)

Page 3 of 4

DEPARTMENT OF HOMELAND SECURITY
Federal Emergency Management Agency
National Flood Insurance Program

OMB No.: 1660-0008
Expiration: 11/30/2022

## FLOODPROOFING CERTIFICATE FOR NON-RESIDENTIAL STRUCTURES

### Instructions for Completingthe Floodproofing Certificate for Non-Residential Structures

To receive credit for floodproofing, a completed Floodproofing Certificate for Non-Residential Structures is required for non-residential and business buildings in the Regular Program communities, located in zones A1–A30, AE, AR, AR Dual, AO, AH, and A with BFE.

In order to ensure compliance and provide reasonable assurance that due diligence had been applied in designing and constructing floodproofing measures, the following information must be provided with the completed Floodproofing Certificate:

- Photographs of shields, gates, barriers, or components designed to provide floodproofing protection to the structure.
- Written certification that all portions of the structure below the BFE that will render it watertight or substantially impermeable to the passage of water and must perform in accordance with Title 44 Code of Federal Regulations (44 CFR 60.3 (c)(3)).
- A comprehensive Maintenance Plan for the entire structure to include but not limited to:
    - Exterior envelope of the structure
    - All penetrations to the exterior of the structure
    - All shields, gates, barriers, or components designed to provide floodproofing protection to the structure
    - All seals or gaskets for shields, gates, barriers, or components
    - Location of all shields, gates, barriers, and components as well as all associated hardware, and any materials or specialized tools necessary to seal the structure.

FEMA Form 086-0-34 (12/19) Page 4 of 4

## VII. NFIP Elevation Certificate and Instructions

# FEMA

*NATIONAL FLOOD INSURANCE PROGRAM*

# ELEVATION CERTIFICATE

## AND

## INSTRUCTIONS

**2019 EDITION**

**ONLINE** The NFIP Elevation Certificate and Instructions, FEMA Form 086-0-33, is available at https://www.fema.gov/media-library/assets/documents/160?id=1383

OMB No. 1660-0008
Expiration Date: November 30, 2022

U.S. DEPARTMENT OF HOMELAND SECURITY
Federal Emergency Management Agency
National Flood Insurance Program

## ELEVATION CERTIFICATE AND INSTRUCTIONS

### Paperwork Reduction Act Notice

Public reporting burden for this data collection is estimated to average 3.75 hours per response. The burden estimate includes the time for reviewing instructions, searching existing data sources, gathering and maintaining the data needed, and completing and submitting this form. You are not required to respond to this collection of information unless a valid OMB control number is displayed on this form. Send comments regarding the accuracy of the burden estimate and any suggestions for reducing the burden to: Information Collections Management, Department of Homeland Security, Federal Emergency Management Agency, 500 C Street SW, Washington, DC 20742, Paperwork Reduction Project (1660-0008). **NOTE: Do not send your completed form to this address.**

### Privacy Act Statement

**Authority:** Title 44 CFR § 61.7 and 61.8

**Principal Purpose(s):** This information is being collected for the primary purpose of estimating the risk premium rates necessary to provide flood insurance for new or substantially improved structures in designated Special Flood Hazard Areas.

**Routine Use(s):** The information on this form may be disclosed as generally permitted under 5 U.S.C. § 552a(b) of the Privacy Act of 1974, as amended. This includes using this information as necessary and authorized by the routine uses published in DHS/FEMA-003 – National Flood Insurance Program Files System or Records Notice 73 Fed. Reg. 77747 (December 19, 2008); DHS/FEMA/NFIP/LOMA-1 – National Flood Insurance Program (NFIP) Letter of Map Amendment (LOMA) System of Records Notice 71 Fed. Reg. 7990 (February 15, 2006); and upon written request, written consent, by agreement, or as required by law.

**Disclosure:** The disclosure of information on this form is voluntary; however, failure to provide the information requested may result in the inability to obtain flood insurance through the National Flood Insurance Program or the applicant may be subject to higher premium rates for flood insurance. Information will only be released as permitted by law.

### Purpose of the Elevation Certificate

The Elevation Certificate is an important administrative tool of the National Flood Insurance Program (NFIP). It is to be used to provide elevation information necessary to ensure compliance with community floodplain management ordinances, to determine the proper insurance premium rate, and to support a request for a Letter of Map Amendment (LOMA) or Letter of Map Revision based on fill (LOMR-F).

The Elevation Certificate is required in order to properly rate Post-FIRM buildings, which are buildings constructed after publication of the Flood Insurance Rate Map (FIRM), located in flood insurance Zones A1–A30, AE, AH, A (with BFE), VE, V1–V30, V (with BFE), AR, AR/A, AR/AE, AR/A1–A30, AR/AH, and AR/AO. The Elevation Certificate is not required for Pre-FIRM buildings unless the building is being rated under the optional Post-FIRM flood insurance rules.

As part of the agreement for making flood insurance available in a community, the NFIP requires the community to adopt floodplain management regulations that specify minimum requirements for reducing flood losses. One such requirement is for the community to obtain the elevation of the lowest floor (including basement) of all new and substantially improved buildings, and maintain a record of such information. The Elevation Certificate provides a way for a community to document compliance with the community's floodplain management ordinance.

Use of this certificate does not provide a waiver of the flood insurance purchase requirement. Only a LOMA or LOMR-F from the Federal Emergency Management Agency (FEMA) can amend the FIRM and remove the Federal mandate for a lending institution to require the purchase of flood insurance. However, the lending institution has the option of requiring flood insurance even if a LOMA/LOMR-F has been issued by FEMA. The Elevation Certificate may be used to support a LOMA or LOMR-F request. Lowest floor and lowest adjacent grade elevations certified by a surveyor or engineer will be required if the certificate is used to support a LOMA or LOMR-F request. A LOMA or LOMR-F request must be submitted with either a completed FEMA MT-EZ or MT-1 package, whichever is appropriate.

This certificate is used only to certify building elevations. A separate certificate is required for floodproofing. Under the NFIP, non-residential buildings can be floodproofed up to or above the Base Flood Elevation (BFE). A floodproofed building is a building that has been designed and constructed to be watertight (substantially impermeable to floodwaters) below the BFE. Floodproofing of residential buildings is not permitted under the NFIP unless FEMA has granted the community an exception for residential floodproofed basements. The community must adopt standards for design and construction of floodproofed basements before FEMA will grant a basement exception. For both floodproofed non-residential buildings and residential floodproofed basements in communities that have been granted an exception by FEMA, a floodproofing certificate is required.

Additional guidance can be found in FEMA Publication 467-1, Floodplain Management Bulletin: Elevation Certificate, available on FEMA's website at https://www.fema.gov/media-library/assets/documents/3539?id=1727.

FEMA Form 086-0-33 (12/19) Replaces all previous editions. F-053

U.S. DEPARTMENT OF HOMELAND SECURITY
Federal Emergency Management Agency
National Flood Insurance Program

OMB No. 1660-0008
Expiration Date: November 30, 2022

# ELEVATION CERTIFICATE

**Important:** Follow the instructions on pages 1–9.

Copy all pages of this Elevation Certificate and all attachments for (1) community official, (2) insurance agent/company, and (3) building owner.

| SECTION A – PROPERTY INFORMATION | | FOR INSURANCE COMPANY USE |
|---|---|---|
| A1. Building Owner's Name | | Policy Number: |
| A2. Building Street Address (including Apt., Unit, Suite, and/or Bldg. No.) or P.O. Route and Box No. | | Company NAIC Number: |
| City | State | ZIP Code |
| A3. Property Description (Lot and Block Numbers, Tax Parcel Number, Legal Description, etc.) | | |

A4. Building Use (e.g., Residential, Non-Residential, Addition, Accessory, etc.) ____________

A5. Latitude/Longitude: Lat ____________ Long. ____________ Horizontal Datum: ☐ NAD 1927 ☐ NAD 1983

A6. Attach at least 2 photographs of the building if the Certificate is being used to obtain flood insurance.

A7. Building Diagram Number ______

A8. For a building with a crawlspace or enclosure(s):

a) Square footage of crawlspace or enclosure(s) ____________ sq ft

b) Number of permanent flood openings in the crawlspace or enclosure(s) within 1.0 foot above adjacent grade ____________

c) Total net area of flood openings in A8.b ____________ sq in

d) Engineered flood openings? ☐ Yes ☐ No

A9. For a building with an attached garage:

a) Square footage of attached garage ____________ sq ft

b) Number of permanent flood openings in the attached garage within 1.0 foot above adjacent grade ____________

c) Total net area of flood openings in A9.b ____________ sq in

d) Engineered flood openings? ☐ Yes ☐ No

**SECTION B – FLOOD INSURANCE RATE MAP (FIRM) INFORMATION**

| B1. NFIP Community Name & Community Number | B2. County Name | B3. State |
|---|---|---|
| | | |

| B4. Map/Panel Number | B5. Suffix | B6. FIRM Index Date | B7. FIRM Panel Effective/ Revised Date | B8. Flood Zone(s) | B9. Base Flood Elevation(s) (Zone AO, use Base Flood Depth) |
|---|---|---|---|---|---|
| | | | | | |

B10. Indicate the source of the Base Flood Elevation (BFE) data or base flood depth entered in Item B9:
☐ FIS Profile ☐ FIRM ☐ Community Determined ☐ Other/Source: ____________

B11. Indicate elevation datum used for BFE in Item B9: ☐ NGVD 1929 ☐ NAVD 1988 ☐ Other/Source: ____________

B12. Is the building located in a Coastal Barrier Resources System (CBRS) area or Otherwise Protected Area (OPA)? ☐ Yes ☐ No

Designation Date: ____________ ☐ CBRS ☐ OPA

FEMA Form 086-0-33 (12/19) Replaces all previous editions. Form Page 1 of 6

## ELEVATION CERTIFICATE

OMB No. 1660-0008
Expiration Date: November 30, 2022

| IMPORTANT: In these spaces, copy the corresponding information from Section A. | | | FOR INSURANCE COMPANY USE |
|---|---|---|---|
| Building Street Address (including Apt., Unit, Suite, and/or Bldg. No.) or P.O. Route and Box No. | | | Policy Number: |
| City | State | ZIP Code | Company NAIC Number |

### SECTION C – BUILDING ELEVATION INFORMATION (SURVEY REQUIRED)

C1. Building elevations are based on: ☐ Construction Drawings* ☐ Building Under Construction* ☐ Finished Construction

*A new Elevation Certificate will be required when construction of the building is complete.

C2. Elevations – Zones A1–A30, AE, AH, A (with BFE), VE, V1–V30, V (with BFE), AR, AR/A, AR/AE, AR/A1–A30, AR/AH, AR/AO. Complete Items C2.a–h below according to the building diagram specified in Item A7. In Puerto Rico only, enter meters.

Benchmark Utilized: ____________ Vertical Datum: ____________

Indicate elevation datum used for the elevations in items a) through h) below.

☐ NGVD 1929 ☐ NAVD 1988 ☐ Other/Source: ____________

Datum used for building elevations must be the same as that used for the BFE.

| | | Check the measurement used. |
|---|---|---|
| a) Top of bottom floor (including basement, crawlspace, or enclosure floor) | ____________ | ☐ feet ☐ meters |
| b) Top of the next higher floor | ____________ | ☐ feet ☐ meters |
| c) Bottom of the lowest horizontal structural member (V Zones only) | ____________ | ☐ feet ☐ meters |
| d) Attached garage (top of slab) | ____________ | ☐ feet ☐ meters |
| e) Lowest elevation of machinery or equipment servicing the building (Describe type of equipment and location in Comments) | ____________ | ☐ feet ☐ meters |
| f) Lowest adjacent (finished) grade next to building (LAG) | ____________ | ☐ feet ☐ meters |
| g) Highest adjacent (finished) grade next to building (HAG) | ____________ | ☐ feet ☐ meters |
| h) Lowest adjacent grade at lowest elevation of deck or stairs, including structural support | ____________ | ☐ feet ☐ meters |

### SECTION D – SURVEYOR, ENGINEER, OR ARCHITECT CERTIFICATION

This certification is to be signed and sealed by a land surveyor, engineer, or architect authorized by law to certify elevation information. *I certify that the information on this Certificate represents my best efforts to interpret the data available. I understand that any false statement may be punishable by fine or imprisonment under 18 U.S. Code, Section 1001.*

Were latitude and longitude in Section A provided by a licensed land surveyor? ☐ Yes ☐ No ☐ Check here if attachments.

| | | | |
|---|---|---|---|
| Certifier's Name | License Number | | Place Seal Here |
| Title | | | |
| Company Name | | | |
| Address | | | |
| City | State | ZIP Code | |
| Signature | Date | Telephone | Ext. |

Copy all pages of this Elevation Certificate and all attachments for (1) community official, (2) insurance agent/company, and (3) building owner.

Comments (including type of equipment and location, per C2(e), if applicable)

FEMA Form 086-0-33 (12/19) Replaces all previous editions. Form Page 2 of 6

## ELEVATION CERTIFICATE

OMB No. 1660-0008
Expiration Date: November 30, 2022

| IMPORTANT: In these spaces, copy the corresponding information from Section A. | | | FOR INSURANCE COMPANY USE |
|---|---|---|---|
| Building Street Address (including Apt., Unit, Suite, and/or Bldg. No.) or P.O. Route and Box No. | | | Policy Number: |
| City | State | ZIP Code | Company NAIC Number |

### SECTION E – BUILDING ELEVATION INFORMATION (SURVEY NOT REQUIRED) FOR ZONE AO AND ZONE A (WITHOUT BFE)

For Zones AO and A (without BFE), complete Items E1–E5. If the Certificate is intended to support a LOMA or LOMR-F request, complete Sections A, B,and C. For Items E1–E4, use natural grade, if available. Check the measurement used. In Puerto Rico only, enter meters.

E1. Provide elevation information for the following and check the appropriate boxes to show whether the elevation is above or below the highest adjacent grade (HAG) and the lowest adjacent grade (LAG).

a) Top of bottom floor (including basement, crawlspace, or enclosure) is ______ ☐ feet ☐ meters ☐ above or ☐ below the HAG.

b) Top of bottom floor (including basement, crawlspace, or enclosure) is ______ ☐ feet ☐ meters ☐ above or ☐ below the LAG.

E2. For Building Diagrams 6–9 with permanent flood openings provided in Section A Items 8 and/or 9 (see pages 1–2 of Instructions), the next higher floor (elevation C2.b in the diagrams) of the building is ______ ☐ feet ☐ meters ☐ above or ☐ below the HAG.

E3. Attached garage (top of slab) is ______ ☐ feet ☐ meters ☐ above or ☐ below the HAG.

E4. Top of platform of machinery and/or equipment servicing the building is ______ ☐ feet ☐ meters ☐ above or ☐ below the HAG.

E5. Zone AO only: If no flood depth number is available, is the top of the bottom floor elevated in accordance with the community's floodplain management ordinance? ☐ Yes ☐ No ☐ Unknown. The local official must certify this information in Section G.

### SECTION F – PROPERTY OWNER (OR OWNER'S REPRESENTATIVE) CERTIFICATION

The property owner or owner's authorized representative who completes Sections A, B, and E for Zone A (without a FEMA-issued or community-issued BFE) or Zone AO must sign here. The statements in Sections A, B, and E are correct to the best of my knowledge.

| Property Owner or Owner's Authorized Representative's Name | | | |
|---|---|---|---|
| Address | City | State | ZIP Code |
| Signature | Date | Telephone | |

Comments

☐ Check here if attachments.

FEMA Form 086-0-33 (12/19) Replaces all previous editions. Form Page 3 of 6

**ELEVATION CERTIFICATE**

OMB No. 1660-0008
Expiration Date: November 30, 2022

| **IMPORTANT: In these spaces, copy the corresponding information from Section A.** | | | FOR INSURANCE COMPANY USE |
|---|---|---|---|
| Building Street Address (including Apt., Unit, Suite, and/or Bldg. No.) or P.O. Route and Box No. | | | Policy Number: |
| City | State | ZIP Code | Company NAIC Number |

**SECTION G – COMMUNITY INFORMATION (OPTIONAL)**

The local official who is authorized by law or ordinance to administer the community's floodplain management ordinance can complete Sections A, B, C (or E), and G of this Elevation Certificate. Complete the applicable item(s) and sign below. Check the measurement used in Items G8–G10. In Puerto Rico only, enter meters.

G1. ☐ The information in Section C was taken from other documentation that has been signed and sealed by a licensed surveyor, engineer, or architect who is authorized by law to certify elevation information. (Indicate the source and date of the elevation data in the Comments area below.)

G2. ☐ A community official completed Section E for a building located in Zone A (without a FEMA-issued or community-issued BFE) or Zone AO.

G3. ☐ The following information (Items G4–G10) is provided for community floodplain management purposes.

| G4. Permit Number | G5. Date Permit Issued | G6. Date Certificate of Compliance/Occupancy Issued |
|---|---|---|
| | | |

G7. This permit has been issued for: ☐ New Construction ☐ Substantial Improvement

G8. Elevation of as-built lowest floor (including basement) of the building: ________ ☐ feet ☐ meters Datum ________

G9. BFE or (in Zone AO) depth of flooding at the building site: ________ ☐ feet ☐ meters Datum ________

G10. Community's design flood elevation: ________ ☐ feet ☐ meters Datum ________

| Local Official's Name | Title |
|---|---|
| Community Name | Telephone |
| Signature | Date |

Comments (including type of equipment and location, per C2(e), if applicable)

☐ Check here if attachments.

FEMA Form 086-0-33 (12/19) Replaces all previous editions. Form Page 4 of 6

## BUILDING PHOTOGRAPHS

**ELEVATION CERTIFICATE**

See Instructions for Item A6.

OMB No. 1660-0008
Expiration Date: November 30, 2022

| **IMPORTANT: In these spaces, copy the corresponding information from Section A.** | | | FOR INSURANCE COMPANY USE |
|---|---|---|---|
| Building Street Address (including Apt., Unit, Suite, and/or Bldg. No.) or P.O. Route and Box No. | | | Policy Number: |
| City | State | ZIP Code | Company NAIC Number |

If using the Elevation Certificate to obtain NFIP flood insurance, affix at least 2 building photographs below according to the instructions for Item A6. Identify all photographs with date taken; "Front View" and "Rear View"; and, if required, "Right Side View" and "Left Side View." When applicable, photographs must show the foundation with representative examples of the flood openings or vents, as indicated in Section A8. If submitting more photographs than will fit on this page, use the Continuation Page.

Photo One

Photo One

Photo One Caption | Clear Photo One

Photo Two

Photo Two

Photo Two Caption | Clear Photo Two

FEMA Form 086-0-33 (12/19) | Replaces all previous editions. | Form Page 5 of 6

**ELEVATION CERTIFICATE**

**BUILDING PHOTOGRAPHS**
Continuation Page

OMB No. 1660-0008
Expiration Date: November 30, 2022

| **IMPORTANT: In these spaces, copy the corresponding information from Section A.** | | | FOR INSURANCE COMPANY USE |
|---|---|---|---|
| Building Street Address (including Apt., Unit, Suite, and/or Bldg. No.) or P.O. Route and Box No. | | | Policy Number: |
| City | State | ZIP Code | Company NAIC Number |

If submitting more photographs than will fit on the preceding page, affix the additional photographs below. Identify all photographs with: date taken; "Front View" and "Rear View"; and, if required, "Right Side View" and "Left Side View." When applicable, photographs must show the foundation with representative examples of the flood openings or vents, as indicated in Section A8.

Photo Three

Photo Three

Photo Three Caption    Clear Photo Three

Photo Four

Photo Four

Photo Four Caption    Clear Photo Four

FEMA Form 086-0-33 (12/19)    Replaces all previous editions.    Form Page 6 of 6

U.S. DEPARTMENT OF HOMELAND SECURITY
Federal Emergency Management Agency
National Flood Insurance Program

OMB No. 1660-0008
Expiration Date: November 30, 2022

## Instructions for Completing the Elevation Certificate

The Elevation Certificate is to be completed by a land surveyor, engineer, or architect who is authorized by law to certify elevation information when elevation information is required for Zones A1–A30, AE, AH, A (with BFE), VE, V1–V30, V (with BFE), AR, AR/A, AR/AE, AR/A1–A30, AR/AH, or AR/AO. Community officials who are authorized by law or ordinance to provide floodplain management information may also complete this form. For Zones AO and A (without BFE), a community official, a property owner, or an owner's representative may provide information on this certificate, unless the elevations are intended for use in supporting a request for a LOMA or LOMR-F. Certified elevations must be included if the purpose of completing the Elevation Certificate is to obtain a LOMA or LOMR-F.

The property owner, the owner's representative, or local official who is authorized by law to administer the community floodplain ordinance can complete Section A and Section B. The partially completed form can then be given to the land surveyor, engineer, or architect to complete Section C. The land surveyor, engineer, or architect should verify the information provided by the property owner or owner's representative to ensure that this certificate is complete.

In Puerto Rico only, elevations for building information and flood hazard information may be entered in meters.

### SECTION A – PROPERTY INFORMATION

**Items A1–A4.** This section identifies the building, its location, and its owner. Enter the name(s) of the building owner(s), the building's complete street address, and the lot and block numbers. If the building's address is different from the owner's address, enter the address of the building being certified. If the address is a rural route or a Post Office box number, enter the lot and block numbers, the tax parcel number, the legal description, or an abbreviated location description based on distance and direction from a fixed point of reference. For the purposes of this certificate, "building" means both a building and a manufactured (mobile) home.

A map may be attached to this certificate to show the location of the building on the property. A tax map, FIRM, or detailed community map is appropriate. If no map is available, provide a sketch of the property location, and the location of the building on the property. Include appropriate landmarks such as nearby roads, intersections, and bodies of water. For building use, indicate whether the building is residential, non-residential, an addition to an existing residential or non-residential building, an accessory building (e.g., garage), or other type of structure. Use the Comments area of the appropriate section if needed, or attach additional comments.

**Item A5.** Provide latitude and longitude coordinates for the center of the front of the building. Use either decimal degrees (e.g., 39.5043°, −110.7585°) or degrees, minutes, seconds (e.g., 39° 30' 15.5", −110° 45' 30.7") format. If decimal degrees are used, provide coordinates to at least 5 decimal places or better. When using degrees, minutes, seconds, provide seconds to at least 1 decimal place or better. The latitude and longitude coordinates must be accurate within 66 feet. When the latitude and longitude are provided by a surveyor, check the "Yes" box in Section D and indicate the method used to determine the latitude and longitude in the Comments area of Section D. If the Elevation Certificate is being certified by other than a licensed surveyor, engineer, or architect, this information is not required. Provide the type of datum used to obtain the latitude and longitude. FEMA prefers the use of NAD 1983.

**Item A6.** If the Elevation Certificate is being used to obtain flood insurance through the NFIP, the certifier must provide at least 2 photographs showing the front and rear of the building taken within 90 days from the date of certification. The photographs must be taken with views confirming the building description and diagram number provided in Section A. To the extent possible, these photographs should show the entire building including foundation. If the building has split-level or multi-level areas, provide at least 2 additional photographs showing side views of the building. In addition, when applicable, provide a photograph of the foundation showing a representative example of the flood openings or vents. All photographs must be in color and measure at least 3" × 3". Digital photographs are acceptable.

**Item A7.** Select the diagram on pages 7–9 that best represents the building. Then enter the diagram number and use the diagram to identify and determine the appropriate elevations requested in Items C2.a–h. If you are unsure of the correct diagram, select the diagram that most closely resembles the building being certified.

**Item A8.a.** Provide the square footage of the crawlspace or enclosure(s) below the lowest elevated floor of an elevated building with or without permanent flood openings. Take the measurement from the outside of the crawlspace or enclosure(s). Examples of elevated buildings constructed with crawlspace and enclosure(s) are shown in Diagrams 6–9

FEMA Form 086-0-33 (12/19) NFIP Elevation Certificate Instructions – Page 1 of 9

**Instructions for Completing the Elevation Certificate** (continued)

on pages 8–9. Diagrams 2A, 2B, 4, and 9 should be used for a building constructed with a crawlspace floor that is below the exterior grade on all sides.

**Items A8.b–d.** Enter in Item A8.b the number of permanent flood openings in the crawlspace or enclosure(s) that are no higher than 1.0 foot above the higher of the exterior or interior grade or floor immediately below the opening. (A permanent flood opening is a flood vent or other opening that allows the free passage of water automatically in both directions without human intervention.) If the interior grade elevation is used, note this in the Comments area of Section D. Estimate the total net area of all such permanent flood openings in square inches, excluding any bars, louvers, or other covers of the permanent flood openings, and enter the total in Item A8.c. If the net area cannot be reasonably estimated, provide the size of the flood openings without consideration of any covers and indicate in the Comments area the type of cover that exists in the flood openings. Indicate in Item A8.d whether the flood openings are engineered. If applicable, attach a copy of the Individual Engineered Flood Openings Certification or an Evaluation Report issued by the International Code Council Evaluation Service (ICC ES), if you have it. If the crawlspace or enclosure(s) have no permanent flood openings, or if the openings are not within 1.0 foot above adjacent grade, enter "N/A" for not applicable in Items A8.b–c.

**Item A9.a.** Provide the square footage of the attached garage with or without permanent flood openings. Take the measurement from the outside of the garage.

**Items A9.b–d.** Enter in Item A9.b the number of permanent flood openings in the attached garage that are no higher than 1.0 foot above the higher of the exterior or interior grade or floor immediately below the opening. (A permanent flood opening is a flood vent or other opening that allows the free passage of water automatically in both directions without human intervention.) If the interior grade elevation is used, note this in the Comments area of Section D. This includes any openings that are in the garage door that are no higher than 1.0 foot above the adjacent grade. Estimate the total net area of all such permanent flood openings in square inches and enter the total in Item A9.c. If the net area cannot be reasonably estimated, provide the size of the flood openings without consideration of any covers and indicate in the Comments area the type of cover that exists in the flood openings. Indicate in Item A9.d whether the flood openings are engineered. If applicable, attach a copy of the Individual Engineered Flood Openings Certification or an Evaluation Report issued by the International Code Council Evaluation Service (ICC ES), if you have it. If the garage has no permanent flood openings, or if the openings are not within 1.0 foot above adjacent grade, enter "N/A" for not applicable in Items A9.b–c.

**SECTION B – FLOOD INSURANCE RATE MAP (FIRM) INFORMATION**

Complete the Elevation Certificate on the basis of the FIRM in effect at the time of the certification.

The information for Section B is obtained by reviewing the FIRM panel that includes the building's location. Information about the current FIRM is available from the Federal Emergency Management Agency (FEMA) by calling 1-800-358-9616. If a Letter of Map Amendment (LOMA) or Letter of Map Revision (LOMR-F) has been issued by FEMA, please provide the letter date and case number in the Comments area of Section D or Section G, as appropriate.

For a building in an area that has been annexed by one community but is shown on another community's FIRM, enter the community name and 6-digit number of the annexing community in Item B1, the name of the county or new county, if necessary, in Item B2, and the FIRM index date for the annexing community in Item B6. Enter information from the actual FIRM panel that shows the building location, even if it is the FIRM for the previous jurisdiction, in Items B4, B5, B7, B8, and B9.

If the map in effect at the time of the building's construction was other than the current FIRM, and you have the past map information pertaining to the building, provide the information in the Comments area of Section D.

**Item B1.** NFIP Community Name & Community Number. Enter the complete name of the community in which the building is located and the associated 6-digit community number. For a newly incorporated community, use the name and 6-digit number of the new community. Under the NFIP, a "community" is any State or area or political subdivision thereof, or any Indian tribe or authorized native organization, that has authority to adopt and enforce floodplain management regulations for the areas within its jurisdiction. To determine the current community number, see the NFIP *Community Status Book*, available on FEMA's web site at https://www.fema.gov/national-flood-insurance-program/national-flood-insurance-program-community-status-book, or call 1-800-358-9616.

FEMA Form 086-0-33 (12/19) NFIP Elevation Certificate Instructions – Page 2 of 9

**Instructions for Completing the Elevation Certificate** (continued)

**Item B2.** County Name. Enter the name of the county or counties in which the community is located. For an unincorporated area of a county, enter "unincorporated area." For an independent city, enter "independent city."

**Item B3.** State. Enter the 2-letter state abbreviation (for example, VA, TX, CA).

**Items B4–B5.** Map/Panel Number and Suffix. Enter the 10-character "Map Number" or "Community Panel Number" shown on the FIRM where the building or manufactured (mobile) home is located. For maps in a county-wide format, the sixth character of the "Map Number" is the letter "C" followed by a 4-digit map number. For maps not in a county-wide format, enter the "Community Panel Number" shown on the FIRM.

**Item B6.** FIRM Index Date. Enter the effective date or the map revised date shown on the FIRM Index.

**Item B7.** FIRM Panel Effective/Revised Date. Enter the map effective date or the map revised date shown on the FIRM panel. This will be the latest of all dates shown on the map. The current FIRM panel effective date can be determined by calling 1-800-358-9616.

**Item B8.** Flood Zone(s). Enter the flood zone, or flood zones, in which the building is located. All flood zones containing the letter "A" or "V" are considered Special Flood Hazard Areas. The flood zones are A, AE, A1–A30, V, VE, V1–V30, AH, AO, AR, AR/A, AR/AE, AR/A1–A30, AR/AH, and AR/AO. Each flood zone is defined in the legend of the FIRM panel on which it appears.

**Item B9.** Base Flood Elevation(s). Using the appropriate Flood Insurance Study (FIS) Profile, Floodway Data Table, or FIRM panel, locate the property and enter the BFE (or base flood depth) of the building site. If the building is located in more than 1 flood zone in Item B8, list all appropriate BFEs in Item B9. BFEs are shown on a FIRM or FIS Profile for Zones A1–A30, AE, AH, V1–V30, VE, AR, AR/A, AR/AE, AR/A1–A30, AR/AH, and AR/AO; flood depth numbers are shown for Zone AO. Use the AR BFE if the building is located in any of Zones AR/A, AR/AE, AR/A1–A30, AR/AH, or AR/AO. In A or V zones where BFEs are not provided on the FIRM, BFEs may be available from another source. For example, the community may have established BFEs or obtained BFE data from other sources for the building site. For subdivisions and other developments of more than 50 lots or 5 acres, establishment of BFEs is required by the community's floodplain management ordinance. If a BFE is obtained from another source, enter the BFE in Item B9. In an A Zone where BFEs are not available, complete Section E and enter N/A for Section B, Item B9. Enter the BFE to the nearest tenth of a foot (nearest tenth of a meter, in Puerto Rico).

**Item B10.** Indicate the source of the BFE that you entered in Item B9. If the BFE is from a source other than FIS Profile, FIRM, or community, describe the source of the BFE.

**Item B11.** Indicate the elevation datum to which the elevations on the applicable FIRM are referenced as shown on the map legend. The vertical datum is shown in the Map Legend and/or the Notes to Users on the FIRM.

**Item B12.** Indicate whether the building is located in a Coastal Barrier Resources System (CBRS) area or Otherwise Protected Area (OPA). (OPAs are portions of coastal barriers that are owned by Federal, State, or local governments or by certain non-profit organizations and used primarily for natural resources protection.) Federal flood insurance is prohibited in designated CBRS areas or OPAs for buildings or manufactured (mobile) homes built or substantially improved after the date of the CBRS or OPA designation. For the first CBRS designations, that date is October 1, 1983. Information about CBRS areas and OPAs may be obtained on the FEMA web site at https://www.fema.gov/national-flood-insurance-program/coastal-barrier-resources-system.

**SECTION C – BUILDING ELEVATION INFORMATION (SURVEY REQUIRED)**

Complete Section C if the building is located in any of Zones A1–A30, AE, AH, A (with BFE), VE, V1–V30, V (with BFE), AR, AR/A, AR/AE, AR/A1–A30, AR/AH, or AR/AO, or if this certificate is being used to support a request for a LOMA or LOMR-F. If the building is located in Zone AO or Zone A (without BFE), complete Section E instead. To ensure that all required elevations are obtained, it may be necessary to enter the building (for instance, if the building has a basement or sunken living room, split-level construction, or machinery and equipment).

Surveyors may not be able to gain access to some crawlspaces to shoot the elevation of the crawlspace floor. If access to the crawlspace is limited or cannot be gained, follow one of these procedures.

- Use a yardstick or tape measure to measure the height from the floor of the crawlspace to the "next higher floor," and then subtract the crawlspace height from the elevation of the "next higher floor." If there is no access to the

**Instructions for Completing the Elevation Certificate** (continued)

crawlspace, use the exterior grade next to the structure to measure the height of the crawlspace to the "next higher floor."

- Contact the local floodplain administrator of the community in which the building is located. The community may have documentation of the elevation of the crawlspace floor as part of the permit issued for the building.
- If the property owner has documentation or knows the height of the crawlspace floor to the next higher floor, try to verify this by looking inside the crawlspace through any openings or vents.

In all 3 cases, use the Comments area of Section D to provide the elevation and a brief description of how the elevation was obtained.

**Item C1.** Indicate whether the elevations to be entered in this section are based on construction drawings, a building under construction, or finished construction. For either of the first 2 choices, a post-construction Elevation Certificate will be required when construction is complete. If the building is under construction, include only those elevations that can be surveyed in Items C2.a–h. Use the Comments area of Section D to provide elevations obtained from the construction plans or drawings. Select "Finished Construction" only when all machinery and/or equipment such as furnaces, hot water heaters, heat pumps, air conditioners, and elevators and their associated equipment have been installed and the grading around the building is completed.

**Item C2.** A field survey is required for Items C2.a–h. Most control networks will assign a unique identifier for each benchmark. For example, the National Geodetic Survey uses the Permanent Identifier (PID). For the benchmark utilized, provide the PID or other unique identifier assigned by the maintainer of the benchmark. For GPS survey, indicate the benchmark used for the base station, the Continuously Operating Reference Stations (CORS) sites used for an On-line Positioning User Service (OPUS) solution (also attach the OPUS report), or the name of the Real Time Network used.

Also provide the vertical datum for the benchmark elevation. All elevations for the certificate, including the elevations for Items C2.a–h, must use the same datum on which the BFE is based. Show the conversion from the field survey datum used if it differs from the datum used for the BFE entered in Item B9 and indicate the conversion software used. Show the datum conversion, if applicable, in the Comments area of Section D.

For property experiencing ground subsidence, the most recent reference mark elevations must be used for determining building elevations. However, when subsidence is involved, the BFE should not be adjusted. Enter elevations in Items C2.a–h to the nearest tenth of a foot (nearest tenth of a meter, in Puerto Rico).

**Items C2.a–d.** Enter the building elevations (excluding the attached garage) indicated by the selected building diagram (Item A7) in Items C2.a–c. If there is an attached garage, enter the elevation for top of attached garage slab in Item C2.d. (Because elevation for top of attached garage slab is self-explanatory, attached garages are not illustrated in the diagrams.) If the building is located in a V zone on the FIRM, complete Item C2.c. If the flood zone cannot be determined, enter elevations for all of Items C2.a–h. For buildings in A zones, elevations a, b, d, and e should be measured at the top of the floor. For buildings in V zones, elevation c must be measured at the bottom of the lowest horizontal structural member of the floor (see drawing below). For buildings elevated on a crawlspace, Diagrams 8 and 9, enter the elevation

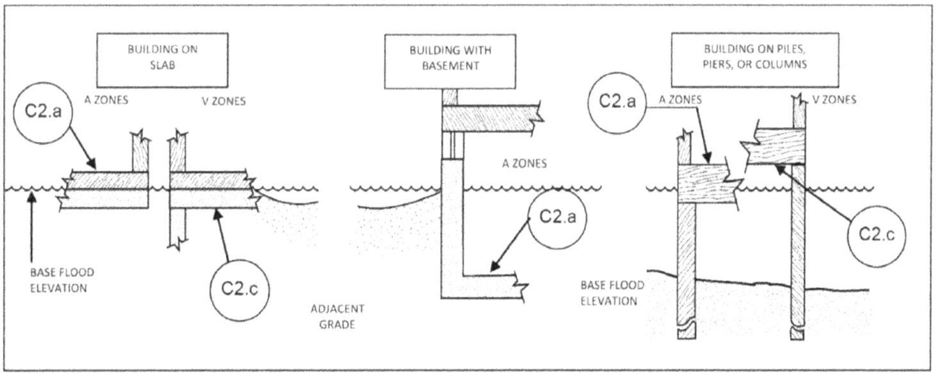


FEMA Form 086-0-33 (12/19) NFIP Elevation Certificate Instructions – Page 4 of 9

**Instructions for Completing the Elevation Certificate** (continued)

of the top of the crawlspace floor in Item C2.a, whether or not the crawlspace has permanent flood openings (flood vents). *If any item does not apply to the building, enter "N/A" for not applicable.*

**Item C2.e.** Enter the lowest platform elevation of at least 1 of the following machinery and equipment items: elevators and their associated equipment, furnaces, hot water heaters, heat pumps, and air conditioners in an attached garage or enclosure or on an open utility platform that provides utility services for the building. Note that elevations for these specific machinery and equipment items are required in order to rate the building for flood insurance. Local floodplain management officials are required to ensure that all machinery and equipment servicing the building are protected from flooding. Thus, local officials may require that elevation information for all machinery and equipment, including ductwork, be documented on the Elevation Certificate. If the machinery and/or equipment is mounted to a wall, pile, etc., enter the platform elevation of the machinery and/or equipment. Indicate machinery/equipment type and its general location, e.g., on floor inside garage or on platform affixed to exterior wall, in the Comments area of Section D or Section G, as appropriate. *If this item does not apply to the building, enter "N/A" for not applicable.*

**Items C2.f–g.** Enter the elevation of the ground, sidewalk, or patio slab immediately next to the building. For Zone AO, use the natural grade elevation, if available. This measurement must be to the nearest tenth of a foot (nearest tenth of a meter, in Puerto Rico) if this certificate is being used to support a request for a LOMA or LOMR-F.

**Item C2.h.** Enter the lowest grade elevation at the deck support or stairs. For Zone AO, use the natural grade elevation, if available. This measurement must be to the nearest tenth of a foot (nearest tenth of a meter, in Puerto Rico) if this certificate is being used to support a request for a LOMA or LOMR-F.

**SECTION D – SURVEYOR, ENGINEER, OR ARCHITECT CERTIFICATION**

Complete as indicated. This section of the Elevation Certificate may be signed by only a land surveyor, engineer, or architect who is authorized by law to certify elevation information. Place your license number, your seal (as allowed by the State licensing board), your signature, and the date in the box in Section D. You are certifying that the information on this certificate represents your best efforts to interpret the data available and that you understand that any false statement may be punishable by fine or imprisonment under 18 U.S. Code, Section 1001. Use the Comments area of Section D to provide datum, elevation, openings, or other relevant information not specified elsewhere on the certificate.

**SECTION E – BUILDING ELEVATION INFORMATION (SURVEY NOT REQUIRED) FOR ZONE AO AND ZONE A (WITHOUT BFE)**

Complete Section E if the building is located in Zone AO or Zone A (without BFE). Otherwise, complete Section C instead. Explain in the Section F Comments area if the measurement provided under Items E1–E4 is based on the "natural grade."

**Items E1.a and b.** Enter in Item E1.a the height to the nearest tenth of a foot (tenth of a meter in Puerto Rico) of the top of the bottom floor (as indicated in the applicable diagram) above or below the highest adjacent grade (HAG). Enter in Item E1.b the height to the nearest tenth of a foot (tenth of a meter in Puerto Rico) of the top of the bottom floor (as indicated in the applicable diagram) above or below the lowest adjacent grade (LAG). For buildings in Zone AO, the community's floodplain management ordinance requires the lowest floor of the building be elevated above the highest adjacent grade at least as high as the depth number on the FIRM. Buildings in Zone A (without BFE) may qualify for a lower insurance rate if an engineered BFE is developed at the site.

**Item E2.** For Building Diagrams 6–9 with permanent flood openings (see pages 8–9), enter the height to the nearest tenth of a foot (tenth of a meter in Puerto Rico) of the next higher floor or elevated floor (as indicated in the applicable diagram) above or below the highest adjacent grade (HAG).

**Item E3.** Enter the height to the nearest tenth of a foot (tenth of a meter in Puerto Rico), in relation to the highest adjacent grade next to the building, for the top of attached garage slab. (Because elevation for top of attached garage slab is self-explanatory, attached garages are not illustrated in the diagrams.) *If this item does not apply to the building, enter "N/A" for not applicable.*

**Item E4.** Enter the height to the nearest tenth of a foot (tenth of a meter in Puerto Rico), in relation to the highest adjacent grade next to the building, of the platform elevation that supports the machinery and/or equipment servicing the building. Indicate machinery/equipment type in the Comments area of Section F. *If this item does not apply to the building, enter "N/A" for not applicable.*

FEMA Form 086-0-33 (12/19) NFIP Elevation Certificate Instructions – Page 5 of 9

**Instructions for Completing the Elevation Certificate** (continued)

**Item E5.** For those communities where this base flood depth is not available, the community will need to determine whether the top of the bottom floor is elevated in accordance with the community's floodplain management ordinance.

**SECTION F – PROPERTY OWNER (OR OWNER'S REPRESENTATIVE) CERTIFICATION**

Complete as indicated. This section is provided for certification of measurements taken by a property owner or property owner's representative when responding to Sections A, B, and E. The address entered in this section must be the actual mailing address of the property owner or property owner's representative who provided the information on the certificate.

**SECTION G – COMMUNITY INFORMATION (OPTIONAL)**

Complete as indicated. The community official who is authorized by law or ordinance to administer the community's floodplain management ordinance can complete Sections A, B, C (or E), and G of this Elevation Certificate. Section C may be filled in by the local official as provided in the instructions below for Item G1. If the authorized community official completes Sections C, E, or G, complete the appropriate item(s) and sign this section.

Check **Item G1** if Section C is completed with elevation data from other documentation that has been signed and sealed by a licensed surveyor, engineer, or architect who is authorized by law to certify elevation information. Indicate the source of the elevation data and the date obtained in the Comments area of Section G. If you are both a community official and a licensed land surveyor, engineer, or architect authorized by law to certify elevation information, and you performed the actual survey for a building in Zones A1–A30, AE, AH, A (with BFE), VE, V1–V30, V (with BFE), AR, AR/A, AR/A1–A30, AR/AE, AR/AH, or AR/AO, you must also complete Section D.

Check **Item G2** if information is entered in Section E by the community for a building in Zone A (without a FEMA-issued or community-issued BFE) or Zone AO.

Check **Item G3** if the information in Items G4–G10 has been completed for community floodplain management purposes to document the as-built lowest floor elevation of the building. Section C of the Elevation Certificate records the elevation of various building components but does not determine the lowest floor of the building or whether the building, as constructed, complies with the community's floodplain management ordinance. This must be done by the community. Items G4–G10 provide a way to document these determinations.

**Item G4.** Permit Number. Enter the permit number or other identifier to key the Elevation Certificate to the permit issued for the building.

**Item G5.** Date Permit Issued. Enter the date the permit was issued for the building.

**Item G6.** Date Certificate of Compliance/Occupancy Issued. Enter the date that the Certificate of Compliance or Occupancy or similar written official documentation of as-built lowest floor elevation was issued by the community as evidence that all work authorized by the floodplain development permit has been completed in accordance with the community's floodplain management laws or ordinances.

**Item G7.** New Construction or Substantial Improvement. Check the applicable box. "Substantial Improvement" means any reconstruction, rehabilitation, addition, or other improvement of a building, the cost of which equals or exceeds 50 percent of the market value of the building before the start of construction of the improvement. The term includes buildings that have incurred substantial damage, regardless of the actual repair work performed.

**Item G8.** As-built lowest floor elevation. Enter the elevation of the lowest floor (including basement) when the construction of the building is completed and a final inspection has been made to confirm that the building is built in accordance with the permit, the approved plans, and the community's floodplain management laws or ordinances. Indicate the elevation datum used.

**Item G9.** BFE. Using the appropriate FIRM panel, FIS Profile, or other data source, locate the property and enter the BFE (or base flood depth) of the building site. Indicate the elevation datum used.

**Item G10.** Community's design flood elevation. Enter the elevation (including freeboard above the BFE) to which the community requires the lowest floor to be elevated. Indicate the elevation datum used.

Enter your name, title, and telephone number, and the name of the community. Sign and enter the date in the appropriate blanks.

FEMA Form 086-0-33 (12/19) NFIP Elevation Certificate Instructions – Page 6 of 9

## Building Diagrams

The following diagrams illustrate various types of buildings. Compare the features of the building being certified with the features shown in the diagrams and select the diagram most applicable. Enter the diagram number in Item A7, the square footage of crawlspace or enclosure(s) and the area of flood openings in square inches in Items A8.a–c, the square footage of attached garage and the area of flood openings in square inches in Items A9.a–c, and the elevations in Items C2.a–h.

In A zones, the floor elevation is taken at the top finished surface of the floor indicated; in V zones, the floor elevation is taken at the bottom of the lowest horizontal structural member (see drawing in instructions for Section C).

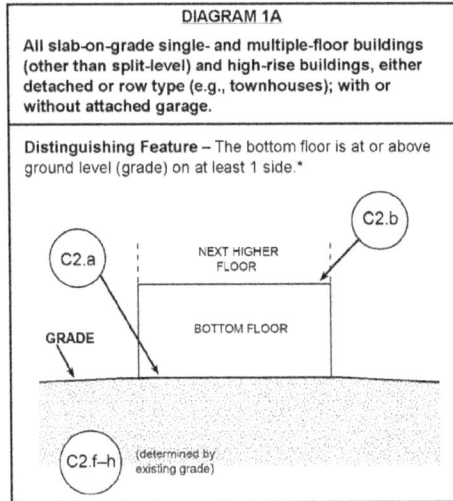

### DIAGRAM 1A

**All slab-on-grade single- and multiple-floor buildings (other than split-level) and high-rise buildings, either detached or row type (e.g., townhouses); with or without attached garage.**

**Distinguishing Feature** – The bottom floor is at or above ground level (grade) on at least 1 side.*

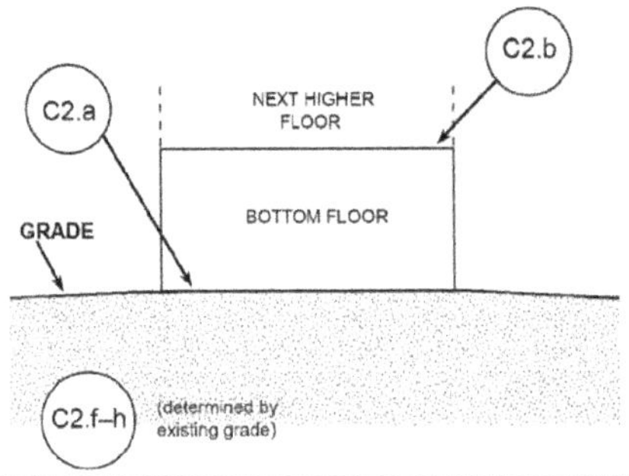

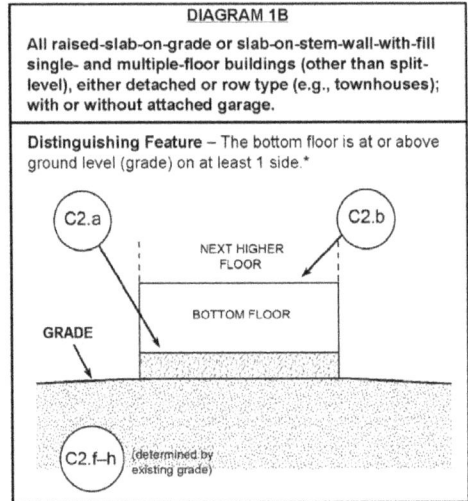

### DIAGRAM 1B

**All raised-slab-on-grade or slab-on-stem-wall-with-fill single- and multiple-floor buildings (other than split-level), either detached or row type (e.g., townhouses); with or without attached garage.**

**Distinguishing Feature** – The bottom floor is at or above ground level (grade) on at least 1 side.*

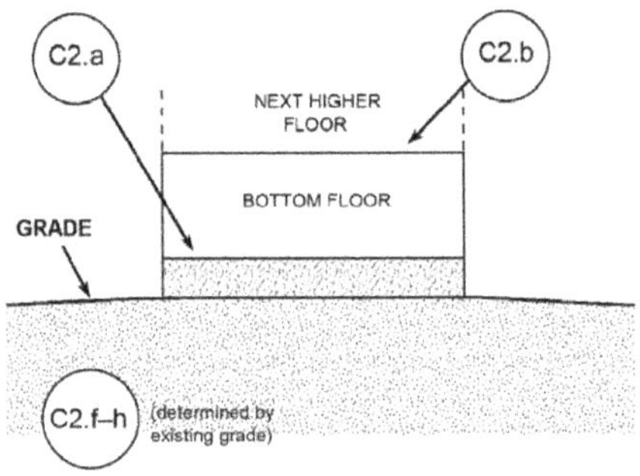

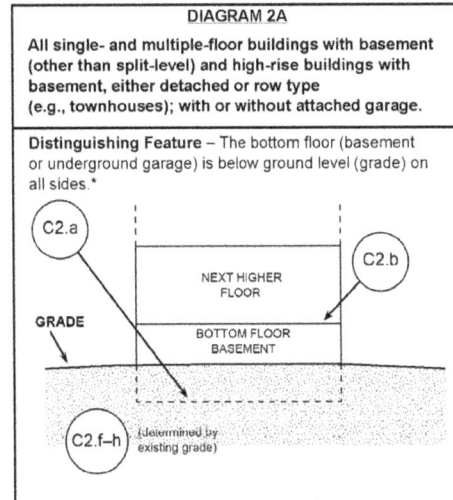

### DIAGRAM 2A

**All single- and multiple-floor buildings with basement (other than split-level) and high-rise buildings with basement, either detached or row type (e.g., townhouses); with or without attached garage.**

**Distinguishing Feature** – The bottom floor (basement or underground garage) is below ground level (grade) on all sides.*

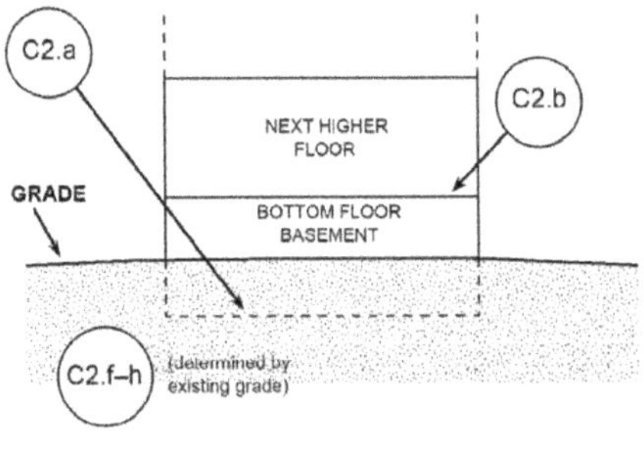

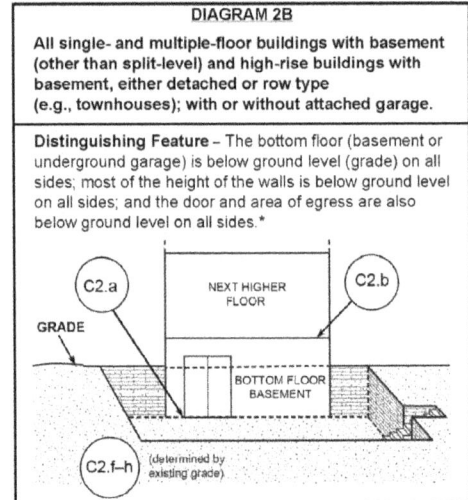

### DIAGRAM 2B

**All single- and multiple-floor buildings with basement (other than split-level) and high-rise buildings with basement, either detached or row type (e.g., townhouses); with or without attached garage.**

**Distinguishing Feature** – The bottom floor (basement or underground garage) is below ground level (grade) on all sides; most of the height of the walls is below ground level on all sides; and the door and area of egress are also below ground level on all sides.*

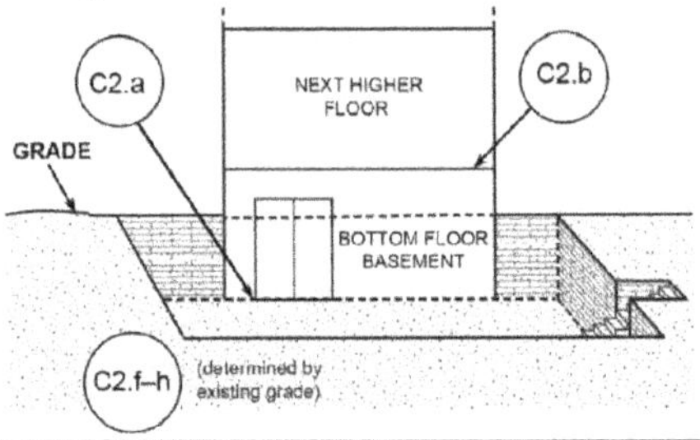


* A floor that is below ground level (grade) on all sides is considered a basement even if the floor is used for living purposes, or as an office, garage, workshop, etc.

FEMA Form 086-0-33 (12/19) NFIP Elevation Certificate Instructions – Page 7 of 9

## Building Diagrams

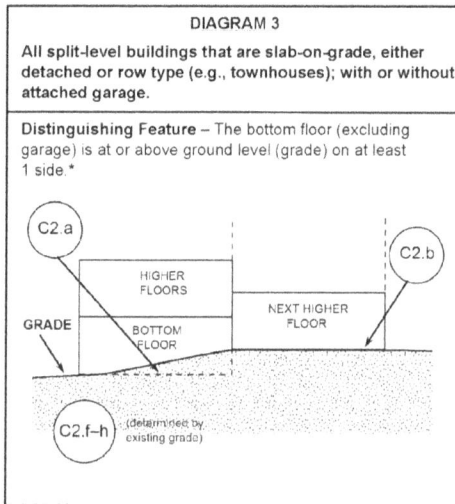

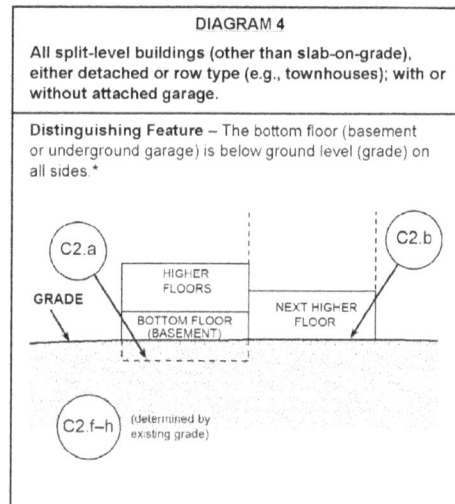

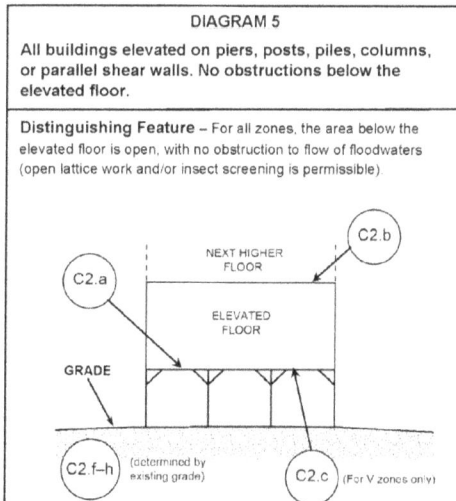

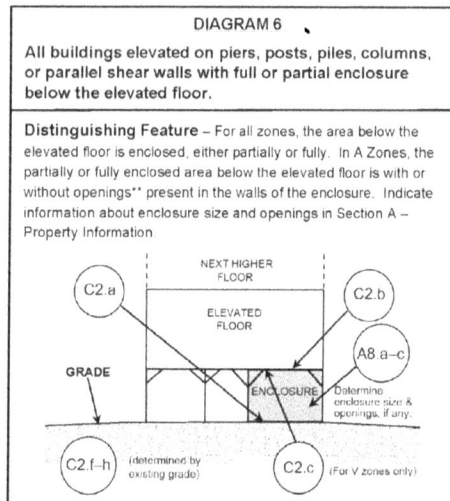

### DIAGRAM 3

**All split-level buildings that are slab-on-grade, either detached or row type (e.g., townhouses); with or without attached garage.**

**Distinguishing Feature** – The bottom floor (excluding garage) is at or above ground level (grade) on at least 1 side.*

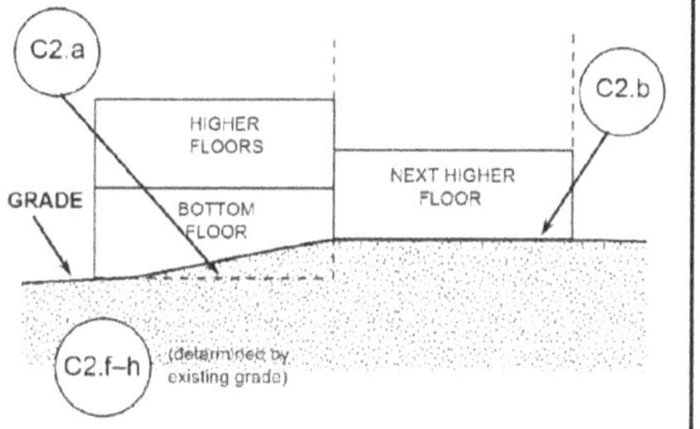


### DIAGRAM 4

**All split-level buildings (other than slab-on-grade), either detached or row type (e.g., townhouses); with or without attached garage.**

**Distinguishing Feature** – The bottom floor (basement or underground garage) is below ground level (grade) on all sides.*

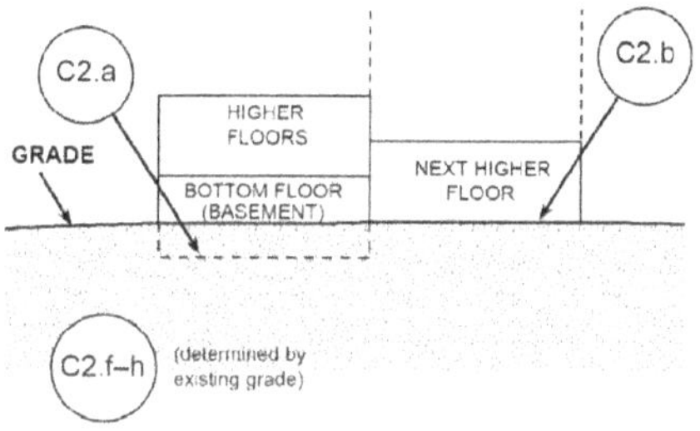


### DIAGRAM 5

**All buildings elevated on piers, posts, piles, columns, or parallel shear walls. No obstructions below the elevated floor.**

**Distinguishing Feature** – For all zones, the area below the elevated floor is open, with no obstruction to flow of floodwaters (open lattice work and/or insect screening is permissible).

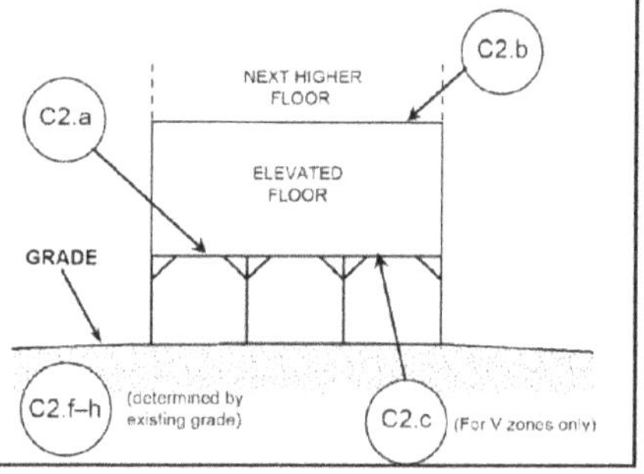


### DIAGRAM 6

**All buildings elevated on piers, posts, piles, columns, or parallel shear walls with full or partial enclosure below the elevated floor.**

**Distinguishing Feature** – For all zones, the area below the elevated floor is enclosed, either partially or fully. In A Zones, the partially or fully enclosed area below the elevated floor is with or without openings** present in the walls of the enclosure. Indicate information about enclosure size and openings in Section A – Property Information.

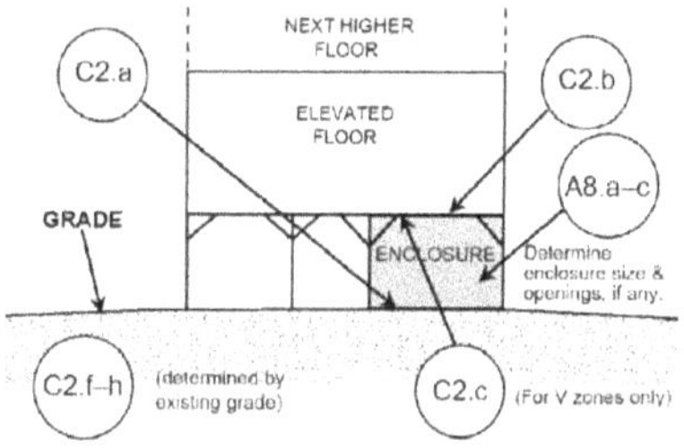


* A floor that is below ground level (grade) on all sides is considered a basement even if the floor is used for living purposes, or as an office, garage, workshop, etc.

** An "opening" is a permanent opening that allows for the free passage of water automatically in both directions without human intervention. Under the NFIP, a minimum of 2 openings is required for enclosures or crawlspaces. The openings shall provide a total net area of not less than 1 square inch for every square foot of area enclosed, excluding any bars, louvers, or other covers of the opening. Alternatively, an Individual Engineered Flood Openings Certification or an Evaluation Report issued by the International Code Council Evaluation Service (ICC ES) must be submitted to document that the design of the openings will allow for the automatic equalization of hydrostatic flood forces on exterior walls. A window, a door, or a garage door is not considered an opening; openings may be installed in doors. Openings shall be on at least 2 sides of the enclosed area. If a building has more than 1 enclosed area, each area must have openings to allow floodwater to directly enter. The bottom of the openings must be no higher than 1.0 foot above the higher of the exterior or interior grade or floor immediately below the opening. For more guidance on openings, see NFIP Technical Bulletin 1.

FEMA Form 086-0-33 (12/19) NFIP Elevation Certificate Instructions – Page 8 of 9

## Building Diagrams

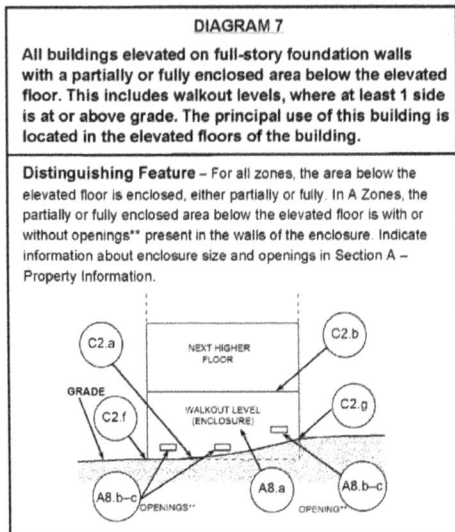

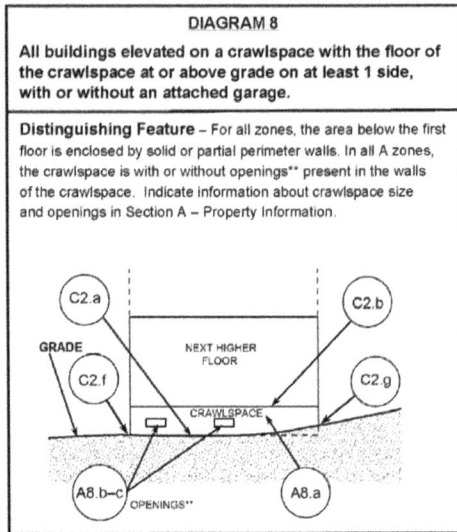

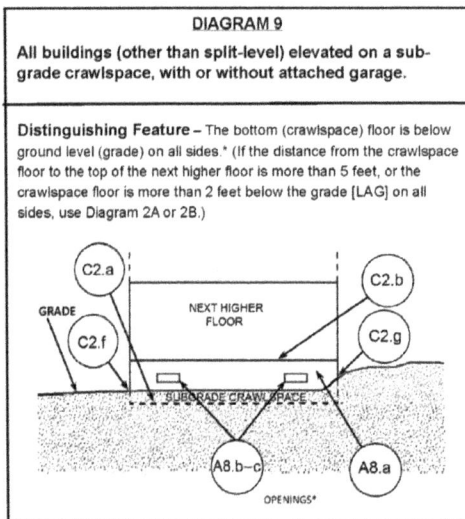

**DIAGRAM 7**

**All buildings elevated on full-story foundation walls with a partially or fully enclosed area below the elevated floor. This includes walkout levels, where at least 1 side is at or above grade. The principal use of this building is located in the elevated floors of the building.**

**Distinguishing Feature** – For all zones, the area below the elevated floor is enclosed, either partially or fully. In A Zones, the partially or fully enclosed area below the elevated floor is with or without openings** present in the walls of the enclosure. Indicate information about enclosure size and openings in Section A – Property Information.

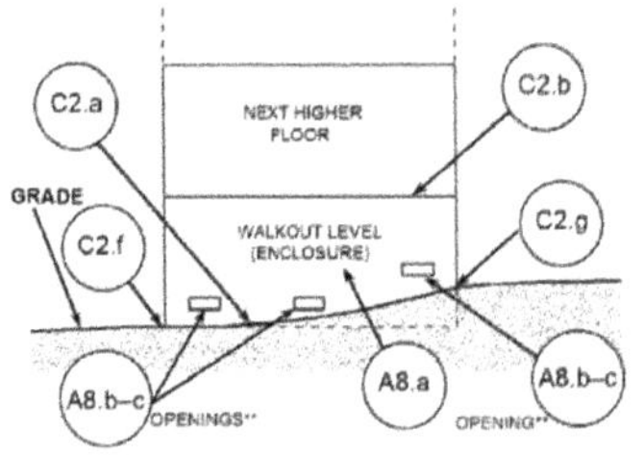


**DIAGRAM 8**

**All buildings elevated on a crawlspace with the floor of the crawlspace at or above grade on at least 1 side, with or without an attached garage.**

**Distinguishing Feature** – For all zones, the area below the first floor is enclosed by solid or partial perimeter walls. In all A zones, the crawlspace is with or without openings** present in the walls of the crawlspace. Indicate information about crawlspace size and openings in Section A – Property Information.

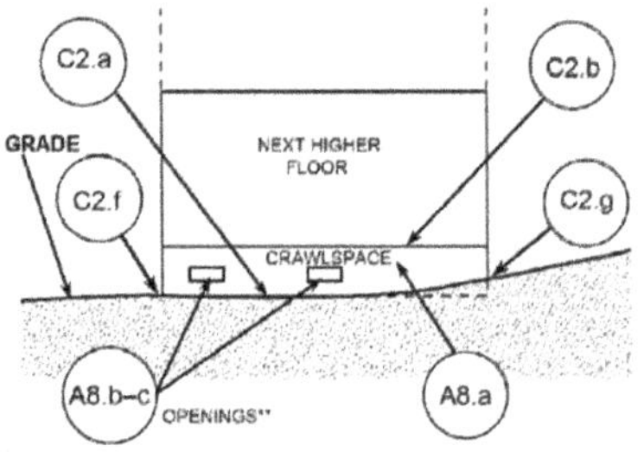


**DIAGRAM 9**

**All buildings (other than split-level) elevated on a sub-grade crawlspace, with or without attached garage.**

**Distinguishing Feature** – The bottom (crawlspace) floor is below ground level (grade) on all sides.* (If the distance from the crawlspace floor to the top of the next higher floor is more than 5 feet, or the crawlspace floor is more than 2 feet below the grade [LAG] on all sides, use Diagram 2A or 2B.)

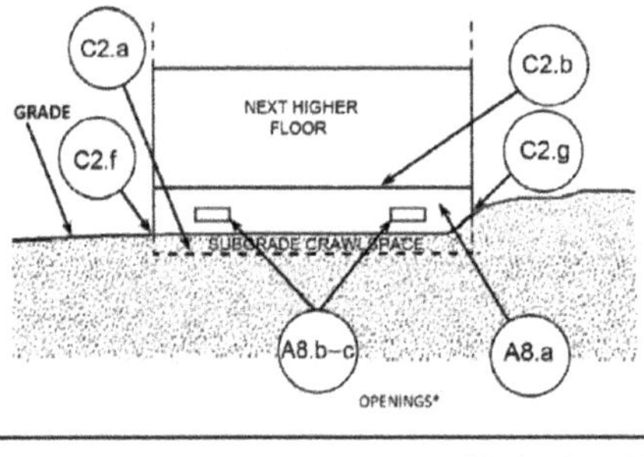


* A floor that is below ground level (grade) on all sides is considered a basement even if the floor is used for living purposes, or as an office, garage, workshop, etc.

** An "opening" is a permanent opening that allows for the free passage of water automatically in both directions without human intervention. Under the NFIP, a minimum of 2 openings is required for enclosures or crawlspaces. The openings shall provide a total net area of not less than 1 square inch for every square foot of area enclosed, excluding any bars, louvers, or other covers of the opening. Alternatively, an Individual Engineered Flood Openings Certification or an Evaluation Report issued by the International Code Council Evaluation Service (ICC ES) must be submitted to document that the design of the openings will allow for the automatic equalization of hydrostatic flood forces on exterior walls. A window, a door, or a garage door is not considered an opening; openings may be installed in doors. Openings shall be on at least 2 sides of the enclosed area. If a building has more than 1 enclosed area, each area must have openings to allow floodwater to directly enter. The bottom of the openings must be no higher than 1.0 foot above the higher of the exterior or interior grade or floor immediately below the opening. For more guidance on openings, see NFIP Technical Bulletin 1.

FEMA Form 086-0-33 (12/19) NFIP Elevation Certificate Instructions – Page 9 of 9

# Lowest Floor Guide

## PUTTING IT INTO PERSPECTIVE...

Section A and C of the Elevation Certificate (EC) provide fields for entering numerous measurements that the surveyor must record in completing an elevation survey. This data will be used to not only help insurance agents accurately rate a flood insurance policy, but also assist FEMA and the local communities with their floodplain management compliance issues.

The EC does not specifically identify for the insurance agent the Lowest Floor Elevation (LFE) that must be used for rating purposes. This guide must be used in conjunction with information provided on the Flood Insurance Application form for rating purposes.

This guide will provide you with some helpful information and hints.

## WHERE TO GET HELP

The Lowest Floor Guide will assist you in determining the LFE for the majority of your business. However, if you are unable to make the determination, contact your Write Your Own (WYO) company underwriting staff or, for NFIP Direct Policies, the NFIP Direct underwriting department for assistance.

## WHERE TO START...

The following are guidelines for interpreting the elevation information in Section C of the EC.

**STEP 1:** Review the EC. Find the referenced Building Diagram Number in Section A, Item A7. This diagram number refers to one of the building diagrams located on Instructions Pages 7–9 of the EC.

**STEP 2:** Once the correct building diagram has been determined, review the data contained in Section C, Item C2 of the EC. The circled letters and numbers on the building diagram correspond to the elevations entered in Items C2. a-h in Section C, Item C2.

**STEP 3:** Review the Elevation in Item C2.a. If the elevation in Item C2.a is lower than the elevation in Item C2.f, then you have a building with a basement. The correct LFE rating will be Item C2.a (Building Diagrams 2A, 2B, 4, or 9).

- For Building Diagrams 1A, 1B, and 3, if Item C2.a is higher than C2.f, the building is slab on grade, or a walkout first level. Rate as no basement and use Item C2.a as the LFE.
- If Item C2.c is given, and the property is in a V Zone, Item C2.c will be the correct LFE if there are no enclosures (Building Diagram 5).
- If Item C2.c is higher than Item C2.a, then you have an elevated building with enclosure(s) below the elevated level. Use Item C2.c as the LFE for V Zones if the enclosure is less than 300 sq. ft., the walls are breakaway, and machinery and equipment are elevated at or above the Base Flood Elevation (BFE). Otherwise use the bottom of Item C2.a if the enclosure is 300 sq. ft. or greater, the walls are supporting walls, or machinery and equipment are below the BFE and an enclosure of any size exists (Building Diagram 6).

## IMPORTANT HINT:

If Item A8 and/or Item A9 shows flood openings, and the openings are adequate for the square footage of the enclosed area, then you have an elevated building with proper venting. The LFE is Item C2.b, top of the next higher floor, as long as the building is not located in a V Zone (Building Diagrams 7 and 8).

### Lowest Floor Guide for Zones AO and A (without Estimated BFE)

**BUILDING DIAGRAMS**

**Distinguishing Feature:** All buildings

**Lowest Floor for Rating:** Difference between the top of the bottom floor and highest adjacent grade

**Elevation Needed for Rating from FEMA EC:** Use the measurement provided in Item E1. If the top of the bottom floor is below the highest adjacent grade, show this difference as a negative number on the application. For buildings similar to diagrams 6-9 with proper openings, use the measurement provided in Item E2.

## Lowest Floor Guide for Zones A, AE, A1-A30, AH, AR, AR Dual

### BUILDING DIAGRAM #1A

**Distinguishing Feature:** The bottom floor is at or above ground level (grade) on at least one side.

**Lowest Floor for Rating:** Top of slab or lower attached garage if it has machinery and equipment below BFE unless the garage is properly vented

**Elevation Needed for Rating from FEMA EC:** Item C2.a or Item C2.d (if structure has attached garage)

**All slab-on-grade single- and multiple-floor buildings (other than split-level) and high-rise buildings, either detached or row type (e.g., townhouses); with or without attached garage.**

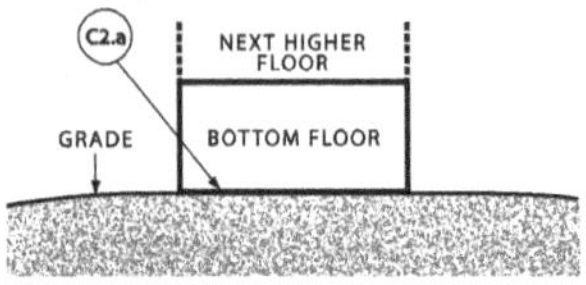


### BUILDING DIAGRAM #1B

**Distinguishing Feature:** The bottom floor is at or above ground level (grade) on at least one side.

**Lowest Floor for Rating:** Top of slab or lower attached garage if it has machinery and equipment below BFE unless the garage is properly vented

**Elevation Needed for Rating from FEMA EC:** Item C2.a or Item C2.d (if structure has attached garage)

**All raised slab-on-grade or slab-on-stem-wall-with-fill single- and multiple-floor buildings (other than split-level) and high-rise buildings, either detached or row type (e.g., townhouses); with or without attached garage.**

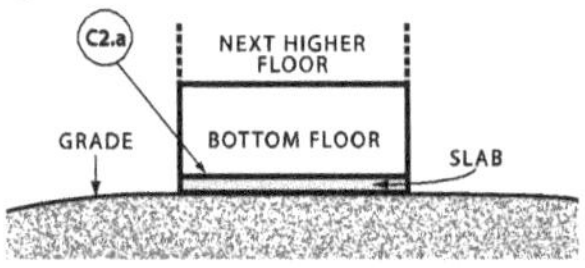


### BUILDING DIAGRAM #2A

**Distinguishing Feature:** The bottom floor (basement or underground garage) is below ground level (grade) on all sides.[1]

**Lowest Floor for Rating:** Top of basement floor

**Elevation Needed for Rating from FEMA EC:** Item C2.a

**All single- and multiple-floor buildings with basement (other than split-level) and high-rise buildings with basement, either detached or row type (e.g., townhouses); with or without attached garage.**

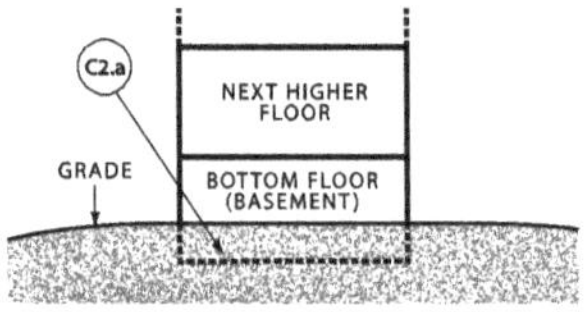


### BUILDING DIAGRAM #2B

**Distinguishing Feature:** The bottom floor (basement or underground garage) is below ground level (grade) on all sides; most of the height of the walls are below ground level on all sides and the door and area of egress is also below ground level on all sides.[1]

**Lowest Floor for Rating:** Top of basement floor

**Elevation Needed for Rating from FEMA EC:** Item C2.a

**All single- and multiple-floor buildings with basement (other than split-level) and high-rise buildings with basement, either detached or row type (e.g., townhouses); with or without attached garage.**

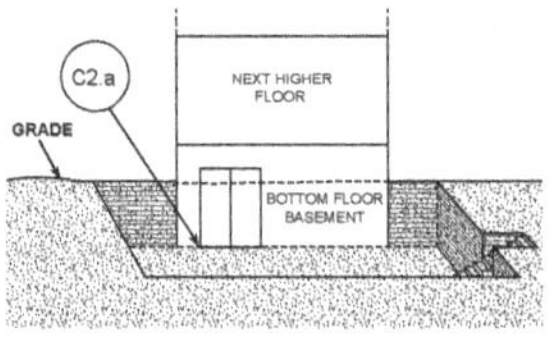


### BUILDING DIAGRAM #3

**Distinguishing Feature:** The bottom floor (excluding garage) is at or above ground level (grade) on at least one side.

**Lowest Floor for Rating:** Top of slab

**Elevation Needed for Rating from FEMA EC:** Item C2.a

**All split-level buildings that are slab-on-grade, either detached or row type (e.g., townhouses); with or without attached garage.**

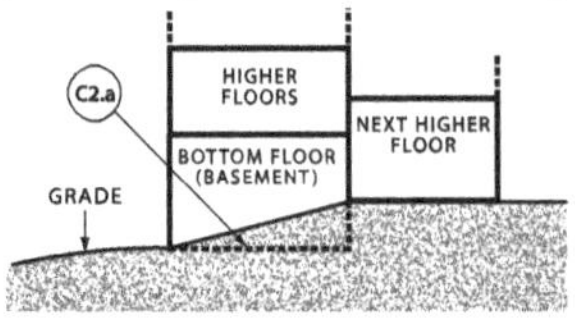


### BUILDING DIAGRAM #4

**Distinguishing Feature:** The bottom floor (basement or underground garage) is below ground level (grade) on all sides.[1]

**Lowest Floor for Rating:** Top of slab (basement floor)

**Elevation Needed for Rating from FEMA EC:** Item C2.a

**All split-level buildings (other than slab-on-grade), either detached or row type (e.g., townhouses); with or without attached garage.**

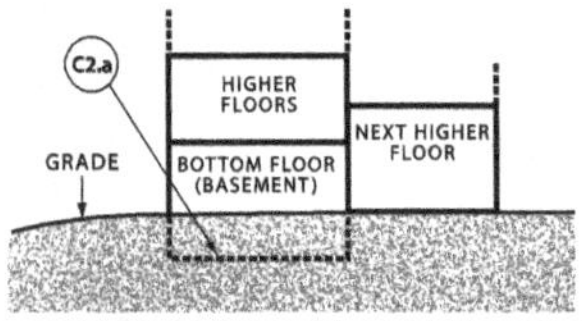


1 A floor that is below ground level (grade) on all sides is considered a basement even if the floor is used for living purposes, or as an office, garage, workshop, etc.

## Lowest Floor Guide for Zones A, AE, A1-A30, AH, AR, AR Dual

### BUILDING DIAGRAM #5

**Distinguishing Feature:** The area below the elevated floor is open, with no obstruction to flow of floodwaters (open lattice work and/or insect screening is permissible).

**Lowest Floor for Rating:** Lowest elevated floor

**Elevation Needed for Rating from FEMA EC:** Item C2.a

**All buildings elevated on piers, posts, piles, columns, or parallel shear walls. No obstructions below the elevated floor.**

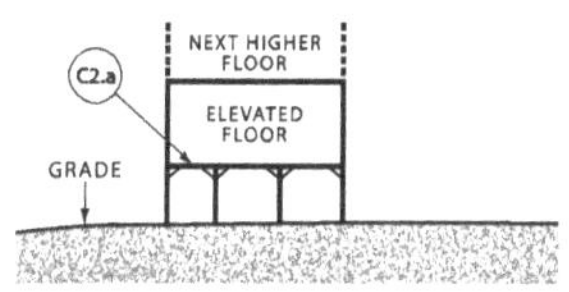


### BUILDING DIAGRAM #6

**Distinguishing Feature:** The area below the elevated floor is enclosed, either partially or fully. In A Zones, the partially or fully enclosed area below the elevated floor is with or without openings[1] present in the walls of the enclosure.

**Lowest Floor for Rating:** Lowest elevated floor or top of bottom floor if conditions in the *FIM* are met

**Elevation Needed for Rating from FEMA EC:** Item C2.a or Item C2.b

**All buildings elevated on piers, posts, piles, columns, or parallel shear walls with full or partial enclosure below the elevated floor.**

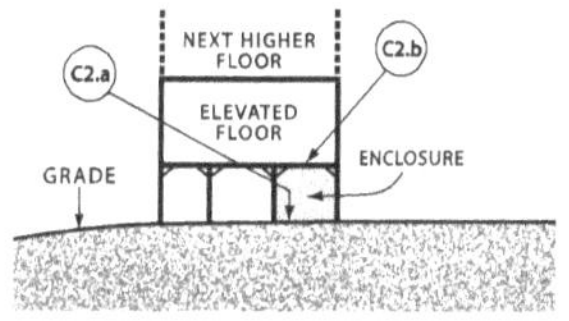


### BUILDING DIAGRAM #7

**Distinguishing Feature:** The area below the elevated floor is enclosed, either partially or fully. In A Zones, the partially or fully enclosed area below the elevated floor is with or without openings[1] present in the walls of the enclosure.

**Lowest Floor for Rating:** Lowest elevated floor or top of bottom floor if conditions in the *FIM* are met

**Elevation Needed for Rating from FEMA EC:** Item C2.a or Item C2.b

**All buildings elevated on full-story foundation walls with a partially or fully enclosed area below the elevated floor. This includes walkout levels, where at least one side is at or above grade. The principal use of this building is located in the elevated floors of the building.**

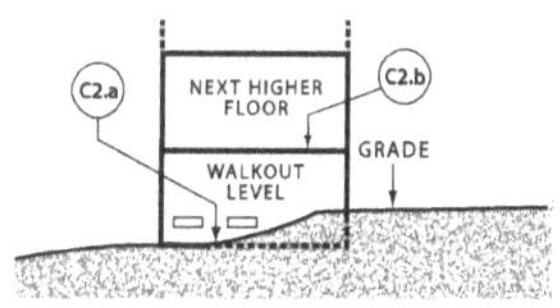


### BUILDING DIAGRAM #8

**Distinguishing Feature:** The area below the first floor is enclosed by solid or partial perimeter walls. In A Zones, the crawlspace is with or without openings[1] present in the walls of the crawlspace.

**Lowest Floor for Rating:** Next higher floor or top of bottom floor if conditions in the *FIM* (Lowest Floor Determination) for A zones are met

**Elevation Needed for Rating from FEMA EC:** Item C2.a or Item C2.b

**All buildings elevated on a crawlspace with the floor of the crawlspace at or above grade on at least one side, with or without attached garage.**

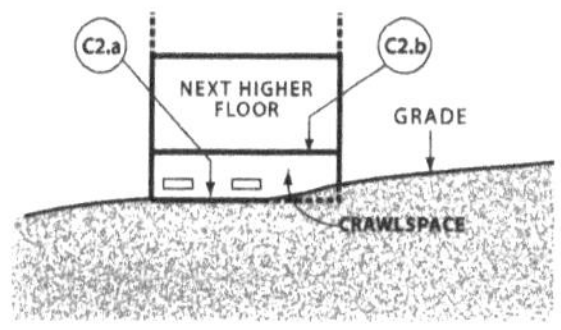


### BUILDING DIAGRAM #9

**Distinguishing Feature:** The bottom (crawlspace) floor is at or below ground level (grade) on all sides.[2] Note: If the distance from the crawlspace floor to the top of the next higher floor is more than 5 feet, or the crawlspace floor is more than 2 feet below the Lowest Adjacent Grade (LAG) on all sides, use Diagram 2.

**Lowest Floor for Rating:** Top of subgrade crawlspace

**Elevation Needed for Rating from FEMA EC:** Item C2.a or Item C2.b

**All buildings (other than split-level) elevated on a subgrade crawlspace with or without attached garage.**

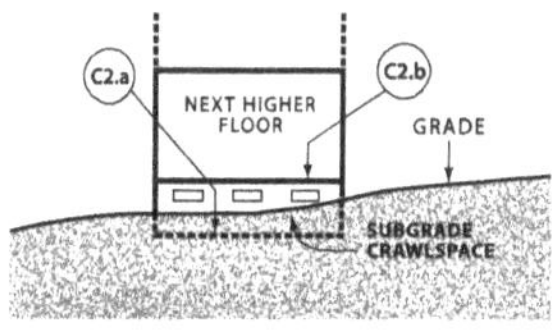


1 An "opening" is a permanent opening that allows for the free passage of water automatically in both directions without human intervention. Under the NFIP, a minimum of two openings is required for enclosures or crawlspaces. The openings shall provide a total net area of not less than 1 square inch for every square foot of area enclosed, excluding any bars, louvers, or other covers of the opening. Alternatively, an Individual Engineered Flood Openings Certification or an Evaluation Report issued by the International Code Council Evaluation Service (ICC ES) must be submitted to document that the design of the openings will allow for the automatic equalization of hydrostatic flood forces on exterior walls. A window, a door, or a garage door is not considered an opening; openings may be installed in doors. Openings shall be on at least two sides of the enclosed area. If a building has more than one enclosed area, each area must have openings to allow floodwater to directly enter. The bottom of the openings must be no higher than 1 foot above the higher of the exterior or interior grade or floor immediately below the opening. For more guidance on openings see NFIP Technical Bulletin 1.

2 A floor that is below ground level (grade) on all sides is considered a basement even if the floor is used for living purposes, or as an office, garage, workshop, etc.

## Lowest Floor Guide for Zones V, VE, V1-V30

### BUILDING DIAGRAM #1A

**Distinguishing Feature:** The bottom floor is at or above ground level (grade) on at least one side.

**Lowest Floor for Rating:** Bottom of slab

**Elevation Needed for Rating from FEMA EC:** Item C2.a[2]

**All slab-on-grade single- and multiple-floor buildings (other than split-level) and high-rise buildings, either detached or row type (e.g., townhouses); with or without attached garage.**

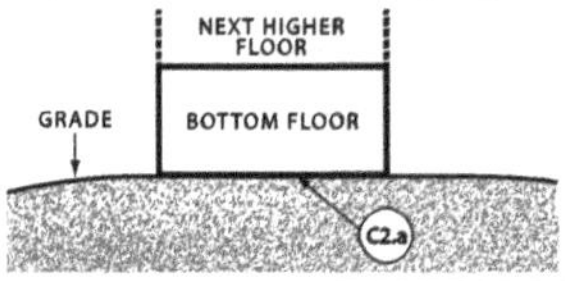


### BUILDING DIAGRAM #1B

**Distinguishing Feature:** The bottom floor is at or above ground level (grade) on at least one side.

**Lowest Floor for Rating:** Bottom of slab

**Elevation Needed for Rating from FEMA EC:** Item C2.a[2]

**All raised slab-on-grade or slab-on-stem-wall-with-fill single- and multiple-floor buildings (other than split-level) and high-rise buildings, either detached or row type (e.g., townhouses); with or without attached garage.**

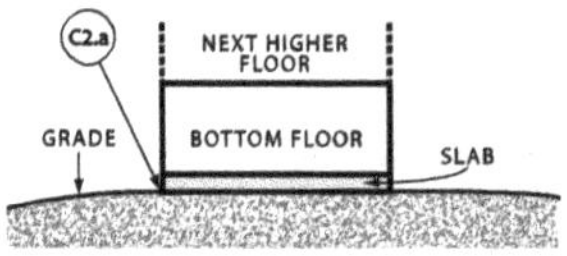


### BUILDING DIAGRAM #2A

**Distinguishing Feature:** The bottom floor (basement or underground garage) is below ground level (grade) on all sides.[1]

**Lowest Floor for Rating:** Bottom of slab (basement floor)

**Elevation Needed for Rating from FEMA EC:** Item C2.a[2]

**All single- and multiple-floor buildings with basement (other than split-level) and high-rise buildings with basement, either detached or row type (e.g., townhouses); with or without attached garage.**

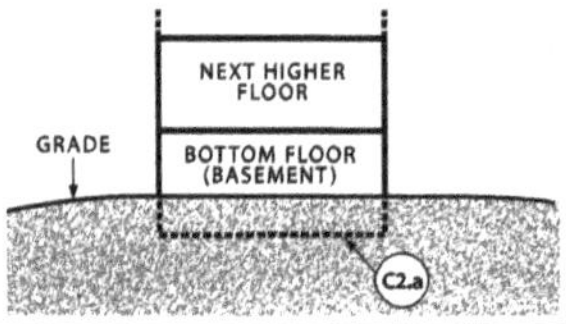


### BUILDING DIAGRAM #2B

**Distinguishing Feature:** The bottom floor (basement or underground garage) is below ground level (grade) on all sides; most of the height of the walls are below ground level on all sides and the door and area of egress is also below ground level on all sides.[1]

**Lowest Floor for Rating:** Bottom of slab (basement floor)

**Elevation Needed for Rating from FEMA EC:** Item C2.a[2]

**All single- and multiple-floor buildings with basement (other than split-level) and high-rise buildings with basement, either detached or row type (e.g., townhouses); with or without attached garage.**

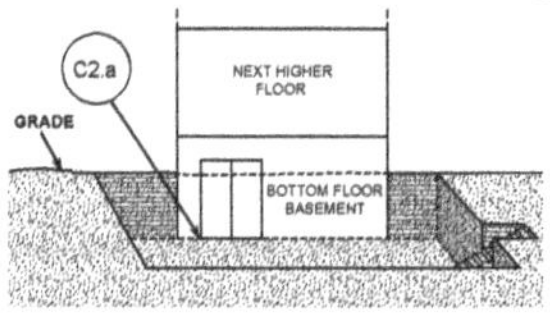


### BUILDING DIAGRAM #3

**Distinguishing Feature:** The bottom floor (excluding garage) is at or above ground level (grade) on at least one side.

**Lowest Floor for Rating:** Bottom of slab (lowest floor)

**Elevation Needed for Rating from FEMA EC:** Item C2.a[2]

**All split-level buildings that are slab-on-grade, either detached or row type (e.g., townhouses); with or without attached garage.**

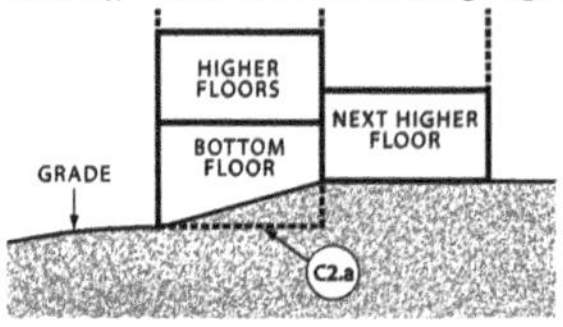


### BUILDING DIAGRAM #4

**Distinguishing Feature:** The bottom floor (basement or underground garage) is below ground level (grade) on all sides. Buildings constructed above crawlspaces that are below grade on all sides should also use this diagram.[1]

**Lowest Floor for Rating:** Bottom of slab (basement floor)

**Elevation Needed for Rating from FEMA EC:** Item C2.a[2]

**All split-level buildings (other than slab-on-grade), either detached or row type (e.g., townhouses); with or without attached garage.**

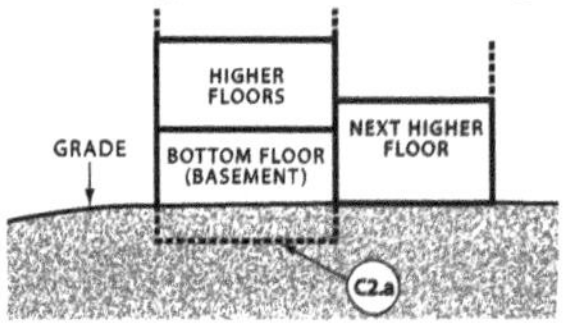


1 A floor that is below ground level (grade) on all sides is considered a basement even if the floor is used for living purposes, or as an office, garage, workshop, etc.

2 Use Item C2.c if available; otherwise subtract 12 inches from Item C2.a for one-to-four family residences. For buildings other than one-to-four family residences subtract 18 inches from Item C2.a.

## Lowest Floor Guide for Zones V, VE, V1-V30

### BUILDING DIAGRAM #5

**Distinguishing Feature:** The area below the elevated floor is open, with no obstruction to flow of floodwaters. Insect screening is permissible, as are wooden or plastic lattice, slats, or shutters if at least 40 percent of their area is open. Maximum thickness is ½ inch for lattice, 1 inch for slats or shutters. Any machinery or equipment below the lowest elevated floor must be at or above the BFE.

**Lowest Floor for Rating:** Bottom of lowest horizontal structural member

**Elevation Needed for Rating from FEMA EC:** Item C2.c.

**All buildings elevated on piers, posts, piles, columns, or parallel shear walls. No obstructions below the elevated floor.**

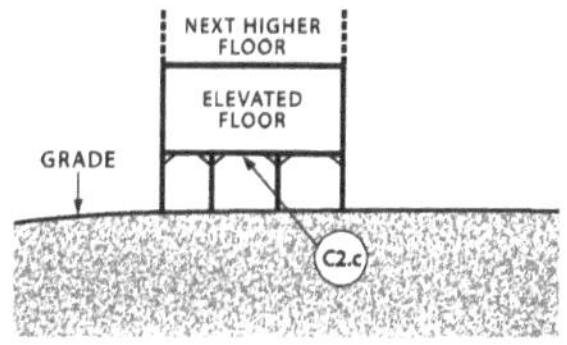


### BUILDING DIAGRAM #6

**Distinguishing Feature:** The area below the elevated floor is enclosed, either partially or fully.

**Lowest Floor for Rating:** Bottom of lowest horizontal structural member, or bottom of slab if conditions in the *Flood Insurance Manual* are met

**Elevation Needed for Rating from FEMA EC:** Item C2.a or Item C2.c.[2]

**All buildings elevated on piers, posts, piles, columns, or parallel shear walls with full or partial enclosure below the elevated floor.**

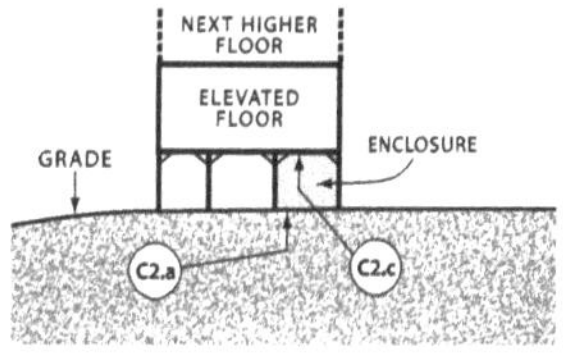


### BUILDING DIAGRAM #7

**Distinguishing Feature:** The area below the elevated floor is enclosed, either partially or fully.

**Lowest Floor for Rating:** Bottom of slab (lowest floor)

**Elevation Needed for Rating from FEMA EC:** Item C2.a.[2]

**All buildings elevated on full-story foundation walls with a partially or fully enclosed area below the elevated floor. This includes walkout levels, where at least one side is at or above grade. The principal use of this building is located in the elevated floors of the building.**

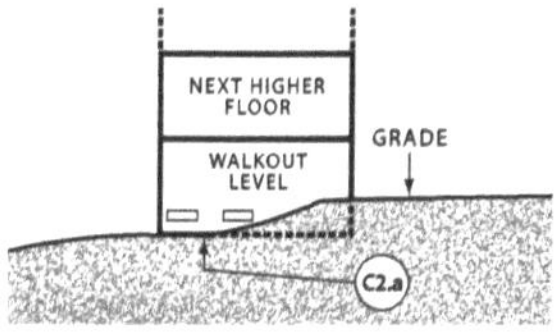


### BUILDING DIAGRAM #8

**Distinguishing Feature:** The area below the first floor is enclosed by solid or partial perimeter walls.

**Lowest Floor for Rating:** Bottom floor

**Elevation Needed for Rating from FEMA EC:** Item C2.a.[2]

**All buildings elevated on a crawlspace with the floor of the crawlspace at or above grade on at least one side, with or without attached garage.**

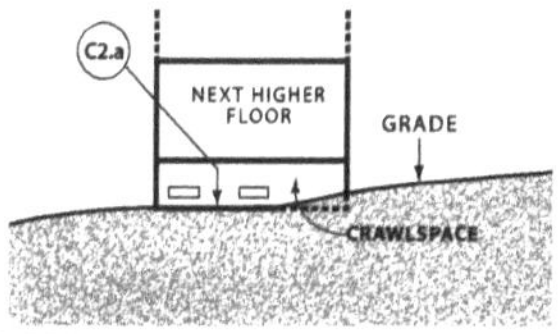


### BUILDING DIAGRAM #9

**Distinguishing Feature:** The bottom (crawlspace) floor is at or below ground level (grade) on all sides.[1] (If the distance from the crawlspace to the top of the next higher floor is more than 5 feet, or the crawlspace floor is more than 2 feet below the grade (LAG) on all sides, use Diagram 2.)

**Lowest Floor for Rating:** Bottom of subgrade crawlspace

**Elevation Needed for Rating from FEMA EC:** Item C2.a. and Item C2.b.

**All buildings (other than split-level) elevated on a subgrade crawlspace with or without attached garage.**

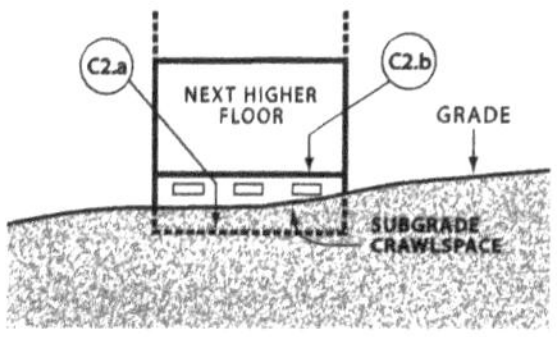


1 A floor that is below ground level (grade) on all sides is considered a basement even if the floor is used for living purposes, or as an office, garage, workshop, etc.

2 Use Item C2.c if available; otherwise subtract 12 inches from Item C2.a for one-to-four family residences. For buildings other than one-to-four family residences subtract 18 inches from Item C2.a.

This page is intentionally left blank.

# I. Specific Building Drawings

## Table of Contents


| SECTION | PAGE |
|---|---|
| Elevated Buildings for Pre- and Post-FIRM Risks in Flood Zones B, C, X, A99, and D (Drawings 1 to 4) | C-8 – C-11 |
| Non-Elevated Buildings for Pre- and Post-FIRM Risks in Flood Zones B, C, X, A99, and D (Drawings 5 to 8) | C-12 – C-15 |
| Elevated Buildings for Pre- and Post-FIRM Risks in Flood Zones A, AO, and AH (Drawings 9 to 15) | C-16 – C-22 |
| Non-Elevated Buildings for Pre- and Post-FIRM Risks in Flood Zones A, AO, and AH (Drawings 16 to 20) | C-23 – C-27 |
| Non-Elevated Buildings for Pre- and Post-FIRM Risks in Flood Zones AE and A1–A30 (Drawings 21 to 29) | C-28 – C-36 |
| Elevated Buildings for Pre- and Post-FIRM Risks in Flood Zones AE and A1–A30 (Drawings 30 to 44) | C-37 – C-51 |
| Non-Elevated Buildings for Pre- and Post-FIRM Risks with Construction Dates of 1975 to September 30, 1981, in Flood Zones VE and V1–V30 (Drawings 45 to 50) | C-52 – C-57 |
| Elevated Buildings for Pre- and Post-FIRM Risks with Construction Dates of 1975 to September 30, 1981, in Flood Zones VE and V1–V30 (Drawings 51 to 63) | C-58 – C-70 |
| Elevated Buildings for Post-FIRM Risks in Flood Zones VE and V1–V30, Construction Date October 1, 1981, and After (Drawings 64 to 75) | C-71 – C-82 |
| Non-Elevated Buildings for Post-FIRM Risks in Flood Zones VE and V1–V30, Construction Date October 1, 1981, and After (Drawing 76) | C-83 |

## ELEVATED BUILDINGS

### 1. Pre- and Post-FIRM Risks In Flood Zones B, C, X, A99, and D

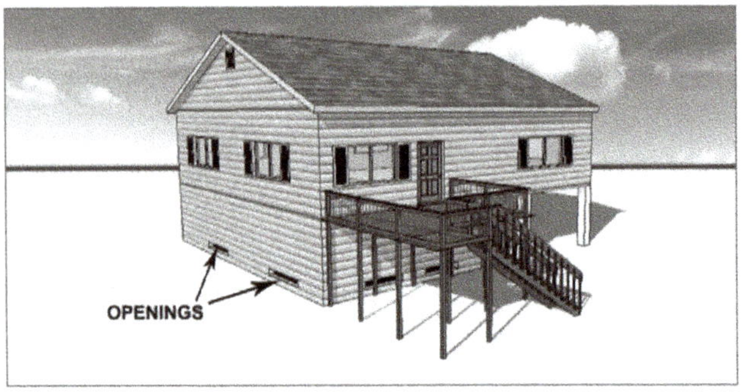


| | |
|---|---|
| **Building Description** | 1 floor with unfinished enclosed area |
| **Elevating Foundation of Building** | Piers, posts, piles, or columns |
| **Type of Enclosure** | Unfinished enclosure<br>With proper openings[3] |
| **Machinery or Equipment Servicing Building** | With or without machinery or equipment below the lowest elevated floor |
| **Lowest Floor for Rating** | No EC required |
| **Application Should Show** | Building type — 1 floor<br>Is building elevated? — Yes<br>Is area below the elevated floor enclosed? — No |
| **Pre-FIRM Rating** | Use Pre-FIRM rate table ***No Basement/Enclosure*** category. |
| **Post-FIRM Rating** | Use Post-FIRM rate table ***No Basement/Enclosure*** category. |

1 LF — Lowest Floor
2 BFE — Base Flood Elevation
3 See Proper Flood Openings Requirement located in the How to Write section for an explanation
4 HAG — Highest Adjacent Grade
5 Pre-FIRM buildings may be rated using Post-FIRM rating, including Submit-for-Rate, if more favorable to the insured
6 Non-elevated buildings with construction dates of October 1, 1981, and after are Submit-for-Rate

NOTE: *Above references may not apply to this page.*

ELEVATED BUILDINGS

## 2. Pre- and Post-FIRM Risks In Flood Zones B, C, X, A99, and D

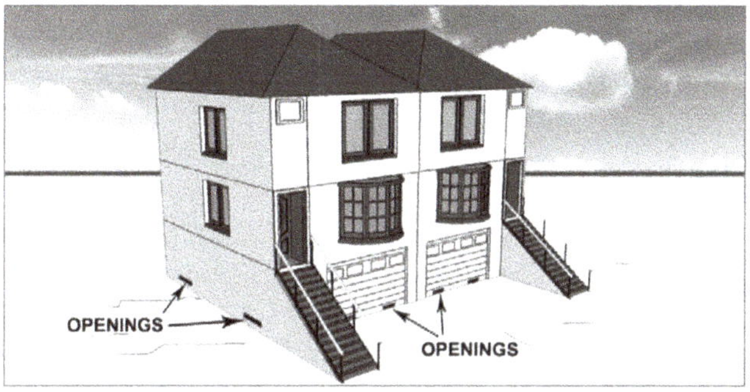


| | |
|---|---|
| **Building Description** | 2 floors with unfinished enclosed area |
| **Elevating Foundation of Building** | Piers, posts, piles, or columns |
| **Type of Enclosure** | Unfinished enclosure<br>With proper openings[3] |
| **Machinery or Equipment Servicing Building** | With or without machinery or equipment below the lowest elevated floor |
| **Lowest Floor for Rating** | No EC required |
| **Application Should Show** | Building type — 2 floors<br>Is building elevated? — Yes<br>Is area below the elevated floor enclosed? — No |
| **Pre-FIRM Rating** | Use Pre-FIRM rate table ***No Basement/Enclosure*** category. |
| **Post-FIRM Rating** | Use Post-FIRM rate table ***No Basement/Enclosure*** category. |

1 LF — Lowest Floor
2 BFE — Base Flood Elevation
3 See Proper Flood Openings Requirement located in the How to Write section for an explanation
4 HAG — Highest Adjacent Grade
5 Pre-FIRM buildings may be rated using Post-FIRM rating, including Submit-for-Rate, if more favorable to the insured
6 Non-elevated buildings with construction dates of October 1, 1981, and after are Submit-for-Rate

NOTE: *Above references may not apply to this page.*

ELEVATED BUILDINGS

## 3. Pre- and Post-FIRM Risks In Flood Zones B, C, X, A99, and D

| | |
|---|---|
| **Building Description** | 2 floors with unfinished enclosed area |
| **Elevating Foundation of Building** | Solid foundation walls |
| **Type of Enclosure** | Unfinished enclosure (garage) and crawlspace<br>No proper openings[3] |
| **Machinery or Equipment Servicing Building** | With or without machinery or equipment below the lowest elevated floor |
| **Lowest Floor for Rating** | No EC required |
| **Application Should Show** | Building type — 3 or more floors<br>Is building elevated? — Yes<br>Is area below the elevated floor enclosed? — Yes |
| **Pre-FIRM Rating** | Use Pre-FIRM rate table ***With Enclosure*** category. |
| **Post-FIRM Rating** | Use Pre-FIRM rate table ***Elevated on Crawlspace*** category. |

1 LF — Lowest Floor
2 BFE — Base Flood Elevation
3 See Proper Flood Openings Requirement located in the How to Write section for an explanation
4 HAG — Highest Adjacent Grade
5 Pre-FIRM buildings may be rated using Post-FIRM rating, including Submit-for-Rate, if more favorable to the insured
6 Non-elevated buildings with construction dates of October 1, 1981, and after are Submit-for-Rate

NOTE: *Above references may not apply to this page.*

## ELEVATED BUILDINGS

## 4. Pre- and Post-FIRM Risks In Flood Zones B, C, X, A99, and D

| | |
|---|---|
| **Building Description** | 1 floor with finished or unfinished enclosed area |
| **Elevating Foundation of Building** | Piers, posts, piles, or columns |
| **Type of Enclosure** | Non-load-bearing walls<br>No proper openings[3] |
| **Machinery or Equipment Servicing Building** | With or without machinery or equipment below the lowest elevated floor |
| **Lowest Floor for Rating** | No EC required |
| **Application Should Show** | Building type — 2 floors<br>Is building elevated? — Yes<br>Is area below the elevated floor enclosed? — Yes |
| **Pre-FIRM Rating** | Use Pre-FIRM rate table ***With Enclosure*** category. |
| **Post-FIRM Rating** | Use Post-FIRM rate table ***With Enclosure*** category. |

1 LF — Lowest Floor
2 BFE — Base Flood Elevation
3 See Proper Flood Openings Requirement located in the How to Write section for an explanation
4 HAG — Highest Adjacent Grade
5 Pre-FIRM buildings may be rated using Post-FIRM rating, including Submit-for-Rate, if more favorable to the insured
6 Non-elevated buildings with construction dates of October 1, 1981, and after are Submit-for-Rate

NOTE: *Above references may not apply to this page.*

NON-ELEVATED BUILDINGS

## 5. Pre- and Post-FIRM Risks In Flood Zones B, C, X, A99, and D

| | |
|---|---|
| **Building Description** | 1 floor on slab |
| **Machinery or Equipment Servicing Building** | N/A |
| **Lowest Floor for Rating** | No EC required |
| **Application Should Show** | Building type — 1 floor<br>Basement — None<br>Is building elevated? — No |
| **Pre-FIRM Rating** | Use Pre-FIRM rate table ***No Basement/Enclosure*** category. |
| **Post-FIRM Rating** | Use Post-FIRM rate table ***No Basement/Enclosure*** category. |

1 LF — Lowest Floor
2 BFE — Base Flood Elevation
3 See Proper Flood Openings Requirement located in the How to Write section for an explanation
4 HAG — Highest Adjacent Grade
5 Pre-FIRM buildings may be rated using Post-FIRM rating, including Submit-for-Rate, if more favorable to the insured
6 Non-elevated buildings with construction dates of October 1, 1981, and after are Submit-for-Rate

NOTE: *Above references may not apply to this page.*

NON-ELEVATED BUILDINGS

## 6. Pre- and Post-FIRM Risks In Flood Zones B, C, X, A99, and D

| | |
|---|---|
| **Building Description** | 3 or more floors on slab |
| **Machinery or Equipment Servicing Building** | N/A |
| **Lowest Floor for Rating** | No EC required |
| **Application Should Show** | Building type — 3 or more floors<br>Basement — None<br>Is building elevated? — No |
| **Pre-FIRM Rating** | Use Pre-FIRM rate table ***No Basement/Enclosure*** category. |
| **Post-FIRM Rating** | Use Post-FIRM rate table ***No Basement/Enclosure*** category. |

1 LF — Lowest Floor
2 BFE — Base Flood Elevation
3 See Proper Flood Openings Requirement located in the How to Write section for an explanation
4 HAG — Highest Adjacent Grade
5 Pre-FIRM buildings may be rated using Post-FIRM rating, including Submit-for-Rate, if more favorable to the insured
6 Non-elevated buildings with construction dates of October 1, 1981, and after are Submit-for-Rate

NOTE: *Above references may not apply to this page.*

## NON-ELEVATED BUILDINGS

# 7. Pre- and Post-FIRM Risks In Flood Zones B, C, X, A99, and D

| | |
|---|---|
| **Building Description** | 2 floors on raised-slab-on-grade or slab-on-stem-wall-with-fill |
| **Machinery or Equipment Servicing Building** | N/A |
| **Lowest Floor for Rating** | No EC required |
| **Application Should Show** | Building type — 2 floors<br>Basement — None<br>Is building elevated? — No |
| **Pre-FIRM Rating** | Use Pre-FIRM rate table ***No Basement/Enclosure*** category. |
| **Post-FIRM Rating** | Use Post-FIRM rate table ***No Basement/Enclosure*** category. |

1 LF — Lowest Floor
2 BFE — Base Flood Elevation
3 See Proper Flood Openings Requirement located in the How to Write section for an explanation
4 HAG — Highest Adjacent Grade
5 Pre-FIRM buildings may be rated using Post-FIRM rating, including Submit-for-Rate, if more favorable to the insured
6 Non-elevated buildings with construction dates of October 1, 1981, and after are Submit-for-Rate

NOTE: *Above references may not apply to this page.*

NON-ELEVATED BUILDINGS

## 8. Pre- and Post-FIRM Risks In Flood Zones B, C, X, A99, and D

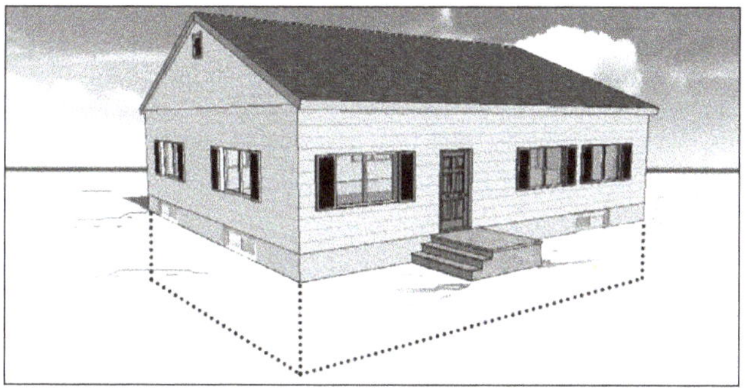

| | |
|---|---|
| **Building Description** | 1 floor with finished or unfinished basement |
| **Machinery or Equipment Servicing Building** | With or without machinery or equipment in basement |
| **Lowest Floor for Rating** | No EC required |
| **Application Should Show** | Building type — 2 floors<br>Basement — Finished or unfinished<br>Is building elevated? — No |
| **Pre-FIRM Rating** | Use Pre-FIRM rate table ***With Basement*** category. |
| **Post-FIRM Rating** | Use Post-FIRM rate table ***With Basement*** category. |

1 LF — Lowest Floor
2 BFE — Base Flood Elevation
3 See Proper Flood Openings Requirement located in the How to Write section for an explanation
4 HAG — Highest Adjacent Grade
5 Pre-FIRM buildings may be rated using Post-FIRM rating, including Submit-for-Rate, if more favorable to the insured
6 Non-elevated buildings with construction dates of October 1, 1981, and after are Submit-for-Rate

NOTE: *Above references may not apply to this page.*

## ELEVATED BUILDINGS

## 9. Pre- and Post-FIRM Risks In Flood Zones A, AO, and AH

| | |
|---|---|
| **Building Description** | 1 floor without enclosed area (see EC, Diagram 5) |
| **Elevating Foundation of Building** | Piers, posts, piles, or columns |
| **Type of Enclosure** | No enclosure |
| **Machinery or Equipment Servicing Building** | None |
| **Lowest Floor for Rating** | Top of lowest elevated floor |
| **Application Should Show** | Building type — 1 floor<br>Is building elevated? — Yes<br>Is area below the elevated floor enclosed? — No |
| **Pre-FIRM Subsidized Rating[5]** | **AO Zone:** Use Pre-FIRM rate table ***No Basement/Enclosure*** category.<br>**AH Zone:** Use Pre-FIRM rate table ***No Basement/Enclosure*** category.<br>**A Zone with BFE[2]:** Use Pre-FIRM rate table ***No Basement/Enclosure*** category.<br>**A Zone without BFE[2]:** Use Pre-FIRM rate table ***No Basement/Enclosure*** category. |
| **Pre-FIRM Full-Risk Rating** (Use Post-FIRM Rate Tables) | **AO Zone:** If difference between LF[1] and HAG[4] is equal to or greater than Base Flood Depth, use ***With Certification of Compliance or Elevation Certificate*** rate. If not, use ***Without Certification of Compliance or Elevation Certificate*** rate.<br>**AH Zone:** If LF[1] elevation is greater than or equal to the BFE[2], use ***With Certification of Compliance or Elevation Certificate*** rate. If not, use ***Without Certification of Compliance or Elevation Certificate*** rate.<br>**A Zone with BFE[2]:** Use Post-FIRM rate table ***With Base Flood Elevation*** category. If LF[1] elevation is 2 or more feet below the BFE[2], submit the Application to the insurer for a rate.<br>**A Zone without BFE[2]:** If difference between the LF[1] and HAG[4] is 1 foot or more, use Post-FIRM rate table ***No Base Flood Elevation*** category. If difference is 0 feet or less, submit the Application to the insurer for a rate. |
| **Post-FIRM Rating** | **AO Zone:** If difference between LF[1] and HAG[4] is equal to or greater than Base Flood Depth, use ***With Certification of Compliance or Elevation Certificate*** rate. If not, use ***Without Certification of Compliance or Elevation Certificate*** rate.<br>**AH Zone:** If LF[1] elevation is greater than or equal to the BFE[2], use ***With Certification of Compliance or Elevation Certificate*** rate. If not, use ***Without Certification of Compliance or Elevation Certificate*** rate.<br>**A Zone with BFE[2]:** Use Post-FIRM rate table ***With Base Flood Elevation*** category. If LF[1] elevation is 2 or more feet below the BFE[2], submit the Application to the insurer for a rate.<br>**A Zone without BFE[2]:** If difference between the LF[1] and HAG[4] is 1 foot or more, use Post-FIRM rate table ***No Base Flood Elevation*** category. If difference is 0 feet or less, submit the Application to the insurer for a rate. |

1 LF — Lowest Floor
2 BFE — Base Flood Elevation
3 See Proper Flood Openings Requirement located in the How to Write section for an explanation
4 HAG — Highest Adjacent Grade
5 Pre-FIRM buildings may be rated using Post-FIRM rating, including Submit-for-Rate, if more favorable to the insured
6 Non-elevated buildings with construction dates of October 1, 1981, and after are Submit-for-Rate

NOTE: *Above references may not apply to this page.*

## ELEVATED BUILDINGS

## 10. Pre- and Post-FIRM Risks In Flood Zones A, AO, and AH

| | |
|---|---|
| **Building Description** | 2 floors, including hanging floor (see EC, Diagram 5) |
| **Elevating Foundation of Building** | Piers, posts, piles, or columns |
| **Type of Enclosure** | No enclosure |
| **Machinery or Equipment Servicing Building** | With or without machinery or equipment below the lowest elevated floor |
| **Lowest Floor for Rating** | Top of lowest elevated floor |
| **Application Should Show** | Building type — 2 floors<br>Is building elevated? — Yes<br>Is area below the elevated floor enclosed? — No |
| **Pre-FIRM Subsidized Rating**[5] | **AO Zone:** Use Pre-FIRM rate table ***No Basement/Enclosure*** category.<br>**AH Zone:** Use Pre-FIRM rate table ***No Basement/Enclosure*** category.<br>**A Zone with BFE**[2]**:** Use Pre-FIRM rate table ***No Basement/Enclosure*** category.<br>**A Zone without BFE**[2]**:** Use Pre-FIRM rate table ***No Basement/Enclosure*** category. |
| **Pre-FIRM Full-Risk Rating** (Use Post-FIRM Rate Tables) | **AO Zone:** If difference between LF[1] and HAG[4] is equal to or greater than Base Flood Depth, use ***With Certification of Compliance or Elevation Certificate*** rate. If not, use ***Without Certification of Compliance or Elevation Certificate*** rate.<br>**AH Zone:** If LF[1] elevation is greater than or equal to the BFE[2], use ***With Certification of Compliance or Elevation Certificate*** rate. If not, use ***Without Certification of Compliance or Elevation Certificate*** rate.<br>**A Zone with BFE**[2]**:** Use Post-FIRM rate table ***With Base Flood Elevation*** category. If LF[1] elevation is 2 or more feet below the BFE[2], submit the Application to the insurer for a rate.<br>**A Zone without BFE**[2]**:** If difference between the LF[1] and HAG[4] is 1 foot or more, use Post-FIRM rate table ***No Base Flood Elevation*** category. If difference is 0 feet or less, submit the Application to the insurer for a rate. |
| **Post-FIRM Rating** | **AO Zone:** If difference between LF[1] and HAG[4] is equal to or greater than Base Flood Depth, use ***With Certification of Compliance or Elevation Certificate*** rate. If not, use ***Without Certification of Compliance or Elevation Certificate*** rate.<br>**AH Zone:** If LF[1] elevation is greater than or equal to the BFE[2], use ***With Certification of Compliance or Elevation Certificate*** rate. If not, use ***Without Certification of Compliance or Elevation Certificate*** rate.<br>**A Zone with BFE**[2]**:** Use Post-FIRM rate table ***With Base Flood Elevation*** category. If LF[1] elevation is 2 or more feet below the BFE[2], submit the Application to the insurer for a rate.<br>**A Zone without BFE**[2]**:** If difference between the LF[1] and HAG[4] is 1 foot or more, use Post-FIRM rate table ***No Base Flood Elevation*** category. If difference is 0 feet or less, submit the Application to the insurer for a rate. |

1 LF — Lowest Floor
2 BFE — Base Flood Elevation
3 See Proper Flood Openings Requirement located in the How to Write section for an explanation
4 HAG — Highest Adjacent Grade
5 Pre-FIRM buildings may be rated using Post-FIRM rating, including Submit-for-Rate, if more favorable to the insured
6 Non-elevated buildings with construction dates of October 1, 1981, and after are Submit-for-Rate

NOTE: *Above references may not apply to this page.*

ELEVATED BUILDINGS

## 11. Pre- and Post-FIRM Risks In Flood Zones A, AO, and AH

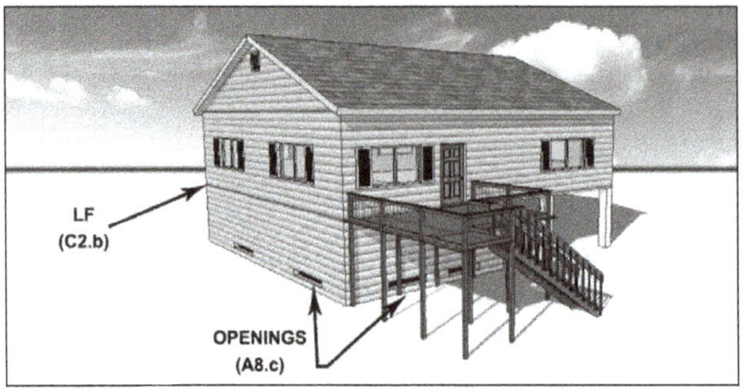


| | |
|---|---|
| **Building Description** | 1 floor with unfinished enclosed area (see EC, Diagram 6) |
| **Elevating Foundation of Building** | Piers, posts, piles, or columns |
| **Type of Enclosure** | Unfinished enclosure<br>With proper openings[3] |
| **Machinery or Equipment Servicing Building** | With or without machinery or equipment below the lowest elevated floor |
| **Lowest Floor for Rating** | Top of next-higher floor (elevated floor) |
| **Application Should Show** | Building type — 1 floor<br>Is building elevated? — Yes<br>Is area below the elevated floor enclosed? — No |
| **Pre-FIRM Subsidized Rating[5]** | **AO Zone:** Use Pre-FIRM rate table ***No Basement/Enclosure*** category.<br>**AH Zone:** Use Pre-FIRM rate table ***No Basement/Enclosure*** category.<br>**A Zone with BFE[2]:** Use Pre-FIRM rate table ***No Basement/Enclosure*** category.<br>**A Zone without BFE[2]:** Use Pre-FIRM rate table ***No Basement/Enclosure*** category. |
| **Pre-FIRM Full-Risk Rating** (Use Post-FIRM Rate Tables) | **AO Zone:** If difference between LF[1] and HAG[4] is equal to or greater than Base Flood Depth, use ***With Certification of Compliance or Elevation Certificate*** rate. If not, use ***Without Certification of Compliance or Elevation Certificate*** rate.<br>**AH Zone:** If LF[1] elevation is greater than or equal to the BFE[2], use ***With Certification of Compliance or Elevation Certificate*** rate. If not, use ***Without Certification of Compliance or Elevation Certificate*** rate.<br>**A Zone with BFE[2]:** Use Post-FIRM rate table ***With Base Flood Elevation*** category. If LF[1] elevation is 2 or more feet below the BFE[2], submit the Application to the insurer for a rate.<br>**A Zone without BFE[2]:** If difference between the LF[1] and HAG[4] is 1 foot or more, use Post-FIRM rate table ***No Base Flood Elevation*** category. If difference is 0 feet or less, submit the Application to the insurer for a rate. |
| **Post-FIRM Rating** | **AO Zone:** If difference between LF[1] and HAG[4] is equal to or greater than Base Flood Depth, use ***With Certification of Compliance or Elevation Certificate*** rate. If not, use ***Without Certification of Compliance or Elevation Certificate*** rate.<br>**AH Zone:** If LF[1] elevation is greater than or equal to the BFE[2], use ***With Certification of Compliance or Elevation Certificate*** rate. If not, use ***Without Certification of Compliance or Elevation Certificate*** rate.<br>**A Zone with BFE[2]:** Use Post-FIRM rate table ***With Base Flood Elevation*** category. If LF[1] elevation is 2 or more feet below the BFE[2], submit the Application to the insurer for a rate.<br>**A Zone without BFE[2]:** If difference between the LF[1] and HAG[4] is 1 foot or more, use Post-FIRM rate table ***No Base Flood Elevation*** category. If the difference is 0 feet or less, submit the Application to the insurer for a rate. |

1 LF — Lowest Floor
2 BFE — Base Flood Elevation
3 See Proper Flood Openings Requirement located in the How to Write section for an explanation
4 HAG — Highest Adjacent Grade
5 Pre-FIRM buildings may be rated using Post-FIRM rating, including Submit-for-Rate, if more favorable to the insured
6 Non-elevated buildings with construction dates of October 1, 1981, and after are Submit-for-Rate

NOTE: *Above references may not apply to this page.*

ELEVATED BUILDINGS

## 12. Pre- and Post-FIRM Risks In Flood Zones A, AO, and AH

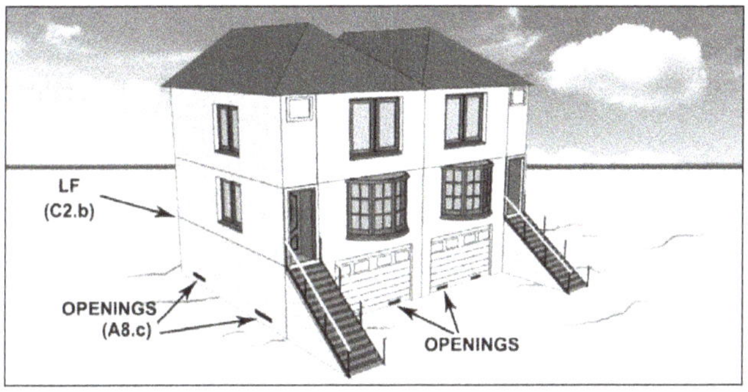


| | |
|---|---|
| **Building Description** | 2 floors with unfinished enclosed area (see EC, Diagram 6) |
| **Elevating Foundation of Building** | Piers, posts, piles, or columns |
| **Type of Enclosure** | Unfinished enclosure<br>With proper openings[3] |
| **Machinery or Equipment Servicing Building** | With or without machinery or equipment below the lowest elevated floor |
| **Lowest Floor for Rating** | Lowest elevated floor |
| **Application Should Show** | Building type — 2 floors<br>Is building elevated? — Yes<br>Is area below the elevated floor enclosed? — No |
| **Pre-FIRM Subsidized Rating**[5] | **AO Zone:** Use Pre-FIRM rate table ***No Basement/Enclosure*** category.<br>**AH Zone:** Use Pre-FIRM rate table ***No Basement/Enclosure*** category.<br>**A Zone with BFE**[2]**:** Use Pre-FIRM rate table ***No Basement/Enclosure*** category.<br>**A Zone without BFE**[2]**:** Use Post-FIRM rate table ***No Basement/Enclosure*** category. |
| **Pre-FIRM Full-Risk Rating** (Use Post-FIRM Rate Tables) | **AO Zone:** If difference between LF[1] and HAG[4] is equal to or greater than Base Flood Depth, use ***With Certification of Compliance or Elevation Certificate*** rate. If not, use ***Without Certification of Compliance or Elevation Certificate*** rate.<br>**AH Zone:** If LF[1] elevation is greater than or equal to the BFE[2], use ***With Certification of Compliance or Elevation Certificate*** rate. If not, use ***Without Certification of Compliance or Elevation Certificate*** rate.<br>**A Zone with BFE**[2]**:** Use Post-FIRM rate table ***With Base Flood Elevation*** category. If LF[1] elevation is 2 or more feet below the BFE[2], submit the Application to the insurer for a rate.<br>**A Zone without BFE**[2]**:** If difference between the LF[1] and HAG[4] is 1 foot or more, use Post-FIRM rate table ***No Base Flood Elevation*** category. If difference is 0 feet or less, submit the Application to the insurer for a rate. |
| **Post-FIRM Rating** | **AO Zone:** If difference between LF[1] and HAG[4] is equal to or greater than Base Flood Depth, use ***With Certification of Compliance or Elevation Certificate*** rate. If not, use ***Without Certification of Compliance or Elevation Certificate*** rate.<br>**AH Zone:** If LF[1] elevation is greater than or equal to the BFE[2], use ***With Certification of Compliance or Elevation Certificate*** rate. If not, use ***Without Certification of Compliance or Elevation Certificate*** rate.<br>**A Zone with BFE**[2]**:** Use Post-FIRM rate table ***With Base Flood Elevation*** category. If LF[1] elevation is 2 or more feet below the BFE[2], submit the Application to the insurer for a rate.<br>**A Zone without BFE**[2]**:** If difference between the LF[1] and HAG[4] is 1 foot or more, use Post-FIRM rate table ***No Base Flood Elevation*** category. If the difference is 0 feet or less, submit the Application to the insurer for a rate. |

1 LF — Lowest Floor
2 BFE — Base Flood Elevation
3 See Proper Flood Openings Requirement located in the How to Write section for an explanation
4 HAG — Highest Adjacent Grade
5 Pre-FIRM buildings may be rated using Post-FIRM rating, including Submit-for-Rate, if more favorable to the insured
6 Non-elevated buildings with construction dates of October 1, 1981, and after are Submit-for-Rate

NOTE: *Above references may not apply to this page.*

## ELEVATED BUILDINGS

## 13. Pre- and Post-FIRM Risks In Flood Zones A, AO, and AH

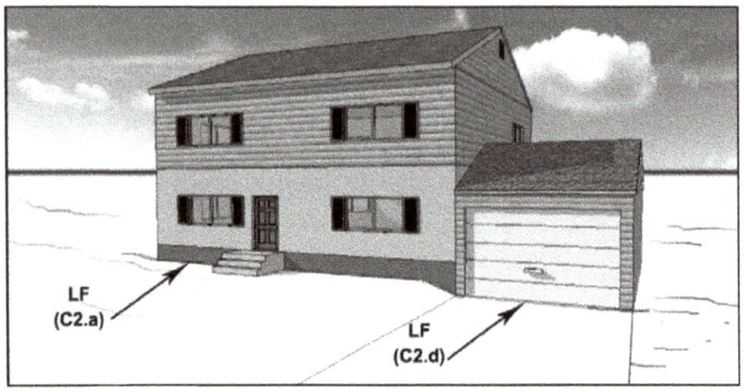


| | |
|---|---|
| **Building Description** | 2 floors with unfinished enclosed area (see EC, Diagram 8) |
| **Elevating Foundation of Building** | Solid foundation walls |
| **Type of Enclosure** | Unfinished enclosure (garage) and crawlspace<br>No openings |
| **Machinery or Equipment Servicing Building** | With or without machinery or equipment below the lowest elevated floor |
| **Lowest Floor for Rating** | Top of bottom floor (lower of crawlspace or garage) |
| **Application Should Show** | Building type — 3 or more floors<br>Is building elevated? — Yes<br>Is area below the elevated floor enclosed? — Yes |
| **Pre-FIRM Subsidized Rating**[5] | **AO Zone:** Use Pre-FIRM rate table ***Elevated on Crawlspace*** category.<br>**AH Zone:** Use Pre-FIRM rate table ***Elevated on Crawlspace*** category.<br>**A Zone:** Use Pre-FIRM rate table ***Elevated on Crawlspace*** category. |
| **Pre-FIRM Full-Risk Rating** (Use Post-FIRM Rate Tables) | Submit the Application to the insurer for a rate. |
| **Post-FIRM Rating** | Submit the Application to the insurer for a rate. |

1 LF — Lowest Floor
2 BFE — Base Flood Elevation
3 See Proper Flood Openings Requirement located in the How to Write section for an explanation
4 HAG — Highest Adjacent Grade
5 Pre-FIRM buildings may be rated using Post-FIRM rating, including Submit-for-Rate, if more favorable to the insured
6 Non-elevated buildings with construction dates of October 1, 1981, and after are Submit-for-Rate

NOTE: *Above references may not apply to this page.*

ELEVATED BUILDINGS

## 14. Pre- and Post-FIRM Risks In Flood Zones A, AO, and AH

| | |
|---|---|
| **Building Description** | 1 floor with finished or unfinished enclosed area (see EC, Diagram 6) |
| **Elevating Foundation of Building** | Piers, posts, piles, or columns |
| **Type of Enclosure** | Unfinished enclosure<br>Non-load-bearing walls<br>No openings |
| **Machinery or Equipment Servicing Building** | With or without machinery or equipment below the lowest elevated floor |
| **Lowest Floor for Rating** | Top of bottom floor (including basement or enclosure) |
| **Application Should Show** | Building type — 2 floors<br>Is building elevated? — Yes<br>Is area below the elevated floor enclosed? — Yes |
| **Pre-FIRM Subsidized Rating**[5] | **AO Zone:** Use Pre-FIRM rate table ***With Enclosure*** category.<br>**AH Zone:** Use Pre FIRM rate table ***With Enclosure*** category.<br>**A Zone:** Use Pre-FIRM rate table ***With Enclosure*** category. |
| **Pre-FIRM Full-Risk Rating** (Use Post-FIRM Rate Tables) | Submit the Application to the insurer for a rate. |
| **Post-FIRM Rating** | Submit the Application to the insurer for a rate. |

1 LF — Lowest Floor
2 BFE — Base Flood Elevation
3 See Proper Flood Openings Requirement located in the How to Write section for an explanation
4 HAG — Highest Adjacent Grade
5 Pre-FIRM buildings may be rated using Post-FIRM rating, including Submit-for-Rate, if more favorable to the insured
6 Non-elevated buildings with construction dates of October 1, 1981, and after are Submit-for-Rate

NOTE: *Above references may not apply to this page.*

## ELEVATED BUILDINGS

## 15. Pre- and Post-FIRM Risks in Flood Zones A, AO, and AH

| | |
|---|---|
| **Building Description** | Mobile home without enclosed area (see EC, Diagram 5) |
| **Elevating Foundation of Building** | Piers, posts, piles, or columns |
| **Type of Enclosure** | Vinyl or aluminum skirting |
| **Machinery or Equipment Servicing Building** | With or without machinery or equipment below the lowest elevated floor |
| **Lowest Floor for Rating** | Top of lowest elevated floor |
| **Application Should Show** | Building type — Mobile home<br>Is building elevated? — Yes<br>Is area below the elevated floor enclosed? — No |
| **Pre-FIRM Subsidized Rating[5]** | **AO Zone:** Use Pre-FIRM rate table ***Manufactured (Mobile) Home*** category.<br>**AH Zone:** Use Pre-FIRM rate table ***Manufactured (Mobile) Home*** category.<br>**A Zone with BFE[2]:** Use Pre-FIRM rate table ***No Basement/Enclosure*** category.<br>**A Zone without BFE[2]:** Use Pre-FIRM rate table ***No Basement/Enclosure*** category. |
| **Pre-FIRM Full-Risk Rating** (Use Post-FIRM Rate Tables) | **AO Zone:** If difference between LF[1] and HAG[4] is equal to or greater than Base Flood Depth, use ***With Certification of Compliance or Elevation Certificate*** rate. If not, use ***Without Certification of Compliance or Elevation Certificate*** rate.<br>**AH Zone:** If LF[1] elevation is greater than or equal to the BFE[2], use ***With Certification of Compliance or Elevation Certificate*** rate. If not, use ***Without Certification of Compliance or Elevation Certificate*** rate.<br>**A Zone with BFE[2]:** Use Post-FIRM rate table ***With Base Flood Elevation*** category. If LF[1] elevation is 2 or more feet below the BFE[2], submit the Application to the insurer for a rate.<br>**A Zone without BFE[2]:** If difference between the LF[1] and HAG[4] is 1 foot or more, use Post-FIRM rate table ***No Base Flood Elevation*** category. If difference is 0 feet or less, submit the Application to the insurer for a rate. |
| **Post-FIRM Rating** | **AO Zone:** If difference between LF[1] and HAG[4] is equal to or greater than Base Flood Depth, use ***With Certification of Compliance or Elevation Certificate*** rate. If not, use ***Without Certification of Compliance or Elevation Certificate*** rate.<br>**AH Zone:** If LF[1] elevation is greater than or equal to the BFE[2], use ***With Certification of Compliance or Elevation Certificate*** rate. If not, use ***Without Certification of Compliance or Elevation Certificate*** rate.<br>**A Zone with BFE[2]:** Use Post-FIRM rate table ***With Base Flood Elevation*** category. If LF[1] elevation is 2 or more feet below the BFE[2], submit the Application to the insurer for a rate.<br>**A Zone without BFE[2]:** If difference between the LF[1] and HAG[4] is 1 foot or more, use Post-FIRM rate table ***No Base Flood Elevation*** category. If difference is 0 feet or less, submit the Application to the insurer for a rate. |

1 LF — Lowest Floor
2 BFE — Base Flood Elevation
3 See Proper Flood Openings Requirement located in the How to Write section for an explanation
4 HAG — Highest Adjacent Grade
5 Pre-FIRM buildings may be rated using Post-FIRM rating, including Submit-for-Rate, if more favorable to the insured
6 Non-elevated buildings with construction dates of October 1, 1981, and after are Submit-for-Rate

NOTE: *Above references may not apply to this page.*

NON-ELEVATED BUILDINGS

## 16. Pre- and Post-FIRM Risks In Flood Zones A, AO, and AH

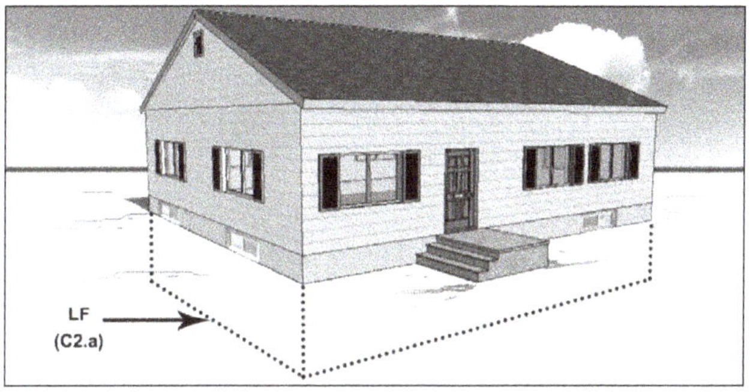


| | |
|---|---|
| **Building Description** | 1 floor with finished or unfinished basement (see EC, Diagram 2A) |
| **Machinery or Equipment Servicing Building** | With or without machinery or equipment in the basement |
| **Lowest Floor for Rating** | Top of bottom floor (including basement) |
| **Application Should Show** | Building type — 2 floors<br>Basement — Finished or unfinished<br>Is building elevated? — No |
| **Pre-FIRM Subsidized Rating**[5] | **AO Zone:** Use Pre-FIRM rate table ***With Basement*** category.<br>**AH Zone:** Use Pre-FIRM rate table ***With Basement*** category.<br>**A Zone:** Use Pre-FIRM rate table ***With Basement*** category. |
| **Pre-FIRM Full-Risk Rating** (Use Post-FIRM Rate Tables) | Submit the Application to the insurer for a rate. |
| **Post-FIRM Rating** | Submit the Application to the insurer for a rate. |

1 LF — Lowest Floor
2 BFE — Base Flood Elevation
3 See Proper Flood Openings Requirement located in the How to Write section for an explanation
4 HAG — Highest Adjacent Grade
5 Pre-FIRM buildings may be rated using Post-FIRM rating, including Submit-for-Rate, if more favorable to the insured
6 Non-elevated buildings with construction dates of October 1, 1981, and after are Submit-for-Rate

NOTE: *Above references may not apply to this page.*

## NON-ELEVATED BUILDINGS

## 17. Pre- and Post-FIRM Risks In Flood Zones A, AO, and AH

| | |
|---|---|
| **Building Description** | 1 floor on slab (see EC, Diagram 1A) |
| **Machinery or Equipment Servicing Building** | N/A |
| **Lowest Floor for Rating** | Top of bottom floor |
| **Application Should Show** | Building type — 1 floor<br>Basement — None<br>Is building elevated? — No |
| **Pre-FIRM Subsidized Rating**[5] | **AO Zone:** Use Pre-FIRM rate table ***No Basement/Enclosure*** category.<br>**AH Zone:** Use Pre-FIRM rate table ***No Basement/Enclosure*** category.<br>**A Zone with BFE**[2]**:** Use Pre-FIRM rate table ***No Basement/Enclosure*** category.<br>**A Zone without BFE**[2]**:** Use Pre-FIRM rate table ***No Basement/Enclosure*** category. |
| **Pre-FIRM Full-Risk Rating** (Use Post-FIRM Rate Tables) | **AO Zone:** If difference between LF[1] and HAG[4] is equal to or greater than Base Flood Depth, use ***With Certification of Compliance or Elevation Certificate*** rate. If not, use ***Without Certification of Compliance or Elevation Certificate*** rate.<br>**AH Zone:** If LF[1] elevation is greater than or equal to the BFE[2], use ***With Certification of Compliance or Elevation Certificate*** rate. If not, use ***Without Certification of Compliance or Elevation Certificate*** rate.<br>**A Zone with BFE**[2]**:** Use Post-FIRM rate table ***With Base Flood Elevation*** category. If LF[1] elevation is 2 or more feet below the BFE[2], submit the Application to the insurer for a rate.<br>**A Zone without BFE**[2]**:** If difference between the LF[1] and HAG[4] is 1 foot or more, use Post-FIRM rate table ***No Base Flood Elevation*** category. If difference is 0 feet or less, submit the Application to the insurer for a rate. |
| **Post-FIRM Rating** | **AO Zone:** If difference between LF[1] and HAG[4] is equal to or greater than Base Flood Depth, use ***With Certification of Compliance or Elevation Certificate*** rate. If not, use ***Without Certification of Compliance or Elevation Certificate*** rate.<br>**AH Zone:** If LF[1] elevation is greater than or equal to the BFE[2], use ***With Certification of Compliance or Elevation Certificate*** rate. If not, use ***Without Certification of Compliance or Elevation Certificate*** rate.<br>**A Zone with BFE**[2]**:** Use Post-FIRM rate table ***With Base Flood Elevation*** category. If LF[1] elevation is 2 or more feet below the BFE[2], submit the Application to the insurer for a rate.<br>**A Zone without BFE**[2]**:** If difference between the LF[1] and HAG[4] is 1 foot or more, use Post-FIRM rate table ***No Base Flood Elevation*** category. If difference is 0 feet or less, submit the Application to the insurer for a rate. |

1 LF — Lowest Floor
2 BFE — Base Flood Elevation
3 See Proper Flood Openings Requirement located in the How to Write section for an explanation
4 HAG — Highest Adjacent Grade
5 Pre-FIRM buildings may be rated using Post-FIRM rating, including Submit-for-Rate, if more favorable to the insured
6 Non-elevated buildings with construction dates of October 1, 1981, and after are Submit-for-Rate

NOTE: *Above references may not apply to this page.*

## NON-ELEVATED BUILDINGS

## 18. Pre- and Post-FIRM Risks In Flood Zones A, AO, and AH

| | |
|---|---|
| **Building Description** | 3 or more floors on slab (see EC, Diagram 1A) |
| **Machinery or Equipment Servicing Building** | N/A |
| **Lowest Floor for Rating** | Top of bottom floor |
| **Application Should Show** | Building type — 3 or more floors<br>Basement — None<br>Is building elevated? — No |
| **Pre-FIRM Subsidized Rating**[5] | **AO Zone:** Use Pre-FIRM rate table ***No Basement/Enclosure*** category.<br>**AH Zone:** Use Pre-FIRM rate table ***No Basement/Enclosure*** category.<br>**A Zone with BFE**[2]**:** Use Pre-FIRM rate table ***No Basement/Enclosure*** category.<br>**A Zone without BFE**[2]**:** Use Pre-FIRM rate table ***No Basement/Enclosure*** category. |
| **Pre-FIRM Full-Risk Rating** (Use Post-FIRM Rate Tables) | **AO Zone:** If difference between LF[1] and HAG[4] is equal to or greater than Base Flood Depth, use ***With Certification of Compliance or Elevation Certificate*** rate. If not, use ***Without Certification of Compliance or Elevation Certificate*** rate.<br>**AH Zone:** If LF[1] elevation is greater than or equal to the BFE[2], use ***With Certification of Compliance or Elevation Certificate*** rate. If not, use ***Without Certification of Compliance or Elevation Certificate*** rate.<br>**A Zone with BFE**[2]**:** Use Post-FIRM rate table ***No Base Flood Elevation*** category. If LF[1] elevation is 2 or more feet below the BFE[2], submit the Application to the insurer for a rate.<br>**A Zone without BFE**[2]**:** If difference between the LF[1] and HAG[4] is 1 foot or more, use Post-FIRM rate table ***With Base Flood Elevation*** category. If difference is 0 feet or less, submit the Application to the insurer for a rate. |
| **Post-FIRM Rating** | **AO Zone:** If difference between LF[1] and HAG[4] is equal to or greater than Base Flood Depth, use ***With Certification of Compliance or Elevation Certificate*** rate. If not, use ***Without Certification of Compliance or Elevation Certificate*** rate.<br>**AH Zone:** If LF[1] elevation is greater than or equal to the BFE[2], use ***With Certification of Compliance or Elevation Certificate*** rate. If not, use ***Without Certification of Compliance or Elevation Certificate*** rate.<br>**A Zone with BFE**[2]**:** Use Post-FIRM rate table ***No Base Flood Elevation*** category. If LF[1] elevation is 2 or more feet below the BFE[2], submit the Application to the insurer for a rate.<br>**A Zone without BFE**[2]**:** If difference between the LF[1] and HAG[4] is 1 foot or more, use Post-FIRM rate table ***With Base Flood Elevation*** category. If difference is 0 feet or less, submit the Application to the insurer for a rate. |

1 LF — Lowest Floor
2 BFE — Base Flood Elevation
3 See Proper Flood Openings Requirement located in the How to Write section for an explanation
4 HAG — Highest Adjacent Grade
5 Pre-FIRM buildings may be rated using Post-FIRM rating, including Submit-for-Rate, if more favorable to the insured
6 Non-elevated buildings with construction dates of October 1, 1981, and after are Submit-for-Rate

NOTE: *Above references may not apply to this page.*

## NON-ELEVATED BUILDINGS

## 19. Pre- and Post-FIRM Risks In Flood Zones A, AO, and AH

| | |
|---|---|
| **Building Description** | 2 floors on raised-slab-on-grade or slab-on-stem-wall-with-fill (see EC, Diagram 1B) |
| **Machinery or Equipment Servicing Building** | N/A |
| **Lowest Floor for Rating** | Top of bottom floor |
| **Application Should Show** | Building type — 2 floors<br>Basement — None<br>Is building elevated? — No |
| **Pre-FIRM Subsidized Rating**[5] | **AO Zone:** Use Pre-FIRM rate table ***No Basement/Enclosure*** category.<br>**AH Zone:** Use Pre-FIRM rate table ***No Basement/Enclosure*** category.<br>**A Zone with BFE**[2]**:** Use Pre-FIRM rate table ***No Basement/Enclosure*** category.<br>**A Zone without BFE**[2]**:** Use Pre-FIRM rate table ***No Basement/Enclosure*** category. |
| **Pre-FIRM Full-Risk Rating** (Use Post-FIRM Rate Tables) | **AO Zone:** If difference between LF[1] and HAG[4] is equal to or greater than Base Flood Depth, use ***With Certification of Compliance or Elevation Certificate*** rate. If not, use ***Without Certification of Compliance or Elevation Certificate*** rate.<br>**AH Zone:** If LF[1] elevation is greater than or equal to the BFE[2], use ***With Certification of Compliance or Elevation Certificate*** rate. If not, use ***Without Certification of Compliance or Elevation Certificate*** rate.<br>**A Zone with BFE**[2]**:** Use Post-FIRM rate table ***No Base Flood Elevation*** category. If LF[1] elevation is 2 or more feet below the BFE[2], submit the Application to the insurer for a rate.<br>**A Zone without BFE**[2]**:** If difference between the LF[1] and HAG[4] is 1 foot or more, use Post-FIRM rate table ***With Base Flood Elevation*** category. If difference is 0 feet or less, submit the Application to the insurer for a rate. |
| **Post-FIRM Rating** | **AO Zone:** If difference between LF[1] and HAG[4] is equal to or greater than Base Flood Depth, use ***With Certification of Compliance or Elevation Certificate*** rate. If not, use ***Without Certification of Compliance or Elevation Certificate*** rate.<br>**AH Zone:** If LF[1] elevation is greater than or equal to the BFE[2], use ***With Certification of Compliance or Elevation Certificate*** rate. If not, use ***Without Certification of Compliance or Elevation Certificate*** rate.<br>**A Zone with BFE**[2]**:** Use Post-FIRM rate table ***No Base Flood Elevation*** category. If LF[1] elevation is 2 or more feet below the BFE[2], submit the Application to the insurer for a rate.<br>**A Zone without BFE**[2]**:** If difference between the LF[1] and HAG[4] is 1 foot or more, use Post-FIRM rate table ***With Base Flood Elevation*** category. If difference is 0 feet or less, submit the Application to the insurer for a rate. |

1 LF — Lowest Floor
2 BFE — Base Flood Elevation
3 See Proper Flood Openings Requirement located in the How to Write section for an explanation
4 HAG — Highest Adjacent Grade
5 Pre-FIRM buildings may be rated using Post-FIRM rating, including Submit-for-Rate, if more favorable to the insured
6 Non-elevated buildings with construction dates of October 1, 1981, and after are Submit-for-Rate

NOTE: *Above references may not apply to this page.*

NON-ELEVATED BUILDINGS

## 20. Pre- and Post-FIRM Risks In Flood Zones A, AO, and AH

| | |
|---|---|
| **Building Description** | 2 floors on slab with attached garage (see EC, Diagram 1A) |
| **Machinery or Equipment Servicing Building** | Machinery or equipment in garage |
| **Lowest Floor for Rating** | If attached garage has no proper openings[3], and has machinery or equipment below the BFE[2], use the garage floor for rating. Otherwise, use the top of the finished floor for rating. |
| **Application Should Show** | Building type — 2 floors<br>Basement — None<br>Is building elevated? — No |
| **Pre-FIRM Subsidized Rating[6]** | **AO Zone:** Use Pre-FIRM rate table ***No Basement/Enclosure*** category.<br>**AH Zone:** Use Pre-FIRM rate table ***No Basement/Enclosure*** category.<br>**A Zone with BFE[2]:** Use Pre-FIRM rate table ***No Basement/Enclosure*** category.<br>**A Zone without BFE[2]:** Use Pre-FIRM rate table ***No Basement/Enclosure*** category. |
| **Pre-FIRM Full-Risk Rating** (Use Post-FIRM Rate Tables) | **AO Zone**: If difference between LF[1] and HAG[4] is equal to or greater than Base Flood Depth, use ***With Certification of Compliance or Elevation Certificate*** rate. If not, use ***Without Certification of Compliance or Elevation Certificate*** rate.<br>**AH Zone:** If LF[1] elevation is greater than or equal to the BFE[2], use ***With Certification of Compliance or Elevation Certificate*** rate. If not, use ***Without Certification of Compliance or Elevation Certificate*** rate.<br>**A Zone with BFE[2]**: Use Post-FIRM rate table ***With Base Flood Elevation*** category. If LF[1] elevation is 2 or more feet below the BFE[2], submit the Application to the insurer for a rate.<br>**A Zone without BFE[2]**: If difference between the LF[1] and HAG[4] is 1 foot or more, use Post-FIRM rate table ***No Base Flood Elevation*** category. If difference is 0 feet or less, submit the Application to the insurer for a rate. |
| **Post-FIRM Rating** | **AO Zone**: If difference between LF[1] and HAG[4] is equal to or greater than Base Flood Depth, use ***With Certification of Compliance or Elevation Certificate*** rate. If not, use ***Without Certification of Compliance or Elevation Certificate*** rate.<br>**AH Zone:** If LF[1] elevation is greater than or equal to the BFE[2], use ***With Certification of Compliance or Elevation Certificate*** rate. If not, use ***Without Certification of Compliance or Elevation Certificate*** rate.<br>**A Zone with BFE[2]**: Use Post-FIRM rate table ***With Base Flood Elevation*** category. If LF[1] elevation is 2 or more feet below the BFE[2], submit the Application to the insurer for a rate.<br>**A Zone without BFE[2]**: If difference between the LF[1] and HAG[4] is 1 foot or more, use Post-FIRM rate table ***No Base Flood Elevation*** category. If difference is 0 feet or less, submit the Application to the insurer for a rate. |

1 LF — Lowest Floor
2 BFE — Base Flood Elevation
3 See Proper Flood Openings Requirement located in the How to Write section for an explanation
4 HAG — Highest Adjacent Grade
5 Pre-FIRM buildings may be rated using Post-FIRM rating, including Submit-for-Rate, if more favorable to the insured
6 Non-elevated buildings with construction dates of October 1, 1981, and after are Submit-for-Rate

NOTE: *Above references may not apply to this page.*

NON-ELEVATED BUILDINGS

## 21. Pre- and Post-FIRM Risks In Flood Zones AE and A1–A30

| | |
|---|---|
| **Building Description** | 1 floor on slab (see EC, Diagram 1A) |
| **Machinery or Equipment Servicing Building** | N/A |
| **Lowest Floor for Rating** | Top of bottom floor |
| **Application Should Show** | Building type — 1 floor<br>Basement — None<br>Is building elevated? — No |
| **Pre-FIRM Subsidized Rating**[5] | Use Pre-FIRM rate table ***No Basement/Enclosure*** category. |
| **Pre-FIRM Full-Risk Rating** (Use Post-FIRM Rate Tables) | Use Post-FIRM rate table ***1 Floor No Basement/Enclosure/Crawlspace*** category. If LF[1] elevation is 2 or more feet below the BFE[2], submit the Application to the insurer for a rate. |
| **Post-FIRM Rating** | Use Post-FIRM rate table ***1 Floor No Basement/Enclosure/Crawlspace*** category. If LF[1] elevation is 2 or more feet below the BFE[2], submit the Application to the insurer for a rate. |

1 LF — Lowest Floor
2 BFE — Base Flood Elevation
3 See Proper Flood Openings Requirement located in the How to Write section for an explanation
4 HAG — Highest Adjacent Grade
5 Pre-FIRM buildings may be rated using Post-FIRM rating, including Submit-for-Rate, if more favorable to the insured
6 Non-elevated buildings with construction dates of October 1, 1981, and after are Submit-for-Rate

NOTE: *Above references may not apply to this page.*

NON-ELEVATED BUILDINGS

## 22. Pre- and Post-FIRM Risks In Flood Zones AE and A1–A30

| | |
|---|---|
| **Building Description** | 3 or more floors on slab (see EC, Diagram 1A) |
| **Machinery or Equipment Servicing Building** | N/A |
| **Lowest Floor for Rating** | Top of bottom floor |
| **Application Should Show** | Building type — 3 or more floors<br>Basement — None<br>Is building elevated? — No |
| **Pre-FIRM Subsidized Rating5** | Use Pre-FIRM rate table ***No Basement/Enclosure*** category. |
| **Pre-FIRM Full-Risk Rating** (Use Post-FIRM Rate Tables) | Use Post-FIRM rate table ***More Than 1 Floor No Basement/Enclosure/Crawlspace*** category. If LF[1] elevation is 2 or more feet below the BFE[2], submit the Application to the insurer for a rate. |
| **Post-FIRM Rating** | Use Post-FIRM rate table ***More Than 1 Floor No Basement/Enclosure/Crawlspace*** category. If LF[1] elevation is 2 or more feet below the BFE[2], submit the Application to the insurer for a rate. |

1 LF — Lowest Floor
2 BFE — Base Flood Elevation
3 See Proper Flood Openings Requirement located in the How to Write section for an explanation
4 HAG — Highest Adjacent Grade
5 Pre-FIRM buildings may be rated using Post-FIRM rating, including Submit-for-Rate, if more favorable to the insured
6 Non-elevated buildings with construction dates of October 1, 1981, and after are Submit-for-Rate

NOTE: *Above references may not apply to this page.*

## NON-ELEVATED BUILDINGS

## 23. Pre- and Post-FIRM Risks In Flood Zones AE and A1–A30

| | |
|---|---|
| **Building Description** | 2 floors on raised-slab-on-grade or slab-on-stem-wall-with-fill (see EC, Diagram 1B) |
| **Machinery or Equipment Servicing Building** | N/A |
| **Lowest Floor for Rating** | Top of bottom floor |
| **Application Should Show** | Building type — 2 floors<br>Basement — None<br>Is building elevated? — No |
| **Pre-FIRM Subsidized Rating**[5] | Use Pre-FIRM rate table ***No Basement/Enclosure*** category. |
| **Pre-FIRM Full-Risk Rating** (Use Post-FIRM Rate Tables) | Use Post-FIRM rate table ***More Than 1 Floor No Basement/Enclosure/Crawlspace*** category. If LF[1] elevation is 2 or more feet below the BFE[2], submit the Application to the insurer for a rate. |
| **Post-FIRM Rating** | Use Post-FIRM rate table ***More Than 1 Floor No Basement/Enclosure/Crawlspace*** category. If LF[1] elevation is 2 or more feet below the BFE[2], submit the Application to the insurer for a rate. |

1 LF — Lowest Floor
2 BFE — Base Flood Elevation
3 See Proper Flood Openings Requirement located in the How to Write section for an explanation
4 HAG — Highest Adjacent Grade
5 Pre-FIRM buildings may be rated using Post-FIRM rating, including Submit-for-Rate, if more favorable to the insured
6 Non-elevated buildings with construction dates of October 1, 1981, and after are Submit-for-Rate

NOTE: *Above references may not apply to this page.*

NON-ELEVATED BUILDINGS

## 24. Pre- and Post-FIRM Risks In Flood Zones AE and A1–A30

| | |
|---|---|
| **Building Description** | 2 floors on slab with attached garage (see EC, Diagram 1A) |
| **Machinery or Equipment Servicing Building** | Machinery or equipment in garage |
| **Lowest Floor for Rating** | If attached garage has no proper openings[3], and has machinery or equipment below the BFE[2], use the garage floor for rating. Otherwise, use the top of the finished floor for rating. |
| **Application Should Show** | Building type — 2 floors<br>Basement — None<br>Is building elevated? — No |
| **Pre-FIRM Subsidized Rating[5]** | Use Pre-FIRM rate table ***No Basement/Enclosure*** category. |
| **Pre-FIRM Full-Risk Rating** (Use Post-FIRM Rate Tables) | Use Post-FIRM rate table ***More Than 1 Floor No Basement/Enclosure/Crawlspace*** category. If LF[1] elevation is 2 or more feet below the BFE[2], submit the Application to the insurer for a rate. |
| **Post-FIRM Rating** | Use Post-FIRM rate table ***More Than 1 Floor No Basement/Enclosure/Crawlspace*** category. If LF[1] elevation is 2 or more feet below the BFE[2], submit the Application to the insurer for a rate. |

1 LF — Lowest Floor
2 BFE — Base Flood Elevation
3 See Proper Flood Openings Requirement located in the How to Write section for an explanation
4 HAG — Highest Adjacent Grade
5 Pre-FIRM buildings may be rated using Post-FIRM rating, including Submit-for-Rate, if more favorable to the insured
6 Non-elevated buildings with construction dates of October 1, 1981, and after are Submit-for-Rate

NOTE: *Above references may not apply to this page.*

NON-ELEVATED BUILDINGS

## 25. Pre- and Post-FIRM Risks In Flood Zones AE and A1–A30

| | |
|---|---|
| **Building Description** | 2 floors with subgrade crawlspace with or without openings (see EC, Diagram 9)<br>Subgrade crawlspace floor is no more than 2 feet below grade, and the distance between the subgrade crawlspace floor and the top of the next-higher floor is no more than 5 feet. |
| **Machinery or Equipment Servicing Building** | With or without machinery or equipment |
| **Lowest Floor for Rating** | Top of bottom floor (including subgrade crawlspace) |
| **Application Should Show** | Building type — 3 or more floors<br>Is building elevated? — No<br>Subgrade crawlspace |
| **Pre-FIRM Subsidized Rating**[5] | Use Pre-FIRM rate table ***Non-Elevated With Subgrade Crawlspace*** category. |
| **Pre-FIRM Full-Risk Rating** (Use Post-FIRM Rate Tables) | Use Post-FIRM rate table ***More Than 1 Floor With Basement/Enclosure/Crawlspace*** category. If LF[1] elevation is 1 or more feet below the BFE[2], submit the Application to the insurer for a rate. Refer to the Special Rates subsection located in the How to Write section. |
| **Post-FIRM Rating** | Use Post-FIRM rate table ***More Than 1 Floor With Basement/Enclosure/Crawlspace*** category. If LF[1] elevation is 1 or more feet below the BFE[2], submit the Application to the insurer for a rate. Refer to the Special Rates subsection located in the How to Write section. |

1 LF — Lowest Floor
2 BFE — Base Flood Elevation
3 See Proper Flood Openings Requirement located in the How to Write section for an explanation
4 HAG — Highest Adjacent Grade
5 Pre-FIRM buildings may be rated using Post-FIRM rating, including Submit-for-Rate, if more favorable to the insured
6 Non-elevated buildings with construction dates of October 1, 1981, and after are Submit-for-Rate

NOTE: *Above references may not apply to this page.*

NON-ELEVATED BUILDINGS

## 26. Pre- and Post-FIRM Risks In Flood Zones AE and A1–A30

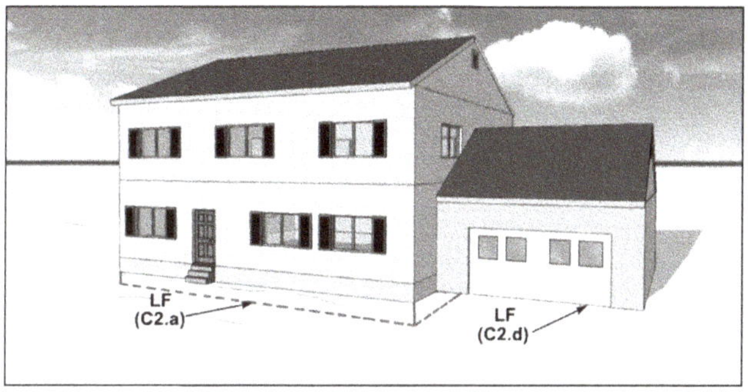


| | |
|---|---|
| **Building Description** | 2 floors with subgrade crawlspace with or without proper openings in crawlspace and attached enclosure (garage). (see EC, Diagram 9)<br>Subgrade crawlspace floor is no more than 2 feet below grade, and the distance between the subgrade crawlspace floor and the top of the next higher floor is no more than 5 feet. |
| **Machinery or Equipment Servicing Building** | With or without machinery or equipment |
| **Lowest Floor for Rating** | Top of bottom floor (including subgrade crawlspace) |
| **Application Should Show** | Building type — 3 or more floors<br>Is building elevated? — No<br>Subgrade crawlspace |
| **Pre-FIRM Subsidized Rating**[6] | Use Pre-FIRM rate table ***Non-Elevated With Subgrade Crawlspace*** category. |
| **Pre-FIRM Full-Risk Rating** (Use Post-FIRM Rate Tables) | Use Post-FIRM rate table ***More Than 1 Floor With Basement/Enclosure/Crawlspace*** category. If LF[1] elevation is 1 or more feet below the BFE[2], submit the Application to the insurer for a rate. Refer to the Special Rates subsection located in the How to Write section. |
| **Post-FIRM Rating** | Use Post-FIRM rate table ***More Than 1 Floor With Basement/Enclosure/Crawlspace*** category. If LF[1] elevation is 1 or more feet below the BFE[2], submit the Application to the insurer for a rate. Refer to the Special Rates subsection located in the How to Write section. |

1 LF — Lowest Floor
2 BFE — Base Flood Elevation
3 See Proper Flood Openings Requirement located in the How to Write section for an explanation
4 HAG — Highest Adjacent Grade
5 Pre-FIRM buildings may be rated using Post-FIRM rating, including Submit-for-Rate, if more favorable to the insured
6 Non-elevated buildings with construction dates of October 1, 1981, and after are Submit-for-Rate

NOTE: *Above references may not apply to this page.*

## NON-ELEVATED BUILDINGS

## 27. Pre- and Post-FIRM Risks In Flood Zones AE and A1–A30

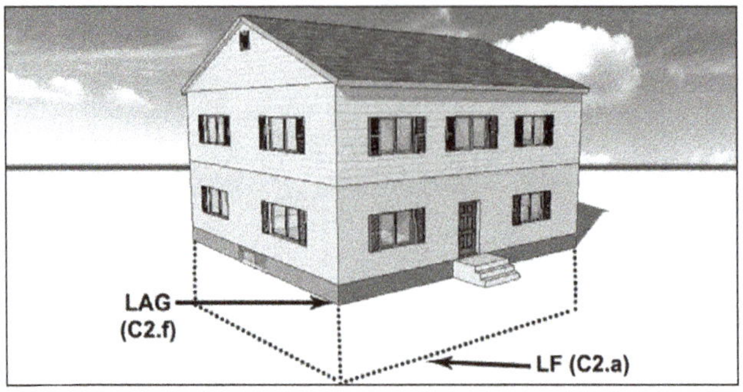


| | |
|---|---|
| **Building Description** | 2 floors with unfinished basement (see EC, Diagram 2A)<br>Basement floor is subgrade more than 2 feet, or subgrade no more than 2 feet and the distance between the basement floor and the top of the next-higher floor is more than 5 feet. |
| **Machinery or Equipment Servicing Building** | With or without machinery or equipment |
| **Lowest Floor for Rating** | Top of bottom floor (including basement) |
| **Application Should Show** | Building type — 3 or more floors<br>Is building elevated? — No<br>Basement — Finished or unfinished |
| **Pre-FIRM Subsidized Rating**[5] | Use Pre-FIRM rate table ***With Basement*** category. |
| **Pre-FIRM Full-Risk Rating** (Use Post-FIRM Rate Tables) | Use Post-FIRM rate table ***More Than 1 Floor With Basement/Enclosure/Crawlspace*** category. If LF[1] elevation is 2 or more feet below the BFE[2], submit the Application to the insurer for a rate. Refer to the Special Rates subsection located in the How to Write section. |
| **Post-FIRM Rating** | Use Post-FIRM rate table ***More Than 1 Floor With Basement/Enclosure/Crawlspace*** category. If LF[1] elevation is 2 or more feet below the BFE[2], submit the Application to the insurer for a rate. Refer to the Special Rates subsection located in the How to Write section. |

1 LF — Lowest Floor
2 BFE — Base Flood Elevation
3 See Proper Flood Openings Requirement located in the How to Write section for an explanation
4 HAG — Highest Adjacent Grade
5 Pre-FIRM buildings may be rated using Post-FIRM rating, including Submit-for-Rate, if more favorable to the insured
6 Non-elevated buildings with construction dates of October 1, 1981, and after are Submit-for-Rate

NOTE: *Above references may not apply to this page.*

NON-ELEVATED BUILDINGS

## 28. Pre- and Post-FIRM Risks In Flood Zones AE and A1–A30

| | |
|---|---|
| **Building Description** | 1 floor with attached garage<br>Garage is at lower elevation than principal building area (see EC, Diagram 1A) |
| **Machinery or Equipment Servicing Building** | Machinery or equipment in garage |
| **Lowest Floor for Rating** | If attached garage has no proper openings[3], and has machinery or equipment below the BFE[2], use the garage floor for rating. Otherwise, use the top of the finished floor for rating. |
| **Application Should Show** | Building type — 1 floor<br>Basement — None<br>Is building elevated? — No |
| **Pre-FIRM Subsidized Rating[5]** | Use Pre-FIRM rate table ***No Basement/Enclosure*** category. |
| **Pre-FIRM Full-Risk Rating** (Use Post-FIRM Rate Tables) | Use Post-FIRM rate table ***1 Floor No Basement/Enclosure/Crawlspace*** category. If LF[1] elevation is 2 or more feet below the BFE[2], submit the Application to the insurer for a rate. |
| **Post-FIRM Rating** | Use Post-FIRM rate table ***1 Floor No Basement/Enclosure/Crawlspace*** category. If LF[1] elevation is 2 or more feet below the BFE[2], submit the Application to the insurer for a rate. |

1 LF — Lowest Floor
2 BFE — Base Flood Elevation
3 See Proper Flood Openings Requirement located in the How to Write section for an explanation
4 HAG — Highest Adjacent Grade
5 Pre-FIRM buildings may be rated using Post-FIRM rating, including Submit-for-Rate, if more favorable to the insured
6 Non-elevated buildings with construction dates of October 1, 1981, and after are Submit-for-Rate

NOTE: *Above references may not apply to this page.*

## NON-ELEVATED BUILDINGS

## 29. Pre- and Post-FIRM Risks In Flood Zones AE and A1–A30

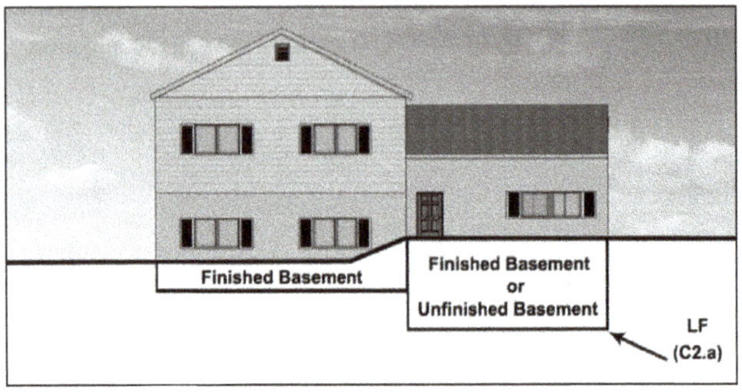


| | |
|---|---|
| **Building Description** | Split level with unfinished or finished basement (see EC, Diagram 4) |
| **Machinery or Equipment Servicing Building** | With or without machinery or equipment in basement |
| **Lowest Floor for Rating** | Top of bottom floor (including basement) |
| **Application Should Show** | Building type — Split level<br>Basement — Finished or unfinished<br>Is building elevated? — No |
| **Pre-FIRM Subsidized Rating**[5] | Use Pre-FIRM rate table ***With Basement*** category. |
| **Pre-FIRM Full-Risk Rating** (Use Post-FIRM Rate Tables) | Use Post-FIRM rate table ***More Than 1 Floor With Basement/Enclosure/Crawlspace*** category. If LF[1] elevation is 2 or more feet below the BFE[2], submit the Application to the insurer for a rate. |
| **Post-FIRM Rating** | Use Post-FIRM rate table ***More Than 1 Floor With Basement/Enclosure/Crawlspace*** category. If LF[1] elevation is 2 or more feet below the BFE[2], submit the Application to the insurer for a rate. |

1 LF — Lowest Floor
2 BFE — Base Flood Elevation
3 See Proper Flood Openings Requirement located in the How to Write section for an explanation
4 HAG — Highest Adjacent Grade
5 Pre-FIRM buildings may be rated using Post-FIRM rating, including Submit-for-Rate, if more favorable to the insured
6 Non-elevated buildings with construction dates of October 1, 1981, and after are Submit-for-Rate

NOTE: *Above references may not apply to this page.*

## ELEVATED BUILDINGS

## 30. Pre- and Post-FIRM Risks in Flood Zones AE And A1–A30

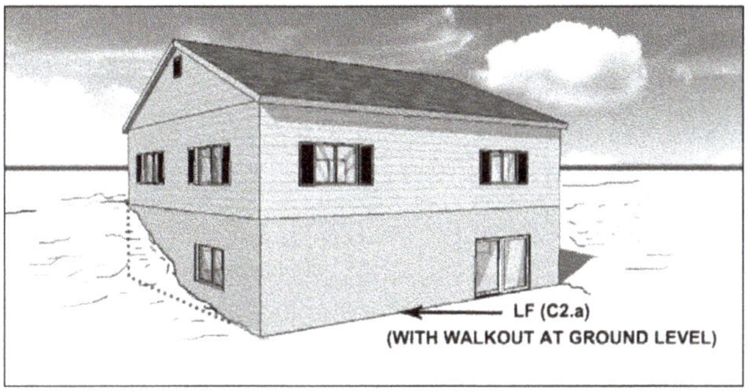


| | |
|---|---|
| **Building Description** | 2 floors with walkout at ground level<br>Lower floor is not below grade on all sides<br>Principal use of the building is on the elevated floor (see EC, Diagram 7) |
| **Elevating Foundation of Building** | Solid foundation walls |
| **Type of Enclosure** | Finished or unfinished lower level<br>No openings |
| **Machinery or Equipment Servicing Building** | With or without machinery or equipment at ground level |
| **Lowest Floor for Rating** | Top of bottom floor (enclosure) |
| **Application Should Show** | Building type — 2 floors<br>Is building elevated? — Yes<br>Is area below the elevated floor enclosed? — Yes |
| **Pre-FIRM Subsidized Rating**[5] | Use Pre-FIRM rate table ***With Enclosure*** category. |
| **Pre-FIRM Full-Risk Rating** (Use Post-FIRM Rate Tables) | Use Post-FIRM rate table ***More Than 1 Floor No Basement/Enclosure/Crawlspace*** category. If LF[1] elevation is 2 or more feet below the BFE[2], submit the Application to the insurer for a rate. |
| **Post-FIRM Rating** | Use Post-FIRM rate table ***More Than 1 Floor With Basement/Enclosure/Crawlspace*** category. If LF[1] elevation is 1 or more feet below the BFE[2], submit the Application to the insurer for a rate. |

1 LF — Lowest Floor
2 BFE — Base Flood Elevation
3 See Proper Flood Openings Requirement located in the How to Write section for an explanation
4 HAG — Highest Adjacent Grade
5 Pre-FIRM buildings may be rated using Post-FIRM rating, including Submit-for-Rate, if more favorable to the insured
6 Non-elevated buildings with construction dates of October 1, 1981, and after are Submit-for-Rate

NOTE: *Above references may not apply to this page.*

## ELEVATED BUILDINGS

## 31. Pre- and Post-FIRM Risks In Flood Zones AE and A1–A30

| | |
|---|---|
| **Building Description** | 1 floor without enclosed area (see EC, Diagram 5) |
| **Elevating Foundation of Building** | Piers, posts, piles, or columns |
| **Type of Enclosure** | No enclosure |
| **Machinery or Equipment Servicing Building** | With or without machinery or equipment below the lowest elevated floor |
| **Lowest Floor for Rating** | Top of lowest elevated floor |
| **Application Should Show** | Building type — 1 floor<br>Is building elevated? — Yes<br>Is area below the elevated floor enclosed? — No |
| **Pre-FIRM Subsidized Rating**[5] | Use Pre-FIRM rate table ***No Basement/Enclosure*** category. |
| **Pre-FIRM Full-Risk Rating** (Use Post-FIRM Rate Tables) | Use Post-FIRM rate table ***1 Floor No Basement/Enclosure/Crawlspace*** category. If LF[1] elevation is 2 or more feet below the BFE[2], submit the Application to the insurer for a rate. |
| **Post-FIRM Rating** | Use Post-FIRM rate table ***1 Floor No Basement/Enclosure/Crawlspace*** category. If LF[1] elevation is 2 or more feet below the BFE[2], submit the Application to the insurer for a rate. |

1 LF — Lowest Floor
2 BFE — Base Flood Elevation
3 See Proper Flood Openings Requirement located in the How to Write section for an explanation
4 HAG — Highest Adjacent Grade
5 Pre-FIRM buildings may be rated using Post-FIRM rating, including Submit-for-Rate, if more favorable to the insured
6 Non-elevated buildings with construction dates of October 1, 1981, and after are Submit-for-Rate

NOTE: *Above references may not apply to this page.*

ELEVATED BUILDINGS

## 32. Pre- and Post-FIRM Risks In Flood Zones AE and A1–A30

| | |
|---|---|
| **Building Description** | Elevated on piers, posts, piles, or columns with hanging floor<br>2 floors, including hanging floor (see EC, Diagram 5) |
| **Elevating Foundation of Building** | Piers, posts, piles, or columns |
| **Type of Enclosure** | No enclosure |
| **Machinery or Equipment Servicing Building** | With or without machinery or equipment below the lowest elevated floor |
| **Lowest Floor for Rating** | Top of lowest elevated floor |
| **Application Should Show** | Building type — 2 floors<br>Is building elevated? — Yes<br>Is area below the elevated floor enclosed? — No |
| **Pre-FIRM Subsidized Rating**[5] | Use Pre-FIRM rate table ***No Basement/Enclosure*** category. |
| **Pre-FIRM Full-Risk Rating** (Use Post-FIRM Rate Tables) | Elevated buildings on posts, piers, pilings, or columns and the lowest elevated floor below the BFE[2] is unfinished and used for storage or building access only, use ***More Than 1 Floor No Basement/Enclosure/Crawlspace*** category. If LF[1] elevation is 2 or more feet below the BFE[2], submit the Application to the insurer for a rate. |
| **Post-FIRM Rating** | Elevated buildings on posts, piers, pilings, or columns and the lowest elevated floor below the BFE[2] is unfinished and used for storage or building access only, use ***More Than 1 Floor No Basement/Enclosure/Crawlspace*** category. If LF[1] elevation is 2 or more feet below the BFE[2], submit the Application to the insurer for a rate. |

1 LF — Lowest Floor
2 BFE — Base Flood Elevation
3 See Proper Flood Openings Requirement located in the How to Write section for an explanation
4 HAG — Highest Adjacent Grade
5 Pre-FIRM buildings may be rated using Post-FIRM rating, including Submit-for-Rate, if more favorable to the insured
6 Non-elevated buildings with construction dates of October 1, 1981, and after are Submit-for-Rate

NOTE: *Above references may not apply to this page.*

## ELEVATED BUILDINGS

## 33. Pre- and Post-FIRM Risks In Flood Zones AE and A1–A30

| | |
|---|---|
| **Building Description** | 1 floor with unfinished enclosed area (see EC, Diagram 6) |
| **Elevating Foundation of Building** | Piers, posts, piles, or columns |
| **Type of Enclosure** | Unfinished enclosure<br>With proper openings[3] |
| **Machinery or Equipment Servicing Building** | With or without machinery or equipment below the lowest elevated floor |
| **Lowest Floor for Rating** | Top of next-higher floor (elevated floor) |
| **Application Should Show** | Building type — 1 floor<br>Is building elevated? — Yes<br>Is area below the elevated floor enclosed? — No |
| **Pre-FIRM Subsidized Rating**[5] | Use Pre-FIRM rate table ***No Basement/Enclosure*** category. |
| **Pre-FIRM Full-Risk Rating** (Use Post-FIRM Rate Tables) | Use Post-FIRM rate table ***1 Floor No Basement/Enclosure/Crawlspace*** category. If LF[1] elevation is 2 or more feet below the BFE[2], submit the Application to the insurer for a rate. |
| **Post-FIRM Rating** | Use Post-FIRM rate table ***1 Floor No Basement/Enclosure/Crawlspace*** category. If LF[1] elevation is 2 or more feet below the BFE[2], submit the Application to the insurer for a rate. |

1 LF — Lowest Floor
2 BFE — Base Flood Elevation
3 See Proper Flood Openings Requirement located in the How to Write section for an explanation
4 HAG — Highest Adjacent Grade
5 Pre-FIRM buildings may be rated using Post-FIRM rating, including Submit-for-Rate, if more favorable to the insured
6 Non-elevated buildings with construction dates of October 1, 1981, and after are Submit-for-Rate

NOTE: *Above references may not apply to this page.*

ELEVATED BUILDINGS

## 34. Pre- and Post-FIRM Risks In Flood Zones AE and A1–A30

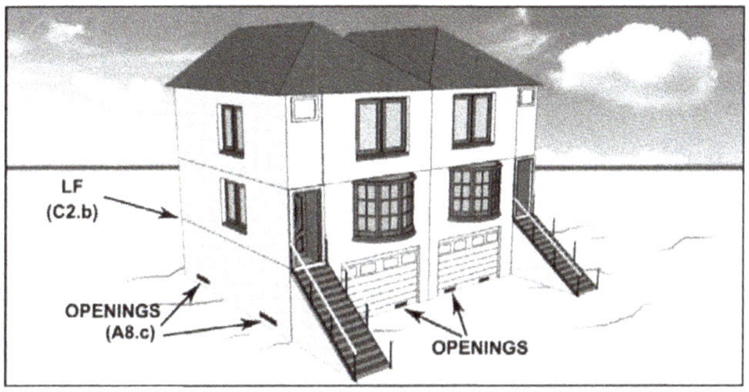


| | |
|---|---|
| **Building Description** | 2 floors with unfinished enclosed area (see EC, Diagram 6) |
| **Elevating Foundation of Building** | Piers, posts, piles, or columns |
| **Type of Enclosure** | Unfinished enclosure<br>With proper openings[3] |
| **Machinery or Equipment Servicing Building** | With or without machinery or equipment below the lowest elevated floor |
| **Lowest Floor for Rating** | Top of next-higher floor (elevated floor) |
| **Application Should Show** | Building type — 2 floors<br>Is building elevated? — Yes<br>Is area below the elevated floor enclosed? — No |
| **Pre-FIRM Subsidized Rating[5]** | Use Pre-FIRM rate table ***No Basement/Enclosure*** category. |
| **Pre-FIRM Full-Risk Rating** (Use Post-FIRM Rate Tables) | Use Post-FIRM rate table ***More Than 1 Floor No Basement/Enclosure/Crawlspace*** category. If LF[1] elevation is 2 or more feet below the BFE[2], submit the Application to the insurer for a rate. |
| **Post-FIRM Rating** | Use Post-FIRM rate table ***More Than 1 Floor No Basement/Enclosure/Crawlspace*** category. If LF[1] elevation is 2 or more feet below the BFE[2], submit the Application to the insurer for a rate. |

1 LF — Lowest Floor
2 BFE — Base Flood Elevation
3 See Proper Flood Openings Requirement located in the How to Write section for an explanation
4 HAG — Highest Adjacent Grade
5 Pre-FIRM buildings may be rated using Post-FIRM rating, including Submit-for-Rate, if more favorable to the insured
6 Non-elevated buildings with construction dates of October 1, 1981, and after are Submit-for-Rate

NOTE: *Above references may not apply to this page.*

ELEVATED BUILDINGS

## 35. Pre- and Post-FIRM Risks In Flood Zones AE and A1–A30

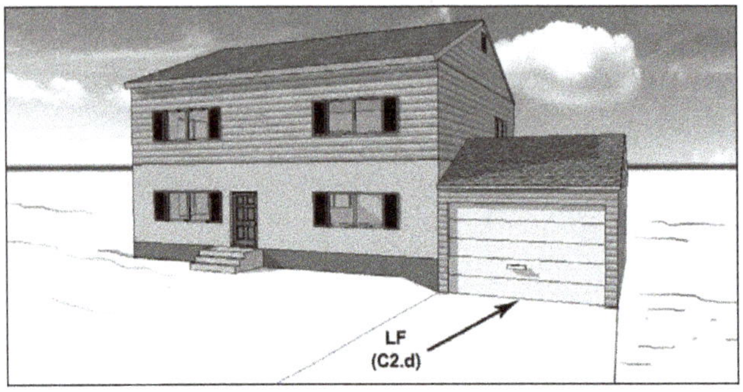


| | |
|---|---|
| **Building Description** | 2 floors with unfinished enclosure/crawlspace (see EC, Diagram 8) |
| **Elevating Foundation of Building** | Solid foundation walls |
| **Type of Enclosure** | Unfinished enclosure (garage) and crawlspace<br>No proper openings[3] |
| **Machinery or Equipment Servicing Building** | With or without machinery or equipment below the lowest elevated floor |
| **Lowest Floor for Rating** | Top of bottom floor (garage) |
| **Application Should Show** | Building type — 3 or more floors<br>Is building elevated? — Yes<br>Is area below the elevated floor enclosed? — Yes |
| **Pre-FIRM Subsidized Rating[5]** | Use Pre-FIRM rate table ***Elevated on Crawlspace*** category. |
| **Pre-FIRM Full-Risk Rating** (Use Post-FIRM Rate Tables) | Use Post-FIRM rate table ***More Than 1 Floor No Basement/Enclosure/Crawlspace*** category. If LF[1] elevation is 2 or more feet below the BFE[2], submit the Application to the insurer for a rate. |
| **Post-FIRM Rating** | Use Post-FIRM rate table ***More Than 1 Floor With Basement/Enclosure/Crawlspace*** category. If LF[1] elevation is 1 or more feet below the BFE[2], submit the Application to the insurer for a rate. |

1 LF — Lowest Floor
2 BFE — Base Flood Elevation
3 See Proper Flood Openings Requirement located in the How to Write section for an explanation
4 HAG — Highest Adjacent Grade
5 Pre-FIRM buildings may be rated using Post-FIRM rating, including Submit-for-Rate, if more favorable to the insured
6 Non-elevated buildings with construction dates of October 1, 1981, and after are Submit-for-Rate

NOTE: *Above references may not apply to this page.*

## ELEVATED BUILDINGS
## 36. Pre- and Post-FIRM Risks In Flood Zones AE and A1–A30

| | |
|---|---|
| **Building Description** | 1 floor with finished or unfinished enclosed area (see EC, Diagram 6) |
| **Elevating Foundation of Building** | Piers, posts, piles, or columns |
| **Type of Enclosure** | Non-load-bearing walls<br>No openings |
| **Machinery or Equipment Servicing Building** | With or without machinery or equipment below the lowest elevated floor |
| **Lowest Floor for Rating** | Top of bottom floor (including basement or enclosure) |
| **Application Should Show** | Building type — 2 floors<br>Is building elevated? — Yes<br>Is area below the elevated floor enclosed? — Yes |
| **Pre-FIRM Subsidized Rating**[5] | Use Pre-FIRM rate table ***With Enclosure*** category. |
| **Pre-FIRM Full-Risk Rating** (Use Post-FIRM Rate Tables) | Use Post-FIRM rate table ***More Than 1 Floor No Basement/Enclosure/Crawlspace*** category. If LF[1] elevation is 2 or more feet below the BFE[2], submit the Application to the insurer for a rate. |
| **Post-FIRM Rating** | Use Post-FIRM rate table ***More Than 1 Floor With Basement/Enclosure/Crawlspace*** category. If LF[1] elevation is 1 or more feet below the BFE[2], submit the Application to the insurer for a rate. |

1 LF — Lowest Floor
2 BFE — Base Flood Elevation
3 See Proper Flood Openings Requirement located in the How to Write section for an explanation
4 HAG — Highest Adjacent Grade
5 Pre-FIRM buildings may be rated using Post-FIRM rating, including Submit-for-Rate, if more favorable to the insured
6 Non-elevated buildings with construction dates of October 1, 1981, and after are Submit-for-Rate

NOTE: *Above references may not apply to this page.*

## ELEVATED BUILDINGS

## 37. Pre- and Post-FIRM Risks In Flood Zones AE and A1–A30

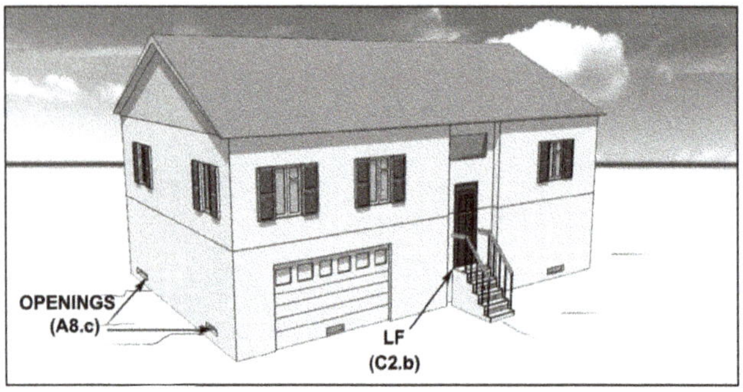


| | |
|---|---|
| **Building Description** | 1-floor Mid-Level Entry with unfinished enclosure (see EC, Diagram 7) |
| **Elevating Foundation of Building** | Solid foundation walls |
| **Type of Enclosure** | Enclosure garage and storage area<br>Proper openings in garage and enclosure |
| **Machinery or Equipment Servicing Building** | With or without machinery or equipment below the lowest elevated floor |
| **Lowest Floor for Rating** | Top of next-higher floor (elevated floor)<br>Mid-Level Entry elevation |
| **Application Should Show** | Building type — 2 floors<br>Is building elevated? — Yes<br>Is area below the elevated floor enclosed? — No |
| **Pre-FIRM Subsidized Rating**[5] | Use Pre-FIRM rate table ***No Enclosure*** category. |
| **Pre-FIRM Full-Risk Rating** (Use Post-FIRM Rate Tables) | Use Post-FIRM rate table ***More Than 1 Floor No Basement/Enclosure/Crawlspace*** category. If LF[1] elevation is 2 or more feet below the BFE[2], submit the Application to the insurer for a rate. |
| **Post-FIRM Rating** | Use Post-FIRM rate table ***More Than 1 Floor No Basement/Enclosure/Crawlspace*** category. If LF[1] elevation is 2 or more feet below the BFE[2], submit the Application to the insurer for a rate. |

1 LF — Lowest Floor
2 BFE — Base Flood Elevation
3 See Proper Flood Openings Requirement located in the How to Write section for an explanation
4 HAG — Highest Adjacent Grade
5 Pre-FIRM buildings may be rated using Post-FIRM rating, including Submit-for-Rate, if more favorable to the insured
6 Non-elevated buildings with construction dates of October 1, 1981, and after are Submit-for-Rate

NOTE: *Above references may not apply to this page.*

## ELEVATED BUILDINGS

## 38. Pre- and Post-FIRM Risks In Flood Zones AE and A1–A30

| | |
|---|---|
| **Building Description** | 2-floor Mid-Level Entry with unfinished enclosure (see EC, Diagram 7) |
| **Elevating Foundation of Building** | Solid foundation walls |
| **Type of Enclosure** | Enclosure garage and storage area<br>No proper openings[3] |
| **Machinery or Equipment Servicing Building** | With or without machinery or equipment below the lowest elevated floor |
| **Lowest Floor for Rating** | Floor of garage and storage area |
| **Application Should Show** | Building type — 2 floors<br>Is building elevated? — Yes<br>Is area below the elevated floor enclosed? — Yes |
| **Pre-FIRM Subsidized Rating**[5] | Use Pre-FIRM rate table ***With Enclosure*** category. |
| **Pre-FIRM Full-Risk Rating** (Use Post-FIRM Rate Tables) | Use Post-FIRM rate table ***More Than 1 Floor No Basement/Enclosure/Crawlspace*** category. If LF[1] elevation is 2 or more feet below the BFE[2], submit the Application to the insurer for a rate. |
| **Post-FIRM Rating** | Use Post-FIRM rate table ***More Than 1 Floor With Basement/Enclosure/Crawlspace*** category. If LF[1] elevation is 1 or more feet below the BFE[2], submit the Application to the insurer for a rate. |

1 LF — Lowest Floor
2 BFE — Base Flood Elevation
3 See Proper Flood Openings Requirement located in the How to Write section for an explanation
4 HAG — Highest Adjacent Grade
5 Pre-FIRM buildings may be rated using Post-FIRM rating, including Submit-for-Rate, if more favorable to the insured
6 Non-elevated buildings with construction dates of October 1, 1981, and after are Submit-for-Rate

NOTE: *Above references may not apply to this page.*

## ELEVATED BUILDINGS

## 39. Pre- and Post-FIRM Risks In Flood Zones AE and A1–A30

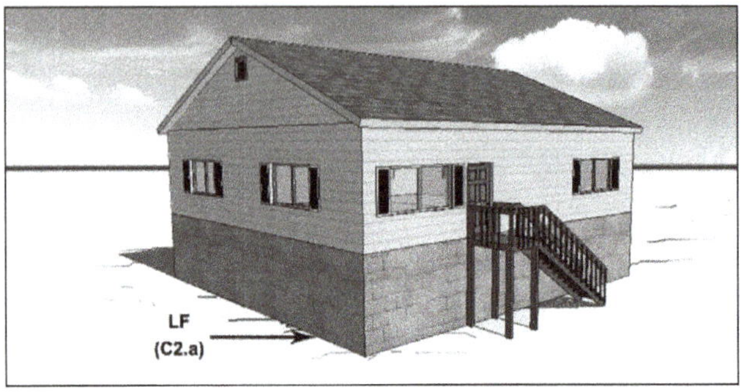


| | |
|---|---|
| **Building Description** | 1 floor with unfinished enclosed area (see EC, Diagram 7) |
| **Elevating Foundation of Building** | Solid foundation walls |
| **Type of Enclosure** | Unfinished enclosure<br>No proper openings[3] |
| **Machinery or Equipment Servicing Building** | With or without machinery or equipment below the lowest elevated floor |
| **Lowest Floor for Rating** | Top of bottom floor (including basement or enclosure) |
| **Application Should Show** | Building type — 2 floors<br>Is building elevated? — Yes<br>Is area below the elevated floor enclosed? — Yes |
| **Pre-FIRM Subsidized Rating**[5] | Use Pre-FIRM rate table ***With Enclosure*** category. |
| **Pre-FIRM Full-Risk Rating** (Use Post-FIRM Rate Tables) | Use Post-FIRM rate table ***More Than 1 Floor No Basement/Enclosure/Crawlspace*** category. If LF[1] elevation is 2 or more feet below the BFE[2], submit the Application to the insurer for a rate. |
| **Post-FIRM Rating** | Use Post-FIRM rate table ***More Than 1 Floor With Basement/Enclosure/Crawlspace*** category. If LF[1] elevation is 1 or more feet below the BFE[2], submit the Application to the insurer for a rate. |

1 LF — Lowest Floor
2 BFE — Base Flood Elevation
3 See Proper Flood Openings Requirement located in the How to Write section for an explanation
4 HAG — Highest Adjacent Grade
5 Pre-FIRM buildings may be rated using Post-FIRM rating, including Submit-for-Rate, if more favorable to the insured
6 Non-elevated buildings with construction dates of October 1, 1981, and after are Submit-for-Rate

NOTE: *Above references may not apply to this page.*

ELEVATED BUILDINGS

## 40. Pre- and Post-FIRM Risks In Flood Zones AE and A1–A30

| | |
|---|---|
| **Building Description** | 2 floors with unfinished enclosure/crawlspace (see EC, Diagram 8) |
| **Elevating Foundation of Building** | Solid foundation walls |
| **Type of Enclosure** | Enclosed garage at same level as crawlspace<br>Unfinished enclosure/crawlspace<br>No proper openings[3] in crawlspace or garage<br>Floor of crawlspace/garage is at or above lowest adjacent grade |
| **Machinery or Equipment Servicing Building** | With or without machinery or equipment below the lowest elevated floor |
| **Lowest Floor for Rating** | Floor of crawlspace and garage |
| **Application Should Show** | Building type — 3 or more floors<br>Is building elevated? — Yes<br>Is area below the elevated floor enclosed? — Yes |
| **Pre-FIRM Subsidized Rating[5]** | Use Pre-FIRM rate table ***Elevated on Crawlspace*** category. |
| **Pre-FIRM Full-Risk Rating** (Use Post-FIRM Rate Tables) | Use Post-FIRM rate table ***More Than 1 Floor No Basement/Enclosure/Crawlspace*** category. If LF[1] elevation is 2 or more feet below the BFE[2], submit the Application to the insurer for a rate. |
| **Post-FIRM Rating** | Use Post-FIRM rate table ***More Than 1 Floor With Basement/Enclosure/Crawlspace*** category. If LF[1] elevation is 1 or more feet below the BFE[2], submit the Application to the insurer for a rate. |

1 LF — Lowest Floor
2 BFE — Base Flood Elevation
3 See Proper Flood Openings Requirement located in the How to Write section for an explanation
4 HAG — Highest Adjacent Grade
5 Pre-FIRM buildings may be rated using Post-FIRM rating, including Submit-for-Rate, if more favorable to the insured
6 Non-elevated buildings with construction dates of October 1, 1981, and after are Submit-for-Rate

NOTE: *Above references may not apply to this page.*

## ELEVATED BUILDINGS

## 41. Pre- and Post-FIRM Risks In Flood Zones AE and A1–A30

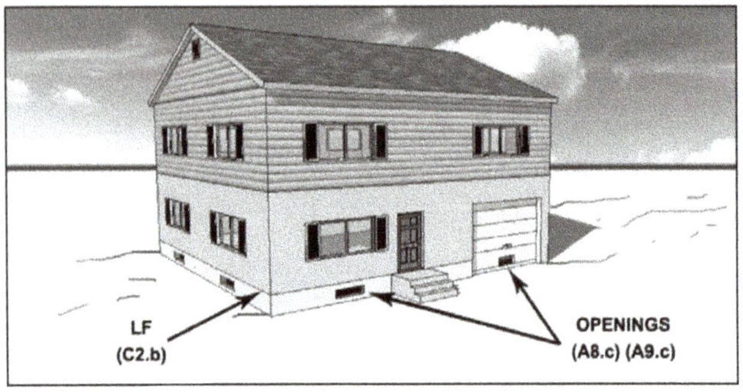


| | |
|---|---|
| **Building Description** | 2 floors with crawlspace (see EC, Diagram 8) |
| **Elevating Foundation of Building** | Solid foundation walls |
| **Type of Enclosure** | Unfinished crawlspace<br>Proper openings[3] in crawlspace and garage<br>Floor of crawlspace/garage is at or above lowest adjacent grade |
| **Machinery or Equipment Servicing Building** | Without machinery or equipment in crawlspace or garage |
| **Lowest Floor for Rating** | Top of next-higher floor (elevated floor) |
| **Application Should Show** | Building type — 2 floors<br>Is building elevated? — Yes<br>Is area below the elevated floor enclosed? — No |
| **Pre-FIRM Subsidized Rating[5]** | Use Pre-FIRM rate table ***No Basement/Enclosure*** category. |
| **Pre-FIRM Full-Risk Rating** (Use Post-FIRM Rate Tables) | Use Post-FIRM rate table ***More Than 1 Floor No Basement/Enclosure/Crawlspace*** category. If LF[1] elevation is 2 or more feet below the BFE[2], submit the Application to the insurer for a rate. |
| **Post-FIRM Rating** | Use Post-FIRM rate table ***More Than 1 Floor No Basement/Enclosure/Crawlspace*** category. If LF[1] elevation is 2 or more feet below the BFE[2], submit the Application to the insurer for a rate. |

1 LF — Lowest Floor
2 BFE — Base Flood Elevation
3 See Proper Flood Openings Requirement located in the How to Write section for an explanation
4 HAG — Highest Adjacent Grade
5 Pre-FIRM buildings may be rated using Post-FIRM rating, including Submit-for-Rate, if more favorable to the insured
6 Non-elevated buildings with construction dates of October 1, 1981, and after are Submit-for-Rate

NOTE: *Above references may not apply to this page.*

ELEVATED BUILDINGS

## 42. Pre- and Post-FIRM Risks In Flood Zones AE and A1–A30

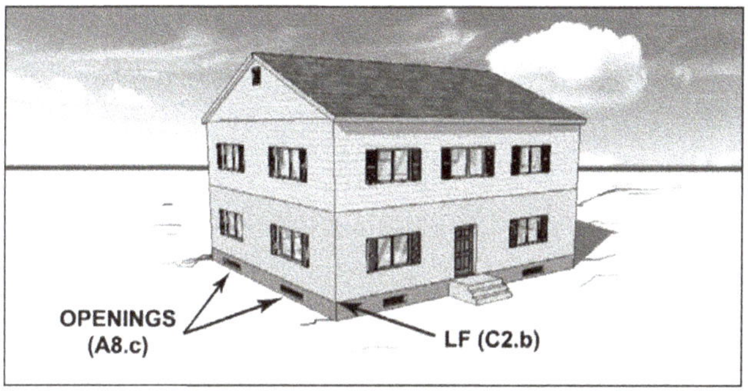


| | |
|---|---|
| **Building Description** | 2 floors with crawlspace (see EC, Diagram 8) |
| **Elevating Foundation of Building** | Solid foundation walls |
| **Type of Enclosure** | Unfinished crawlspace<br>With proper openings[3]<br>Floor of crawlspace is at or above lowest adjacent grade |
| **Machinery or Equipment Servicing Building** | With or without machinery or equipment in crawlspace |
| **Lowest Floor for Rating** | Top of next-higher floor (elevated floor) |
| **Application Should Show** | Building type — 2 floors<br>Is building elevated? — Yes<br>Is area below the elevated floor enclosed? — No |
| **Pre-FIRM Subsidized Rating**[5] | Use Pre-FIRM rate table ***No Basement/Enclosure*** category. |
| **Pre-FIRM Full-Risk Rating** (Use Post-FIRM Rate Tables) | Use Post-FIRM rate table ***More Than 1 Floor No Basement/Enclosure/Crawlspace*** category. If LF[1] elevation is 2 or more feet below the BFE[2], submit the Application to the insurer for a rate. |
| **Post-FIRM Rating** | Use Post-FIRM rate table ***More Than 1 Floor No Basement/Enclosure/Crawlspace*** category. If LF[1] elevation is 2 or more feet below the BFE[2], submit the Application to the insurer for a rate. |

1 LF — Lowest Floor
2 BFE — Base Flood Elevation
3 See Proper Flood Openings Requirement located in the How to Write section for an explanation
4 HAG — Highest Adjacent Grade
5 Pre-FIRM buildings may be rated using Post-FIRM rating, including Submit-for-Rate, if more favorable to the insured
6 Non-elevated buildings with construction dates of October 1, 1981, and after are Submit-for-Rate

NOTE: *Above references may not apply to this page.*

ELEVATED BUILDINGS

## 43. Pre- and Post-FIRM Risks In Flood Zones AE and A1–A30

| | |
|---|---|
| **Building Description** | 2 floors with crawlspace (see EC, Diagram 8) |
| **Elevating Foundation of Building** | Solid foundation walls |
| **Type of Enclosure** | Unfinished crawlspace<br>No proper openings[3]<br>Floor of crawlspace is at or above lowest adjacent grade |
| **Machinery or Equipment Servicing Building** | With or without machinery or equipment in crawlspace |
| **Lowest Floor for Rating** | Top of bottom floor (crawlspace) |
| **Application Should Show** | Building type — 3 or more floors<br>Is building elevated? — Yes<br>Is area below the elevated floor enclosed? — Yes |
| **Pre-FIRM Subsidized Rating**[5] | Use Pre-FIRM rate table ***Elevated on Crawlspace*** category. |
| **Pre-FIRM Full-Risk Rating** (Use Post-FIRM Rate Tables) | Use Post-FIRM rate table ***More Than 1 Floor No Basement/Enclosure/Crawlspace*** category. If LF[1] elevation is 1 or more feet below the BFE[2], submit the Application to the insurer for a rate. |
| **Post-FIRM Rating** | Use Post-FIRM rate table ***More Than 1 Floor With Basement/Enclosure/Crawlspace*** category. If LF[1] elevation is 1 or more feet below the BFE[2], submit the Application to the insurer for a rate. |

1 LF — Lowest Floor
2 BFE — Base Flood Elevation
3 See Proper Flood Openings Requirement located in the How to Write section for an explanation
4 HAG — Highest Adjacent Grade
5 Pre-FIRM buildings may be rated using Post-FIRM rating, including Submit-for-Rate, if more favorable to the insured
6 Non-elevated buildings with construction dates of October 1, 1981, and after are Submit-for-Rate

NOTE: *Above references may not apply to this page.*

ELEVATED BUILDINGS

## 44. Pre- and Post-FIRM Risks In Flood Zones AE and A1–A30

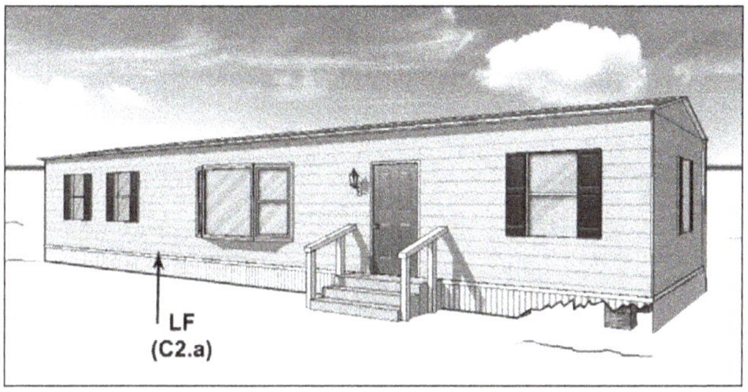


| | |
|---|---|
| **Building Description** | Mobile home without enclosed area (see EC, Diagram 5) |
| **Elevating Foundation of Building** | Piers, posts, piles, or columns |
| **Type of Enclosure** | Vinyl or aluminum skirting |
| **Machinery or Equipment Servicing Building** | With or without machinery or equipment below the lowest elevated floor |
| **Lowest Floor for Rating** | Top of lowest elevated floor |
| **Application Should Show** | Building type — Mobile home<br>Is building elevated? — Yes<br>Is area below the elevated floor enclosed? — No |
| **Pre-FIRM Subsidized Rating**[5] | Use Pre-FIRM rate table ***Manufactured (Mobile) Home*** category. |
| **Pre-FIRM Full-Risk Rating** (Use Post-FIRM Rate Tables) | Use Post-FIRM ***Manufactured (Mobile) Home*** rates. If LF[1] elevation is 1 or more feet below the BFE[2], submit the Application to the insurer for a rate. |
| **Post-FIRM Rating** | Use Post-FIRM ***Manufactured (Mobile) Home*** rates. If LF[1] elevation is 1 or more feet below the BFE[2], submit the Application to the insurer for a rate. |

1 LF — Lowest Floor
2 BFE — Base Flood Elevation
3 See Proper Flood Openings Requirement located in the How to Write section for an explanation
4 HAG — Highest Adjacent Grade
5 Pre-FIRM buildings may be rated using Post-FIRM rating, including Submit-for-Rate, if more favorable to the insured
6 Non-elevated buildings with construction dates of October 1, 1981, and after are Submit-for-Rate

NOTE: *Above references may not apply to this page.*

NON-ELEVATED BUILDINGS

## 45. Pre- and Post-FIRM Risks with Construction Dates of 1975 to September 30, 1981, In Flood Zones VE and V1–V30[6]

| | |
|---|---|
| **Building Description** | 1 floor<br>No basement (see EC, Diagram 1A) |
| **Lowest Floor for Rating** | Bottom of slab<br>In V Zones, the LFE should reflect the bottom of the lowest horizontal structural member. If the surveyor used item C2.a in lieu of C2.c of the EC, and the top of the bottom floor is at or above grade, deduct (for 1–4 family residences) 12 inches from the elevation figure found in item C2.a. For buildings other than 1–4 family, deduct 18 inches from the elevation figure found in item C2.a. |
| **Application Should Show** | Building type — 1 floor<br>Basement — None<br>Is building elevated? — No |
| **Pre-FIRM Subsidized Rating[5]** | Use Pre-FIRM rate table ***No Basement/Enclosure*** category. |
| **Pre-FIRM Full-Risk Rating** (Use Post-FIRM Rate Tables) | Use Post-FIRM '75–'81 VE, V1–V30 Zone ***1 Floor No Basement/Enclosure/Crawlspace*** rates. If LF[1] elevation is 2 or more feet below the BFE[2], submit the Application to the insurer for a rate. |
| **Post-FIRM Rating 1975 to September 30, 1981, Construction Date** | Use Post-FIRM '75–'81 VE, V1–V30 Zone ***1 Floor No Basement/Enclosure/Crawlspace*** rates. If LF[1] elevation is 2 or more feet below the BFE[2], submit the Application to the insurer for a rate. |

1 LF — Lowest Floor
2 BFE — Base Flood Elevation
3 See Proper Flood Openings Requirement located in the How to Write section for an explanation
4 HAG — Highest Adjacent Grade
5 Pre-FIRM buildings may be rated using Post-FIRM rating, including Submit-for-Rate, if more favorable to the insured
6 Non-elevated buildings with construction dates of October 1, 1981, and after are Submit-for-Rate

NOTE: *Above references may not apply to this page.*

NON-ELEVATED BUILDINGS

## 46. Pre- and Post-FIRM Risks with Construction Dates of 1975 to September 30, 1981, In Flood Zones VE and V1–V30[6]

| | |
|---|---|
| **Building Description** | 3 or more floors<br>No basement (see EC, Diagram 1A) |
| **Lowest Floor for Rating** | Bottom of slab<br>In V Zones, the LFE should reflect the bottom of the lowest horizontal structural member. If the surveyor used item C2.a in lieu of C2.c of the EC, and the top of the bottom floor is at or above grade, deduct (for 1–4 family residences) 12 inches from the elevation figure found in item C2.a. For buildings other than 1–4 family, deduct 18 inches from the elevation figure found in item C2.a. |
| **Application Should Show** | Building type — 3 or more floors<br>Basement — None<br>Is building elevated? — No |
| **Pre-FIRM Subsidized Rating[5]** | Use Pre-FIRM rate table ***No Basement/Enclosure*** category. |
| **Pre-FIRM Full-Risk Rating** (Use Post-FIRM Rate Tables) | Use Post-FIRM '75–'81 VE, V1–V30 Zone ***More Than 1 Floor No Basement/Enclosure/ Crawlspace*** rates. If LF[1] elevation is 2 or more feet below the BFE[2], submit the Application to the insurer for a rate. |
| **Post-FIRM Rating 1975 to September 30, 1981, Construction Date** | Use Post-FIRM '75–'81 VE, V1–V30 Zone ***More Than 1 Floor No Basement/Enclosure/ Crawlspace*** rates. If LF[1] elevation is 2 or more feet below the BFE[2], submit the Application to the insurer for a rate. |

1 LF — Lowest Floor
2 BFE — Base Flood Elevation
3 See Proper Flood Openings Requirement located in the How to Write section for an explanation
4 HAG — Highest Adjacent Grade
5 Pre-FIRM buildings may be rated using Post-FIRM rating, including Submit-for-Rate, if more favorable to the insured
6 Non-elevated buildings with construction dates of October 1, 1981, and after are Submit-for-Rate

NOTE: *Above references may not apply to this page.*

## NON-ELEVATED BUILDINGS

## 47. Pre- and Post-FIRM Risks with Construction Dates of 1975 to September 30, 1981, In Flood Zones VE and V1–V30[6]

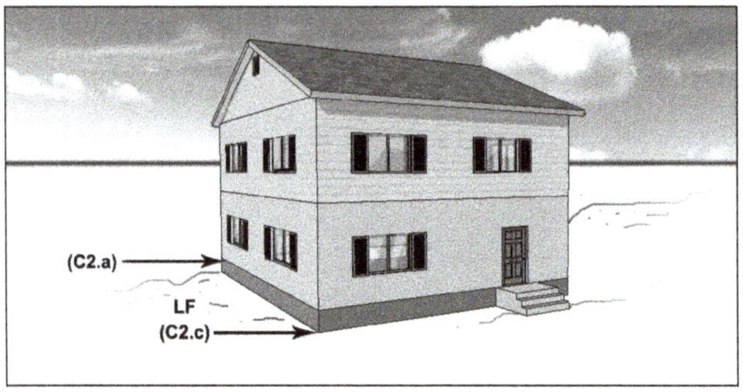


| | |
|---|---|
| **Building Description** | 2 floors on raised-slab-on-grade or slab-on-stem-wall-with-fill (see EC, Diagram 1B) |
| **Lowest Floor for Rating** | Bottom of lowest horizontal structural member (C2.c) |
| **Application Should Show** | Building type — 2 floors<br>Basement — None<br>Is building elevated? — No |
| **Pre-FIRM Subsidized Rating**[5] | Use Pre-FIRM rate table ***No Basement/Enclosure*** category. |
| **Pre-FIRM Full-Risk Rating** (Use Post-FIRM Rate Tables) | Use Post-FIRM '75–'81 VE, V1–V30 Zone ***More Than 1 Floor No Basement/Enclosure/ Crawlspace*** rates. If LF[1] elevation is 2 or more feet below the BFE[2], submit the Application to the insurer for a rate. |
| **Post-FIRM Rating 1975 to September 30, 1981, Construction Date** | Use Post-FIRM '75–'81 VE, V1–V30 Zone ***More Than 1 Floor No Basement/Enclosure/ Crawlspace*** rates. If LF[1] elevation is 2 or more feet below the BFE[2], submit the Application to the insurer for a rate. |

1 LF — Lowest Floor
2 BFE — Base Flood Elevation
3 See Proper Flood Openings Requirement located in the How to Write section for an explanation
4 HAG — Highest Adjacent Grade
5 Pre-FIRM buildings may be rated using Post-FIRM rating, including Submit-for-Rate, if more favorable to the insured
6 Non-elevated buildings with construction dates of October 1, 1981, and after are Submit-for-Rate

NOTE: *Above references may not apply to this page.*

NON-ELEVATED BUILDINGS

## 48. Pre- and Post-FIRM Risks with Construction Dates of 1975 to September 30, 1981, In Flood Zones VE and V1–V30[6]

| | |
|---|---|
| **Building Description** | 1 floor with attached garage<br>Garage is at lower elevation than principal building area (see EC, Diagram 1) |
| **Lowest Floor for Rating** | In V Zones, the LFE should reflect the bottom of the slab. If the surveyor used item C2. a or d (attached garage/top of slab) in lieu of C2.c of the EC, and the top of the bottom floor is at or above the lowest adjacent grade (C2.f), deduct (for 1–4 family residences) 12 inches from the elevation figure found in item C2. a or d, whichever is lower. For buildings other than 1–4 family, deduct 18 inches from the elevation figure found in item C2. a or d, whichever is lower. |
| **Application Should Show** | Building type — 1 floor<br>Basement — None<br>Is building elevated? — No |
| **Pre-FIRM Subsidized Rating[5]** | Use Pre-FIRM rate table ***No Basement/Enclosure*** category. |
| **Pre-FIRM Full-Risk Rating** (Use Post-FIRM Rate Tables) | Use Post-FIRM '75–'81 VE, V1–V30 Zone ***1 Floor No Basement/Enclosure*** rates. If LF[1] elevation is 2 or more feet below the BFE[2], submit the Application to the insurer for a rate. |
| **Post-FIRM Rating 1975 to September 30, 1981, Construction Date** | Use Post-FIRM '75–'81 VE, V1–V30 Zone ***1 Floor No Basement/Enclosure*** rates. If LF[1] elevation is 2 or more feet below the BFE[2], submit the Application to the insurer for a rate. |

1 LF — Lowest Floor
2 BFE — Base Flood Elevation
3 See Proper Flood Openings Requirement located in the How to Write section for an explanation
4 HAG — Highest Adjacent Grade
5 Pre-FIRM buildings may be rated using Post-FIRM rating, including Submit-for-Rate, if more favorable to the insured
6 Non-elevated buildings with construction dates of October 1, 1981, and after are Submit-for-Rate

NOTE: *Above references may not apply to this page.*

NON-ELEVATED BUILDINGS

## 49. Pre- and Post-FIRM Risks with Construction Dates of 1975 to September 30, 1981, In Flood Zones VE and V1–V30[6]

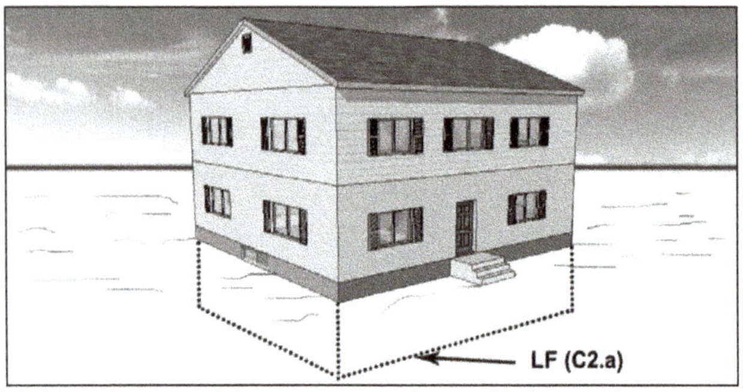


| | |
|---|---|
| **Building Description** | 3 floors<br>Finished basement (see EC, Diagram 2A) |
| **Lowest Floor for Rating** | Bottom of slab (basement)<br>In V Zones, the LFE should reflect the bottom of the lowest horizontal structural member. If the surveyor used item C2.a in lieu of C2.c of the EC, and the top of the bottom floor is indicated in the EC, deduct (for 1–4 family residences) 12 inches from the elevation figure found in item C2.a. For buildings other than 1–4 family, deduct 18 inches from the elevation figure found in item C2.a. |
| **Application Should Show** | Building type — 3 or more floors<br>Basement — Finished<br>Is building elevated? — No |
| **Pre-FIRM Subsidized Rating[5]** | Use Pre-FIRM rate table ***With Basement*** category. |
| **Pre-FIRM Full-Risk Rating** (Use Post-FIRM Rate Tables) | Use Post-FIRM '75–'81 VE, V1–V30 Zone ***More Than 1 Floor With Basement/Enclosure/ Crawlspace*** rates. If LF[1] elevation is 2 or more feet below the BFE[2], submit the Application to the insurer for a rate. |
| **Post-FIRM Rating 1975 to September 30, 1981, Construction Date** | Use Post-FIRM '75–'81 VE, V1–V30 Zone ***More Than 1 Floor With Basement/Enclosure/ Crawlspace*** rates. If LF[1] elevation is 2 or more feet below the BFE[2], submit the Application to the insurer for a rate. |

1 LF — Lowest Floor
2 BFE — Base Flood Elevation
3 See Proper Flood Openings Requirement located in the How to Write section for an explanation
4 HAG — Highest Adjacent Grade
5 Pre-FIRM buildings may be rated using Post-FIRM rating, including Submit-for-Rate, if more favorable to the insured
6 Non-elevated buildings with construction dates of October 1, 1981, and after are Submit-for-Rate

NOTE: *Above references may not apply to this page.*

NON-ELEVATED BUILDINGS

## 50. Pre- and Post-FIRM Risks with Construction Dates of 1975 to September 30, 1981, In Flood Zones VE and V1–V30[6]

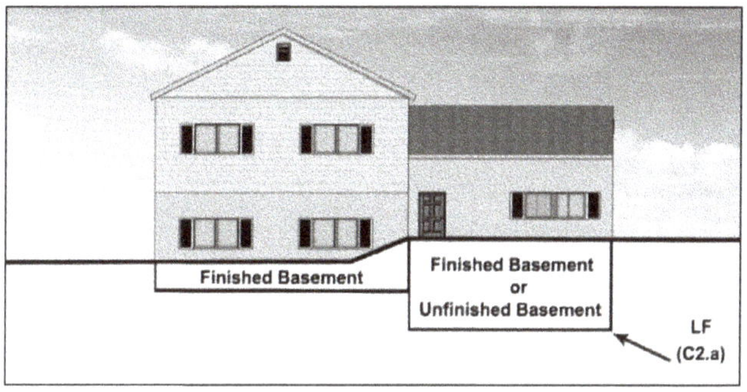


| | |
|---|---|
| **Building Description** | Split level<br>Unfinished basement (see EC, Diagram 4) |
| **Lowest Floor for Rating** | Bottom of slab (basement)<br>In V Zones, the LFE should reflect the bottom of the lowest horizontal structural member. If the surveyor used item C2.a in lieu of C2.c of the EC, and the top of the bottom floor is indicated in the EC, deduct (for 1–4 family residences) 12 inches from the elevation figure found in item C2.a. For buildings other than 1–4 family, deduct 18 inches from the elevation figure found in item C2.a. |
| **Application Should Show** | Building type — Split level<br>Basement — Unfinished<br>Is building elevated? — No |
| **Pre-FIRM Subsidized Rating**[5] | Use Pre-FIRM rate table ***With Basement*** category. |
| **Pre-FIRM Full-Risk Rating** (Use Post-FIRM Rate Tables) | Use Post-FIRM '75–'81 VE, V1–V30 Zone ***More Than 1 Floor With Basement/Enclosure/Crawlspace*** rates. If LF[1] elevation is 2 or more feet below the BFE[2], submit the Application to the insurer for a rate. |
| **Post-FIRM Rating 1975 to September 30, 1981, Construction Date** | Use Post-FIRM '75–'81 VE, V1–V30 Zone ***More Than 1 Floor With Basement/Enclosure/Crawlspace*** rates. If LF[1] elevation is 2 or more feet below the BFE[2], submit the Application to the insurer for a rate. |

1 LF — Lowest Floor
2 BFE — Base Flood Elevation
3 See Proper Flood Openings Requirement located in the How to Write section for an explanation
4 HAG — Highest Adjacent Grade
5 Pre-FIRM buildings may be rated using Post-FIRM rating, including Submit-for-Rate, if more favorable to the insured
6 Non-elevated buildings with construction dates of October 1, 1981, and after are Submit-for-Rate

NOTE: *Above references may not apply to this page.*

ELEVATED BUILDINGS

## 51. Pre- and Post-FIRM Risks with Construction Dates of 1975 to September 30, 1981, In Flood Zones VE and V1–V30

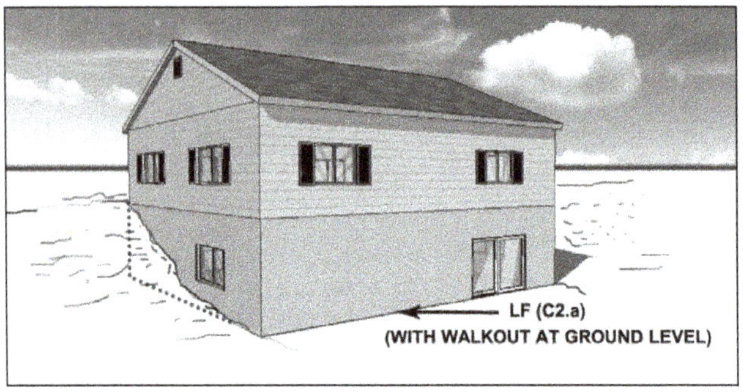


| | |
|---|---|
| **Building Description** | 2 floors with walkout at ground level<br>Lower floor is not below grade on all sides<br>Principal use of the building is on the elevated floor (see EC, Diagram 7) |
| **Elevating Foundation of Building** | Solid foundation walls |
| **Type of Enclosure** | Finished or unfinished lower level |
| **Machinery or Equipment Servicing Building** | With or without machinery or equipment below the lowest elevated floor |
| **Lowest Floor for Rating** | Bottom of slab<br>In V Zones, the LFE should reflect the bottom of the lowest horizontal structural member. If the surveyor used item C2.a in lieu of C2.c of the EC, and the top of the bottom floor is at or above the lowest adjacent grade (C2.f), deduct (for 1–4 family residences) 12 inches from the elevation figure found in item C2.a. For buildings other than 1–4 family, deduct 18 inches from the elevation figure found in item C2.a. |
| **Application Should Show** | Building type — 2 floors<br>Is building elevated? — Yes<br>Is area below the elevated floor enclosed? — Yes |
| **Pre-FIRM Subsidized Rating**[5] | Use Pre-FIRM rate table ***With Enclosure*** category. |
| **Pre-FIRM Full-Risk Rating** (Use Post-FIRM Rate Tables) | Use Post-FIRM '75–'81 VE, V1–V30 Zone ***More Than 1 Floor No Basement/Enclosure/ Crawlspace*** rates. If LF[1] elevation is 2 or more feet below the BFE[2], submit the Application to the insurer for a rate. |
| **Post-FIRM Rating 1975 to September 30, 1981, Construction Date** | Use Post-FIRM '75–'81 VE, V1–V30 Zone ***More Than 1 Floor With Basement/Enclosure/ Crawlspace*** rates. If LF[1] elevation is 1 or more feet below the BFE[2], submit the Application to the insurer for a rate. |

1 LF — Lowest Floor
2 BFE — Base Flood Elevation
3 See Proper Flood Openings Requirement located in the How to Write section for an explanation
4 HAG — Highest Adjacent Grade
5 Pre-FIRM buildings may be rated using Post-FIRM rating, including Submit-for-Rate, if more favorable to the insured
6 Non-elevated buildings with construction dates of October 1, 1981, and after are Submit-for-Rate

NOTE: *Above references may not apply to this page.*

## ELEVATED BUILDINGS

## 52. Pre- and Post-FIRM Risks with Construction Dates of 1975 to September 30, 1981, In Flood Zones VE and V1–V30

| | |
|---|---|
| **Building Description** | 1 floor without enclosed area (see EC, Diagram 5) |
| **Elevating Foundation of Building** | Piers, posts, piles, or columns |
| **Type of Enclosure** | The space below the lowest elevated floor either has no enclosure or has:<br>(1) Insect screening, provided that no additional supports are required for the screening; *or*<br>(2) Wooden or plastic lattice with at least 40% of its area open and made of material no thicker than ½ inch; *or*<br>(3) Wooden or plastic slats or shutters with at least 40% of their area open and made of material no thicker than 1 inch; *or*<br>(4) The area below the lowest elevated floor is enclosed by a combination of 1 solid breakaway wall or garage door, and the other sides of the enclosure are insect screening, or wooden or plastic lattice, slats, or shutters.<br>Any of these systems must be designed and installed to collapse under stress without jeopardizing the structural support of the building, so that the impact on the building of abnormally high tides or wind-driven water is minimized. |
| **Machinery or Equipment Servicing Building** | Any machinery or equipment below elevated floor is at or above the BFE[2] |
| **Lowest Floor for Rating** | Bottom of lowest horizontal structural member |
| **Application Should Show** | Building type — 1 floor<br>Is building elevated? — Yes<br>Is area below the elevated floor enclosed? — No |
| **Pre-FIRM Subsidized Rating[5]** | Use Pre-FIRM rate table ***No Basement/Enclosure*** category. |
| **Pre-FIRM Full-Risk Rating** (Use Post-FIRM Rate Tables) | Use Post-FIRM '75–'81 VE, V1–V30 Zone ***1 Floor No Basement/Enclosure/Crawlspace*** rates. If LF[1] elevation is 2 or more feet below the BFE[2], submit the Application to the insurer for a rate. |
| **Post-FIRM Rating 1975 to September 30, 1981, Construction Date** | Use Post-FIRM '75–'81 VE, V1–V30 Zone ***1 Floor No Basement/Enclosure/Crawlspace*** rates. If LF[1] elevation is 2 or more feet below the BFE[2], submit the Application to the insurer for a rate. |

1 LF — Lowest Floor
2 BFE — Base Flood Elevation
3 See Proper Flood Openings Requirement located in the How to Write section for an explanation
4 HAG — Highest Adjacent Grade
5 Pre-FIRM buildings may be rated using Post-FIRM rating, including Submit-for-Rate, if more favorable to the insured
6 Non-elevated buildings with construction dates of October 1, 1981, and after are Submit-for-Rate

NOTE: *Above references may not apply to this page.*

## ELEVATED BUILDINGS

## 53. Pre- and Post-FIRM Risks with Construction Dates of 1975 to September 30, 1981, In Flood Zones VE and V1–V30

| | |
|---|---|
| **Building Description** | 2 floors, including hanging floor (see EC, Diagram 5) |
| **Elevating Foundation of Building** | Piers, posts, piles, or columns |
| **Type of Enclosure** | No enclosure |
| **Machinery or Equipment Servicing Building** | With or without machinery or equipment below the lowest elevated floor |
| **Lowest Floor for Rating** | Bottom of lowest horizontal structural member |
| **Application Should Show** | Building type — 2 floors<br>Is building elevated? — Yes<br>Is area below the elevated floor enclosed? — No |
| **Pre-FIRM Subsidized Rating5** | Use Pre-FIRM rate table ***No Basement/Enclosure*** category. |
| **Pre-FIRM Full-Risk Rating** (Use Post-FIRM Rate Tables) | Use Post-FIRM '75–'81 VE, V1–V30 Zone ***More Than 1 Floor No Basement/Enclosure/ Crawlspace*** rates. If LF[1] elevation is 2 or more feet below the BFE[2], submit the Application to the insurer for a rate. |
| **Post-FIRM Rating 1975 to September 30, 1981, Construction Date** | Use Post-FIRM '75–'81 VE, V1–V30 Zone ***More Than 1 Floor No Basement/Enclosure/ Crawlspace*** rates. If LF[1] elevation is 2 or more feet below the BFE[2], submit the Application to the insurer for a rate. |

1 LF — Lowest Floor
2 BFE — Base Flood Elevation
3 See Proper Flood Openings Requirement located in the How to Write section for an explanation
4 HAG — Highest Adjacent Grade
5 Pre-FIRM buildings may be rated using Post-FIRM rating, including Submit-for-Rate, if more favorable to the insured
6 Non-elevated buildings with construction dates of October 1, 1981, and after are Submit-for-Rate

NOTE: *Above references may not apply to this page.*

## ELEVATED BUILDINGS

## 54. Pre- and Post-FIRM Risks with Construction Dates of 1975 to September 30, 1981, In Flood Zones VE and V1–V30

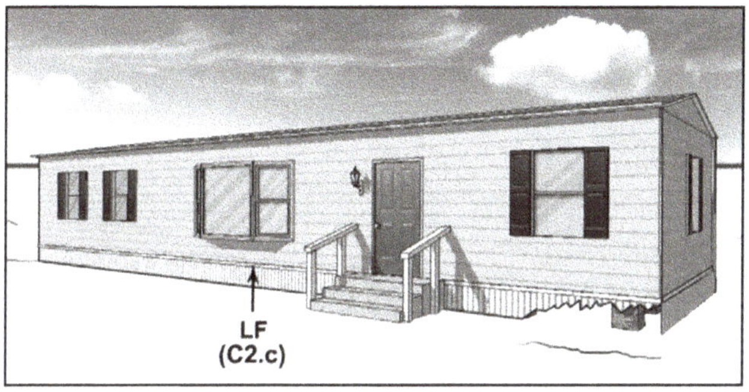


| | |
|---|---|
| **Building Description** | Mobile home without enclosed area (see EC, Diagram 5) |
| **Elevating Foundation of Building** | Piers, posts, piles, or columns |
| **Type of Enclosure** | Vinyl or aluminum skirting |
| **Machinery or Equipment Servicing Building** | With or without machinery or equipment below the lowest elevated floor |
| **Lowest Floor for Rating** | Bottom of lowest horizontal structural member |
| **Application Should Show** | Building type — Mobile home<br>Is building elevated? — Yes<br>Is area below the elevated floor enclosed? — No |
| **Pre-FIRM Subsidized Rating**[5] | Use Pre-FIRM rate table ***No Basement/Enclosure*** category. |
| **Pre-FIRM Full-Risk Rating** (Use Post-FIRM Rate Tables) | Use Post-FIRM '75–'81 VE, V1–V30 Zone ***Manufactured (Mobile) Home*** rates. If LF[1] elevation is 1 or more feet below the BFE[2], submit the Application to the insurer for a rate. |
| **Post-FIRM Rating 1975 to September 30, 1981, Construction Date** | Use Post-FIRM '75–'81 VE, V1–V30 Zone ***Manufactured (Mobile) Home*** rates. If LF[1] elevation is 1 or more feet below the BFE[2], submit the Application to the insurer for a rate. |

1 LF — Lowest Floor
2 BFE — Base Flood Elevation
3 See Proper Flood Openings Requirement located in the How to Write section for an explanation
4 HAG — Highest Adjacent Grade
5 Pre-FIRM buildings may be rated using Post-FIRM rating, including Submit-for-Rate, if more favorable to the insured
6 Non-elevated buildings with construction dates of October 1, 1981, and after are Submit-for-Rate

NOTE: *Above references may not apply to this page.*

## ELEVATED BUILDINGS

## 55. Pre- and Post-FIRM Risks with Construction Dates of 1975 to September 30, 1981, In Flood Zones VE and V1–V30

| | |
|---|---|
| **Building Description** | 2 floors with unfinished enclosed area (see EC, Diagram 6) |
| **Elevating Foundation of Building** | Piers, posts, piles, or columns |
| **Type of Enclosure** | Enclosure (total area less than 300 sq. ft.) with breakaway walls |
| **Machinery or Equipment Servicing Building** | No machinery or equipment below elevated floor |
| **Lowest Floor for Rating** | Bottom of lowest horizontal structural member |
| **Application Should Show** | <table><tr><td></td><td><u>Pre-FIRM</u></td><td><u>Post-FIRM</u></td></tr><tr><td>Building type</td><td>2 floors</td><td>2 floors</td></tr><tr><td>Is building elevated?</td><td>Yes</td><td>Yes</td></tr><tr><td>Is area below the elevated floor enclosed?</td><td>Yes</td><td>No</td></tr></table> |
| **Pre-FIRM Subsidized Rating**[5] | Use Pre-FIRM rate table ***With Enclosure*** category and describe the building as an elevated building with enclosure. |
| **Pre-FIRM Full-Risk Rating** (Use Post-FIRM Rate Tables) | Use Post-FIRM '75–'81 VE, V1–V30 Zone ***More Than 1 Floor No Basement/Enclosure/ Crawlspace*** rate category. If LF[1] elevation is 2 or more feet below the BFE[2], submit the Application to the insurer for a rate. |
| **Post-FIRM Rating 1975 to September 30, 1981, Construction Date** | Use Post-FIRM '75–'81 VE, V1–V30 Zone ***More Than 1 Floor No Basement/Enclosure/ Crawlspace*** rate category. If LF[1] elevation is 2 or more feet below the BFE[2], submit the Application to the insurer for a rate. |

1 LF — Lowest Floor
2 BFE — Base Flood Elevation
3 See Proper Flood Openings Requirement located in the How to Write section for an explanation
4 HAG — Highest Adjacent Grade
5 Pre-FIRM buildings may be rated using Post-FIRM rating, including Submit-for-Rate, if more favorable to the insured
6 Non-elevated buildings with construction dates of October 1, 1981, and after are Submit-for-Rate

NOTE: *Above references may not apply to this page.*

ELEVATED BUILDINGS

## 56. Pre- and Post-FIRM Risks with Construction Dates of 1975 to September 30, 1981, In Flood Zones VE and V1–V30

| | |
|---|---|
| **Building Description** | 1 floor with unfinished enclosed area (see EC, Diagram 6) |
| **Elevating Foundation of Building** | Piers, posts, piles, or columns |
| **Type of Enclosure** | Enclosure (total area less than 300 sq. ft.) with breakaway walls |
| **Machinery or Equipment Servicing Building** | No machinery or equipment below elevated floor |
| **Lowest Floor for Rating** | Bottom of lowest horizontal structural member |
| **Application Should Show** | |

| | Pre-FIRM | Post-FIRM |
|---|---|---|
| Building type | 2 floors | 1 floor |
| Is building elevated? | Yes | Yes |
| Is area below the elevated floor enclosed? | Yes | No |

| | |
|---|---|
| **Pre-FIRM Subsidized Rating[5]** | Use Pre-FIRM rate table ***With Enclosure*** category and describe the building as an elevated building with enclosure. |
| **Pre-FIRM Full-Risk Rating** (Use Post-FIRM Rate Tables) | Use Post-FIRM '75–'81 VE, V1–V30 Zone ***More Than 1 Floor No Basement*** rate category. If LF[1] elevation is 1 or more feet below the BFE[2], submit the Application to the insurer for a rate. |
| **Post-FIRM Rating 1975 to September 30, 1981, Construction Date** | Use Post-FIRM '75–'81 VE, V1–V30 Zone ***1 Floor No Basement/Enclosure/Crawlspace*** rate category. If LF[1] elevation is 2 or more feet below the BFE[2], submit the Application to the insurer for a rate. |

1 LF — Lowest Floor
2 BFE — Base Flood Elevation
3 See Proper Flood Openings Requirement located in the How to Write section for an explanation
4 HAG — Highest Adjacent Grade
5 Pre-FIRM buildings may be rated using Post-FIRM rating, including Submit-for-Rate, if more favorable to the insured
6 Non-elevated buildings with construction dates of October 1, 1981, and after are Submit-for-Rate

NOTE: *Above references may not apply to this page.*

ELEVATED BUILDINGS

## 57. Pre- and Post-FIRM Risks with Construction Dates of 1975 to September 30, 1981, In Flood Zones VE and V1–V30

| | |
|---|---|
| **Building Description** | 1 floor with unfinished enclosed area (see EC, Diagram 6) |
| **Elevating Foundation of Building** | Piers, posts, piles, or columns |
| **Type of Enclosure** | Enclosure (total area less than 300 sq. ft.) with breakaway walls |
| **Machinery or Equipment Servicing Building** | With machinery or equipment below elevated floor |
| **Lowest Floor for Rating** | Bottom of slab<br>In V Zones, the LFE should reflect the bottom of the lowest horizontal structural member. If the surveyor used item C2.a in lieu of C2.c of the EC, and the top of the bottom floor is at or above the lowest adjacent grade (C2.f), deduct (for 1–4 family residences) 12 inches from the elevation figure found in item C2.a. For buildings other than 1–4 family, deduct 18 inches from the elevation figure found in item C2.a. |
| **Application Should Show** | Building Type — 2 floors<br>Is building elevated? — Yes<br>Is area below the elevated floor enclosed? — Yes |
| **Pre-FIRM Subsidized Rating**[5] | Use Pre-FIRM rate table ***With Enclosure*** category. |
| **Pre-FIRM Full-Risk Rating** (Use Post-FIRM Rate Tables) | Use Post-FIRM '75–'81 VE, V1–V30 Zone ***More Than 1 Floor No Basement/Enclosure/ Crawlspace*** rate category. If LF[1] elevation is 1 or more feet below the BFE[2], submit the Application to the insurer for a rate. |
| **Post-FIRM Rating 1975 to September 30, 1981, Construction Date** | Use Post-FIRM '75–'81 VE, V1–V30 Zone ***More Than 1 Floor With Basement/Enclosure/ Crawlspace*** rate category. If LF[1] elevation is 1 or more feet below the BFE[2], submit the Application to the insurer for a rate. |

1 LF — Lowest Floor
2 BFE — Base Flood Elevation
3 See Proper Flood Openings Requirement located in the How to Write section for an explanation
4 HAG — Highest Adjacent Grade
5 Pre-FIRM buildings may be rated using Post-FIRM rating, including Submit-for-Rate, if more favorable to the insured
6 Non-elevated buildings with construction dates of October 1, 1981, and after are Submit-for-Rate

NOTE: *Above references may not apply to this page.*

ELEVATED BUILDINGS

## 58. Pre- and Post-FIRM Risks with Construction Dates of 1975 to September 30, 1981, In Flood Zones VE and V1–V30

| | |
|---|---|
| **Building Description** | 1 floor with finished enclosed area (see EC, Diagram 6) |
| **Elevating Foundation of Building** | Piers, posts, piles, or columns |
| **Type of Enclosure** | Enclosure (total area 300 sq. ft. or more) with non-breakaway walls or with breakaway walls |
| **Machinery or Equipment Servicing Building** | With or without machinery or equipment below the lowest elevated floor |
| **Lowest Floor for Rating** | Bottom of slab<br>In V Zones, the LFE should reflect the bottom of the lowest horizontal structural member. If the surveyor used item C2.a in lieu of C2.c of the EC, and the top of the bottom floor is at or above the lowest adjacent grade (C2.f), deduct (for 1–4 family residences) 12 inches from the elevation figure found in item C2.a. For buildings other than 1–4 family, deduct 18 inches from the elevation figure found in item C2.a. |
| **Application Should Show** | Building type — 2 floors<br>Is building elevated? — Yes<br>Is area below the elevated floor enclosed? — Yes |
| **Pre-FIRM Subsidized Rating**[5] | Use Pre-FIRM rate table ***With Enclosure*** category. |
| **Pre-FIRM Full-Risk Rating** (Use Post-FIRM Rate Tables) | Use Post-FIRM '75–'81 VE, V1–V30 Zone ***More Than 1 Floor No Basement/Enclosure/ Crawlspace*** rate category. If LF[1] elevation is 2 or more feet below the BFE[2], submit the Application to the insurer for a rate. |
| **Post-FIRM Rating 1975 to September 30, 1981, Construction Date** | Use Post-FIRM '75–'81 VE, V1–V30 Zone ***More Than 1 Floor With Basement/Enclosure/ Crawlspace*** rate category. If LF[1] elevation is 1 or more feet below the BFE[2], submit the Application to the insurer for a rate. |

1 LF — Lowest Floor
2 BFE — Base Flood Elevation
3 See Proper Flood Openings Requirement located in the How to Write section for an explanation
4 HAG — Highest Adjacent Grade
5 Pre-FIRM buildings may be rated using Post-FIRM rating, including Submit-for-Rate, if more favorable to the insured
6 Non-elevated buildings with construction dates of October 1, 1981, and after are Submit-for-Rate

NOTE: *Above references may not apply to this page.*

ELEVATED BUILDINGS

## 59. Pre- and Post-FIRM Risks with Construction Dates of 1975 to September 30, 1981, In Flood Zones VE and V1–V30

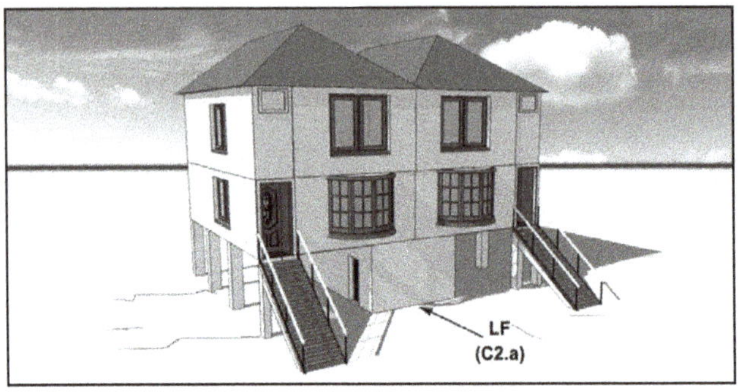


| | |
|---|---|
| **Building Description** | 2 floors with unfinished enclosed area (see EC, Diagram 6) |
| **Elevating Foundation of Building** | Piers, posts, piles, or columns |
| **Type of Enclosure** | Enclosure (total area less than 300 sq. ft.) with non-breakaway walls |
| **Machinery or Equipment Servicing Building** | With or without machinery or equipment below the lowest elevated floor |
| **Lowest Floor for Rating** | Bottom of slab<br>In V Zones, the LFE should reflect the bottom of the lowest horizontal structural member. If the surveyor used item C2.a in lieu of C2.c of the EC, and the top of the bottom floor is at or above the lowest adjacent grade (C2.f), deduct (for 1–4 family residences) 12 inches from the elevation figure found in item C2.a. For buildings other than 1–4 family, deduct 18 inches from the elevation figure found in item C2.a. |
| **Application Should Show** | Building Type — 3 floors<br>Is building elevated? — Yes<br>Is area below the elevated floor enclosed? — Yes |
| **Pre-FIRM Subsidized Rating[5]** | Use Pre-FIRM rate table ***With Enclosure*** category. |
| **Pre-FIRM Full-Risk Rating (Use Post-FIRM Rate Tables)** | Use Post-FIRM '75–'81 VE, V1-V30 Zone ***More Than 1 Floor No Basement/Enclosure/ Crawlspace*** rate category. If LF[1] elevation is 1 or more feet below the BFE[2], submit the Application to the insurer for a rate. |
| **Post-FIRM Rating 1975 to September 30, 1981, Construction Date** | Use Post-FIRM '75–'81 VE, V1–V30 Zone ***More Than 1 Floor With Basement/Enclosure/ Crawlspace*** rate category. If LF[1] elevation is 1 or more feet below the BFE[2], submit the Application to the insurer for a rate. |

1 LF — Lowest Floor
2 BFE — Base Flood Elevation
3 See Proper Flood Openings Requirement located in the How to Write section for an explanation
4 HAG — Highest Adjacent Grade
5 Pre-FIRM buildings may be rated using Post-FIRM rating, including Submit-for-Rate, if more favorable to the insured
6 Non-elevated buildings with construction dates of October 1, 1981, and after are Submit-for-Rate

NOTE: *Above references may not apply to this page.*

ELEVATED BUILDINGS

## 60. Pre- and Post-FIRM Risks with Construction Dates of 1975 to September 30, 1981, In Flood Zones VE and V1–V30

| | |
|---|---|
| **Building Description** | 3 or more floors with unfinished enclosed area (see EC, Diagram 6) |
| **Elevating Foundation of Building** | Piers, posts, piles, or columns |
| **Type of Enclosure** | Enclosure (total area 300 sq. ft. or more) with non-breakaway walls or with breakaway walls |
| **Machinery or Equipment Servicing Building** | With or without machinery or equipment below the lowest elevated floor |
| **Lowest Floor for Rating** | Bottom of slab<br>In V Zones, the LFE should reflect the bottom of the lowest horizontal structural member. If the surveyor used item C2.a in lieu of C2.c of the EC, and the top of the bottom floor is at or above the lowest adjacent grade (C2.f), deduct (for 1–4 family residences) 12 inches from the elevation figure found in item C2.a. For buildings other than 1–4 family, deduct 18 inches from the elevation figure found in item C2.a. |
| **Application Should Show** | Building type — 3 or more floors<br>Is building elevated? — Yes<br>Is area below the elevated floor enclosed? — Yes |
| **Pre-FIRM Subsidized Rating**[5] | Use Pre-FIRM rate table ***With Enclosure*** category. |
| **Pre-FIRM Full-Risk Rating** (Use Post-FIRM Rate Tables) | Use Post-FIRM '75–'81 VE, V1–V30 Zone ***More Than 1 Floor No Basement/Enclosure/ Crawlspace*** rate category. If LF[1] elevation is 1 or more feet below the BFE[2], submit the Application to the insurer for a rate. |
| **Post-FIRM Rating 1975 to September 30, 1981, Construction Date** | Use Post-FIRM '75–'81 VE, V1–V30 Zone ***More Than 1 Floor With Basement/Enclosure/ Crawlspace*** rate category. If LF[1] elevation is 1 or more feet below the BFE[2], submit the Application to the insurer for a rate. |

1 LF — Lowest Floor
2 BFE — Base Flood Elevation
3 See Proper Flood Openings Requirement located in the How to Write section for an explanation
4 HAG — Highest Adjacent Grade
5 Pre-FIRM buildings may be rated using Post-FIRM rating, including Submit-for-Rate, if more favorable to the insured
6 Non-elevated buildings with construction dates of October 1, 1981, and after are Submit-for-Rate

NOTE: *Above references may not apply to this page.*

## ELEVATED BUILDINGS

## 61. Pre- and Post-FIRM Risks with Construction Dates of 1975 to September 30, 1981, In Flood Zones VE and V1–V30

| | |
|---|---|
| **Building Description** | 1 floor with finished or unfinished enclosed area (see EC, Diagram 6) |
| **Elevating Foundation of Building** | Shear walls parallel to the expected flow of floodwaters |
| **Type of Enclosure** | Both ends enclosed with nonbreakaway walls or breakaway walls (total enclosed area 300 sq. ft. or more) |
| **Machinery or Equipment Servicing Building** | With or without machinery or equipment below the lowest elevated floor |
| **Lowest Floor for Rating** | Bottom of slab<br>In V Zones, the LFE should reflect the bottom of the lowest horizontal structural member. If the surveyor used item C2.a in lieu of C2.c of the EC, and the top of the bottom floor is at above the lowest adjacent grade (C2.f), deduct (for 1–4 family residences) 12 inches from the elevation figure found in item C2.a. For buildings other than 1–4 family, deduct 18 inches from the elevation figure found in item C2.a. |
| **Application Should Show** | Building type — 2 floors<br>Is building elevated? — Yes<br>Is area below the elevated floor enclosed? — Yes |
| **Pre-FIRM Subsidized Rating**[5] | Use Pre-FIRM rate table ***With Enclosure*** category. |
| **Pre-FIRM Full-Risk Rating** (Use Post-FIRM Rate Tables) | Use Post-FIRM '75–'81 VE, V1–V30 Zone ***More Than 1 Floor No Basement/Enclosure/ Crawlspace*** rate category. If LF[1] elevation is 2 or more feet below the BFE[2], submit the Application to the insurer for a rate. |
| **Post-FIRM Rating 1975 to September 30, 1981, Construction Date** | Use Post-FIRM '75–'81 VE, V1–V30 Zone ***More Than 1 Floor With Basement/Enclosure/ Crawlspace*** rate category. If LF[1] elevation is 1 or more feet below the BFE[2], submit the Application to the insurer for a rate. |

1 LF — Lowest Floor
2 BFE — Base Flood Elevation
3 See Proper Flood Openings Requirement located in the How to Write section for an explanation
4 HAG — Highest Adjacent Grade
5 Pre-FIRM buildings may be rated using Post-FIRM rating, including Submit-for-Rate, if more favorable to the insured
6 Non-elevated buildings with construction dates of October 1, 1981, and after are Submit-for-Rate

NOTE: *Above references may not apply to this page.*

ELEVATED BUILDINGS

## 62. Pre- and Post-FIRM Risks with Construction Dates of 1975 to September 30, 1981, In Flood Zones VE and V1–V30

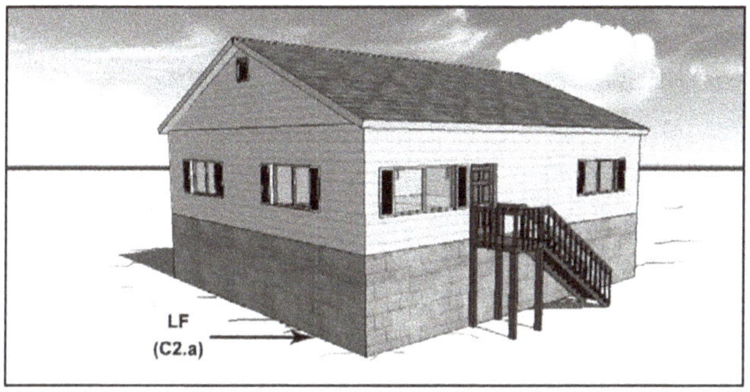


| | |
|---|---|
| Building Description | 1 floor with finished or unfinished enclosed area (see EC, Diagram 7) |
| Elevating Foundation of Building | Solid foundation walls |
| Type of Enclosure | Finished or unfinished enclosure |
| Machinery or Equipment Servicing Building | With or without machinery or equipment below the lowest elevated floor |
| Lowest Floor for Rating | Bottom of slab<br>In V Zones, the LFE should reflect the bottom of the lowest horizontal structural member. If the surveyor used item C2.a in lieu of C2.c of the EC, and the top of the bottom floor is at or above the lowest adjacent grade (C2.f), deduct (for 1–4 family residences) 12 inches from the elevation figure found in item C2.a. For buildings other than 1–4 family, deduct 18 inches from the elevation figure found in item C2.a. |
| Application Should Show | Building type — 2 floors<br>Is building elevated? — Yes<br>Is area below the elevated floor enclosed? — Yes |
| Pre-FIRM Subsidized Rating[5] | Use Pre-FIRM rate table ***With Enclosure*** category. |
| Pre-FIRM Full-Risk Rating (Use Post-FIRM Rate Tables) | Use Post-FIRM '75–'81 VE, V1–V30 Zone ***More Than 1 Floor No Basement/Enclosure/ Crawlspace*** rate category. If LF[1] elevation is 2 or more feet below the BFE[2], submit the Application to the insurer for a rate. |
| Post-FIRM Rating 1975 to September 30, 1981, Construction Date | Use Post-FIRM '75–'81 VE, V1–V30 Zone ***More Than 1 Floor With Basement/Enclosure/ Crawlspace*** rate category. If LF[1] elevation is 1 or more feet below the BFE[2], submit the Application to the insurer for a rate. |

1 LF — Lowest Floor
2 BFE — Base Flood Elevation
3 See Proper Flood Openings Requirement located in the How to Write section for an explanation
4 HAG — Highest Adjacent Grade
5 Pre-FIRM buildings may be rated using Post-FIRM rating, including Submit-for-Rate, if more favorable to the insured
6 Non-elevated buildings with construction dates of October 1, 1981, and after are Submit-for-Rate

NOTE: *Above references may not apply to this page.*

## ELEVATED BUILDINGS

## 63. Pre- and Post-FIRM Risks with Construction Dates of 1975 to September 30, 1981, In Flood Zones VE and V1–V30

| | |
|---|---|
| **Building Description** | 2 floors with crawlspace (see EC, Diagram 8) |
| **Elevating Foundation of Building** | Solid foundation walls |
| **Type of Enclosure** | Unfinished crawlspace |
| **Machinery or Equipment Servicing Building** | With or without machinery or equipment below the lowest elevated floor |
| **Lowest Floor for Rating** | Bottom of foundation wall |
| **Application Should Show** | Building type — 3 or more floors<br>Is building elevated? — Yes<br>Is area below the elevated floor enclosed? — Yes |
| **Pre-FIRM Subsidized Rating**[5] | Use Pre-FIRM rate table ***Elevated On Crawlspace*** category. |
| **Pre-FIRM Full-Risk Rating** (Use Post-FIRM Rate Tables) | Use Post-FIRM '75–'81 VE, V1–V30 Zone ***More Than 1 Floor No Basement/Enclosure/ Crawlspace*** rate category. If LF[1] elevation is 2 or more feet below the BFE[2], submit the Application to the insurer for a rate. |
| **Post-FIRM Rating 1975 to September 30, 1981, Construction Date** | Use Post-FIRM '75–'81 VE, V1–V30 Zone ***More Than 1 Floor With Basement/Enclosure/ Crawlspace*** rate category. If LF[1] elevation is 1 or more feet below the BFE[2], submit the Application to the insurer for a rate. |

1 LF — Lowest Floor
2 BFE — Base Flood Elevation
3 See Proper Flood Openings Requirement located in the How to Write section for an explanation
4 HAG — Highest Adjacent Grade
5 Pre-FIRM buildings may be rated using Post-FIRM rating, including Submit-for-Rate, if more favorable to the insured
6 Non-elevated buildings with construction dates of October 1, 1981, and after are Submit-for-Rate

NOTE: *Above references may not apply to this page.*

ELEVATED BUILDINGS

## 64. Post-FIRM Risks in Flood Zones VE and V1–V30 — Construction Date October 1, 1981, and After

| | |
|---|---|
| **Building Description** | 1 floor without enclosed area (see EC, Diagram 5) |
| **Elevating Foundation of Building** | Piers, posts, piles, or columns |
| **Type of Enclosure** | The space below the lowest elevated floor either has no enclosure or has:<br>(1) Insect screening, provided that no additional supports are required for the screening; *or*<br>(2) Wooden or plastic lattice with at least 40% of its area open and made of material no thicker than ½ inch; *or*<br>(3) Wooden or plastic slats or shutters with at least 40% of their area open and made of material no thicker than 1 inch; *or*<br>(4) The area below the lowest elevated floor is enclosed by a combination of 1 solid breakaway wall or garage door, and the other sides of the enclosure are insect screening, or wooden or plastic lattice, slats, or shutters.<br>Any of these systems must be designed and installed to collapse under stress without jeopardizing the structural support of the building, so that the impact on the building of abnormally high tides or wind-driven water is minimized. |
| **Machinery or Equipment Servicing Building** | No machinery or equipment below elevated floor |
| **Lowest Floor for Rating** | Bottom of lowest horizontal structural member |
| **Application Should Show** | Building type — 1 floor<br>Is building elevated? — Yes<br>Is area below the elevated floor enclosed? — No |
| **V-Zone Rating; Construction Date October 1, 1981, and After** | Use 1981 Post-FIRM V1–V30, VE Zone ***Free of Obstruction*** rates. If LF[1] elevation is 4 or more feet below the BFE[2], submit the Application to the insurer for a rate. |

1 LF — Lowest Floor
2 BFE — Base Flood Elevation
3 See Proper Flood Openings Requirement located in the How to Write section for an explanation
4 HAG — Highest Adjacent Grade
5 Pre-FIRM buildings may be rated using Post-FIRM rating, including Submit-for-Rate, if more favorable to the insured
6 Non-elevated buildings with construction dates of October 1, 1981, and after are Submit-for-Rate

NOTE: *Above references may not apply to this page.*

## ELEVATED BUILDINGS

## 65. Post-FIRM Risks in Flood Zones VE and V1–V30 — Construction Date October 1, 1981, and After

| | |
|---|---|
| **Building Description** | 1 floor without enclosed area (see EC, Diagram 5) |
| **Elevating Foundation of Building** | Piers, posts, piles, or columns |
| **Type of Enclosure** | No enclosure or open-wood latticework or insect screening |
| **Machinery or Equipment Servicing Building** | With machinery or equipment at or above the BFE |
| **Lowest Floor for Rating** | Bottom of lowest horizontal structural member |
| **Application Should Show** | Building type — 1 floor<br>Is building elevated? — Yes<br>Is area below the elevated floor enclosed? — No |
| **V-Zone Rating; Construction Date October 1, 1981, and After** | Use 1981 Post-FIRM V1–V30, VE Zone ***Free of Obstruction*** rates. If LF[1] elevation is 4 or more feet below the BFE[2], submit the Application to the insurer for a rate. |

1 LF — Lowest Floor
2 BFE — Base Flood Elevation
3 See Proper Flood Openings Requirement located in the How to Write section for an explanation
4 HAG — Highest Adjacent Grade
5 Pre-FIRM buildings may be rated using Post-FIRM rating, including Submit-for-Rate, if more favorable to the insured
6 Non-elevated buildings with construction dates of October 1, 1981, and after are Submit-for-Rate

NOTE: *Above references may not apply to this page.*

ELEVATED BUILDINGS

## 66. Post-FIRM Risks in Flood Zones VE and V1–V30 — Construction Date October 1, 1981, and After

| | |
|---|---|
| Building Description | 2 floors, including hanging floor (see EC, Diagram 5) |
| Elevating Foundation of Building | Piers, posts, piles, or columns |
| Type of Enclosure | No enclosure |
| Machinery or Equipment Servicing Building | Without machinery or equipment below the lowest elevated floor |
| Lowest Floor for Rating | Bottom of lowest horizontal structural member |
| Application Should Show | Building type — 2 floors<br>Is building elevated? — Yes<br>Is area below the elevated floor enclosed? — No |
| V-Zone Rating; Construction Date October 1, 1981, and After | Use 1981 Post-FIRM V1–V30, VE Zone ***Free of Obstruction*** rates. If LF[1] elevation is 4 or more feet below the BFE[2], submit the Application to the insurer for a rate. |

1 LF — Lowest Floor
2 BFE — Base Flood Elevation
3 See Proper Flood Openings Requirement located in the How to Write section for an explanation
4 HAG — Highest Adjacent Grade
5 Pre-FIRM buildings may be rated using Post-FIRM rating, including Submit-for-Rate, if more favorable to the insured
6 Non-elevated buildings with construction dates of October 1, 1981, and after are Submit-for-Rate

NOTE: *Above references may not apply to this page.*

ELEVATED BUILDINGS

## 67. Post-FIRM Risks in Flood Zones VE and V1–V30 — Construction Date October 1, 1981, and After

| | |
|---|---|
| **Building Description** | 1 floor with unfinished enclosed area (see EC, Diagram 6) |
| **Elevating Foundation of Building** | Piers, posts, piles, or columns |
| **Type of Enclosure** | Enclosure (total area less than 300 sq. ft.) with breakaway walls |
| **Machinery or Equipment Servicing Building** | Without machinery or equipment below elevated floor |
| **Lowest Floor for Rating** | Bottom of lowest horizontal structural member |
| **Application Should Show** | Building type — 2 floors<br>Is building elevated? — Yes<br>Is area below the elevated floor enclosed? — Yes |
| **V-Zone Rating; Construction Date October 1, 1981, and After** | Use 1981 Post-FIRM V1–V30, VE Zone ***With Obstruction*** rates. If LF[1] elevation is 4 or more feet below the BFE[2], submit the Application to the insurer for a rate. |

1 LF — Lowest Floor
2 BFE — Base Flood Elevation
3 See Proper Flood Openings Requirement located in the How to Write section for an explanation
4 HAG — Highest Adjacent Grade
5 Pre-FIRM buildings may be rated using Post-FIRM rating, including Submit-for-Rate, if more favorable to the insured
6 Non-elevated buildings with construction dates of October 1, 1981, and after are Submit-for-Rate

NOTE: *Above references may not apply to this page.*

## ELEVATED BUILDINGS

## 68. Post-FIRM Risks in Flood Zones VE and V1–V30 — Construction Date October 1, 1981, and After

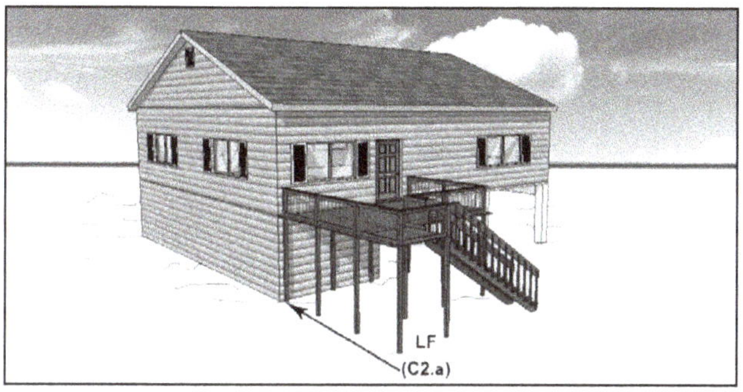


| | |
|---|---|
| **Building Description** | 1 floor with unfinished enclosed area (see EC, Diagram 6) |
| **Elevating Foundation of Building** | Piers, posts, piles, or columns |
| **Type of Enclosure** | Enclosure (total area less than 300 sq. ft.) with breakaway walls |
| **Machinery or Equipment Servicing Building** | With machinery or equipment below the BFE |
| **Lowest Floor for Rating** | Bottom of slab<br>In V Zones, the LFE should reflect the bottom of the lowest horizontal structural member. If the surveyor used item C2.a in lieu of C2.c of the EC, and the top of the bottom floor is at or above the lowest adjacent grade, deduct (for 1–4 family residences) 12 inches from the elevation figure found in item C2.a. For buildings other than 1–4 family, deduct 18 inches from the elevation figure found in item C2.a. |
| **Application Should Show** | Building type — 2 floors<br>Is building elevated? — Yes<br>Is area below the elevated floor enclosed? — Yes |
| **V-Zone Rating; Construction Date October 1, 1981, and After** | Submit the Application to the insurer for a rate. |

1 LF — Lowest Floor
2 BFE — Base Flood Elevation
3 See Proper Flood Openings Requirement located in the How to Write section for an explanation
4 HAG — Highest Adjacent Grade
5 Pre-FIRM buildings may be rated using Post-FIRM rating, including Submit-for-Rate, if more favorable to the insured
6 Non-elevated buildings with construction dates of October 1, 1981, and after are Submit-for-Rate

NOTE: *Above references may not apply to this page.*

ELEVATED BUILDINGS

## 69. Post-FIRM Risks in Flood Zones VE and V1–V30 — Construction Date October 1, 1981, and After

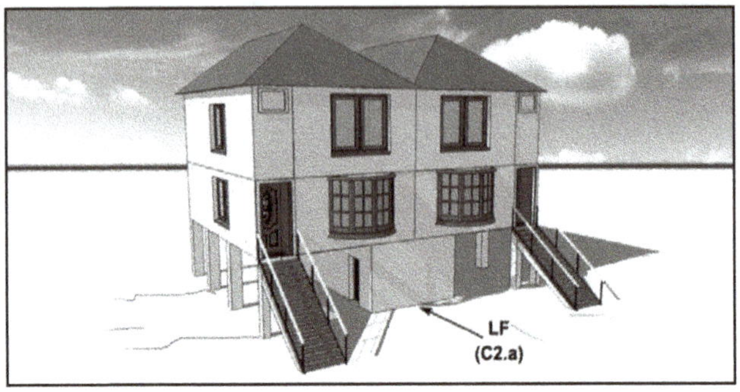


| | |
|---|---|
| **Building Description** | 2 floors with finished or unfinished enclosed area (see EC, Diagram 6) |
| **Elevating Foundation of Building** | Piers, posts, piles, or columns |
| **Type of Enclosure** | Enclosure (total area less than 300 sq. ft.) with breakaway walls |
| **Machinery or Equipment Servicing Building** | With machinery or equipment below the BFE |
| **Lowest Floor for Rating** | Bottom of slab<br>In V Zones, the LFE should reflect the bottom of the lowest horizontal structural member. If the surveyor used item C2.a in lieu of C2.c of the EC, and the top of the bottom floor is at or above the lowest adjacent grade, deduct (for 1–4 family residences) 12 inches from the elevation figure found in item C2.a. For buildings other than 1–4 family, deduct 18 inches from the elevation figure found in item C2.a. |
| **Application Should Show** | Building type — 3 floors<br>Is building elevated? — Yes<br>Is area below the elevated floor enclosed? — Yes |
| **V-Zone Rating; Construction Date October 1, 1981, and After** | Submit the Application to the insurer for a rate. |

1 LF — Lowest Floor
2 BFE — Base Flood Elevation
3 See Proper Flood Openings Requirement located in the How to Write section for an explanation
4 HAG — Highest Adjacent Grade
5 Pre-FIRM buildings may be rated using Post-FIRM rating, including Submit-for-Rate, if more favorable to the insured
6 Non-elevated buildings with construction dates of October 1, 1981, and after are Submit-for-Rate

NOTE: *Above references may not apply to this page.*

## ELEVATED BUILDINGS

## 70. Post-FIRM Risks in Flood Zones VE and V1–V30 — Construction Date October 1, 1981, and After

| | |
|---|---|
| **Building Description** | 1 floor with finished or unfinished enclosed area (see EC, Diagram 6) |
| **Elevating Foundation of Building** | Piers, posts, piles, or columns |
| **Type of Enclosure** | Enclosure (total area 300 sq. ft. or more) with nonbreakaway walls or breakaway walls |
| **Machinery or Equipment Servicing Building** | With or without machinery or equipment below the lowest elevated floor |
| **Lowest Floor for Rating** | Bottom of slab<br>In V Zones, the LFE should reflect the bottom of the lowest horizontal structural member. If the surveyor used item C2.a in lieu of C2.c of the EC, and the top of the bottom floor is at or above the lowest adjacent grade (C2.f), deduct (for 1–4 family residences) 12 inches from the elevation figure found in item C2.a. For buildings other than 1–4 family, deduct 18 inches from the elevation figure found in item C2.a. |
| **Application Should Show** | Building type — 2 floors<br>Is building elevated? — Yes<br>Is area below the elevated floor enclosed? — Yes |
| **V-Zone Rating; Construction Date October 1, 1981, and After** | Submit the Application to the insurer for a rate. |

1 LF — Lowest Floor
2 BFE — Base Flood Elevation
3 See Proper Flood Openings Requirement located in the How to Write section for an explanation
4 HAG — Highest Adjacent Grade
5 Pre-FIRM buildings may be rated using Post-FIRM rating, including Submit-for-Rate, if more favorable to the insured
6 Non-elevated buildings with construction dates of October 1, 1981, and after are Submit-for-Rate

NOTE: *Above references may not apply to this page.*

## ELEVATED BUILDINGS

## 71. Post-FIRM Risks in Flood Zones VE and V1–V30 — Construction Date October 1, 1981, and After

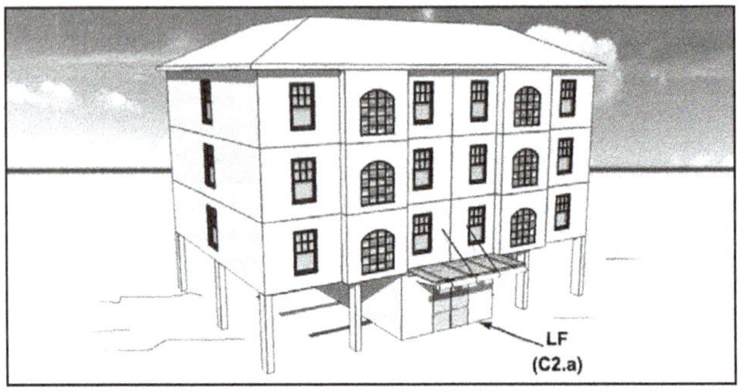


| | |
|---|---|
| **Building Description** | 3 or more floors with finished or unfinished enclosed area (see EC, Diagram 6) |
| **Elevating Foundation of Building** | Piers, posts, piles, or columns |
| **Type of Enclosure** | Enclosure (total area 300 sq. ft. or more) with nonbreakaway walls or breakaway walls |
| **Machinery or Equipment Servicing Building** | With or without machinery or equipment below the lowest elevated floor |
| **Lowest Floor for Rating** | Bottom of slab<br>In V Zones, the LFE should reflect the bottom of the lowest horizontal structural member. If the surveyor used item C2.a in lieu of C2.c of the EC, and the top of the bottom floor is at or above the lowest adjacent grade (C2.f), deduct (for 1–4 family residences) 12 inches from the elevation figure found in item C2.a. For buildings other than 1–4 family, deduct 18 inches from the elevation figure found in item C2.a. |
| **Application Should Show** | Building type — 3 or more floors<br>Is building elevated? — Yes<br>Is area below the elevated floor enclosed? — Yes |
| **V-Zone Rating; Construction Date October 1, 1981, and After** | Submit the Application to the insurer for a rate. |

1 LF — Lowest Floor
2 BFE — Base Flood Elevation
3 See Proper Flood Openings Requirement located in the How to Write section for an explanation
4 HAG — Highest Adjacent Grade
5 Pre-FIRM buildings may be rated using Post-FIRM rating, including Submit-for-Rate, if more favorable to the insured
6 Non-elevated buildings with construction dates of October 1, 1981, and after are Submit-for-Rate

NOTE: *Above references may not apply to this page.*

## ELEVATED BUILDINGS

## 72. Post-FIRM Risks in Flood Zones VE and V1–V30 — Construction Date October 1, 1981, and After

| | |
|---|---|
| **Building Description** | 1 floor with finished or unfinished enclosed area (see EC, Diagram 6) |
| **Elevating Foundation of Building** | Shear walls parallel to the expected flow of floodwaters |
| **Type of Enclosure** | Both ends enclosed with breakaway walls (total enclosed area 300 sq. ft. or more) |
| **Machinery or Equipment Servicing Building** | With or without machinery or equipment below the lowest elevated floor |
| **Lowest Floor for Rating** | Bottom of slab<br>In V Zones, the LFE should reflect the bottom of the lowest horizontal structural member. If the surveyor used item C2.a in lieu of C2.c of the EC, and the top of the bottom floor is at or above the lowest adjacent grade (C2.f), deduct (for 1–4 family residences) 12 inches from the elevation figure found in item C2.a. For buildings other than 1–4 family, deduct 18 inches from the elevation figure found in item C2.a. |
| **Application Should Show** | Building type — 2 floors<br>Is building elevated? — Yes<br>Is area below the elevated floor enclosed? — Yes |
| **V-Zone Rating; Construction Date October 1, 1981, and After** | Submit the Application to the insurer for a rate. |

1 LF — Lowest Floor
2 BFE — Base Flood Elevation
3 See Proper Flood Openings Requirement located in the How to Write section for an explanation
4 HAG — Highest Adjacent Grade
5 Pre-FIRM buildings may be rated using Post-FIRM rating, including Submit-for-Rate, if more favorable to the insured
6 Non-elevated buildings with construction dates of October 1, 1981, and after are Submit-for-Rate

NOTE: *Above references may not apply to this page.*

## ELEVATED BUILDINGS

## 73. Post-FIRM Risks In Flood Zones VE and V1–V30 — Construction Date October 1, 1981, And After

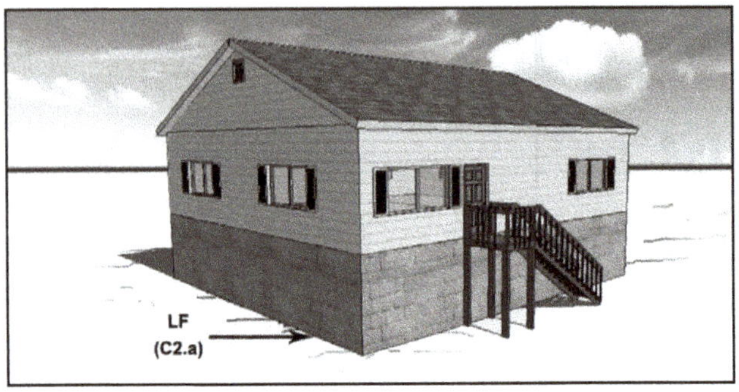


| | |
|---|---|
| **Building Description** | 1 floor with finished or unfinished enclosed area (see EC, Diagram 7) |
| **Elevating Foundation of Building** | Solid foundation walls |
| **Type of Enclosure** | Finished or unfinished enclosure |
| **Machinery or Equipment Servicing Building** | With or without machinery or equipment below the lowest elevated floor |
| **Lowest Floor for Rating** | Bottom of slab<br>In V Zones, the LFE should reflect the bottom of the lowest horizontal structural member. If the surveyor used item C2.a in lieu of C2.c of the EC, and the top of the bottom floor is at or above the lowest adjacent grade (C2.f), deduct (for 1–4 family residences) 12 inches from the elevation figure found in item C2.a. For buildings other than 1–4 family, deduct 18 inches from the elevation figure found in item C2.a |
| **Application Should Show** | Building type — 2 floors<br>Is building elevated? — Yes<br>Is area below the elevated floor enclosed? — Yes |
| **V-Zone Rating; Construction Date October 1, 1981, and After** | Submit the Application to the insurer for a rate. |

1 LF — Lowest Floor
2 BFE — Base Flood Elevation
3 See Proper Flood Openings Requirement located in the How to Write section for an explanation
4 HAG — Highest Adjacent Grade
5 Pre-FIRM buildings may be rated using Post-FIRM rating, including Submit-for-Rate, if more favorable to the insured
6 Non-elevated buildings with construction dates of October 1, 1981, and after are Submit-for-Rate

NOTE: *Above references may not apply to this page.*

## ELEVATED BUILDINGS

## 74. Post-FIRM Risks in Flood Zones VE and V1–V30 — Construction Date October 1, 1981, and After

| | |
|---|---|
| Building Description | 2 floors with crawlspace (see EC, Diagram 8) |
| Elevating Foundation of Building | Solid foundation walls |
| Type of Enclosure | Unfinished crawlspace |
| Machinery or Equipment Servicing Building | With or without machinery or equipment below the lowest elevated floor |
| Lowest Floor for Rating | Bottom of foundation wall |
| Application Should Show | Building type — 3 or more floors<br>Is building elevated? — Yes<br>Is area below the elevated floor enclosed? — Yes |
| V-Zone Rating; Construction Date October 1, 1981, and After | Submit the Application to the insurer for a rate. |

1 LF — Lowest Floor
2 BFE — Base Flood Elevation
3 See Proper Flood Openings Requirement located in the How to Write section for an explanation
4 HAG — Highest Adjacent Grade
5 Pre-FIRM buildings may be rated using Post-FIRM rating, including Submit-for-Rate, if more favorable to the insured
6 Non-elevated buildings with construction dates of October 1, 1981, and after are Submit-for-Rate

NOTE: *Above references may not apply to this page.*

## ELEVATED BUILDINGS

## 75. Post-FIRM Risks in Flood Zones VE and V1–V30 — Construction Date October 1, 1981, and After

| | |
|---|---|
| **Building Description** | 1 floor Mid-Level Entry with unfinished enclosure (see EC, Diagram 6) |
| **Elevating Foundation of Building** | Piers, posts, piles, or columns |
| **Type of Enclosure** | Enclosure garage<br>Enclosure (total area 300 sq. ft. or more) with nonbreakaway walls or breakaway walls |
| **Machinery or Equipment Servicing Building** | With or without machinery or equipment below the lowest elevated floor |
| **Lowest Floor for Rating** | Bottom of slab<br>In V Zones, the LFE should reflect the bottom of the lowest horizontal structural member. If the surveyor used item C2.a in lieu of C2.c of the EC, and the top of the bottom floor is at or above the lowest adjacent grade (C2.f), deduct (for 1–4 family residences) 12 inches from the elevation figure found in item C2.a. For buildings other than 1–4 family, deduct 18 inches from the elevation figure found in item C2.a |
| **Application Should Show** | Building type — 2 floors<br>Is building elevated? — Yes<br>Is area below the elevated floor enclosed? — Yes |
| **V-Zone Rating; Construction Date October 1, 1981, and After** | Submit the Application to the insurer for a rate. |

1 LF — Lowest Floor
2 BFE — Base Flood Elevation
3 See Proper Flood Openings Requirement located in the How to Write section for an explanation
4 HAG — Highest Adjacent Grade
5 Pre-FIRM buildings may be rated using Post-FIRM rating, including Submit-for-Rate, if more favorable to the insured
6 Non-elevated buildings with construction dates of October 1, 1981, and after are Submit-for-Rate

NOTE: *Above references may not apply to this page.*

NON-ELEVATED BUILDINGS

## 76. Post-FIRM Risks in Flood Zones VE and V1–V30 — Construction Date October 1, 1981, and After

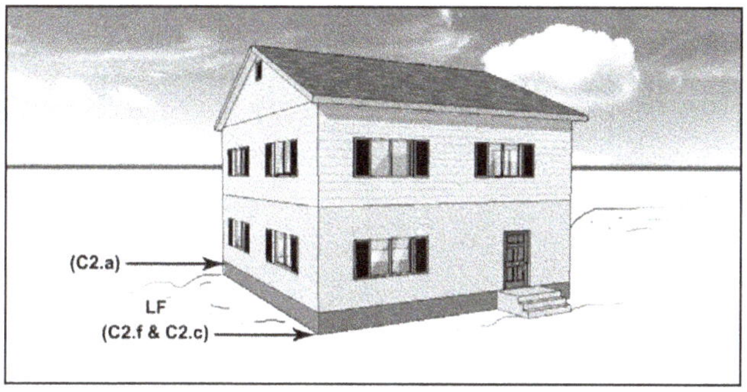


| | |
|---|---|
| **Building Description** | 2 floors on raised-slab-on-grade or slab-on-stem-wall-with-fill (see EC, Diagram 1B) |
| **Lowest Floor for Rating** | Lowest adjacent grade (C2.f) |
| **Application Should Show** | Building type — 2 floors<br>Basement — None<br>Is building elevated? — No |
| **V-Zone Rating; Construction Date October 1, 1981, and After** | Submit the Application to the insurer for a rate. |

1 LF — Lowest Floor
2 BFE — Base Flood Elevation
3 See Proper Flood Openings Requirement located in the How to Write section for an explanation
4 HAG — Highest Adjacent Grade
5 Pre-FIRM buildings may be rated using Post-FIRM rating, including Submit-for-Rate, if more favorable to the insured
6 Non-elevated buildings with construction dates of October 1, 1981, and after are Submit-for-Rate

NOTE: *Above references may not apply to this page.*

This page is intentionally left blank.

# Appendix D: Coastal Barrier Resources System

## I. General Information

- The Coastal Barrier Resources Act (CBRA) (16 U.S.C. 3501 et seq.) established the John H. Chafee Coastal Barrier Resources System (CBRS), a defined set of geographic units located along the Atlantic, Gulf of Mexico, Great Lakes, U.S. Virgin Islands, and Puerto Rico coasts.
- The CBRS contains two types of units, System Units and Otherwise Protected Areas (OPAs). OPAs are denoted with a "P" at the end of the unit number (e.g., FL-64P, P10P). With limited exceptions, the NFIP may not provide flood insurance for buildings located in a System Unit or an OPA established under the CBRA. System Units carry additional restrictions on federal funding and financial assistance.
- The purpose of the CBRA is to minimize the loss of human life, wasteful expenditure of federal revenues, and the damage to fish, wildlife, and other natural resources associated with the coastal barriers by restricting most new federal expenditures and financial assistance that have the effect of encouraging development.
- OPAs are predominantly comprised of conservation and/or recreation areas such as national wildlife refuges, state and national parks, local conservation areas, and private conservation areas, though they may also contain private areas that are not held for conservation and/or recreation.
- The CBRS units are depicted on a set of maps maintained by the U.S. Fish & Wildlife Service (USFWS). The public may access the maps via the CBRS Mapper at https://www.fws.gov/cbra/maps/Mapper.html.
- Flood Insurance Rate Maps (FIRMs) have historically displayed System Units and OPAs of the CBRS. Beginning in late 2018, CBRS boundaries will no longer appear on new FIRMs. The CBRS boundaries will continue to be accessible through the National Flood Hazard Layer Viewer and are visible on FIRM downloads and FIRMette exports through the Map Service Center.

## II. Determining Eligibility

Buildings in System Units or OPAs are eligible for a federal flood insurance policy if they meet the criteria outlined in this section. Eligibility depends on:

- The date of the building's permitting and construction.
- The location of the building (cannot be in areas where the prohibition applies).
- For buildings in OPAs, the building's use.

### A. Determine if Community has a System Unit or OPA

System Units and OPAs currently exist in 23 states and territories along the Atlantic, Gulf of Mexico, Great Lakes, U.S. Virgin Islands, and Puerto Rico coasts. To identify communities that contain System Units and/or OPAs, refer to the CBRS Mapper on the USFWS website listed in II.B. The information provided in the CBRS Mapper indicates whether a community contains a System Unit or OPA, but does not determine flood insurance eligibility. If the

CBRS Mapper does not identify any System Units or OPAs in the community, no further action is required. To determine flood insurance eligibility and write a policy for a structure located in a community that has System Units or OPAs identified in the CBRS Mapper, please follow the steps outlined below.

## B. Determine if the Property is Located in a System Unit or OPA

To determine if a property is located in a System Unit or OPA, visit the CBRS Mapper on the USFWS website (https://www.fws.gov/cbra/maps/Mapper.html) and use the "CBRS Validation Tool."

The CBRS Validation Tool is an automated tool accessible through the CBRS Mapper that allows any user (surveyors, property owners, insurance agents, real estate agents, federal agencies, etc.) to select a particular location and produce a document entitled "CBRS Mapper Documentation" that indicates whether that location is within or outside of the CBRS. For locations within the CBRS, the documentation will also indicate the unit type (System Unit or OPA) and date the prohibition on federal flood insurance went into effect.

For guidance on using the CBRS Validation Tool, please review the user guide at: https://www.fws.gov/cbra/documents/CBRS-Validation-Tool-User-Guide.pdf.

### *1. Unable to Determine Building Location*

An agent may need to utilize one of the following if unable to locate the building using the CBRS Validation Tool in the CBRS Mapper:

- A copy of a plat survey or tax map.
- A copy of a county or municipal street map that shows the area surrounding the property's location and has the risk's location clearly marked.
- An aerial photograph that shows the property in question.
- A metes-and-bounds description of the location, and/or the latitude and longitude of the property.

The agent may contact the insurer for guidance.

### *2. Building Located in the CBRS Buffer Zone*

The CBRS Buffer Zone represents the area immediately adjacent to the CBRS boundary. Agents should send requests for CBRS determinations for properties within the CBRS Buffer Zone to the insurer. The insurer will send the request to FEMA by email to: NFIPUnderwritingMailbox@fema.dhs.gov. FEMA will submit the case to the USFWS for an official determination letter as to whether the property is located "in" or "out" of the CBRS.

USFWS requires the following documentation to complete the determination:

- A valid address; *and*
- The output from the CBRS Validation Tool indicating that the building is within the CBRS Buffer Zone.

Additional documentation that USFWS may need to confirm the location of the property includes the following:

- A map showing the location of the building;
- A property record card;

- Property survey;
- Property deed; *and/or*
- Elevation Certificate (EC).

## C. Determine Building Eligibility

To be eligible for federal flood insurance, the building must not be constructed, substantially improved, or substantially damaged on or after the System Unit's or OPA's prohibition effective date. See below to determine if a building located within a System Unit or OPA is eligible for federal flood insurance:

**For a building located in a System Unit or OPA added to the CBRS under the original CBRA ("1982 Act") to be eligible for federal flood insurance it must:**

- Have a legally valid building construction permit issued prior to October 1, 1983;
- Be built (walled and roofed) prior to October 1, 1983; *and*
- Not be substantially improved or substantially damaged on or after October 1, 1983.

**For a building located in a System Unit or OPA added to the CBRS under the Coastal Zone Act Reauthorization Amendments of 1990 ("1990 Act") to be eligible for federal flood insurance it must:**

For System Units:

- Have a legally valid building construction permit issued prior to November 16, 1990;
- Building construction must have started prior to November 16, 1990; *and*
- Not be substantially improved or substantially damaged on or after November 16, 1990.

For OPAs:

- Have a legally valid building construction permit issued prior to November 16, 1991;
- Building constructed (walled and roofed) prior to November 16, 1991; *and*
- Not substantially improved or substantially damaged on or after November 16, 1991.

; or

- Building use is consistent with the purpose of the protected area, regardless of the date of construction. **Note:** This exception only applies to OPAs.

## D. Proof of Eligibility

If a building is located in a community with System Units or OPAs, then insurers must receive evidence demonstrating that the building is not subject to the CBRA's insurance prohibition, as described below.

### *1. Buildings Not Located in a System Unit or OPA*

If a building is located in a community with System Units or OPAs, but the building itself is not located in a System Unit or OPA, any of the following documentation can be used to verify that the building is eligible for federal flood insurance:

- The CBRS Mapper Documentation produced through the CBRS Validation Tool with the building location marked showing that it is not in the CBRS or the CBRS Buffer Zone;
- A CBRS Property Determination, which is an official letter from the USFWS that indicates whether a specific property or project site is located within or outside of the CBRS. As of December 1, 2018, the USFWS only provides such determinations for properties that are within 20 feet of a CBRS boundary (i.e., areas within the "CBRS Buffer Zone" depicted in the CBRS Mapper).
- An EC; *or*
- A Standard Flood Hazard Determination Form (SFHDF).

If using an EC or an SFHDF, the surveyor or flood hazard determination company must have one of the CBRS documents listed above attached to the form or on file to substantiate the information that pertains to the CBRS determination shown on the EC or SFHDF.

**NOTE:** Buildings that are completely outside of the CBRS are eligible for flood insurance (even if a portion of the property is within the CBRS).

### *2. Buildings Located in a System Unit or OPA*

If a building is located in a System Unit or OPA, but the subject building was constructed (or permitted and under construction) before the effective date of the insurance prohibition, then all of the following documentation is needed to verify that the building is eligible for federal flood insurance:

**a. Proof of building permit date, as evidenced by either:**

- A legally valid building permit; *or*
- A written statement signed by the community building permit official indicating the date of construction.

**b. Proof of building construction date, as evidenced by a written statement from the community building permit official that:**

- The building was not substantially improved or substantially damaged on or after the date the insurance prohibition became effective; *and*
- The building meets one of the following criteria:
  - The walls and roof of the building were in place prior to October 1, 1983 (1982 Act);
  - The start of construction took place prior to November 16, 1990 (in System Units and OPAs per the 1990 Act); *or*
  - The walls and roof of the building were in place prior to November 16, 1991 (in OPAs per the 1990 Act).

**c. Proof of building location in a System Unit or OPA:**

- CBRS Mapper Documentation produced through the CBRS Validation Tool with the building location marked; *or*

- A letter from the USFWS indicating the building is in a System Unit or OPA and the flood insurance prohibition date.

If one or more of the documents are not available, insurers may make CBRA eligibility determinations using other acceptable documentation supporting eligibility, such as:

- First mortgage financing records.
- Property tax records.
- Electrical permit records.
- On-site septic or sewer system records.
- State Coastal Zone Management Agency records.
- State Wetlands Program permit records.

**NOTE:** Buildings, including attached decks and stairs, located partially within the CBRS boundary (i.e., building is bisected by CBRS boundary line) are considered to be located within the CBRS.

### 3. *Buildings Eligible Because of Conforming Use*

If a building is located in an OPA, but its use is consistent with the protection purpose of the area, then the following documentation is needed to verify that the building is eligible for federal flood insurance:

- A certification from the governmental body or other qualified organization (e.g., tax-exempt conservation organization) overseeing the OPA indicating that the building's use is consistent with the protection purpose of the area. Examples of structures that may meet these criteria include, but are not limited to:
  - Restroom facilities in a state or local park;
  - Park visitor's center; *or*
  - Park employee housing within a park or protected area; *and*
- Documentation of the building's location in an OPA, in the form of either:
  - CBRS Mapper Documentation produced through the CBRS Validation Tool with the building location marked; *or*
  - A letter from USFWS indicating the building is in an OPA.

This page is intentionally left blank.

# Appendix E: Claims

## I. Information for Insureds after a Flood

The Standard Flood Insurance Policy (SFIP) covers direct physical loss by or from a flood to a property insured by the NFIP. The NFIP pays an insured's flood claim if the insured paid the correct premium, complied with all terms and conditions of the SFIP, and furnished accurate information and statements.

For more information regarding the NFIP claims process, please review the *NFIP Flood Insurance Claims Handbook* and the NFIP Claims Fact Sheet. They are available through the FEMA website using the following links:

- *NFIP Flood Insurance Claims Handbook* – https://www.fema.gov/media-library/assets/documents/6659
- NFIP Fact Sheet: The Flood Claim Process – https://www.fema.gov/media-library/assets/documents/114402

Insureds may also reference the Claims Guidelines In Case of a Flood included with their SFIP form for additional information (see the Policy Appendix).

## II. Claim Process

Following a flood loss, the insured must provide prompt written notice to the insurer to start the claims process. Upon notification, the insurer assigns an adjuster to assist the insured with the claim. Generally, the adjuster contacts the insured within 24 to 48 hours after receiving the notice of loss. However, assigning an adjuster may take more time depending upon the severity of flooding and local conditions.

### A. Damage Estimate

The adjuster visits the property to inspect the extent of the flood loss, assess the damage, and review the insured's documentation to prepare a detailed estimate of the covered damages. Subsequently, the adjuster provides the insured with a copy of his or her estimate, which the insured may compare to a licensed contractor's damage repair cost estimate. The insured and the adjuster then submit a Proof of Loss (POL) to request payment for the covered flood loss amount.

> **RESOURCE**
>
> The Proof of Loss Form (086-0-9) and other Claims Adjuster Forms are available online at: https://www.fema.gov/claimsadjuster-forms.

The completed, signed, and sworn-to POL form represents the insured's statement of the amount of flood loss they are claiming. The insurer must have the POL form and documentation that supports the requested covered loss amount prior to paying the claim. The adjuster coordinates with the insured to agree on the covered loss amount and may assist in completing and/or updating the POL form that the insured signs and swears to. Even if the insured does not agree with the adjuster, the insured must still prepare, sign, and swear to a POL, and ensure the insurer receives the POL along with supporting documentation within 60 days following the flood loss date.

The insured retains the right to amend the original POL to request additional covered loss amounts after they have submitted the original POL. Similarly, the insured must prepare, sign, and swear to the amended POL, as well as ensure the insurer receives the amended POL along with supporting documentation within 60 days following the flood loss date. Following review of the amended POL, the insurer may make additional payments for the additional identified flood damage. Please note that an insured may initiate only one claim for a flood loss event, but can submit multiple POLs for that claim.

In severe flood events, FEMA may authorize an extension of the 60-day submission requirement to provide a POL to the insurer. Specifically, the Federal Insurance & Mitigation Administration (FIMA) Associate Administrator may authorize and publish extensions in writing through media outlets and direct correspondence to insureds.

### B. Claim Payment

Once the insured receives final payment for the loss, the claim process is complete. If the insurer underwrote the policy correctly, the insurer pays the claim subject to the coverage limits and deductibles at the time of loss.

Insurers must reform any incorrectly rated policies discovered during the claim process in accordance with the SFIP and *NFIP Flood Insurance Manual* guidance in the Before You Start section under the Reforming the Policy heading.

## III. Disputed Claims

Insureds may take the following steps to resolve disputed claims:

### A. Work with the Adjuster

If the insured does not agree with the reported covered loss amount in the adjuster's report, the insured should identify disputed items, work with the adjuster to reach agreement on the covered loss amount, and submit supporting documentation to justify the differing position. As part of this effort, the insured may also consult a general contractor to support the requested covered loss amount for the flood damages.

### B. Contact the Adjusting Firm

If the insured is unable to agree with the adjuster, the insured should contact the adjusting firm and the adjuster's supervisor. The supervisor can work with the insured to reach agreement on the covered loss amounts in the adjuster's report.

### C. Work with the Insurer

If the insured and the adjuster's supervisor cannot reach agreement, they should contact the insurer's claims department to discuss the covered loss amount difference or coverage issue with a claim examiner.

### D. File a Proof of Loss with the Insurer

If the insured does not agree with the adjusting firm's report, the insured should complete a POL form for the total covered loss amount requested (undisputed amount plus additional amount) and send the signed and sworn-to POL with supporting documentation to the insurer. If the insurer agrees with the form and supporting documentation, it will pay the total covered loss amount requested. If the insurer disagrees, it will issue payment for the undisputed amount and provide the insured with a written denial letter. Following the denial of any part of the claim, the insured may file an appeal if not in agreement with the decision.

## IV. Appealing a Claim

Any insured with a denied or partially denied claim, or an authorized representative of the insured, may file an appeal to FEMA. Insureds must submit appeals within 60 days of the date of the insured's denial letter.

Insureds submitting an appeal to FEMA do not lose the right to file suit against the insurer, but the appeal process does not change the one-year statute of limitations for filing suit. Once the insured sues the insurer, FEMA cannot consider any appeals. In addition, FEMA cannot consider an appeal from an insured invoking the appraisal option under the SFIP.

### A. Filing an Appeal

An insured must submit an appeal request in writing. The request must include the following:

- Insured name(s)
- Property address
- The flood insurance policy number (shown on the policy's Declarations Page)
- Contact information (i.e., mailing address, telephone number, e-mail)
- A copy of the denial letter from the insurer
- A summary of the issues with the underlying claim including supporting documentation, prior history, and names of the individuals involved in the claim to date

Without the above elements, FEMA may reject appeals as ineligible.

If the insured wishes to authorize a third party (e.g., family member, public adjuster, or attorney) to discuss the appeal with FEMA, the insured must provide a written authorization including the following information:

- Insured's full name
- Current address
- Date and place of birth
- Representative's name
- Insured's signature

The authorization must include the following statement:

- "I expressly grant permission to FEMA to release my records to this third party representative."

The insured must have the authorization notarized and signed, or include the following language:

- "I declare under penalty of perjury that the foregoing is true and correct."
- Executed on (date)
- Signature of insured

The insured must send the appeal request and documentation to:

- By Mail:

  Federal Insurance and Mitigation Administration
  Federal Insurance Administrator
  400 C Street SW
  Washington, DC 20472-3010

- By E-Mail:

  FEMA-NFIP-Appeals@fema.dhs.gov

### B. Appeal Process

Insureds may send appeals via mail or email. Due to delivery delays and federal mail screening requirements, FEMA may not immediately receive all appeals submitted. However, upon receipt, FEMA begins its appeal review as expeditiously as possible. FEMA may request the insured to provide any missing information within 14 calendar days.

FEMA assigns each appeal it receives to a multi-disciplinary team that conducts a review of the entire claim file. The typical appeal requires an initial review to ensure the submission complies with policy requirements and to conduct careful review of the file documentation. The team works directly with the insured, the insurer, and other relevant parties to ensure compliance with the SFIP's terms and conditions. Following the team's review, FEMA determines whether the insurer properly evaluated and paid the claim.

FEMA keeps insureds informed of the status of the appeal during the review process. Typically, FEMA makes a determination within 90 days of receiving all necessary documentation and sends its appeal decision to the insured and the insurer, explaining FEMA's decision to either uphold or overturn the insurer's denial or disallowance.

For more information regarding flood claim appeals, please refer to: https://www.fema.gov/flood-claim-appeals-and-guidance.

## V. Litigation

If the insured does not agree with the insurer's claim decision, the insured may file a lawsuit within one year of the insurer's first written denial letter. The insured must file the lawsuit in United States District Court in the district where the property is located at the time of the loss. The appeal process does not extend the one-year period to file suit that begins with the original written denial by the insurer. Subsequent written denials do not restart the one-year period.

## VI. Increased Cost of Compliance (ICC) Claims

The NFIP defines a building as substantially damaged when the value of the damage or the cost to repair the damage caused directly by or from flood is 50 percent (or a lower threshold if adopted and enforced by the community) or more of the value of the building at the time of the flood. When the local community declares a building substantially damaged, the insured may initiate a request for payment under the SFIP Coverage – D, ICC, by providing a copy of the local community's notice of substantial damage determination to the insurer. Effective on January 1, 2011, insureds have up to six years from the date of the flood loss to complete the approved mitigation activity (floodproofing, relocation, elevation, demolition, or any combination of these activities).

If a state or community adopts and enforces a cumulative substantial damage provision or repetitive loss provision requiring action by property owners to comply with floodplain management laws or ordinances, this may also qualify a structure for an ICC claim after a flood loss. The community must declare the structure to be substantially damaged and the structure must meet the NFIP's repetitive loss structure definition. The NFIP defines a repetitive loss structure as an NFIP-insured building that has incurred flood-related damages on two occasions during a 10-year period ending on the date of the event for which the insured makes a second claim. The cost of repairing the flood damage, on average, must equal or exceed 25 percent of the market value of the building at the time of each flood. The insurer must verify that the NFIP paid a claim for both qualifying losses and that the state or community is enforcing a cumulative substantial damage or repetitive loss provision in its law or ordinance and declared the building substantially damaged on that basis.

Beginning a mitigation project prior to receiving the substantial damage letter from the community official may jeopardize eligibility to receive an ICC payment.

The insured may not transfer or assign ICC benefits to another party, such as through a sales transaction, unless the prospective buyer is the local community or the state, which is purchasing the property under a FEMA-funded buy-out program.

This page is intentionally left blank.

# Appendix F: Community Rating System

## I. General Information

The Community Rating System (CRS) is a voluntary program for communities participating in the NFIP. The CRS offers NFIP policy premium discounts in communities that develop and execute extra measures beyond minimum floodplain management requirements to provide protection from flooding.

## II. Community Eligibility

A community's eligibility for the CRS depends upon participating in the Regular Program and maintaining full compliance with the NFIP. CRS flood insurance policy premium discounts range from 0 percent to 45 percent depending on the community's floodplain management measures and activities.

## III. CRS Premium Discount Eligibility

### A. Premium Discount Eligibility by Policy Rating Category

**Table 1** highlights CRS premium discount eligibility by policy rating category.

**Table 1. CRS Premium Discount Eligibility by Policy Rating Category**

| Flood Zone | Eligible for CRS Premium Discount | Not Eligible for CRS Premium Discount |
|---|---|---|
| All Flood Zones | Pre-Flood Insurance Rate Map (FIRM) Buildings | N/A |
| B, C, X, D, A99, AR, and AR Dual Zones (AR/A, AR/AE, AR/ A1–A30, AR/ AH, and AR/AO) | Post-FIRM Buildings | N/A |
| A Zones (AE, A1–A30, Unnumbered A, AO, AH) | Post-FIRM **Non-Elevated** Buildings where the elevation difference used for rating is 0 feet or higher or with subgrade crawlspace certification from a community official | Post-FIRM **Non-Elevated** Buildings where the elevation difference used for rating is –1 foot or lower or with no subgrade crawlspace certification from a community official |
| A Zones (AE, A1–A30, Unnumbered A, AO, AH) | Post-FIRM **Elevated** Buildings[1] where the elevation difference used for rating is 0 feet or higher | Post-FIRM Elevated Buildings where the elevation difference used for rating is –1 foot or lower |
| V Zones (VE, V1–V30, Unnumbered V) | '75–'81 and Post–'81 Post-FIRM **Non-Elevated** Buildings where the elevation difference used for rating is 0 feet or higher | '75–'81 and Post–'81 Post-FIRM **Non-Elevated** Buildings where the elevation difference used for rating is –1 foot or lower |

**Table 1. CRS Premium Discount Eligibility by Policy Rating Category** *continued*

| Flood Zone | Eligible for CRS Premium Discount | Not Eligible for CRS Premium Discount |
|---|---|---|
| V Zones (VE, V1–V30, Unnumbered V) | '75–'81 and Post–'81 Post-FIRM **Elevated** Buildings where the elevation difference used for rating is 0 feet or higher.<br>'75–'81 and Post–'81 Post-FIRM **Elevated** Buildings with:<br>• Unfinished enclosure where the elevation difference used for rating is 0 feet or higher, with no machinery or equipment below the Base Flood Elevation (BFE); *or*<br>• Unfinished enclosure used only for parking, access, or storage with breakaway walls regardless of size, with no machinery or equipment below the BFE. | '75–'81 and Post–'81 post-FIRM **Elevated** Buildings where the elevation difference used for rating is –1 foot or lower<br>'75–'81 and Post–'81 Post-FIRM **Elevated** Buildings with:<br>• No enclosure where the elevation difference used for rating is –1 foot or lower; *or*<br>• Enclosure with non-breakaway walls where the elevation difference used for rating is –1 foot or lower; *or*<br>• Machinery or equipment below the BFE; *or*<br>• Finished enclosure below the BFE. |

1. Contact the insurer for CRS discount eligibility for Post-FIRM Elevated Buildings having an elevator below the BFE.

### B. Ineligible for CRS Premium Discounts

The following policies are not eligible for CRS premium discounts:

- Emergency Program Policies
- Preferred Risk Policies (PRP)
- Newly Mapped Policies
- Mortgage Portfolio Protection Program Policies (MPPP)
- Group Flood Insurance Policies
- Post-FIRM buildings located in a Special Flood Hazard Area (SFHA) where the elevation difference used for rating is at least 1 foot or more below the BFE, with the following exceptions:
  - Post-FIRM V-Zone buildings with unfinished breakaway wall enclosures and machinery or equipment at or above the BFE.
  - A building with a subgrade crawlspace with certification from a community official. The letter signed by the community official that certifies a subgrade crawlspace exception must contain the following statement:

  "I certify that the building located at __________________________ has a crawlspace that was built in compliance with the NFIP requirements for crawlspace construction as outlined in FEMA Technical Bulletin 11-01, Crawlspace Construction for Buildings Located in Special Flood Hazard Areas."

## IV. CRS Classes and Discounts

The CRS recognizes measures for flood protection and flood loss reduction. The four main activity categories include Public Information, Mapping and Regulation, Flood Damage Reduction, and Flood Preparedness.

In order to participate in the CRS, a community must complete and submit an application to FEMA. Subsequently, FEMA reviews the community's floodplain management efforts and assigns the appropriate CRS classification based on credit points earned for various activities. A community's classification may change depending on the level of continued floodplain management efforts. Classifications range from 1 to 10 and determine the premium discount for eligible flood insurance policies (see Table 2 below). All community assignments begin at Class 10 with no premium discount. Communities with a Class 1 designation receive the maximum 45 percent premium discount.

**Note:** If a community's CRS class changes, or a given policy's eligibility for a CRS discount changes, midway through a policy term, any resulting adjustment to the CRS discount applies only at the next policy renewal.

**Table 2** highlights the available CRS premium discounts organized by class and flood zone.

**Table 2. CRS Premium Discounts by Class and Flood Zone**

| Class | Discount | Class | Discount |
|---|---|---|---|
| **Zones A, AE, A1–A30, V, V1–V30, AO, and AH (SFHA)** | | | |
| 1 | 45% | 6 | 20% |
| 2 | 40% | 7 | 15% |
| 3 | 35% | 8 | 10% |
| 4 | 30% | 9 | 5% |
| 5 | 25% | 10 | — |
| **Zones B, C, X, D (Non-SFHA); A99, AR, AR Dual (SFHA)[1]** | | | |
| 1 | 10% | 6 | 10% |
| 2 | 10% | 7 | 5% |
| 3 | 10% | 8 | 5% |
| 4 | 10% | 9 | 5% |
| 5 | 10% | 10 | — |

1. For the purpose of determining CRS discounts, all AR and A99 Zones are treated as non-SFHAs.

## V. Elevation Certificates and Map Information for Agents

- After the date of application for CRS classification, communities must maintain FEMA ECs and Floodproofing Certificates for new and substantially improved construction in the SFHA.
- Some CRS communities receive credit for completing ECs for Post-FIRM buildings constructed prior to the CRS application date. Agents may request copies of these certificates from the community.
- Many CRS communities receive credit for providing residents, agents, and others with information that includes a property's flood risk zone and BFE from the community's FIRM. The community, if receiving this credit, must publicize the availability of the service once a year.

## VI. CRS Eligible Communities

A list of all current CRS eligible communities and their status can be found at: https://www.fema.gov/flood-insurance/rules-legislation/community-rating-system.

This page is intentionally blank.

# Appendix G: Leased Federal Properties

## I. General Information

FEMA must charge full-risk rates for flood insurance for residential or non-residential properties leased from the Federal Government, referred to as Leased Federal Properties (LFPs), that the Administrator determines are located:

- On the river-facing side of any dike, levee, or other riverine flood-control structure; *or*
- Seaward of any seawall or other coastal flood-control structure.

The U.S. Army Corps of Engineers provided a list of property addresses meeting these criteria to FEMA.

## II. Requirements

NFIP insurers must determine whether property addresses for new or existing business are LFPs. Specifically, prior to selling an NFIP policy or at least 120 days prior to renewing an NFIP policy, NFIP insurers must make this determination by comparing the property address with a list of LFP addresses provided by FEMA.

**Table 1** describes what an NFIP insurer must do if it determines that a property for either new or existing business is an LFP.

### Table 1. Requirements for LFP Properties

| Requirement | New Business | Existing Business |
|---|---|---|
| **Notification** | The NFIP insurer must notify the applicant (as well as the applicant's agent and lender) of the LFP determination. The notice must explain:<br>• Why the property is an LFP;<br>• That the NFIP may only insure LFPs using full-risk rates; *and*<br>• That the applicant may challenge the property's designation as an LFP.<br>The NFIP insurer may base this notice on the examples provided at the end of this section. | The NFIP insurer must notify the insured (as well as the insured's agent and lender) of the LFP determination no later than 120 days before the renewal date. The notice must explain:<br>• Why the property is an LFP;<br>• That the NFIP may only insure LFPs using full-risk rates; *and*<br>• That the insured may challenge the property's designation as an LFP.<br>The NFIP insurer may base this notice on the examples provided at the end of this section. |
| **Request Information for Full-Risk Rating**[1] | The NFIP insurer must obtain information necessary to establish full-risk rates for the LFP, including requesting the applicant submit an Elevation Certificate (EC) to the NFIP insurer (refer to the Elevation Certificate heading under Certifications in the How to Write section). | The NFIP insurer must obtain information necessary to establish full-risk rates for the LFP, including requesting the insured submit an EC to the NFIP insurer (refer to the Elevation Certificate heading under Certifications in the How to Write section). |

**Table 1. Requirements for LFP Properties, *continued***

| Requirement | New Business | Existing Business |
|---|---|---|
| **If Information for Full-Risk Rating Is Not Received within 45 Days from the Date of Notice** | The NFIP insurer must either:<br>• Decline to write the policy; *or*<br>• Write the policy for only a single policy term using tentative rates (see the Tentative Rates heading in the How to Write section). | The NFIP insurer must either:<br>• Decline to renew the policy; or<br>• Renew the policy for only a single policy term using tentative rates (see the Tentative Rates heading in the How to Write section). |
| **If Property Added to the LFP List Near Renewal** | N/A | Properties added to the LFP list within the 120-day window prior to policy renewal will not receive the LFP notice until the subsequent renewal. |

1. Note that unlike most categories of properties, there is no cap on annual premium rate increases for LFPs.

## III. Correcting an LFP Designation

Insureds may challenge the designation of their property as an LFP by submitting information showing that the property is not an LFP. Examples of acceptable documentation include the following:

- A letter from a community official or land surveyor stating that the property does qualify as an LFP; *or*
- Documentation showing that the Federal Government does not own the property, such as a deed or rental agreement.

Insureds must submit their request to change their property's LFP designation to their NFIP insurer. The NFIP insurer must then review the request and recommend whether FEMA should change the property's LFP designation. If FEMA approves the request, it will remove the property from the LFP list, and the building may be rated under the general NFIP rating procedures described in the How to Write section.

If the insured does not provide acceptable documentation, or FEMA denies the request, the property remains on the list. See Table 1 above for information on the insurer's responsibilities and options.

## IV. Settling a Claim

The insurer may not process claims relating to a tentatively-rated policy until the insurer receives the underwriting information establishing a full-risk rate for the policy. Once the insurer notifies an insured of the property's inclusion on the LFP list, it cannot settle any subsequent flood loss until it receives the appropriate underwriting documentation (e.g., new EC and photographs) or FEMA approves a request to correct the property's LFP designation and remove it from the list.

## V. Sample Letters

### A. Sample Insured Notification Letter

**IMPORTANT FLOOD INSURANCE POLICY INFORMATION**

Insured's Name:

Property Address:

Policy Number:

Dear Policyholder:

This letter is to inform you that your property, which is covered by flood insurance, meets the criteria for a new subset of properties that must be charged actuarial rates, in accordance with the provisions of the Flood Insurance Reform Act of 2004, Sec. 106.

In accordance with the law, the Federal Emergency Management Agency (FEMA) must charge actuarial rates for any property meeting the following criteria:

(1) Leased from the Federal Government, and

(2) Located on the river-facing side of any dike, levee, or other riverine flood control structure, or seaward of any seawall or other coastal flood control structure.

In order for an actuarial rate to be developed, proper underwriting documentation, including a FEMA Elevation Certificate using current Flood Insurance Rate Map data and two photographs showing the front and back of the building, must be submitted to your flood insurer. The insurer must receive this information within 45 days of receipt of this notice to allow for rate calculation and processing of the renewal bill.

If your insurer does not receive the requested underwriting information in sufficient time to meet their renewal billing cycle, they can only renew the flood policy using tentative rates. Please be advised that a policy with tentative rates cannot be endorsed to increase limits or be renewed. In the event of a loss a tentatively rated policy will not receive a claim settlement until actuarial rates are determined. These rates, along with the amount of premium originally submitted, will determine the coverage available.

You may appeal this determination by furnishing your insurer with documentation verifying that your property does not meet the criteria listed above.

Your insurance agent has also received this notice concerning your property.

If you have questions about the information in this letter, please contact (your company name and telephone number).

## B. Sample Agent Notification Letter

### IMPORTANT FLOOD INSURANCE POLICY INFORMATION

Insured's Name:

Property Address:

Policy Number:

Dear Agent:

This letter is to inform you that your client's property, which is covered by flood insurance, meets the criteria for a new subset of properties that must be charged actuarial rates, in accordance with the provisions of the Flood Insurance Reform Act of 2004, Sec. 106.

In accordance with the law, the Federal Emergency Management Agency (FEMA) must charge actuarial rates for any property meeting the following criteria:

(1) Leased from the Federal Government, and

(2) Located on the river-facing side of any dike, levee, or other riverine flood control structure, or seaward of any seawall or other coastal flood control structure.

In order for an actuarial rate to be developed, proper underwriting documentation, including a FEMA Elevation Certificate using current Flood Insurance Rate Map data and two photographs showing the front and back of the building, must be submitted to the writing company. The writing company must receive this information within 45 days of receipt of this notice to allow for rate calculation and processing of the renewal bill.

A writing company that does not receive the requested underwriting information in sufficient time to meet their renewal billing cycle can only renew the flood policy using tentative rates. Please be advised that a policy with tentative rates cannot be endorsed to increase limits or be renewed. In the event of a loss a tentatively rated policy will not receive a claim settlement until actuarial rates are determined. These rates, along with the amount of premium originally submitted, will determine the coverage available.

Your client may appeal this determination by furnishing the writing company with documentation verifying that the property does not meet the criteria listed above.

This notice has also been sent to your client.

If you have questions about the information in this letter, please contact (your company name and telephone number).

## C. Sample Lender Notification Letter

**IMPORTANT FLOOD INSURANCE POLICY INFORMATION**

Insured's Name:

Property Address:

Policy Number:

Dear Lender:

This letter is to inform you that your client's property, which is covered by flood insurance, meets the criteria for a new subset of properties that must be charged actuarial rates, in accordance with the provisions of the Flood Insurance Reform Act of 2004, Sec. 106.

In accordance with the law, the Federal Emergency Management Agency (FEMA) must charge actuarial rates for any property meeting the following criteria:

(1) Leased from the Federal Government, and

(2) Located on the river-facing side of any dike, levee, or other riverine flood control structure, or seaward of any seawall or other coastal flood control structure.

In order for an actuarial rate to be developed, proper underwriting documentation, including a FEMA Elevation Certificate using current Flood Insurance Rate Map data and two photographs showing the front and back of the building, must be submitted to the writing company. The writing company must receive this information within 45 days of receipt of this notice to allow for rate calculation and processing of the renewal bill.

A writing company that does not receive the requested underwriting information in sufficient time to meet their renewal billing cycle can only renew the flood policy using tentative rates. Please be advised that a policy with tentative rates cannot be endorsed to increase limits or be renewed. In the event of a loss a tentatively rated policy will not receive a claim settlement until actuarial rates are determined. These rates, along with the amount of premium originally submitted, will determine the coverage available.

Your client may appeal this determination by furnishing the writing company with documentation verifying that the property does not meet the criteria listed above.

This notice has also been sent to your client and their insurance agent.

If you have questions about the information in this letter, please contact (your company name and telephone number).

This page is intentionally left blank.

# Appendix H: Flood Maps

## I. Flood Map Service Center

The FEMA Flood Map Service Center (MSC) and its website (http://msc.fema.gov) serve as the official public source for flood hazard information produced in support of the NFIP.

Individuals and communities can view and download flood maps and related products free of charge through the MSC website. The integrated "Search All Products" feature allows users to find and download all products for a geographic area and, using the "Search by Address" feature, download all Flood Insurance Rate Maps (FIRMs) and Letters of Map Change directly from the search results page.

Map Specialists are available to answer questions Monday through Friday from 8:00 a.m. to 7:00 p.m. ET by calling the FEMA Mapping and Insurance eXchange (FMIX) toll-free information line at 1-877-FEMA-MAP (1-877-336-2627).

## II. Flood Hazard Maps

FEMA produces two types of maps for rating flood insurance:

- Flood Hazard Boundary Map (FHBM) – Initial flood hazard identification generally used for Emergency Program communities.
- FIRM (See an example in **Figure 1** at the end of this appendix) – Generally used for Regular Program communities. Some Regular Program communities may use a map originally published as an FHBM. When a community converts to the Regular Program, FEMA sends a letter accompanying the map stating that FEMA considers the map to be a FIRM.

Countywide FIRMs supersede all previous versions of the FEMA flood hazard maps for covered communities. Countywide FIRMs show flooding information for the entire county's geographic area, including incorporated communities.

### A. Map Information

Insureds or agents may obtain the date of their current effective map version by calling their local community official or by going to the MSC. Maps provide the community name, community number, suffix, panel number, map type, and map effective date. (See FIRM panel example at the end of this section.)

- The maps may have one panel or multiple panels.
  - Flat maps generally consist of only one panel.
  - For multiple-panel maps, the community map index identifies individual panels.
  - Panel numbers for a community's map are in numerical order.
- Each panel has a panel number and community number. When there is only one panel (i.e., a flat map), the community number will consist of only six digits.
  - Example: Monterey County, CA 060195-1025

  - The first two digits of the number identify the state and the next four digits identify the community. The last four digits identify the map panel.

- FHBMs and FIRMs show:
  - Community boundaries.
  - Special Flood Hazard Areas (SFHAs).
  - Areas not included in a community's map.
    - > A community may be physically located within the overall geographical area covered by the map, but may actually be a separate community. This community would have a separate map.
- Most FIRMs also show:
  - Flood Zones,
  - Base Flood Elevations (BFEs) and/or,
  - Base Flood Depths (BFDs).

### B. Communities with Unpublished Maps

Communities with unpublished maps are communities where local flooding is too small to map but that offer flood insurance coverage. The NFIP considers all areas within these communities in the Regular Program as Zone C or X.

### C. Unmapped Areas in Communities with Maps

Zone D designates flood hazard areas within mapped communities that remain undetermined and unmapped. In addition, agents may use Zone D for rating when a community incorporates portions of another community's area where no map has been prepared.

## III. Map Zones

### A. SFHAs

#### *1. Zone A*

Areas subject to inundation by the 1-percent-annual-chance flood event generally determined using approximate methodologies. Because detailed hydraulic analyses have not been performed, no BFEs or flood depths are shown on the map. Mandatory flood insurance purchase requirements and floodplain management standards apply.

#### *2. Zones A1–A30*

Areas subject to inundation by the 1-percent-annual-chance flood event determined by detailed methods. The maps show the BFEs. Mandatory flood insurance purchase requirements and floodplain management standards apply.

#### *3. Zone AE*

Areas subject to inundation by the 1-percent-annual-chance flood event determined by detailed methods. The maps show the BFEs. Mandatory flood insurance purchase requirements and floodplain management standards apply. Some maps use AE in place of A1-A30.

### *4. Zone AH*

Areas subject to inundation by 1-percent-annual-chance shallow flooding (usually areas of ponding) where average depths are between 1 and 3 feet. In this zone the maps show BFEs derived from detailed hydraulic analyses. Mandatory flood insurance purchase requirements and floodplain management standards apply.

### *5. Zone AO*

Areas subject to inundation by 1-percent-annual-chance shallow flooding (usually sheet flow on sloping terrain) where average depths are between 1 and 3 feet. Maps show the average flood depths derived from detailed hydraulic analyses in this zone. Mandatory flood insurance purchase requirements and floodplain management standards apply.

### *6. Zone A99*

The A99 zone applies to areas with sufficient progress on the construction or repair of a protective system including features such as dikes, dams, and levees, to consider it complete for insurance rating purposes. The map does not have BFEs. Treat A99 Zones as non-SFHAs when determining Community Rating System (CRS) premium discounts. Mandatory flood insurance purchase requirements and floodplain management standards apply.

### *7. Zone AR*

The AR zone reflects the decertification of a previously accredited flood protection system that the community is in the process of restoring to provide base flood protection. Treat all AR Zones as non-SFHAs to determine CRS premium discounts. Mandatory flood insurance purchase requirements and floodplain management standards apply

### *8. Zones AR/AE, AR/AH, AR/AO, AR/A1–A30, AR/A*

These are dual flood zones subject to flooding from other water sources that the restored flood protection system does not contain. Treat all AR Zones as non-SFHAs when determining CRS premium discounts and determining mandatory purchase requirements.

### *9. Zone V*

The V zones are areas along coasts subject to inundation by the 1-percent-annual-chance flood event with additional hazards associated with storm-induced waves. The map does not have BFEs or flood depths because detailed hydraulic analyses were not performed. Mandatory flood insurance purchase requirements and floodplain management standards apply.

### *10. Zones V1–V30*

Areas along coasts subject to inundation by the 1-percent-annual-chance flood event with additional hazards due to storm-induced velocity wave action. The maps show BFEs derived from detailed hydraulic analyses. Mandatory flood insurance purchase requirements and floodplain management standards apply.

### *11. Zone VE*

Used in place of V1-V30 on some maps. Zone VE areas are subject to inundation by the 1-percent-annual-chance flood event with additional hazards due to storm-induced velocity wave action. The maps show BFEs derived from detailed hydraulic analyses. Mandatory flood insurance purchase requirements and floodplain management standards apply.

## B. Moderate or Minimal Hazard Areas

### *1. Zones B, C, and X*

B, C, and X zones designate areas of moderate or minimal flooding hazard resulting from severe storm activity or local drainage problems. Zone X equals the designation for B and C zones on some maps.

### *2. Zone D*

The D zone reflects an area where the flood hazard is undetermined and where there is sparse population. Agents may use Zone D for rating when a community incorporates portions of another community's area where no map has been prepared. Agents also use Zone D if the map shows an area as being unmapped.

# IV. Locating a Property on a Map

- Check the map index to identify the correct map panel.
- Directly locate the property by the address or other information. Comparing the FHBM or FIRM to an assessor's map or a community street map helps locate properties precisely.
- Note the map color where the property is located.
  - On FHBMs and FIRMs, darkly shaded areas are the SFHAs. When viewing a map through the MSC, they are blue (or blue with a red stripe if in the regulatory floodway).
  - On an FHBM, no other zone data may be given.
- On a FIRM, zones have an alpha designation and the entire area within the boundaries indicated for the zone carries that specific zone designation.
- BFEs in SFHA zones (A1-A30 [or AE], AH, V1-V30 [or VE]) are shown within wavy lines. In some SFHA zones, the BFE is in parentheses because the BFE does not vary within the entire zone.
- An agent may interpolate a BFE for the property using the closest BFE indicators. In this case, the agent must document use of this method.

# V. Changing or Correcting a Flood Map

There are three procedures that can be used to change or correct a flood map:

## A. Letter of Map Amendment (LOMA)

A LOMA is a determination FEMA makes for a property and/or building as to whether it is located within the SFHA. An applicant/insured may apply for a LOMA if he or she believes the requirement to purchase flood insurance is in error and there is evidence that the building is not in the SFHA on the effective FIRM.

In order to determine whether or not to grant a LOMA, FEMA examiners follow the following steps as necessary:

### 1. *Compare the location of the property to the SFHA*

If the FEMA examiner finds, after plotting the location on the FIRM, that the property and/or building is not located in the SFHA, then the Determination will be "Out-As-Shown" rather than "Removed." The FEMA Out-As-Shown Determination will state that the property or building is outside the SFHA and, therefore, the mandatory flood insurance requirement does not apply.

An Out-As-Shown Determination does not require elevation information. The minimum requirements to make an Out-As-Shown Determination follow:

- A photocopy of the FIRM panel (including the title block) that shows the location of the property.
- Section A of the MT-EZ form, found in the MT-EZ application package. It is available from FEMA at https://www.fema.gov/media-library/assets/documents/8001, or by calling the toll-free number 1-877-336-2627.
- A copy of the subdivision plat map of the area, showing the recordation data (i.e., book/volume and page numbers) and the recorder's seal.

  OR
- A copy of the property's deed, showing the data recorded (i.e., book/volume and page numbers) and the recorder's seal; a tax assessor's or other suitable map showing the surveyed location of the property; and at least two street intersections shown on FEMA's FIRM.

### 2. *Compare the elevation of the property to the 1-percent-annual-chance flood elevation*

In some cases, FEMA may require additional information to make a determination.

## B. Letter of Map Revision (LOMR)

A LOMR is an official revision to the currently effective FEMA map. It changes flood zones, floodplain and floodway delineations, flood elevations, and planimetric features. An insured should make all LOMR requests to FEMA through the chief executive officer of the community, as the community must adopt any changes and revisions to the map resulting from a LOMR. A physical map revision usually follows a LOMR.

## C. Physical Map Revision

A physical map revision is an official republication of a map changing flood insurance zones, floodplain delineations, flood elevations, floodways, and planimetric features.

The community's chief executive officer can submit scientific and technical data to FEMA requesting a map revision. FEMA will analyze the data and revise the map if warranted.

**NOTE:** Community officials should retain old maps to verify past rating determinations and to establish floodplain management compliance requirements.

**Figure 1. Example FIRM**

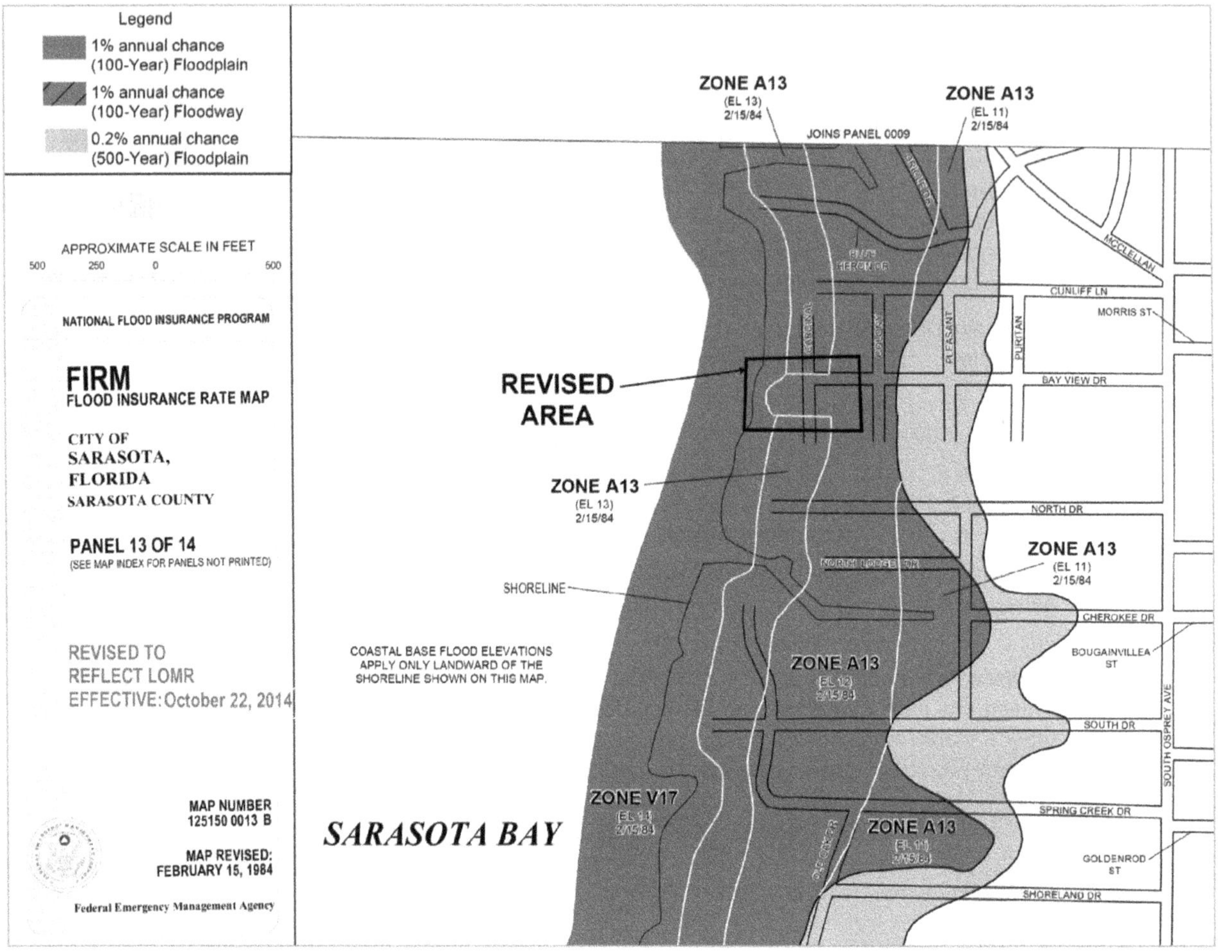

# Appendix I: Severe Repetitive Loss Properties

## I. General Information

FEMA designates as Severe Repetitive Loss (SRL) any NFIP-insured single-family or multi-family residential building:

1. That has incurred flood-related damage for which four or more separate claims payments have been made, with the amount of each claim (including building and contents payments) exceeding $5,000, and with the cumulative amount of such claims payments exceeding $20,000; *or*
2. For which at least two separate claims payments (building payments only) have been made under such coverage, with the cumulative amount of such claims exceeding the market value of the building.

In both instances, at least two of the claims must be within 10 years of each other, and claims made within 10 days of each other will be counted as one claim. In determining SRL status, FEMA considers the loss history since 1978, or from the building's construction if it was built after 1978, regardless of any changes in the ownership of the building. The term "SRL property" refers to either an SRL building or the contents within an SRL building, or both.

The writing company must transfer SRL policies to the Special Direct Facility (SDF) operated by NFIP Direct as they reach their renewal date. The NFIP monitors all transferred SRL policies located at the SDF for targeted mitigation actions.

SRL properties may obtain renewal or new business coverage only through the SDF. The agent of record remains in that capacity while the policy remains in the SDF.

NFIP Direct can provide additional assistance on the handling of SRL properties. You can contact NFIP Direct at 1-800-638-6620.

## II. New Business

If the insurer determines a property to be an SRL property, the insurer must submit the completed application and the required documentation to the SDF at the following address:

NFIP Special Direct Facility
P.O. Box 913111
Denver, CO 80291-3111

Alternatively, the insured's agent can access the NFIP Direct online portal (https://www.nfipdirect.fema.gov/Membership/SignIn/), enter the application information, and upload supporting documentation directly into the SDF.

## III. Notification Requirements

A request to transfer a policy occurs when the NFIP identifies a property as meeting the SRL criteria.

- The NFIP notifies the Write Your Own (WYO) company at least 150 days prior to the policy expiration date.

- The company notifies the affected insured, agent, and lender 90 days before expiration of the policy. This notice explains that the policy must be written with the SDF. (See agent, lender, and insured SDF Notification Letters in this section.)
- The SDF issues a renewal offer for the SRL policy approximately 45 days prior to the expiration date.

## IV. Underwriting Requirements

The WYO company must provide the SDF sufficient policy documentation for all SRL policies transferred to the SDF. The SDF will process and issue policies based upon the current rates, flood zone, and other map information unless the property meets the NFIP grandfathering eligibility rules. The SDF will re-underwrite all transferred policies by their next renewal in order to validate rating elements and calculate the premium.

**RESOURCE**

See Appendix B: Forms for the NFIP Flood Insurance Application (page B-1) and the NFIP Elevation Certificate and Instructions (page B-20)

Required documentation consists of the following:

- An NFIP Flood Insurance Application;
- Front and rear photographs of the building (if applicable);
- NFIP Elevation Certificate (EC) (if applicable); *and*
- Any additional documents to ensure the accuracy of current policy and rating information.

Companies must submit this documentation at least 120 days prior to the policy expiration date. If documentation is not received, the insured may be notified of non-renewal or billed with tentative rates or Pre-FIRM rates (if eligible).

## V. Process for Correcting or Updating a Property's SRL Status

FEMA designates a property as SRL based on the information it has on file. The insured may request that FEMA correct the property's SRL status if the insured believes that the claims history or the market value used to determine loss history is inaccurate. The insured may request that FEMA update the property's SRL status if property mitigation has occurred to reduce future flooding potential. The policy remains with the SDF during the review.

### A. Required Documentation

Documentation required to correct or update a property's SRL status includes but is not limited to the following:

- Invalid Loss History Association — Documentation that shows:
  - Incorrectly linked addresses and/or losses; *or*
  - A second address added to a Property Locator Record.
- Property Value Updates — The property value is based on market value, which must be shown on one of the following documents:
  - Property tax assessment; *or*
  - Property appraisal.

- Mitigation Action
  - EC based on finished construction of the new or improved building;
  - Color photographs of the building before the improvement;
  - Color photographs of the building after the improvement;
  - Photographs of the flood vents/openings (if applicable);
  - Source of funding for the mitigation action (state, local or individual);
  - Demolition permit (if the building was demolished and rebuilt);
  - Building permit (if the building was elevated or rebuilt); *and*
  - In Zone B, C, or X, a signed statement from a community official that shows mitigation was approved by the community.

Required documents should be emailed to NFIPUnderwritingMailbox@fema.dhs.gov.

## B. SDF Process After FEMA Determination

FEMA notifies the SDF, insured, and agent of record regarding the review results when completed. If FEMA determined that correction or update of the property's SRL status is not justified, the policy stays with the SDF. If FEMA agreed to correct or update the property's SRL status, the possible actions the SDF may take include:

- If an invalid loss history association or incorrect property valuation justified correction of the property's SRL status, the SDF will coordinate with the agent of record to transfer the policy back to the former insurer, or another NFIP insurer the insured chooses, at the next policy renewal. The insurer renews the policy using the SDF's effective dates ensuring continuous coverage with no overlap. If the insured does not want to wait until the next renewal, the SDF will cancel the current policy and send the premium to the former insurer, or another NFIP insurer the insured chooses, to issue a new policy.
- If a mitigation action other than a buyout or demolition justified update of the property's SRL status, the SDF will coordinate with the agent of record to transfer the policy back to the former insurer, or another NFIP insurer the insured chooses, at the next policy renewal. The insurer renews the policy using the SDF's effective dates ensuring continuous coverage with no overlap.
- If a buyout or demolition justified update of the property's SRL status, the SDF will coordinate policy cancellation with the agent of record. The SDF cancels the policy and refunds the pro-rata premium (less Federal Policy Fee and Probation Surcharge, if applicable). There is no commission chargeback if FEMA approves the specific property buyout or demolition under an approved FEMA mitigation project.
- If a loss occurs both in the current term and before the policy transfers to the former or new insurer, the SDF will continue to service the claim and transfer the policy to the insurer at the next renewal unless the new claim qualifies the property for the SDF again.

## VI. Flood Mitigation Assistance (FMA) Program

The FMA Program makes funding available for a variety of flood mitigation activities. Under the FMA Program, FEMA provides funds to state and local governments assisting NFIP-insured property owners to conduct mitigation projects that reduce future flood losses, such as:

- Acquisition or relocation of at-risk structures and conversion of the property to open space;
- Elevation of existing structures; *or*
- Dry floodproofing of historic properties.

Eligible applicants (states, territories, and tribes) that receive FMA mitigation grants provide subgrants to local governments or communities. The applicant must have a FEMA-approved mitigation plan at the time of project award.

State and local officials prioritize NFIP-insured properties within their jurisdictions to award FMA grants. They may contact insureds directly to determine the appropriate mitigation activity that most effectively reduces future flood losses and advise them of their inclusion in the FMA grant application.

Property owners should contact their local floodplain manager or state hazard mitigation officer, or go to the FEMA Hazard Mitigation Assistance webpage at https://www.fema.gov/hazard-mitigation-assistance to obtain additional information on the FMA Program and other mitigation grant programs for residential and non-residential properties.

## VII. Sample Letters

### A. Agent Notification Letter

U.S. Department of Homeland Security
500 C Street, SW
Washington, DC 20472

FEMA

**IMPORTANT FLOOD INSURANCE POLICY INFORMATION**

Insured's Name:

Property Address:

Policy Number:

Dear Agent:

As you may be aware, your client's property, which is covered by flood insurance, has experienced repetitive flood losses under FEMA's National Flood Insurance Program (NFIP). This letter is to inform you that your client's property meets the criteria for a subset of repetitive loss structures: insured properties with a high frequency of losses or a high value of claims. These properties are designated as Severe Repetitive Loss (SRL) properties.

Congress recognized that SRL properties represent the greatest risk of sustaining repeated flood losses and, through the Flood Insurance Reform Act of 2004, made it a top priority to reduce the number of SRL properties nationwide. As of January 2013, FEMA has identified approximately 11,900 properties that meet the designation for SRL. The loss characteristics of an SRL property must meet one of the following criteria based on paid flood losses since 1978, regardless of ownership:

(1) Four or more separate claim payments of more than $5,000 each (building and/or contents payments); or

(2) Two or more separate claim payments (building payments only) where the total of the payments exceeds the current value of the property.

In either case, two of the claim payments must have occurred within 10 years of each other. If there are multiple losses at the same location within 10 days of each other, they are counted as one loss, with the payment amounts added collectively.

The strategy for reducing the number of SRL properties is twofold: First, the NFIP has centralized the processing of all flood insurance policies for SRL properties in order for FEMA to obtain additional underwriting information, verify loss information, and collect information about the flood risk to the SRL properties. Second, FEMA implements the Flood Mitigation Assistance (FMA) grant program annually to mitigate SRL properties. You need to be aware of the following:

- The Write Your Own (WYO) Insurance Companies that sell and service flood insurance under the NFIP will assign flood insurance policies for SRL properties, upon renewal, to a centralized processing center operated by the NFIP Servicing Agent. This center is the Special Direct Facility (SDF).

www.fema.gov

Agent Notification Letter, Page 2

Agent
Date
Page 2

- As a result, your client's policy will not be processed by the chosen WYO Company or by the traditional NFIP Direct Program. You will, however, continue to be the agent of record throughout the process.

- Approximately 45 days prior to the renewal date of the policy, your client will receive a premium bill from the NFIP Servicing Agent. **This bill is the only bill that should be paid by your client.**

- For the time being, the SDF will be the only source of NFIP flood insurance coverage for your client's property. As always, the full premium amount and any related fees should be paid by the date indicated. The policy sent to your client will meet all the requirements of any mortgage company to the same extent as the current policy.

- You should encourage your client to continue to contact you directly for any service needs on the policy because you will remain the agent of record.

- The NFIP provides a procedure for your client to follow if he or she believes that FEMA has incorrectly included his or her insured property on its list of SRL properties.

The FMA Program was authorized by the National Flood Insurance Reform Act of 1994 and amended by the Biggert-Waters Flood Insurance Reform Act of 2012. The FMA Program may provide Federal grant funds to pay for up to 100 percent of the cost of eligible mitigation activities, such as elevating your client's NFIP-insured structure. Mitigated properties may qualify for reduced flood insurance rates. To obtain additional information on the FMA Program and other mitigation grant programs for residential and non-residential properties, please contact your local floodplain manager or state hazard mitigation officer, or go to the FEMA Hazard Mitigation Assistance webpage at www.fema.gov/hazard-mitigation-assistance.

FEMA's goal is to reduce the devastating effects of repetitive flood losses. If you have questions about this letter and the SRL procedures, please contact the NFIP Help Center by telephone at the toll-free number 1-866-395-7496.

Sincerely,

National Flood Insurance Program

## B. Lender Notification Letter

U.S. Department of Homeland Security
500 C Street, SW
Washington, DC 20472

FEMA

**IMPORTANT FLOOD INSURANCE POLICY INFORMATION**

Insured's Name:

Property Address:

Policy Number:

Dear Lender:

As you may be aware, your client's property, which is covered by flood insurance, has experienced repetitive flood losses under FEMA's National Flood Insurance Program (NFIP). This letter is to inform you that your client's property meets the criteria for a subset of repetitive loss structures: insured properties with a high frequency of losses or a high value of claims. These properties are designated as Severe Repetitive Loss (SRL) properties.

Congress recognized that SRL properties represent the greatest risk of sustaining repeated flood losses and, through the Flood Insurance Reform Act of 2004, made it a top priority to reduce the number of SRL properties nationwide. As of January 2013, FEMA has identified approximately 11,900 properties that meet the designation for SRL. The loss characteristics of an SRL property must meet one of the following criteria based on paid flood losses since 1978, regardless of ownership:

(1) Four or more separate claim payments of more than $5,000 each (building and/or contents payments); or

(2) Two or more separate claim payments (building payments only) where the total of the payments exceeds the current value of the property.

In either case, two of the claim payments must have occurred within 10 years of each other. If there are multiple losses at the same location within 10 days of each other, they are counted as one loss, with the payment amounts added collectively.

The strategy for reducing the number of SRL properties is twofold. First, the NFIP has centralized the processing of all flood insurance policies for SRL properties in order for FEMA to obtain additional underwriting information, verify loss information, and collect information about the flood risk to the SRL properties. Second, FEMA implements the Flood Mitigation Assistance (FMA) grant program annually to mitigate SRL properties. You need to be aware of the following:

- The Write Your Own (WYO) Insurance Companies that sell and service flood insurance under the NFIP will assign flood insurance policies for SRL properties, upon renewal, to a centralized processing center operated by the NFIP Servicing Agent. This center is the Special Direct Facility (SDF).

www.fema.gov

Lender Notification Letter, Page 2

Lender
Date
Page 2

- As a result, your client's policy will not be processed by the chosen WYO Company or by the traditional NFIP Direct Program.
- Approximately 45 days prior to the renewal date of the policy, your client will receive a premium bill from the NFIP Servicing Agent. **This bill is the only bill that should be paid by your client.**
- For the time being, the SDF will be the only source of NFIP flood insurance coverage for your client's property. As always, the full premium amount and any related fees should be paid by the date indicated. The policy sent to your client will meet all the requirements of any mortgage company to the same extent as the current policy.
- The NFIP provides a procedure for your client to follow if he or she believes that FEMA has incorrectly included his or her insured property on its list of SRL properties.

The FMA Program was authorized by the National Flood Insurance Reform Act of 1994 and amended by the Biggert-Waters Flood Insurance Reform Act of 2012. The FMA Program may provide Federal grant funds to pay for up to 100 percent of the cost of eligible mitigation activities, such as elevating your client's NFIP-insured structure. Mitigated properties may qualify for reduced flood insurance rates. To obtain additional information on the FMA Program and other mitigation grant programs for residential and non-residential properties, please contact your local floodplain manager or state hazard mitigation officer, or go to the FEMA Hazard Mitigation Assistance webpage at www.fema.gov/hazard-mitigation-assistance.

FEMA's goal is to reduce the devastating effects of repetitive flood losses. If you have questions about this letter and the SRL procedures, please contact the NFIP Help Center by telephone at the toll-free number 1-866-395-7496.

Sincerely,

National Flood Insurance Program

## C. Insured Notification Letter

*National Flood Insurance Program*
**U.S. Department of Homeland Security**
P.O. Box 2966
Shawnee Mission, KS 66201-1366

FEMA

**IMPORTANT FLOOD INSURANCE POLICY INFORMATION**

Insured's Name:

Property Address:

Policy Number:

Dear Policyholder:

As you may be aware, your property, which is covered by flood insurance, has experienced repetitive flood losses under FEMA's National Flood Insurance Program (NFIP). This letter is to inform you that your property meets the criteria for a subset of repetitive loss structures: insured properties with a high frequency of losses or a high value of claims. These properties are designated as Severe Repetitive Loss (SRL) properties.

Congress recognized that SRL properties represent the greatest risk of sustaining repeated flood losses and, through the Flood Insurance Reform Act of 2004, made it a top priority to reduce the number of SRL properties nationwide. As of January 2013, FEMA has identified approximately 11,900 properties that meet the designation for SRL. The loss characteristics of an SRL property must meet one of the following criteria based on paid flood losses since 1978, regardless of ownership:

(1) Four or more separate claim payments of more than $5,000 each (building and/or contents payments); or

(2) Two or more separate claim payments (building payments only) where the total of the payments exceeds the current value of the property.

In either case, two of the claim payments must have occurred within 10 years of each other. If there are multiple losses at the same location within 10 days of each other, they are counted as one loss, with the payment amounts added collectively.

The strategy for reducing the number of SRL properties is twofold. First, the NFIP has centralized the processing of all flood insurance policies for SRL properties in order for FEMA to obtain additional underwriting information, verify loss information, and collect information about the flood risk to the SRL properties. Second, FEMA implements the Flood Mitigation Assistance (FMA) grant program annually to mitigate SRL properties. You need to be aware of the following:

- The Write Your Own (WYO) Insurance Companies that sell and service flood insurance under the NFIP will assign flood insurance policies for SRL properties, upon renewal, to a centralized processing center operated by the NFIP Servicing Agent. This center is the Special Direct Facility (SDF).

www.fema.gov

Policyholder Notification Letter, Page 2

Policyholder
Date
Page 2

- As a result, your policy will not be processed by your chosen WYO Company or by the traditional NFIP Direct Program. Your agent, however, will continue to be the agent of record throughout the process.
- Approximately 45 days prior to the renewal date of your policy, you will receive a premium bill from the NFIP Servicing Agent. **This bill is the only bill that you should pay.**
- For the time being, the SDF will be the only source of NFIP flood insurance coverage for your property. As always, the full premium amount and any related fees should be paid by the date indicated. The policy sent to you will meet all the requirements of any mortgage company to the same extent as your current policy.
- You may continue to contact your agent directly for any service needs on the policy because he or she will remain the agent of record.
- The NFIP provides a procedure for you to follow if you believe that FEMA has incorrectly included your insured property on its list of SRL properties.

The FMA Program was authorized by the National Flood Insurance Reform Act of 1994 and amended by the Biggert-Waters Flood Insurance Reform Act of 2012. The FMA Program may provide Federal grant funds to pay for up to 100 percent of the cost of eligible mitigation activities, such as elevating your NFIP-insured structure. Mitigated properties may qualify for reduced flood insurance rates. To obtain additional information on the FMA Program and other mitigation grant programs for residential and non-residential properties, please contact your local floodplain manager or state hazard mitigation officer, or go to the FEMA Hazard Mitigation Assistance webpage at www.fema.gov/hazard-mitigation-assistance.

FEMA's goal is to reduce the devastating effects of repetitive flood losses. If you have questions about this letter and the SRL procedures, please contact the NFIP Help Center by telephone at the toll-free number 1-866-395-7496.

Sincerely,

National Flood Insurance Program

# Appendix J: Rate Tables

## I. Effective Date of Rates

FEMA updates its flood insurance rates once a year, but on occasion the effective date varies. Most of the following tables present rates that become effective April 1, 2021. However, some Preferred Risk Policy (PRP) and Newly Mapped (NM) tables have effective dates of Jan. 1, 2021 or Jan. 1, 2022. Affected tables will include the January dates above the table title.

## II. Rates for Standard NFIP Policies

**Table 1** presents annual rates per $100 of coverage for properties in Emergency Program communities. **Tables 1–5** show annual rates per $100 of coverage for properties in Regular Program communities, according to Pre-FIRM premium rates, or Post-FIRM/full-risk premium rates for each zone classification. **Table 6** provides tentative rates (for more information, refer to the Tentative Rates subsection in the How to Write section). Tables **7A–7C** detail the Federal Policy Fee, Probation Surcharge, Reserve Fund Assessment, and HFIAA Surcharge.

**RATE TABLE 1. EMERGENCY PROGRAM RATES**

ANNUAL RATES PER $100 OF COVERAGE

| | BUILDING | CONTENTS |
|---|---|---|
| Residential | 1.27 | 1.60 |
| Non-Residential Business, Other Non-Residential | 1.38 | 2.70 |

**IMPORTANT TO NOTE**

The rate tables in this Appendix have the same numbering as the tables in the April 2018 *NFIP Flood Insurance Manual* sections from which they came. These table numbers are tied to Pivot reporting requirements and cannot be modified at this time. We have included the section abbreviation used in the April 2018 manual (e.g., RATE, CONDO, etc.) before the word "Table" in the titles in this appendix.

## RATE TABLE 2A. REGULAR PROGRAM – PRE-FIRM CONSTRUCTION RATES[1, 2, 3]

ANNUAL RATES PER $100 OF COVERAGE (Basic/Additional)

### FIRM ZONES A, AE, A1–A30, AO, AH, D[4]

| | OCCUPANCY | SINGLE FAMILY | | 2-4 FAMILY | | OTHER RESIDENTIAL | | NON-RESIDENTIAL BUSINESS[5] | | OTHER NON-RESIDENTIAL[5] | |
|---|---|---|---|---|---|---|---|---|---|---|---|
| | | Building | Contents | Building | Contents | Building | Contents | Building | Contents | Building | Contents |
| BUILDING TYPE | No Basement/Enclosure | 1.27 /1.17 | 1.60 /2.08 | 1.27 /1.17 | | 1.27 /2.45 | | 3.60 /6.76 | | 1.38 /2.55 | |
| | With Basement | 1.36 /1.71 | 1.60 /1.76 | 1.36 /1.71 | | 1.27 /2.04 | | 3.79 /6.60 | | 1.46 /2.51 | |
| | With Enclosure[6] | 1.36 /2.05 | 1.60 /2.08 | 1.36 /2.05 | | 1.36 /2.53 | | 3.79 /8.35 | | 1.46 /3.15 | |
| | Elevated on Crawlspace | 1.27 /1.17 | 1.60 /2.08 | 1.27 /1.17 | | 1.27 /2.45 | | 3.60 /6.76 | | 1.38 /2.55 | |
| | Non-Elevated with Subgrade Crawlspace | 1.27 /1.17 | 1.60 /1.76 | 1.27 /1.17 | | 1.27 /2.45 | | 3.60 /6.76 | | 1.38 /2.55 | |
| | Manufactured (Mobile) Home[7] | 1.27 /1.17 | 1.60 /2.08 | | | | | 3.60 /6.76 | | 1.38 /2.55 | |
| CONTENTS LOCATION | Basement & Above[8] | | | | 1.60 /1.76 | | 1.60 /1.76 | | 7.15/11.33 | | 2.70 / 4.27 |
| | Enclosure & Abov | | | | 1.60 /2.08 | | 1.60 /2.08 | | 7.15/13.60 | | 2.70 / 5.10 |
| | Lowest Floor Only – Above Ground Level | | | | 1.60 /2.08 | | 1.60 /2.08 | | 7.15/ 5.93 | | 2.70 / 2.25 |
| | Lowest Floor Above Ground Level and Higher Floors | | | | 1.60 /1.46 | | 1.60 /1.46 | | 7.15/ 5.06 | | 2.70 / 1.94 |
| | Above Ground Level – More Than 1 Full Floor | | | | .35 / .12 | | .35 / .12 | | .24/ .12 | | .24 / .12 |
| | Manufactured (Mobile) Home[7] | | | | | | | | 7.15/ 5.93 | | 2.70 / 2.25 |

### FIRM ZONES V, VE, V1–V30

| | OCCUPANCY | SINGLE FAMILY | | 2-4 FAMILY | | OTHER RESIDENTIAL | | NON-RESIDENTIAL BUSINESS[5] | | OTHER NON-RESIDENTIAL[5] | |
|---|---|---|---|---|---|---|---|---|---|---|---|
| | | Building | Contents | Building | Contents | Building | Contents | Building | Contents | Building | Contents |
| BUILDING TYPE | No Basement/Enclosure | 1.65 /2.91 | 2.05 /4.95 | 1.65 /2.91 | | 1.65 /5.33 | | 4.79 /16.43 | | 1.84 /6.16 | |
| | With Basement | 1.77 /4.29 | 2.05 /4.20 | 1.77 /4.29 | | 1.77 /7.92 | | 5.06 /24.43 | | 1.94 /9.13 | |
| | With Enclosure[6] | 1.77 /5.07 | 2.05 /4.93 | 1.77 /5.07 | | 1.77 /8.85 | | 5.06 /25.00 | | 1.94 /10.20 | |
| | Elevated on Crawlspace | 1.65 /2.91 | 2.05 /4.95 | 1.65 /2.91 | | 1.65 /5.33 | | 4.79 /16.43 | | 1.84 /6.16 | |
| | Non-Elevated with Subgrade Crawlspace | 1.65 /2.91 | 2.05 /4.20 | 1.65 /2.91 | | 1.65 /5.33 | | 4.79 /16.43 | | 1.84 /6.16 | |
| | Manufactured (Mobile) Home[7] | 1.65 /9.02 | 2.05 /4.93 | | | | | 4.79 /25.00 | | 1.84 /17.31 | |
| CONTENTS LOCATION | Basement & Above[8] | | | | 2.05 /4.20 | | 2.05 /4.20 | | 9.43 /25.00 | | 3.54 /10.77 |
| | Enclosure & Above[9] | | | | 2.05 /4.93 | | 2.05 /4.93 | | 9.43 /25.00 | | 3.54 /11.63 |
| | Lowest Floor Only – Above Ground Level | | | | 2.05 /4.93 | | 2.05 /4.93 | | 9.43 /25.00 | | 3.54 /9.77 |
| | Lowest Floor Above Ground Level and Higher Floors | | | | 2.05 /4.34 | | 2.05 /4.34 | | 9.43 /22.54 | | 3.54 /8.43 |
| | Above Ground Level – More Than 1 Full Floor | | | | .54 / .47 | | .54 / .47 | | .52/ .67 | | .52/ .67 |
| | Manufactured (Mobile) Home[7] | | | | | | | | 9.43 /25.00 | | 3.54 /16.19 |

### FIRM ZONES A99, B, C, X

| | OCCUPANCY | SINGLE FAMILY | | 2-4 FAMILY | | OTHER RESIDENTIAL | | NON-RESIDENTIAL BUSINESS[5] | | OTHER NON-RESIDENTIAL[5] | |
|---|---|---|---|---|---|---|---|---|---|---|---|
| | | Building | Contents | Building | Contents | Building | Contents | Building | Contents | Building | Contents |
| BUILDING TYPE | No Basement/Enclosure | 1.12 / .32 | 1.73 / .55 | 1.12 / .32 | | 1.06 / .32 | | 1.06 / .32 | | 1.06 / .32 | |
| | With Basement | 1.25 / .44 | 1.93 / .64 | 1.25 / .44 | | 1.34 / .44 | | 1.34 / .44 | | 1.34 / .44 | |
| | With Enclosure[6] | 1.25 / .48 | 1.93 / .72 | 1.25 / .48 | | 1.34 / .48 | | 1.34 / .48 | | 1.34 / .48 | |
| | Elevated on Crawlspace | 1.12 / .32 | 1.73 / .55 | 1.12 / .32 | | 1.06 / .32 | | 1.06 / .32 | | 1.06 / .32 | |
| | Non-Elevated with Subgrade Crawlspace | 1.12 / .32 | 1.73 / .55 | 1.12 / .32 | | 1.06 / .32 | | 1.06 / .32 | | 1.06 / .32 | |
| | Manufactured (Mobile) Home[7] | 1.12 / .56 | 1.73 / .55 | | | | | 1.34 / .60 | | 1.34 / .60 | |
| CONTENTS LOCATION | Basement & Above[8] | | | | 2.17 / .82 | | 2.17 / .82 | | 2.22 / .89 | | 2.22 / .89 |
| | Enclosure & Above[9] | | | | 2.17 / .93 | | 2.17 / .93 | | 2.22 /1.03 | | 2.22 /1.03 |
| | Lowest Floor Only – Above Ground Level | | | | 1.73 / .86 | | 1.73 / .86 | | 1.37 / .64 | | 1.37 / .64 |
| | Lowest Floor Above Ground Level and Higher Floors | | | | 1.73 / .55 | | 1.73 / .55 | | 1.37 / .45 | | 1.37 / .45 |
| | Above Ground Level – More Than 1 Full Floor | | | | .35 / .12 | | .35 / .12 | | .22 / .12 | | .22 / .12 |
| | Manufactured (Mobile) Home[7] | | | | | | | | 1.20 / .77 | | 1.20 / .77 |

1. Pre-FIRM construction refers to a building that has a date of construction or substantial improvement date on or before 12/31/74, or before the effective date of the initial Flood Insurance Rate Map (FIRM), whichever is later. If there has been a lapse in coverage, refer to Table 10, Pre-FIRM Subsidized Rate Ineligibility Determination, to confirm whether Pre-FIRM subsidized rates can be used.
2. Refer to Table 11, Pre-FIRM Rate Table Hierarchy, to determine which Pre-FIRM rate table to use.
3. Any policy designated as Severe Repetitive Loss (SRL) is subject to the SRL premium. Refer to Table 7D, Severe Repetitive Loss Premium, in this section.
4. Pre-FIRM buildings may use Post-FIRM elevation rating if more favorable to the insured. However, when the lowest floor elevation is below the Base Flood Elevation (BFE), follow the Submit-for-Rate procedures for policy processing.
5. For further guidance on Non-Residential Business and Other Non-Residential occupancies, refer to the Before You Start section of this manual.
6. For an elevated building on a crawlspace with an attached garage without openings, use "Elevated on Crawlspace" rates.
7. Manufactured (Mobile) Homes include travel trailers that meet the definition of a building; refer to Appendix L: Definitions in this manual.
8. Includes subgrade crawlspace.
9. Includes crawlspace.

## RATE TABLE 2B. REGULAR PROGRAM – PRE-FIRM CONSTRUCTION RATES[1, 2] NON-PRIMARY RESIDENCE[3,4]

ANNUAL RATES PER $100 OF COVERAGE (Basic/Additional)

### FIRM ZONES A, AE, A1–A30, AO, AH, D[5]

| | OCCUPANCY | SINGLE FAMILY | | 2–4 FAMILY (CONDO UNIT)[6] | | OTHER RESIDENTIAL (CONDO UNIT)[6] | |
|---|---|---|---|---|---|---|---|
| | | Building | Contents | Building | Contents | Building | Contents |
| BUILDING TYPE | No Basement/Enclosure | 4.82 / 4.18 | 6.11 / 7.55 | 4.82 / 4.18 | | 4.82 / 4.18 | |
| | With Basement | 5.17 / 6.17 | 6.11 / 6.28 | 5.17 / 6.17 | | 5.17 / 6.17 | |
| | With Enclosure[7] | 5.17 / 7.43 | 6.11 / 7.55 | 5.17 / 7.43 | | 5.17 / 7.43 | |
| | Elevated on Crawlspace | 4.82 / 4.18 | 6.11 / 7.55 | 4.82 / 4.18 | | 4.82 / 4.18 | |
| | Non-Elevated with Subgrade Crawlspace | 4.82 / 4.18 | 6.11 / 6.28 | 4.82 / 4.18 | | 4.82 / 4.18 | |
| | Manufactured (Mobile) Home[8] | 3.34 / 2.88 | 4.20 / 5.23 | | | | |
| CONTENTS LOCATION | Basement & Above[9] | | | | 6.11 / 6.28 | | 6.11 / 6.28 |
| | Enclosure & Above[10] | | | | 6.11 / 7.55 | | 6.11 / 7.55 |
| | Lowest Floor Only – Above Ground Level | | | | 6.11 / 7.55 | | 6.11 / 7.55 |
| | Lowest Floor Above Ground Level and Higher Floors | | | | 6.11 / 5.23 | | 6.11 / 5.23 |
| | Above Ground Level – More Than 1 Full Floor | | | | .35 / .12 | | .35 / .12 |
| | Manufactured (Mobile) Home[8] | | | | | | |

### FIRM ZONES V, VE, V1–V30

| | OCCUPANCY | SINGLE FAMILY | | 2–4 FAMILY (CONDO UNIT)[6] | | OTHER RESIDENTIAL (CONDO UNIT)[6] | |
|---|---|---|---|---|---|---|---|
| | | Building | Contents | Building | Contents | Building | Contents |
| BUILDING TYPE | No Basement/Enclosure | 6.28 / 10.82 | 7.87 / 18.54 | 6.28 / 10.82 | | 6.28 / 10.82 | |
| | With Basement | 6.70 / 16.10 | 7.87 / 15.69 | 6.70 / 16.10 | | 6.70 / 16.10 | |
| | With Enclosure[7] | 6.70 / 19.05 | 7.87 / 18.47 | 6.70 / 19.05 | | 6.70 / 19.05 | |
| | Elevated on Crawlspace | 6.28 / 10.82 | 7.87 / 18.54 | 6.28 / 10.82 | | 6.28 / 10.82 | |
| | Non-Elevated with Subgrade Crawlspace | 6.28 / 10.82 | 7.87 / 15.69 | 6.28 / 10.82 | | 6.28 / 10.82 | |
| | Manufactured (Mobile) Home[8] | 6.28 / 25.00 | 7.87 / 18.47 | | | | |
| CONTENTS LOCATION | Basement & Above[9] | | | | 7.87 / 15.69 | | 7.87 / 15.69 |
| | Enclosure & Above[10] | | | | 7.87 / 18.47 | | 7.87 / 18.47 |
| | Lowest Floor Only – Above Ground Level | | | | 7.87 / 18.47 | | 7.87 / 18.47 |
| | Lowest Floor Above Ground Level and Higher Floors | | | | 7.87 / 16.24 | | 7.87 / 16.24 |
| | Above Ground Level – More Than 1 Full Floor | | | | .68 / .59 | | .68 / .59 |
| | Manufactured (Mobile) Home[8] | | | | | | |

### FIRM ZONES A99, B, C, X

| | OCCUPANCY | SINGLE FAMILY | | 2–4 FAMILY (UNIT ONLY)[6] | | OTHER RESIDENTIAL (UNIT ONLY)[6] | |
|---|---|---|---|---|---|---|---|
| | | Building | Contents | Building | Contents | Building | Contents |
| BUILDING TYPE | No Basement/Enclosure | 1.12 / .32 | 1.73 / .55 | 1.12 / .32 | | 1.06 / .32 | |
| | With Basement | 1.25 / .44 | 1.93 / .64 | 1.25 / .44 | | 1.34 / .44 | |
| | With Enclosure[7] | 1.25 / .48 | 1.93 / .72 | 1.25 / .48 | | 1.34 / .48 | |
| | Elevated on Crawlspace | 1.12 / .32 | 1.73 / .55 | 1.12 / .32 | | 1.06 / .32 | |
| | Non-Elevated with Subgrade Crawlspace | 1.12 / .32 | 1.73 / .55 | 1.12 / .32 | | 1.06 / .32 | |
| | Manufactured (Mobile) Home[8] | 1.12 / .56 | 1.73 / .55 | | | | |
| CONTENTS LOCATION | Basement & Above[9] | | | | 2.17 / .82 | | 2.17 / .82 |
| | Enclosure & Above[10] | | | | 2.17 / .93 | | 2.17 / .93 |
| | Lowest Floor Only – Above Ground Level | | | | 1.73 / .86 | | 1.73 / .86 |
| | Lowest Floor Above Ground Level and Higher Floors | | | | 1.73 / .55 | | 1.73 / .55 |
| | Above Ground Level – More Than 1 Full Floor | | | | .35 / .12 | | .35 / .12 |
| | Manufactured (Mobile) Home[8] | | | | | | |

1. Pre-FIRM construction refers to a building that has a date of construction or substantial improvement date on or before 12/31/74, or before the effective date of the initial Flood Insurance Rate Map (FIRM), whichever is later. If there has been a lapse in coverage, refer to Table 10, Pre-FIRM Subsidized Rate Ineligibility Determination, to confirm whether Pre-FIRM subsidized rates can be used.
2. Refer to Table 11, Pre-FIRM Rate Table Hierarchy, to determine which Pre-FIRM rate table to use.
3. For rating purposes only, FEMA defines a non-primary residence as a building that will not be lived in by an insured or an insured's spouse for more than 50% of the 365 days following the policy effective date.
4. Any policy designated as SRL is subject to the SRL premium. Refer to Table 7D, Severe Repetitive Loss Premium, in this section.
5. Pre-FIRM buildings may use Post-FIRM elevation rating if more favorable to the insured. However, when the lowest floor elevation is below the BFE, follow the Submit-for-Rate procedures for policy processing.
6. Individually owned unit in the condominium form of ownership located within a multi-unit building.
7. For an elevated building on a crawlspace with an attached garage without openings, use "Elevated on Crawlspace" rates.
8. Manufactured (Mobile) Homes include travel trailers that meet the definition of a building; refer to Appendix L: Definitions in this manual.
9. Includes subgrade crawlspace.
10. Includes crawlspace.

## RATE TABLE 2C. REGULAR PROGRAM – PRE-FIRM CONSTRUCTION RATES SEVERE REPETITIVE LOSS PROPERTIES[1, 2, 3, 4]

ANNUAL RATES PER $100 OF COVERAGE (Basic/Additional)

### FIRM ZONES A, AE, A1–A30, AO, AH, D[5]

| | OCCUPANCY | SINGLE FAMILY | | 2-4 FAMILY | |
|---|---|---|---|---|---|
| | | Building | Contents | Building | Contents |
| BUILDING TYPE | No Basement/Enclosure | 3.33 / 3.40 | 4.25 / 6.12 | 3.33 / 3.40 | |
| | With Basement | 3.55 / 5.03 | 4.25 / 5.09 | 3.55 / 5.03 | |
| | With Enclosure[6] | 3.55 / 6.03 | 4.25 / 6.12 | 3.55 / 6.03 | |
| | Elevated on Crawlspace | 3.33 / 3.40 | 4.25 / 6.12 | 3.33 / 3.40 | |
| | Non-Elevated with Subgrade Crawlspace | 3.33 / 3.40 | 4.25 / 5.09 | 3.33 / 3.40 | |
| | Manufactured (Mobile) Home[7] | 3.33 / 3.40 | 4.25 / 6.12 | | |
| CONTENTS LOCATION | Basement & Above[8] | | | | 4.25 / 5.09 |
| | Enclosure & Above[9] | | | | 4.25 / 6.12 |
| | Lowest Floor Only – Above Ground Level | | | | 4.25 / 6.12 |
| | Lowest Floor Above Ground Level and Higher Floors | | | | 4.25 / 4.25 |
| | Above Ground Level – More Than 1 Full Floor | | | | .35 / .12 |
| | Manufactured (Mobile) Home[7] | | | | |

### FIRM ZONES V, VE, V1–V30

| | OCCUPANCY | SINGLE FAMILY | | 2-4 FAMILY | |
|---|---|---|---|---|---|
| | | Building | Contents | Building | Contents |
| BUILDING TYPE | No Basement/Enclosure | 4.33 / 8.57 | 5.41 / 14.70 | 4.33 / 8.57 | |
| | With Basement | 4.66 / 12.77 | 5.41 / 12.44 | 4.66 / 12.77 | |
| | With Enclosure[6] | 4.66 / 15.12 | 5.41 / 14.64 | 4.66 / 15.12 | |
| | Elevated on Crawlspace | 4.33 / 8.57 | 5.41 / 14.70 | 4.33 / 8.57 | |
| | Non-Elevated with Subgrade Crawlspace | 4.33 / 8.57 | 5.41 / 12.44 | 4.33 / 8.57 | |
| | Manufactured (Mobile) Home[7] | 4.33 / 27.12 | 5.41 / 14.64 | | |
| CONTENTS LOCATION | Basement & Above[8] | | | | 5.41 / 12.44 |
| | Enclosure & Above[9] | | | | 5.41 / 14.64 |
| | Lowest Floor Only – Above Ground Level | | | | 5.41 / 14.64 |
| | Lowest Floor Above Ground Level and Higher Floors | | | | 5.41 / 12.89 |
| | Above Ground Level – More Than 1 Full Floor | | | | .78 / .65 |
| | Manufactured (Mobile) Home[7] | | | | |

### FIRM ZONES A99, B, C, X

| | OCCUPANCY | SINGLE FAMILY | | 2-4 FAMILY | |
|---|---|---|---|---|---|
| | | Building | Contents | Building | Contents |
| BUILDING TYPE | No Basement/Enclosure | 1.12 / .32 | 1.73 / .55 | 1.12 / .32 | |
| | With Basement | 1.25 / .44 | 1.93 / .64 | 1.25 / .44 | |
| | With Enclosure[6] | 1.25 / .48 | 1.93 / .72 | 1.25 / .48 | |
| | Elevated on Crawlspace | 1.12 / .32 | 1.73 / .55 | 1.12 / .32 | |
| | Non-Elevated with Subgrade Crawlspace | 1.12 / .32 | 1.73 / .55 | 1.12 / .32 | |
| | Manufactured (Mobile) Home[7] | 1.12 / .56 | 1.73 / .55 | | |
| CONTENTS LOCATION | Basement & Above[8] | | | | 2.17 / .82 |
| | Enclosure & Above[9] | | | | 2.17 / .93 |
| | Lowest Floor Only – Above Ground Level | | | | 1.73 / .86 |
| | Lowest Floor Above Ground Level and Higher Floors | | | | 1.73 / .55 |
| | Above Ground Level – More Than 1 Full Floor | | | | .35 / .12 |
| | Manufactured (Mobile) Home[7] | | | | |

1. Pre-FIRM construction refers to a building that has a date of construction or substantial improvement date on or before 12/31/74, or before the effective date of the initial Flood Insurance Rate Map (FIRM), whichever is later. Refer to the rating guidance hierarchy and chart in Table 10 to determine which Pre-FIRM rate table to use. If there has been a lapse in coverage, refer to Table 10, Pre-FIRM Subsidized Rate Ineligibility Determination, to confirm whether Pre-FIRM subsidized rates can be used.
2. Refer to Table 11, Pre-FIRM Rate Table Hierarchy, to determine which Pre-FIRM rate table to use.
3. For additional guidance, refer to Appendix I: Severe Repetitive Loss Properties in this manual.
4. Any policy designated as SRL is subject to the SRL premium. Refer to Table 7D, Severe Repetitive Loss Premium, in this section.
5. Pre-FIRM buildings may use Post-FIRM elevation rating if more favorable to the insured. However, when the lowest floor elevation is below the BFE, follow the Submit-for-Rate procedures for policy processing.
6. For an elevated building on a crawlspace with an attached garage without openings, use "Elevated on Crawlspace" rates.
7. Manufactured (Mobile) Homes include travel trailers that meet the definition of a building; refer to Appendix L: Definitions in this manual.
8. Includes subgrade crawlspace.
9. Includes crawlspace.

## RATE TABLE 2D. REGULAR PROGRAM – PRE-FIRM CONSTRUCTION RATES [1, 2]
## SUBSTANTIAL IMPROVEMENT ON OR AFTER APRIL 1, 2015[3,4]

ANNUAL RATES PER $100 OF COVERAGE (Basic/Additional)

### FIRM ZONES A, AE, A1–A30, AO, AH, D[3]

| | OCCUPANCY | SINGLE FAMILY | | 2-4 FAMILY | | OTHER RESIDENTIAL | | NON-RESIDENTIAL BUSINESS[5] | | OTHER NON-RESIDENTIAL[5] | |
|---|---|---|---|---|---|---|---|---|---|---|---|
| | | Building | Contents | Building | Contents | Building | Contents | Building | Contents | Building | Contents |
| BUILDING TYPE | No Basement/Enclosure | 3.60 / 3.30 | 4.52 / 5.93 | 3.60 / 3.30 | | 3.60 / 7.00 | | 3.93 / 7.36 | | 3.93 / 7.36 | |
| | With Basement | 3.83 / 4.88 | 4.50 / 4.97 | 3.83 / 4.88 | | 3.60 / 5.83 | | 4.13 / 7.16 | | 4.13 / 7.16 | |
| | With Enclosure[6] | 3.83 / 5.84 | 4.52 / 5.93 | 3.83 / 5.84 | | 3.83 / 7.30 | | 4.13 / 9.08 | | 4.13 / 9.08 | |
| | Elevated on Crawlspace | 3.60 / 3.30 | 4.52 / 5.93 | 3.60 / 3.30 | | 3.60 / 7.00 | | 3.93 / 7.36 | | 3.93 / 7.36 | |
| | Non-Elevated with Subgrade Crawlspace | 3.60 / 3.30 | 4.52 / 4.97 | 3.60 / 3.30 | | 3.60 / 7.00 | | 3.93 / 7.36 | | 3.93 / 7.36 | |
| | Manufactured (Mobile) Home[7] | 3.60 / 3.30 | 4.52 / 5.93 | | | | | 3.93 / 7.36 | | 3.93 / 7.36 | |
| CONTENTS LOCATION | Basement & Above[8] | | | | 4.52 / 4.97 | | 4.52 / 4.97 | | 7.74 / 12.36 | | 7.74 / 12.36 |
| | Enclosure & Above[9] | | | | 4.52 / 5.93 | | 4.52 / 5.93 | | 7.74 / 14.76 | | 7.74 / 14.76 |
| | Lowest Floor Only – Above Ground Level | | | | 4.52 / 5.93 | | 4.52 / 5.93 | | 7.74 / 6.46 | | 7.74 / 6.46 |
| | Lowest Floor Above Ground Level and Higher Floors | | | | 4.52 / 4.13 | | 4.52 / 4.13 | | 7.74 / 5.51 | | 7.74 / 5.51 |
| | Above Ground Level – More Than 1 Full Floor | | | | .35 / .12 | | .35 / .12 | | .24 / .12 | | .24 / .12 |
| | Manufactured (Mobile) Home[7] | | | | | | | | 7.74 / 6.46 | | 7.74 / 6.46 |

### FIRM ZONES V, VE, V1–V30

| | OCCUPANCY | SINGLE FAMILY | | 2-4 FAMILY | | OTHER RESIDENTIAL | | NON-RESIDENTIAL BUSINESS[5] | | OTHER NON-RESIDENTIAL[5] | |
|---|---|---|---|---|---|---|---|---|---|---|---|
| | | Building | Contents | Building | Contents | Building | Contents | Building | Contents | Building | Contents |
| BUILDING TYPE | No Basement/Enclosure | 4.67 / 8.35 | 5.84 / 14.30 | 4.67 / 8.35 | | 4.67 / 15.48 | | 5.23 / 17.89 | | 5.23 / 17.89 | |
| | With Basement | 5.03 / 12.43 | 5.84 / 12.14 | 5.03 / 12.43 | | 5.03 / 23.08 | | 5.51 / 25.00 | | 5.51 / 25.00 | |
| | With Enclosure[6] | 5.03 / 14.65 | 5.84 / 14.29 | 5.03 / 14.65 | | 5.03 / 25.00 | | 5.51 / 25.00 | | 5.51 / 25.00 | |
| | Elevated on Crawlspace | 4.67 / 8.35 | 5.84 / 14.30 | 4.67 / 8.35 | | 4.67 / 15.48 | | 5.23 / 17.89 | | 5.23 / 17.89 | |
| | Non-Elevated with Subgrade Crawlspace | 4.67 / 8.35 | 5.84 / 12.14 | 4.67 / 8.35 | | 4.67 / 15.48 | | 5.23 / 17.89 | | 5.23 / 17.89 | |
| | Manufactured (Mobile) Home[7] | 4.67 / 25.00 | 5.84 / 14.29 | | | | | 5.23 / 25.00 | | 5.23 / 25.00 | |
| CONTENTS LOCATION | Basement & Above[8] | | | | 5.84 / 12.14 | | 5.84 / 12.14 | | 10.20 / 25.00 | | 10.20 / 25.00 |
| | Enclosure & Above[9] | | | | 5.84 / 14.29 | | 5.84 / 14.29 | | 10.20 / 25.00 | | 10.20 / 25.00 |
| | Lowest Floor Only – Above Ground Level | | | | 5.84 / 14.29 | | 5.84 / 14.29 | | 10.20 / 25.00 | | 10.20 / 25.00 |
| | Lowest Floor Above Ground Level and Higher Floors | | | | 5.84 / 12.55 | | 5.84 / 12.55 | | 10.20 / 24.52 | | 10.20 / 24.52 |
| | Above Ground Level – More Than 1 Full Floor | | | | .59 / .51 | | .59 / .51 | | .57 / .73 | | .57 / .73 |
| | Manufactured (Mobile) Home[7] | | | | | | | | 10.20 / 25.00 | | 10.20 / 25.00 |

### FIRM ZONES A99, B, C, X

| | OCCUPANCY | SINGLE FAMILY | | 2-4 FAMILY | | OTHER RESIDENTIAL | | NON-RESIDENTIAL BUSINESS[5] | | OTHER NON-RESIDENTIAL[5] | |
|---|---|---|---|---|---|---|---|---|---|---|---|
| | | Building | Contents | Building | Contents | Building | Contents | Building | Contents | Building | Contents |
| BUILDING TYPE | No Basement/Enclosure | 1.12 / .32 | 1.73 / .55 | 1.12 / .32 | | 1.06 / .32 | | 1.06 / .32 | | 1.06 / .32 | |
| | With Basement | 1.25 / .44 | 1.93 / .64 | 1.25 / .44 | | 1.34 / .44 | | 1.34 / .44 | | 1.34 / .44 | |
| | With Enclosure[6] | 1.25 / .48 | 1.93 / .72 | 1.25 / .48 | | 1.34 / .48 | | 1.34 / .48 | | 1.34 / .48 | |
| | Elevated on Crawlspace | 1.12 / .32 | 1.73 / .55 | 1.12 / .32 | | 1.06 / .32 | | 1.06 / .32 | | 1.06 / .32 | |
| | Non-Elevated with Subgrade Crawlspace | 1.12 / .32 | 1.73 / .55 | 1.12 / .32 | | 1.06 / .32 | | 1.06 / .32 | | 1.06 / .32 | |
| | Manufactured (Mobile) Home[7] | 1.12 / .56 | 1.73 / .55 | | | | | 1.34 / .60 | | 1.34 / .60 | |
| CONTENTS LOCATION | Basement & Above[8] | | | | 2.17 / .82 | | 2.17 / .82 | | 2.22 / .89 | | 2.22 / .89 |
| | Enclosure & Above[9] | | | | 2.17 / .93 | | 2.17 / .93 | | 2.22 / 1.03 | | 2.22 / 1.03 |
| | Lowest Floor Only – Above Ground Level | | | | 1.73 / .86 | | 1.73 / .86 | | 1.37 / .64 | | 1.37 / .64 |
| | Lowest Floor Above Ground Level and Higher Floors | | | | 1.73 / .55 | | 1.73 / .55 | | 1.37 / .45 | | 1.37 / .45 |
| | Above Ground Level – More Than 1 Full Floor | | | | .35 / .12 | | .35 / .12 | | .22 / .12 | | .22 / .12 |
| | Manufactured (Mobile) Home[7] | | | | | | | | 1.20 / .77 | | 1.20 / .77 |

1. Use this table to rate a Pre-FIRM building that has been substantially improved on or after April 1, 2015. However, Post-FIRM rating may always be used if beneficial to the insured. If there has been a lapse in coverage, refer to Table 10, Pre-FIRM Subsidized Rate Ineligibility Determination, to confirm whether Pre-FIRM subsidized rates can be used.
2. Refer to Table 11, Pre-FIRM Rate Table Hierarchy, to determine which Pre-FIRM rate table to use.
3. Pre-FIRM buildings may use Post-FIRM elevation rating if more favorable to the insured. However, when the lowest floor elevation is below the BFE, follow the Submit-for-Rate procedures for policy processing.
4. Any policy designated as SRL is subject to the SRL premium. Refer to Table 7D, Severe Repetitive Loss Premium, in this section.
5. For further guidance on Non-Residential Business and Other Non-Residential occupancies, refer to the Before You Start section of this manual.
6. For an elevated building on a crawlspace with an attached garage without openings, use "Elevated on Crawlspace" rates.
7. Manufactured (Mobile) Homes include travel trailers that meet the definition of a building; refer to Appendix L: Definitions in this manual.
8. Includes subgrade crawlspace.
9. Includes crawlspace.

## RATE TABLE 3A. REGULAR PROGRAM – POST-FIRM CONSTRUCTION RATES[1]

ANNUAL RATES PER $100 OF COVERAGE (Basic/Additional)

### FIRM ZONES A99, B, C, X

| | OCCUPANCY | SINGLE FAMILY | | 2-4 FAMILY | | OTHER RESIDENTIAL | | NON-RESIDENTIAL BUSINESS, OTHER NON-RESIDENTIAL[2] | |
|---|---|---|---|---|---|---|---|---|---|
| | | Building | Contents | Building | Contents | Building | Contents | Building | Contents |
| BUILDING TYPE | No Basement/Enclosure | 1.12 / .32 | 1.73 / .55 | 1.12 / .32 | | 1.06 / .32 | | 1.06 / .32 | |
| | With Basement | 1.25 / .44 | 1.93 / .64 | 1.25 / .44 | | 1.34 / .44 | | 1.34 / .44 | |
| | With Enclosure[3] | 1.25 / .48 | 1.93 / .72 | 1.25 / .48 | | 1.34 / .48 | | 1.34 / .48 | |
| | Elevated on Crawlspace | 1.12 / .32 | 1.73 / .55 | 1.12 / .32 | | 1.06 / .32 | | 1.06 / .32 | |
| | Non-Elevated with Subgrade Crawlspace | 1.12 / .32 | 1.73 / .55 | 1.12 / .32 | | 1.06 / .32 | | 1.06 / .32 | |
| | Manufactured (Mobile) Home[4] | 1.12 / .56 | 1.73 / .55 | | | | | 1.34 / .60 | |
| CONTENTS LOCATION | Basement & Above[5] | | | | 2.17 / .82 | | 2.17 / .82 | | 2.22 / .89 |
| | Enclosure & Above[6] | | | | 2.17 / .93 | | 2.17 / .93 | | 2.22 / 1.03 |
| | Lowest Floor Only – Above Ground Level | | | | 1.73 / .86 | | 1.73 / .86 | | 1.37 / .64 |
| | Lowest Floor Above Ground Level and Higher Floors | | | | 1.73 / .55 | | 1.73 / .55 | | 1.37 / .45 |
| | Above Ground Level – More Than 1 Full Floor | | | | .35 / .12 | | .35 / .12 | | .22 / .12 |
| | Manufactured (Mobile) Home[4] | | | | | | | | 1.20 / .77 |

### FIRM ZONE D

| | OCCUPANCY | SINGLE FAMILY | | 2-4 FAMILY | | OTHER RESIDENTIAL | | NON-RESIDENTIAL BUSINESS, OTHER NON-RESIDENTIAL[2] | |
|---|---|---|---|---|---|---|---|---|---|
| | | Building | Contents | Building | Contents | Building | Contents | Building | Contents |
| BUILDING TYPE | No Basement/Enclosure | 3.30 / .28 | 1.45 / .29 | 3.30 / .24 | | 2.75 / .46 | | 2.75 / .46 | |
| | With Basement | *** | *** | *** | | *** | | *** | |
| | With Enclosure[3] | *** | *** | *** | | *** | | *** | |
| | Elevated on Crawlspace | 3.30 / .28 | 1.45 / .29 | 3.30 / .24 | | 2.75 / .46 | | 2.75 / .46 | |
| | Non-Elevated with Subgrade Crawlspace | 3.30 / .28 | 1.45 / .29 | 3.30 / .24 | | 2.75 / .46 | | 2.75 / .46 | |
| | Manufactured (Mobile) Home[4] | 3.73 / .90 | 1.89 / .41 | | | | | 3.34 / 1.70 | |
| CONTENTS LOCATION | Basement & Above[5] | | | | *** | | *** | | *** |
| | Enclosure & Above[6] | | | | *** | | *** | | *** |
| | Lowest Floor Only – Above Ground Level | | | | 1.57 / .29 | | 1.57 / .29 | | 1.38 / .23 |
| | Lowest Floor Above Ground Level and Higher Floors | | | | 1.18 / .18 | | 1.18 / .18 | | 1.10 / .22 |
| | Above Ground Level – More Than 1 Full Floor | | | | .35 / .12 | | .35 / .12 | | .22 / .12 |
| | Manufactured (Mobile) Home[4] | | | | | | | | 1.82 / .59 |

### FIRM ZONES AO, AH (No Basement/Enclosure/Crawlspace/Subgrade Crawlspace Buildings Only)[7]

| OCCUPANCY | BUILDING | | CONTENTS | |
|---|---|---|---|---|
| | 1-4 Family | Other Residential, Non-Residential Business, Other Non-Residential[2] | Residential | Non-Residential Business, Other Non-Residential[2] |
| With Certification of Compliance or Elevation Certificate (EC)[8] | .30 / .09 | .26 / .09 | .38 / .12 | .22 / .12 |
| Without Certification of Compliance or EC[9,10] | 1.71 / .20 | 1.56 / .26 | .84 / .15 | 1.20 / .16 |

1. Any policy designated as SRL is subject to the SRL premium. Refer to Table 7D, Severe Repetitive Loss Premium, in this section.
2. For further guidance on Non-Residential Business and Other Non-Residential occupancies, refer to the Before You Start section of this manual.
3. For an elevated building on a crawlspace with an attached garage without openings, use "Elevated on Crawlspace" rates.
4. Manufactured (Mobile) Homes include travel trailers that meet the definition of a building; refer to Appendix L: Definitions in this manual.
5. Includes subgrade crawlspace.
6. Includes crawlspace.
7. Zones AO, AH Buildings with Basement/Enclosure/Crawlspace/Subgrade Crawlspace: follow Submit-for-Rate procedures. Pre-FIRM buildings with basement/enclosure/crawlspace/subgrade crawlspace at or above the BFE or Base Flood Depth are to use the "With Certification of Compliance or EC" rates and would not have to follow Submit-for-Rate procedures.
8. "With Certification of Compliance or EC" rates are to be used when the EC shows that the lowest floor elevation used for rating is equal to or greater than the community's elevation requirement, or when there is a Letter of Compliance from the community.
9. "Without Certification of Compliance or EC" rates are to be used on Post-FIRM buildings when the EC shows that the lowest floor elevation is less than the community's elevation requirement. These rates may be used for Pre-FIRM buildings when more favorable to the insured than Pre-FIRM subsidized rates even without an EC or Letter of Compliance.
10. For transfers and renewals of existing business where there is no Letter of Compliance or EC in the company's file, these rates can continue to be used. Provisional or tentative rates are to be used for new business without an EC or Letter of Compliance. For new business effective on or after Oct. 1, 2011, the provisions of footnote 8 apply.

*** **Use the *Specific Rating Guidelines* (SRG) manual.**

## RATE TABLE 3B. REGULAR PROGRAM – POST-FIRM CONSTRUCTION RATES[1,2]

ANNUAL RATES PER $100 OF COVERAGE (Basic/Additional)

### FIRM ZONES AE, A1–A30 — BUILDING RATES

| ELEVATION OF LOWEST FLOOR ABOVE OR BELOW THE BFE[3,4] | 1 FLOOR No Basement/Enclosure/ Crawlspace[5,6] | | MORE THAN 1 FLOOR No Basement/Enclosure/ Crawlspace[5,6] | | MORE THAN 1 FLOOR With Basement/Enclosure/ Crawlspace[5,6] | | MANUFACTURED (MOBILE) HOME[7,8] | |
|---|---|---|---|---|---|---|---|---|
| | 1-4 Family | Other Residential, Non-Residential Business, Other Non-Residential[9] | 1-4 Family | Other Residential, Non-Residential Business, Other Non-Residential[9] | 1-4 Family | Other Residential, Non-Residential Business, Other Non-Residential[9] | Single Family | Non-Residential Business, Other Non-Residential[9] |
| +4 | .31 / .09 | .28 / .13 | .27 / .08 | .22 / .08 | .24 / .08 | .20 / .08 | .32 / .16 | .31 / .29 |
| +3 | .35 / .09 | .32 / .15 | .31 / .08 | .25 / .08 | .27 / .08 | .23 / .09 | .37 / .18 | .35 / .33 |
| +2 | .51 / .11 | .46 / .20 | .44 / .08 | .36 / .08 | .32 / .08 | .28 / .10 | .54 / .24 | .50 / .44 |
| +1 | .96 / .17 | .84 / .31 | .80 / .08 | .66 / .09 | .46 / .08 | .36 / .12 | 1.02 / .40 | .95 / .76 |
| 0 | 2.25 / .27 | 1.92 / .50 | 1.79 / .08 | 1.44 / .14 | .68 / .08 | .58 / .14 | 2.39 / .71 | 2.16 / 1.34 |
| –1 | 5.47 / .36 | 4.58 / .69 | 4.40 / .08 | 3.54 / .15 | 1.17 / .08 | .86 / .17 | 5.83 / 1.13 | 5.17 / 2.15 |
| –2[8] | 8.07 / .70 | 6.88 / 1.35 | 6.53 / .13 | 5.25 / .26 | *** | *** | 8.61 / 2.19 | 7.87 / 4.14 |
| –3[8] | 10.00 / 1.20 | 8.76 / 2.30 | 8.32 / .22 | 6.77 / .47 | *** | *** | 10.59 / 3.41 | 9.89 / 6.43 |
| –4[8] | 12.06 / 1.80 | 10.76 / 3.45 | 10.26 / .36 | 8.46 / .77 | *** | *** | 12.68 / 4.77 | 12.00 / 8.97 |
| –5[8] | 13.61 / 2.41 | 12.34 / 4.60 | 11.79 / .57 | 9.88 / 1.16 | *** | *** | 14.21 / 6.00 | 13.58 / 11.27 |
| –6[8] | 13.96 / 2.96 | 12.86 / 5.63 | 12.36 / .84 | 10.56 / 1.69 | *** | *** | 14.51 / 6.84 | 13.99 / 12.81 |
| –7[8] | 14.20 / 3.49 | 13.34 / 6.53 | 12.87 / 1.11 | 11.15 / 2.21 | *** | *** | 14.85 / 7.50 | 14.38 / 14.04 |
| –8[8] | 14.26 / 3.99 | 13.44 / 7.46 | 13.23 / 1.40 | 11.59 / 2.75 | *** | *** | 14.89 / 8.04 | 14.43 / 15.06 |
| –9[8] | 14.31 / 4.29 | 13.54 / 8.04 | 13.27 / 1.68 | 11.67 / 3.31 | *** | *** | 14.93 / 8.25 | 14.48 / 15.48 |
| –10[8] | 14.36 / 4.45 | 13.64 / 8.36 | 13.28 / 1.89 | 11.75 / 3.74 | *** | *** | 14.97 / 8.50 | 14.53 / 15.55 |
| –11[8] | 14.41 / 4.95 | 13.74 / 9.32 | 13.29 / 2.32 | 12.02 / 4.46 | *** | *** | 15.01 / 8.69 | 14.56 / 16.40 |
| –12[8] | 14.46 / 5.38 | 13.84 / 10.08 | 13.52 / 2.63 | 12.31 / 5.03 | *** | *** | 15.05 / 9.05 | 14.60 / 17.03 |
| –13[8] | 14.57 / 5.65 | 13.98 / 10.58 | 13.67 / 2.86 | 12.49 / 5.46 | *** | *** | 15.08 / 9.28 | 14.65 / 17.40 |
| –14[8] | 14.61 / 5.97 | 14.07 / 11.17 | 13.78 / 3.14 | 12.67 / 5.98 | *** | *** | 15.11 / 9.51 | 14.69 / 17.84 |
| –15[8] | 14.91 / 6.29 | 14.38 / 11.76 | 14.08 / 3.40 | 13.00 / 6.45 | *** | *** | 15.19 / 9.87 | 14.97 / 18.39 |
| –16[8] | *** | *** | *** | *** | *** | *** | *** | *** |

1. Pre-FIRM elevated buildings with or without enclosure/crawlspace must use the "No Basement/Enclosure/Crawlspace" columns. Use Appendix C: Lowest Floor Guide to determine the lowest floor elevation for rating. Unfinished partial enclosures below a Pre-FIRM building that are used solely for parking, storage, and building access and are located below the BFE are eligible for Special Rate Consideration.
2. Any policy designated as SRL is subject to the SRL premium. Refer to Table 7D, Severe Repetitive Loss Premium, in this section.
3. If the Lowest Floor is –1 because of an attached garage and the building is described and rated as a single-family dwelling, refer to the Lowest Floor Determination subsection in Appendix C: Lowest Floor Guide in this manual or contact the insurer for rating guidance; rate may be lower.
4. If the lowest floor of a crawlspace or subgrade crawlspace is –1, use Submit-For-Rate procedures (Pre-FIRM or Post-FIRM). If the lowest floor of an enclosure below the elevated floor of a Post-FIRM building is –1, also use Submit-For-Rate procedures.
5. Includes subgrade crawlspace.
6. Use Submit-for-Rate procedures if there is an elevator below the BFE regardless of whether there is an enclosure or not.
7. Manufactured (Mobile) Homes include travel trailers that meet the definition of a building; refer to Appendix L: Definitions in this manual.
8. For elevations of –2 and below and –1 and below for Manufactured (Mobile) Homes, follow Submit-for-Rate procedures in this manual. These rates supersede the rates in the SRG manual.
9. For further guidance on Non-Residential Business and Other Non-Residential occupancies, refer to the Before You Start section of this manual.

*** **Use the SRG manual.**

## RATE TABLE 3B. REGULAR PROGRAM – POST-FIRM CONSTRUCTION RATES[1,2]

ANNUAL RATES PER $100 OF COVERAGE (Basic/Additional)

### FIRM ZONES AE, A1–A30 — CONTENTS RATES

| ELEVATION OF LOWEST FLOOR ABOVE OR BELOW THE BFE[3,4] | LOWEST FLOOR ONLY – ABOVE GROUND LEVEL No Basement/Enclosure/ Crawlspace[5] | | LOWEST FLOOR ABOVE GROUND LEVEL & HIGHER FLOORS No Basement/Enclosure/ Crawlspace[5] | | MORE THAN 1 FLOOR With Basement/Enclosure/ Crawlspace[5] | | MANUFACTURED (MOBILE) HOME[7,8] | |
|---|---|---|---|---|---|---|---|---|
| | Residential | Non-Residential Business, Other Non-Residential[9] | Residential | Non-Residential Business, Other Non-Residential[9] | Residential | Non-Residential Business, Other Non-Residential[9] | Single Family | Non-Residential Business, Other Non-Residential[9] |
| +4 | .38 / .12 | .22 / .12 | .38 / .12 | .22 / .12 | .38 / .12 | .22 / .12 | .38 / .12 | .24 / .15 |
| +3 | .38 / .12 | .22 / .12 | .38 / .12 | .22 / .12 | .38 / .12 | .22 / .12 | .38 / .12 | .28 / .16 |
| +2 | .38 / .12 | .26 / .12 | .38 / .12 | .22 / .12 | .38 / .12 | .22 / .12 | .38 / .15 | .37 / .22 |
| +1 | .54 / .12 | .46 / .12 | .41 / .12 | .34 / .12 | .38 / .12 | .22 / .12 | .66 / .22 | .65 / .34 |
| 0 | 1.03 / .12 | .91 / .12 | .77 / .12 | .65 / .12 | .38 / .12 | .22 / .12 | 1.27 / .34 | 1.24 / .53 |
| –1 | 2.37 / .12 | 2.09 / .12 | 1.80 / .12 | 1.54 / .12 | .59 / .12 | .22 / .12 | 2.81 / .44 | 2.67 / .69 |
| –2[8] | 3.75 / .13 | 3.30 / .12 | 2.80 / .12 | 2.36 / .12 | *** | *** | 4.73 / .84 | 4.53 / 1.32 |
| –3[8] | 5.10 / .24 | 4.43 / .17 | 3.87 / .12 | 3.22 / .12 | *** | *** | 6.53 / 1.48 | 6.34 / 2.33 |
| –4[8] | 6.62 / .40 | 5.71 / .26 | 5.11 / .12 | 4.22 / .15 | *** | *** | 8.42 / 2.29 | 8.25 / 3.57 |
| –5[8] | 7.95 / .61 | 6.85 / .41 | 6.24 / .17 | 5.16 / .24 | *** | *** | 9.97 / 3.13 | 9.84 / 4.87 |
| –6[8] | 8.73 / .87 | 7.56 / .67 | 7.03 / .28 | 5.87 / .39 | *** | *** | 10.70 / 3.89 | 10.63 / 6.03 |
| –7[8] | 9.37 / 1.12 | 8.19 / .94 | 7.69 / .42 | 6.49 / .57 | *** | *** | 11.29 / 4.52 | 11.27 / 6.98 |
| –8[8] | 9.86 / 1.35 | 8.69 / 1.23 | 8.21 / .58 | 7.03 / .79 | *** | *** | 11.69 / 5.03 | 11.71 / 7.75 |
| –9[8] | 10.07 / 1.57 | 8.97 / 1.51 | 8.52 / .73 | 7.39 / 1.02 | *** | *** | 11.78 / 5.38 | 11.83 / 8.30 |
| –10[8] | 10.10 / 1.76 | 9.09 / 1.77 | 8.67 / .89 | 7.63 / 1.24 | *** | *** | 11.88 / 5.57 | 11.95 / 8.70 |
| –11[8] | 10.52 / 2.02 | 9.55 / 2.10 | 9.16 / 1.08 | 8.15 / 1.51 | *** | *** | 11.98 / 6.15 | 12.10 / 9.47 |
| –12[8] | 10.84 / 2.22 | 9.91 / 2.37 | 9.52 / 1.24 | 8.56 / 1.74 | *** | *** | 12.22 / 6.52 | 12.36 / 10.02 |
| –13[8] | 11.03 / 2.35 | 10.14 / 2.55 | 9.74 / 1.36 | 8.82 / 1.91 | *** | *** | 12.40 / 6.73 | 12.55 / 10.34 |
| –14[8] | 11.25 / 2.52 | 10.41 / 2.78 | 10.02 / 1.50 | 9.14 / 2.11 | *** | *** | 12.54 / 7.02 | 12.71 / 10.79 |
| –15[8] | 11.57 / 2.67 | 10.75 / 2.98 | 10.35 / 1.62 | 9.49 / 2.29 | *** | *** | 12.83 / 7.31 | 13.01 / 11.23 |
| –16[8] | *** | *** | *** | *** | *** | *** | *** | *** |

### FIRM ZONES AE, A1–A30 — CONTENTS RATES

| ELEVATION OF LOWEST FLOOR ABOVE OR BELOW THE BFE[3] | ABOVE GROUND LEVEL MORE THAN 1 FULL FLOOR | | | | |
|---|---|---|---|---|---|
| | Single Family | 2-4 Family | Other Residential | Non-Residential Business[9] | Other Non-Residential[9] |
| +4 | | .35 / .12 | .35 / .12 | .22 / .12 | .22 / .12 |
| +3 | | .35 / .12 | .35 / .12 | .22 / .12 | .22 / .12 |
| +2 | | .35 / .12 | .35 / .12 | .22 / .12 | .22 / .12 |
| +1 | | .35 / .12 | .35 / .12 | .22 / .12 | .22 / .12 |
| 0 | | .35 / .12 | .35 / .12 | .22 / .12 | .22 / .12 |
| –1 | | .35 / .12 | .35 / .12 | .22 / .12 | .22 / .12 |
| –2 | | .35 / .12 | .35 / .12 | .22 / .12 | .22 / .12 |

1. Pre-FIRM elevated buildings with or without enclosure/crawlspace must use the "No Basement/Enclosure/Crawlspace" columns. Use Appendix C: Lowest Floor Guide to determine the lowest floor elevation for rating. Unfinished partial enclosures below a Pre-FIRM building that are used solely for parking, storage, and building access and are located below the BFE are eligible for Special Rate Consideration.
2. Any policy designated as SRL is subject to the SRL premium. Refer to Table 7D, Severe Repetitive Loss Premium, in this section.
3. If the Lowest Floor is –1 because of an attached garage and the building is described and rated as a single-family dwelling, refer to the Lowest Floor Determination subsection in Appendix C: Lowest Floor Guide in this manual or contact the insurer for rating guidance; rate may be lower.
4. If the lowest floor of a crawlspace or subgrade crawlspace is –1, use Submit-For-Rate procedures (Pre-FIRM or Post-FIRM). If the lowest floor of an enclosure below the elevated floor of a Post-FIRM building is –1, also use Submit-For-Rate procedures.
5. Includes subgrade crawlspace.
6. Use Submit-for-Rate procedures if there is an elevator below the BFE regardless of whether there is an enclosure or not.
7. Manufactured (Mobile) Homes include travel trailers that meet the definition of a building; refer to Appendix L: Definitions in this manual.
8. For elevations of –2 and below and –1 and below for Manufactured (Mobile) Homes, follow Submit-for-Rate procedures in this manual. These rates supersede the rates in the SRG manual.
9. For further guidance on Non-Residential Business and Other Non-Residential occupancies, refer to the Before You Start section of this manual.

***** Use the SRG manual.**

## RATE TABLE 3C. REGULAR PROGRAM – POST-FIRM CONSTRUCTION RATES

ANNUAL RATES PER $100 OF COVERAGE (Basic/Additional)

### UNNUMBERED ZONE A — WITHOUT BASEMENT/ENCLOSURE/CRAWLSPACE/SUBGRADE CRAWLSPACE[1,2,3]

| ELEVATION DIFFERENCE | BUILDING RATES | | CONTENTS RATES | | TYPE OF EC |
|---|---|---|---|---|---|
| | Occupancy | | Occupancy | | |
| | 1-4 Family | Other Residential, Non-Residential Business, Other Non-Residential[4] | Residential[5] | Non-Residential Business, Other Non-Residential[4,5] | |
| +5 or more | .59 / .12 | .51 / .19 | .34 / .08 | .29 / .08 | No BFE[6] |
| +2 to +4 | 1.71 / .19 | 1.44 / .35 | .80 / .08 | .70 / .08 | |
| +1 | 3.30 / .24 | 2.75 / .47 | 1.45 / .10 | 1.58 / .14 | |
| 0 or below | *** | *** | *** | *** | |
| +2 or more | .58 / .10 | .50 / .18 | .33 / .08 | .28 / .09 | With BFE[7] |
| 0 to +1 | 2.72 / .21 | 2.28 / .39 | 1.22 / .09 | 1.06 / .10 | |
| −1 | 6.44 / .35 | 5.33 / .67 | 2.75 / .16 | 2.41 / .33 | |
| −2 or below | *** | *** | *** | *** | |
| No EC[8] | 8.05 /1.30 | 6.67 / .90 | 3.52 / .80 | 3.01 / .96 | No EC |

1. Buildings with basement, enclosure, crawlspace, or subgrade crawlspace: follow Submit-for-Rate procedures. Unfinished partial enclosures below a Pre-FIRM building that are used solely for parking, storage, and building access and are located below the BFE are eligible for Special Rate Consideration.
2. Pre-FIRM buildings may use this table if the rates are more favorable to the insured.
3. Any policy designated as SRL is subject to the SRL premium. Refer to Table 7D, Severe Repetitive Loss Premium, in this section.
4. For further guidance on Non-Residential Business and Other Non-Residential occupancies, refer to the Before You Start section of this manual.
5. For elevation-rated risks other than Single Family, when contents are located 1 floor or more above lowest floor used for rating – use Table 3B, Contents Rates, Above Ground Level More Than 1 Full Floor.
6. Elevation difference is the measured distance between the highest adjacent grade next to the building and the lowest floor of the building.
7. In A Zones where BFEs are not available, the BFE may be provided by Federal, state, or local government agencies, such as the United States Geological Survey, United States Army Corps of Engineers, Department of Transportation, or Division of Water Resources. In these cases, the insurer should document in the policy file the source of the BFE used for rating.
8. For policies with effective dates on or after Oct. 1, 2011, the No EC rates apply only to renewals and transfers. Provisional or tentative rates are to be used for new business without an EC.

*** **Use the SRG manual.**

## RATE TABLE 3D. REGULAR PROGRAM – POST-FIRM CONSTRUCTION RATES[1,2]

ANNUAL RATES PER $100 OF COVERAGE (Basic/Additional)

### FIRM ZONES '75–'81, V1–V30, VE — BUILDING RATES[3]

| ELEVATION OF LOWEST FLOOR ABOVE OR BELOW THE BFE | 1 FLOOR No Basement/Enclosure/ Crawlspace[4,5] | | MORE THAN 1 FLOOR No Basement/Enclosure/ Crawlspace[4,5] | | MORE THAN 1 FLOOR With Basement/Enclosure/ Crawlspace[4,5] | | MANUFACTURED (MOBILE) HOME[6] | |
|---|---|---|---|---|---|---|---|---|
| | 1-4 Family | Other Residential, Non-Residential Business, Other Non-Residential[7] | 1-4 Family | Other Residential, Non-Residential Business, Other Non-Residential[7] | 1-4 Family | Other Residential, Non-Residential Business, Other Non-Residential[7] | Single Family | Non-Residential Business, Other Non-Residential[7] |
| 0[8] | 8.60 / 1.50 | 10.38 / 3.96 | 6.97 / 1.50 | 7.56 / 3.71 | 6.01 / 1.50 | 6.76 / 2.99 | 10.50 / 1.94 | 10.50 / 2.27 |
| –1[9] | 11.43 / 9.98 | 11.43 / 14.73 | 11.43 / 9.98 | 11.43 / 12.58 | 11.43 / 8.56 | 11.43 / 12.04 | *** | *** |
| –2 | *** | *** | *** | *** | *** | *** | *** | *** |

### FIRM ZONES '75–'81, V1–V30, VE — CONTENTS RATES

| ELEVATION OF LOWEST FLOOR ABOVE OR BELOW THE BFE | LOWEST FLOOR ONLY – ABOVE GROUND LEVEL No Basement/Enclosure/ Crawlspace[4] | | LOWEST FLOOR ABOVE GROUND LEVEL & HIGHER FLOORS No Basement/Enclosure/ Crawlspace[4] | | MORE THAN 1 FLOOR With Basement/Enclosure/ Crawlspace[4] | | MANUFACTURED (MOBILE) HOME[6] | |
|---|---|---|---|---|---|---|---|---|
| | Residential | Non-Residential Business, Other Non-Residential[7] | Residential | Non-Residential Business, Other Non-Residential[7] | Residential | Non-Residential Business, Other Non-Residential[7] | Single Family | Non-Residential Business, Other Non-Residential[7] |
| 0[8] | 4.71 / 3.26 | 5.16 / 5.16 | 4.71 / 2.99 | 5.16 / 5.16 | 3.90 / 2.41 | 3.90 / 2.52 | 4.71 / 3.63 | 5.16 / 5.77 |
| –1[9] | 9.79 / 7.34 | 9.61 / 12.11 | 5.97 / 5.97 | 6.83 / 7.64 | 4.61 / 2.47 | 6.14 / 4.08 | *** | *** |
| –2 | *** | *** | *** | *** | *** | *** | *** | *** |

### FIRM ZONES '75–'81, V1–V30, VE — CONTENTS RATES

| ELEVATION OF LOWEST FLOOR ABOVE OR BELOW THE BFE | ABOVE GROUND LEVEL MORE THAN 1 FULL FLOOR | | | |
|---|---|---|---|---|
| | Single Family | 2-4 Family | Other Residential | Non-Residential Business, Other Non-Residential[7] |
| 0[8] | | .56 / .25 | .56 / .25 | .42 / .25 |
| –1[9] | | .56 / .25 | .56 / .25 | .42 / .25 |
| –2 | | .56 / .25 | .56 / .25 | .46 / .25 |

1. Pre-FIRM elevated buildings with or without enclosure/crawlspace must use the "No Basement/Enclosure/Crawlspace" columns. Use Appendix C: Lowest Floor Guide to determine the lowest floor elevation for rating. Unfinished partial enclosures below a Pre-FIRM building that are used solely for parking, storage, and building access and are located below the BFE are eligible for Special Rate Consideration.
2. Any policy designated as SRL is subject to the SRL premium. Refer to Table 7D, Severe Repetitive Loss Premium, in this section.
3. Policies for 1975 through 1981 Post-FIRM and Pre-FIRM buildings in zones VE and V1–V30 will be allowed to use the Post-'81 V-Zone rate table if the rates are more favorable to the insured. Refer to instructions in the How to Write section for V-Zone Optional Rating.
4. Includes subgrade crawlspace.
5. Use Submit-for-Rate procedures if there is an elevator below the BFE regardless of whether there is an enclosure or not.
6. Manufactured (Mobile) Homes include travel trailers that meet the definition of a building; refer to Appendix L: Definitions in this manual.
7. For further guidance on Non-Residential Business and Other Non-Residential occupancies, refer to the Before You Start section of this manual.
8. These rates are to be used if the lowest floor of the building is at or above the BFE.
9. Use Submit-for-Rate procedures if the enclosure below the lowest elevated floor of an elevated building, which is used for rating, is 1 or more feet below the BFE.

*** **Use the SRG manual.**

### FIRM ZONES '75–'81, UNNUMBERED V ZONE

| SUBMIT FOR RATING |
|---|

## RATE TABLE 3E. REGULAR PROGRAM – POST-FIRM CONSTRUCTION RATES

ANNUAL RATES PER $100 OF COVERAGE

### 1981 POST-FIRM V1–V30, VE ZONE RATES[1,2]

| ELEVATION OF THE LOWEST FLOOR ABOVE OR BELOW BFE ADJUSTED FOR WAVE HEIGHT[3] | ELEVATED BUILDINGS FREE OF OBSTRUCTION[4] | | | | |
|---|---|---|---|---|---|
| | CONTENTS | | BUILDING | | |
| | Residential | Non-Residential Business, Other Non-Residential[5] | Replacement Cost Ratio .75 or More[6] | Replacement Cost Ratio .50 to .74[6] | Replacement Cost Ratio Under .50[6] |
| +4 or more | .93 | .95 | 1.51 | 1.83 | 2.45 |
| +3 | 1.08 | 1.08 | 1.79 | 2.19 | 2.91 |
| +2 | 1.47 | 1.52 | 2.18 | 2.65 | 3.43 |
| +1 | 1.95 | 2.01 | 2.68 | 3.19 | 4.02 |
| 0 | 2.55 | 2.64 | 3.29 | 3.85 | 4.72 |
| −1 | 3.29 | 3.41 | 4.04 | 4.67 | 5.59 |
| −2 | 4.14 | 4.27 | 4.88 | 5.63 | 6.70 |
| −3 | 5.10 | 5.26 | 5.85 | 6.68 | 7.89 |
| −4 or below | *** | *** | *** | *** | *** |

1. Policies for 1975 through 1981 Post-FIRM and Pre-FIRM buildings in zones VE and V1–V30 will be allowed to use the Post-'81 V-Zone rate table if the rates are more favorable to the insured. Refer to instructions in the How to Write section for V-Zone Optional Rating.
2. Any policy designated as SRL is subject to the SRL premium. Refer to Table 7D, Severe Repetitive Loss Premium, in this section.
3. Wave height adjustment is not required in those cases where the FIRM indicates that the map includes wave height.
4. FREE OF OBSTRUCTION – The space below the lowest elevated floor must be completely free of obstructions or any attachment to the building, or may have:
   (1) Insect screening, provided that no additional supports are required for the screening; *or*
   (2) Wooden or plastic lattice with at least 40% of its area open and made of material no thicker than ½ inch; *or*
   (3) Wooden or plastic slats or shutters with at least 40% of their area open and made of material no thicker than 1 inch.
   (4) One solid breakaway wall or a garage door, with the remaining sides of the enclosure constructed of insect screening, wooden or plastic lattice, slats, or shutters. Any of these systems must be designed and installed to collapse under stress without jeopardizing the structural support of the building, so that the impact on the building of abnormally high tides or wind-driven water is minimized.
   (5) Any machinery or equipment below the lowest elevated floor must be at or above the BFE.
5. For further guidance on Non-Residential Business and Other Non-Residential occupancies, refer to the Before You Start section of this manual.
6. These percentages represent building replacement cost ratios, which are determined by dividing the amount of building coverage being purchased through the NFIP by the replacement cost. Refer to the Replacement Cost Ratio subsection in the How to Write section for more details.

**NOTE:** Use Submit-for-Rate procedures if there is an elevator below the BFE enclosed with lattice, slats, or shutters (including louvers).

*** **Use the SRG manual.**

### 1981 POST-FIRM V1–V30, VE ZONE NON-ELEVATED BUILDINGS

| SUBMIT FOR RATING |
|---|

### 1981 POST-FIRM UNNUMBERED V ZONE

| SUBMIT FOR RATING |
|---|

## RATE TABLE 3F. REGULAR PROGRAM – POST-FIRM CONSTRUCTION RATES

ANNUAL RATES PER $100 OF COVERAGE

### 1981 POST-FIRM V1–V30, VE ZONE RATES[1,2,3]

| ELEVATION OF THE LOWEST FLOOR ABOVE OR BELOW BFE ADJUSTED FOR WAVE HEIGHT[4] | ELEVATED BUILDINGS WITH OBSTRUCTION[5] | | | | |
|---|---|---|---|---|---|
| | CONTENTS | | BUILDING | | |
| | Residential | Non-Residential Business, Other Non-Residential[6] | Replacement Cost Ratio .75 or More[7] | Replacement Cost Ratio .50 to .74[7] | Replacement Cost Ratio Under .50[7] |
| +4 or more | 1.35 | 1.43 | 2.26 | 2.83 | 3.95 |
| +3 | 1.42 | 1.52 | 2.72 | 3.43 | 4.76 |
| +2 | 1.91 | 2.05 | 3.27 | 4.09 | 5.56 |
| +1 | 2.41 | 2.67 | 3.85 | 4.73 | 6.30 |
| 0 | 3.14 | 3.44 | 4.46 | 5.39 | 7.00 |
| –1[8] | 3.98 | 4.09 | 5.03 | 6.00 | 7.62 |
| –2[8] | 4.68 | 4.82 | 5.75 | 6.76 | 8.39 |
| –3[8] | 5.57 | 5.75 | 6.66 | 7.73 | 9.39 |
| –4 or below[8] | *** | *** | *** | *** | *** |

1. Policies for 1975 through 1981 Post-FIRM and Pre-FIRM buildings in zones VE and V1–V30 will be allowed to use the Post-'81 V-Zone rate table if the rates are more favorable to the insured. Refer to instructions in the How to Write section for V-Zone Optional Rating.
2. Rates provided are only for elevated buildings, except those elevated on solid foundation walls. For buildings elevated on solid foundation walls, and for non-elevated buildings, follow the Submit-for-Rate procedures.
3. Any policy designated as SRL is subject to the SRL premium. Refer to Table 7D, Severe Repetitive Loss Premium, in this section.
4. Wave height adjustment is not required in those cases where the FIRM indicates that the map includes wave height.
5. WITH OBSTRUCTION – The space below has an area of less than 300 square feet with breakaway solid walls or contains machinery or equipment below the BFE. If the space below has an area of 300 square feet or more, or if any portion of the space below the elevated floor is enclosed with non-breakaway walls, submit for rating. If the enclosure is at or above the BFE, use the "Free of Obstruction" rate table on the preceding page. The elevation of the bottom enclosure floor is the lowest floor for rating (LFE). Refer to Elevated Buildings – Post-FIRM V-Zone Construction in the How to Write section for more details.
6. For further guidance on Non-Residential Business and Other Non-Residential occupancies, refer to the Before You Start section of this manual.
7. These percentages represent building replacement cost ratios, which are determined by dividing the amount of building coverage being purchased through the NFIP by the replacement cost. Refer to the Replacement Cost Ratio subsection in the How to Write section for more details.
8. For buildings with obstruction, use Submit-for-Rate procedures if the enclosure below the lowest elevated floor of an elevated building, which is used for rating, is 1 or more feet below the BFE.

**NOTE:** Use Submit-for-Rate procedures if there is an elevator below the BFE.

*** **Use the SRG manual.**

### 1981 POST-FIRM UNNUMBERED V ZONE

| SUBMIT FOR RATING |
|---|

## RATE TABLE 4. REGULAR PROGRAM – FIRM ZONE AR AND AR DUAL ZONES[1,2]
## NOT ELEVATION-RATED RATES

ANNUAL RATES PER $100 OF COVERAGE (Basic/Additional)

### PRE-FIRM RATES[3]

| | OCCUPANCY | SINGLE FAMILY | | 2-4 FAMILY | | OTHER RESIDENTIAL | | NON-RESIDENTIAL BUSINESS, OTHER NON-RESIDENTIAL[4] | |
|---|---|---|---|---|---|---|---|---|---|
| | | Building | Contents | Building | Contents | Building | Contents | Building | Contents |
| BUILDING TYPE | No Basement/Enclosure | 1.12 / .32 | 1.73 / .55 | 1.12 / .32 | | 1.06 / .32 | | 1.06 / .32 | |
| | With Basement | 1.25 / .44 | 1.93 / .64 | 1.25 / .44 | | 1.34 / .44 | | 1.34 / .44 | |
| | With Enclosure | 1.25 / .48 | 1.93 / .72 | 1.25 / .48 | | 1.34 / .48 | | 1.34 / .48 | |
| | Elevated on Crawlspace | 1.12 / .32 | 1.73 / .55 | 1.12 / .32 | | 1.06 / .32 | | 1.06 / .32 | |
| | Non-Elevated with Subgrade Crawlspace | 1.12 / .32 | 1.73 / .55 | 1.12 / .32 | | 1.06 / .32 | | 1.06 / .32 | |
| | Manufactured (Mobile) Home[5] | 1.12 / .56 | 1.73 / .55 | | | | | 1.34 / .60 | |
| CONTENTS LOCATION | Basement & Above | | | | 2.17 / .82 | | 2.17 / .82 | | 2.22 / .89 |
| | Enclosure & Above | | | | 2.17 / .93 | | 2.17 / .93 | | 2.22 /1.03 |
| | Lowest Floor Only – Above Ground Level | | | | 1.73 / .86 | | 1.73 / .86 | | 1.37/ .64 |
| | Lowest Floor Above Ground Level and Higher Floors | | | | 1.73 / .55 | | 1.73 / .55 | | 1.37 / .45 |
| | Above Ground Level – More Than 1 Full Floor | | | | .35 / .12 | | .35 / .12 | | .22 / .12 |
| | Manufactured (Mobile) Home[5] | | | | | | | | 1.20 / .77 |

### POST-FIRM RATES

| | OCCUPANCY | SINGLE FAMILY | | 2-4 FAMILY | | OTHER RESIDENTIAL | | NON-RESIDENTIAL BUSINESS, OTHER NON-RESIDENTIAL[4] | |
|---|---|---|---|---|---|---|---|---|---|
| | | Building | Contents | Building | Contents | Building | Contents | Building | Contents |
| BUILDING TYPE | No Basement/Enclosure | 1.12 / .32 | 1.73 / .55 | 1.12 / .32 | | 1.06 / .32 | | 1.06 / .32 | |
| | With Basement | 1.25 / .44 | 1.93 / .64 | 1.25 / .44 | | 1.34 / .44 | | 1.34 / .44 | |
| | With Enclosure | 1.25 / .48 | 1.93 / .72 | 1.25 / .48 | | 1.34 / .48 | | 1.34 / .48 | |
| | Elevated on Crawlspace | 1.12 / .32 | 1.73 / .55 | 1.12 / .32 | | 1.06 / .32 | | 1.06 / .32 | |
| | Non-Elevated with Subgrade Crawlspace | 1.12 / .32 | 1.73 / .55 | 1.12 / .32 | | 1.06 / .32 | | 1.06 / .32 | |
| | Manufactured (Mobile) Home[5] | 1.12 / .56 | 1.73 / .55 | | | | | 1.34 / .60 | |
| CONTENTS LOCATION | Basement & Above | | | | 2.17 / .82 | | 2.17 / .82 | | 2.22 / .89 |
| | Enclosure & Above | | | | 2.17 / .93 | | 2.17 / .93 | | 2.22 /1.03 |
| | Lowest Floor Only – Above Ground Level | | | | 1.73 / .86 | | 1.73 / .86 | | 1.37/ .64 |
| | Lowest Floor Above Ground Level and Higher Floors | | | | 1.73 / .55 | | 1.73 / .55 | | 1.37 / .45 |
| | Above Ground Level – More Than 1 Full Floor | | | | .35 / .12 | | .35 / .12 | | .22 / .12 |
| | Manufactured (Mobile) Home[5] | | | | | | | | 1.20 / .77 |

1. Properties in AR zones may be eligible for the PRP. Refer to the PRP section in the How to Write section of this manual.
2. Any policy designated as SRL is subject to the SRL premium. Refer to Table 7D, Severe Repetitive Loss Premium, in this section.
3. Pre-FIRM construction refers to a building that has a date of construction or substantial improvement date on or before 12/31/74, or before the effective date of the initial FIRM, whichever is later.
4. For further guidance on Non-Residential Business and Other Non-Residential occupancies, refer to the Before You Start section of this manual.
5. Manufactured (Mobile) Homes include travel trailers that meet the definition of a building; refer to Appendix L: Definitions in this manual.

## RATE TABLE 5. REGULAR PROGRAM – PRE-FIRM AND POST-FIRM ELEVATION-RATED RATES[1]

ANNUAL RATES PER $100 OF COVERAGE (Basic/Additional)

### FIRM ZONES AR AND AR DUAL ZONES[2] — BUILDING RATES

| ELEVATION OF LOWEST FLOOR ABOVE OR BELOW THE BFE | 1 FLOOR No Basement/Enclosure/ Crawlspace[3] | | MORE THAN 1 FLOOR No Basement/Enclosure/ Crawlspace[3] | | MORE THAN 1 FLOOR With Basement/Enclosure/ Crawlspace[3] | | MANUFACTURED (MOBILE) HOME[4] | |
|---|---|---|---|---|---|---|---|---|
| | 1-4 Family | Other Residential, Non-Residential Business, Other Non-Residential[5] | 1-4 Family | Other Residential, Non-Residential Business, Other Non-Residential[5] | 1-4 Family | Other Residential, Non-Residential Business, Other Non-Residential[5] | Single Family | Non-Residential Business, Other Non-Residential[5] |
| +4 | .31 / .09 | .28 / .13 | .27 / .08 | .22 / .08 | .24 / .08 | .20 / .08 | .32 / .16 | .31 / .29 |
| +3 | .35 / .09 | .32 / .15 | .31 / .08 | .25 / .08 | .27 / .08 | .23 / .09 | .37 / .18 | .35 / .33 |
| +2 | .51 / .11 | .46 / .20 | .44 / .08 | .36 / .08 | .32 / .08 | .28 / .10 | .54 / .24 | .50 / .44 |
| +1 | .96 / .17 | .84 / .31 | .80 / .08 | .66 / .09 | .46 / .08 | .36 / .12 | 1.02 / .32 | .95 / .60 |
| 0 | 1.12 / .32 | 1.06/ .32 | 1.12 / .32 | 1.06 / .32 | .68 / .08 | .58 / .14 | 1.12 / .32 | 1.34 / .60 |
| −1[6] | SEE FOOTNOTE 5 | | | | | | | |

### FIRM ZONES AR AND AR DUAL ZONES[2] — CONTENTS RATES

| ELEVATION OF LOWEST FLOOR ABOVE OR BELOW THE BFE | LOWEST FLOOR ONLY - ABOVE GROUND LEVEL No Basement/Enclosure/ Crawlspace[3] | | LOWEST FLOOR ABOVE GROUND LEVEL & HIGHER FLOORS No Basement/Enclosure/ Crawlspace[3] | | MORE THAN 1 FLOOR With Basement/Enclosure/ Crawlspace[3] | | MANUFACTURED (MOBILE) HOME[4] | |
|---|---|---|---|---|---|---|---|---|
| | Residential | Non-Residential Business, Other Non-Residential[5] | Residential | Non-Residential Business, Other Non-Residential[5] | Residential | Non-Residential Business, Other Non-Residential[5] | Single Family | Non-Residential Business, Other Non-Residential[5] |
| +4 | .38 / .12 | .22 / .12 | .38 / .12 | .22 / .12 | .38 / .12 | .22 / .12 | .38 / .12 | .24 / .15 |
| +3 | .38 / .12 | .22 / .12 | .38 / .12 | .22 / .12 | .38 / .12 | .22 / .12 | .38 / .12 | .28 / .16 |
| +2 | .38 / .12 | .26 / .12 | .38 / .12 | .22 / .12 | .38 / .12 | .22 / .12 | .38 / .15 | .37 / .22 |
| +1 | .54 / .12 | .46 / .12 | .41 / .12 | .34 / .12 | .38 / .12 | .22 / .12 | .66 / .22 | .65 / .34 |
| 0 | 1.03 / .12 | .91 / .12 | .77 / .12 | .65 / .12 | .38 / .12 | .22 / .12 | 1.27 / .34 | 1.20 / .55 |
| −1[6] | SEE FOOTNOTE 5 | | | | | | | |

### FIRM ZONES AR AND AR DUAL ZONES[2] — CONTENTS RATES

| ELEVATION OF LOWEST FLOOR ABOVE OR BELOW THE BFE | ABOVE GROUND LEVEL MORE THAN 1 FULL FLOOR | | | |
|---|---|---|---|---|
| | Single Family | 2-4 Family | Other Residential | Non-Residential Business, Other Non-Residential[5] |
| +4 | | .35 / .12 | .35 / .12 | .22 / .12 |
| +3 | | .35 / .12 | .35 / .12 | .22 / .12 |
| +2 | | .35 / .12 | .35 / .12 | .22 / .12 |
| +1 | | .35 / .12 | .35 / .12 | .22 / .12 |
| 0 | | .35 / .12 | .35 / .12 | .22 / .12 |
| −1[7] | | .35 / .12 | .35 / .12 | .22 / .12 |
| −2[7] | | .35 / .12 | .35 / .12 | .22 / .12 |

1. Any policy designated as SRL is subject to the SRL premium. Refer to Table 7D, Severe Repetitive Loss Premium, in this section.
2. Properties in AR zones may be eligible for the PRP. Refer to the PRP subsection in the How to Write section of this manual.
3. Includes subgrade crawlspace.
4. Manufactured (Mobile) Homes include travel trailers that meet the definition of a building; refer to Appendix L: Definitions in this manual.
5. For further guidance on Non-Residential Business and Other Non-Residential occupancies, refer to the Before You Start section of this manual.
6. For elevation for −1 and below, refer to Table 4.
7. These rates are applicable only to contents-only policies.

## RATE TABLE 6. TENTATIVE RATES[1,2]

RATES PER $100 OF COVERAGE (Basic/Additional)

### FIRM ZONES A, AE, A1–A30, AO, AH RATES

| BUILDING TYPE | BUILDING | | CONTENTS | |
|---|---|---|---|---|
| **Non-Elevated, No Basement** | **Basic Limits** | **Additional Limits** | **Basic Limits** | **Additional Limits** |
| 1-4 Family | 5.00 | 3.00 | 6.00 | 4.00 |
| Other Residential | 7.00 | 4.00 | 7.00 | 4.00 |
| Non-Residential Business, Other Non-Residential[3] | 7.00 | 4.00 | 8.00 | 8.00 |
| **Post-FIRM Non-Elevated with Basement and Post-FIRM Elevated Building[4]** | **Basic Limits** | **Additional Limits** | **Basic Limits** | **Additional Limits** |
| 1-4 Family | 3.00 | 2.00 | 3.00 | 2.00 |
| Other Residential | 5.00 | 3.00 | 3.00 | 3.00 |
| Non-Residential Business, Other Non-Residential[3] | 5.00 | 3.00 | 5.00 | 3.00 |

### FIRM ZONES V, V1–V30, VE RATES

| BUILDING TYPE | BUILDING | | CONTENTS | |
|---|---|---|---|---|
| **Non-Elevated, No Basement** | **Basic Limits** | **Additional Limits** | **Basic Limits** | **Additional Limits** |
| 1-4 Family | 11.00 | 11.00 | 12.00 | 12.00 |
| Other Residential | 12.00 | 12.00 | 12.00 | 12.00 |
| Non-Residential Business, Other Non-Residential[3] | 12.00 | 12.00 | 12.00 | 12.00 |
| **Post-FIRM Non-Elevated with Basement and Post-FIRM Elevated Building[4]** | **Basic Limits** | **Additional Limits** | **Basic Limits** | **Additional Limits** |
| 1-4 Family | 6.00 | 6.00 | 6.00 | 6.00 |
| Other Residential | 8.00 | 8.00 | 6.00 | 6.00 |
| Non-Residential Business, Other Non-Residential[3] | 8.00 | 8.00 | 8.00 | 8.00 |

1. Use of this table is subject to the provisions found in the Tentative Rates subsection in the How to Write section of this manual.
2. Use Pre-/Post-FIRM full-risk deductible factors (Table 8B) and ICC premiums (Table 9) for all tentatively rated buildings.
3. For further guidance on Non-Residential Business and Other Non-Residential occupancies, refer to the Before You Start section of this manual.
4. The basement/elevated building rates should be used only if the submitted information indicates that the risk is constructed as a Post-FIRM elevated building or has a basement as defined by the NFIP (coverage restrictions apply).

## RATE TABLE 7A. FEDERAL POLICY FEE AND PROBATION SURCHARGE

| FEDERAL POLICY FEE[1, 2] | PROBATION SURCHARGE |
|---|---|
| $50 | $50 |

1. For the PRP, the Federal Policy Fee is $25.
2. For tenants' contents-only policies (except for RCBAP) the Federal Policy Fee is $25.

## RATE TABLE 7B. RESERVE FUND ASSESSMENT[1]

| ASSESSED POLICIES | RESERVE FUND ASSESSMENT |
|---|---|
| GFIP[2] | 0% |
| PRP | 18% |
| Newly Mapped | 18% |
| All Other Policies | 18% |

1. Apply the Reserve Fund Assessment percentage to the Total Premium after the ICC Premium and CRS Premium discount have been calculated.
2. The GFIP is only available to recipients of federal disaster assistance and is serviced by the NFIP Direct Servicing Agent.

## RATE TABLE 7C. HFIAA SURCHARGE[1]

| PROPERTY TYPE | HFIAA SURCHARGE |
|---|---|
| Primary Residences[2,3] | $25 |
| All Other NFIP policies, including Non-Primary Residences, Non-Residential Business, Other Non-Residential Buildings/Non-Condominium Multi-Family Buildings[4,5] | $250 |

1. The Homeowner Flood Insurance Affordability Act of 2014 (HFIAA) surcharge is an annual surcharge for all new and renewal policies.
2. Dwelling Form policies covering single-family primary residences, individual residential condominium units, or contents-only for apartments used as a primary residence by the named insured in non-condominium buildings.
3. A 2–4 family building may be considered a primary residence if the policyholder provides primary residence documentation.
4. A non-primary residence is a residential building that is not the primary residence of the policyholder.
5. Policies covering 2–4 family non-primary residences, non-residential business, other non-residential, multi-family (other residential), or non-condominium multi-family buildings.

## RATE TABLE 7D. SEVERE REPETITIVE LOSS PREMIUM[1]

| PROPERTY DESIGNATION | PREMIUM |
|---|---|
| Severe Repetitive Loss (SRL) | 15% |

1. For all SRL policies add the SRL Premium after the annual premium subtotal and before the ICC premium.

## RATE TABLE 8A. MINIMUM DEDUCTIBLES[1]

| PROGRAM TYPE | RATING | MINIMUM DEDUCTIBLE FOR COVERAGE OF $100,000 OR LESS[2] | MINIMUM DEDUCTIBLE FOR COVERAGE OVER $100,000 |
|---|---|---|---|
| EMERGENCY | All | $1,500 | $2,000[3] |
| REGULAR | All Pre-FIRM Subsidized[4] zones: A, AE, A1–A30, AH, AO, V, VE, and V1–V30, AR/AR Dual zones without Elevation Data | $1,500 | $2,000 |
| | All Full-Risk[5] zones: A, AE, A1–A30, AH, AO, V, VE, and V1–V30, AR/AR Dual zones with Elevation Data and B, C, X, A99, and D | $1,000 | $1,250 |
| | Tentative and Provisional | $1,000 | $1,250 |

1. The deductible for the PRP, MPPP and Newly Mapped policies will be $1,000 for both building and contents if the building coverage is less than or equal to $100,000 and $1,250 if building coverage is over $100,000. A contents-only policy will have a $1,000 deductible.
2. Use this column if building coverage is $100,000 or less, regardless of the contents coverage amount. This includes policies issued with contents coverage only.
3. In Alaska, Guam, Hawaii, and U.S. Virgin Islands, the coverage amount available is $150,000.
4. Pre-FIRM subsidized policies are those policies covering a Pre-FIRM building that are rated in zones Unnumbered A, AE, A1–A30, AH, AO, VE, and V1–V30 without elevation data from an EC. Also included among Pre-FIRM subsidized policies are policies covering certain Pre-FIRM buildings rated in zones D and Unnumbered V, for which the Pre-FIRM subsidized rate remains more favorable than full-risk rating in zone D or Unnumbered V.
5. Full-Risk rates apply to all policies rated with elevation data from an EC in zones Unnumbered A, AE, A1–A30, AH, AO, VE, and V1–V30, regardless of whether the building is Pre-FIRM or Post-FIRM. Post-FIRM buildings rated in zones D or Unnumbered V, and Pre-FIRM buildings in zones D or Unnumbered V using Post-FIRM rate tables are considered Full-Risk. Full-Risk rates are also applied to all policies rated in zones B, C, or X, regardless of product type or the building classification as Pre-FIRM or Post-FIRM. Grandfathered standard-X zone policies, and grandfathered policies using elevation data from an EC are considered Full-Risk.

**NOTE**

When a building under construction, alteration, or repair does not have at least two rigid exterior walls and a fully secured roof at the time of loss, the deductible amount will be two times the deductible that would otherwise apply to a completed building.

## RATE TABLE 8B. DEDUCTIBLE FACTORS[1,2,3]

### Single-Family and 2–4 Family Building and Contents Policies[4]

| DEDUCTIBLE OPTIONS: Building/Contents | PRE-/POST-FIRM Full-Risk | PRE-FIRM Subsidized | DEDUCTIBLE OPTIONS: Building/Contents | PRE-/POST-FIRM Full-Risk | PRE-FIRM Subsidized |
|---|---|---|---|---|---|
| $1,000/$1,000 | 1.000[5] | N/A | $3,000/$3,000 | .850 | .925 |
| $1,250/$1,000 | .995[5] | N/A | $4,000/$1,000 | .925[5] | N/A |
| $1,250/$1,250 | .980 | N/A | $4,000/$1,250 | .915 | N/A |
| $1,500/$1,000 | .990[5] | N/A | $4,000/$1,500 | .900 | .975[5] |
| $1,500/$1,250 | .975 | N/A | $4,000/$2,000 | .875 | .950 |
| $1,500/$1,500 | .965 | 1.050[5] | $4,000/$3,000 | .825 | .900 |
| $2,000/$1,000 | .975[5] | N/A | $4,000/$4,000 | .775 | .850 |
| $2,000/$1,250 | .965 | N/A | $5,000/$1,000 | .900[5] | N/A |
| $2,000/$1,500 | .950 | 1.025[5] | $5,000/$1,250 | .890 | N/A |
| $2,000/$2,000 | .925 | 1.000 | $5,000/$1,500 | .875 | .955[5] |
| $3,000/$1,000 | .950[5] | N/A | $5,000/$2,000 | .850 | .930 |
| $3,000/$1,250 | .940 | N/A | $5,000/$3,000 | .800 | .880 |
| $3,000/$1,500 | .925 | 1.000[5] | $5,000/$4,000 | .760 | .830 |
| $3,000/$2,000 | .900 | .975 | $5,000/$5,000 | .750 | .810 |
| | | | $10,000/$10,000 | .600 | .650 |

### Single-Family and 2–4 Family Building-Only or Contents-Only Policies[4]

| BUILDING | PRE-/POST-FIRM Full-Risk | PRE-FIRM Subsidized |
|---|---|---|
| $1,000 | 1.000[5] | N/A |
| $1,250 | .985 | N/A |
| $1,500 | .970 | 1.040[5] |
| $2,000 | .935 | 1.000 |
| $3,000 | .885 | .945 |
| $4,000 | .835 | .890 |
| $5,000 | .785 | .840 |
| $10,000 | .650 | .700 |

| CONTENTS[6] | PRE-/POST-FIRM Full-Risk | PRE-FIRM Subsidized |
|---|---|---|
| $1,000 | 1.000 | N/A |
| $1,250 | .975 | N/A |
| $1,500 | .950 | 1.050 |
| $2,000 | .900 | 1.000 |
| $3,000 | .825 | .915 |
| $4,000 | .750 | .830 |
| $5,000 | .675 | .750 |
| $10,000 | .475 | .525 |

### Other Residential, Non-Residential Business, or Other Non-Residential Policies[7]

| | DISCOUNT FROM | | | BUILDING ONLY | | CONTENTS ONLY | |
|---|---|---|---|---|---|---|---|
| BUILDING/CONTENTS | PRE-/POST-FIRM Full-Risk | PRE-FIRM Subsidized | AMOUNT | PRE-/POST-FIRM Full-Risk | PRE-FIRM Subsidized | PRE-/POST-FIRM Full-Risk | PRE-FIRM Subsidized |
| $1,000/$1,000 | 1.000[5] | N/A | $1,000 | 1.000[5] | N/A | 1.000 | N/A |
| $1,250/$1,250 | .990 | N/A | $1,250 | .990 | N/A | .990 | N/A |
| $1,500/$1,500 | .980 | 1.025[5] | $1,500 | .980 | 1.025[5] | .985 | 1.025 |
| $2,000/$2,000 | .960 | 1.000 | $2,000 | .960 | 1.000 | .965 | 1.000 |
| $3,000/$3,000 | .930 | .970 | $3,000 | .925 | .965 | .940 | .975 |
| $4,000/$4,000 | .910 | .950 | $4,000 | .900 | .935 | .915 | .950 |
| $5,000/$5,000 | .890 | .930 | $5,000 | .875 | .910 | .890 | .925 |
| $10,000/$10,000 | .815 | .855 | $10,000 | .775 | .800 | .815 | .850 |
| $15,000/$15,000 | .765 | .800 | $15,000 | .700 | .725 | .740 | .775 |
| $20,000/$20,000 | .715 | .750 | $20,000 | .625 | .650 | .670 | .700 |
| $25,000/$25,000 | .665 | .700 | $25,000 | .575 | .600 | .620 | .650 |
| $50,000/$50,000 | .565 | .600 | $50,000 | .475 | .500 | .550 | .575 |

1. Deductible factors for the RCBAP are located are located in CONDO Table 7. Any combination not provided in regulation may be submitted for rating to the NFIP, subject to the minimum statutory deductibles.
2. The ICC Premium is not eligible for the deductible discount.
3. Pre-FIRM/Post-FIRM deductibles apply to all buildings receiving full-risk rates, including Pre-FIRM buildings rated with elevation data, or in the non-SFHA. Pre-FIRM deductibles apply only to policies receiving Pre-FIRM subsidized premium rates.
4. These deductible factors apply to condominium unit owners.
5. Only available if building coverage is $100,000 or less.
6. These deductible factors apply to residential unit contents in an Other Residential building or in a multi-unit condominium building.
7. For further guidance on Other Residential, Non-Residential Business and Other Non-Residential occupancies, refer to the Before You Start section of this manual.

## RATE TABLE 9. STANDARD FLOOD INSURANCE POLICY INCREASED COST OF COMPLIANCE (ICC) COVERAGE

**Premiums for $30,000 ICC Coverage**

All Except RCBAP, MPPP, and Submit-for-Rate Policies

| | | | | 1–4 FAMILY | | OTHER RESIDENTIAL, NON-RESIDENTIAL BUSINESS, OTHER NON-RESIDENTIAL | |
|---|---|---|---|---|---|---|---|
| | | | | Building Amount of Insurance | | Building Amount of Insurance | |
| RATE TABLE | RATED ZONE | BUILDING TYPE | ELEVATION DIFFERENCE | $1–$230,000 | $230,001–$250,000 | $1–$480,000 | $480,001–$500,000 |
| Table 1 | N/A | All Emergency Program | N/A | $0 | $0 | $0 | $0 |
| Table 2A, 2B, 2C, and 2D | A, AE, A1–A30, AO, AH, V, VE, and V1–V30 | All Pre-FIRM | N/A | $56 | $49 | $56 | $49 |
| | A99, B, C, X, D | All Pre-FIRM | N/A | $8 | $6 | $8 | $6 |
| Table 3A | A99, B, C, and X | All Pre-FIRM and Post-FIRM | N/A | $8 | $6 | $8 | $6 |
| | AO, AH, and D | All Post-FIRM without basement/enclosure or All Pre-FIRM Optional Rating | N/A | $8 | $6 | $8 | $6 |
| Table 3B | AE, A1–A30 | All Post-FIRM and Pre-FIRM Optional Rating | > –2 | $8 | $6 | $8 | $6 |
| | | Post-FIRM Non-Elevated; Pre-FIRM Non-Elevated or Elevated with full enclosure | < –1 | $45 | $34 | $45 | $34 |
| | | Post-FIRM Elevated; Pre-FIRM Elevated, partial or no enclosure | < –1 | $12 | $9 | $12 | $9 |
| Table 3C | Unnumbered A | All Post-FIRM without basement/enclosure or All Pre-FIRM Optional Rating | N/A (All) | $8 | $6 | $8 | $6 |
| Table 3D | ('75-'81) VE, V1–V30 | All Post-FIRM and Pre-FIRM Optional Rating | > –2 | $33 | $25 | $33 | $25 |
| Table 3E | (Post '81) VE, V1–V30 | Post-FIRM Elevated no enclosure and Pre-FIRM Elevated no obstruction (no enclosure) and '75–'81 Post-FIRM no obstruction | > –4 | $21 | $16 | $21 | $16 |
| Table 3F | (Post '81) VE, V1–V30 | Post-FIRM Elevated with enclosure < 300 SF breakaway and Pre-FIRM or '75–'81 Post-FIRM Optional rating Elevated with enclosure < 300 SF breakaway | > –4 | $21 | $16 | $21 | $16 |
| Table 4 | AR and AR Dual | All (rated without elevation) | N/A | $8 | $6 | $8 | $6 |
| Table 5 | AR and AR Dual | All (rated with elevation) | > –1 | $8 | $6 | $8 | $6 |
| Table 6 | A, AE, A1–A30, AO, AH, V, VE, V1–V30 | All Tentative Rate | N/A | $8 | $6 | $8 | $6 |
| PRP | B, C, X, AR, A99 | All | N/A | $8 | $6 | $8 | $6 |
| Newly Mapped | N/A | All | N/A | $8 | $6 | $8 | $6 |
| Provisionally Rated | N/A | All | N/A | $8 | $6 | N/A | N/A |

**NOTES:**

(1) ICC coverage does not apply to the Emergency Program, individually owned condominium units located within a multi-unit building and insured under the Dwelling Form, contents-only policies, and GFIPs.

(2) The ICC Premium is not eligible for the deductible discount.

(3) For RCBAP and MPPP policies, use the ICC Premiums contained in applicable sections of this manual.

(4) Use the ICC Premiums above for Table 3B for elevations of –2 and below. For all other Submit-for-Rate policies, refer to the SRG manual.

(5) For further guidance on Other Residential, Non-Residential Business and Other Non-Residential occupancies, refer to the Before You Start section of this manual.

## RATE TABLE 10. PRE-FIRM SUBSIDIZED RATES INELIGIBILITY DETERMINATION[1,2]

| WAS THERE A PRIOR NFIP POLICY FOR THIS PROPERTY IN APPLICANT'S NAME? | WAS THE PRIOR NFIP POLICY REQUIRED BY A LENDER? | DID THE PRIOR NFIP POLICY LAPSE WHILE REQUIRED BY A LENDER? | WAS THE LAPSE THE RESULT OF A COMMUNITY SUSPENSION? | WAS THE COMMUNITY REINSTATED WITHIN THE LAST 180 DAYS? | **ELIGIBLE FOR PRE-FIRM SUBSIDIZED RATES** |
|---|---|---|---|---|---|
| YES | YES | YES | YES | NO | **NO** |
| YES | YES | YES | NO | YES | **NO** |
| YES | YES | YES | NO | NO | **NO** |

1. Use this table for all applications for Pre-FIRM buildings.
2. Also use this table for policy reinstatements by means of renewal, where coverage has lapsed more than 30 days after the prior policy expiration or cancellation date, and where the named insured has not maintained continuous coverage on the property from April 1, 2016 to the prior policy expiration or cancellation date.

## RATE TABLE 11. PRE-FIRM RATE TABLE HIERARCHY[1,2]

| PRE-FIRM PRIMARY RESIDENCE | PRE-FIRM NON-PRIMARY RESIDENCE | PRE-FIRM SRL | PRE-FIRM SUBSTANTIALLY IMPROVED | TABLE FOR RATING |
|---|---|---|---|---|
| YES | NO | NO | NO | **Table 2A** |
| NO | YES | NO | NO | **Table 2B** |
| YES | NO | YES | NO | **Table 2C** |
| NO | YES | YES | NO | **Table 2C** |
| YES | NO | NO | YES | **Table 2D** |
| NO | YES | NO | YES | **Table 2B** |
| NO | YES | YES | YES | **Table 2C** |
| YES | NO | YES | YES | **Table 2C** |

1. For primary residence single-family, 2–4 family, and other residential buildings where the entire building is being insured, use Table 2A.
2. For non-primary residence single-family buildings and condominium units in 2–4 family and other residential buildings, use Table 2B.

**PLEASE NOTE:**

RATE Table 12A. Contents Location In Non-Elevated Buildings and RATE Table 12B, Contents Location In Elevated Buildings do not provide rates. They provide descriptions of contents locations and are included in the How to Write Section of this manual.

## PROVISIONAL RATING

## NATIONAL FLOOD INSURANCE PROGRAM
## PROVISIONAL RATING QUESTIONNAIRE

1–4 Family Post-FIRM Zones A with BFE[1], AE, A1–A30, AO, and AH
(To be attached to the Flood Insurance Application)

NAME ______________________ POLICY NUMBER ______________________

PROPERTY ADDRESS ______________________ POLICY PERIOD IS FROM __________ TO __________

CITY ______________________ STATE __________ ZIP CODE __________

Answer the questions below. Use the rates associated with the first "yes" response. These rates are to be used on the Flood Insurance Application.

| Yes | No | |
|---|---|---|
| ☐ | ☐ | 1. Is there a basement or subgrade crawlspace? |
| ☐ | ☐ | 2. Is the house built on fill[2] or with a crawlspace or solid perimeter foundation walls? |
| ☐ | ☐ | 3. Is the house elevated on pilings, piers, columns, or parallel shear walls? If yes, determine whether there is an enclosed area underneath the building. |
| ☐ | ☐ | 4. Were the answers to the previous questions all no? Then the house is assumed to be slab on natural grade. |

| FOUNDATION TYPE | BUILDING TYPE | | CONTENTS LOCATION | | | |
|---|---|---|---|---|---|---|
| | 1 Floor (No Basement) | More Than 1 Floor (Basement or No Basement) | Basement and Above | Lowest Floor Only - Above Ground Level (Not in Basement) | Lowest Floor Above Ground Level and Higher (Not in Basement) | Above[3] Ground Level - More Than 1 Full Floor |
| **Basement or Subgrade Crawlspace** | N/A | 3.00 / 2.00 | 3.00 / 2.00 | 3.00 / 2.00 | 3.00 / 2.00 | 3.00 / 2.00 |
| **Slab on Fill, Crawlspace, or Solid Perimeter Foundation Walls** | 5.00 / 3.00 | 5.00 / 3.00 | N/A | 6.00 / 4.00 | 6.00 / 4.00 | 3.00 / 2.00 |
| **Piles, Piers, Columns, or Parallel Shear Walls** | | | | | | |
| With Enclosure | 5.00 / 3.00 | 5.00 / 3.00 | N/A | 6.00 / 4.00 | 6.00 / 4.00 | 3.00 / 2.00 |
| No Enclosure | 5.00 / 3.00 | 5.00 / 3.00 | N/A | 6.00 / 4.00 | 6.00 / 4.00 | 3.00 / 2.00 |
| **Slab on Natural Grade** | 5.00 / 3.00 | 5.00 / 3.00 | N/A | 6.00 / 4.00 | 6.00 / 4.00 | 3.00 / 2.00 |

1. Provisional rates can be used in Unnumbered A Zones only where communities provide BFEs.
2. For information on how to determine whether a house is built on fill, refer to the guidelines for Provisional Rating within the How to Write section of the manual.
3. The "Above Ground Level – More Than 1 Full Floor" rates are applicable to 2–4 family buildings only.

**NOTE:** The ICC Premium is $8 for residential coverage up to $230,000 and $6 for coverage over $230,000. The Reserve Fund Assessment is 18%, and the Federal Policy Fee is $50. Add either a $25.00 or a $250.00 surcharge to the premium in accordance with the Homeowner Flood Insurance Affordability Act of 2014 (HFIAA). The HFIAA surcharge is $25.00 for policies covering single-family primary residences, 2–4 family primary residences, individual residential condominium units, or contents-only policies for apartments used as a primary residence by the named insured in non-condominium buildings. For all other policies, the HFIAA surcharge is $250.00. If applicable, also add the $50 Probation Surcharge.

## III. Preferred Risk Policy (PRP) Rates

**EFFECTIVE JAN. 1, 2021**
**PRP TABLE 3A. PRP COVERAGE LIMITS AND BASE PREMIUMS FOR PROPERTIES CURRENTLY MAPPED IN B, C, X, AR, OR A99 ZONES[1]**

**1–4 FAMILY RESIDENTIAL BUILDING AND CONTENTS COVERAGE COMBINATIONS**

| WITH BASEMENT OR ENCLOSURE[2] | | | WITHOUT BASEMENT OR ENCLOSURE[3] | | |
|---|---|---|---|---|---|
| BUILDING | CONTENTS | PREMIUM | BUILDING | CONTENTS | PREMIUM |
| $ 20,000 | $ 8,000 | $161 | $ 20,000 | $ 8,000 | $127 |
| $ 30,000 | $ 12,000 | $203 | $ 30,000 | $ 12,000 | $168 |
| $ 50,000 | $ 20,000 | $271 | $ 50,000 | $ 20,000 | $236 |
| $ 75,000 | $ 30,000 | $326 | $ 75,000 | $ 30,000 | $286 |
| $100,000 | $ 40,000 | $361 | $100,000 | $ 40,000 | $323 |
| $125,000 | $ 50,000 | $382 | $125,000 | $ 50,000 | $342 |
| $150,000 | $ 60,000 | $405 | $150,000 | $ 60,000 | $367 |
| $200,000 | $ 80,000 | $452 | $200,000 | $ 80,000 | $405 |
| $250,000 | $100,000 | $488 | $250,000 | $100,000 | $436 |

**RESIDENTIAL CONTENTS-ONLY COVERAGE**

| CONTENTS ABOVE GROUND LEVEL MORE THAN 1 FLOOR | | ALL OTHER LOCATIONS (BASEMENT-ONLY NOT ELIGIBLE) | |
|---|---|---|---|
| CONTENTS | PREMIUM | CONTENTS | PREMIUM |
| $ 8,000 | $ 25 | $ 8,000 | $ 50 |
| $ 12,000 | $ 47 | $ 12,000 | $ 84 |
| $ 20,000 | $ 88 | $ 20,000 | $132 |
| $ 30,000 | $108 | $ 30,000 | $158 |
| $ 40,000 | $123 | $ 40,000 | $181 |
| $ 50,000 | $140 | $ 50,000 | $204 |
| $ 60,000 | $157 | $ 60,000 | $226 |
| $ 80,000 | $188 | $ 80,000 | $253 |
| $100,000 | $221 | $100,000 | $281 |

**NOTE:** Base Premium does not include the Multiplier, ICC Premium, Reserve Fund Assessment, HFIAA Surcharge, Probation Surcharge, or Federal Policy Fee. To determine the total amount due, refer to the How to Write section of this manual.

1. Use this table for eligible properties in AR or A99 zones on or after Oct. 1, 2016.
2. Use this section of the table for buildings with crawlspaces or subgrade crawlspaces with an attached garage without proper openings.
3. Use this section of the table for buildings with crawlspaces or subgrade crawlspaces, including those with an attached garage that has proper openings.

EFFECTIVE JAN. 1, 2022

## PRP TABLE 3A. PRP COVERAGE LIMITS AND BASE PREMIUMS FOR PROPERTIES CURRENTLY MAPPED IN B, C, X, AR, OR A99 ZONES[1]

### 1–4 FAMILY RESIDENTIAL BUILDING AND CONTENTS COVERAGE COMBINATIONS

| WITH BASEMENT OR ENCLOSURE[2] | | | WITHOUT BASEMENT OR ENCLOSURE[3] | | |
|---|---|---|---|---|---|
| BUILDING | CONTENTS | PREMIUM | BUILDING | CONTENTS | PREMIUM |
| $ 20,000 | $ 8,000 | $185 | $ 20,000 | $ 8,000 | $146 |
| $ 30,000 | $ 12,000 | $233 | $ 30,000 | $ 12,000 | $193 |
| $ 50,000 | $ 20,000 | $312 | $ 50,000 | $ 20,000 | $271 |
| $ 75,000 | $ 30,000 | $375 | $ 75,000 | $ 30,000 | $329 |
| $100,000 | $ 40,000 | $415 | $100,000 | $ 40,000 | $371 |
| $125,000 | $ 50,000 | $439 | $125,000 | $ 50,000 | $393 |
| $150,000 | $ 60,000 | $466 | $150,000 | $ 60,000 | $422 |
| $200,000 | $ 80,000 | $520 | $200,000 | $ 80,000 | $466 |
| $250,000 | $100,000 | $561 | $250,000 | $100,000 | $501 |

### RESIDENTIAL CONTENTS-ONLY COVERAGE

| CONTENTS ABOVE GROUND LEVEL MORE THAN 1 FLOOR | | ALL OTHER LOCATIONS (BASEMENT-ONLY NOT ELIGIBLE) | |
|---|---|---|---|
| CONTENTS | PREMIUM | CONTENTS | PREMIUM |
| $ 8,000 | $ 29 | $ 8,000 | $ 58 |
| $ 12,000 | $ 54 | $ 12,000 | $ 97 |
| $ 20,000 | $101 | $ 20,000 | $152 |
| $ 30,000 | $124 | $ 30,000 | $182 |
| $ 40,000 | $141 | $ 40,000 | $208 |
| $ 50,000 | $161 | $ 50,000 | $235 |
| $ 60,000 | $180 | $ 60,000 | $260 |
| $ 80,000 | $216 | $ 80,000 | $291 |
| $100,000 | $254 | $100,000 | $323 |

**NOTE:** Base Premium does not include the Multiplier, ICC Premium, Reserve Fund Assessment, HFIAA Surcharge, Probation Surcharge, or Federal Policy Fee. To determine the total amount due, refer to the How to Write section of this manual.

1. Use this table for eligible properties in AR or A99 zones on or after Oct. 1, 2016.
2. Use this section of the table for buildings with crawlspaces or subgrade crawlspaces with an attached garage without proper openings.
3. Use this section of the table for buildings with crawlspaces or subgrade crawlspaces, including those with an attached garage that has proper openings.

## EFFECTIVE JAN. 1, 2021
## PRP TABLE 3B. PRP COVERAGE LIMITS AND BASE PREMIUMS FOR PROPERTIES CURRENTLY MAPPED IN B, C, X, AR, OR A99 ZONES[1]

### OTHER RESIDENTIAL BUILDING AND CONTENTS COVERAGE COMBINATIONS

With Basement or Enclosure[2]

| | CONTENTS COVERAGE | $8,000 | $12,000 | $20,000 | $30,000 | $40,000 | $50,000 | $60,000 | $80,000 | $100,000 |
|---|---|---|---|---|---|---|---|---|---|---|
| BUILDING COVERAGE | $ 20,000 | $180 | $198 | $215 | $233 | $250 | $264 | $279 | $291 | $306 |
| | $ 30,000 | $198 | $216 | $234 | $252 | $268 | $283 | $298 | $310 | $325 |
| | $ 50,000 | $243 | $263 | $281 | $298 | $314 | $329 | $344 | $356 | $371 |
| | $ 75,000 | $265 | $284 | $302 | $319 | $335 | $351 | $366 | $377 | $392 |
| | $100,000 | $295 | $314 | $332 | $349 | $366 | $380 | $394 | $408 | $421 |
| | $125,000 | $302 | $320 | $336 | $354 | $371 | $385 | $401 | $414 | $427 |
| | $150,000 | $308 | $326 | $344 | $361 | $376 | $392 | $407 | $420 | $433 |
| | $200,000 | $349 | $368 | $385 | $403 | $419 | $433 | $448 | $460 | $474 |
| | $250,000 | $372 | $391 | $408 | $426 | $441 | $455 | $470 | $485 | $496 |
| | $300,000 | $391 | $408 | $424 | $440 | $455 | $469 | $485 | $496 | $510 |
| | $350,000 | $408 | $426 | $441 | $457 | $472 | $486 | $501 | $512 | $524 |
| | $400,000 | $424 | $440 | $456 | $473 | $487 | $500 | $515 | $525 | $539 |
| | $450,000 | $439 | $455 | $470 | $487 | $500 | $513 | $528 | $540 | $551 |
| | $500,000 | $452 | $468 | $485 | $500 | $512 | $524 | $540 | $551 | $562 |

### OTHER RESIDENTIAL BUILDING AND CONTENTS COVERAGE COMBINATIONS

Without Basement or Enclosure[3]

| | CONTENTS COVERAGE | $8,000 | $12,000 | $20,000 | $30,000 | $40,000 | $50,000 | $60,000 | $80,000 | $100,000 |
|---|---|---|---|---|---|---|---|---|---|---|
| BUILDING COVERAGE | $ 20,000 | $141 | $158 | $171 | $187 | $202 | $214 | $226 | $239 | $250 |
| | $ 30,000 | $166 | $181 | $195 | $209 | $224 | $236 | $250 | $262 | $272 |
| | $ 50,000 | $213 | $228 | $242 | $256 | $271 | $284 | $297 | $308 | $319 |
| | $ 75,000 | $240 | $254 | $269 | $283 | $297 | $309 | $323 | $334 | $345 |
| | $100,000 | $264 | $279 | $292 | $307 | $320 | $334 | $347 | $357 | $370 |
| | $125,000 | $273 | $288 | $304 | $315 | $329 | $342 | $353 | $366 | $375 |
| | $150,000 | $283 | $298 | $312 | $325 | $338 | $351 | $363 | $374 | $385 |
| | $200,000 | $320 | $334 | $349 | $363 | $375 | $389 | $401 | $410 | $422 |
| | $250,000 | $339 | $354 | $370 | $383 | $395 | $408 | $420 | $431 | $441 |
| | $300,000 | $371 | $382 | $395 | $407 | $419 | $431 | $440 | $450 | $461 |
| | $350,000 | $391 | $401 | $416 | $426 | $437 | $446 | $457 | $467 | $477 |
| | $400,000 | $409 | $419 | $432 | $441 | $451 | $463 | $473 | $483 | $493 |
| | $450,000 | $427 | $436 | $446 | $456 | $467 | $476 | $487 | $495 | $507 |
| | $500,000 | $441 | $449 | $461 | $470 | $478 | $491 | $500 | $508 | $520 |

**NOTE:** Base Premium does not include the Multiplier, ICC Premium, Reserve Fund Assessment, HFIAA Surcharge, Probation Surcharge, or Federal Policy Fee. To determine the total amount due, refer to the How to Write section of this manual.

1. Use this table for eligible properties in AR or A99 zones on or after Oct. 1, 2016.
2. Use this section of the table for buildings with crawlspaces or subgrade crawlspaces with an attached garage without proper openings.
3. Use this section of the table for buildings with crawlspaces or subgrade crawlspaces, including those with an attached garage that has proper openings.

EFFECTIVE JAN. 1, 2022

## PRP TABLE 3B. PRP COVERAGE LIMITS AND BASE PREMIUMS FOR PROPERTIES CURRENTLY MAPPED IN B, C, X, AR, OR A99 ZONES[1]

### OTHER RESIDENTIAL BUILDING AND CONTENTS COVERAGE COMBINATIONS

With Basement or Enclosure[2]

| | CONTENTS COVERAGE | $8,000 | $12,000 | $20,000 | $30,000 | $40,000 | $50,000 | $60,000 | $80,000 | $100,000 |
|---|---|---|---|---|---|---|---|---|---|---|
| BUILDING COVERAGE | $ 20,000 | $207 | $228 | $247 | $268 | $288 | $304 | $321 | $335 | $352 |
| | $ 30,000 | $228 | $248 | $269 | $290 | $308 | $325 | $343 | $357 | $374 |
| | $ 50,000 | $279 | $302 | $323 | $343 | $361 | $378 | $396 | $409 | $427 |
| | $ 75,000 | $305 | $327 | $347 | $367 | $385 | $404 | $421 | $434 | $451 |
| | $100,000 | $339 | $361 | $382 | $401 | $421 | $437 | $453 | $469 | $484 |
| | $125,000 | $347 | $368 | $386 | $407 | $427 | $443 | $461 | $476 | $491 |
| | $150,000 | $354 | $375 | $396 | $415 | $432 | $451 | $468 | $483 | $498 |
| | $200,000 | $401 | $423 | $443 | $463 | $482 | $498 | $515 | $529 | $545 |
| | $250,000 | $428 | $450 | $469 | $490 | $507 | $523 | $541 | $558 | $570 |
| | $300,000 | $450 | $469 | $488 | $506 | $523 | $539 | $558 | $570 | $587 |
| | $350,000 | $469 | $490 | $507 | $526 | $543 | $559 | $576 | $589 | $603 |
| | $400,000 | $488 | $506 | $524 | $544 | $560 | $575 | $592 | $604 | $620 |
| | $450,000 | $505 | $523 | $541 | $560 | $575 | $590 | $607 | $621 | $634 |
| | $500,000 | $520 | $538 | $558 | $575 | $589 | $603 | $621 | $634 | $646 |

### OTHER RESIDENTIAL BUILDING AND CONTENTS COVERAGE COMBINATIONS

Without Basement or Enclosure[3]

| | CONTENTS COVERAGE | $8,000 | $12,000 | $20,000 | $30,000 | $40,000 | $50,000 | $60,000 | $80,000 | $100,000 |
|---|---|---|---|---|---|---|---|---|---|---|
| BUILDING COVERAGE | $ 20,000 | $162 | $182 | $197 | $215 | $232 | $246 | $260 | $275 | $288 |
| | $ 30,000 | $191 | $208 | $224 | $240 | $258 | $271 | $288 | $301 | $313 |
| | $ 50,000 | $245 | $262 | $278 | $294 | $312 | $327 | $342 | $354 | $367 |
| | $ 75,000 | $276 | $292 | $309 | $325 | $342 | $355 | $371 | $384 | $397 |
| | $100,000 | $304 | $321 | $336 | $353 | $368 | $384 | $399 | $411 | $426 |
| | $125,000 | $314 | $331 | $350 | $362 | $378 | $393 | $406 | $421 | $431 |
| | $150,000 | $325 | $343 | $359 | $374 | $389 | $404 | $417 | $430 | $443 |
| | $200,000 | $368 | $384 | $401 | $417 | $431 | $447 | $461 | $472 | $485 |
| | $250,000 | $390 | $407 | $426 | $440 | $454 | $469 | $483 | $496 | $507 |
| | $300,000 | $427 | $439 | $454 | $468 | $482 | $496 | $506 | $518 | $530 |
| | $350,000 | $450 | $461 | $478 | $490 | $503 | $513 | $526 | $537 | $549 |
| | $400,000 | $470 | $482 | $497 | $507 | $519 | $532 | $544 | $555 | $567 |
| | $450,000 | $491 | $501 | $513 | $524 | $537 | $547 | $560 | $569 | $583 |
| | $500,000 | $507 | $516 | $530 | $541 | $550 | $565 | $575 | $584 | $598 |

**NOTE:** Base Premium does not include the Multiplier, ICC Premium, Reserve Fund Assessment, HFIAA Surcharge, Probation Surcharge, or Federal Policy Fee. To determine the total amount due, refer to the How to Write section of this manual.

1. Use this table for eligible properties in AR or A99 zones on or after Oct. 1, 2016.
2. Use this section of the table for buildings with crawlspaces or subgrade crawlspaces with an attached garage without proper openings.
3. Use this section of the table for buildings with crawlspaces or subgrade crawlspaces, including those with an attached garage that has proper openings.

## EFFECTIVE JAN. 1, 2021
## PRP TABLE 3C. PRP COVERAGE LIMITS AND BASE PREMIUMS FOR PROPERTIES CURRENTLY MAPPED IN B, C, X, AR, OR A99 ZONES[1]

**Non-Residential Business or Other Non-Residential Building And Contents Coverage Combinations**
With Basement or Enclosure[2]

| BUILDING COVERAGE | CONTENTS COVERAGE | $50,000 | $100,000 | $150,000 | $200,000 | $250,000 | $300,000 | $350,000 | $400,000 | $450,000 | $500,000 |
|---|---|---|---|---|---|---|---|---|---|---|---|
| | $ 50,000 | $1,160 | $1,510 | $1,842 | $2,160 | $2,464 | $2,752 | $3,025 | $3,283 | $3,525 | $3,753 |
| | $100,000 | $1,664 | $2,013 | $2,345 | $2,663 | $2,966 | $3,254 | $3,527 | $3,786 | $4,026 | $4,254 |
| | $150,000 | $2,014 | $2,359 | $2,689 | $3,003 | $3,303 | $3,588 | $3,858 | $4,114 | $4,352 | $4,579 |
| | $200,000 | $2,212 | $2,559 | $2,887 | $3,201 | $3,502 | $3,788 | $4,059 | $4,312 | $4,553 | $4,777 |
| | $250,000 | $2,353 | $2,698 | $3,028 | $3,341 | $3,642 | $3,927 | $4,197 | $4,451 | $4,693 | $4,918 |
| | $300,000 | $2,508 | $2,852 | $3,182 | $3,496 | $3,796 | $4,081 | $4,351 | $4,607 | $4,845 | $5,071 |
| | $350,000 | $2,679 | $3,023 | $3,352 | $3,668 | $3,966 | $4,252 | $4,520 | $4,776 | $5,016 | $5,242 |
| | $400,000 | $2,791 | $3,135 | $3,464 | $3,779 | $4,078 | $4,365 | $4,633 | $4,888 | $5,127 | $5,354 |
| | $450,000 | $2,918 | $3,264 | $3,592 | $3,908 | $4,207 | $4,491 | $4,760 | $5,016 | $5,255 | $5,480 |
| | $500,000 | $3,058 | $3,404 | $3,732 | $4,047 | $4,347 | $4,632 | $4,901 | $5,155 | $5,395 | $5,620 |

**Non-Residential Business or Other Non-Residential Building And Contents Coverage Combinations**
Without Basement or Enclosure[3]

| BUILDING COVERAGE | CONTENTS COVERAGE | $50,000 | $100,000 | $150,000 | $200,000 | $250,000 | $300,000 | $350,000 | $400,000 | $450,000 | $500,000 |
|---|---|---|---|---|---|---|---|---|---|---|---|
| | $ 50,000 | $ 712 | $ 898 | $1,077 | $1,247 | $1,409 | $1,561 | $1,707 | $1,844 | $1,973 | $2,094 |
| | $100,000 | $ 972 | $1,158 | $1,335 | $1,505 | $1,667 | $1,820 | $1,967 | $2,103 | $2,232 | $2,354 |
| | $150,000 | $1,152 | $1,336 | $1,513 | $1,682 | $1,840 | $1,992 | $2,137 | $2,274 | $2,400 | $2,521 |
| | $200,000 | $1,351 | $1,536 | $1,710 | $1,880 | $2,040 | $2,191 | $2,335 | $2,472 | $2,600 | $2,719 |
| | $250,000 | $1,484 | $1,669 | $1,844 | $2,013 | $2,173 | $2,324 | $2,467 | $2,605 | $2,732 | $2,852 |
| | $300,000 | $1,625 | $1,810 | $1,986 | $2,155 | $2,314 | $2,465 | $2,610 | $2,746 | $2,873 | $2,994 |
| | $350,000 | $1,701 | $1,886 | $2,063 | $2,230 | $2,391 | $2,542 | $2,686 | $2,821 | $2,949 | $3,070 |
| | $400,000 | $1,786 | $1,970 | $2,146 | $2,314 | $2,474 | $2,626 | $2,770 | $2,906 | $3,034 | $3,154 |
| | $450,000 | $1,878 | $2,063 | $2,238 | $2,406 | $2,566 | $2,718 | $2,863 | $2,997 | $3,125 | $3,246 |
| | $500,000 | $1,977 | $2,162 | $2,337 | $2,507 | $2,666 | $2,817 | $2,961 | $3,098 | $3,224 | $3,344 |

**Non-Residential Business or Other Non-Residential Contents-Only Coverage**

| CONTENTS ABOVE GROUND LEVEL MORE THAN 1 FLOOR | | ALL OTHER LOCATIONS (BASEMENT-ONLY NOT ELIGIBLE) | |
|---|---|---|---|
| CONTENTS | PREMIUM | CONTENTS | PREMIUM |
| $ 50,000 | $ 173 | $ 50,000 | $ 423 |
| $100,000 | $ 275 | $100,000 | $ 654 |
| $150,000 | $ 372 | $150,000 | $ 870 |
| $200,000 | $ 470 | $200,000 | $1,095 |
| $250,000 | $ 570 | $250,000 | $1,319 |
| $300,000 | $ 671 | $300,000 | $1,546 |
| $350,000 | $ 771 | $350,000 | $1,771 |
| $400,000 | $ 870 | $400,000 | $1,996 |
| $450,000 | $ 967 | $450,000 | $2,221 |
| $500,000 | $1,066 | $500,000 | $2,447 |

**NOTE:** : Base Premium does not include the Multiplier, ICC Premium, Reserve Fund Assessment, HFIAA Surcharge, Probation Surcharge, or Federal Policy Fee. To determine the total amount due, refer to the How to Write section of this manual.

1. Use this table for eligible properties in AR or A99 zones on or after Oct. 1, 2016.
2. Use this section of the table for buildings with crawlspaces or subgrade crawlspaces with an attached garage without proper openings.
3. Use this section of the table for buildings with crawlspaces or subgrade crawlspaces, including those with an attached garage that has proper openings.

EFFECTIVE JAN. 1, 2022

## PRP TABLE 3C. PRP COVERAGE LIMITS AND BASE PREMIUMS FOR PROPERTIES CURRENTLY MAPPED IN B, C, X, AR, OR A99 ZONES[1]

### Non-Residential Business or Other Non-Residential Building And Contents Coverage Combinations

With Basement or Enclosure[2]

| BUILDING COVERAGE / CONTENTS COVERAGE | $50,000 | $100,000 | $150,000 | $200,000 | $250,000 | $300,000 | $350,000 | $400,000 | $450,000 | $500,000 |
|---|---|---|---|---|---|---|---|---|---|---|
| $ 50,000 | $1,334 | $1,737 | $2,118 | $2,484 | $2,834 | $3,165 | $3,479 | $3,775 | $4,054 | $4,316 |
| $100,000 | $1,914 | $2,315 | $2,697 | $3,062 | $3,411 | $3,742 | $4,056 | $4,354 | $4,630 | $4,892 |
| $150,000 | $2,316 | $2,713 | $3,092 | $3,453 | $3,798 | $4,126 | $4,437 | $4,731 | $5,005 | $5,266 |
| $200,000 | $2,544 | $2,943 | $3,320 | $3,681 | $4,027 | $4,356 | $4,668 | $4,959 | $5,236 | $5,494 |
| $250,000 | $2,706 | $3,103 | $3,482 | $3,842 | $4,188 | $4,516 | $4,827 | $5,119 | $5,397 | $5,656 |
| $300,000 | $2,884 | $3,280 | $3,659 | $4,020 | $4,365 | $4,693 | $5,004 | $5,298 | $5,572 | $5,832 |
| $350,000 | $3,081 | $3,476 | $3,855 | $4,218 | $4,561 | $4,890 | $5,198 | $5,492 | $5,768 | $6,028 |
| $400,000 | $3,210 | $3,605 | $3,984 | $4,346 | $4,690 | $5,020 | $5,328 | $5,621 | $5,896 | $6,157 |
| $450,000 | $3,356 | $3,754 | $4,131 | $4,494 | $4,838 | $5,165 | $5,474 | $5,768 | $6,043 | $6,302 |
| $500,000 | $3,517 | $3,915 | $4,292 | $4,654 | $4,999 | $5,327 | $5,636 | $5,928 | $6,204 | $6,463 |

### Non-Residential Business or Other Non-Residential Building And Contents Coverage Combinations

Without Basement or Enclosure[3]

| BUILDING COVERAGE / CONTENTS COVERAGE | $50,000 | $100,000 | $150,000 | $200,000 | $250,000 | $300,000 | $350,000 | $400,000 | $450,000 | $500,000 |
|---|---|---|---|---|---|---|---|---|---|---|
| $ 50,000 | $ 819 | $1,033 | $1,239 | $1,434 | $1,620 | $1,795 | $1,963 | $2,121 | $2,269 | $2,408 |
| $100,000 | $1,118 | $1,332 | $1,535 | $1,731 | $1,917 | $2,093 | $2,262 | $2,418 | $2,567 | $2,707 |
| $150,000 | $1,325 | $1,536 | $1,740 | $1,934 | $2,116 | $2,291 | $2,458 | $2,615 | $2,760 | $2,899 |
| $200,000 | $1,554 | $1,766 | $1,967 | $2,162 | $2,346 | $2,520 | $2,685 | $2,843 | $2,990 | $3,127 |
| $250,000 | $1,707 | $1,919 | $2,121 | $2,315 | $2,499 | $2,673 | $2,837 | $2,996 | $3,142 | $3,280 |
| $300,000 | $1,869 | $2,082 | $2,284 | $2,478 | $2,661 | $2,835 | $3,002 | $3,158 | $3,304 | $3,443 |
| $350,000 | $1,956 | $2,169 | $2,372 | $2,565 | $2,750 | $2,923 | $3,089 | $3,244 | $3,391 | $3,531 |
| $400,000 | $2,054 | $2,266 | $2,468 | $2,661 | $2,845 | $3,020 | $3,186 | $3,342 | $3,489 | $3,627 |
| $450,000 | $2,160 | $2,372 | $2,574 | $2,767 | $2,951 | $3,126 | $3,292 | $3,447 | $3,594 | $3,733 |
| $500,000 | $2,274 | $2,486 | $2,688 | $2,883 | $3,066 | $3,240 | $3,405 | $3,563 | $3,708 | $3,846 |

### Non-Residential Business or Other Non-Residential Contents-Only Coverage

| CONTENTS ABOVE GROUND LEVEL MORE THAN 1 FLOOR | | ALL OTHER LOCATIONS (BASEMENT-ONLY NOT ELIGIBLE) | |
|---|---|---|---|
| CONTENTS | PREMIUM | CONTENTS | PREMIUM |
| $ 50,000 | $ 199 | $ 50,000 | $ 486 |
| $100,000 | $ 316 | $100,000 | $ 752 |
| $150,000 | $ 428 | $150,000 | $1,001 |
| $200,000 | $ 541 | $200,000 | $1,259 |
| $250,000 | $ 656 | $250,000 | $1,517 |
| $300,000 | $ 772 | $300,000 | $1,778 |
| $350,000 | $ 887 | $350,000 | $2,037 |
| $400,000 | $1,001 | $400,000 | $2,295 |
| $450,000 | $1,112 | $450,000 | $2,554 |
| $500,000 | $1,226 | $500,000 | $2,814 |

**NOTE:** : Base Premium does not include the Multiplier, ICC Premium, Reserve Fund Assessment, HFIAA Surcharge, Probation Surcharge, or Federal Policy Fee. To determine the total amount due, refer to the How to Write section of this manual.

1. Use this table for eligible properties in AR or A99 zones on or after Oct. 1, 2016.
2. Use this section of the table for buildings with crawlspaces or subgrade crawlspaces with an attached garage without proper openings.
3. Use this section of the table for buildings with crawlspaces or subgrade crawlspaces, including those with an attached garage that has proper openings.

## IV. Newly Mapped Procedure Rates

**EFFECTIVE JAN. 1, 2021**
**NEWLY MAPPED TABLE 3. COVERAGE LIMITS AND BASE PREMIUMS FOR PROPERTIES NEWLY MAPPED INTO AN SFHA ON OR AFTER OCT. 1, 2008[1]**

**1–4 FAMILY RESIDENTIAL BUILDING AND CONTENTS COVERAGE COMBINATIONS**

| WITH BASEMENT OR ENCLOSURE[2] | | | WITHOUT BASEMENT OR ENCLOSURE[3] | | |
|---|---|---|---|---|---|
| BUILDING | CONTENTS | PREMIUM | BUILDING | CONTENTS | PREMIUM |
| $ 20,000 | $ 8,000 | $161 | $ 20,000 | $ 8,000 | $127 |
| $ 30,000 | $ 12,000 | $203 | $ 30,000 | $ 12,000 | $168 |
| $ 50,000 | $ 20,000 | $271 | $ 50,000 | $ 20,000 | $236 |
| $ 75,000 | $ 30,000 | $326 | $ 75,000 | $ 30,000 | $286 |
| $100,000 | $ 40,000 | $361 | $100,000 | $ 40,000 | $323 |
| $125,000 | $ 50,000 | $382 | $125,000 | $ 50,000 | $342 |
| $150,000 | $ 60,000 | $405 | $150,000 | $ 60,000 | $367 |
| $200,000 | $ 80,000 | $452 | $200,000 | $ 80,000 | $405 |
| $250,000 | $100,000 | $488 | $250,000 | $100,000 | $436 |

**RESIDENTIAL CONTENTS-ONLY COVERAGE**

| CONTENTS ABOVE GROUND LEVEL MORE THAN 1 FLOOR | | ALL OTHER LOCATIONS (BASEMENT-ONLY NOT ELIGIBLE) | |
|---|---|---|---|
| CONTENTS | PREMIUM | CONTENTS | PREMIUM |
| $ 8,000 | $ 25 | $ 8,000 | $ 50 |
| $ 12,000 | $ 47 | $ 12,000 | $ 84 |
| $ 20,000 | $ 88 | $ 20,000 | $132 |
| $ 30,000 | $108 | $ 30,000 | $158 |
| $ 40,000 | $123 | $ 40,000 | $181 |
| $ 50,000 | $140 | $ 50,000 | $204 |
| $ 60,000 | $157 | $ 60,000 | $226 |
| $ 80,000 | $188 | $ 80,000 | $253 |
| $100,000 | $221 | $100,000 | $281 |

**NOTE:** Base Premium does not include the Multiplier, ICC Premium, Reserve Fund Assessment, HFIAA Surcharge, Probation Surcharge, or Federal Policy Fee. To determine the total amount due, refer to the How to Write section of this manual.

1. Use this table for eligible properties in AR or A99 zones on or after Oct. 1, 2016.
2. Use this section of the table for buildings with crawlspaces or subgrade crawlspaces with an attached garage without proper openings.
3. Use this section of the table for buildings with crawlspaces or subgrade crawlspaces, including those with an attached garage that has proper openings.

EFFECTIVE JAN. 1, 2022

## NEWLY MAPPED TABLE 3. COVERAGE LIMITS AND BASE PREMIUMS FOR PROPERTIES NEWLY MAPPED INTO AN SFHA ON OR AFTER OCT. 1, 2008[1]

### 1–4 FAMILY RESIDENTIAL BUILDING AND CONTENTS COVERAGE COMBINATIONS

| WITH BASEMENT OR ENCLOSURE[2] | | | WITHOUT BASEMENT OR ENCLOSURE[3] | | |
|---|---|---|---|---|---|
| BUILDING | CONTENTS | PREMIUM | BUILDING | CONTENTS | PREMIUM |
| $ 20,000 | $ 8,000 | $185 | $ 20,000 | $ 8,000 | $146 |
| $ 30,000 | $ 12,000 | $233 | $ 30,000 | $ 12,000 | $193 |
| $ 50,000 | $ 20,000 | $312 | $ 50,000 | $ 20,000 | $271 |
| $ 75,000 | $ 30,000 | $375 | $ 75,000 | $ 30,000 | $329 |
| $100,000 | $ 40,000 | $415 | $100,000 | $ 40,000 | $371 |
| $125,000 | $ 50,000 | $439 | $125,000 | $ 50,000 | $393 |
| $150,000 | $ 60,000 | $466 | $150,000 | $ 60,000 | $422 |
| $200,000 | $ 80,000 | $520 | $200,000 | $ 80,000 | $466 |
| $250,000 | $100,000 | $561 | $250,000 | $100,000 | $501 |

### RESIDENTIAL CONTENTS-ONLY COVERAGE

| CONTENTS ABOVE GROUND LEVEL MORE THAN 1 FLOOR | | ALL OTHER LOCATIONS (BASEMENT-ONLY NOT ELIGIBLE) | |
|---|---|---|---|
| CONTENTS | PREMIUM | CONTENTS | PREMIUM |
| $ 8,000 | $ 29 | $ 8,000 | $ 58 |
| $ 12,000 | $ 54 | $ 12,000 | $ 97 |
| $ 20,000 | $101 | $ 20,000 | $152 |
| $ 30,000 | $124 | $ 30,000 | $182 |
| $ 40,000 | $141 | $ 40,000 | $208 |
| $ 50,000 | $161 | $ 50,000 | $235 |
| $ 60,000 | $180 | $ 60,000 | $260 |
| $ 80,000 | $216 | $ 80,000 | $291 |
| $100,000 | $254 | $100,000 | $323 |

**NOTE:** Base Premium does not include the Multiplier, ICC Premium, Reserve Fund Assessment, HFIAA Surcharge, Probation Surcharge, or Federal Policy Fee. To determine the total amount due, refer to the How to Write section of this manual.

1. Use this table for eligible properties in AR or A99 zones on or after Oct. 1, 2016.
2. Use this section of the table for buildings with crawlspaces or subgrade crawlspaces with an attached garage without proper openings.
3. Use this section of the table for buildings with crawlspaces or subgrade crawlspaces, including those with an attached garage that has proper openings.

## EFFECTIVE JAN. 1, 2021
## NEWLY MAPPED TABLE 4. COVERAGE LIMITS AND BASE PREMIUMS FOR PROPERTIES NEWLY MAPPED INTO AN SFHA ON OR AFTER OCT. 1, 2008[1]

### OTHER RESIDENTIAL BUILDING AND CONTENTS COVERAGE COMBINATIONS

With Basement or Enclosure[2]

| BUILDING COVERAGE | CONTENTS COVERAGE | $8,000 | $12,000 | $20,000 | $30,000 | $40,000 | $50,000 | $60,000 | $80,000 | $100,000 |
|---|---|---|---|---|---|---|---|---|---|---|
| | $ 20,000 | $180 | $198 | $215 | $233 | $250 | $264 | $279 | $291 | $306 |
| | $ 30,000 | $198 | $216 | $234 | $252 | $268 | $283 | $298 | $310 | $325 |
| | $ 50,000 | $243 | $263 | $281 | $298 | $314 | $329 | $344 | $356 | $371 |
| | $ 75,000 | $265 | $284 | $302 | $319 | $335 | $351 | $366 | $377 | $392 |
| | $100,000 | $295 | $314 | $332 | $349 | $366 | $380 | $394 | $408 | $421 |
| | $125,000 | $302 | $320 | $336 | $354 | $371 | $385 | $401 | $414 | $427 |
| | $150,000 | $308 | $326 | $344 | $361 | $376 | $392 | $407 | $420 | $433 |
| | $200,000 | $349 | $368 | $385 | $403 | $419 | $433 | $448 | $460 | $474 |
| | $250,000 | $372 | $391 | $408 | $426 | $441 | $455 | $470 | $485 | $496 |
| | $300,000 | $391 | $408 | $424 | $440 | $455 | $469 | $485 | $496 | $510 |
| | $350,000 | $408 | $426 | $441 | $457 | $472 | $486 | $501 | $512 | $524 |
| | $400,000 | $424 | $440 | $456 | $473 | $487 | $500 | $515 | $525 | $539 |
| | $450,000 | $439 | $455 | $470 | $487 | $500 | $513 | $528 | $540 | $551 |
| | $500,000 | $452 | $468 | $485 | $500 | $512 | $524 | $540 | $551 | $562 |

### OTHER RESIDENTIAL BUILDING AND CONTENTS COVERAGE COMBINATIONS

Without Basement or Enclosure[3]

| BUILDING COVERAGE | CONTENTS COVERAGE | $8,000 | $12,000 | $20,000 | $30,000 | $40,000 | $50,000 | $60,000 | $80,000 | $100,000 |
|---|---|---|---|---|---|---|---|---|---|---|
| | $ 20,000 | $141 | $158 | $171 | $187 | $202 | $214 | $226 | $239 | $250 |
| | $ 30,000 | $166 | $181 | $195 | $209 | $224 | $236 | $250 | $262 | $272 |
| | $ 50,000 | $213 | $228 | $242 | $256 | $271 | $284 | $297 | $308 | $319 |
| | $ 75,000 | $240 | $254 | $269 | $283 | $297 | $309 | $323 | $334 | $345 |
| | $100,000 | $264 | $279 | $292 | $307 | $320 | $334 | $347 | $357 | $370 |
| | $125,000 | $273 | $288 | $304 | $315 | $329 | $342 | $353 | $366 | $375 |
| | $150,000 | $283 | $298 | $312 | $325 | $338 | $351 | $363 | $374 | $385 |
| | $200,000 | $320 | $334 | $349 | $363 | $375 | $389 | 401 | $410 | $422 |
| | $250,000 | $339 | $354 | $370 | $383 | $395 | $408 | $420 | $431 | $441 |
| | $300,000 | $371 | $382 | $395 | $407 | $419 | $431 | $440 | $450 | $461 |
| | $350,000 | $391 | $401 | $416 | $426 | $437 | $446 | $457 | $467 | $477 |
| | $400,000 | $409 | $419 | $432 | $441 | $451 | $463 | $473 | $483 | $493 |
| | $450,000 | $427 | $436 | $446 | $456 | $467 | $476 | $487 | $495 | $507 |
| | $500,000 | $441 | $449 | $461 | $470 | $478 | $491 | $500 | $508 | $520 |

**NOTE:** Base Premium does not include the Multiplier, ICC Premium, Reserve Fund Assessment, HFIAA Surcharge, Probation Surcharge, or Federal Policy Fee. To determine the total amount due, refer to the How to Write section of this manual.

1. Use this table for properties newly mapped into SFHA zones excluding AR and A99 on or after Oct. 1, 2016.
2. Use this section of the table for buildings with crawlspaces or subgrade crawlspaces with an attached garage without proper openings.
3. Use this section of the table for buildings with crawlspaces or subgrade crawlspaces, including those with an attached garage that has proper openings.

EFFECTIVE JAN. 1, 2022

## NEWLY MAPPED TABLE 4. COVERAGE LIMITS AND BASE PREMIUMS FOR PROPERTIES NEWLY MAPPED INTO AN SFHA ON OR AFTER OCT. 1, 2008[1]

### OTHER RESIDENTIAL BUILDING AND CONTENTS COVERAGE COMBINATIONS

With Basement or Enclosure[2]

| BUILDING COVERAGE / CONTENTS COVERAGE | $8,000 | $12,000 | $20,000 | $30,000 | $40,000 | $50,000 | $60,000 | $80,000 | $100,000 |
|---|---|---|---|---|---|---|---|---|---|
| $ 20,000 | $207 | $228 | $247 | $268 | $288 | $304 | $321 | $335 | $352 |
| $ 30,000 | $228 | $248 | $269 | $290 | $308 | $325 | $343 | $357 | $374 |
| $ 50,000 | $279 | $302 | $323 | $343 | $361 | $378 | $396 | $409 | $427 |
| $ 75,000 | $305 | $327 | $347 | $367 | $385 | $404 | $421 | $434 | $451 |
| $100,000 | $339 | $361 | $382 | $401 | $421 | $437 | $453 | $469 | $484 |
| $125,000 | $347 | $368 | $386 | $407 | $427 | $443 | $461 | $476 | $491 |
| $150,000 | $354 | $375 | $396 | $415 | $432 | $451 | $468 | $483 | $498 |
| $200,000 | $401 | $423 | $443 | $463 | $482 | $498 | $515 | $529 | $545 |
| $250,000 | $428 | $450 | $469 | $490 | $507 | $523 | $541 | $558 | $570 |
| $300,000 | $450 | $469 | $488 | $506 | $523 | $539 | $558 | $570 | $587 |
| $350,000 | $469 | $490 | $507 | $526 | $543 | $559 | $576 | $589 | $603 |
| $400,000 | $488 | $506 | $524 | $544 | $560 | $575 | $592 | $604 | $620 |
| $450,000 | $505 | $523 | $541 | $560 | $575 | $590 | $607 | $621 | $634 |
| $500,000 | $520 | $538 | $558 | $575 | $589 | $603 | $621 | $634 | $646 |

### OTHER RESIDENTIAL BUILDING AND CONTENTS COVERAGE COMBINATIONS

Without Basement or Enclosure[3]

| BUILDING COVERAGE / CONTENTS COVERAGE | $8,000 | $12,000 | $20,000 | $30,000 | $40,000 | $50,000 | $60,000 | $80,000 | $100,000 |
|---|---|---|---|---|---|---|---|---|---|
| $ 20,000 | $162 | $182 | $197 | $215 | $232 | $246 | $260 | $275 | $288 |
| $ 30,000 | $191 | $208 | $224 | $240 | $258 | $271 | $288 | $301 | $313 |
| $ 50,000 | $245 | $262 | $278 | $294 | $312 | $327 | $342 | $354 | $367 |
| $ 75,000 | $276 | $292 | $309 | $325 | $342 | $355 | $371 | $384 | $397 |
| $100,000 | $304 | $321 | $336 | $353 | $368 | $384 | $399 | $411 | $426 |
| $125,000 | $314 | $331 | $350 | $362 | $378 | $393 | $406 | $421 | $431 |
| $150,000 | $325 | $343 | $359 | $374 | $389 | $404 | $417 | $430 | $443 |
| $200,000 | $368 | $384 | $401 | $417 | $431 | $447 | $461 | $472 | $485 |
| $250,000 | $390 | $407 | $426 | $440 | $454 | $469 | $483 | $496 | $507 |
| $300,000 | $427 | $439 | $454 | $468 | $482 | $496 | $506 | $518 | $530 |
| $350,000 | $450 | $461 | $478 | $490 | $503 | $513 | $526 | $537 | $549 |
| $400,000 | $470 | $482 | $497 | $507 | $519 | $532 | $544 | $555 | $567 |
| $450,000 | $491 | $501 | $513 | $524 | $537 | $547 | $560 | $569 | $583 |
| $500,000 | $507 | $516 | $530 | $541 | $550 | $565 | $575 | $584 | $598 |

NOTE: Base Premium does not include the Multiplier, ICC Premium, Reserve Fund Assessment, HFIAA Surcharge, Probation Surcharge, or Federal Policy Fee. To determine the total amount due, refer to the How to Write section of this manual.

1. Use this table for properties newly mapped into SFHA zones excluding AR and A99 on or after Oct. 1, 2016.
2. Use this section of the table for buildings with crawlspaces or subgrade crawlspaces with an attached garage without proper openings.
3. Use this section of the table for buildings with crawlspaces or subgrade crawlspaces, including those with an attached garage that has proper openings.

## EFFECTIVE JAN. 1, 2021
## NEWLY MAPPED TABLE 5. COVERAGE LIMITS AND BASE PREMIUMS FOR PROPERTIES NEWLY MAPPED INTO AN SFHA ON OR AFTER OCT. 1, 2008[1]

### Non-Residential Business or Other Non-Residential Building And Contents Coverage Combinations
With Basement or Enclosure[2]

| | CONTENTS COVERAGE | $50,000 | $100,000 | $150,000 | $200,000 | $250,000 | $300,000 | $350,000 | $400,000 | $450,000 | $500,000 |
|---|---|---|---|---|---|---|---|---|---|---|---|
| BUILDING COVERAGE | $ 50,000 | $1,160 | $1,510 | $1,842 | $2,160 | $2,464 | $2,752 | $3,025 | $3,283 | $3,525 | $3,753 |
| | $100,000 | $1,664 | $2,013 | $2,345 | $2,663 | $2,966 | $3,254 | $3,527 | $3,786 | $4,026 | $4,254 |
| | $150,000 | $2,014 | $2,359 | $2,689 | $3,003 | $3,303 | $3,588 | $3,858 | $4,114 | $4,352 | $4,579 |
| | $200,000 | $2,212 | $2,559 | $2,887 | $3,201 | $3,502 | $3,788 | $4,059 | $4,312 | $4,553 | $4,777 |
| | $250,000 | $2,353 | $2,698 | $3,028 | $3,341 | $3,642 | $3,927 | $4,197 | $4,451 | $4,693 | $4,918 |
| | $300,000 | $2,508 | $2,852 | $3,182 | $3,496 | $3,796 | $4,081 | $4,351 | $4,607 | $4,845 | $5,071 |
| | $350,000 | $2,679 | $3,023 | $3,352 | $3,668 | $3,966 | $4,252 | $4,520 | $4,776 | $5,016 | $5,242 |
| | $400,000 | $2,791 | $3,135 | $3,464 | $3,779 | $4,078 | $4,365 | $4,633 | $4,888 | $5,127 | $5,354 |
| | $450,000 | $2,918 | $3,264 | $3,592 | $3,908 | $4,207 | $4,491 | $4,760 | $5,016 | $5,255 | $5,480 |
| | $500,000 | $3,058 | $3,404 | $3,732 | $4,047 | $4,347 | $4,632 | $4,901 | $5,155 | $5,395 | $5,620 |

### Non-Residential Business or Other Non-Residential Building And Contents Coverage Combinations
Without Basement or Enclosure[3]

| | CONTENTS COVERAGE | $50,000 | $100,000 | $150,000 | $200,000 | $250,000 | $300,000 | $350,000 | $400,000 | $450,000 | $500,000 |
|---|---|---|---|---|---|---|---|---|---|---|---|
| BUILDING COVERAGE | $ 50,000 | $ 712 | $ 898 | $1,077 | $1,247 | $1,409 | $1,561 | $1,707 | $1,844 | $1,973 | $2,094 |
| | $100,000 | $ 972 | $1,158 | $1,335 | $1,505 | $1,667 | $1,820 | $1,967 | $2,103 | $2,232 | $2,354 |
| | $150,000 | $1,152 | $1,336 | $1,513 | $1,682 | $1,840 | $1,992 | $2,137 | $2,274 | $2,400 | $2,521 |
| | $200,000 | $1,351 | $1,536 | $1,710 | $1,880 | $2,040 | $2,191 | $2,335 | $2,472 | $2,600 | $2,719 |
| | $250,000 | $1,484 | $1,669 | $1,844 | $2,013 | $2,173 | $2,324 | $2,467 | $2,605 | $2,732 | $2,852 |
| | $300,000 | $1,625 | $1,810 | $1,986 | $2,155 | $2,314 | $2,465 | $2,610 | $2,746 | $2,873 | $2,994 |
| | $350,000 | $1,701 | $1,886 | $2,063 | $2,230 | $2,391 | $2,542 | $2,686 | $2,821 | $2,949 | $3,070 |
| | $400,000 | $1,786 | $1,970 | $2,146 | $2,314 | $2,474 | $2,626 | $2,770 | $2,906 | $3,034 | $3,154 |
| | $450,000 | $1,878 | $2,063 | $2,238 | $2,406 | $2,566 | $2,718 | $2,863 | $2,997 | $3,125 | $3,246 |
| | $500,000 | $1,977 | $2,162 | $2,337 | $2,507 | $2,666 | $2,817 | $2,961 | $3,098 | $3,224 | $3,344 |

### Non-Residential Business or Other Non-Residential Contents-Only Coverage

| CONTENTS ABOVE GROUND LEVEL MORE THAN 1 FLOOR | | ALL OTHER LOCATIONS (BASEMENT-ONLY NOT ELIGIBLE) | |
|---|---|---|---|
| CONTENTS | PREMIUM | CONTENTS | PREMIUM |
| $ 50,000 | $ 173 | $ 50,000 | $ 423 |
| $100,000 | $ 275 | $100,000 | $ 654 |
| $150,000 | $ 372 | $150,000 | $ 870 |
| $200,000 | $ 470 | $200,000 | $1,095 |
| $250,000 | $ 570 | $250,000 | $1,319 |
| $300,000 | $ 671 | $300,000 | $1,546 |
| $350,000 | $ 771 | $350,000 | $1,771 |
| $400,000 | $ 870 | $400,000 | $1,996 |
| $450,000 | $ 967 | $450,000 | $2,221 |
| $500,000 | $1,066 | $500,000 | $2,447 |

**NOTE:** Base Premium does not include the Multiplier, ICC Premium, Reserve Fund Assessment, HFIAA Surcharge, Probation Surcharge, or Federal Policy Fee. To determine the total amount due, refer to the How to Write section of this manual.

1. Use this table for properties newly mapped into SFHA zones excluding AR and A99 on or after Oct. 1, 2016.
2. Use this section of the table for buildings with crawlspaces or subgrade crawlspaces with an attached garage without proper openings.
3. Use this section of the table for buildings with crawlspaces or subgrade crawlspaces, including those with an attached garage that has proper openings.

EFFECTIVE JAN. 1, 2022

## NEWLY MAPPED TABLE 5. COVERAGE LIMITS AND BASE PREMIUMS FOR PROPERTIES NEWLY MAPPED INTO AN SFHA ON OR AFTER OCT. 1, 2008[1]

### Non-Residential Business or Other Non-Residential Building And Contents Coverage Combinations

With Basement or Enclosure[2]

| | CONTENTS COVERAGE | $50,000 | $100,000 | $150,000 | $200,000 | $250,000 | $300,000 | $350,000 | $400,000 | $450,000 | $500,000 |
|---|---|---|---|---|---|---|---|---|---|---|---|
| BUILDING COVERAGE | $ 50,000 | $1,334 | $1,737 | $2,118 | $2,484 | $2,834 | $3,165 | $3,479 | $3,775 | $4,054 | $4,316 |
| | $100,000 | $1,914 | $2,315 | $2,697 | $3,062 | $3,411 | $3,742 | $4,056 | $4,354 | $4,630 | $4,892 |
| | $150,000 | $2,316 | $2,713 | $3,092 | $3,453 | $3,798 | $4,126 | $4,437 | $4,731 | $5,005 | $5,266 |
| | $200,000 | $2,544 | $2,943 | $3,320 | $3,681 | $4,027 | $4,356 | $4,668 | $4,959 | $5,236 | $5,494 |
| | $250,000 | $2,706 | $3,103 | $3,482 | $3,842 | $4,188 | $4,516 | $4,827 | $5,119 | $5,397 | $5,656 |
| | $300,000 | $2,884 | $3,280 | $3,659 | $4,020 | $4,365 | $4,693 | $5,004 | $5,298 | $5,572 | $5,832 |
| | $350,000 | $3,081 | $3,476 | $3,855 | $4,218 | $4,561 | $4,890 | $5,198 | $5,492 | $5,768 | $6,028 |
| | $400,000 | $3,210 | $3,605 | $3,984 | $4,346 | $4,690 | $5,020 | $5,328 | $5,621 | $5,896 | $6,157 |
| | $450,000 | $3,356 | $3,754 | $4,131 | $4,494 | $4,838 | $5,165 | $5,474 | $5,768 | $6,043 | $6,302 |
| | $500,000 | $3,517 | $3,915 | $4,292 | $4,654 | $4,999 | $5,327 | $5,636 | $5,928 | $6,204 | $6,463 |

### Non-Residential Business or Other Non-Residential Building And Contents Coverage Combinations

Without Basement or Enclosure[3]

| | CONTENTS COVERAGE | $50,000 | $100,000 | $150,000 | $200,000 | $250,000 | $300,000 | $350,000 | $400,000 | $450,000 | $500,000 |
|---|---|---|---|---|---|---|---|---|---|---|---|
| BUILDING COVERAGE | $ 50,000 | $ 819 | $1,033 | $1,239 | $1,434 | $1,620 | $1,795 | $1,963 | $2,121 | $2,269 | $2,408 |
| | $100,000 | $1,118 | $1,332 | $1,535 | $1,731 | $1,917 | $2,093 | $2,262 | $2,418 | $2,567 | $2,707 |
| | $150,000 | $1,325 | $1,536 | $1,740 | $1,934 | $2,116 | $2,291 | $2,458 | $2,615 | $2,760 | $2,899 |
| | $200,000 | $1,554 | $1,766 | $1,967 | $2,162 | $2,346 | $2,520 | $2,685 | $2,843 | $2,990 | $3,127 |
| | $250,000 | $1,707 | $1,919 | $2,121 | $2,315 | $2,499 | $2,673 | $2,837 | $2,996 | $3,142 | $3,280 |
| | $300,000 | $1,869 | $2,082 | $2,284 | $2,478 | $2,661 | $2,835 | $3,002 | $3,158 | $3,304 | $3,443 |
| | $350,000 | $1,956 | $2,169 | $2,372 | $2,565 | $2,750 | $2,923 | $3,089 | $3,244 | $3,391 | $3,531 |
| | $400,000 | $2,054 | $2,266 | $2,468 | $2,661 | $2,845 | $3,020 | $3,186 | $3,342 | $3,489 | $3,627 |
| | $450,000 | $2,160 | $2,372 | $2,574 | $2,767 | $2,951 | $3,126 | $3,292 | $3,447 | $3,594 | $3,733 |
| | $500,000 | $2,274 | $2,486 | $2,688 | $2,883 | $3,066 | $3,240 | $3,405 | $3,563 | $3,708 | $3,846 |

### Non-Residential Business or Other Non-Residential Contents-Only Coverage

| CONTENTS ABOVE GROUND LEVEL MORE THAN 1 FLOOR | | ALL OTHER LOCATIONS (BASEMENT-ONLY NOT ELIGIBLE) | |
|---|---|---|---|
| CONTENTS | PREMIUM | CONTENTS | PREMIUM |
| $ 50,000 | $ 199 | $ 50,000 | $ 486 |
| $100,000 | $ 316 | $100,000 | $ 752 |
| $150,000 | $ 428 | $150,000 | $1,001 |
| $200,000 | $ 541 | $200,000 | $1,259 |
| $250,000 | $ 656 | $250,000 | $1,517 |
| $300,000 | $ 772 | $300,000 | $1,778 |
| $350,000 | $ 887 | $350,000 | $2,037 |
| $400,000 | $1,001 | $400,000 | $2,295 |
| $450,000 | $1,112 | $450,000 | $2,554 |
| $500,000 | $1,226 | $500,000 | $2,814 |

**NOTE:** Base Premium does not include the Multiplier, ICC Premium, Reserve Fund Assessment, HFIAA Surcharge, Probation Surcharge, or Federal Policy Fee. To determine the total amount due, refer to the How to Write section of this manual.

1. Use this table for properties newly mapped into SFHA zones excluding AR and A99 on or after Oct. 1, 2016.
2. Use this section of the table for buildings with crawlspaces or subgrade crawlspaces with an attached garage without proper openings.
3. Use this section of the table for buildings with crawlspaces or subgrade crawlspaces, including those with an attached garage that has proper openings.

## NEWLY MAPPED TABLE 6A. NEWLY MAPPED MULTIPLIER FOR POLICIES EFFECTIVE APRIL 1, 2016 THROUGH DEC. 31, 2016

| MAP EFFECTIVE DATE | ELIGIBLE TRANSACTION | MULTIPLIER |
|---|---|---|
| Oct 2008-Dec 2014 | 1. Renewal of a policy written, in its prior term, as a Newly Mapped policy | 1.000 |
| Jan 2015-Dec 2015 | 1. New business if policy effective date is within 12 months of map effective date<br>2. Renewal of a policy written, in its prior term, as a Newly Mapped policy<br>3. Renewal of a policy written, in its prior term, as a PRP | 1.000 |
| Jan 2016-Dec 2016 | 1. New business<br>2. Renewal of a policy written, in its prior term, as a PRP | 1.000 |

## NEWLY MAPPED TABLE 6B. NEWLY MAPPED MULTIPLIER FOR POLICIES EFFECTIVE JAN. 1, 2017 THROUGH DEC. 31, 2017

| MAP EFFECTIVE DATE | ELIGIBLE TRANSACTION | MULTIPLIER |
|---|---|---|
| Oct 2008-Dec 2014 | 1. Renewal of a policy written, in its prior term, as a Newly Mapped policy | 1.150 |
| Jan 2015-Dec 2015 | 1. Renewal of a policy written, in its prior term, as a Newly Mapped policy | 1.150 |
| Jan 2016-Dec 2016 | 1. New business if policy effective date is within 12 months of map effective date<br>2. Renewal of a policy written, in its prior term, as a PRP<br>3. Renewal of a policy written, in its prior term, as a Newly Mapped policy | 1.000 |
| Jan 2017-Dec 2017 | 1. New business if policy effective date is within 12 months of map effective date<br>2. Renewal of a policy written, in its prior term, as a PRP | 1.000 |

## NEWLY MAPPED TABLE 6C. NEWLY MAPPED MULTIPLIER FOR POLICIES EFFECTIVE JAN. 1, 2018 THROUGH DEC. 31, 2018

| MAP EFFECTIVE DATE | ELIGIBLE TRANSACTION | MULTIPLIER |
|---|---|---|
| Oct 2008-Dec 2014 | 1. Renewal of a policy written, in its prior term, as a Newly Mapped policy | 1.325 |
| Jan 2015-Dec 2015 | 1. Renewal of a policy written, in its prior term, as a Newly Mapped policy | 1.325 |
| Jan 2016-Dec 2016 | 1. Renewal of a policy written, in its prior term, as a Newly Mapped policy | 1.150 |
| Jan 2017-Dec 2017 | 1. New business if policy effective date is within 12 months of map effective date<br>2. Renewal of a policy written, in its prior term, as a PRP<br>3. Renewal of a policy written, in its prior term, as a Newly Mapped policy | 1.000 |
| Jan 2018-Dec 2018 | 1. New business if policy effective date is within 12 months of map effective date<br>2. Renewal of a policy written, in its prior term, as a PRP | 1.000 |

## NEWLY MAPPED TABLE 6D. NEWLY MAPPED MULTIPLIER FOR POLICIES EFFECTIVE JAN. 1, 2019 THROUGH DEC. 31, 2019

| MAP EFFECTIVE DATE | ELIGIBLE TRANSACTION | MULTIPLIER |
|---|---|---|
| Oct 2008-Dec 2014 | 1. Renewal of a policy written, in its prior term, as a Newly Mapped Policy | 1.415 |
| Jan 2015-Dec 2015 | 1. Renewal of a policy written, in its prior term, as a Newly Mapped Policy | 1.415 |
| Jan 2016-Dec 2016 | 1. Renewal of a policy written, in its prior term, as a Newly Mapped Policy | 1.230 |
| Jan 2017-Dec 2017 | 1. Renewal of a policy written, in its prior term, as a Newly Mapped Policy | 1.070 |
| Jan 2018-Dec 2018 | 1. New business if policy effective date is within 12 months of map effective date<br>2. Renewal of a policy written, in its prior term, as a Newly Mapped Policy<br>3. Renewal of a policy written, in its prior term, as a PRP | 1.000 |
| Jan 2019-Dec 2019 | 1. New business, if policy effective date is within 12 months of map effective date<br>2. Renewal of a policy written, in its prior term, as a PRP | 1.000 |

### NEWLY MAPPED TABLE 6E. NEWLY MAPPED MULTIPLIER FOR POLICIES EFFECTIVE JAN. 1, 2020 THROUGH DEC. 31, 2020

| MAP EFFECTIVE DATE | ELIGIBLE TRANSACTION | MULTIPLIER |
|---|---|---|
| Oct 2008 - Dec 2014 | 1. Renewal of a policy written, in its prior term, as a Newly Mapped Policy | 1.550 |
| Jan 2015 - Dec 2015 | 1. Renewal of a policy written, in its prior term, as a Newly Mapped Policy | 1.550 |
| Jan 2016 - Dec 2016 | 1. Renewal of a policy written, in its prior term, as a Newly Mapped Policy | 1.350 |
| Jan 2017 - Dec 2017 | 1. Renewal of a policy written, in its prior term, as a Newly Mapped Policy | 1.170 |
| Jan 2018 - Dec 2018 | 1. Renewal of a policy written, in its prior term, as a Newly Mapped Policy | 1.100 |
| Jan 2019 - Dec 2019 | 1. New business if policy effective date is within 12 months of map effective date<br>2. Renewal of a policy written, in its prior term, as a Newly Mapped policy<br>3. Renewal of a policy written, in its prior term, as a PRP | 1.000 |
| Jan 2020 - Dec 2020 | 1. New business, if policy effective date is within 12 months of map effective date<br>2. Renewal of a policy written, in its prior term, as a PRP | 1.000 |

### NEWLY MAPPED TABLE 6F. NEWLY MAPPED MULTIPLIER FOR POLICIES EFFECTIVE JAN. 1, 2021 THROUGH DEC. 31, 2021

| MAP EFFECTIVE DATE | ELIGIBLE TRANSACTION | MULTIPLIER |
|---|---|---|
| Oct 2008 - Dec 2014 | 1. Renewal of a policy written, in its prior term, as a Newly Mapped Policy | 1.550 |
| Jan 2015 - Dec 2015 | 1. Renewal of a policy written, in its prior term, as a Newly Mapped Policy | 1.550 |
| Jan 2016 - Dec 2016 | 1. Renewal of a policy written, in its prior term, as a Newly Mapped Policy | 1.350 |
| Jan 2017 - Dec 2017 | 1. Renewal of a policy written, in its prior term, as a Newly Mapped Policy | 1.170 |
| Jan 2018 - Dec 2018 | 1. Renewal of a policy written, in its prior term, as a Newly Mapped Policy | 1.100 |
| Jan 2019 - Dec 2019 | 1. Renewal of a policy written, in its prior term, as a Newly Mapped Policy | 1.000 |
| Jan 2020 - Dec 2020 | 1. New business if policy effective date is within 12 months of map effective date<br>2. Renewal of a policy written, in its prior term, as a Newly Mapped policy<br>3. Renewal of a policy written, in its prior term, as a PRP | 1.000 |
| Jan 2021 - Dec 2021 | 1. New business, if policy effective date is within 12 months of map effective date<br>2. Renewal of a policy written, in its prior term, as a PRP | 1.000 |

### NEWLY MAPPED TABLE 6G. NEWLY MAPPED MULTIPLIER FOR POLICIES EFFECTIVE JAN. 1, 2022 THROUGH DEC. 31, 2022

| MAP EFFECTIVE DATE | ELIGIBLE TRANSACTION | MULTIPLIER |
|---|---|---|
| Oct 2008 - Dec 2014 | 1. Renewal of a policy written, in its prior term, as a Newly Mapped Policy | 1.550 |
| Jan 2015 - Dec 2015 | 1. Renewal of a policy written, in its prior term, as a Newly Mapped Policy | 1.550 |
| Jan 2016 - Dec 2016 | 1. Renewal of a policy written, in its prior term, as a Newly Mapped Policy | 1.350 |
| Jan 2017 - Dec 2017 | 1. Renewal of a policy written, in its prior term, as a Newly Mapped Policy | 1.170 |
| Jan 2018 - Dec 2018 | 1. Renewal of a policy written, in its prior term, as a Newly Mapped Policy | 1.100 |
| Jan 2019 - Dec 2019 | 1. Renewal of a policy written, in its prior term, as a Newly Mapped Policy | 1.000 |
| Jan 2020 - Dec 2020 | 1. Renewal of a policy written, in its prior term, as a Newly Mapped Policy | 1.000 |
| Jan 2021 - Dec 2021 | 1. New business if policy effective date is within 12 months of map effective date<br>2. Renewal of a policy written, in its prior term, as a Newly Mapped policy<br>3. Renewal of a policy written, in its prior term, as a PRP | 1.000 |
| Jan 2022 - Dec 2022 | 1. New business, if policy effective date is within 12 months of map effective date<br>2. Renewal of a policy written, in its prior term, as a PRP | 1.000 |

## V. Mortgage Portfolio Protection Program (MPPP) Rates

**MPPP RATE AND INCREASED COST OF COMPLIANCE (ICC) [1,2]**

| ZONE | MPPP RATES PER $100 OF BUILDING COVERAGE[3] | MPPP RATES PER $100 OF CONTENTS COVERAGE[3] | ICC PREMIUM FOR $30,000 COVERAGE[4,5] |
|---|---|---|---|
| Emergency Program Community | 5.00 | 5.00 | N/A |
| A Zones - All building & occupancy types, except A99, AR, AR Dual Zones | 5.00 / 3.00 | 5.00 / 3.00 | $56 |
| V Zones - All building & occupancy types | 11.00 / 11.00 | 11.00 / 11.00 | $56 |
| A99 Zone, AR, AR Dual Zones | 1.12 / .67 | 1.42 / .60 | $8 |

1. Include the Reserve Fund Assessment, Probation Surcharge, Homeowner Flood Insurance Affordability Act of 2014 (HFIAA) surcharge, and Federal Policy Fee, if applicable, when calculating the Total Amount Due.
2. MPPP policies are not eligible for Community Rating System premium discounts.
3. For basic and additional insurance limits, refer to the How to Write section of this manual.
4. ICC coverage does not apply to contents-only policies or to individually owned condominium units insured under the Dwelling Form or General Property Form.
5. The ICC premium is not eligible for the deductible discount. First calculate the deductible discount, then add in the ICC premium.

## VI. Residential Condominium Building Association Policy (RCBAP) Rates

### CONDO TABLE 2B. PRE-FIRM SUBSIDIZED RATES INELIGIBILITY DETERMINATION[1,2]

| WAS THERE A PRIOR NFIP POLICY FOR THIS PROPERTY IN APPLICANT'S NAME? | WAS THE PRIOR NFIP POLICY REQUIRED BY A LENDER? | DID THE PRIOR NFIP POLICY LAPSE WHILE REQUIRED BY A LENDER? | WAS THE LAPSE THE RESULT OF A COMMUNITY SUSPENSION? | WAS THE COMMUNITY REINSTATED WITHIN THE LAST 180 DAYS? | **ELIGIBLE FOR PRE-FIRM SUBSIDIZED RATES** |
|---|---|---|---|---|---|
| YES | YES | YES | YES | NO | **NO** |
| YES | YES | YES | NO | YES | **NO** |
| YES | YES | YES | NO | NO | **NO** |

1. Use this table for all applications for Pre-FIRM buildings.
2. Also use this table for policy reinstatements by means of renewal, where coverage has lapsed more than 30 days after the prior policy expiration or cancellation date, and where the named insured has not maintained continuous coverage on the property from April 1, 2016 to the prior policy expiration or cancellation date.

### CONDO TABLE 2C. CONDOMINIUM PRE-FIRM RATE TABLE HIERARCHY

| PRE-FIRM | PRE-FIRM SRL | PRE-FIRM SUBSTANTIALLY IMPROVED | **HIGH-RISE TABLE FOR RATING** | **LOW-RISE TABLE FOR RATING** |
|---|---|---|---|---|
| YES | YES | NO | **N/A** | **4B** |
| YES | NO | YES | **3B** | **4C** |
| YES | YES | YES | **N/A** | **4B** |

## CONDO TABLE 3A. RCBAP HIGH-RISE CONDOMINIUM RATES[1]

ANNUAL RATES PER $100 OF COVERAGE (Basic/Additional)

### BUILDING

| BUILDING TYPE | REGULAR PROGRAM PRE-FIRM[2,3,4] | | | REGULAR PROGRAM POST-FIRM | |
|---|---|---|---|---|---|
| | A, A1–A30, AE, AO, AH, D | V, VE | A99, B, C, X | A99, B, C, X | D |
| NO BASEMENT/ENCLOSURE | 1.45 / .412 | 1.86 / .988 | 1.33 / .075 | 1.33 / .075 | 1.94 / .346 |
| WITH BASEMENT | 1.56 / .550 | 1.96 / 2.068 | 1.61 / .099 | 1.61 / .099 | SUBMIT FOR RATE |
| WITH ENCLOSURE | 1.56 / .412 | 1.96 / 1.015 | 1.40 / .075 | 1.40 / .075 | |
| ELEVATED ON CRAWLSPACE | 1.45 / .412 | 1.86 / .988 | 1.33 / .075 | 1.33 / .075 | |
| NON-ELEVATED WITH SUBGRADE CRAWLSPACE | 1.45 / .412 | 1.86 / .988 | 1.33 / .075 | 1.33 / .075 | |

### CONTENTS

| CONTENTS LOCATION | REGULAR PROGRAM PRE-FIRM[2,3,4] | | | REGULAR PROGRAM POST-FIRM | |
|---|---|---|---|---|---|
| | A, A1–A30, AE, AO, AH, D | V, VE | A99, B, C, X | A99, B, C, X | D |
| BASEMENT/SUBGRADE CRAWLSPACE AND ABOVE | 1.60 / 1.76 | 2.05 / 4.20 | 2.17 / .82 | 2.17 / .82 | SUBMIT FOR RATE |
| ENCLOSURE/CRAWLSPACE AND ABOVE | 1.60 / 2.08 | 2.05 / 4.93 | 2.17 / .93 | 2.17 / .93 | |
| LOWEST FLOOR ONLY - ABOVE GROUND LEVEL | 1.60 / 2.08 | 2.05 / 4.93 | 1.73 / .86 | 1.73 / .86 | 1.57 / .29 |
| LOWEST FLOOR ABOVE GROUND LEVEL AND HIGHER FLOORS | 1.60 / 1.46 | 2.05 / 4.34 | 1.73 / .55 | 1.73 / .55 | 1.18 / .18 |
| ABOVE GROUND LEVEL MORE THAN 1 FULL FLOOR | .38 / .12 | .54 / .47 | .35 / .12 | .35 / .12 | .35 / .12 |

### BUILDING — A1–A30, AE · POST-FIRM[5]

| ELEVATION DIFFERENCE | 3 OR MORE FLOORS NO BASEMENT/ENCLOSURE/CRAWLSPACE[5,6] | 3 OR MORE FLOORS WITH BASEMENT/ENCLOSURE/CRAWLSPACE[5,6] |
|---|---|---|
| +4 | .35 / .048 | .30 / .048 |
| +3 | .40 / .048 | .34 / .048 |
| +2 | .58 / .048 | .40 / .048 |
| +1 | 1.05 / .064 | .56 / .064 |
| 0 | 2.40 / .078 | 1.44 / .078 |
| −1[6,7] | 6.10 / .180 | 3.48 / .152 |
| −2 | SUBMIT FOR RATE | |

### CONTENTS — A1–A30, AE · POST-FIRM[5]

| ELEVATION DIFFERENCE | LOWEST FLOOR ONLY - ABOVE GROUND LEVEL (NO BASEMENT/ ENCLOSURE/CRAWLSPACE[6]) | LOWEST FLOOR ABOVE GROUND LEVEL AND HIGHER (NO BASEMENT/ENCLOSURE/ CRAWLSPACE[6]) | BASEMENT/ENCLOSURE/ CRAWLSPACE[6] AND ABOVE | ABOVE GROUND LEVEL MORE THAN 1 FULL FLOOR |
|---|---|---|---|---|
| +4 | .38 / .12 | .38 / .12 | .38 / .12 | .35 / .12 |
| +3 | .38 / .12 | .38 / .12 | .38 / .12 | .35 / .12 |
| +2 | .38 / .12 | .38 / .12 | .38 / .12 | .35 / .12 |
| +1 | .54 / .12 | .41 / .12 | .38 / .12 | .35 / .12 |
| 0 | 1.03 / .12 | .77 / .12 | .38 / .12 | .35 / .12 |
| −1[7,8] | 2.37 / .27 | 1.80 / .18 | .59 / .12 | .35 / .12 |
| −2 | SUBMIT FOR RATE | | | .35 / .12 |

1. Any policy designated as SRL is subject to the SRL premium. Refer to Table 7D, Severe Repetitive Loss Premium, in this section.
2. Pre-FIRM construction refers to a building that has a start of construction date or substantial improvement date on or before 12/31/74, or before the effective date of the initial FIRM, whichever is later. If there has been a lapse in coverage, refer to Condo Table 2B, Pre-FIRM Subsidized Rate Ineligibility Determination, to confirm whether Pre-FIRM subsidized rates can be used.
3. Refer to the Pre-FIRM rating hierarchy guidance and chart in Condo Table 2C to determine which Pre-FIRM rate table to use.
4. Pre-FIRM buildings may use Post-FIRM elevation rating if more favorable to the insured. However, when the lowest floor elevation is below the BFE, follow the Submit-for-Rate procedures for policy processing.
5. Pre-FIRM elevated buildings with or without enclosure/crawlspace must use the "No Basement/Enclosure/Crawlspace" columns. Use Appendix C: Lowest Floor Guide in this manual to determine the lowest floor elevation for rating. Unfinished partial enclosures below a Pre-FIRM building that are used solely for parking, storage, and building access and are located below the BFE are eligible for Special Rate Consideration.
6. Includes subgrade crawlspace.
7. Use Submit-for-Rate procedures if there is an elevator below the BFE regardless of whether there is an enclosure or not.
8. If the lowest floor of a crawlspace or subgrade crawlspace is −1, use submit-for-rate procedures (Pre-FIRM or Post-FIRM). If the lowest floor of an enclosure below the elevated floor of a Post-FIRM building is −1, also use submit-for-rate procedures.

## CONDO TABLE 3B. RCBAP HIGH-RISE CONDOMINIUM RATES PRE-FIRM SUBSTANTIAL IMPROVEMENT ON OR AFTER APRIL 1, 2015[1,2,3,4]

ANNUAL RATES PER $100 OF COVERAGE (Basic/Additional)

### BUILDING

**REGULAR PROGRAM PRE-FIRM**

| BUILDING TYPE | A, A1-A30, AE, AO, AH, D | V, VE | A99, B, C, X |
|---|---|---|---|
| NO BASEMENT/ENCLOSURE | 4.02 /1.103 | 5.11 /2.750 | 1.33 / .075 |
| WITH BASEMENT | 4.24 /1.554 | 5.43 /5.862 | 1.61 / .099 |
| WITH ENCLOSURE | 4.24 /1.103 | 5.43 /2.838 | 1.40 / .075 |
| ELEVATED ON CRAWLSPACE | 4.02 /1.103 | 5.11 /2.750 | 1.33 / .075 |
| NON-ELEVATED WITH SUBGRADE CRAWLSPACE | 4.02 /1.103 | 5.11 /2.750 | 1.33 / .075 |

### CONTENTS

**REGULAR PROGRAM PRE-FIRM**

| CONTENTS LOCATION | A, A1-A30, AE, AO, AH, D | V, VE | A99, B, C, X |
|---|---|---|---|
| BASEMENT/SUBGRADE CRAWLSPACE AND ABOVE | 4.52 / 4.89 | 5.84 /11.94 | 2.17 / .82 |
| ENCLOSURE/CRAWLSPACE AND ABOVE | 4.52 / 5.84 | 5.84 /14.06 | 2.17 / .93 |
| LOWEST FLOOR ONLY - ABOVE GROUND LEVEL | 4.52 / 5.84 | 5.84 /14.06 | 1.73 / .86 |
| LOWEST FLOOR ABOVE GROUND LEVEL AND HIGHER FLOORS | 4.52 / 4.04 | 5.84 /12.37 | 1.73 / .55 |
| ABOVE GROUND LEVEL MORE THAN 1 FULL FLOOR | .35 / .12 | .59 /51 | .35 / .12 |

1. Use this table to rate a Pre-FIRM building that has been substantially improved on or after April 1, 2015. If there has been a lapse in coverage, refer to Condo Table 3A, Pre-FIRM Subsidized Rate Ineligibility Determination, to confirm whether Pre-FIRM subsidized rates can be used.
2. Refer to the Pre-FIRM rating guidance hierarchy and chart in Condo Table 2C to determine which Pre-FIRM rate table to use.
3. Pre-FIRM buildings may use Post-FIRM elevation rating if more favorable to the insured. However, when the lowest floor elevation is below the BFE, follow the Submit-for-Rate procedures for policy processing.
4. Any policy designated as SRL is subject to the SRL premium. Refer to Table 7D, Severe Repetitive Loss Premium, in this section.

## CONDO TABLE 3C. RCBAP HIGH-RISE CONDOMINIUM RATES[1]

ANNUAL RATES PER $100 OF COVERAGE (Basic/Additional)

### AO, AH POST-FIRM
### NO BASEMENT/ENCLOSURE/CRAWLSPACE/SUBGRADE CRAWLSPACE BUILDINGS[2]

| | BUILDING | CONTENTS |
|---|---|---|
| WITH CERTIFICATION OF COMPLIANCE OR EC[3] | .95 / .058 | .47 / .12 |
| WITHOUT CERTIFICATION OF COMPLIANCE OR EC[4,9] | 2.88 / .094 | 1.05 / .15 |

### POST-FIRM UNNUMBERED A ZONE
### WITHOUT BASEMENT/ENCLOSURE/CRAWLSPACE/SUBGRADE CRAWLSPACE[2,5]

| ELEVATION DIFFERENCE | BUILDING | CONTENTS[6] | TYPE OF EC |
|---|---|---|---|
| +5 OR MORE | .88 / .070 | .34 / .08 | NO BFE[7] |
| +2 TO +4 | 1.80 / .082 | .80 / .09 | |
| +1 | 3.44 / .190 | 1.45 / .10 | |
| 0 OR BELOW | *** | *** | |
| +2 OR MORE | .75 / .058 | .33 / .08 | WITH BFE[8] |
| 0 TO +1 | 2.85 / .082 | 1.22 / .09 | |
| -1 | 6.66 / .240 | 2.75 / .16 | |
| -2 OR BELOW | *** | *** | |
| NO EC[9] | 8.34 / 1.30 | 3.52 / .80 | NO EC |

1. Any policy designated as SRL is subject to the SRL premium. Refer to Table 7D, Severe Repetitive Loss Premium, in this section.
2. Post-FIRM buildings in zones A, AO, or AH with basement, enclosure, crawlspace, or subgrade crawlspace: follow Submit-for-Rate procedures. Pre-FIRM buildings in AO or AH Zones with basement/enclosure/crawlspace/subgrade crawlspace at or above the BFE or Base Flood Depth are to use the "With Certification of Compliance or EC" rates and would not have to follow Submit- for-Rate procedures.
3. "With Certification of Compliance or EC" rates are to be used when the EC shows that the lowest floor elevation used for rating is equal to or greater than the community's elevation requirement, or when there is a Letter of Compliance. This rule applies to all building types, including buildings with basement/enclosure/crawlspace/subgrade crawlspace.
4. "Without Certification of Compliance or EC" rates are to be used on Post-FIRM buildings when the EC shows that the lowest floor elevation is less than the community's elevation requirement. These rates may be used for Pre-FIRM buildings when more favorable to the insured than Pre-FIRM subsidized rates.
5. Pre-FIRM buildings in Unnumbered A Zones with basement, enclosure, or crawlspace may use this table if the rates are more favorable to the insured. For buildings with subgrade crawlspace, follow the optional Submit-for-Rate procedures.
6. For elevation-rated policies, when contents are located 1 floor or more above the lowest floor used for rating, use .35/.12.
7. NO BFE: Elevation difference is the measured distance between the lowest floor of the building and the highest adjacent grade next to the building.
8. WITH BFE: Elevation difference is the measured distance between the lowest floor of the building and the BFE provided by the community or registered professional engineer, surveyor, or architect.
9. For policies with effective dates on or after Oct. 1, 2011, the NO EC rates apply only to renewals and transfers.

***Use the ***Specific Rating Guidelines*** (SRG) manual.**

## CONDO TABLE 3D. RCBAP HIGH-RISE CONDOMINIUM RATES

ANNUAL RATES PER $100 OF COVERAGE (Basic/Additional)

### AR AND AR DUAL ZONES[1]

#### BUILDING – PRE-FIRM[2] AND POST-FIRM NOT ELEVATION-RATED

| BUILDING TYPE | RATES |
|---|---|
| No Basement/Enclosure | 1.33 / .075 |
| With Basement | 1.61 / .099 |
| With Enclosure | 1.40 / .075 |
| Elevated on Crawlspace | 1.33 / .075 |
| Non-Elevated with Subgrade Crawlspace | 1.33 / .075 |

#### CONTENTS – PRE-FIRM[2] AND POST-FIRM NOT ELEVATION-RATED

| CONTENTS LOCATION | RATES |
|---|---|
| Basement/Subgrade Crawlspace and above | 2.17 / .82 |
| Enclosure/Crawlspace and above | 2.17 / .93 |
| Lowest floor only – above ground level | 1.73 / .86 |
| Lowest floor above ground level and higher floors | 1.73 / .55 |
| Above ground level more than 1 full floor | .35 / .12 |

#### BUILDING – PRE-FIRM AND POST-FIRM ELEVATION-RATED

| ELEVATION DIFFERENCE | 3 OR MORE FLOORS NO BASEMENT/ENCLOSURE/CRAWLSPACE[3] | 3 OR MORE FLOORS WITH BASEMENT/ENCLOSURE/CRAWLSPACE[3] |
|---|---|---|
| +4 | .35 / .048 | .30 / .048 |
| +3 | .40 / .048 | .34 / .048 |
| +2 | .58 / .048 | .40 / .048 |
| +1 | 1.05 / .064 | .56 / .064 |
| 0 | 1.33 / .075 | 1.44 / .078 |
| −1[4] | SEE FOOTNOTE 4 | |

#### CONTENTS – PRE-FIRM AND POST-FIRM ELEVATION-RATED

| ELEVATION DIFFERENCE | LOWEST FLOOR ONLY – ABOVE GROUND LEVEL (NO BASEMENT/ENCLOSURE/CRAWLSPACE[2]) | LOWEST FLOOR ABOVE GROUND LEVEL AND HIGHER (NO BASEMENT/ENCLOSURE/CRAWLSPACE[2]) | BASEMENT/ENCLOSURE/CRAWLSPACE[2] AND ABOVE | ABOVE GROUND LEVEL – MORE THAN 1 FULL FLOOR |
|---|---|---|---|---|
| +4 | .38 / .12 | .38 / .12 | .38 / .12 | .35 / .12 |
| +3 | .38 / .12 | .38 / .12 | .38 / .12 | .35 / .12 |
| +2 | .38 / .12 | .38 / .12 | .38 / .12 | .35 / .12 |
| +1 | .54 / .12 | .41 / .12 | .38 / .12 | .35 / .12 |
| 0 | 1.03 / .12 | .77 / .12 | .38 / .12 | .35 / .12 |
| −1[4] | SEE FOOTNOTE 4 | | | |

1. Any policy designated as SRL is subject to the SRL premium. Refer to Table 7D, Severe Repetitive Loss Premium, in this section.
2. Pre-FIRM construction refers to a building that has a start of construction date or substantial improvement date on or before 12/31/74, or before the effective date of the initial FIRM, whichever is later.
3. Includes subgrade crawlspace.
4. Use Pre-FIRM Not Elevation-Rated AR and AR Dual Zones Rate Table above.

## CONDO TABLE 3E. RCBAP HIGH-RISE CONDOMINIUM RATES [1,2]

ANNUAL RATES PER $100 OF COVERAGE (Basic/Additional)

### REGULAR PROGRAM — 1975–1981[3] POST-FIRM CONSTRUCTION[4]
### FIRM ZONES V1–V30, VE — BUILDING RATES

| ELEVATION OF LOWEST FLOOR ABOVE OR BELOW THE BFE | BUILDING TYPE | |
|---|---|---|
| | 3 OR MORE FLOORS NO BASEMENT/ ENCLOSURE/CRAWLSPACE[5,6] | 3 OR MORE FLOORS WITH BASEMENT/ ENCLOSURE/CRAWLSPACE[5,6] |
| 0[7] | 7.23 / .475 | 7.23 / .475 |
| −1[8] | 11.00 /1.775 | 11.00 / 1.363 |
| −2 | *** | *** |

### 1975–1981 POST-FIRM CONSTRUCTION
### FIRM ZONES V1–V30, VE — CONTENTS RATES

| ELEVATION OF LOWEST FLOOR ABOVE OR BELOW THE BFE | CONTENTS LOCATION | | | |
|---|---|---|---|---|
| | LOWEST FLOOR ONLY – ABOVE GROUND LEVEL (NO BASEMENT/ ENCLOSURE/CRAWLSPACE[5]) | LOWEST FLOOR ABOVE GROUND LEVEL AND HIGHER FLOORS (NO BASEMENT/ ENCLOSURE/CRAWLSPACE[5]) | BASEMENT/ ENCLOSURE/ CRAWLSPACE[54] AND ABOVE | ABOVE GROUND LEVEL – MORE THAN 1 FULL FLOOR |
| 0[7] | 5.87 /2.85 | 5.87 /2.74 | 3.99 /2.42 | .56 /.25 |
| −1[8] | 8.92 /8.92 | 8.92 /8.92 | 4.70 /2.53 | .56 /.25 |
| −2 | *** | *** | *** | *** |

1. Pre-FIRM elevated buildings with or without enclosure/crawlspace must use the "No Basement/Enclosure/Crawlspace" columns. Use Appendix C: Lowest Floor Guide to determine the lowest floor elevation for rating. Unfinished partial enclosures below a Pre-FIRM building that are used solely for parking, storage and building access and are located below the BFE are eligible for Special Rate Consideration.
2. Any policy designated as SRL is subject to the SRL premium. Refer to Table 7D, Severe Repetitive Loss Premium, in this section.
3. Policies for 1975 through 1981 Post-FIRM and Pre-FIRM buildings in zones VE and V1–V30 will be allowed to use the Post-'81 V-Zone rate table if the rates are more favorable to the insured. Refer to instructions in the How to Write section of this manual for V-Zone Optional Rating.
4. For 1981 Post-FIRM construction rating, refer to Condo Table 5A.
5. Includes subgrade crawlspace.
6. Use Submit-for-Rate procedures if there is an elevator below the BFE regardless of whether there is an enclosure or not.
7. These rates are to be used if the lowest floor of the building is at or above the BFE.
8. Use Submit-for-Rate procedures if the enclosure below the lowest floor of an elevated building, which is used for rating, is 1 or more feet below the BFE

*****Use the SRG manual.**

### REGULAR PROGRAM 1975–1981 POST-FIRM CONSTRUCTION
### UNNUMBERED V ZONE — ELEVATED BUILDINGS

| SUBMIT FOR RATING |
|---|

## CONDO TABLE 4A. RCBAP LOW-RISE CONDOMINIUM RATES[1]

(Including Townhouse/Rowhouse)

ANNUAL RATES PER $100 OF COVERAGE (Basic/Additional)

### REGULAR PROGRAM – PRE-FIRM CONSTRUCTION RATES[2,3,4]

For Pre-FIRM 1–4 Family SRL property renewals, use Table 4B.

| | FIRM ZONES: | A, A1–A30, AE, AO, AH, D | | V, VE | | A99, B, C, X | |
|---|---|---|---|---|---|---|---|
| | | BUILDING | CONTENTS | BUILDING | CONTENTS | BUILDING | CONTENTS |
| BUILDING TYPE | NO BASEMENT/ENCLOSURE | 1.17 /1.16 | 1.64 /2.19 | 1.59 /2.93 | 2.10 /5.38 | .83 /.25 | 1.31 /.42 |
| | WITH BASEMENT | 1.29 /1.43 | 1.64 /2.19 | 1.69 /5.08 | 2.10 /5.08 | .90 /.35 | 1.48 /.51 |
| | WITH ENCLOSURE | 1.29 /1.69 | 1.64 /2.19 | 1.69 /5.51 | 2.10 /5.51 | .90 /.39 | 1.48 /.61 |
| | ELEVATED ON CRAWLSPACE | 1.17 /1.16 | 1.64 /2.19 | 1.59 /2.93 | 2.10 /5.38 | .83 /.25 | 1.31 /.42 |
| | NON-ELEVATED WITH SUBGRADE CRAWLSPACE | 1.17 /1.16 | 1.64 /2.19 | 1.59 /2.93 | 2.10 /5.38 | .83 /.25 | 1.31 /.42 |

### REGULAR PROGRAM – POST-FIRM CONSTRUCTION RATES

| | FIRM ZONES: | A99, B, C, X | | D | |
|---|---|---|---|---|---|
| | | BUILDING | CONTENTS | BUILDING | CONTENTS |
| BUILDING TYPE | NO BASEMENT/ENCLOSURE | .83 / .25 | 1.31 /.42 | 2.75 / .46 | 1.57 / .29 |
| | WITH BASEMENT | .90 / .35 | 1.48 /.51 | *** | *** |
| | WITH ENCLOSURE | .90 / .39 | 1.48 /.61 | *** | *** |
| | ELEVATED ON CRAWLSPACE | .83 / .25 | 1.31 /.42 | 2.75 / .46 | 1.57 / .29 |
| | NON-ELEVATED WITH SUBGRADE CRAWLSPACE | .83 / .25 | 1.31 /.42 | 2.75 / .46 | 1.57 / .29 |

| FIRM ZONES: | AO, AH (NO BASEMENT/ENCLOSURE/CRAWLSPACE BUILDINGS ONLY[4]) | |
|---|---|---|
| | BUILDING | CONTENTS |
| WITH CERTIFICATION OF COMPLIANCE OR EC[6] | .24 / .08 | .38 / .12 |
| WITHOUT CERTIFICATION OF COMPLIANCE OR EC[7,8] | 1.56 / .26 | .84 / .15 |

1. Any policy designated as SRL is subject to the SRL premium. Refer to Table 7D, Severe Repetitive Loss Premium, in this section.
2. Pre-FIRM construction refers to a building that has a start of construction date or substantial improvement date on or before 12/31/74, or before the effective date of the initial FIRM, whichever is later. If there has been a lapse in coverage, refer to Condo Table 2B, Pre-FIRM Subsidized Rate Ineligibility Determination, to confirm whether Pre-FIRM subsidized rates can be used.
3. Refer to the Pre-FIRM rating hierarchy guidance and chart in Condo Table 3A to determine which Pre-FIRM rate table to use.
4. Pre-FIRM buildings may use Post-FIRM elevation rating if more favorable to the insured. However, when the lowest floor elevation is below the BFE, follow the Submit-for-Rate procedures for policy processing.
5. Zones AO, AH Buildings with basement/enclosure/crawlspace/subgrade crawlspace: follow Submit-for-Rate procedures. Pre-FIRM buildings in AO or AH Zones with basement/enclosure/crawlspace/subgrade crawlspace at or above the BFE or Base Flood Depth are to use the "With Certification of Compliance or EC" rates and would not have to follow Submit-for-Rate procedures.
6. "With Certification of Compliance or EC" rates are to be used when the EC shows that the lowest floor elevation used for rating is equal to or greater than the community's elevation requirement, or when there is a Letter of Compliance. This rule applies to all building types, including buildings with basement/enclosure/crawlspace/subgrade crawlspace.
7. "Without Certification of Compliance or EC" rates are to be used on Post-FIRM buildings when the EC shows that the lowest floor elevation is less than the community's elevation requirement. These rates may be used for Pre-FIRM buildings when more favorable to the insured than Pre-FIRM subsidized rates.
8. For transfers and renewals of existing business where there is no Letter of Compliance or EC in the company's file, these rates can continue to be used. For new business effective on or after Oct. 1, 2011, the provisions of footnote 4 apply.

*****Use the SRG manual.**

## CONDO TABLE 4B. RCBAP LOW-RISE CONDOMINIUM RATES 1–4 FAMILY SRL PROPERTIES[1]

(Including Townhouse/Rowhouse)

ANNUAL RATES PER $100 OF COVERAGE (Basic/Additional)

### REGULAR PROGRAM – PRE-FIRM CONSTRUCTION RATES[2,3,4,5]

| | FIRM ZONES: | A, A1-A30, AE, AO, AH, D | | V, VE | | A99, B, C, X | |
|---|---|---|---|---|---|---|---|
| | | BUILDING | CONTENTS | BUILDING | CONTENTS | BUILDING | CONTENTS |
| BUILDING TYPE | NO BASEMENT/ENCLOSURE | 3.04 /3.31 | 4.24 /6.17 | 4.07 / 8.42 | 5.39 /15.50 | .83 /.25 | 1.31 /.42 |
| | WITH BASEMENT | 3.29 /4.07 | 4.24 /5.18 | 4.34 /14.59 | 5.39 /14.58 | .90 /.35 | 1.48 /.51 |
| | WITH ENCLOSURE | 3.29 /4.85 | 4.24 /5.30 | 4.34 /15.92 | 5.39 /15.89 | .90 /.39 | 1.48 /.61 |
| | ELEVATED ON CRAWLSPACE | 3.04 /3.31 | 4.24 /6.17 | 4.07 / 8.42 | 5.39 /15.50 | .83 /.25 | 1.31 /.42 |
| | NON-ELEVATED WITH SUBGRADE CRAWLSPACE | 3.04 /3.31 | 4.24 /6.17 | 4.07 / 8.42 | 5.39 /15.50 | .83 /.25 | 1.31 /.42 |

1. For additional guidance, refer to Appendix I: Severe Repetitive Loss Properties in this manual.
2. Pre-FIRM construction refers to a building that has a date of construction or substantial improvement date on or before 12/31/74, or before the effective date of the initial FIRM, whichever is later. If there has been a lapse in coverage, refer to Condo Table 3A, Pre-FIRM Subsidized Rate Ineligibility Determination, to confirm whether Pre-FIRM subsidized rates can be used.
3. Refer to Condo Table 3A, Pre-FIRM Rate Table Hierarchy, to determine which Pre-FIRM rate table to use.
4. Pre-FIRM buildings may use Post-FIRM elevation rating if more favorable to the insured. However, when the lowest floor elevation is below the BFE, follow the Submit-for-Rate procedures for policy processing.
5. Any policy designated as SRL is subject to the SRL premium. Refer to Table 7D, Severe Repetitive Loss Premium, in this section.

## CONDO TABLE 4C. RCBAP LOW-RISE CONDOMINIUM RATES PRE-FIRM SUBSTANTIAL IMPROVEMENT ON OR AFTER APRIL 1, 2015[1,2,3,4]

ANNUAL RATES PER $100 OF COVERAGE (Basic/Additional)

### REGULAR PROGRAM – PRE-FIRM CONSTRUCTION RATES

| | FIRM ZONES: | A, A1–A30, AE, AO, AH, D | | V, VE | | A99, B, C, X | |
|---|---|---|---|---|---|---|---|
| | | BUILDING | CONTENTS | BUILDING | CONTENTS | BUILDING | CONTENTS |
| BUILDING TYPE | NO BASEMENT/ENCLOSURE | 3.28 /3.20 | 4.52 /6.06 | 4.39 / 8.21 | 5.84 /15.11 | .83 /.25 | 1.31 /.42 |
| | WITH BASEMENT | 3.49 /3.95 | 4.52 /5.06 | 4.69 /14.20 | 5.84 /14.20 | .90 /.35 | 1.48 /.51 |
| | WITH ENCLOSURE | 3.49 /4.69 | 4.52 /5.21 | 4.69 /15.46 | 5.84 /15.46 | .90 /.39 | 1.48 /.61 |
| | ELEVATED ON CRAWLSPACE | 3.28 /3.20 | 4.52 /6.06 | 4.39 / 8.21 | 5.84 /15.11 | .83 /.25 | 1.31 /.42 |
| | NON-ELEVATED WITH SUBGRADE CRAWLSPACE | 3.28 /3.20 | 4.52 /6.06 | 4.39 / 8.21 | 5.84 /15.11 | .83 /.25 | 1.31 /.42 |

1. Use this table to rate a Pre-FIRM building that has been substantially improved on or after April 1, 2015. If there has been a lapse in coverage, refer to Condo Table 3A in this section of the manual, Pre-FIRM Subsidized Rate Ineligibility Determination to confirm whether Pre- FIRM subsidized rates can be used.
2. Refer to the Pre-FIRM rating guidance hierarchy and chart in Condo Table 3A to determine which Pre-FIRM rate table to use.
3. Pre-FIRM buildings may use Post-FIRM elevation rating if more favorable to the insured. However, when the lowest floor elevation is below the BFE, follow the Submit-for-Rate procedures for policy processing.
4. Any policy designated as SRL is subject to the SRL premium. Refer to Table 7D, Severe Repetitive Loss Premium, in this section.

## CONDO TABLE 4D. RCBAP LOW-RISE CONDOMINIUM RATES[1,2]

(Including Townhouse/Rowhouse)

ANNUAL RATES PER $100 OF COVERAGE (Basic/Additional)

### REGULAR PROGRAM – POST-FIRM CONSTRUCTION
### FIRM ZONES A1–A30, AE — BUILDING RATES

| ELEVATION OF LOWEST FLOOR ABOVE OR BELOW THE BFE[3] | BUILDING TYPE | | |
|---|---|---|---|
| | 1 FLOOR NO BASEMENT/ ENCLOSURE/CRAWLSPACE[4] | MORE THAN 1 FLOOR NO BASEMENT/ENCLOSURE/ CRAWLSPACE[4] | MORE THAN 1 FLOOR WITH BASEMENT/ENCLOSURE/ CRAWLSPACE[4] |
| +4 | .28 / .13 | .27 / .08 | .22 / .08 |
| +3 | .32 / .13 | .31 / .08 | .25 / .08 |
| +2 | .46 / .13 | .44 / .08 | .36 / .08 |
| +1 | .84 / .18 | .80 / .08 | .64 / .09 |
| 0 | 1.92 / .30 | 1.79 / .08 | 1.13 / .14 |
| −1[5] | 4.58 / .69 | 4.40 / .14 | 1.50 / .15 |
| −2 | *** | *** | *** |

### FIRM ZONES A1–A30, AE — CONTENTS RATES

| ELEVATION OF LOWEST FLOOR ABOVE OR BELOW THE BFE[3] | CONTENTS LOCATION | | | |
|---|---|---|---|---|
| | LOWEST FLOOR ONLY – ABOVE GROUND LEVEL (NO BASEMENT/ENCLOSURE/ CRAWLSPACE[4]) | LOWEST FLOOR ABOVE GROUND LEVEL AND HIGHER FLOORS (NO BASEMENT/ ENCLOSURE/CRAWLSPACE[4]) | BASEMENT/ ENCLOSURE/ CRAWLSPACE[4] AND ABOVE | ABOVE GROUND LEVEL – MORE THAN 1 FULL FLOOR |
| +4 | .38 /.12 | .31 /.12 | .38 /.12 | .29 /.12 |
| +3 | .38 /.12 | .31 /.12 | .38 /.12 | .29 /.12 |
| +2 | .38 /.12 | .31 /.12 | .38 /.12 | .29 /.12 |
| +1 | .54 /.12 | .46 /.12 | .41 /.12 | .34 /.12 |
| 0 | 1.03 /.12 | .91 /.12 | .50 /.12 | .45 /.12 |
| −1[5] | 2.37 /.28 | 2.09 /.18 | .72 /.12 | .45 /.12 |
| −2 | *** | *** | *** | .45 /.12 |

1. Pre-FIRM elevated buildings with or without enclosure/crawlspace must use the "No Basement/Enclosure/Crawlspace" columns. Use Appendix C: Lowest Floor Guide to determine the lowest floor elevation for rating. Unfinished partial enclosures below a Pre-FIRM building that are used solely for parking, storage and building access and are located below the BFE are eligible for Special Rate Consideration.
2. Any policy designated as SRL is subject to the SRL premium. Refer to Table 7D, Severe Repetitive Loss Premium, in this section.
3. If the Lowest Floor is −1 or lower because of an attached garage and the building is described and rated as a single-family dwelling, refer to the Lowest Floor Determination subsection in Appendix C: Lowest Floor Guide in this manual or contact the insurer for rating guidance; rate may be lower.
4. Includes subgrade crawlspace.
5. If the lowest floor of a crawlspace or subgrade crawlspace is −1, use submit-for-rate procedures (Pre-FIRM or Post-FIRM). If the lowest floor of an enclosure below the elevated floor of a Post-FIRM building is −1, also use submit-for-rate procedures.

***Use the SRG manual.**

## CONDO TABLE 4E. RCBAP LOW-RISE CONDOMINIUM RATES

**(Including Townhouse/Rowhouse)**

ANNUAL RATES PER $100 OF COVERAGE (Basic/Additional)

### REGULAR PROGRAM – POST-FIRM CONSTRUCTION RATES
### UNNUMBERED ZONE A – WITHOUT BASEMENT/ENCLOSURE/CRAWLSPACE[1,2,3]

| ELEVATION DIFFERENCE | BUILDING | CONTENTS[4] | TYPE OF EC |
|---|---|---|---|
| +5 OR MORE | .59 / .12 | .57 / .10 | NO BFE[5] |
| +2 TO +4 | 1.71 / .19 | .97 / .10 | |
| +1 | 3.30 / .24 | 1.99 / .12 | |
| 0 OR BELOW | *** | *** | |
| +2 OR MORE | .58 / .10 | .57 / .10 | WITH BFE[6] |
| 0 TO +1 | 2.72 / .21 | 1.51 / .11 | |
| −1 | 6.44 / .36 | 3.62 / .16 | |
| −2 OR BELOW | *** | *** | |
| NO EC[7] | 8.05 / 1.30 | 5.17 / .80 | NO EC |

1. Zone A buildings with basement/enclosure without proper openings/crawlspace without proper openings/subgrade crawlspace: follow Submit-for-Rate procedures in the How to Write section of this manual.
2. Pre-FIRM buildings with basement, enclosure, or crawlspace may use this table if the rates are more favorable to the insured. For buildings with subgrade crawlspace, follow the optional Submit-for-Rate procedures.
3. Any policy designated as SRL is subject to the SRL premium. Refer to Table 7D, Severe Repetitive Loss Premium, in this section.
4. For elevation-rated policies, when contents are located 1 floor or more above lowest floor used for rating, use .35/.12.
5. No BFE: Elevation difference is the measured distance between the lowest floor of the building and the highest adjacent grade next to the building.
6. With BFE: Elevation difference is the measured distance between the lowest floor of the building and the BFE provided by the community or registered professional engineer, surveyor, or architect.
7. For policies with effective dates on or after Oct. 1, 2011, the No EC rates apply only to renewals and transfers.

*****Use the SRG manual.**

## CONDO TABLE 4F. RCBAP LOW-RISE CONDOMINIUM RATES[1]

(Including Townhouse/Rowhouse)

ANNUAL RATES PER $100 OF COVERAGE (Basic/Additional)

### AR AND AR DUAL ZONES

### REGULAR PROGRAM – PRE-FIRM[2] AND POST-FIRM NOT ELEVATION-RATED RATES

| BUILDING TYPE | BUILDING | CONTENTS |
|---|---|---|
| NO BASEMENT/ENCLOSURE | .83 / .25 | 1.31 / .42 |
| WITH BASEMENT | .90 / .35 | 1.48 / .51 |
| WITH ENCLOSURE | .90 / .39 | 1.48 / .61 |
| ELEVATED ON CRAWLSPACE | .83 / .25 | 1.31 / .42 |
| NON-ELEVATED WITH SUBGRADE CRAWLSPACE | .83 / .25 | 1.31 / .42 |

### REGULAR PROGRAM – PRE-FIRM AND POST-FIRM ELEVATION-RATED RATES

#### BUILDING RATES

| ELEVATION OF LOWEST FLOOR ABOVE OR BELOW THE BFE | BUILDING TYPE | | |
|---|---|---|---|
| | 1 FLOOR NO BASEMENT/ ENCLOSURE/CRAWLSPACE[2] | MORE THAN 1 FLOOR NO BASEMENT/ENCLOSURE/ CRAWLSPACE[3] | MORE THAN 1 FLOOR WITH BASEMENT/ENCLOSURE/ CRAWLSPACE[3] |
| +4 | .28 / .13 | .27 / .08 | .22 / .08 |
| +3 | .32 / .13 | .31 / .08 | .25 / .08 |
| +2 | .46 / .13 | .44 / .08 | .36 / .08 |
| +1 | .83 / .18 | .80 / .08 | .64 / .09 |
| 0 | .83 / .25 | .83 / .15 | .90 / .14 |
| −1[4] | SEE FOOTNOTE 4 | | |

#### CONTENTS RATES

| ELEVATION OF LOWEST FLOOR ABOVE OR BELOW THE BFE | CONTENTS LOCATION | | | |
|---|---|---|---|---|
| | LOWEST FLOOR ONLY – ABOVE GROUND LEVEL (NO BASEMENT/ ENCLOSURE/ CRAWLSPACE[3]) | LOWEST FLOOR ABOVE GROUND LEVEL AND HIGHER FLOORS (NO BASEMENT/ENCLOSURE/ CRAWLSPACE[3]) | BASEMENT/ENCLOSURE/ CRAWLSPACE[3] AND ABOVE | ABOVE GROUND LEVEL – MORE THAN 1 FULL FLOOR |
| +4 | .38 / .12 | .31 / .12 | .38 / .12 | .29 / .12 |
| +3 | .38 / .12 | .31 / .12 | .38 / .12 | .29 / .12 |
| +2 | .38 / .12 | .31 / .12 | .38 / .12 | .29 / .12 |
| +1 | .54 / .12 | .46 / .12 | .41 / .12 | .34 / .12 |
| 0 | 1.03 / .12 | .91 / .12 | .50 / .12 | .45 / .12 |
| −1[4] | SEE FOOTNOTE 4 | | | |

1. Any policy designated as SRL is subject to the SRL premium. Refer to Table 7D, Severe Repetitive Loss Premium, in this section.
2. Pre-FIRM construction refers to a building that has a start of construction date or substantial improvement date on or before 12/31/74, or before the effective date of the initial FIRM, whichever is later.
3. Includes subgrade crawlspace.
4. Use Pre-FIRM Not Elevation-Rated AR and AR Dual Zones Rate Table above.

## CONDO TABLE 4G. RCBAP LOW-RISE CONDOMINIUM RATES[1,2]

(Including Townhouse/Rowhouse)

ANNUAL RATES PER $100 OF COVERAGE (Basic/Additional)

### REGULAR PROGRAM — 1975–1981 POST-FIRM CONSTRUCTION[3,4] FIRM ZONES V1–V30, VE — BUILDING RATES

| ELEVATION OF LOWEST FLOOR ABOVE OR BELOW THE BFE | BUILDING TYPE | | |
|---|---|---|---|
| | 1 FLOOR NO BASEMENT/ ENCLOSURE/CRAWLSPACE[5] | MORE THAN 1 FLOOR NO BASEMENT/ENCLOSURE/ CRAWLSPACE[5] | MORE THAN 1 FLOOR WITH BASEMENT/ENCLOSURE/ CRAWLSPACE[5] |
| 0[6] | 7.23 / 1.60 | 6.98 / 1.60 | 6.02 / 1.60 |
| –1[7] | 11.00 / 6.64 | 11.00 / 6.64 | 8.32 / 6.03 |
| –2 | *** | *** | *** |

### REGULAR PROGRAM — 1975–1981 POST-FIRM CONSTRUCTION[3,4] FIRM ZONES V1–V30, VE — CONTENTS RATES

| ELEVATION OF LOWEST FLOOR ABOVE OR BELOW THE BFE | CONTENTS LOCATION | | | |
|---|---|---|---|---|
| | LOWEST FLOOR ONLY – ABOVE GROUND LEVEL (NO BASEMENT/ENCLOSURE/ CRAWLSPACE[5]) | LOWEST FLOOR ABOVE GROUND LEVEL AND HIGHER FLOORS (NO BASEMENT/ ENCLOSURE/CRAWLSPACE[5]) | BASEMENT/ ENCLOSURE/ CRAWLSPACE[5] AND ABOVE | ABOVE GROUND LEVEL – MORE THAN 1 FULL FLOOR |
| 0[6] | 5.87 / 2.99 | 5.87 / 2.87 | 4.18 / 2.53 | .56 / .25 |
| –1[7] | 8.92 / 8.92 | 8.92 / 8.92 | 4.93 / 2.65 | .56 / .25 |
| –2 | *** | *** | *** | .56 / .25 |

1. Pre-FIRM elevated buildings with or without enclosure/crawlspace must use the "No Basement/Enclosure/Crawlspace" columns. Use Appendix C: Lowest Floor Guide to determine the lowest floor elevation for rating. Unfinished partial enclosures below a Pre-FIRM building that are used solely for parking, storage, and building access and are located below the BFE are eligible for Special Rate Consideration.
2. Any policy designated as SRL is subject to the SRL premium. Refer to Table 7D, Severe Repetitive Loss Premium, in this section.
3. Policies for 1975 through 1981 Post-FIRM and Pre-FIRM buildings in zones VE and V1–V30 will be allowed to use the Post-'81 V Zone rate table if the rates are more favorable to the insured. Refer to instructions in the How to Write section for V-Zone Optional Rating.
4. For 1981 Post-FIRM construction rating, refer to Condo Tables 5A and 5B.
5. Includes subgrade crawlspace.
6. These rates are to be used if the lowest floor of the building is at or above the BFE.
7. Use Submit-for-Rate procedures if the enclosure below the lowest floor of an elevated building, which is used for rating, is 1 or more feet below the BFE.

***Use the SRG manual.**

### REGULAR PROGRAM — 1975–1981 POST-FIRM CONSTRUCTION UNNUMBERED V ZONE — ELEVATED BUILDINGS

| SUBMIT FOR RATING |
|---|

## CONDO TABLE 5A. RCBAP HIGH-RISE AND LOW-RISE CONDOMINIUM RATES

(Including Townhouse/Rowhouse)

ANNUAL RATES PER $100 OF COVERAGE

### 1981 POST-FIRM V1–V30, VE ZONE RATES[1,2] ELEVATED BUILDINGS FREE OF OBSTRUCTION[3] BELOW THE BEAM SUPPORTING THE BUILDING'S LOWEST FLOOR

| ELEVATION OF THE BOTTOM OF THE FLOOR BEAM OF THE LOWEST FLOOR ABOVE OR BELOW THE BFE ADJUSTED FOR WAVE HEIGHT AT BUILDING SITE[4] | BUILDING RATE | CONTENTS RATE |
|---|---|---|
| +4 or more | 1.49 | 0.93 |
| +3 | 1.71 | 1.03 |
| +2 | 2.33 | 1.47 |
| +1 | 2.98 | 1.95 |
| 0 | 3.67 | 2.55 |
| −1 | 4.46 | 3.29 |
| −2 | 5.37 | 4.14 |
| −3 | 6.29 | 5.10 |
| −4 or lower | *** | *** |

**Rates above are only for elevated buildings.**
**Use the *Specific Rating Guidelines* manual for non-elevated buildings.**

1. Policies for 1975 through 1981 Post-FIRM and Pre-FIRM buildings in zones VE and V1–V30 will be allowed to use the Post-'81 V-Zone rate table if the rates are more favorable to the insured. Refer to instructions in the How to Write section for V-Zone Optional Rating.
2. Any policy designated as SRL is subject to the SRL premium. Refer to Table 7D, Severe Repetitive Loss Premium, in this section.
3. FREE OF OBSTRUCTION – The space below the lowest elevated floor must be completely free of obstructions or any attachment to the building, or may have:
   a. Insect screening, provided that no additional supports are required for the screening; *or*
   b. Wooden or plastic lattice with at least 40% of its area open and made of material no thicker than ½ inch; *or*
   c. Wooden or plastic slats or shutters with at least 40% of their area open and made of material no thicker than 1 inch.
   d. One solid breakaway wall or a garage door, with the remaining sides of the enclosure constructed of insect screening, wooden or plastic lattice, slats, or shutters.

   Any of these systems must be designed and installed to collapse under stress without jeopardizing the structural support of the building, so that the impact on the building of abnormally high tides or wind-driven water is minimized. Any machinery or equipment below the lowest elevated floor must be at or above the BFE.
4. Wave height adjustment is not required in those cases where the Flood Insurance Rate Map indicates that the map includes wave height.

**NOTE:** For high-rise only, use Submit-for-Rate procedures if there is an elevator below the BFE enclosed with lattice, slats, or shutters (including louvers).

***__Use the SRG manual.__

## CONDO TABLE 5B. RCBAP HIGH-RISE AND LOW-RISE CONDOMINIUM RATES

(Including Townhouse/Rowhouse)

ANNUAL RATES PER $100 OF COVERAGE

### 1981 POST-FIRM V1–V30, VE ZONE RATES[1,2,3] ELEVATED BUILDINGS WITH OBSTRUCTION[4] BELOW THE BEAM SUPPORTING THE BUILDING'S LOWEST FLOOR

| ELEVATION OF THE BOTTOM OF THE FLOOR BEAM OF THE LOWEST FLOOR ABOVE OR BELOW THE BFE ADJUSTED FOR WAVE HEIGHT AT BUILDING SITE[5] | BUILDING RATE | CONTENTS RATE |
|---|---|---|
| +4 or more | 2.49 | 1.27 |
| +3 | 2.95 | 1.34 |
| +2 | 3.50 | 1.82 |
| +1 | 3.99 | 2.29 |
| 0 | 4.74 | 2.98 |
| −1[6] | 5.39 | 3.90 |
| −2[6] | 6.20 | 4.68 |
| −3[6] | 7.08 | 5.57 |
| −4 or lower[5] | *** | *** |

1. Policies for 1975 through 1981 Post-FIRM and Pre-FIRM buildings in zones VE and V1–V30 will be allowed to use the Post-'81 V-Zone rate table if the rates are more favorable to the insured. Refer to instructions in the How to Write section for V-Zone Optional Rating.
2. Rates provided are only for elevated buildings, except those elevated on solid perimeter foundation walls. For buildings elevated on solid perimeter foundation walls, and for non-elevated buildings, use the *Specific Rating Guidelines* manual.
3. Any policy designated as SRL is subject to the SRL premium. Refer to Table 7D, Severe Repetitive Loss Premium, in this section.
4. WITH OBSTRUCTION – The space below has an area of less than 300 square feet with breakaway solid walls or contains equipment below the BFE. If the space below has an area of 300 square feet or more, or if any portion of the space below the elevated floor is enclosed with non-breakaway walls, submit for rating. If the enclosure is at or above the BFE, use the "Free of Obstruction" rate table on the preceding page. The elevation of the bottom enclosure floor is the lowest floor for rating (LFE). Refer to the How to Write section of this manual for details.
5. Wave height adjustment is not required in those cases where the Flood Insurance Rate Map indicates that the map includes wave height.
6. For buildings with obstruction, use Submit-for-Rate procedures if the enclosure below the lowest elevated floor of an elevated building, which is used for rating, is 1 or more feet below the BFE.

*****Use the SRG manual.**

## TABLE 5C. RCBAP HIGH-RISE AND LOW-RISE BUILDING RATES

(Including Townhouse/Rowhouse)

ANNUAL RATES PER $100 OF COVERAGE

### 1981 POST-FIRM V-ZONE RATES

| SUBMIT FOR RATING |
|---|

## CONDO TABLE 6. RCBAP HIGH-RISE AND LOW-RISE CONDOMINIUM RATES

(Including Townhouse/Rowhouse)

### INCREASED COST OF COMPLIANCE (ICC) COVERAGE

All Except Submit-for-Rate Policies[1]
Premiums for $30,000 ICC Coverage

| CONDO RATE TABLE | RATED ZONE | BUILDING TYPE | ELEVATION DIFFERENCE | RCBAP ICC PREMIUM |
|---|---|---|---|---|
| Table 3A | A, AE, A1–A30, AO, AH, V, VE, and V1–V30 | Pre-FIRM subsidized High Rise (HR) rated without elevation | N/A | $56 |
| | A99, B, C, and X | All HR | N/A | $8 |
| | D | Post-FIRM HR No Basement/Enclosure | N/A | $8 |
| | A, AE, A1–A30, AO, AH, V, VE, and V1–V30 | All HR full-risk rated with elevation | > −2 | $8 |
| Table 3B | A, AE, A1–A30, AO, AH, V, VE, and V1–V30 | All HR | N/A | $56 |
| Table 3C | AO and AH | All Post-FIRM HR No Basement/ Enclosure or Pre-FIRM Optional Rating | Any | $8 |
| | Unnumbered A | Post-FIRM No Basement/Enclosure HR and All Pre-FIRM HR Optional Rating | > 0 With no BFE, or > −2 with BFE | $8 |
| Table 3D | AR and AR Dual | All HR rated without elevation | N/A | $8 |
| | AR and AR Dual | All HR rated with elevation | > −1 | $8 |
| Table 3E | ('75-'81) VE, V1-V30 | All HR | > −2 | $33 |
| Table 4A | A, AE, A1-A30, AO, AH, V, VE, and V1–V30 | Pre-FIRM LR rated without elevation | N/A | $56 |
| | A99, B, C, and X | All LR | N/A | $8 |
| | AO and AH | Post-FIRM LR No Basement/Enclosure or Pre-FIRM Optional Rating | Any | $8 |
| | D | Post-FIRM LR No Basement/Enclosure | N/A | $8 |
| Table 4B (SRL) | A, AE, A1-A30, AO, AH, V, VE, and V1–V30 | Pre-FIRM subsidized LR rated without elevation | N/A | $56 |
| Table 4C (substantial improvement) | A, AE, A1-A30, AO, AH, V, VE, and V1–V30 | Pre-FIRM subsidized LR rated without elevation | N/A | $56 |
| Table 4D | AE, A1-A30 | Post-FIRM LR and Pre-FIRM LR Optional Rating | > −2 | $8 |
| Table 4E | Unnumbered A | Post-FIRM No Basement/Enclosure LR and All Pre-FIRM HR Optional Rating | > 0 With no BFE, or > −2 with BFE | $8 |
| Table 4F | AR and AR Dual | All LR rated without elevation | N/A | $8 |
| | AR and AR Dual | All LR rated with elevation | > −1 | $8 |
| Table 4G | ('75-'81) VE, V1-V30 | All LR | > −2 | $33 |
| Table 5A | (Post '81) VE, V1-V30 | Post-FIRM LR and LR Elevated no enclosure and Pre-FIRM HR and LR Elevated no enclosure and Post-FIRM '75-'81 | > −4 | $21 |
| Table 5B | (Post '81) VE, V1-V30 | Post-FIRM LR and LR Elevated with enclosure and Pre-FIRM LR and LR Elevated with enclosure and Post-FIRM '75-'81 | > −4 | $21 |

1. Use the ICC Premium Table contained in the *Specific Rating Guidelines* manual.

## CONDO TABLE 7. RCBAP DEDUCTIBLE FACTORS – ALL ZONES[1,2,3]

### CATEGORY 1 – LOW-RISE CONDOMINIUM BUILDING-AND-CONTENTS POLICIES

| DEDUCTIBLE OPTIONS | DEDUCTIBLE FACTOR | | | | | |
|---|---|---|---|---|---|---|
| | SINGLE FAMILY | | 2-4 UNITS | | 5 OR MORE UNITS | |
| BUILDING/CONTENTS | PRE-/POST-FIRM Full Risk | PRE-FIRM Subsidized | PRE-/POST-FIRM Full Risk | PRE-FIRM Subsidized | PRE-/POST-FIRM Full Risk | PRE-FIRM Subsidized |
| $1,000/$1,000 | 1.000[2] | N/A | 1.000[2] | N/A | 1.000[2] | N/A |
| $1,250/$1,250 | .980 | N/A | .990 | N/A | .995 | N/A |
| $1,500/$1,500 | .965 | 1.050[2] | .980 | 1.025[2] | .990 | 1.025[2] |
| $2,000/$2,000 | .925 | 1.000 | .960 | 1.000 | .975 | 1.000 |
| $3,000/$3,000 | .850 | .925 | .930 | .965 | .950 | .975 |
| $4,000/$4,000 | .775 | .850 | .900 | .930 | .925 | .950 |
| $5,000/$5,000 | .750 | .810 | .880 | .910 | .915 | .930 |
| $10,000/$10,000 | .600 | .650 | .735 | .765 | .840 | .860 |
| $25,000/$25,000 | .500 | .550 | .635 | .665 | .740 | .760 |

### CATEGORY 2 – LOW-RISE CONDOMINIUM BUILDING-ONLY POLICIES

| | DEDUCTIBLE FACTOR | | | | | |
|---|---|---|---|---|---|---|
| | SINGLE FAMILY | | 2-4 UNITS | | 5 OR MORE UNITS | |
| DEDUCTIBLE OPTIONS | PRE-/POST-FIRM Full Risk | PRE-FIRM Subsidized | PRE-/POST-FIRM Full Risk | PRE-FIRM Subsidized | PRE-/POST-FIRM Full Risk | PRE-FIRM Subsidized |
| $1,000 | 1.000[3] | N/A | 1.000[3] | N/A | 1.000[3] | N/A |
| $1,250 | .980 | N/A | .990 | N/A | .995 | N/A |
| $1,500 | .965 | 1.050[3] | .975 | 1.040[3] | .985 | 1.025[3] |
| $2,000 | .925 | 1.000 | .950 | 1.000 | .970 | 1.000 |
| $3,000 | .865 | .935 | .910 | .960 | .940 | .970 |
| $4,000 | .815 | .880 | .870 | .920 | .920 | .950 |
| $5,000 | .765 | .830 | .835 | .880 | .900 | .930 |
| $10,000 | .630 | .685 | .650 | .690 | .830 | .860 |
| $25,000 | .530 | .580 | .550 | .585 | .730 | .760 |

### CATEGORY 3 – HIGH-RISE CONDOMINIUM POLICIES, BUILDING-AND-CONTENTS AND BUILDING-ONLY

The deductible factors are multipliers, and total deductible amounts are subject to a maximum dollar discount per annual premium.

**BUILDING/CONTENTS**

| DEDUCTIBLE OPTIONS | DEDUCTIBLE FACTOR | | MAXIMUM DISCOUNT |
|---|---|---|---|
| | PRE-/POST-FIRM Full Risk | PRE-FIRM Subsidized | |
| $1,000/ $1,000 | 1.000[3] | N/A | N/A |
| $1,250/ $1,250 | .995 | N/A | $14 |
| $1,500/ $1,500 | .990 | 1.025[3] | $28 |
| $2,000/ $2,000 | .980 | 1.000 | $56 |
| $3,000/ $3,000 | .960 | .980 | $111 |
| $4,000/ $4,000 | .940 | .960 | $166 |
| $5,000/ $5,000 | .920 | .940 | $221 |
| $10,000/$10,000 | .840 | .860 | $476 |
| $25,000/$25,000 | .740 | .760 | $1,001 |

**BUILDING ONLY**

| DEDUCTIBLE OPTIONS | DEDUCTIBLE FACTOR | | MAXIMUM DISCOUNT |
|---|---|---|---|
| | PRE-/POST-FIRM Full Risk | PRE-FIRM Subsidized | |
| $1,000 | 1.000[3] | N/A | N/A |
| $1,250 | .995 | N/A | $13 |
| $1,500 | .985 | 1.025[3] | $27 |
| $2,000 | .970 | 1.000 | $55 |
| $3,000 | .940 | .970 | $110 |
| $4,000 | .920 | .950 | $165 |
| $5,000 | .900 | .930 | $220 |
| $10,000 | .830 | .860 | $475 |
| $25,000 | .730 | .760 | $1,000 |

1. Pre-FIRM/Post-FIRM deductibles apply to all buildings receiving full-risk rates, including Pre-FIRM buildings rated with elevation data, or in the non-SFHA. Pre-FIRM deductibles apply only to policies receiving Pre-FIRM subsidized premium rates.
2. Only available if building coverage is $100,000 or less.
3. Any policy designated as SRL is subject to the SRL premium. Refer to Table 7D, Severe Repetitive Loss Premium, in this section.

This page is intentionally left blank.

# Appendix K: Residential Basement Floodproofing Premium Discount

## I. Approved Communities for Residential Basement Floodproofing Premium Discount

This table lists the only communities approved for the Residential Basement Floodproofing Premium Discount. Refer to the Floodproofing heading under Certifications in the How to Write section for more information on eligibility for premium discounts.

| State | Community Number | Community Name | Effective Date[1] | Status[2] |
|---|---|---|---|---|
| AK | 025009 | Fairbanks N. Star Borough | 2/28/73 | Current |
| ID | 160028 | Ammon, City of | 6/8/90 | Current |
| IA | 190488 | Clive, City of | 4/24/81 | Current |
| IA | 190031 | Independence, City of | 9/7/89 | Current |
| IA | 190309 | La Porte City, City of | 6/12/89 | Current |
| KS | 200484 | Colwich, City of | 1/17/86 | Current |
| KS | 200323 | Derby, City of | 2/15/83[3] | Current |
| KS | 200019 | Great Bend, City of | 8/10/83 | Current |
| KS | 200131 | Halstead, City of | 7/8/83 | Current |
| KS | 200215 | Lindsborg, City of | 11/7/94 | Current |
| KS | 200334 | Rossville, City of | 2/18/92 | Current |
| KS | 200319 | Salina, City of | 3/6/86 | Current |
| KS | 200316 | Saline County | 1/14/86 | Current |
| KS | 200134 | Sedgwick, City of | 5/19/86[3] | Current |
| MN | 270267 | Alvarado, City of | 2/28/85 | Current |
| MN | 275235 | Clay County | 3/28/75 | Current |
| MN | 270080 | Dilworth, City of | 8/29/83 | Current |
| MN | 275236 | East Grand Forks, City of | 5/15/86[3] | Current |
| MN | 275244 | Moorhead, City of | 2/12/76 | Current |
| MN | 270414 | Roseau, City of | 7/14/92 | Current |
| MN | 270273 | Stephen, City of | 5/10/83 | Current |
| MN | 270274 | Warren, City of | 9/24/82 | Current |
| NE | 310069 | Fremont, City of | 1/25/79 | Current |
| NE | 310103 | Grand Island, City of | 7/29/80 | Current |
| NE | 310100 | Hall County | 2/10/80 | Current |
| NE | 310001 | Hastings, City of | 7/8/83 | Current |
| NE | 310239 | North Bend, City of | 10/15/98 | Rescinded 11/1/08 |
| NE | 310046 | Schuyler, City of | 9/17/91 | Current |
| NE | 310039 | Sidney, City of | 12/4/84 | Current |
| NE | 310104 | Wood River, City of | 1/12/82 | Current |
| NY | 360226 | Amherst, Town of | 11/20/78 | Current |

1. Effective date corresponds to the date of the letter from FEMA that granted the community's exception request.
2. The Residential Floodproofing Premium Discount may be grandfathered for those residential buildings with a valid Residential Basement Floodproofing Certificate that were constructed between the effective date and rescission date, but not on or after the rescission date.
3. The date the community adopted floodproofing ordinances.

| State | Community Number | Community Name | Effective Date[1] | Status[2] |
|---|---|---|---|---|
| NY | 360232 | Clarence, Town of | 8/1/00 | Current |
| ND | 380256 | Barnes, Township of | 1/22/82 | Current |
| ND | 380020 | Casselton, City of | 6/18/81 | Current |
| ND | 385364 | Fargo, City of | 3/26/75[3] | Current |
| ND | 380137 | Grafton, City of | 5/21/81 | Current |
| ND | 380338 | Harwood, City of | 12/19/85 | Current |
| ND | 380259 | Harwood, Township of | 1/22/82 | Current |
| ND | 380022 | Horace, City of | 1/22/82 | Current |
| ND | 380023 | Mapleton, City of | 1/22/82[3] | Current |
| ND | 380681 | Oxbow, City of | 6/1/92[3] | Current |
| ND | 380263 | Pleasant, Township of | 5/5/83 | Current |
| ND | 380257 | Reed, Township of | 1/22/82 | Current |
| ND | 380324 | Reiles Acres, City of | 8/23/82 | Current |
| ND | 380258 | Stanley, Township of | 2/8/82 | Current |
| ND | 380024 | West Fargo, City of | 6/5/78 | Current |
| SD | 460044 | Madison, City of | 8/30/83 | Current |
| WI | 550612 | Allouez, Village of | 1/11/93[3] | Current |
| WI | 550600 | Ashwaubenon, Village of | 10/27/78 | Current |
| WI | 550020 | Brown County | 2/21/79[3] | Current |
| WI | 550021 | Depere, City of | 10/27/78 | Current |
| WI | 550022 | Green Bay, City of | 10/27/78 | Current |
| WI | 550023 | Howard, Village of | 10/27/78 | Current |
| WI | 550309 | Shiocton, Village of | 8/1/98 | Current |

1. Effective date corresponds to the date of the letter from FEMA that granted the community's exception request.
2. The Residential Floodproofing Premium Discount may be grandfathered for those residential buildings with a valid Residential Basement Floodproofing Certificate that were constructed between the effective date and rescission date, but not on or after the rescission date.
3. The date the community adopted floodproofing ordinances.

# Appendix L: Definitions and Acronyms

## I. Definitions

This table of terms includes definitions of specific terms/words related to the NFIP. It includes a few standard industry terms for additional focus and emphasis.

| Term | Definition |
|---|---|
| **Actual Cash Value (ACV)** | The cost to replace an insured item of property at the time of loss, less the value of its physical depreciation. |
| **Agricultural Structure** | A structure used exclusively in connection with the production, harvesting, storage, raising, or drying of agricultural commodities. |
| **Alternative Rating** | A rating method used when a building is Pre-FIRM construction, the flood zone is unknown, and the community in which the building is located has no V Zones. May also be used for renewal of policies in communities that have converted from the Emergency Program to the Regular Program during a policy's term. |
| **Anchored** | Adequately secured to prevent flotation, collapse, or lateral movement. |
| **Application** | The statement made and signed by the prospective insured or the agent in applying for an NFIP flood insurance policy. The application gives information used to determine the eligibility of the risk, the kind of policy to be issued, and the correct premium payment. |
| **Base Flood** | A flood having a 1% chance of being equaled or exceeded in any given year. |
| **Base Flood Depth (BFD)** | The depth shown on the Flood Insurance Rate Map (FIRM) for Zone AO that indicates the depth of water above the highest adjacent grade resulting from a flood that has a 1% chance of equaling or exceeding that level in any given year. |
| **Base Flood Elevation (BFE)** | The elevation of surface water resulting from a flood that has a 1% chance of equaling or exceeding that level in any given year. The BFE is shown on the Flood insurance Rate Map (FIRM) for zones AE, AH, A1–A30, AR, AR/A, AR/AE, AR/A1–A30, AR/AH, AR/AO, V1–V30 and VE. |
| **Basement** | Any area of the building, including any sunken room or sunken portion of a room, having its floor below ground level (subgrade) on all sides. |
| **Breakaway Wall** | A wall that is not part of the structural support of a building and is intended through its design and construction to collapse under specific lateral loading forces, without causing damage to the elevated portion of the building or supporting foundation system. |
| **Building** | • A structure with two or more outside rigid walls and a fully secured roof, that is affixed to a permanent site; *or*<br>• A manufactured home (a "manufactured home," also known as a mobile home, is a structure: built on a permanent chassis, transported to its site in one or more sections, and affixed to a permanent foundation); *or*<br>• A travel trailer without wheels, built on a chassis and affixed to a permanent foundation, that is regulated under the community's floodplain management and building ordinances or laws.<br>"Building" does not mean a gas or liquid storage tank or a recreational vehicle, park trailer, or other similar vehicle, except as described above. |
| **Building in the Course of Construction** | A walled and roofed building (see the Before You Start section for exceptions) that is principally above ground and affixed to a permanent site. It does not include building materials or supplies intended for use in construction, alteration, or repair unless such materials or supplies are within an enclosed building on the premises. |

| Term | Definition |
| --- | --- |
| **Business Building** | A building in which the named insured is a commercial enterprise primarily carried out to generate income and the coverage is for:<br>2. A building designed as a non-habitational building;<br>3. A mixed-use building in which the total floor area devoted to residential uses is—<br>• 50% or less of the total floor area within the building if the residential building is a single family property; *or*<br>• 75% or less of the total floor area within the building for all other residential properties; *or*<br>4. A building designed for use as an office or retail space, wholesale space, hospitality space, or for similar uses. |
| **Business Property** | Either a business building or the contents within a business building, or both. |
| **Cancellation** | The termination of the insurance coverage provided by a policy before the expiration date. |
| **Cistern** | A tank for storing water. A cistern eligible for coverage and the water in it are defined as an integral part of an insurable building, meaning under the building or above ground and physically attached to a side of the building with one of the walls of the building and cistern being common to each other. |
| **Coastal Barrier** | A naturally occurring island, sandbar, or other strip of land, including coastal mainland, which protects the coast from severe wave wash. |
| **Coastal Barrier Resources Act (CBRA)** | Legislation designating relatively undeveloped coastal barriers along the Atlantic, Gulf of Mexico, Great Lakes, U.S. Virgin Islands, and Puerto Rico coasts as part of the John H. Chafee Coastal Barrier Resources System (CBRS) and making these areas ineligible for most new federal expenditures and financial assistance. |
| **Coastal Barrier Resources System (CBRS)** | A defined set of geographic units (known as System Units and Otherwise Protected Areas (OPAs)) along the Atlantic, Gulf of Mexico, Great Lakes, U.S. Virgin Islands, and Puerto Rico coasts identified under the CBRA and subsequent amendments. |
| **Community** | A political entity that has the authority to adopt and enforce floodplain ordinances for the area under its jurisdiction. |
| **Community Number** | A 6-digit designation identifying each NFIP community. The first two numbers are the state code. The next four are the FEMA-assigned community number. An alphabetical suffix is added to a community number to identify revisions in the FIRM for that community. |
| **Community Rating System** | A program developed by FEMA to provide incentives for those communities in the Regular Program that have gone beyond the minimum floodplain management requirements to develop extra measures to provide protection from flooding. |
| **Condominium Association** | The entity made up of condominium unit owners responsible for the maintenance and operation of:<br>• Common elements owned in undivided shares by unit owners;<br>• Other real property in which the unit owners have use rights;<br>Where membership in the entity is a required condition of unit ownership. |
| **Condominium Building** | A type of building in the form of ownership in which each unit owner has an undivided interest in common elements of the building. |
| **Countywide Map** | A FIRM that shows flooding information for the entire geographic area of a county, including the incorporated communities within the county. |

| Term | Definition |
|---|---|
| **Crawlspace** | An under-floor space that has its interior floor area (finished or not) no more than 5 feet below the top of the next-higher floor. Crawlspaces generally have solid foundation walls. See Diagram 8 in the NFIP Elevation Certificate and Instructions (a sample of the form can be found in Appendix B: Forms). |
| **Cumulative Damage Property** | Either a cumulative damage building or the contents within a cumulative damage building, or both. |
| **Date of Construction** | The date that the building permit was issued, provided the actual start of construction, repair, reconstruction, or improvement was within 180 days of the permit date. |
| **Deductible** | The fixed amount of an insured loss that is the responsibility of the insured and that is deducted before any amounts are paid for the insured loss under the insurance policy. |
| **Described Location** | The location where the insured building or personal property is found. The described location is shown on the Declarations Page. |
| **Doublewide Manufactured (Mobile) Home** | A manufactured (mobile) home that, when assembled as a non-movable, permanent building, is at least 16 feet wide and has an area within its perimeter walls of at least 600 square feet. |
| **Elevated Building** | A building that has no basement and that has its lowest elevated floor raised above ground level by foundation walls, shear walls, posts, piers, pilings, or columns. Solid (perimeter) foundation walls are not an acceptable means of elevating buildings in V and VE Zones. |
| **Emergency Program** | The initial phase of a community's participation in the NFIP, as prescribed by Section 1306 of the National Flood Insurance Act of 1968 (NFIA) (42 U.S.C. 4056). In this phase, limited amounts of coverage are available. |
| **Enclosure** | That portion of an elevated building below the lowest elevated floor that is either partially or fully shut in by rigid walls. |
| **Erosion** | The collapse, undermining, or subsidence of land along the shore of a lake or other body of water. Erosion is a covered peril if it is caused by waves or currents of water exceeding their cyclical levels, which result in flooding. |
| **Federal Policy Fee** | A flat charge that the policyholder must pay on each new or renewal policy to defray certain administrative expenses incurred in carrying out NFIP operations. |
| **Financial Assistance/ Subsidy Arrangement** | The arrangement between an insurance company and FEMA to initiate the company participation in the Write Your Own (WYO) Program. It establishes the duties of the company and the government. |
| **Finished (Habitable) Area** | An enclosed area having more than 20 linear feet of finished interior walls (paneling, etc.) or used for any purpose other than solely for parking of vehicles, building access, or storage. |
| **Flood** | A general and temporary condition of partial or complete inundation of 2 or more acres of normally dry land area or of 2 or more properties (at least one of which is the policyholder's property) from:<br>• Overflow of inland or tidal waters;<br>• Unusual and rapid accumulation or runoff of surface waters from any source; *or*<br>• Mudflow<br>*OR*<br>Collapse or subsidence of land along the shore of a lake or similar body of water as a result of erosion or undermining caused by waves or currents of water exceeding anticipated cyclical levels that result in a flood as defined above. |

| Term | Definition |
|---|---|
| **Flood Hazard Boundary Map (FHBM)** | Official map of a community issued by FEMA, where the boundaries of the flood, mudflow, and related erosion areas having special hazards have been designated. Typically the initial flood hazard identification used for Emergency Program communities. |
| **Flood Insurance Rate Map (FIRM)** | Official map of a community on which FEMA has delineated the Special Flood Hazard Areas (SFHAs), the BFEs, and the flood zones applicable to the community. |
| **Floodplain Management** | The operation of an overall program of corrective and preventive measures for reducing flood damage, including but not limited to emergency preparedness plans, flood control works, and floodplain management regulations. |
| **Foundation Walls** | Masonry walls, poured concrete walls, or precast concrete walls, regardless of height, that extend above grade and support the loads of a building. |
| **Freeboard** | An additional amount of height above the BFE used as a factor of safety (e.g., 2 feet above the Base Flood) in determining the level at which a building's lowest floor must be elevated or floodproofed to be in accordance with state or community floodplain management regulations. |
| **Full-Risk Premium Rate** | A rate charged to a group of policies that results in aggregate premiums sufficient to pay anticipated losses and expense for that group. |
| **Grade Elevation** | The lowest or highest finished ground level that is immediately adjacent to the walls of the building. Use natural (pre-construction) ground level, if available, for Zone AO and Zone A (without BFE). |
| **Grandfathering** | A rating procedure that enables policyholders to use a prior flood map for rating if the building was built in compliance or continuously insured.<br>• Under NFIP administrative grandfathering, Post-FIRM buildings in the Regular Program built in compliance with the floodplain management regulations in effect at the start of construction will continue to have favorable rate treatment even though higher BFEs or more restrictive, greater risk zone designations result from FIRM revisions.<br>• Policyholders who have remained loyal customers of the NFIP by maintaining continuous coverage (since coverage was first obtained on the building) are also eligible for administrative grandfathering. |
| **Group Flood Insurance Policy (GFIP)** | A GFIP is a policy covering all individuals named by a State as recipients under section 408 of the Robert T. Stafford Disaster Relief and Emergency Assistance Act (Pub. L. No. 93-288, 88 Stat. 143; 42 U.S.C. 5174) of an Individuals and Households Program award for flood damage as a result of a major disaster declaration by the President. |
| **HFIAA Surcharge** | The statutory surcharge imposed by Section 1308A of the NFIA (42 U.S.C. 4015a). |
| **High-Rise Building** | High-rise condominium buildings have five or more units and at least three floors, excluding enclosures even if it is the lowest floor for rating purposes.<br>• An enclosure below an elevated building, even if it is the lowest floor for rating purposes, cannot be counted as a floor to avoid classifying the building as low rise.<br>• Townhouses/rowhouses are not considered high-rise buildings, regardless of the number of floors. |

| Term | Definition |
|---|---|
| **Historic Building** | Any building that is:<br>• Listed individually in the National Register of Historic Places (a listing maintained by the Department of the Interior) or preliminarily determined by the Secretary of the Interior as meeting the requirements for individual listing on the National Register; *or*<br>• Certified or preliminarily determined by the Secretary of the Interior as contributing to the historical significance of a registered historic district or a district preliminarily determined by the Secretary of the Interior to qualify as a registered historic district; *or*<br>• Individually listed in a state inventory of historic places in states with preservation programs that have been approved by the Secretary of the Interior; *or*<br>• Individually listed on a local inventory of historic places in communities with historic preservation programs that have been certified either:<br>– By an approved state program as determined by the Secretary of the Interior; *or*<br>– Directly by the Secretary of the Interior in states without approved programs. |
| **Increased Cost of Compliance (ICC)** | Coverage for expenses that a property owner must incur, above and beyond the cost to repair the physical damage the building actually sustained from a flooding event, to comply with mitigation requirements of state or local floodplain management ordinances or laws. Acceptable mitigation measures are elevation, floodproofing, relocation, demolition, or any combination thereof. |
| **Letter of Determination Review (LODR)** | FEMA's ruling on the determination made by a lender or third party that a borrower's building is in an SFHA. A LODR deals only with the location of a building relative to the SFHA boundary shown on the FIRM. |
| **Letter of Map Amendment (LOMA)** | An amendment to the currently effective FIRM issued by FEMA that establishes that a property is not located in an SFHA. |
| **Letter of Map Revision (LOMR)** | An official amendment to the currently effective FIRM. It is issued by FEMA and changes flood zones, delineations, and elevations. |
| **Lowest Adjacent Grade** | The lowest point of the ground level immediately next to a building. |
| **Low-Rise Building** | A condominium building with fewer than five units regardless of the number of floors or five or more units with fewer than three floors including the basement.<br>• All townhouses/rowhouses, regardless of the number of floors or units, and all single-family detached condominium buildings are classified as low rise.<br>• An enclosure below an elevated building, even if it is the lowest floor for rating purposes, cannot be counted as a floor to avoid classifying the building as low rise. |
| **Mandatory Purchase Requirement** | A statutory requirement under the Flood Disaster Protection Act of 1973 (FDPA) making the purchase of flood insurance mandatory for properties in SFHAs that are located in NFIP participating communities and either secure mortgages from federally-backed lenders or received federal assistance for acquisition or construction. |
| **Manufactured (Mobile) Home** | A structure built on a permanent chassis transported to its site in one or more sections and affixed to a permanent foundation, but not including recreational vehicles. |
| **Map Revision** | A change in the FHBM or FIRM for a community which reflects revised zone, base flood, or other information. |
| **Masonry Walls** | Walls constructed of individual components laid in and bound together with mortar. These components can be brick, stone, concrete block, poured concrete, etc. |
| **Mixed-Use Building** | A building that has both residential and non-residential uses. |
| **Modular Building** | A building that is usually transported to its site on a steel frame or special trailer because it does not have a permanent chassis like a manufactured (mobile) home. A modular building is classified and rated under one of the other building types. |

| Term | Definition |
|---|---|
| Mortgage Portfolio Protection Program (MPPP) | A program designed to help lending institutions maintain compliance with the FDPA. Policies written under the MPPP can be placed only through a WYO company. |
| Mudflow | A river of liquid and flowing mud on the surface of normally dry land areas, as when earth is carried by a current of water. Other earth movements, such as landslide, slope failure, or a saturated soil mass moving by liquidity down a slope, are not mudflows. |
| Natural Grade | The grade unaffected by construction techniques such as fill, landscaping, or berming. |
| New Construction | Buildings for which the "start of construction" commenced on or after the effective date of an initial FIRM or after December 31, 1974, whichever is later, including any subsequent improvements. |
| Newly Mapped (A Property Newly Mapped into the SFHA) | A property that was once designated outside of the SFHA on an effective FIRM, and following a map revision, is designated within the SFHA. Refer to the Newly Mapped section for additional information. |
| NFIP Direct Servicing Agent (NFIP Direct) | An entity contracted with FEMA to sell and service NFIP policies. |
| NFIP Special Direct Facility (SDF) | The NFIP Direct Servicing Agent operates the SDF which services and supports Severe Repetitive Loss (SRL) policies, re-underwrites them, and coordinates with FEMA on necessary policy actions for FEMA-approved mitigation projects. |
| Non-Primary Residence | A residential building that is not the primary residence of the policyholder. |
| Non-Primary Residential Property | Either a non-primary residence or the contents within a non-primary residence, or both. |
| Non-Residential Building | A commercial or mixed-use building where the primary use is commercial or non-habitational. |
| Non-Residential Property | Either a non-residential building, the contents within a non-residential building, or both. |
| Nullification | The act of declaring an insurance contract invalid from its inception so that, from a legal standpoint, the insurance contract never existed. |
| Other Non-Residential Building | A non-habitational building that does not qualify as a business building or residential building. |
| Other Residential Building | A residential building that is designed for use as a residential space for five or more families or a mixed-use building in which the total floor area devoted to non-residential uses is less than 25% of the total floor area within the building. |
| Other Residential Property | Either an other residential building, the contents within an other residential building, or both. |
| Otherwise Protected Area (OPA) | Any undeveloped coastal barrier within the boundaries of an area established under federal, state, or local law, or held by a qualified organization, primarily for wildlife refuge, sanctuary, recreational, or natural resource conservation purposes that is included within the CBRS established by the CBRA (16 U.S.C. 3503). |
| Out-As-Shown Determination | An alternative outcome of the FEMA LOMA review process stating that a specific property is located outside the SFHA as indicated on the FHBM or FIRM. |
| Participating Community | A community for which FEMA has authorized the sale of flood insurance under the NFIP. |

| Term | Definition |
|---|---|
| Policy | The entire written contract between the insured and the insurer. The written contract includes the following:<br>• The printed policy form;<br>• The application and declarations page;<br>• Any endorsement(s) that may be issued; *and*<br>• Any renewal certificate indicating that coverage has been instituted for a new policy and new policy term. |
| Post-FIRM Building | A building for which construction or substantial improvement occurred after December 31, 1974, or on or after the effective date of an initial FIRM, whichever is later. |
| Pre-FIRM Building | A building for which construction or substantial improvement occurred on or before December 31, 1974, or before the effective date of an initial FIRM. |
| Preferred Risk Policy (PRP) | A lower-cost SFIP written under the Dwelling Form or General Property Form. It offers fixed combinations of building/contents coverage limits or contents-only coverage. The PRP is available for properties located in Zones B, C, X, AR, or A99 in a Regular Program community that meet certain loss history requirements. |
| Presentment of Premium Payment | The date of the check or credit card payment by the applicant or applicant's representative if the premium payment is not part of a loan closing, or the date of closing, if the premium payment is part of a loan closing. |
| Primary Residence | A single-family building, condominium unit, apartment unit, or unit within a cooperative building that will be lived in by the policyholder or the policyholder's spouse for:<br>• More than 50% of the 365 calendar days following the current policy effective date; *or*<br>• 50% or less of the 365 calendar days following the current policy effective date if the policyholder has only one residence and does not lease that residence to another party or use it as rental or income property at any time during the policy term. |
| Primary Residential Property | Either a primary residence or the contents within a primary residence, or both. |
| Principal Residence | A single-family dwelling in which, at the time of loss, the named insured or the named insured's spouse has lived for either 80% of the 365 days immediately preceding the loss, or 80% of the period of ownership, if less than 365 days. |
| Probation | A FEMA-imposed change in a community's status resulting from violations and deficiencies in the administration and enforcement of NFIP local floodplain management regulations. |
| Probation Surcharge | A flat surcharge that the policyholder must pay on each new or renewed policy issued covering property in a community that the NFIP has placed on probation under the provisions of 44 CFR 59.24. |
| Proper Openings | (See the Enclosures heading in the How to Write section – applicable to Zones A, A1–A30, AE, AO, AH, AR, and AR Dual.) All enclosures below the lowest elevated floor must be designed to automatically equalize hydrostatic flood forces on exterior walls by allowing for the entry and exit of floodwaters. Requirements for proper openings:<br>• A minimum of 2 openings, with positioning on at least 2 walls;<br>• A total net area of not less than 1 square inch for every square foot of enclosed area subject to flooding; *and*<br>• The bottom of all openings must be no higher than 1 foot above the higher of the exterior or interior grade (adjacent) or floor immediately below the openings. |
| Provisional Rating | A method for placing flood coverage prior to the receipt of a FEMA EC. |
| Regular Program | The final phase of a community's participation in the NFIP. In this phase, a FIRM is in effect and full limits of coverage are available under the NFIA. |

| Term | Definition |
|---|---|
| **Replacement Cost Value (RCV)** | The cost to replace property with the same kind of material and construction without deduction for depreciation. |
| **Reserve Fund Assessment** | An amount dedicated to the NFIP Reserve Fund added to the insured's premium pursuant to section 1310A of the NFIA (42 U.S.C. 4017a). |
| **Residential Building** | A non-commercial building designed for habitation by one or more families or a mixed-use building that qualifies as a single-family, 2-4 family, or other residential building. |
| **Residential Condominium Building** | A building, owned and administered as a condominium, containing one or more family units and in which at least 75% of the total floor area is residential. |
| **Residential Property** | Either a residential building or the contents within a residential building, or both. |
| **Severe Repetitive Loss (SRL) Building** | An NFIP-insured single-family or multi-family residential building:<br>• That has incurred flood-related damage for which four or more separate claims payments have been made, with the amount of each claim (including building and contents payments) exceeding $5,000, and with the cumulative amount of such claims payments exceeding $20,000; *or*<br>• For which at least two separate claims payments (building payments only) have been made under such coverage, with the cumulative amount of such claims exceeding the market value of the building.<br>In both instances, at least two of the claims must be within 10 years of each other, and claims made within 10 days of each other will be counted as one claim. In determining SRL status, FEMA considers the loss history since 1978, or from the building's construction if it was built after 1978, regardless of any changes in the ownership of the building. |
| **Severe Repetitive Loss (SRL) Property** | Either an SRL building or the contents within an SRL building, or both. |
| **Shear Walls** | Walls used for structural support but not structurally joined or enclosed at the ends (except by breakaway walls). Shear walls are parallel, or nearly parallel, to the flow of the water and can be used in any flood zone. |
| **Single Building** | A building that is separated from other buildings by intervening clear space or solid, vertical, load-bearing division walls. |
| **Single-Family Dwelling** | Either:<br>• A residential single-family building in which the total floor area devoted to non-residential uses is less than 50% of the building's total floor area; *or*<br>• A single-family residential unit within a 2–4 family building, other residential building, business, or non-residential building, in which commercial uses within the unit are limited to less than 50% of the unit's total floor area. |
| **Solid (Perimeter) Foundation Walls** | Walls that are used as a means of elevating a building. |
| **Special Flood Hazard Area (SFHA)** | An area having special flood, mudflow, or flood-related erosion hazards, and shown on an FHBM or FIRM as Zone A, AO, A1–A30, AE, A99, AH, AR, AR/A, AR/AE, AR/ AH, AR/ AO, AR/A1–A30, V1–V30, VE, or V. |
| **Split Level** | A foundation with a vertical offset in the floor framing on either side of a common wall. |

| Term | Definition |
|---|---|
| **Standard Flood Insurance Policy (SFIP)** | • **Dwelling Form.** The policy form used to insure a building designed for use as a residence for no more than 4 families or a single-family unit in a residential building under a condominium form of ownership. This form is also used to insure residential contents in any building. The owner of a residential building with 5 or more units can use this form to insure contents only in his or her own residential unit.<br>• **General Property Form.** The policy form used to insure a non-residential building or a 5-or-more-unit residential building not eligible for the RCBAP. This form is also used to insure non-residential contents in any building or a building owner's residential contents located in multiple units within a building with 5 or more units.<br>• **RCBAP.** The policy form used to insure a building, owned and administered as a condominium, containing 1 or more units and in which at least 75% of the total floor area is residential. The building must be located in a Regular Program community. |
| **Start of Construction** | For other than new construction or substantial improvements, this is the date the building permit was issued, provided the actual start of construction, repair, reconstruction, rehabilitation, addition placement, or other improvement was within 180 days of the permit date.<br>• The actual start means either the first placement of permanent construction of a building on site, such as the pouring of slab or footings, the installation of piles, the construction of columns, or any work beyond the stage of excavation; or the placement of a manufactured (mobile) home on a foundation.<br>• For a substantial improvement, the actual start of construction means the first alteration of any wall, ceiling, floor, or other structural part of a building, whether or not that alteration affects the external dimensions of the building.<br>See the CBRS appendix for additional discussion of this concept in that context. |
| **Stock** | Merchandise held in storage or for sale, raw materials, and in-process or finished goods, including supplies used in their packing or shipping. "Stock" does not include any property listed under "Section IV. Property Not Covered" of the General Property Form, except the following:<br>• Parts and equipment for self-propelled vehicles;<br>• Furnishings and equipment for watercraft;<br>• Spas and hot tubs, including their equipment; *and*<br>• Swimming pool equipment. |
| **Subgrade Crawlspace** | A crawlspace foundation where the subgrade under-floor area is no more than 5 feet below the top of the next-higher floor and no more than 2 feet below the lowest adjacent grade on all sides. |
| **Subsidized Premium Rate** | A rate charged to a group of policies that results in aggregate premiums insufficient to pay anticipated losses and expenses for that group. |
| **Substantially Damaged Building** | A building that has incurred damage of any origin whereby the cost of restoring the building to its condition before damage would equal or exceed 50% (or a lower threshold if adopted and enforced by the community) of the market value of the building before the damage occurred. |
| **Substantially Damaged Property** | Either a substantially damaged building or the contents within a substantially damaged building, or both. |

| Term | Definition |
|---|---|
| **Substantially Improved Building** | A building that has undergone reconstruction, rehabilitation, addition, or other improvement, the cost of which equals or exceeds 50% (or a lower threshold if adopted and enforced by the community) of the market value of the building before the "start of construction" of the improvement. This term does not include a building that has undergone reconstruction, rehabilitation, addition, or other improvement related to:<br>• Any project or improvement of a building to correct existing violations of a state or local health, sanitary, or safety code specifications that have been identified by the local code enforcement official and which are the minimum necessary to assure safe living conditions; *or*<br>• Any alteration of a "historic building", provided that the alteration will not preclude the structure's continued designation as a "historic building". |
| **Substantially Improved Property** | Either a substantially improved building or the contents within a substantially improved building, or both. |
| **Suspension** | FEMA's removal of a participating community from the NFIP because the community has not enacted and/or enforced the proper floodplain management regulations required for participation. |
| **Tentative Rates** | NFIP rates used to issue policies for applications that fail to provide the NFIP with valid actuarial rating information. |
| **Travel Trailer** | Under the NFIP, a travel trailer can be considered a building only if it is without wheels, built on a chassis and affixed to a permanent foundation, and regulated under the community's floodplain management and building ordinances or laws. |
| **Two-to-Four-Family Building** | A residential building, including an apartment building, containing 2–4 residential spaces and in which commercial uses are limited to less than 25% of the building's total floor area. |
| **Underground Building** | A building for which 50% or more of the Actual Cash Value (ACV), including machinery and equipment that are part of the building, is below ground. |
| **Unfinished Area** | An enclosed area that is used only for the parking of vehicles, building access, or storage purposes and that does not meet the definition of a finished (habitable) area. Drywall used for fire protection is permitted in unfinished areas. |
| **Unit** | • Under the Dwelling Form: A single-family unit owned by the policyholder in a condominium building.<br>• Under the General Property Form: A unit in a condominium building.<br>• Under the RCBAP Form: A single-family unit in a residential condominium building. |
| **Variance** | A grant of relief by a participating community from the terms of its floodplain management regulations. |
| **Waiting Period** | A waiting period refers to the time an insured must wait before some or all of the purchased flood insurance coverage goes into effect. Only after the waiting period passes does the insured have a right to file a claim for the benefits of the insurance policy. |
| **Walled and Roofed Building** | A building that has two or more exterior rigid walls and a fully secured roof and that is affixed to a permanent site. |
| **Wave Height Adjustment** | A measurement that is added to the BFE for V Zones shown on the FIRM published prior to 1981. For coastal communities, the BFE shown on FIRMs published prior to 1981 are stillwater elevations, which include only the effects of tide and storm surge, and not the height of wind-generated waves, and thus require adjustment. |

| Term | Definition |
|---|---|
| **Write Your Own (WYO) Program** | The program under which FEMA enters into a standard arrangement with private property insurance companies to sell contracts for flood insurance coverage under their own business lines of insurance, and to adjust and pay claims arising under such contracts. |
| **Zone** | A geographical area shown on a FHBM or a FIRM that reflects the severity or type of flooding in the area. |

## II. Acronyms

This table shows acronyms and their full name for specific terms related to the NFIP. The list is arranged alphabetically by the acronym.

| Acronym | Meaning |
|---|---|
| **BFD** | Base Flood Depth |
| **BFE** | Base Flood Elevation |
| **CAP** | Community Assistance Program |
| **CBIA** | Coastal Barrier Improvement Act of 1990 |
| **CBRA** | Coastal Barrier Resources Act |
| **CBRS** | Coastal Barrier Resources System |
| **CRS** | Community Rating System |
| **DFIRM** | Digital Flood Insurance Rate Map |
| **DHS** | U.S. Department of Homeland Security |
| **EC** | Elevation Certificate |
| **FEMA** | Federal Emergency Management Agency |
| **FHBM** | Flood Hazard Boundary Map |
| **FIMA** | Federal Insurance & Mitigation Administration |
| **FIRA** | Flood Insurance Reform Act of 2004 |
| **FIRM** | Flood Insurance Rate Map |
| **FIS** | Flood Insurance Study |
| **FMA** | Flood Mitigation Assistance, Flood Mitigation Assistance Grant Program |
| **FMIX** | FEMA Mapping and Insurance eXchange |
| **GFIP** | Group Flood Insurance Policy |
| **HAG** | Highest Adjacent Grade |
| **HFIAA** | Homeowner Flood Insurance Affordability Act |
| **HMGP** | Hazard Mitigation Grant Program |
| **ICC** | Increased Cost of Compliance |
| **LAG** | Lowest Adjacent Grade |
| **LFE** | Lowest Floor Elevation |
| **LFP** | Leased Federal Property |
| **LODR** | Letter of Determination Review |
| **LOMC** | Letter of Map Change |
| **LOMR** | Letter of Map Revision |

| Acronym | Meaning |
|---|---|
| LOMR-F | Letter of Map Revision Based on Fill |
| LOMR-FW | Letter of Map Revision — Floodway |
| MPPP | Mortgage Portfolio Protection Program |
| MSC | FEMA Flood Map Service Center, Flood Map Service Center |
| NFIA | National Flood Insurance Act of 1968 |
| NFIP | National Flood Insurance Program |
| NFIRA | National Flood Insurance Reform Act of 1994 |
| NM | Newly Mapped rating procedure |
| NSF | Non-sufficient funds |
| OPA | Otherwise Protected Area |
| PDA | Preliminary Damage Assessment |
| PDM | Pre-Disaster Mitigation Grant Program |
| PMR | Physical Map Revision |
| POL | Proof of Loss |
| PRP | Preferred Risk Policy |
| RCBAP | Residential Condominium Building Association Policy |
| RCV | Replacement Cost Value |
| RL | Repetitive Loss |
| SDF | Special Direct Facility |
| SFHA | Special Flood Hazard Area |
| SFHDF | Standard Flood Hazard Determination Form |
| SFIP | Standard Flood Insurance Policy |
| SRL | Severe Repetitive Loss |
| USFWS | U.S. Fish & Wildlife Service |
| WYO | Write Your Own |

www.ingramcontent.com/pod-product-compliance
Lightning Source LLC
Chambersburg PA
CBHW080414030426
42335CB00020B/2448
* 9 7 8 1 9 5 4 2 8 5 3 1 6 *